Spatial Analysis in Field Primatolo

Applying GIS at Varying Scales

MW00843405

From foraging patterns in a single tree to social interactions across a home range, how primates use space is a key question in the field of primate behavioral ecology. Drawing on the latest advances in spatial analysis tools, this book offers practical guidance on applying geographic information systems (GIS) to central questions in primatology. An initial methodological section discusses niche modeling, home range analysis, and agent-based modeling, with a focus on remote data collection. Research-based chapters demonstrate how ecologists apply this technology to a suite of topics including calculating the intensity of use of both range and travel routes, assessing the impacts of logging, mining and hunting, and informing conservation strategies. Offering best-practice guidelines on cutting-edge technologies, this is an indispensable resource for any primatologist or student of animal behavior.

Francine L. Dolins is Associate Professor of Comparative Psychology at the University of Michigan-Dearborn, USA. Her research investigates spatial cognition, navigation and foraging behavior with nonhuman primates in the lab using virtual reality, and she also conducts field research to integrate the understanding of species' cognitive capacities with socioecological factors. She has published two edited books with Cambridge University Press, *Attitudes to Animals: Views in Animal Welfare* (1999) and *Spatial Cognition, Spatial Perception: Mapping the Self and Space* (2010).

Christopher A. Shaffer is Assistant Professor of Anthropology at Grand Valley State University, USA, and Principal Investigator of the Konashen Ecosystem Health Project. His primary research and teaching interests focus on community ecology and behavioral ecology, particularly in the context of human–nonhuman animal interactions and natural resource management.

Leila M. Porter is Professor of Anthropology and Presidential Engagement Professor at Northern Illinois University, USA. She studies the behavior and ecology of tamarins and Goeldi's monkeys in South America, specifically their diet, ranging, and patterns of infant care.

Jena R. Hickey served as the Conservation Scientist for the International Gorilla Conservation Programme (IGCP) for 5 years. With over 20 years of professional experience, Jena has held positions with state and federal agencies, academic institutions, and not-for-profit organizations. She focuses on species occurrence, abundance, spatial distributions, movements, and habitat use, as well as how anthropogenic factors shape these response variables.

Nathan P. Nibbelink is Professor of GIS and Spatial Ecology in the Warnell School of Forestry and Natural Resources, University of Georgia, USA. He serves as Director of the Center for Integrative Conservation Research and the Integrative Conservation PhD program. His research uses spatially explicit models to address landscape connectivity in a changing world, and to inform conservation and management of species and ecosystems.

Spatial Analysis in Field Primatology

Applying GIS at Varying Scales

Edited by

FRANCINE L. DOLINS
University of Michigan-Dearborn

CHRISTOPHER A. SHAFFER
Grand Valley State University

LEILA M. PORTER
Northern Illinois University

JENA R. HICKEY
International Gorilla Conservation Programme

NATHAN P. NIBBELINK
University of Georgia

CAMBRIDGE
UNIVERSITY PRESS

CAMBRIDGE
UNIVERSITY PRESS

University Printing House, Cambridge CB2 8BS, United Kingdom

One Liberty Plaza, 20th Floor, New York, NY 10006, USA

477 Williamstown Road, Port Melbourne, VIC 3207, Australia

314–321, 3rd Floor, Plot 3, Splendor Forum, Jasola District Centre, New Delhi – 110025, India

79 Anson Road, #06–04/06, Singapore 079906

Cambridge University Press is part of the University of Cambridge.

It furthers the University's mission by disseminating knowledge in the pursuit of
education, learning, and research at the highest international levels of excellence.

www.cambridge.org
Information on this title: www.cambridge.org/9781107062306
DOI: 10.1017/9781107449824

© Cambridge University Press 2021

First published 2021

Printed in the United Kingdom by TJ Books Limited, Padstow Cornwall

A catalogue record for this publication is available from the British Library.

Library of Congress Cataloging-in-Publication Data
Names: Dolins, Francine L. (Francine Leigh), 1964– editor.
Title: Spatial analysis in field primatology : applying GIS at varying scales / edited by Francine L. Dolins,
   University of Michigan, Dearborn, Christopher A. Shaffer, Grand Valley State University, Michigan,
   Leila M. Porter, Northern Illinois University, Jena R. Hickey, Nathan P. Nibbelink, University of Georgia.
Description: Cambridge, United Kingdom ; New York : Cambridge University Press, 2020. | Includes index.
Identifiers: LCCN 2019037315 (print) | LCCN 2019037316 (ebook) | ISBN 9781107062306 (hardback) |
   ISBN 9781107694309 (paperback) | ISBN 9781107449824 (epub)
Subjects: LCSH: Primatology–Geographic information systems. | Global Positioning System.
Classification: LCC QL737.P9 S688 2020 (print) | LCC QL737.P9 (ebook) | DDC 599.804526/64–dc23
LC record available at https://lccn.loc.gov/2019037315
LC ebook record available at https://lccn.loc.gov/2019037316

ISBN 978-1-107-06230-6 Hardback
ISBN 978-1-107-69430-9 Paperback

Additional resources for this publication at www.cambridge.org/9781107062306.

Francine L. Dolins, Ph.D.
Francine would like to dedicate this book to Alison Jolly, mentor, friend, and guide to the many wondrous things about lemurs, Madagascar, and the natural world, and teaching her that the best outreach to promote science and conservation is through a thoroughly engaging story.

Christopher A. Shaffer Ph.D.
Christopher would like to dedicate this book to the late Bob Sussman, an incredible mentor and friend, without whom he would have never observed wild bearded sakis or set foot in the Guyanese rainforest.

Leila M. Porter, Ph.D.
Leila would like to thank Sean and Liam Farrell for their continuous support.

Jena R. Hickey, Ph.D.
Jena dedicates this book to L'Équipe de Georgie, the field team who worked tirelessly by her side as they searched for bonobo nests deep in the heart of Congo.

Nathan P. Nibbelink, Ph.D.
Nate would like to dedicate this book to his graduate students, past as present, who have collectively made him a better scientist and human being.

Contents

Color plates can be found between pages 242 and 243.

Contributors

Kyler Abernathy
National Geographic Remote Imaging Team

Simone D. Ban
Department of Biosciences, Félix Houphouët Boigny University, Abidjan, Côte d'Ivoire

Lydia Beaudrot
Department of BioSciences, Program in Ecology & Evolutionary Biology, Rice University, Houston, USA

Adam O. Bebko
Psychology Department, York University, Toronto, Canada
Department of Anthropology, University of Notre Dame, Notre Dame, USA

Mary E. Blair
Center for Biodiversity and Conservation, American Museum of Natural History, New York, USA

Christopher Boesch
Department of Primatology, Max Planck Institute for Evolutionary Anthropology, Leipzig, Germany

Sarah A. Boyle
Department of Biology and Environmental Studies and Sciences Program, Rhodes College, Memphis, USA

Kenneth L. Chiou
Department of Psychology, University of Washington, Seattle, USA
Nathan Shock Center of Excellence in the Basic Biology of Aging, University of Washington, Seattle, USA

Michael J. Conroy
Warnell School of Forestry and Natural Resources, University of Georgia, Athens, USA

Margaret C. Crofoot
Department for the Ecology of Animal Societies, Max Planck Institute of Animal Behavior, Konstanz, Germany

Anthony Di Fiore
Department of Anthropology, Primate Molecular Ecology and Evolution Laboratory, University of Texas at Austin, Austin, USA

Francine L. Dolins
Department of Behavioral Sciences, University of Michigan-Dearborn, Dearborn, USA

Kerry M. Dore
Department of Anthropology, Baylor University, Waco, USA

Agustín Fuentes
Department of Anthropology, Princeton University, Princeton, USA

Paul Garber
Department of Anthropology, Northern Illinois University, DeKalb, USA

Matt Grove
Evolutionary Anthropology Group, Department of Archaeology, Classics and Egyptology, University of Liverpool, Liverpool, UK

Joanna Hatt
New Mexico Department of Game and Fish, Santa Fe, USA

Jena R. Hickey
International Gorilla Conservation Programme, Musanze Field Office, Musanze, Rwanda

Allison Howard
Department of Psychology, University of Georgia, Athens, USA

Mitchell T. Irwin
Department of Anthropology, Northern Illinois University, DeKalb, USA
NGO Sadabe, Antananarivo, Madagascar

Karline R. L. Janmaat
Department of Evolutionary Population Biology, Institute for Biodiversity and Ecosystem Dynamics, University of Amsterdam, Amsterdam, The Netherlands

Lisa Jones-Engel
Department of Anthropology, University of Washington, Seattle, USA

Jason M. Kamilar
Department of Anthropology, University of Massachusetts, Amherst, USA
Graduate Program in Organismic & Evolutionary Biology, University of
Massachusetts, Amherst, USA

Amy Klegarth
Department of Anthropology, University of Notre Dame, Notre Dame, USA

Shawn M. Lehman
Department of Anthropology, University of Toronto, Toronto, Canada

Greg Marshall
National Geographic Remote Imaging Team

Eduardo M. Mattenet
Geospatial Information Independent Consultant, Alcañiz, Teruel, Spain

Roger Mundry
Department of Primatology, Max Planck Institute for Evolutionary Anthropology,
Leipzig, Germany
Department of Psychology, Max Planck Institute for Evolutionary Anthropology,
Leipzig, Germany

Nathan P. Nibbelink
Daniel B. Warnell School of Forestry and Natural Resources, University of Georgia,
Athens, USA

Leila M. Porter
Department of Anthropology, Northern Illinois University, DeKalb, USA

Jean-Luc Raharison
NGO Sadabe, Antananarivo, Madagascar

Stephen R. Ross
Lester E. Fisher Center for the Study and Conservation of Apes, Lincoln Park Zoo,
Chicago, USA

Amy L. Schreier
Department of Biology, Regis University, Denver, USA

Daniel Sewell
University of Iowa, Department of Biostatistics, Iowa City, USA

Christopher A. Shaffer
Department of Anthropology, Grand Valley State University, Allendale, USA

Marisa A. Shender
Lester E. Fisher Center for the Study and Conservation of Apes, Lincoln Park Zoo, Chicago, USA

Travis S. Steffens
Department of Sociology and Anthropology, University of Guelph, Guelph, Canada
Planet Madagascar, Guelph, Canada

Trudy R. Turner
Department of Anthropology, University of Wisconsin-Milwaukee, Milwaukee, USA

Acknowledgments

We very warmly thank our commissioning editor at Cambridge University Press, Megan Keirnan, her delightful colleague, Ilaria Tassistro, and the wonderful editorial team for their help and infinite patience, Jenny van der Meijden and Helen Prasad. We also thank our copy editor, Gary Smith, who identified errors and organized our chapters for excellence. We thank and gratefully acknowledge all of the authors who have submitted their work to create this edited volume. Finally, we thank the primates for being there, and hope that, through our efforts, we are able to keep all primate species from extinction.

Francine Dolins
Leila Porter
Jena Hickey
Nathaniel Nibbelink
Christopher Shaffer

1 Why Place Matters, and its Use in Primate Behavioral and Ecological Research

Francine L. Dolins

Introduction

Almost all behavior can be assessed spatially, paving the way for insights into both the proximate and ultimate causes of expressed behaviors. Field primatologists following their focal group or individual animal identify and record essential data about where salient behaviors occur because behaviors do not occur in random locations, but in relation to what the environment and habitat specifically affords to a primate with regard to traveling, foraging, defending a home range, finding mates, and fulfilling other basic and essential needs. Recording the "where" and also the "when" and the "what" of a traveling primate's behavior in conjunction with the biogeography of the habitat is a multilayered, dynamic problem. The spatial analysis tools, global positioning systems (GPS), and geographic information systems (GIS) analysis provide a stable and powerful means to apply cutting-edge data and analytic methods to the study of free-ranging primate behavior. In this way, primatologists can address Tinbergen's "Four Questions" of mechanism, ontogeny, adaptive value, and phylogeny underlying behaviors (Tinbergen 1963), and develop an overarching picture of their primate species' patterns of behavior, habitat use, and life histories.

Until the recent past, in research with free-ranging primates, behavioral and spatial data were collected using transects, a grid pattern imposed on the forest or landscape generated with compass coordinates to define squares, "quadrats", of often 25 or 30 m within free-ranging primate troops' homes and day ranges. Primatologists record transects and cross-points within the grid to demarcate where their subjects display specific types of behaviors (e.g., "troop fed on figs in D8"). This method was applied directly from archeological methods (i.e., probabilistic sampling strategy: Binford 1964; Drennan 1996) and expanded in scale to encompass larger tracts of forest or landscape, reflecting primates' home ranges (Hester et al. 2009). GPS, however, uses points instead of compass coordinates, and has the potential for greater accuracy. Combined with the digital power for visualization and current statistical analytic methods, GPS and GIS allow for a greater breadth of investigative questions than would have been possible just 20 years ago.

Many of the fundamental questions in primate behavioral ecology involve a spatial component. Whether the scale is a single feeding tree, a 100 ha home range, or a geographic range spanning several countries, understanding primate behavioral ecology is inherently spatial: It requires an understanding of how primates use their habitat, that is, space. The development of powerful spatial data collection and analysis tools, GPS and GIS, in the past two decades has dramatically increased our ability to ask and answer spatial questions. This book, *Spatial Analysis in Field Primatology: Applying GIS at Varying Scales*, aims to fill a gap in the methodological literature and provide field primatologists with a practical guide for conducting spatial analysis. Many primatologists are increasingly recognizing the potential for spatial analysis but are, in many cases, unaware of how to effectively apply the technology to their own research questions. In addition, while the majority of primatologists use GPS units and spatial software to map out animal locations, many struggle with commonly shared issues of applying these technologies to the study of free-ranging primates. Some excellent resources are currently available concerning the general use of GPS and GIS; however, they typically apply to other disciplines (e.g., archeology) rather than to primatology *per se*. The aim of this edited volume is as a guide to scientists working through the unique questions and issues applied to primate behavior and other free-ranging terrestrial and arboreal animals.

This edited volume grew out of a GPS/GIS workshop for primatologists held at the International Primatological Society Congress in Cancun, Mexico. The workshop itself was initiated to disseminate knowledge to primatologists about how to accurately use GPS in the field and also how to analyze those data, correcting for errors. For example, we aimed to address questions such as what is the best type of GPS unit to use, how to reduce error rate in the field, what errors might occur and under what circumstances, and whether GPS collars are more effective for some species than others. The aim was also to present and disseminate ways to more effectively analyze the GPS-generated datasets such that being able to conduct analyses taking into account the different types of errors, primatologists could creatively address research questions that were previously not accessible. The workshop was successful in showing that there was significant interest in primatological circles to better understand the use and application of GPS and GIS. This edited volume was a natural development from that workshop, with the aim of making it possible for the information to reach a wider audience.

Divided into three parts and 20 chapters, *Spatial Analysis in Field Primatology: Applying GIS at Varying Scales* addresses issues and questions related to research in field primatology. At present, no guide exists for best practices in GPS or applying GIS tools to the research questions specific to primatology or studying free-ranging animals. This volume integrates the research of a range of primatologists who have used spatial analyses to address a diverse set of research questions, and their explanations about how they have creatively applied GPS and GIS technology. In this way, this book focuses on spatial research by primatologists, for primatologists, with the objective to advance the field more rapidly. A rapid pace in research in primatology is especially expedient just now, as we face extreme uncertainty about the long-term health and longevity of populations of wild primates globally.

The three parts of this book feature research-based chapters that demonstrate how scientists apply GIS methods to address some of the fundamental research questions about group movement, spatial memory, spatial problem solving, behavior and biogeography, and conservation status in relation to nonhuman and human primate behavior. These sections are: *Part I: Global Positioning Systems for Primatologists*; *Part II: GIS Analysis in Fine-Scale Space*; and *Part III: GIS Analysis in Broad-Scale Space*.

The chapters in Part I discuss the technological advances and applications of GPS and GIS analysis. They introduce the types of spatial data and the basics of mapping, including coordinate systems, projections, and geo-referencing. The chapters offer a practical foundation on which more complex analyses found in later sections of the book are based. Although not designed as a step-by-step tutorial in GIS software, the chapters in this first section present a summary of the primary concepts relevant to any spatial analysis, particularly that of primate data.

In Chapter 2, Nibbelink and Hatt present a history of GPS and GIS technology, a discussion of what a geographic information system is and how GIS analysis is accomplished.

When using the larger datasets generated by GPS, statistical programs such as R (Chapter 5, Howard and Mundry) can correct for errors and create adjustments in relation to scale. In Chapters 3 and 4 respectively, Crofoot and then Klegarth et al. present the debates surrounding studies but also provide advice on best practices for tagging an animal using a tracking device and the ethical issues involved in using GPS collars on primates. In Chapter 6, Janmaat et al. present a field study in which they have collected very detailed GPS data on wild chimpanzee movement and food source locations, comparing their digital data to that collected using more traditional methods (compass). They present their insightful GIS analysis methods for correcting errors, using R to substantially improve the accuracy of their analyses.

In Part II, the authors of these chapters present studies investigating a number of different primate species, both arboreal and terrestrial, New and Old World monkeys, as well as apes (orangutans), and multiple types of spatial behavior, topography, and habitat. Assessing home ranges and ranging behavior are the most common applications of fine-scale spatial analyses, as described in Boyle's chapter (Chapter 7). However, fine-scale analyses can also involve assessments of biogeographical and ecological factors addressing questions that can assist in understanding spatial decision-making by individuals and groups, such as shortest or most optimal paths. Data logging involving specific types of behaviors exhibited at locations is another use for fine-scale analyses, and is represented in a number of the chapters throughout this book and in this part. In particular, for a focus on data-collection methods on primate spatial decision-making and spatial behavior at fine scales, see Chapters 9, 10, 11, and 12 by Irwin and Raharison, Bebko, Porter et al., and Schrier and Grove, respectively. Bebko's chapter (Chapter 10) focuses on orangutans' spatial knowledge of their home ranges, resources available, and route-based navigation in this arboreal species. His use of GPS and GIS and discussion of methods and analysis quintessentially display the effective way in which these spatial tools can inform important theoretical questions about species' ecological knowledge.

In Chapter 11, Porter et al. compare the foraging patterns of two fruit-eating primates living in very different habitats, western chimpanzees and Weddell's saddleback tamarins. The comparison of these primates' foraging behaviors is examined through their knowledge gain in relation to fruit availability (temporal patterns), and their use and re-use of travel routes over time, allowing the authors to calculate daily use of the home range and to determine whether exploration occurred based on distance traveled. This insightful and creative comparison highlights the usefulness of GPS data and effective GIS analyses in these types of cross-species comparisons. Also, it demonstrates how comparative studies such as these can glean important ecological and cognitive differences in relation to species and habitat differences.

Spatial scale is another theme within chapters in this part. Using GIS can address questions such as whether free-ranging primates perceptually parse parts of their home ranges into smaller-scale units, such as foraging patches, compared to units in which to travel. These types of questions are exemplified in Chapter 8 by Shaffer, as well as in Irwin and Raharison's chapter (Chapter 9). Significantly, fine scale is examined in a different way in Ross and Shender's chapter (Chapter 13), instead involving captive environments at a zoo. These authors use GPS data to assess welfare in relation to the size and complexity of enclosures. Modeling social as well as travel behavior of primates, and testing the hypotheses generated by modeling, also falls within the fine-scale type of analyses, as discussed in Chapters 12 and 14, respectively, by Schreier and Grove and by Di Fiore.

In Chapter 12, Schreier and Grove present models of foraging behavior that compare optimal search behavior with that of travel efficiency between multiple sites. Using GPS and GIS, they then evaluate the models with hamadryas baboon spatial and behavioral data, to understand the relevance of the proposed models to species' actual spatial behavior, memory, and learning capabilities. In Di Fiore's chapter, using GIS analyses, he explores the uses of agent-based modeling (ABM), which is spatially construed and allows for investigations about primates' interactions with their environment and with other individuals. The success of ABM using GIS analysis allows identification of emerging patterns from complex, dynamic natural systems through the agents' behavioral decisions.

The third and final section of the book, Part III, explores the use of GIS for large-scale, population-level research questions. The chapters in this part present details on remote sensing methods and how satellite imagery can be used to measure forest change, demonstrating the importance of GIS for informing primate conservation strategies and evaluating successful, ongoing projects. Chapters in this part also demonstrate the range and potential of GIS, for example in assessing the impact of anthropogenic disturbance on primates, including logging and hunting. In particular, Hickey's chapter (Chapter 16) examines the impact of changes in habitat quality on the fauna, caused by human encroachment, especially hunting. Steffens and Lehman's chapter (Chapter 17) presents an investigation into the effects of deforestation on lemurs' survival in a fragmented habitat. In both of these chapters, use of GPS and GIS for large-scale analysis were essential to the success of these studies and for understanding the effects of anthropogenic factors on the health, wellbeing, and consequent behavior of the primate populations.

Part III also has chapters that present details on techniques of niche modeling and habitat distribution, as in Chapter 15 by Chiou and Blair. Ecological niche models are used to produce predictive maps of species distributions; the inherently spatial nature of these niche models requires GPS data and GIS analyses. When compared with species' actual occurrences and environmental variables (e.g., food resources, climate, rainfall), these models help to establish the "ecological tolerances" that shape population distributions. However, very few studies to date have used ecological niche modeling for primate populations, although ecological niche modeling could be an essential tool in various areas, such as for conservation management and population genetics, the spread of pathogens, as well as in addressing theoretical questions about cognitive capacities of species (see Chapter 14 by Di Fiore as an example).

GPS data and GIS analyses are extremely useful in a relatively new branch of investigation in primatology – ethnoprimatology. Chapter 19, by Dore et al., presents the background and a review of the literature on the broad range of environments in which human and nonhuman primates share space and, at times, resources. The focus on how the interaction, which is inherently spatial and for which GPS and GIS are implicitly useful, affects both the human and nonhuman primates also provides insights into how the interaction informs decisions and outcomes for these two populations. For example, crop damage is a major negative interaction between nonhuman and human primates. Dore et al. present data on vervet monkeys' crop raiding in St. Kitts, using a predictive model to project the amount of crop damage. They then use GPS and GIS to measure the actual damage done, for comparison. This type of data and analysis can assist in making informed decisions about any required action for preserving crops, as well as other forms of conservation.

An understanding of the biogeography and macroecology of extant and extinct primate populations and species helps to inform conservation strategies. In their chapter (Chapter 18), Kamilar and Beaudrot discuss methods for applying GPS and GIS to evaluate species' locales and regional distributions. Use of spatial data applied to range maps can be made more accurate and can assist in estimating home ranges and a group's actual habitat use, subtracting terrain not suitable or usable by the primates. This provides more precise spatial data for predictive ecological modeling across space as well as over time. Species distributions analyzed together with environmental datasets (on resource abundance, rainfall, temperature, etc.) provides a method for understanding and predicting dynamics in primate population changes and their presence or absence, geographically. Depending on the types of research questions to be investigated, these types of data can be applied in ecological niche modeling and phylogenetic comparative methods.

As a guide to understanding certain spatial terms throughout this volume, I introduce a brief caveat about the chapter authors' use of "fine-scale" and "broad-scale space," and "small-scale" and "large-scale space," respectively. These terms are used interchangeably as concepts, which appears to depend on the author's background training and experience, and the influence of other scientists (e.g., Poucet 1993; Garber & Dolins 2010; Hickey et al. 2012; Noser & Byrne 2013; Garber & Dolins 2014; Garber & Porter 2014).

In summary, the objectives of this edited volume are to encourage and disseminate best practices in GPS data collection and GIS analyses of primate behavior, for the purposes of theoretical investigations and practical applications, and to improve conservation monitoring and outcomes for primate populations. The geographical range of field sites and species, different habitats, types of landscape, and terrain presented in these 20 chapters, and the creative application of GIS in research questions, should hopefully contribute to readers' application of "best practices" to their own studies. The ultimate aim is to assist the primatology community in its quest to better understand our primate subjects and species, their relationship to their environments, and the cognitive capacities they have for understanding and navigating their own social and physical environments, and to aid primate conservation in this changing and uncertain world.

References

Binford, L. 1964. A consideration of archaeological research design. *American Antiquity* **29**: 425–441.

Drennan, R. D. 1996. *Statistics for Archaeologists: A Common Sense Approach*. Plenum Press, New York.

Garber, P. A. and Dolins, F. L. 2010. Examining spatial cognitive strategies in small-scale and large-scale space in tamarin monkeys. In *Spatial Cognition, Spatial Perception: Mapping the Self and Space*. F. L. Dolins and R. W. Mitchell (Eds.). Cambridge University Press, Cambridge.

Garber, P. A. and Dolins, F. L. 2014. Primate spatial strategies and cognition: introduction to the special issue. *American Journal of Primatology*. DOI: 10.1002/ajp.22257.

Garber, P. A. and Porter, L. M. 2014. Navigating in small-scale space: the role of landmarks and resource monitoring in understanding saddleback tamarin travel. *American Journal of Primatology* **76**: 447–459. DOI: 10.1002/ajp.22196.

Hester, T. R., Shafer, H. J., and Feder, K. L. 2009. *Field Methods in Archeology*, 7th edition. Routledge, New York.

Hickey, J. R., Carroll, J. P., and Nibbelink, N. P. 2012. Applying landscape metrics to characterize potential habitat of bonobos (*Pan paniscus*) in the Maringa-Lopori-Wamba Landscape, Democratic Republic of Congo. *International Journal of Primatology* **33**: 381–400.

Noser, R. and Byrne, R. W. 2014. Change point analysis of travel routes reveals novel insights into foraging strategies and cognitive maps of wild baboons. *American Journal of Primatology* **76**: 399–409. DOI: 10.1002/ajp.22181.

Poucet, B. 1993. Spatial cognitive maps in animals: new hypotheses on their structure and neural mechanisms. *Psychological Review* **100**(2): 163–182.

Tinbergen, N. 1963. On aims and methods of ethology. *Zeitschrift für Tierpsychologie* **20**: 410–433.

Part I

GPS for Primatologists

Introduction

Leila M. Porter

Over the last two decades, technological advances in GPS (global positioning devices) and GIS (global information systems) have allowed primatologists to dramatically increase the quantity of spatial location data they can gather in the field, and the complexity of the analyses they can perform on these data. Prior to 15 years ago, GPS units did not function well in remote locations and/or under dense foliage, thus they were useless for most field primatologists. In contrast, in the last 15 years, technological advances have made GPS devices functional across the globe and in most environments, allowing field researchers to collect detailed spatial data using this technology. In addition, increased access to and development of GIS software has allowed primatologists around the world to perform complex analyses of these data.

A review of original research articles published at five-year intervals in the *American Journal of Primatology* over the last 20 years documents the dramatic changes that have occurred in primatological spatial research. The methods and analyses authors used to examine primate home ranges are shown in Table 1. Researchers who published articles in 1995 were unable to use GPS technology. As a result, these authors plotted the spatial position of their study subjects on paper maps, cut grid trails in order to document the animals' movements, and used tapes and footsteps to measure the distances the animals traveled. These techniques were both time consuming and produced limited datasets. In 2000 and 2005, GPS technology was still not practical in the field; however, authors began to use spatial analysis software to analyze the data they collected through traditional mapping methods. In subsequent years (2010 and 2015), researchers were able to shift from traditional mapping techniques to GPS devices in order to plot the spatial locations of their study animals. Furthermore, beginning in 2010, all authors who published in the journal used GIS software and multiple types of analyses to analyze the spatial location data. Thus, it is clear that 1995–2015 was a transformative period in spatial research.

As a result of these changes, primatologists can now use GPS and GIS technologies to test hypotheses on a wide variety of topics, including primate biogeography, foraging patterns, habitat use, dispersal patterns, and cognitive abilities (see Parts II and III). However, the introduction of these new technologies into field work also creates new ethical, methodological, and analytical dilemmas. In this part, the authors introduce some of the problems associated with the collection of spatial data, and offer guidelines and techniques for solving some issues, and case studies for evaluating the costs and benefits of these new technologies.

Table 1 Changes in the methods and analyses used for calculating primate home ranges over time (*American Journal of Primatology* 1995, 2000, 2005, 2010 and 2015)

Year	Methods for collecting spatial data	Software used for calculating home range[a]	Citations
1995	Location plotted on trail map, topographic map, or quadrat trail system, distances measured by tape or footsteps	None	Chiarello 1995; Corbin & Schmid 1995; de la Torre et al. 1995; Hill & Agetsuma 1995; Zhang 1995
2000	Location plotted on trail map or topographic map, distances measured by tape	ArcGIS, CAD-All plan 500, or distances measured by tape	Di Bitetti et al. 2000; Fashing & Cords 2000; Schwab 2000; Sprague 2000; Wong & Ni 2000
2005	Location plotted on trail map, distances measured by tape	Ranges V (kernel)	Bayart & Simmen 2005; Pimley et al. 2005; Yepez et al. 2005
2010	GPS	ArcGIS (MCP, kernel)	Phoonjampa et al. 2010; Spehar et al. 2010
2015	GPS	ArcGIS (hull polygons, kernel), QGIS (kernel), BRB/MKDE (kernel)	Asensio et al. 2015; Brockmeyer et al. 2015; Fan et al. 2015; Kurihara & Hanya 2015; José-Dominguez et al. 2015; Van Belle 2015

[a] for a review of home range analyses, see Chapter 8.

Part I Summary

Part I begins with an introduction to the spatial technologies used to collect, analyze, and display spatial information (Chapter 2 by Nibbelink and Hatt). Chapter 2 provides important information for researchers to consider when choosing a GPS unit and an overview of the types of GIS analyses they can conduct once they have gathered spatial data with those units. The chapter provides a clear introduction to spatial technology for the novice and a valuable refresher for experienced researchers on the sources of error which are introduced during the collection and analysis of spatial data and how those errors can be reduced and managed. In Chapter 3, Crofoot reviews the use of animal tracking tags in biological research. Given the risks associated with capturing and tagging an animal, the chapter provides valuable guidance as to how to assess the costs and benefits of using a tracking device. For example, animal tagging may allow researchers to gather data on the behavior and ecology of cryptic species that would be impossible using traditional observational methods. Thus, for cryptic species, the costs of fitting an animal with a tracking tag may be offset by the benefits gained. She further reviews the factors that can affect the accuracy and fix success rate of a GPS device (e.g., vegetation structure), and some ways in which GPS accuracy can be improved. Furthermore, Crofoot offers useful advice as to how to compromise between tag weight, study duration, and sampling. Additionally, she reviews how GPS tags can be integrated with sensors to explore a whole new set of research questions involving how an animal's internal state, such as its body temperature, may influence its movement patterns.

In Chapter 4, Klegarth and colleagues discuss the ethical and methodological issues researchers must consider when placing GPS collars on study animals. For five years, this research team has used GPS and camera units affixed to collars to study human–macaque interactions in Singapore and Gibraltar. Thus, these authors use their own experience to explore the difficulties of trapping animals, as well as the rewards of using these technologies. In particular, they emphasize the need to consider the full range of potential harms a research program may incur on animals before the program begins. Thus, the authors recommend using short-term pilot studies to experiment with collar design, and to evaluate device failure rates in order to redesign or terminate a research project as needed. Primatologists have become increasingly concerned with reducing their impact on study animals (Riley et al. 2014), and this chapter offers useful recommendations as to how this can be accomplished. This chapter therefore is a timely guide for researchers to use for designing new research protocols.

In addition to considering how and when to use GPS devices to study primates, researchers must also consider how they will analyze location data once they are gathered. In Chapter 5, Howard and Mundry discuss the benefits of using the open-source statistics program R (R Core Team 2013) to process and analyze GPS and other geographic data. Howard and Mundry note that most primatologists collect massive amounts of GPS data during field studies (e.g., tracks of daily path lengths, waypoints of feeding sites), leading to the daunting challenge of organizing, converting, and analyzing this information. Howard and Mundry demonstrate how R can be used to read a variety of commonly collected geographical data (GPS files, maps, and shapefiles), and how to automate tasks that primatologists frequently perform on these types of data. For example, Howard and Mundry demonstrate how to save tracks and waypoints as separate files, how to convert between GPS and UTM coordinates, and how to determine the shape and size of an area such as a home range. Howard and Mundry demonstrate that by using R, researchers may perform more efficient analyses than is possible using other software.

Finally, Janmaat and colleagues explore the inaccuracies of GPS data and how these errors can influence the conclusions researchers make from their data (Chapter 6). Janmaat and colleagues collected GPS data as part of a field study on *Pan troglodytes* in the Côte d'Ivoire. They explain how they determined the accuracy of a GPS unit at their field site, including comparing data at a stationary point over time, and checking GPS-based measurements with those done with measuring tapes. They demonstrate that the GPS data they collected often had a wide margin of error. As a result, they developed a set of software programs in R, which can be used to clean and smooth track data. Given the proliferation of studies that use location data collected by GPS units, this chapter offers important analytical measures that can be used to improve the quality of the data used for analyses.

Our intention in this section is to provide readers with a set of issues to consider before beginning a project that involves the collection and analysis of spatial data. Readers may use this section to consider the types of data collection appropriate for a study animal, and new ways of improving data collection and analysis.

References

Asensio, N., Schaffner, C. M., and Aureli, F. 2015. Quality and overlap of individual core areas are related to group tenure in female spider monkeys. *American Journal of Primatology* **77**(7): 777–785.

Bayart, F. and Simmen, B. 2005. Demography, range use, and behavior in black lemurs (*Eule mur macaco macaco*) at Ampasikely, northwest Madagascar. *American Journal of Primatology* **67**(3): 299–312.

Brockmeyer, T., Kappeler, P. M., Willaume, E., et al. 2015. Social organization and space use of a wild mandrill (*Mandrillus sphinx*) group. *American Journal of Primatology* **77**(10): 1036–1048.

Chiarello, A. G. 1995. Role of loud calls in brown howlers, *Alouatta fusca*. *American Journal of Primatology* **36**(3): 213–222.

Corbin, G. D. and Schmid, J. 1995. Insect secretions determine habitat use patterns by a female lesser mouse lemur (*Microcebus murinus*). *American Journal of Primatology* **37**(4): 317–324.

de la Torre, S., Campos, F., and Devries, T. 1995. Home-range and birth seasonality of *Saguinus nicricollis graelssi* in Ecuadorian Amazonia. *American Journal of Primatology* **37**(1): 39–56.

Di Bitetti, M. S., Vidal, E. M. L., Baldovino, M. C., and Benesovsky, V. 2000. Sleeping site preferences in tufted capuchin monkeys (*Cebus apella nigritus*). *American Journal of Primatology* **50**(4): 257–274.

Fan, P. F., Garber, P., Chi, M., et al. 2015. High dietary diversity supports large group size in Indo-Chinese gray langurs in Wuliangshan, Yunnan, China. *American Journal of Primatology* **77**(5): 479–491.

Fashing, P. J. and Cords, M. 2000. Diurnal primate densities and biomass in the Kakamega Forest: an evaluation of census methods and a comparison with other forests. *American Journal of Primatology* **50**(2): 139–152.

Hill, D. A. and Agetsuma, N. 1995. Supra-annual variation in the influence of *Myrica rubra* fruit on the behavior of a troop of Japanese macaques in Yakushima. *American Journal of Primatology* **35**(3): 241–250.

José-Dominguez, J. M., Savini, T., and Asensio, N. 2015. Ranging and site fidelity in northern pigtailed macaques (*Macaca leonina*) over different temporal scales. *American Journal of Primatology* **77**(8): 841–853.

Kurihara, Y. and Hanya, G. 2015. Comparison of feeding behavior between two different-sized groups of Japanese macaques (*Macaca fuscata yakui*). *American Journal of Primatology* **77**(9): 986–1000.

Phoonjampa, R., Koenig, A., Borries, C., Gale, G. A., and Savini, T. 2010. Selection of sleeping trees in pileated gibbons (*Hylobates pileatus*). *American Journal of Primatology* **72**(7): 617–625.

Pimley, E. R., Bearder, S. K., and Dixson, A. F. 2005. Social organization of the Milne-Edward's potto. *American Journal of Primatology* **66**(4): 317–330.

R Core Team 2013. *R: A Language and Environment for Statistical Computing*. R Foundation for Statistical Computing, Vienna.

Riley, E. P., MacKinnon, K. C., Fernandez-Duque, E., Setchell, J. M., and Garber, P. A. 2014. Code of best practices for field primatology. Resource document, International Primatological Society & American Society of Primatologists.

Schwab, D. 2000. A preliminary study of spatial distribution and mating system of pygmy mouse lemurs (*Microcebus* cf *myoxinus*). *American Journal of Primatology* **51**(1): 41–60.

Spehar, S. N., Link, A., and Di Fiore, A. 2010. Male and female range use in a group of white-bellied spider monkeys (*Ateles belzebuth*) in Yasuni National Park, Ecuador. *American Journal of Primatology* **72**(2): 129–141.

Sprague, D. S. 2000. Topographic effects on spatial data at a Japanese macaque study site. *American Journal of Primatology* **52**(3): 143–147.

Van Belle, S. 2015. Female participation in collective group defense in black howler monkeys (*Alouatta pigra*). *American Journal of Primatology* **77**(6): 595–604.

Wong, C. L. and Ni, I. H. 2000. Population dynamics of the feral macaques in the Kowloon Hills of Hong Kong. *American Journal of Primatology* **50**(1): 53–66.

Yepez, P., de la Torre, S., and Snowdon, C. T. 2005. Interpopulation differences in exudate feeding of pygmy marmosets in Ecuadorian Amazonia. *American Journal of Primatology* **66**(2): 145–158.

Zhang, S. Y. 1995. Sleeping habits of brown capuchin monkeys (*Cebus apella*) in French Guiana. *American Journal of Primatology* **36**(4): 327–335.

2 Fundamentals of GIS and GPS

Nathan P. Nibbelink and Joanna Hatt

Introduction

All data are spatial. Try to think of a piece of data that is *not* spatial, and we bet with a little more thought, you could come up with a spatial characteristic of those data! Perhaps the name of a historic figure? That name has a provenance ... it was given in a particular place, and the person may have lived in one or more places, and moved about the surface of the Earth according to some pattern. And the name itself (if written) has a length measured in number of letters, and it has shapes and sizes that affect its perception by others, much like the spatial elements of a map communicate something to its audience.

Of course the spatial information associated with any given object may not always be relevant to the question at hand, but *it is* always present. Particularly in the study of animal behavior and species–environment relationships, spatial information is often of central importance. How large was the area explored? How far did the animal travel? Was the movement straight or convoluted? Particularly in primatology, which integrates the behavior, physiology, and ecology of primates, spatial information is often implicit (if not explicit) in many important research questions. This will be evident in this book as the authors address primate travel routes (Janmaat et al., Chapter 6; Bebko, Chapter 10; Porter et al., Chapter 11), resource dispersion (Shaffer, Chapter 8), niche/habitat modeling (Chiou and Blair, Chapter 15; Hickey and Conroy, Chapter 16), biogeography (Steffens and Lehman, Chapter 17) and more. Spatial concepts, data, and tools are central to addressing each of these important questions in primate behavior and conservation.

What Is Spatial Information?

When I (Nibbelink) ask this question on the first day of class, I get many answers. But, in 12 years of teaching, I do not think I have had a wrong answer (while some are better than others). As we have established, almost everything has *some* spatial component that can be discovered with little difficulty. Asking the class this question accomplishes at least two things. First, it effectively demonstrates how much spatial information permeates our thoughts, actions, and professional areas of study (my students represent more than five natural science disciplines, and many more areas of specialization). Second, it allows me to highlight answers representing the *most common* types of spatial information, and set the stage for the remainder of the course, which Joanna Hatt and I will do now.

One of the most common answers to "What is spatial information?" is "Maps." It is true that while the spatial information we are interested in is often a physical feature of a landscape (or something moving through it), maps, or mapped features, are the way that we *represent* those features. We italicize *represent* to make a key point that we will revisit later in this chapter, that as a *representation* of a feature, a map feature is nothing more than a *model* of that feature. We know that models are subject to assumptions, errors, and biases of which we must be aware in order to properly interpret our data, and we will deal with that abstraction explicitly later in this chapter as we discuss types of spatial data and dealing with uncertainty. For now, most basically, spatial information is any information (data) that can be spatially referenced to a set of known coordinate locations in the real, geographical world (Goodchild 1992).

What Are Spatial Technologies?

Spatial technologies include tools we can use to collect, analyze, and display spatial (geographic) information (Clarke 1986). The most common types of spatial technology we are concerned with in environmental sciences are geographic information systems (GIS), global positioning systems (GPS), remote sensing, and photogrammetry. While remote sensing and photogrammetry are critical fields that contribute significantly to certain types of primate research, they are not a major focus of the work in this book, and thus are not discussed here. In this chapter, we give a brief introduction to both GIS and GPS. Our goal is such that a reader who is unfamiliar with the technology and its application can appreciate some of the definitions, data types, common methods, sources of error, and other challenges in dealing with GIS and GPS technologies and data in their application to primate research. For those interested in more depth on any of the fundamental GIS topics we discuss here, these authors have found the following GIS texts of considerable value for instruction and reference: Bolstad (2016), Burrough et al. (2015), Madden (2009), and Longley et al. (2005). For anyone getting involved in spatial analysis in primate research, we also strongly recommend familiarity with concepts and tools from landscape ecology (Turner et al. 2001). For spatial analysis in environmental research, the list could be extensive, but in terms of population dynamics and interspecific interactions, the volume edited by Tilman and Kareiva (2001) is particularly useful. Finally, a fundamental understanding of spatial scaling (e.g., Wiens 1989) is invaluable for effectively applying spatial tools and analyses with species–environment research.

Global Positioning Systems (GPS)

We start this chapter with a brief overview of GPS, as it is becoming the primary source for information about the locations of individual animals, groups, and sometimes other features of the environment. The aim of this section is to illustrate in a basic way how GPS systems work, what can introduce error into GPS data, and how to select appropriate GPS devices, collection techniques, and account for error. Other chapters in this book elaborate on how error can be accounted for in several specific cases, such as in the study of primate movement routes using both handheld GPS units (Janmaat et al., Chapter 6) and GPS tags/collars (Crofoot, Chapter 3).

A GPS consists of three essential parts: the *satellite segment*, the *control segment*, and the *user segment* (Hofmann-Wellenhof et al. 2001). The system we are most familiar with in the USA is the Navstar (NAVigation Satellite Timing And Ranging) system developed by the US Department of Defense. Navstar's satellite segment consists of 24 satellites that have been placed in six orbital planes at about 17,500 km from Earth. This results in 4–10 satellites that are theoretically visible from any unobstructed location on the Earth's surface at any given time. The USA also typically flies more satellites than the minimum in order to fill slots during outages or decommissioning. Most contemporary GPS chips can also take advantage of the Russian GLONASS (GLObal NAvigation Satellite System) satellites. While for many years GLONASS struggled with funding and other issues, in 2013 the system reached minimum global coverage at 24 satellites, and was fully operational as of December 2015. A third major system is the Galileo system being created by the European Union and the European Space Agency. Like the US and Russian systems, the Galileo project aims to have 24 fully operational satellites and six spares. As of July 2019, 26 satellites are in orbit and the system is expected to be completed by 2020. This system plans to have both a free (low-precision) service and a subscription (high-precision) service available.

The *control segment* of a satellite system consists of ground stations that observe, maintain, and monitor the satellites. The Navstar system is maintained by five control stations in Hawaii, Colorado Springs, Ascension Island, Diego Garcia Atoll, and Kwajalein Atoll.

Finally, the *user segment* consists of users on the Earth's surface (you!) who are operating a GPS receiver. That receiver can be anything from a smartphone to a $10,000+ survey-grade system. Of course these systems vary in their accuracy. In ideal conditions (unobstructed sky and good satellite configuration), vendors typically report accuracies of ±3 m or more for consumer-grade receivers. Mapping-grade receivers, depending on quality, can vary from 0.5 to 5 m (reported accuracy), and survey grade receivers can achieve ±1 cm. The main difference is not the GPS chip itself, but mostly in the size and gain of the antenna and the post-processing capabilities including differential correction (discussed below). For a majority of wildlife applications, either recreational-grade or mapping-grade receivers are sufficient because errors that arise from other sources (land-cover maps, animal movements, etc.) often exceed that of the anticipated mean GPS error. Thus, the user's needs, and ultimately the spatial scale at which the user must draw conclusions about observed patterns, will determine what type of GPS receiver is adequate for a particular application.

GPS Positions and Sources of Error

To collect quality GPS data, it is useful to understand some of the sources of error that can arise in the process. Let us begin with how a GPS position is calculated by software

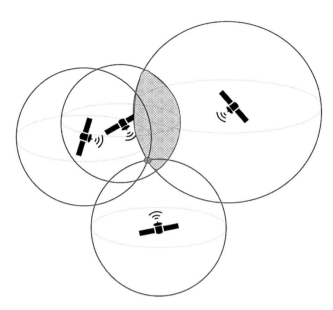

Figure 2.1 Illustration of how a receiver can calculate a single position on Earth via the intersection of spheres from four satellites based on satellite positions and their ranges. Adapted from Bolstad (2016).

in the GPS unit. Satellites generate a code known as the course acquisition code (C/A code; see Hofmann-Wellenhof et al. 2001). Because the GPS unit is calibrated to the same time as the satellite time and also produces the same C/A code, the unit can calculate the time delay between the code generated internally versus that received by the satellite. Since the signal travels at approximately the speed of light (299,792,458 m/s), the distance from each satellite can be calculated. If the receiver knows its distance from at least four satellites (or three plus an accurate elevation measurement), it can theoretically calculate a single position on the surface of the Earth (Figure 2.1).

However, there are some factors that can introduce uncertainty into this estimate, including atmospheric effects on signal travel time and signal distortion from electrical interference. Small errors in satellite positions or satellite clocks can also introduce errors into calculated positions, because in those cases the information the GPS unit has for satellite position and time (ephemeris data) are not correct. This error can be addressed with differential correction (discussed below). Multipath error arises when signals bounce off other surfaces before they are detected by the receiver. And, finally, the geometric configuration of satellites can also affect accuracy (positional dilution of precision, or PDOP). This effect arises because errors in the distance between each satellite and the receiver have a larger effect on positional accuracy when the satellites are clustered (high PDOP) versus when they are spread out (low PDOP) (Figure 2.2). This is similar to the effect of triangulation error in traditional VHF radio-tracking studies. Most GPS units will record (or display) a PDOP value to give an indication of the current precision. Generally, a PDOP of 4 or less is considered excellent, a PDOP of

Table 2.1 Sources of error affecting calculation of GPS positions

Error source	Observed error (meters)
Ionosphere	1–5
Troposphere	≤1
Ephemeris data	2.1
Satellite clock drift	1–2
Multipath	≤1
Receiver error (bias and noise)	≤0.3
Total	~10

Source: summarized from Parkinson (1996).

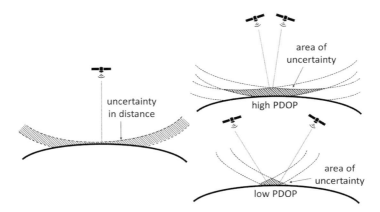

Figure 2.2 Geometric configuration of satellites affecting the position dilution of precision (PDOP), or a measure of 3D position accuracy. Adapted from Bolstad (2016).

5–8 is acceptable, and a PDOP greater than 8 is poor. Some GPS receivers allow you to set a PDOP mask. This will prevent the receiver from storing or reporting positions that are generated from poor satellite configurations. Table 2.1 shows estimated errors from a variety of these sources.

Minimizing Error

There are a few basic recommendations that can be made to reduce error in GPS data. Here, we briefly describe them in no particular order:

- *Select appropriate GPS unit*. Select a GPS unit (or GPS tracking device) that has better antenna gain, more advanced signal processing, and/or built-in mechanisms for controlling for multipath, PDOP, and other sources of error. Trade-offs generally include increased cost, size, and battery drain. External antennas or antenna–receiver combination units can boost the signal and reduce multipath error, but they can consume more battery, and can be unwieldy to carry, particularly through dense forest areas (often a backpack with the antenna sticking out the top). Thus, a smaller handheld unit may be preferable as long as the error can be managed.

• *Post-process your data using differential correction.* Differential correction can account for known errors (e.g., satellite position, clock, atmospheric) by correcting your calculated position based on known offsets recorded at nearby base stations. This is rarely needed for wildlife applications with current levels of accuracy available in commercially available technology, but can improve positional accuracy significantly in some cases.

• *Collect point-averaged positions.* When recording a GPS position, it is ideal to let the receiver collect data in a fixed position for an extended period of time and record a point-average position. For stationary objects like study area boundaries or fixed objects within the study area, this is ideally done with multiple visits, which can help account for differences in satellite configurations. Control over this feature is limited in GPS collar applications, but can be applied when following animals and recording points along the animals' paths. Obvious limitations include the inability to remain in one spot when tracking animals. Generally 30–60 seconds is sufficient to improve your positional estimate, depending on topographic and forest cover conditions. Nonetheless, some primates are fast, and waiting even briefly may cause the researcher to lose the animal. In these cases, the researcher must simply be aware of the amount of error in the data and use intelligent methods for cleaning and analyzing the data. For some excellent guidance, see Janmaat et al. (Chapter 6).

Many GPS devices today combine satellite data with additional information such as previous position, velocity, and direction to improve the accuracy of any given new location (Tao & Li 2007). Indeed, most smart phones can combine sensor information from satellites, cell towers, and Wi-Fi, in addition to data on position, speed, and direction, to deliver a highly accurate position (at times, when all of these data are available). However, with most commercial GPS receivers it is difficult to find information in the advertising or manuals that will reveal what type of algorithm might be used to calculate positions under various conditions. Thus, it is left to the user/ researcher community and demonstrated effectiveness to make decisions about devices that will work well for our particular applications.

Geographic Information Systems

While this chapter (and book) is largely focused on the *systems* (tools and approaches) that allow us to apply GIS to behavioral and environmental research, GIS is also used as an acronym for *geographic information science* (GIScience) (Goodchild 1992). GIScience has been generally described as a form of information science that studies the "fundamental issues arising from geographic information," such as "the creation, handling, storage, and use" of that information (Longley et al. 2005), although exactly what constitutes GIScience has been debated (Mark 2003). A research agenda for

GIScience was proposed by Goodchild in his foundational article in 1992, and that agenda has been evolving since that time, largely led by the University Consortium for Geographic Information Science (UCGIS). It is important to recognize that doing the science on fundamental issues arising from geographic information requires not only questions about how we depict spatial information, but also how that depiction impacts what we can learn about environmental features. Thus, GIScience also involves applied research in disciplines that use the tools of GIS. While at times recognizing what constitutes GIScience and what constitutes the use of GIS tools to do *other* science becomes fuzzy, GIScience and the use of GIS constantly inform and advance each other. Hereafter we will largely discuss the fundamentals of GIS and basic GIS tools and approaches that facilitate our research. A GIS, then, is "an organized collection of computer hardware, software, geographic data, and personnel designed to efficiently capture, store, update, manipulate, analyze, and display all forms of geographically referenced information" (ESRI 1990).

A GIS is composed not only of the software that we often think of when we hear the term GIS, but also of hardware, data, methodologies, and perhaps most importantly, people. Each of these components of a GIS typically require some specialized characteristics, which together contribute both to the ability to deal with spatial information and to the efficiency with which it is done. Although many GIS software solutions can run on nearly any computer these days, *hardware* requirements of a serious GIS analyst often include the latest (and fastest) processors, large amounts of RAM and disk storage, high-end graphics cards, and large, high-resolution monitors. The *people* in a GIS generally are trained professionals who understand the data and methodologies, and can apply GIS tools to one or more fields of study, however, one might argue that *people* could be expanded to include all those who interact with a GIS, as the technology is becoming more seamlessly integrated into daily activities in several professions, and even in citizen science and educational applications. Particularly now that nearly every citizen has a relatively powerful GPS device in their hands at all times (a smartphone), integrated with basic GIS software (e.g., Google Maps, Yelp, Zillow), people are often reliant on these systems for day-to-day activities. They also have an unprecedented ability (opportunity) to be involved in citizen science through custom smartphone apps such as IveGot1, iNaturalist, and numerous others.

GIS Software

GIS software is widely available at varying levels of cost and flexibility. For a concise review of several of the major options and their benefits and limitations, see Bolstad (2016: 15–20). In academic practice, two of the most common GIS software solutions at this time are the ArcGIS suite (ESRI, Redlands, CA) and R (R Core Team 2016), which has several spatial packages available, some specifically focused on animal movement and home range analysis, which may be of particular interest in primate research. The reader will find several useful tools in R presented in this volume (Howard and Mundry, Chapter 5; Janmaat et al., Chapter 6). There are also several open-source packages, the most common ones probably being QGIS (www.qgis.org) and GRASS (grass.osgeo.org), which have both been available for a long time and have an extensive user community. In this chapter, as we introduce basic GIS concepts and tools we attempt to remain largely software-independent, but will draw occasionally on ArcGIS for specific examples when needed as it is the most commonly used GIS software in academic instruction and research, and is responsible for our familiarity with much of the terminology we use to describe features and functions in a GIS.

A (Very) Brief History of GIS

The first computerized GIS system is most often credited to Roger Tomlinson (Chang 2012), who worked with an aerial survey company in Canada in the 1960s when he first conceptualized combining land-use mapping with emerging computational technology. This eventually led to his leadership in the development of the Canada Geographic Information System. Of course, as with other technologies, there was similar work going on in other places. Longley et al. (2001) discuss early European influences, and the conceptual framework of GIS grounded in land management systems and cartography can be traced back to the Romans (Burrough et al. 2015). Modern GIS systems were given a big push with the creation of ArcView (ESRI, Redlands, CA) around 1991, which represented a big step forward in user-friendly GIS. Also contributing to awareness of the technology and growth of its use in research was the explosion of GPS and associated real-time mapping applications around the year 2000 (e.g., online mapping software and automobile navigation systems). This came shortly after the US government's removal of selective availability from the GPS satellite signals, announced by President Clinton in May 2000. Selective availability imposed an intentional degradation of GPS signals for security reasons, but there was a growing realization that the utility for research, civilian applications, and public safety likely exceeded any security concerns. For a more detailed early history of GIS, see Coppock and Rhind (1991). Longley et al. (2005) have an excellent table summarizing major events shaping GIS from 1957 to 2004. But now let's turn to some of the nuts and bolts of GIS – the data.

GIS Data Types

The two major classes of spatial data are vector data and raster data. Vector data consist of points, lines, and polygons – shapes (generally referred to as *features*) that can be constructed from coordinate pairs and (excepting points) the lines that connect them. While each GIS software system may represent features slightly differently, vector data all require the following information. GIS software generally "sees" point features as lists of *coordinate pairs* with individual identifiers (IDs), and can plot them in a Cartesian coordinate plane for the user to view on a flat screen (Figure 2.3a). Similarly, line features consist of a list of coordinate pairs, but also include a second list of *arcs*, the lines that connect each point. This list specifies the arc ID, and a "from" and "to"

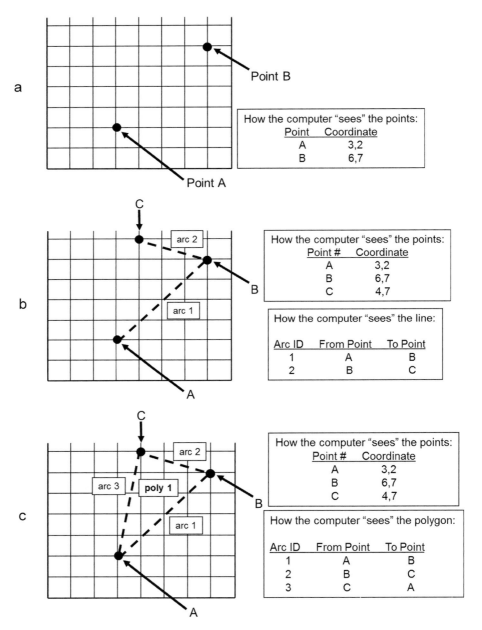

Figure 2.3 Graphical illustration of three types of vector data and how they are represented in GIS: (a) point features and corresponding coordinate information, (b) line features and coordinates, (c) polygon features and coordinates.

point ID, which references those points to connect with arcs from the primary list of coordinate pairs (Figure 2.3b). Finally, polygons can be represented in the same way as lines, but with the added requirement that the final arc connects the final point back to the first point, creating a closed feature, or polygon (Figure 2.3c).

Most vector data formats today support a *topological data structure*. Topology, most simply, refers to the way parts of an object are connected or organized. In a GIS, a vector dataset with a topological data structure shares nodes and boundaries with neighboring features. These shared boundaries have several advantages, including joint feature editing (e.g., moving/correcting a forest plot edge will also automatically correct the edge of the adjacent non-forest polygons). In addition, by sharing adjacent features, the GIS can inherently "know" some of the spatial relationships among features in the map, which economizes spatial queries (see below) and other operations. The "older" data model was referred to as a *spaghetti data structure*, where all features had their own boundaries, even if they were adjacent. This commonly led to problems with "sliver polygons" and other nearly undetectable but frustrating errors in GIS vector datasets. Excellent descriptions of topological data structures are contained in the texts by Longley et al. (2005) and Burrough et al. (2015).

Attribute tables are another very important and useful feature of vector data. Each individual feature has a dedicated record (row) in the attribute table, which can hold a large number of attributes (or fields) associated with the unique feature, such as an individual identifier (Object ID in ArcGIS), geometric properties like length or area, and any other descriptive or numeric value of interest to the user (stream name, water depth, etc.). When studying primates in the field, it might be useful to mark the location of a food tree, for example, and add several useful attributes such as species, fruit ripeness, height, time spent in the tree, etc. These attributes tied to spatially referenced locations will facilitate many useful analyses. Attributes provide the user with the ability to query a large dataset based on a set of criteria, or summarize information for a specific area (see the section Vector Analyses). An exception to the rule that each feature has a record in the attribute table is called a multipart feature. This vector format option was introduced by ESRI in ArcGIS for cases in which the individual features are not important to the user, but all areas composed of a particular landscape feature are important to maintain. For example, if you do not need to isolate or calculate anything based on individual forest patches, but only care whether something is forest or not, you may be able to get away with a multipart feature for a polygon layer of forest cover.

Vector data are very intuitive data types for elements that we typically conceptualize as discrete on the landscape, such as animal locations (points), streams (lines), and land cover types (polygons). Vector data can also be used to represent features that vary continuously across the landscape, such as the elevation contours on a USGS topographic map, or the temperature contours on a weather map that you might see in the newspaper or on television. However, for GIS analysis and/or a more appealing (smooth) map for continuous data, a raster data structure is often preferred.

Raster data (sometimes referred to as field data or grid data) generally consist of a matrix of rows and columns containing a numeric value representing the data of interest (e.g., elevation or land cover type; Figure 2.4). In its most basic form, raster data can be presented using an ASCII (text) data file consisting of a list of values in rows and columns, ordered from top left to bottom right, with each value representing a *cell* of a particular size on the landscape. An ASCII raster file also contains *header* information occupying the top few rows of the text file, consisting of basic information that the GIS software needs in order to depict the data correctly on the map. For example, the ESRI

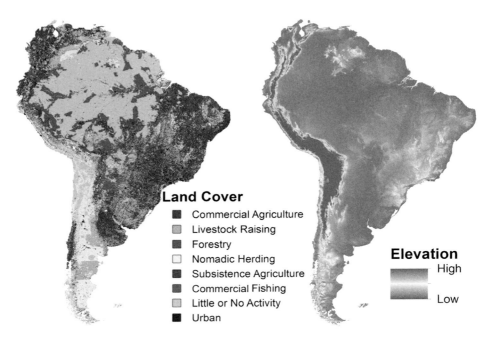

Figure 2.4 Two raster datasets from South America representing gradients of elevation, and land cover types, respectively. Elevation data are a 30 arc-second DEM (US Geological Survey 1996). Land cover data are clipped from a global mosaic of MODIS-derived land cover classification (Channan et al. 2014). (A black and white version of this figure will appear in some formats. For the color version, please refer to the plate section.)

ASCII raster format requires a header that specifies the number of columns and rows, the bounding coordinates, cell size, and the value for cells with no data (Table 2.2).

ASCII raster formats can be useful for transferring data between different software programs and occasionally for inspecting data for certain characteristics or problems in a text editor, but generally ASCII rasters are cumbersome to view in an editor due to their size, and are not efficient for advanced data processing in GIS software. Thus, most GIS systems use some type of binary data format for raster storage and processing. The ESRI GRID format is a proprietary binary raster format commonly used in ArcGIS, but also readable by a handful of other software programs. For digital aerial photographs, satellite images, and other image data, which are also considered raster data, it is common to use one of many available image formats including jpeg, tiff, img, and more.

An important difference between vector data and raster data is the attributes. Vector data can contain a large number of attributes for each feature, whereas raster data are essentially featureless, and each cell contains only one value, which must be numeric. While integer value raster data can be used to represent categorical elements such as land cover types, the patches are not treated discretely with separate identifiers as in vector data. All cells in a raster that represent a single type (e.g., forest) are coded the same, whether they are adjacent or not. However, this is far less of a limitation than it used to be, as several software programs, and the raster data types they use, can

Table 2.2 A description of the parameters used for the header information in an ESRI ASCII raster dataset

Parameter	Description	Requirements
NCOLS	Number of cell columns	Integer > 0
NROWS	Number of cell rows	Integer > 0
XLLCENTER or XLLCORNER	X coordinate of the origin (by center or lower left corner of the cell)	Match with Y coordinate type
YLLCENTER or YLLCORNER	Y coordinate of the origin (by center or lower left corner of the cell)	Match with X coordinate type
CELLSIZE	Cell size (single number to represent both height and width of cell)	> 0
NODATA_VALUE	Values to represent areas with no data (e.g., outside the study area)	Optional (default is –9999)

Source: adapted from ArcMap 10.4 online help (http://desktop.arcgis.com/en/arcmap/latest/manage-data/raster-and-images/esri-ascii-raster-format.htm).

overcome this limitation when an understanding of individual features is needed but raster processing is desired over vector due to speed, scale, and/or data availability issues. For example, ArcGIS can use regions or zones to specify specific areas over which to calculate results, and Fragstats (McGarigal et al. 2012) can be used to calculate several landscape characteristics at several organizational scales, from the individual patch level to the class level, and for the entire landscape. The concept of attributes does apply, however, to most current raster data structures via the use of a value attribute table (VAT). In contrast to vector data, this table contains information unique only to classes (e.g., all cells belonging to a land cover type, regardless of location). The VAT in an ArcGIS GRID contains a unique class ID (OID), the raster value (VALUE), and a count of cells (COUNT) by default. Other fields, such as a text description of the class, and other class characteristics can be added to this table as desired. Continuous raster data containing floating point values (digits beyond the decimal) cannot contain a VAT, as there would theoretically be an infinite number of classes.

So what data type should be used for a given application? It is our opinion that many problems can be addressed using either or both data types, and that the availability of data and the preferences and skills of the user may influence the decision. Nonetheless, there are some general strengths and weaknesses with each type, and some recommendations for analysis that can be made. A major advantage of vector data is individual feature recognition – something that can be important for many types of problems. Point data for animal locations are nearly always dealt with in vector format, even if certain analyses occasionally use background raster transformations when necessary. Whether it be animals or any other features (roads, parcels of land, water bodies, etc.), it can be useful or even necessary to be able to access unique attribute information in order to answer certain important questions. For example, to identify all protected areas that intersect suitable bonobo habitat in the Democratic Republic of Congo (DRC), it might be most effective to use a polygon layer of suitable habitat and a polygon layer of the protected areas to perform a spatial query to generate a list of the affected protected areas. Likewise, when working with elevation data, temperature data, or other data that change continuously across the landscape, raster data are the preferred format. Also when working with large areas, complex analyses can be slow or impossible on typical desktop computers when vector data contain very large numbers of features. Raster data, due to their relatively simple format, can be substantially faster. However, a major consideration when using raster data is the selection of a raster resolution, or cell size. The finer the resolution and larger the study area, the longer it can take to draw on the display, or to run a complex analysis. Thus, there may be a trade-off between the desired resolution and the capabilities of the computer (or patience of the user). Ideally, the selection of a raster resolution will be a function of the species and the research question being asked. For example, 0.86 km^2 resolution was adequate for characterizing elevation zones used by lemurs (Steffens and Lehman, Chapter 17), but finer resolution is needed to address behavior studies in captive settings covering much smaller areas (Ross and Shender, Chapter 13).

Additional advantages of each type may become apparent as we discuss vector and raster analyses, and in further reading of what authors in this book chose to use for their particular problems. Indeed, the application and its commonly accepted methodologies may drive the relative use of vector and raster data types more than anything else.

Converting Between Vector and Raster

Often there is a need to convert data layers from vector to raster format, or vice versa, in order to complete an analysis. This process should be done very carefully in order to avoid the introduction of critical errors into the dataset. When going from vector to raster, you are taking points, lines, and polygons, and converting them to raster cells of a particular size. Along with this comes several assumptions and potentially some loss of accuracy. First and foremost, it represents a simplification of the features, in which the choice of raster cell size has a big influence on whether those features still look the same or are severely distorted. In addition, spatial error can be introduced (Figure 2.5). When converting point data from vector to raster, the exact position of each raster cell will be determined by the extent of the data and the cell size. Converted cells may not be centered on the original point – thus, if back-conversion occurs, the new points will be in a shifted spatial position whose error depends on the cell size and the original position (Figure 2.5a). When converting line data from vector to raster, each cell the original line "touches" becomes part of the raster line. When back-converting, the lines are simplified (Figure 2.5b). ArcGIS has a "generalize lines" option that will smooth the features somewhat, but they will still be subject to positional errors and distortion relative to the cell size and the position of the original features. When converting polygon data from vector to raster, a general rule is that 50 percent of the cell must be covered for the software to assign the vector value to an output raster cell. Simple back-conversion leads to a simplified object, again dependent on the cell size used (Figure 2.5c).

An additional concern with polygon data is that features smaller than the pixel resolution can sometimes be lost. I (Nibbelink) once worked for many hours to figure out why the number of ponds in a hydrologic data layer did not add up to the total

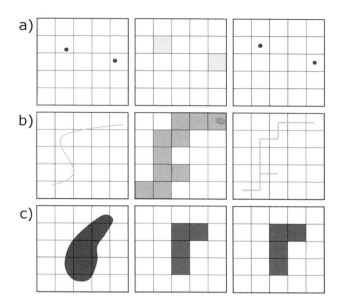

Figure 2.5 Potential errors when converting data from vector (left) to raster (center) and back to vector (right) for: (a) point features, (b) line features and (c) polygon features.

number expected. Finally, in back-tracing the steps, I realized that a conversion from vector to raster at 100-meter resolution resulted in the loss of many small farm ponds whose surface area was less than 50% of the raster cell area. Errors like these can be minimized (at least temporarily) by increasing resolution (reducing cell size). However, as raster resolution increases, so do file size (storage requirements) and processing time for raster operations. Thus, working with a much higher resolution is not always possible. The user simply needs to be aware of the potential for error when doing these conversions, and to make sure that the methods used, cell size chosen, and interpretation of output are appropriate for the specific application. For example, if you were building a niche model (Chiou and Blair, Chapter 15) for primates, and water features were thought to be important, losing the occurrence of a few small ponds in a dry area used by small primates may bias an analysis far more than losing a few small ponds in a wet area used by gorillas. There will always be multiple potential sources of error in GIS data and analyses (see the section Uncertainty in Spatial Information), and those errors are important to recognize and document.

Coordinate Systems (Datums and Projections)

How do we go from a three-dimensional irregular surface (the Earth) to a flat (two-dimensional) map? As we have seen, spatial information for both vector features (points, lines, polygons) and raster data require X and Y coordinate values. In order to make any spatial data useful (and show up on the map in the right place), these coordinates must be in reference to a particular Cartesian *coordinate system*, which is

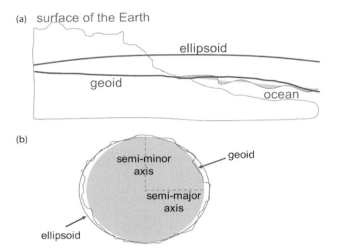

Figure 2.6 Different models depicting the shape of the Earth. (a) The geoid is the hypothetical shape of the Earth as defined by equigravitational force, without wind and tidal influence. (b) The ellipsoid is primarily defined by the semi-major and semi-minor axes.

(1) overlaid on a portion of the Earth's surface that has been *projected* onto a flat map; and (2) referenced to a three-dimensional reference surface specified by a *datum*.

Let's begin with the 3D reference surface specified by the datum. Our 3D reference surface must do three things: it must approximate the shape and size of the Earth with a geometric object of known dimensions; it must have a reference coordinate system; and that coordinate system must be tied to a set of known locations on the surface of the Earth (the datum) in order that each time we reference a particular location, it always references the same point on the surface of the Earth. Although the shape of the Earth has been historically contested to be that of an oyster shell (Babylonians *c.* 3000 BC), a flat disk (Homer, Hesiod *c.* 1100–700 BC), and finally a spherical body (Pythagoras *c.* 570–495 BC), it is now understood to be an ellipsoidal object with irregularities referred to as a geoid. The geoid is the hypothetical shape defined by the Earth's equigravitational force, or the shape that the oceans would take according to gravity and rotation alone, without the influence of wind and tides. This shape is best approximated by an ellipsoid (Figure 2.6), which is defined generally by the semi-major and semi-minor axes, or the radii from the Earth's center of mass to the equator (semi-major axis) and the north pole (semi-minor axis).

A geodetic datum is a reference system defined by an ellipsoid and a set of reference points (known locations on the Earth's surface and their contact points with the ellipsoid). Many different datums have been developed throughout history, and they can differ from one another by more than 100 meters (Table 2.3).

Thus, the important thing to remember is those data must be referenced to a known datum! This is often a problem when using historic data, or data acquired from another source without the datum information included. This leaves the analyst to guess the

Table 2.3 Datums and appropriate regions where they are used

Name	Applicable region
Arc 1950 or 1960	South/Central Africa (1950: Botswana, Lesotho, Malawi, Swaziland, Zaire, Zambia, Zimbabwe; 1960: Kenya, Tanzania)
Indian Datum	Bangladesh, India, Nepal, Thailand, Vietnam
North American Datum of 1983	Canada, Caribbean, Central America, Mexico, USA
South American Datum of 1969	South America
World Geodetic System 1984	Entire globe

correct datum definition based on clues such as date of collection or visual overlap with other data with known provenance, and if it remains arbitrary (as is often the case with animal locations) it may subject the data and subsequent analysis to errors of 10 to more than 100 meters (on top of the already existing error from GPS accuracy and other sources).

The *geographic* coordinate system, using the familiar units of latitude and longitude, is the coordinate system we use in conjunction with the ellipsoid to reference objects on the unprojected Earth. In fact, data that use the geographic coordinate system are described as unprojected, and are limited to units of latitude and longitude, which are measured in degrees of the angles described by arcs connecting the center of the ellipsoid to the equator and the prime meridian, and to the point of interest on the Earth's surface. However, for day-to-day use of spatial data, we need to calculate properties like distance, area, and direction, which cannot be done directly with latitude/ longitude coordinate values, particularly because the measure of one degree longitude is not the same at different latitudes. Thus, we need *map projections.*

Map projections are developed by projecting a portion of the Earth's surface onto a flat map, allowing us to assign coordinate values in useful units (e.g., meters). There are a few basic ways to accomplish a map projection, and each can be visualized by thinking about a light bulb placed in the center of the Earth and placing a sheet of paper of a particular shape onto the Earth in a particular place. The reflection of Earth on the paper, then unrolled onto a flat surface, represents the projection (Figure 2.7). For each projection type, where it touches the Earth's surface represents the point or line of least distortion, and moving away from that line increases the distortion of shape, direction, area, and distance. Thus, projecting a round object onto a flat surface cannot be done without distortion.

It has been said that "all maps lie flat and all flat maps lie." This statement is often attributed to Mark Monmonier. While we could not find a reference for that exact quotation, the concept is dealt with extensively in Monmonier (1996). This is said because no matter which projection method you use, it is impossible to get away from at least some distortion of one or more of the following properties: distance, direction, area, and shape. Thus, a selection of an appropriate projection for your data will often depend on what characteristic you need to preserve the most for a particular application (Table 2.4).

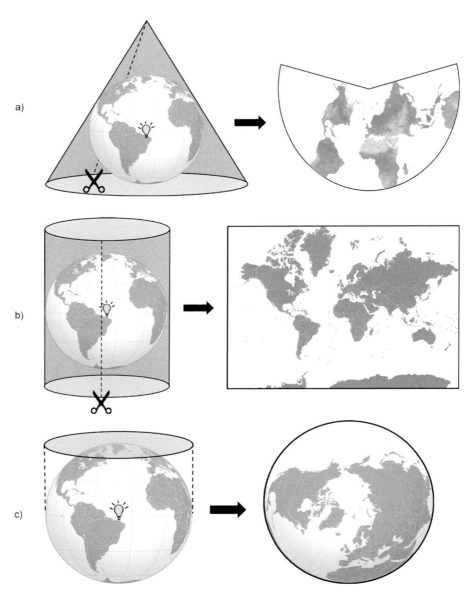

Figure 2.7 Examples of a few different map projections and how they were created: (a) conical projection (e.g., Lambert conformal conic), (b) cylindrical projection (e.g., Mercator), and (c) azimuthal projection (e.g., orthographic). Underlying globe images sourced from Wikimedia Commons. Panel (a–c) left, globe image from Eddo: Location_of_Cape_Verde_in_the_ globe.svg; Derivative work: Luan fala! [CC BY-SA 3.0 (http://creativecommons.org/licenses/by-sa/3.0)], via Wikimedia Commons; https://commons.wikimedia.org/wiki/File%3AGlobe_centered_ in_the_Atlantic_Ocean_(green_and_grey_globe_scheme).svg; panel a and c, right, (panel a modified) from Rob984 (derived from File:Worldmap northern.svg) [CC BY-SA 4.0 (http:// creativecommons.org/licenses/by-sa/4.0)], via Wikimedia Commons https://commons.wikimedia .org/wiki/File%3ANorth_Pole_(orthographic_projection).svg; panel b right, from Geordie Bosanko [CC BY-SA 3.0 (http://creativecommons.org/licenses/by-sa/3.0)], via Wikimedia Commons https:// commons.wikimedia.org/wiki/File%3AMercator_Projection.svg.

Table 2.4 List of terms used to characterize projections and what is preserved

Characteristic of projection	What is preserved?
Azimuthal	Direction
Conformal	Shape
Equidistant	Distance
Equivalent	Area

For example, a map used in a geography text for children aimed at learning states or countries would likely need to be constructed with a conformal projection, such that the shapes were readily identifiable, as they would be on a globe. Alternatively, when needing to calculate animal home ranges, an equivalent projection that minimizes distortion of area is most important.

Once you have selected a map projection, a Cartesian coordinate plane must be applied, using standardized units (e.g., meters), a specific origin (defined using a central meridian and/or standard parallel), and sometimes a false easting and/or false northing, which places the coordinate plane all in positive space so there are no negative coordinates within the region to which the coordinate system applies. The ability to center a projection on a specific area of the globe, and define the coordinate space, releases us from some of the dangers imposed by distortion. Coordinate systems (composed of a projection, a defined coordinate plane, and assigned to a specific datum) are designed to minimize distortion for the area in which they are applied. Thus, one of the most important decisions at the outset of a GIS project is the choice of a projection and coordinate system (often chosen together) whose parameters are appropriate for the geographic location and size of the study area. This is often simplified by easy-to-interpret menu-driven options in GIS software, but the user will quickly discover that what the software can do for you is insufficient to deal with the coordinate system problems you are likely to encounter throughout a project (or career!). GIS analysts must have a thorough understanding of projections, coordinate systems, and how to troubleshoot common problems.

Although there have been many types of coordinate systems developed for different purposes and locations in the world, and certain localities often have their own preferences, there is one coordinate system that has likely become the most commonly used in the world for the spatial scale of many environmental research studies, and that is the Universal Transverse Mercator (UTM) coordinate system. The UTM coordinate system uses a Transverse Mercator projection (as in its name), which is a cylindrical projection in which the axis of the cylinder cuts through the equator. This design conveniently allows UTM to have many zones, each defined by a central meridian and a false easting, where Y coordinates (northings) are measured in meters from the equator (for north zones), or 10,000,000 minus meters from the equator for south zones (south zones have a "false northing" set to 10,000,000 meters). There are a total of 60 zones around the globe, and one can be assured (at least for most natural resources work) that the distortion of shape, direction, distance, and area is minimal within a particular zone. If your study area of interest is substantially larger than a single UTM zone, such as a large state/province, continent, or the globe, then you will need to apply an alternative coordinate system that preserves the features important to your application.

Just to emphasize some practicalities regarding the importance of a basic understanding of projections, coordinate systems, and datums in working with GIS data, we offer the following thoughts. (1) Data are sometimes acquired from sources with unknown coordinate systems and/or datums applied, and the analyst often has to figure out how to get it to show up correctly on the map. (2) Data that are defined incorrectly can cause significant errors in analysis. (3) Any given project should strive to use the same coordinate system and datum for *all* data in the project to avoid confusion and analysis errors. A thorough and effective treatment of map projections and coordinate systems can be found in Bolstad (2016: ch. 3). In addition, the ESRI Support site and numerous other university educator websites offer extensive guidance on the subject.

Map Scale

Scale is a critical part of any GIS data collection, acquisition, or analysis. Here we give a brief introduction to scale, but discuss further implications below in the section on uncertainty. Contrary to how scale is often described, where large scale generally refers to a big area and small scale refers to a small area, map scale is in some ways exactly the opposite. Map scale is expressed as a unitless ratio of map units to real-world units. For example, a map in which 1 cm on the map equals 10,000 cm on the ground would have a map scale of 1:10,000, and a map in which 1 cm on the map equals 50,000 cm on the ground would have a map scale of 1:50,000. The 1:10,000 scale map is a larger scale than the 1:50,000 scale map (1/10,000 = 0.0001 versus 1/50,000 = 0.00002). If printed at the same size, the larger scale (1:10,000) map covers a much smaller area of the Earth's surface, typically in more detail (zoomed in), whereas the smaller scale (1:50,000) map would cover a larger area with less detail (zoomed out). Usefully, landscape ecologists have encouraged a definition of scale that avoids the terms large and small, and instead breaks scale into two parts, grain and extent, which speaks to both the resolution and land area, and encourages researchers to be explicit about each element (Turner et al. 2001).

You may be wondering what map scale has to do with GIS maps, because in GIS you can zoom in and out and view spatial data at any scale. This is correct; however, source data are always collected or created at a particular scale, which has important implications for positional error in any data, and thus any analysis or interpretation that might be derived from those data. The selection of an appropriate scale of data when addressing any spatial problem is *critical* for appropriate analysis and interpretation.

The determination of scale for a particular analysis will be driven by several factors. Perhaps most importantly, the question of interest, and the scale at which the phenomena must be understood in order to answer the question. Secondly, the scale (extent and resolution) of available data may impose constraints on the scale of analysis, and therefore affect your ability to answer specific types of questions. For example, if we wanted to understand social dynamics within a group of primates, which might require positional accuracy on the order of 1 m, or even centimeters, the use of GPS collars whose accuracy is rarely better than 5 m, is not going to work. However, for a group of chimpanzees, 5 m accuracy may be sufficient to capture some types of social interactions. Likewise, in any spatial analysis, it is important to match the scale of the question with the scale of available data and other technology.

We have said nothing so far about temporal scale, but time should not be forgotten! The temporal coherence of available data with the phenomena of interest is also critical in order to draw appropriate conclusions. Abuses of this are common due to limitations of available data. For example, a land cover map from 1992 should probably not be used to model the habitat suitability for a species that was observed in 2015. While this seems obvious, these are real trade-offs faced by GIS analysts daily, and sometimes compromises (with careful interpretations) need to be made.

GIS Analyses

There are huge libraries of spatial analysis tools and approaches (many available in common packages such as ArcGIS and R), which have been developed and used for all types of spatial questions. And for those questions that demand new approaches, it seems there is always a savvy analyst to create a new method based on the fundamental approaches available. Indeed, thinking about what the problem requires in a spatial context, rather than what tools are available, often leads to a creative solution that is more appropriate for the data. Realistically, however, it is a cycle, where the more you learn about what GIS can do, the more you have a body of knowledge to think about new problems in creative ways.

Fundamentally, GIS analyses can be broken down into two major classes, *vector analyses* and *raster analyses*, and it's no coincidence that these analyses generally fall in line with the major data types. While certain analyses were generally developed to work with one or the other data type, GIS software is sometimes capable of using either data type as input for an analysis that is traditionally done with only one type. For example, in ArcGIS if you would like to summarize the areas of different land cover types within one or more zones (such as animal home ranges), the land cover layer and the home range layer can be in either vector or raster format. However, it should be noted that this flexibility is highly software- and tool-specific, and it is often prudent to understand how the software is treating the data. In the above example, ArcGIS converts input vector layers to raster (if needed) to conduct the analysis in the raster environment, and a processing cell size should be chosen to match your desired data resolution.

Vector Analyses

Analyses with vector data can generally be classified into two types, *queries* and *topological operations*. Queries can be further classified into *attribute queries* and *spatial queries*. Both types of queries use expressions using relational operators

($>$, $<$, =, $\geq$, $\leq$) and/or Boolean operators (AND, OR, NOR) to select subsets of the data to match a particular condition.

For example, if we had a polygon layer of a study area consisting of several land cover types, but wanted to perform some operation with only one of the types, let's say "Forest," we could perform an attribute query using the following expression: TYPE = 'Forest'. The exact syntax used in queries is critically important to the operation being carried out successfully, but can vary among software programs. This particular example is from ArcGIS, where TYPE is a column heading in the attribute table and 'Forest' (which is a label in a *text field*) requires single quotes as shown, and all words are case-sensitive. If this had been a numeric query such as HECTARES > 50, no quotation marks are needed. One can likewise use Boolean operators (e.g., AND, OR) to select data. For example, TYPE = 'Forest' OR TYPE = 'Shrub' selects all polygons that contain both types of land cover. Novice users often get confused with the use of AND in these situations, because in their mind if they want to select both types, selecting Forest AND Shrub seems to make sense. But, in a strict query setting, the operation TYPE = 'Forest' AND TYPE = 'Shrub' yields no results because no record can meet both criteria. Therefore, AND is used when selecting based on more than one attribute, for example, TYPE = 'Forest' AND HECTARES > 50. This type of selection might be used, for example, to identify and map bonobo nesting habitat (if research indicated that they were likely to build nests in forest habitat patches larger than 50 ha). In most projects, queries are most useful for data exploration and visualization, whereas modeling habitat for a species might be left to more advanced applications (see Chiou and Blair, Chapter 15); nonetheless, queries are fundamental to understanding features and manipulating data in GIS.

While attribute queries are powerful in that they can take advantage of any tabular information you may have about your data, spatial queries can really harness the power of GIS by assessing spatial relationships across data layers. Spatial queries are designed to select elements from one or more data layers based on a spatial relationship to features in another layer. For example, if we had vector layers of roads and bonobo nest sites, we could test the hypothesis that bonobo nests are more likely to occur far from roads (likely due to human activity; Hickey et al. 2013). Our query could essentially say "select all bonobo nests within 500 meters of roads," and if our hypothesis is correct there would be very few sites selected relative to the total number in the dataset. We could also perform potentially useful queries such as selecting primate locations within a specified distance of a food source, or selecting all movement paths that intersect rivers. As with attribute queries, syntax for spatial queries varies among software programs, and can take many forms depending on the particular question that needs to be answered. Both spatial and attribute queries can be powerful tools to explore your data and understand relationships among elements within and across data layers. However, sometimes queries are insufficient, and study objectives will require combining, transforming, or making new data layers, based on existing layers.

Operations that alter and/or combine vector features are referred to as topological operations (Table 2.5). For example, with a clip operation, which is perhaps the simplest conceptually, you use one layer (e.g., a study area boundary) to clip "excess" data from a thematic layer of interest (e.g., land cover type) and the output produces a land cover

Table 2.5 Common topological operations in GIS

Operation	Function
Buffer	Create polygons around other point, line, or polygon features using a specified distance
Clip	Clip the features of an input layer with those of another layer (e.g., study area boundary)
Erase	Remove the features of an input layer with those of another layer
Intersect	Combine the features and attributes of two input layers for areas where both layers overlap
Union	Combine the features and attributes of two input layers for all areas, regardless of overlap

layer that is neatly clipped to the study area of interest. Several boundaries are altered in the process.

Keeping track of what happens with attributes is also critical to data integrity when performing topological operations, especially in the common case in which several transformations are necessary to reach a final product. Often an attribute field should be added to indicate a new feature that results from the operation. For example, when performing a buffer operation, it is sometimes useful to add a field to the output (buffer) layer to code those polygons as buffers. This can be done by adding an informative field title (e.g., STRM_BUF100m = stream buffered by 100 meters), and calculating the field values to 1, to indicate that those polygons are contained within the stream buffer. In future operations, where additional polygons are added or changed, those features whose STRM_BUF100m value = 1 can always be identified when needed for data summaries, reports, or statistics. It is also critical to be sure that attributes that depend on spatial information are updated as needed when arc lengths or polygon boundaries change. While ArcGIS Geodatabase feature classes will always keep the length, perimeter, and area fields up to date when using these operations, the older ArcView shapefile format will not. Therefore, with geometry fields when using shapefiles, and with other user-calculated fields in any data format, those that depend on the shapes themselves must be recalculated to reflect the new topology.

Raster Analyses

Working with raster data always seems a little less intuitive than working with vector data for beginner students of GIS. This is very likely because vector data are typically used to represent familiar objects in a familiar way (e.g., point for animal location, line for road). Even though rasters are simpler in construct, using them to represent landscape features seems to be more difficult to grasp. However, once the analyst becomes familiar with raster data and the associated tools, it becomes increasingly intuitive. Working with raster data is very powerful, and often preferred (even necessary) for many applications. Here we describe some of the most common raster functions and provide examples from this volume where possible.

Table 2.6 An example of a reclassification table indicating both old values and new values that might be used to turn many classes into fewer classes for a particular analysis

Original land cover type (old values)	Reclassified land cover (new values)
1 = Tropical lowland forest	1 = Forest
2 = Tropical montane forest	1
3 = Mangrove forest	1
4 = Agriculture	0 = Non-forest
5 = Water	0

Basic Raster Functions

Basic raster analysis tools can generally be classified as single-layer analyses (one input) and multilayer analyses (more than one input). We start with a list of the most common single-layer analyses, with some examples of their utility.

Reclassify. Likely the most common operation needed for raster data is a reclassify tool. If, for example, you have a multi-class land cover raster dataset but only need to differentiate forest and non-forest, you could reclassify the original layer into fewer classes by specifying a new code for each of the original codes (Table 2.6). This layer could then be used, for example, to calculate forest fragmentation or patch size (Shaffer, Chapter 8) and test whether it affects primate occupancy (Hickey and Conroy, Chapter 16).

Distance. Distance tools can be used to assign a distance to every cell in a region of interest from a feature of interest. For example, one might be interested in defining a riparian zone along rivers. A raster tool that calculated the Euclidean distance from the rivers to every cell in the area of interest would be an alternative to the equivalent vector-data buffer tool. To create the actual buffer area, you would use a reclassify tool to generate a new raster that was coded "0" for areas greater than your desired zone width, and "1" for areas with the specified distance. Hickey and Conroy (Chapter 16) calculated raster datasets representing distance from fire points and distance from rivers, and these variables were both found to influence bonobo nest presence in the DRC, likely due to their avoidance of human presence (potential threat) associated with fires and rivers.

Neighborhood analysis (moving window). A neighborhood analysis is one that summarizes a landscape gradient within a specified window around each focal cell, such that the output raster layer has cells that represent the region around them, and not just the values within them. For example, if you were interested in the percentage forest cover surrounding animal locations, you could take a forest/non-forest raster (coded 0, 1) and run a neighborhood mean ("focal mean" in ArcGIS). The window size would be chosen to match a relevant characteristic of the animal, such as home range, daily movements, and/or an estimate of the GPS error. Because the mean of ones and zeros within a zone represents the proportion of ones to the total number of cells, the result is a percentage forest raster in which each cell (equal in size to the original raster resolution) contains the value for percentage forest in the specified neighborhood.

Density. A density function can calculate the magnitude per unit area of a particular feature (e.g., points per unit area or length per unit area of lines) for all cells in the area of interest, based on a window around the focal cell (density can be thought of as a special case of the neighborhood analysis). An example might be if you were interested in the impact of trails on occupancy by a particular species, you could calculate trail density (m/m^2 or other units as appropriate), and your selection of a window size might be the home range or other area of interest, as indicated above. Density measures are often more desirable than a simple "distance to feature" because it accounts for the totality of the impact of particular features on the landscape, rather than just the closest one.

Topographic analyses. There is a suite of operations that are particularly useful for characterizing physical landscapes that are mostly based on elevation (or, more specifically, the digital elevation model or DEM). Calculating characteristics like slope and aspect, finding the line of steepest descent (where water would flow), and creating a line of sight (or whole viewshed) are just a few of the characteristics that can be calculated from a DEM. Particularly things like slope and aspect, which often drive biological and ecological relationships in particular locations, can be critical to some applications for animal behavior and ecology. For example, high-slope areas (steep ridges) were avoided by bearded capuchin monkeys in Brazil during regular travel between resource sites (Howard et al. 2015).

Here we list a few of the most commonly applied multilayer raster functions (those requiring multiple input layers).

Map algebra. Combining two or more raster layers using any number of mathematical functions or conditional statements is termed map algebra. The raster calculator tool in ArcGIS is commonly used to accomplish this. The ability to combine information across layers (equivalent to the overlays in vector analysis), is a powerful feature of raster analysis, in particular because it is often much faster to perform these calculations over large areas with many layers than would be practical (or even feasible) in a vector analysis environment. The most common analysis that depends on map algebra is the "suitability analysis," in which the user creates several layers that potentially drive suitability for a desired outcome (e.g., siting a home or, more relevantly, suitable habitat for a species). For example, if sufficient information is known about the limits of a species' use of particular habitat gradients such as elevation, percentage forested habitat, and distance from rivers, you could use reclassify functions to create individual raster layers of suitable/unsuitable (0, 1) for each gradient. Then, using map algebra, you can multiply the layers together; because $1 \times 1 \times 1 = 1$, and anything $\times 0 = 0$, your output will be a map of the areas that are suitable based on all of the input criteria (Figure 2.8). While species may not be so binary in their actual habitat selection, this type of analysis often represents a first cut, or a way to determine outside range limits. Species distribution modeling (SDM), also referred to as niche modeling, is a natural extension of the suitability analysis, and often involves using actual observational data along with statistical algorithms to map relative suitability of habitat. A more extensive treatment of this topic is given by Chiou and Blair (Chapter 15).

Zonal summaries. Another commonly used raster analysis approach involves zonal summaries. As the name indicates, this analysis consists of performing a statistical summary of a gradient of interest based on zones (which in ArcGIS can be specified using either a coded raster or vector polygons). For example, it might be valuable to summarize the mean and standard deviation of elevation and forest cover within animal

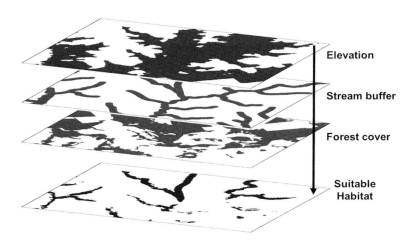

Figure 2.8 Graphical representation of using map algebra to conduct a habitat suitability analysis for a species based on environmental covariates.

home ranges. For this analysis, the layer of interest would be a digital elevation model and the zones would be specified by the calculated animal home range polygons. See Boyle (Chapter 7) for approaches to home range analysis.

Masking (raster clip). Creating a raster mask, which is equivalent to the vector "clip" operation, involves specifying a layer of interest and a "mask" layer that defines the area of interest to be extracted from the layer of interest. The most practical use of this operation is probably in taking several data layers you may need for a project and masking them all to the extent of a desired study area boundary.

Cartographic Models

While several more advanced spatial modeling approaches are covered in this book, we want to briefly cover *cartographic modeling* here, which we believe can help set the stage for any spatial project or analysis, whether simple or complex (Bolstad 2016: ch. 13). A cartographic model, most basically, is a model that uses spatial operations to solve problems. Cartographic models are often depicted using flow diagrams indicating inputs and outputs through a series of operations, resulting in a final output representing the solution to a particular problem. Figure 2.9 shows a diagram for a cartographic model depicting the suitability analysis in Figure 2.8. Cartographic models can also help a user think through a project from start to finish, and thus help determine what data are needed, what software and/or expertise are needed, and help to anticipate potential challenges. Perhaps most useful is the fact that the user must first specify a desired outcome in order to trace back to the data and methods needed to achieve the outcome. The definition of the desired outcome often requires careful specification of the research question or objective. Thus, the use of the flow diagram can be applied more broadly to research questions in general, but certainly to more complex spatial models. For some,

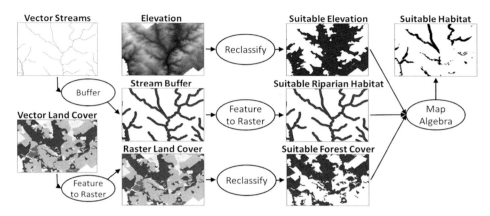

Figure 2.9 Conceptual flow diagram (cartographic model) for suitability analysis shown in Figure 2.8.

the cartographic model becomes an indispensable part of project planning and design. In both undergraduate and graduate courses, I (Nibbelink) require students to use cartographic flow diagrams to design solutions to various hypothetical questions, labs, and/or semester projects.

Uncertainty in Spatial Information

No introduction to GIS would be complete without some explicit attention to the concept of uncertainty, where uncertainty arises in GIS data and analyses, and how to deal with it. For a thoughtful and more thorough treatment of uncertainty in GIS, see Longley et al. (2001), from which we borrow a useful framework to present the concept here. Longley et al. (2001) describe uncertainty in GIS as an all-encompassing term to describe the problems that arise from the process of modeling the real world. They further argue that uncertainty can be characterized and reduced, but not eliminated. In this chapter, we have already described GPS error, and shown how vector to raster conversions can introduce errors into spatial analyses. Those represent just a few of the points at which uncertainty can arise.

Uncertainty can arise in several key areas in a GIS analysis (Figure 2.10): Uncertainty 1 (U1): Conception – our imposition of certain perceptions or classifications which simplify the real world. For example, how we choose to represent objects as vector or raster features with particular units, how we classify elements that have somewhat ambiguous characteristics (e.g., assigning land cover classes such as "mixed pine/hardwood"), and how we impose fuzziness onto our data by drawing a boundary at a particular scale around a feature and treating it like a homogeneous feature that might be more heterogeneous at a fine scale. U2: Measurement – how we measure things, and our choice of scale for that measurement (or acquisition of data). For example, the sources of error in GPS data discussed earlier, and the uncertainty arising from choice of cell size for raster data. U3: Analysis – analysis choices result in additional uncertainty that

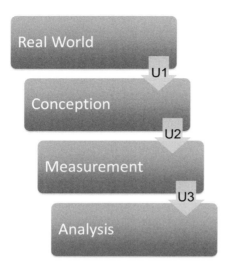

Figure 2.10 Places uncertainty can arise in GIS analysis (adapted from Longley et al. 2001).

can arise both from assumptions made when combining layers (e.g., discipline- or question-specific relevance of certain overlays or other operations), and from compounded error arising from the combination and transformation of layers throughout the analysis process. It is rare that studies consider this cumulative error, but it can be significant.

So, how can we deal with uncertainty in GIS analyses? We close this chapter with some important recommendations. (1) Fully understand your sources of data. Read the metadata and assess whether they can be appropriately used for your purpose. What is the scale, and does it match your other data and the needs of your research objective? What attributes or values exist, and have they been appropriately measured? How recent are the data; were the data collected at an appropriate time for your study? What were the original sources for the data? Trusted, well-documented? (2) Rely on multiple sources. When uncertainties arise, it can be desirable to compare or combine data sources in order to either validate the one you are using, or improve one by "burning in" features of the other that might be absent or improved from the first source. (3) Finally, and perhaps most importantly, acknowledge uncertainty, document it carefully, simulate the consequences if possible, and make decisions and interpretations appropriately. Happy GISing!

References

Bolstad, P. 2016. *GIS Fundamentals: A First Text on Geographic Information Systems*, 5th edition. XanEdu Publishing Inc., Ann Arbor, MI.

Burrough, P. A., McDonnell, R. A., and Lloyd, C. D. 2015. *Principles of Geographical Information Systems*. Oxford University Press, Oxford.

Clarke, K. C. 1986. Advances in geographic information systems. *Computers, Environment and Urban Systems* **10**(3–4): 175–184.

Chang, K. 2012. *Introduction to Geographic Information Systems*, 6th edition. McGraw-Hill, New York.

Channan, S., Collins, K., and Emanuel, W. R. 2014. *Global Mosaics of the Standard MODIS Land Cover Type Data*. University of Maryland and the Pacific Northwest National Laboratory, College Park, MD.

Coppock, J. T. and Rhind, D. W. 1991. The history of GIS. *Geographical Information Systems: Principles and Applications* **1**(1): 21–43.

Environmental Systems Research Institute (ESRI). 1990. *Understanding GIS: The ARC/INFO Method*. ESRI, Redlands, CA.

Goodchild, M. F. 1992. Geographical information science. *International Journal of Geographical Information Systems* **6**(1): 31–45.

Hickey, J. R., Nackoney, J., Nibbelink, N. P., et al. 2013. Human proximity and habitat fragmentation are key drivers of the rangewide bonobo distribution. *Biodiversity and Conservation* **22**: 3085–3104.

Hofmann-Wellenhof, B., Lichtenegger, H., and Collins, J. 2001. *Global Positioning System: Theory and Practice*. Springer Science & Business Media, New York.

Howard, A. M., Nibbelink, N. P., Madden, M., et al. 2015. Landscape influences on the natural and artificially manipulated movements of bearded capuchin monkeys. *Animal Behaviour* **106**: 59–70.

Longley, P. A., Goodchild, M. F., Maguire, D. J., and Rhind, D. W. 2001. *Geographic Information Systems and Science*, Wiley, New York.

Longley, P. A., Goodchild, M. F., Maguire, D. J., and Rhind, D. W. 2005. *Geographic Information Systems and Science*. Wiley, Chichester.

Madden, M. (Ed.) 2009. *Manual of Geographic Information Systems*. American Society for Photogrammetry and Remote Sensing, Bethesda, MD.

Mark, D. M. 2003. Geographic information science: defining the field. Pages 3–18 in *Foundations of Geographic Information Science*. M. Duckham, M. F. Goodchild, and M. Worboys (Eds.). Taylor & Francis, New York.

McGarigal, K., Cushman, S. A., and Ene, E. 2012. FRAGSTATS v4: Spatial Pattern Analysis Program for Categorical and Continuous Maps. Computer software program produced by the authors at the University of Massachusetts, Amherst. Available at: www.umass.edu/landeco/research/fragstats/fragstats.html.

Monmonier, M. 1996. *How to Lie With Maps*, 2nd edition. University of Chicago Press, Chicago, IL.

Parkinson, B. W. 1996. GPS error analysis. Pages 478–483 in *Global Positioning System: Theory and Applications*, Volume II. B. W. Parkinson and J. J. Spilker Jr. (Eds.). American Institute of Astronautics and Aeronautics, Washington, DC.

R Core Team. 2016. *R: A Language and Environment for Statistical Computing*. R Foundation for Statistical Computing, Vienna.

Tao, C. V., and Li, J. 2007. *Advances in Mobile Mapping Technology*. Taylor & Francis, London.

Tilman, D., and Kareiva, P. (Eds.) 2001. *Spatial Ecology*. Princeton University Press, Princeton, NJ.

Tomlinson, R. F. 2007. *Thinking about GIS: Geographic Information System Planning for Managers*. ESRI, Redlands, CA.

Turner, M. G., Gardner, R. H., and O'Neill, R. V. 2001. *Landscape Ecology in Theory and Practice*. Springer, New York.

US Geological Survey. 1996. 30 arc-second DEM of South America. Digital elevation model. US Geological Survey's Center for Earth Resources Observation and Science (EROS).

Wiens, J. A. 1989. Spatial scaling in ecology. *Functional Ecology* **3**(4): 385–397.

3 "Next-Gen" Tracking in Primatology
Opportunities and Challenges

Margaret C. Crofoot

The first troop of *Propithecus verreauxi* that I saw at Berenty, February 11, 1963, and the first that I know saw me, became alarmed, sifakaed, and growled at me. They moved off, but a group of *Lemur catta* barred their path. Four *L. catta* had been playing jump-on-and-wrestle on a springy branch. One of the *Propithecus* leaped on the branch, only to be faced by an adult *L. catta,* who leaned forward and cuffed the air in front of the *Propithecus.* The *Propithecus* promptly swung under the branch and dropped. A second *Propithecus* jumped to the far end of the branch, swinging it down in a long arc; then, on the upswing, it leaped to land directly in front of the *L. catta.* The *L. catta* feinted again with head and body. The *Propithecus* flinched, then suddenly lifted its head to give an alarm roar. The whole *Propithecus* troop roared with him, and the *L. catta* fled precipitously. The *Propithecus* troop crossed out of sight, after which the *L. catta* reoccupied their playground.

Alison Jolly, *Lemur Behavior: A Madagascar Field Study* (1966: 44)

Why would you ever want to rely on electronic sensors when you can collect rich data like these by watching wild primates as they go about their daily lives? Compared to other mammalian species, primates are quite amenable to observational study; most species are diurnal and habituate quickly to the presence of human observers, allowing researchers to directly record data on their behaviors, movements, and interactions. Because, as primatologists, we can directly observe the behavior of our study animals in their natural habitats, we have never relied as heavily on telemetry (i.e., remote data collection) as scientists studying the behavior and ecology of other wild animals. Thus, before launching into specifics about how to GPS-track primates, it is worth asking why (or when) it would ever be worth the expense and the risk (to both the health of the study animal and the researcher) to catch and tag a primate with an electronic monitoring device. There are at least four distinct answers to this question.

(1) Remote sensing allows us to "see" cryptic behaviors and unobservable species. There is a long tradition of using radio-telemetry to locate and monitor the movements of nocturnal primates (Charles Dominique 1977; Gursky 2005; Kappeler 1997; Merker 2006; Thorington et al. 1976), perhaps because the limits of our own perceptual abilities for understanding the behavior of these species are so clear. GPS tracking and other telemetry technologies may be the only way to learn about primate species that range in inaccessible areas or that cannot (or should not, due to concerns about hunting or disease) be habituated. Similarly, remote sensing may be the only way to collect data on some behaviors, like extra-pair copulations or predation events, that are, by their very nature, cryptic.

Box 3.1 You Only Die Once: Tracking the Causes of Primate Mortality

Information about when, where, and how animals die is key to understanding the selective pressures shaping their evolution and to planning effective conservation action to protect threatened populations (Kays et al. 2015; Wilcove & Wikelski 2008). However, determining the causes of animal mortality can pose substantial challenges, particularly in long-lived species. Predation is hypothesized to be a major cause of mortality in wild primate populations, and a primary selective force shaping their social organization (Alexander 1974; Isbell 1994; van Schaik 1983). Few studies, however, have produced reliable data on the interactions between

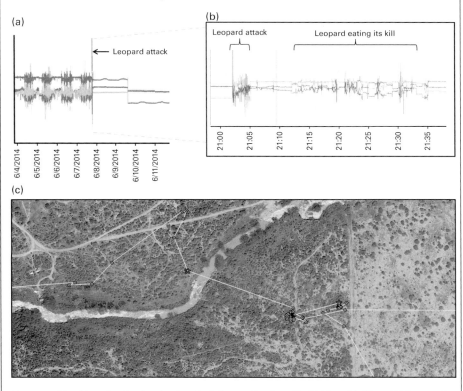

Figure 3.1 Tracking the death of a female baboon. On June 7, 2014 at 21:02, a GPS-tagged female baboon was killed by a GPS-collared leopard. Plots of the baboon's 3D acceleration (sampled for 2 seconds every minute at a rate of 40 Hz) in the days (a) and minutes (b) surrounding her death reveal the exact timing of this predation event, and allow us to infer the amount of time the leopard spent consuming its kill. GPS locations collected at 15-minute intervals (c) show that just prior to the attack (red stars), the baboon (yellow) was stationary on a rocky outcropping (likely asleep, given the time of night), while the leopard was quite a distance away, on the opposite side of a river. In the minutes leading up to the predation event, the leopard (aqua) crossed this river and traveled quickly and directly (>250 meters in 2 minutes) toward the baboon. After the kill, the leopard dragged the baboon approximately 90 meters to another rocky outcropping where the body and collar were eventually recovered. (A black and white version of this figure will appear in some formats. For the color version, please refer to the plate section.)

Box 3.1 (*cont.*)

predators and their primate prey. In part, this is because the very act of conducting behavioral observations appears to influence the likelihood that a study subject falls prey to a predator (Isbell & Young 1993). Further, animals from habituated study groups may vanish, but it is rare that researchers can unambiguously link these disappearances to predator attacks, let alone obtain enough contextual information to understand why one individual, but not another, succumbed.

An exciting new study by Lynne Isbell and colleagues is taking advantage of the recent advances in animal tracking technology to overcome some of these obstacles. By simultaneously tracking the movements and activity patterns of both baboons and leopards, this team is exploring the dynamic patterns of interaction among the hunters and the hunted. They are using GPS tracking data not only to identify when and where predators come into close contact with their primate prey, but also to capture the predation events themselves. Data such as these will make it possible not only to identify individual characteristics that increase (or decrease) predation risk, but also quantify how that risk varies over space and through time.

(2) Telemetry makes it possible to eliminate biases introduced by human observers. Habituation – the process by which animals, with enough "neutral exposure," become accustomed to and eventually ignore human observers (Carpenter 1934) – is the primary method primatologists use to minimize or eliminate observer effects in their research (Crofoot et al. 2010). However, observers almost certainly impact aspects of behavior of even extremely well-habituated study animals (e.g., Caine 1989; Nowak et al. 2014). Of particular concern is the effect we have on interactions between the primates we observe and the other, unhabituated animals in the habitat, including predators (Isbell & Young 1993) and resource competitors (Rasmussen 1991; Zinner et al. 2001). GPS tracking technology provides a way to study important processes like predation and competition, while avoiding the potential biases that human observers introduce (e.g., artificially reducing predation pressure or increasing habituated individuals' competitive ability).

(3) "Wearable" data-collection devices overcome some of the inherent limitations of observational methodologies. Many important aspects of primates' responses to environmental and social stressors are not directly measurable using behavioral observations, but can be monitored with biotelemetry. Loggers that record body temperature may be key to understanding behavioral responses to disease (Adelman et al. 2014). Heart-rate monitors can provide otherwise unobtainable insight into both levels of arousal (Davies et al. 2014) and energetics (Tomlinson et al. 2014), and portable electroencephalograms (EEGs) may help us to uncover the evolutionary importance of sleep (Lesku et al. 2012; Rattenborg et al. 2008). Observational methods are also unsuitable for collecting data on unpredictable or large-scale movements. While many primates have comparatively small, stable ranges, some species and populations conduct seasonal "migrations" between habitats (Abernethy et al. 2002; Singleton & van Schaik 2001; White et al. 2010), which have not been well described and whose causes are poorly understood.

Remote tracking via GPS greatly improves our ability to study the process of juvenile dispersal – currently a major black box in our understanding of primate life history (Fairbanks & Pereira 2002).

Observational methods are also inherently unsuited to answering questions about the dynamics of group behavior, as it is usually impossible to collect data on more than one individual at a time. As Byrne (2000: 501) observed in his review of collective decision-making in primates: "It is an observational task of daunting dimensions to attempt to record the actions of many potential decision-maker animals at once." Remote tracking technology, however, can easily be used to simultaneously monitor the movements and activity patterns of entire primate groups, providing new and exciting opportunities to tackle previously intractable questions about the collective behaviors of primates (Strandburg-Peshkin et al. 2015).

Box 3.2 Moving Collective Behavior Research from the Lab to the Field

The apparent choreography in the flocking of birds, schooling of fish, and swarming of insects has given rise to substantial interest in how groups of animals coordinate their movements. The rapidly growing field of collective animal behavior relies primarily on theoretical models (Conradt & Roper 2003, 2010), computer simulations (Conradt et al. 2009; Couzin et al. 2005), and lab-based experiments (Perez-Escudero & de Polavieja 2011; Strandburg-Peshkin et al. 2013) to investigate how the behaviors of individuals combine to create group movement decisions. However, advances in GPS technology – specifically the ability to monitor the movements of free-ranging animals with sub-meter accuracy and near-continuous resolution – are making it possible to take the study of collective behavior from the lab into the field, dramatically increasing the number of species in which collective phenomena can be studied. Free-flying homing pigeons are quickly becoming a model system for studying consensus decision-making in animal groups on the move (Flack et al. 2013; Nagy et al. 2010, 2013; Pettit et al. 2013; Watts et al. 2016), and whole-group tracking of sheep is shedding light on the anti-predator responses of group-living species (King et al. 2012).

In an effort to understand the emergence of leadership in primate societies, my colleagues and I recently conducted a study in which we fit >80 percent of the adult and subadult members of a troop of wild baboons with high-resolution GPS collars (Crofoot et al. 2015; Farine et al. 2016). Simultaneous tracking of their movements revealed that rather than being led by a despotic leader, the baboons' collective movements were instead driven by a strong majority rule (Strandburg-Peshkin et al. 2015). Studies like this, which expand the focus of collective behavior research from a small set of model organisms that can be easily kept and experimentally manipulated in captivity to a more diverse set of species living in their natural habitat, are key to identifying unifying rules that govern collective behavior across social species, and comparative research is needed to understand how these rules shape the evolution of social complexity.

Box 3.2 (*cont.*)

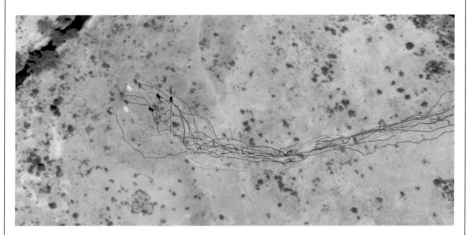

Figure 3.2 Olive baboons (*Papio anubis*) travel together as a more-or-less cohesive unit. High-resolution GPS tracking (1 location/second) of the troop revealed that consensus decision-making governs choices about which direction to move. (A black and white version of this figure will appear in some formats. For the color version, please refer to the plate section.)

(4) Use of remote tracking technology permits increased sample sizes. When groups, rather than individuals, are the unit of analysis, it may not be logistically feasible to obtain a large sample size using traditional observational techniques. With increasing interest in the variation in primate behavior within and between habitats (Kappeler et al. 2013), the workload of habituating and observing social groups becomes a limiting factor. Remote tracking technology can facilitate observational research on multiple groups by making it easier for researchers to find their study subjects (Campbell & Sussman 1994; Juarez et al. 2011). It can also provide standardized data on a range of behavioral and physiological parameters, permitting comparisons of a larger number of groups across a more geographically dispersed area (Crofoot 2013; Markham et al. 2013).

Box 3.3 Inter-Group Conflict in Primates

The relationships between primate social groups have long been of interest to primatologists because of the central role warfare is hypothesized to have played in shaping human evolution (Bowles 2009; Cheney 1987; Crofoot & Wrangham 2010; Manson & Wrangham 1991). However, empirical data have been hard to come by. Primates' intergroup interactions tend to be hectic affairs which often play out in forest environments with poor visibility. Furthermore, data on multiple social groups are needed to answer the most interesting questions about intergroup conflict, but habituating even a single primate group and conducting regular behavioral observations is time-consuming, labor intensive, and expensive. Due to these

Box 3.3 (*cont.*)

logistical difficulties, it has been difficult to determine the factors that influence a group's competitive ability, or investigate the impact that winning (or losing) fights with neighbors has on an individual's behavior, space use, or, ultimately, fitness (Brown & Crofoot 2013).

Advances in tracking technology are creating new opportunities to address these questions. Large-scale tracking projects monitoring the movements of multiple neighboring primate social groups have revealed how the relative size of competing groups affects the outcome of intergroup conflicts (Crofoot et al. 2008; Markham et al. 2012), and demonstrated the important impact that conflict location has in some species (white-faced capuchins [Crofoot et al. 2008], baboons [Markham et al. 2012]), but not others (vervets [Arseneau et al. 2015]). These studies have also documented some of the direct costs that members of losing groups pay (Crofoot 2013; Markham et al. 2012), and shown how relationships with neighbors shape primate ranging behavior and space use patterns (Markham et al. 2013).

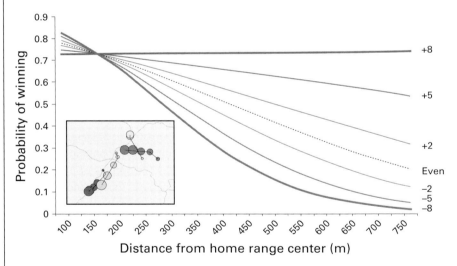

Figure 3.3 Home-field advantage in capuchin intergroup conflict. Automated tracking of six white-faced capuchin (*Cebus capucinus*) social groups revealed that while relative group size (represented by colored lines, top) did influence the odds a group would win in a competitive interaction with a neighbor, the location of the conflict had a larger impact on the outcome (Crofoot 2008). In this study, interactions and their outcomes were defined based on spatial criteria (*see inset*): two groups had to come within 150 m of one another and a clear displacement event had to occur. Using this approach, we identified 58 interactions with a clear winner and loser in 6 months of movement data. In contrast, in 10 months of direct behavioral data collection, we observed 23 intergroup interactions, only 18 of which had a clear outcome (Crofoot 2007). (A black and white version of this figure will appear in some formats. For the color version, please refer to the plate section.)

As the examples above illustrate, the mantra of wildlife telemetry is no longer simply "location, location, location." The development of small, energy-efficient GPS tags capable of tracking animal movement at extremely high spatio-temporal resolution, the integration of diverse sensors capable of monitoring animal behavior, physiology, and communication, and our increasing ability to access these data in near real time via cell tower and satellite networks has fundamentally changed the kinds of questions we can answer using telemetry (Krause et al. 2013; Lynch et al. 2013; Nagy et al. 2010; Sapir et al. 2013; Spiegel et al. 2013; Voirin et al. 2014; Wall et al. 2014; Wilson et al. 2008). "Next-gen" animal tracking tags are both more powerful and more flexible than previous technologies, creating a plethora of new research opportunities. However, they are also more complicated and more expensive, and using them to their fullest extent requires more knowledge on the part of the researcher (Breed et al. 2011; Tomkiewicz et al. 2010). The remainder of this chapter provides an overview of how GPS tracking works, highlights important considerations when planning a GPS tracking study, and briefly reviews some of the sensors that can be integrated into GPS collars to add behavioral or physiological context to animal movement data.

How GPS Tags Work

In recent decades, satellite-based tracking has revolutionized the study of animal movement ecology by allowing automated collection of location data over global scales (Kays et al. 2015; Wikelski et al. 2007). Most satellite-based animal tracking today relies on the Navstar Global Positioning System (GPS), an array of 24 geosynchronous satellites owned and maintained by the US Department of Defense. Rather than emitting signals like radio-transmitters, GPS tags worn by study animals instead act as receivers for the signals broadcast by these 24 satellites. Two kinds of information are needed to calculate the location of a GPS-tagged animal: (1) the distance between each satellite and the tagged animal (derived based on the time lag between radio-signals being transmitted by the satellite and received by the tag); and (2) exact information about the orbital path and position of each satellite (Rodgers 2001). A three-dimensional location (latitude, longitude, altitude) can be estimated by measuring the time it takes for signals from four satellites of known positions to reach a GPS receiver; with data from only three satellites, only a two-dimensional estimate is possible (latitude, longitude). These location estimates are typically stored in the collar's onboard memory and either downloaded remotely, via radio- or satellite-link, or directly when the collar is recovered (Rodgers 2001). The amount of data that collars are capable of storing varies by make and manufacturer, but is more than adequate for the majority of studies. However, users who are sampling GPS locations at extremely high frequency, or who are simultaneously logging data from other, integrated sensors risk losing data if they fail to pay attention to the quantity of data they are collecting in relation to the capacity of their collars' onboard memory. While some collars stop logging data when their memory is full, others will overwrite old data with new.

Sources of Error in GPS Tracking

To be useful as a method for studying primate behavior, GPS collars must produce spatially accurate location estimates in a reliable and unbiased manner. Two main types of error are thus of interest to any researcher planning a tracking-based study: location error (LE) and fix success rate (FSR). The LE of a GPS tag refers to the distance between its real and estimated positions. Fix success rate is a measure of missed data – the frequency with which a tag fails to acquire the necessary satellite signals to estimate its location.

Until recently poor FSRs in forested environments have limited the utility of GPS technology for tracking most primate species (Markham & Altmann 2008; Phillips et al. 1998; Sprague 2004; Sprague et al. 2004). Sprague and colleagues (2004) reported a 20 percent FSR for the GPS collar worn by a female Japanese macaque (*Macaca fuscata*), and noted that all but one instance when the GPS tag failed to obtain a location estimate occurred in forested areas. However, the incorporation of high-sensitivity GPS microcontrollers into the new generations of GPS-collars continues to improve the rate at which tags acquire location estimates, making them appropriate for use in forest habitats. For example, while a 2003 study of Yunnan snub-nosed monkeys reported a fix rate of 82 percent in a temperate, coniferous forest (Ren et al. 2008), a collar deployed on a white-faced capuchin monkey living in much denser lowland tropical forest in Panama in 2008 achieved an 83 percent FSR(Campbell et al. 2011) and a more recent study (2016–2018) at the same site, conducted using the latest version of that collar, obtained >98 percent fix rate (Crofoot, unpublished data).

Having good estimates of LE and FSR is critical for planning GPS tracking studies, and for analyzing the resulting data. Both types of error are influenced by a wide range of environmental, behavioral, and technological factors that impact signal transmission between satellites and receivers, and thus will likely vary substantially depending on study site, the habits of the species being tracked, and even the time of year. For this reason, researchers should pilot test and ground truth the specific equipment they plan to use, at their own study site, rather than relying on published error estimates.

What Determines GPS Accuracy and Fix Success Rate?

The US Department of Defense discontinued its policy of degrading the accuracy of civilian GPS receivers in 2000, decreasing the error of GPS location estimates under ideal conditions to <10 m (Rodgers 2001). In fact, it is possible to achieve sub-meter accuracy by sampling at very high rates (Strandburg-Peshkin et al. 2015), by integrating information from additional sensors (e.g., Wilson et al. 2013), or by post-processing data (differential correction – Kaplan & Hegarty 2005). Nonetheless, because of the myriad factors that influence signal quality, each location estimated by a GPS tag has an associated (but unknown) level of error. Some sources of error, such as changes in atmospheric conditions that impact GPS accuracy by slowing down and deviating satellite signals (Cargnelutti et al. 2007), are of comparatively lesser concern to most users, as their impact on data quality is likely unbiased. Others, however, should be considered more carefully, as they can differentially impact the spatial accuracy of particular tags, of tags in particular habitats, or during particular times of year.

Environmental factors that obstruct or reflect the transmission of satellite signals increase the LE and decrease the FSR of GPS tags (Adams et al. 2013). Rugged topography (Cain et al. 2005; D'Eon et al. 2002; Frair et al. 2010; Hansen & Riggs 2008) and dense, structurally complex vegetation (Adams et al. 2013; D'Eon et al. 2002; Frair et al. 2010; Hulbert & French 2001; Rempel et al. 1995) have particularly important effects. For example, in a recent study, median LE increased nearly six-fold and FSR plummeted when GPS collars were moved from an open site with low vegetation to a native forest with an intact understory (LE = 5 m versus 29.2 m; FSR = 100 percent versus 37 percent; Recio et al. 2011). Not all GPS accuracy tests, however, show such a dramatic impact of forest cover: a similar study found only a small (but significant) increase in LE and no change in the FSR of GPS collars deployed at sites with a range of canopy cover (LE at 0–25 percent versus 75–100 percent canopy cover = 3.03 versus 5.29 m; Williams et al. 2012). It is not clear if the difference in the impact of canopy cover in these two studies is due to a difference in the structure or density of the forest at the two sites, in collar manufacture, or some other factor. However, what these examples illustrate is that both LE and FSR can be highly site- and study-specific. Researchers using GPS tracking technology should test the LE and FSR of their equipment in the range of habitats where their study subjects range, and reporting of this information in publications should become a community standard.

Although less well studied, the behavior of tagged animals can also impact GPS error (Cargnelutti et al. 2007; D'Eon & Delparte 2005; Gau et al. 2004; Hebblewhite et al. 2007). Location error will be higher, and FSR lower, when tagged animals use dens, burrows, or nests, or spend time hiding in dense vegetation where satellite reception is poor. Positional behavior that changes the orientation of the tag antenna can have similar effects. For example, tamandua anteaters (*Tamandua mexicana*) tend to sleep lying on their backs, so their body shields the antenna of tags mounted on backpack-style harnesses (Danielle Brown, personal communication).

In addition to these environmental and behavioral variables, collar model and manu-facturer also influence both the accuracy and precision of GPS location estimates (Frair et al. 2010; Hansen & Riggs 2008; Hebblewhite et al. 2007). All commercially available GPS tags include proprietary firmware that includes an algorithm used to calculate locations and the criteria for using or not using information from specific satellites (Hansen & Riggs 2008). The duty cycle – how frequently and for how long the GPS receiver attempts to obtain a location estimate – also has an important impact on GPS error (Hansen & Riggs 2008). Before a tag can use a satellite for position calculations, it must obtain the latest information about the satellite's orbit (i.e., ephemeris data) – a download process that takes 30 seconds or more. However, when fix rates are high, tags are in a "hot start" condition: the current almanac, time, location, and ephemeris infor-mation for each satellite in sight is already stored in memory, and more accurate location estimates can be obtained in shorter periods of time (Recio et al. 2011; Tomkiewicz et al. 2010). Importantly, the duty cycle of GPS tags can often be controlled by the user, allowing researchers to tailor their sampling protocol to local conditions.

Because of the errors in GPS data that arise from environmental, behavioral, and technological factors, researchers must keep in mind that the movement path recorded by a GPS tag does not represent the actual path a study animal traveled. Instead, it should be thought of as one possible set of locations from among a distribution whose size is determined by the magnitude of the LE and the number of missing fixes. Two main approaches exist for addressing this error: identifying and eliminating "bad" fixes, and explicitly accounting for error or incorporating uncertainty into analyses (e.g., dynamic Brownian bridge models – Kranstauber et al. 2012).

How Can GPS Accuracy be Improved?

As discussed in the previous section, many factors contribute to the performance of GPS tags used in wildlife tracking, and the spatial accuracy and FSR achieved will be highly dependent on local conditions. Capturing and fitting wild primates with GPS collars is an inherently risky and unavoidably stressful procedure. It is therefore incumbent upon us, before initiating such research, to carefully consider whether our study merits imposing these costs (see Chapter 4 on the ethics of primate tracking) and, if so, (1) what data are needed to address our research questions, (2) how much error is acceptable, and (3) whether GPS technology can provide the requisite data at the proposed study site and with the proposed study species. *This requires thorough pilot testing.*

GPS tags are expensive (often more than $1000) and, with limited funding, it may seem like a waste of resources to use them for testing. However, pilot tests are not only necessary for estimating the spatial accuracy of GPS location estimates, but are key to optimizing the GPS duty cycle to minimize error and maximize the likelihood a research project will succeed. "Time to fix" – how long a tag searches for satellite signals before powering down to conserve battery – is probably the most important user-defined parameter, and can be the difference between the success and failure of a project. If the "time to fix" is too short the GPS tag will not be able to acquire information from enough satellites to produce a (high-quality) location estimate, resulting in a low FSR and lots of missing data. If, on the other hand, it is too long, the tag can burn through its battery searching for satellite signals when none are available (e.g., when the animal is in a burrow or shielding the antenna of the GPS tag with its body), substantially shortening the data-collection period. In my experience, "time to fix" values of 60–90 seconds provide the right balance for arboreal primates in lowland tropical forests. If at all possible, however, researchers should decide on a duty cycle for their GPS tags based on their own testing of the specific equipment they plan to use, at their study site, simulating, as closely as possible, the behavior of their study species (e.g., placing tags in trees to simulate the conditions experienced by arboreal primates).

The level of spatial accuracy a study needs will depend critically on the kinds of questions it is trying to address. For example, depending on the scale of habitat heterogeneity, a resolution of ±50 meters may be sufficient for some habitat selection studies; when heterogeneity is more fine-grained, however, much higher levels of spatial accuracy will be required. Several strategies exist for reducing GPS location error. If extremely high levels of spatial resolution (<1 m) are desired, specialized GPS tags that store the complete satellite information required for differential correction may be necessary (Kaplan & Hegarty 2005). I have found it possible to achieve ~1 m error

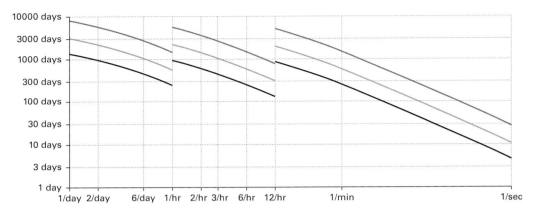

Figure 3.4 Trade-off between sampling frequency and sampling duration. To illustrate this trade-off, I estimated the life span (in days) of GPS collars with small (black; capacity ~2500 mAh), medium (red; capacity ~5800 mAh), and large (blue; capacity ~15,000 mAh) capacity batteries for sampling rates ranging from one location estimate per day to one location estimate per second. Time-to-fix (TTF – the latency between a GPS tag turning on and obtaining a fix) varies with sampling frequency. To account for this, I varied TTF in three stages: TTF = 60 seconds for rates from 1 to 12 fixes/day; TTF decreases monotonically from 60 seconds to 30 seconds for rates from 1 to 12 fixes/hour; TTF = 1 second for rates from 1 fix/5 minutes to 1 fix/second. Note that battery performance varies depending on environmental factors (e.g., temperature), and TTF will be highly dependent on the study site. Predicted collar life spans for low-frequency sampling regimes are likely overestimates. (A black and white version of this figure will appear in some formats. For the color version, please refer to the plate section.)

without specialized equipment or data post-processing by near-continuous sampling (1 GPS fix/second – Strandburg-Peshkin et al. 2015). For most primate tracking applications, however, these levels of spatial resolution are unnecessary. A more broadly useful, "low cost" strategy for minimizing LE is to collect a sequence of GPS fixes at each sampling interval (rather than a single location estimate). When more satellites contribute to a location estimate, the error associated with that estimate tends to be lower (Hansen & Riggs 2008). However, most GPS tags are programmed to take a fix as soon as they have the minimum number of satellites in view (four) to save battery power. By programming a tag to collect a burst of data – for example, 10 fixes in 10 seconds – the tag has time to find and integrate information from additional satellites, which can reduce the associated error. Furthermore, these repeated samples make it possible to determine the precision of the estimated location.

The Fundamental Tracking Trade-off: Life Span versus Sampling Frequency versus Weight

Studies that use GPS tracking are faced with an unavoidable trade-off between tag weight, sampling frequency, and study duration (Figure 3.4). Battery size is the main determinant of the weight of GPS tags and the number of location estimates they can record. Thus, for a given size battery, researchers are faced with a choice between recording more fixes per day for a shorter period of time or adopting a lower sampling rate to extend the life span of the GPS tag. Higher capacity batteries make it possible to collect data more frequently or for longer periods, but come at the cost of increased tag size and weight.

The size of the study species places an upper limit on this parameter, as tags that are too large or too heavy may substantially alter the behavior of the individuals carrying the GPS unit. A commonly cited guideline is that tags should weigh <5 percent of an individual's body weight (Macdonald & Amlaner 1980), but what constitutes a reasonable tag weight for a particular species will vary depending on factors such as mode of locomotion and attachment type and location. According to this guideline, for example, a male orangutan weighing 80 kg could be fitted with a 4 kg GPS tag! While this amount of weight might not be overly burdensome if it could be attached near the individual's center of mass – for example, using a backpack-style harness or even a collar – neither of these attachment methods is appropriate for a species whose locomotor behavior depends on unimpeded flexibility at the shoulder and hip joint (Shumaker 2007), and which also has pendulous throat sacs used to produces long calls (Rodman & Mitani 1987). As this example illustrates, a thorough knowledge of the study species and good judgment on the part of researchers is critical when designing tag attachments. While not exceeding specific target weights is important, a better "best-practice" goal might be minimizing the weight and size of telemetry tags as much as is possible while still achieving the scientific goals of the study.

Assuming that weight is a limiting factor, as it will almost certainly be for any primate species, what options exist for increasing the battery life of GPS tags? Alternative energy sources are one potential way to get around these limitations. Rechargeable, solar-powered GPS tags exist, and have been successfully used to overcome tag life and sampling frequency limitations in studies of bird movement (Bridge et al. 2011; Burger & Shaffer 2008; Flack et al. 2016; Sapir et al. 2013). A major challenge in translating these solar tags designed for birds into a package appropriate for a primate lies in figuring out how to keep the solar panel oriented toward the sun and unobscured by dust or hair. To my knowledge, no one has successfully used solar-powered tags on primates, and while species that live in open habitats (e.g., savannah-living baboons) might receive enough exposure to solar radiation to make this a viable alternative power source, it is doubtful that such tags would be an effective research tool for forest-living species.

Targeted sampling schedules are another way to extend the battery life of GPS tags. At its simplest, this involves limiting data collection to particular times of day when the behaviors of interest to the researcher occur – for example, only turning on the GPS tag of a diurnal species during daylight hours. For studies that need to sample over relatively long periods of time (e.g., an annual cycle), but do not necessarily need continuous data, sampling for a limited number of days at regularly spaced intervals (e.g., 10 days/month) may be an effective approach. However, new methods for dynamically varying GPS sampling rate promise even greater control and power savings. Accelerometer-informed scheduling, for example, makes it possible to auto-matically switch back and forth between sampling protocols based on the activity levels of the tagged individual (Brown et al. 2012). Tags can be programmed to collect GPS location data at a relatively low rate (e.g., 1 location/hour) when study animals are inactive, but increase sampling effort (for example, to 6 locations/hour) when they start to move. For species that spend substantial amounts of time resting in a single location, this approach can lead to substantial power savings (Brown et al. 2012). Similarly, some tags are now capable of varying their sampling schedule based on location (geofencing – Jachowski et al. 2014; Wall et al. 2014), making it possible to collect movement data at a high temporal resolution in particular areas of interest, while conserving battery power by sampling a lower rate in other parts of the range.

Movement in Context: Sensor Integration in GPS Tags

A multitude of sensors can be integrated into modern GPS tags, meaning that the decision to remotely track primate movement also presents an opportunity to collect additional environmental, behavioral, and physiological data. Video cameras can be used to monitor foraging behavior (Fuentes et al. 2014; Moil et al. 2007; Newmaster et al. 2013; Rutz & Troscianko 2013) and social interactions (Yoda et al. 2011). Heart-rate monitors provide insight into individual physiology (Sapir et al. 2010), and may also permit scientists to track arousal (Davies et al. 2014). Sensors that log body temperature are central to efforts to understand immune and behavioral responses to infectious disease in wild animal populations (Adelman et al. 2014). However, accelerometers may be the most generally useful sensor for studies of primate behavior, in part because they are integrated, by default, into many commercially available GPS collars.

Accelerometers are small, light, inexpensive, and energy-efficient, and can be used in GPS tracking studies to provide additional insight into the behavior and energetics of study animals. These spring-like sensors work by generating a voltage signal proportional to their acceleration (i.e., change in velocity) when they are deformed. An accelerometer attached to an animal measures two distinct types of acceleration that can be used to infer different aspects of behavior. The first of these, known as static or gravitational acceleration, results from the force of the Earth's gravity field (which deforms the sensor) and how the sensor is positioned with respect to that field. Static acceleration can thus be used to determine the spatial orientation of tagged study animals. Dynamic (or inertial) acceleration, in contrast, is due to movements of the animal's body. An integrated measure of three-dimensional body movement, termed overall dynamic body acceleration (ODBA; Qasem et al. 2012; Shepard et al. 2009), has been shown to correlate strongly with energy expenditure in many species (Gleiss et al. 2011; Halsey et al. 2009a, 2009b; Wilson et al. 2006), providing a means to monitor the energetics of free-ranging animals over large spatial and temporal scales. In addition, many behaviors have distinctive acceleration profiles (e.g., imagine a horse that is walking versus trotting versus galloping), and so data on dynamic acceleration can also be used to infer the behavioral state of tagged individuals (Brown et al. 2013; Nathan et al. 2012). While these methods hold great promise for expanding the kinds of questions we can ask about the behavior and energetics of wild primates, they are not without their challenges. To get the most out of accelerometers, remote data collection has to be paired with direct observations of study animals, and substantial effort must be invested in calibration and validation, as well as in managing and analyzing the large quantities of data these sensors produce (Brown et al. 2013).

"Next-Gen" Tracking: Moving Beyond "Where" and "When" to "How" and "Why"

The majority of research on primate movement to date has been essentially descriptive in nature: How far do groups travel? What is the size of their home range? When do neighboring groups share space? The emerging field of movement ecology provides an intellectual framework for linking these patterns of space use to the movement processes that drive them (Nathan et al. 2008). Primatology's next challenge is to move beyond monitoring where our study animals go, and to investigate, at a mechanistic level, how they get there and why. Developing predictive movement models must be a priority if we hope to mitigate the impacts of human-induced rapid environmental change on wild primate populations (Sih 2013).

Together, "next-gen" tracking and GIS-based analytical tools create a methodological toolkit for exploring how internal states and external factors combine to shape primate movement decisions (Figure 3.5). However, they also present some unprecedented challenges for our field. Most critically, automated data-collection methods yield "big data," which are often unsuited to off-the-shelf statistics. Primatologists often lack the analytical training and computational skills to implement such solutions. In addition,

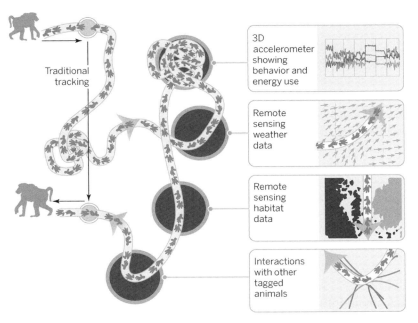

Figure 3.5 "Next-gen" animal tracking. High spatio-temporal resolution tracking combined with remotely sensed information about study animals' behavior and physiology, interactions with hetero- or conspecifics, habitat characteristics and environmental variables such as temperature or wind direction is shedding light on the causes and consequences of animal movement.
Source: Terrestrial animal tracking as an eye on life and planet by Kays et al., Science 12 Jun 2015: Vol. 348, Issue 6240, aaa2478, DOI: 10.1126/science.aaa2478).

there is reason to be concerned that the high costs of GPS collars lead researchers to reduce their sample sizes, limiting the power of tracking studies to provide strong tests of competing hypotheses (Hebblewhite & Haydon 2010). Finally, projects that make use of tracking technology unavoidably involve the capture of wild primates. A lack of consensus exists within our community about the ethics of capturing and collaring primates (see Chapter 4). Nonetheless, I hope we can agree that if primates are going to be captured, we want it to be done in the safest manner possible. This places an obligation on those of us performing animal capture to report our methods – both our successes *and* our failures – so others can learn from our experiences. The broader primate community also has a responsibility; reviewers and editors must be willing to publish studies that report undesirable outcomes of animal capture, as well as the success stories. Furthermore, as a community we need to be willing to invest in studies designed to improve capture, collaring, and tracking practices. Among other things, this means recognizing the importance of pilot testing and being willing to fund such activities, and investing the time to test and the money to develop and integrate appropriate "break-away" mechanisms so that study animals do not have to be recaptured at the end of a study to remove their collars. Too often, such activities seem to be perceived as peripheral to the "real" science.

An Ethical Note on Data Sharing

To end, I want to encourage all primatologists conducting GPS tracking to permanently archive the movement data they collect and consider publishing their data and/or making it otherwise publicly available. High-quality information on primate movement is key to addressing a number of the major outstanding questions in primatology, as well as for confronting the conservation challenges we currently face. GPS tracking is a powerful tool for collecting such data, but is conducted at an unavoidable risk to the animals being studied, and is generally paid for by the public. GPS tracking datasets often have substantial value beyond the original goals of the study for which they were collected. Thus, making them easily available to policy-makers, conservation organizations, and other scientists via online data repositories such as MoveBank (Wikelski & Kays 2011; www.movebank.org) can greatly increase the scientific return on our investment and promote primate welfare by reducing the need for new data collection.

Acknowledgments

Thanks to Damien Farine and Lynne Isbell for contributions to and helpful feedback on a previous draft of this chapter. I also wish to acknowledge the support from the National Science Foundation under grants IOS-1250895, BCS-1440755, III-1514174, and SMA-1620391.

References

Abernethy, K. A., White, L. J. T., and Wickings, E. J. 2002. Hordes of mandrills (*Mandrillus sphinx*): extreme group size and seasonal male presence. *Journal of Zoology* **258**: 131–137.

Adams, A. L., Dickinson, K. J. M., Robertson, B. C., and van Heezik, Y. 2013. An evaluation of the accuracy and performance of lightweight GPS collars in a suburban environment. *PLoS ONE* **8**. DOI: 10.1371/journal.pone.0068496.

Adelman, J. S., Moyers, S. C., and Hawley, D. M. 2014. Using remote biomonitoring to understand heterogeneity in immune-responses and disease-dynamics in small, free-living animals. *Integrative and Comparative Biology* **54**: 377–386.

Alexander, R. D. 1974. The evolution of social behavior. *Annual Review of Ecology and Systematics* **5**: 325–383.

Arseneau, T. J. M., Taucher, A.-L., van Schaik, C. P., and Willems, E. P. 2015. Male monkeys fight in between-group conflicts as protective parents and reluctant recruits. *Animal Behaviour* **110**: 39–50.

Bowles, S. 2009. Did warfare among ancestral hunter-gatherers affect the evolution of human social behaviors? *Science* **324**: 1293–1298.

Breed, G. A., Costa, D. P., Goebel, M. E., and Robinson, P. W. 2011. Electronic tracking tag programming is critical to data collection for behavioral time-series analysis. *Ecosphere* **2**. DOI: 10.1890/ES10-00021.1.

Bridge, E. S., Thorup, K., Bowlin, M. S., et al. 2011. Technology on the move: recent and forthcoming innovations for tracking migratory birds. *BioScience* **61**: 689–698.

Brown, D., LaPoint, S., Kays, R., et al. 2012. Accelerometer-informed GPS telemetry: reducing the trade-off between resolution and longevity. *Wildlife Society Bulletin* **36**: 139–146.

Brown, D., Kays, R., Wikelski, M., Wilson, R., and Klimley, A. 2013. Observing the unwatchable through acceleration logging of animal behavior. *Animal Biotelemetry* **1**: 1–16.

Brown, M. and Crofoot, M. C. 2013. Social and spatial relationships between primate groups. Pages 151–176 in *Primate Ecology and Conservation: A Handbook of Techniques*. E. J. Sterling, N. Bynum, and M. E. Blair (Eds.). Oxford University Press, Oxford.

Burger, A. E. and Shaffer, S. A. 2008. Application of tracking and data-logging technology in research and conservation of seabirds. *Auk* **125**: 253–264.

Byrne, R. W. 2000. How monkeys find their way: leadership, coordination, and cognitive maps of African baboons. Pages 491–518 in *On the Move: How and Why Animals Travel in Groups*. S. Boinski and P. Garber. Chicago University Press, Chicago, IL.

Cain, J. W., Krausman, P. R., Jansen, B. D., and Morgart, J. R. 2005. Influence of topography and GPS fix interval on GPS collar performance. *Wildlife Society Bulletin* **33**: 926–934.

Caine, N. G. 1989. Unrecognized anti-predator behaviour can bias observational data. *Animal Behaviour* **39**: 195–197.

Campbell, A. F. and Sussman, R. W. 1994. The value of radio tracking in the study of neotropical rain-forest monkeys. *American Journal of Primatology* **32**: 291–301.

Campbell, C. J., Crofoot, M. C., MacKinnon, J. R., and Stumpf, R. 2011. Behavioral data collection in primate field studies. Pages 358–367 in *Primates in Perspective*. R. Stumpf, C. J. Campbell, A. Fuentes, J. R. MacKinnon, and S. K. Bearder (Eds.). Oxford University Press, Oxford.

Cargnelutti, B., Coulon, A., Hewison, A. J. M., et al. 2007. Testing global positioning system performance for wildlife monitoring using mobile collars and known reference points. *Journal of Wildlife Management* **71**: 1380–1387.

Carpenter, C. R. 1934. A field study of the behavioral and social relations of howling monkeys (*Alouatta palliata*). *Comparative Psychology Monographs* **10**: 1–168.

Charles Dominique, P. 1977. Urine marking and territoriality in *Galago alleni*: field-study by radio-telemetry. *Zeitschrift Fur Tierpsychologie – Journal of Comparative Ethology* **43**: 113–138.

Cheney, D. L. 1987. Interactions and relations between groups. Pages 267–281 in *Primate Societies*. B. B. Smuts, D. L. Cheney, R. M. Seyfarth, et al. (Eds.). University of Chicago Press, Chicago, IL.

Conradt, L. and Roper, T. J. 2003. Group decision-making in animals. *Nature* **421**: 155–158.

Conradt, L. and Roper, T. J. 2010. Deciding group movements: where and when to go. *Behavioural Processes* **84**: 675–677.

Conradt, L., Krause, J., Couzin, I. D., and Roper, T. J. 2009. Leading according to need in self-organizing groups. *American Naturalist* 173: 304–312.

Couzin, I. D., Krause, J., Franks, N. R., and Levin, S. A. 2005. Effective leadership and decision-making in animal groups on the move. *Nature* **433**: 513–516.

Crofoot, M. C. 2007. Mating and feeding competition in white-faced capuchins (*Cebus capucinus*): the importance of short- and long-term strategies. *Behaviour* **144**: 1473–1495.

Crofoot, M. C. 2008. *Intergroup Competition in White-Faced Capuchin Monkeys (*Cebus capucinus*): Automated Radio-Telemetry Reveals How Intergroup Relationships Shape Space-Use and Foraging Success*. Harvard University, Cambridge, MA.

Crofoot, M. C. 2013. The cost of defeat: capuchin groups travel further, faster and later after losing conflicts with neighbors. *American Journal of Physical Anthropology* **152**: 79–85.

Crofoot, M. C. and Wrangham, R. W. 2010. Intergroup aggression in primates and humans: the case for a unified theory. Pages 171–195 in *Mind the Gap*. P. M. Kappeler and J. Silk (Eds.). Springer, New York.

Crofoot, M. C., Gilby, I. C., Wikelski, M. C., and Kays, R. W. 2008. Interaction location outweighs the competitive advantage of numerical superiority in *Cebus capucinus* intergroup contests. *Proceedings of the National Academy of Sciences of the United States of America* **105**: 577–581.

Crofoot, M. C., Lambert, T. D., Kays, R., and Wikelski, M. C. 2010. Does watching a monkey change its behaviour? Quantifying observer effects in habituated wild primates using automated radiotelemetry. *Animal Behaviour* **80**: 475–480.

Crofoot, M. C., Kays, R. W., and Wikelski, M. 2015. Shared decision-making drives collective movement in wild baboons. Movebank data repository.

Davies, A., Radford, A., and Nicol, C. 2014. Behavioural and physiological expression of arousal during decision-making in laying hens. *Physiology & Behavior* **123**: 93–99.

D'Eon, R. G. and Delparte, D. 2005. Effects of radio-collar position and orientation on GPS radio-collar performance, and the implications of PDOP in data screening. *Journal of Applied Ecology* **42**: 383–388.

D'Eon, R. G., Serrouya, R., Smith, G., and Kochanny, C. O. 2002. GPS radiotelemetry error and bias in mountainous terrain. *Wildlife Society Bulletin* **30**: 430–439.

Fairbanks, L. A. and Pereira, M. E. 2002. Juvenile primates: dimensions for future research. Pages 359–366 in *Juvenile Primates: Life History, Development and Behavior*. M. E. Pereira and L. A. Fairbanks (Eds.). University of Chicago Press, Chicago, IL.

Farine, D. R., Strandburg-Peshkin, A., Berger-Wolf, T., et al. 2016. Both nearest neighbours and long-term affiliates predict individual locations during collective movement in wild baboons. *Scientific Reports* **6**: 27704.

Flack, A., Ákos, Z., Nagy, M., Vicsek, T., and Biro, D. 2013. Robustness of flight leadership relations in pigeons. *Animal Behaviour* **86**: 723–732.

Flack, A., Fiedler, W., Blas, J., et al. 2016. Costs of migratory decisions: a comparison across eight white stork populations. *Science Advances* **2**: e1500931.

Frair, J. L., Fieberg, J., Hebblewhite, M., et al. 2010. Resolving issues of imprecise and habitat-biased locations in ecological analyses using GPS telemetry data. *Philosophical Transactions of the Royal Society B: Biological Sciences* **365**: 2187–2200.

Fuentes, A., Klegarth, A., Jones-Engel, L., et al. 2014. "Seeing the world through their eyes": analyses of the first National Geographic Crittercam (TM) deployments on macaques in Singapore and Gibraltar. *American Journal of Physical Anthropology* **153**: 122.

Gau, R. J., Mulders, R., Ciarniello, L. J., et al. 2004. Uncontrolled field performance of Televilt GPS-Simplex (TM) collars on grizzly bears in western and northern Canada. *Wildlife Society Bulletin* **32**: 693–701.

Gleiss, A. C., Wilson, R. P., and Shepard, E. L. C. 2011. Making overall dynamic body acceleration work: on the theory of acceleration as a proxy for energy expenditure. *Methods in Ecology and Evolution* **2**: 23–33.

Gursky, S. 2005. Associations between adult spectral tarsiers. *American Journal of Physical Anthropology* **128**: 74–83.

Halsey, L. G., Green, J. A., Wilson, R. P., and Frappell, P. B. 2009a. Accelerometry to estimate energy expenditure during activity: best practice with data loggers. *Physiological and Biochemical Zoology* **82**: 396–404.

Halsey, L. G., Shepard, E. L. C., Quintana, F., et al. 2009b. The relationship between oxygen consumption and body acceleration in a range of species. *Comparative Biochemistry and Physiology A: Molecular & Integrative Physiology* **152**: 197–202.

Hansen, M. C. and Riggs, R. A. 2008. Accuracy, precision, and observation rates of global positioning system telemetry collars. *Journal of Wildlife Management* **72**: 518–526.

Hebblewhite, M. and Haydon, D. T. 2010. Distinguishing technology from biology: a critical review of the use of GPS telemetry data in ecology. *Philosophical Transactions of the Royal Society B: Biological Sciences* **365**: 2303–2312.

Hebblewhite, M., Percy, M., and Merrill, E. H. 2007. Are all global positioning system collars created equal? Correcting habitat-induced bias using three brands in the Central Canadian Rockies. *Journal of Wildlife Management* **71**: 2026–2033.

Hulbert, I. A. R. and French, J. 2001. The accuracy of GPS for wildlife telemetry and habitat mapping. *Journal of Applied Ecology* **38**: 869–878.

Isbell, L. A. 1994. Predation on primates: ecological patterns and evolutionary consequences. *Evolutionary Anthropology: Issues, News, and Reviews* **3**: 61–71.

Isbell, L. A. and Young, T. P. 1993. Human presence reduces predation in a free-ranging vervet monkey population in Kenya. *Animal Behaviour* **45**: 1233–1235.

Jachowski, D. S., Slotow, R., and Millspaugh, J. J. 2014. Good virtual fences make good neighbors: opportunities for conservation. *Animal Conservation* **17**: 187–196.

Jolly, A. 1966. *Lemur Behavior: A Madagascar Field Study.* University of Chicago Press, Chicago, IL.

Juarez, C. P., Rotundo, M. A., Berg, W., and Fernandez-Duque, E. 2011. Costs and benefits of radio-collaring on the behavior, demography, and conservation of owl monkeys (*Aotus azarai*) in Formosa, Argentina. *International Journal of Primatology* **32**: 69–82.

Kaplan, E. D. and Hegarty, C. J. 2005. *Understanding GPS: Principles and Applications.* Artech House, London.

Kappeler, P. 1997. Intrasexual selection in *Mirza coquereli*: evidence for scramble competition polygyny in a solitary primate. *Behavioral Ecology and Sociobiology* **41**: 115–127.

Kappeler, P., Barrett, L., Blumstein, D. T., and Clutton-Brock, T. H. E. 2013. Flexibility and constraint in the evolution of mammalian social behaviour. *Philosophical Transactions of the Royal Society B: Biological Sciences* **368**: 20120337.

Kays, R., Crofoot, M. C., Jetz, W., and Wikelski, M. 2015. Terrestrial animal tracking as an eye on life and planet. *Science* **348**: DOI: 10.1126/science.aaa2478.

King, A. J., Wilson, A. M., Wilshin, S. D., et al. 2012. Selfish-herd behaviour of sheep under threat. *Current Biology* **22**: R561–R562.

Kranstauber, B., Kays, R., LaPoint, S. D., Wikelski, M., and Safi, K. 2012. A dynamic Brownian bridge movement model to estimate utilization distributions for heterogeneous animal movement. *Journal of Animal Ecology* **81**: 738–746.

Krause, J., Krause, S., Arlinghaus, R., et al. 2013. Reality mining of animal social systems. *Trends in Ecology & Evolution* **28**: 541–551.

Lesku, J. A., Rattenborg, N. C., Valcu, M., et al. 2012. You snooze, you lose: adaptive sleep loss in polygynous pectoral sandpipers. *Journal of Sleep Research* **21**: 5.

Lynch, E., Angeloni, L., Fristrup, K., Joyce, D., and Wittemyer, G. 2013. The use of on-animal acoustical recording devices for studying animal behavior. *Ecology and Evolution* **3**: 2030–2037.

Macdonald, D. W. and Amlaner, C. J. 1980. A practical guide to radio tracking. Pages 143–159 in A *Handbook on Biotelemetry and Radio Tracking*. C. J. Amlaner and D. W. MacDonald (Eds.). Pergamon Press, Oxford.

Manson, J. H. and Wrangham, R. W. 1991. Intergroup aggression in chimpanzees and humans. *Current Anthropology* **32**: 369–390.

Markham, A. C. and Altmann, J. 2008. Remote monitoring of primates using automated GPS technology in open habitats. *American Journal of Primatology* **70**: 1–5.

Markham, A. C., Alberts, S. C., and Altmann, J. 2012. Intergroup conflict: ecological predictors of winning and consequences of defeat in a wild primate population. *Animal Behaviour* **84**: 399–403.

Markham, A. C., Guttal, V., Alberts, S. C., and Altmann, J. 2013. When good neighbors don't need fences: temporal landscape partitioning among baboon social groups. *Behavioral Ecology and Sociobiology* **67**: 875–884.

Merker, S. 2006. Habitat-specific ranging patterns of Dian's tarsiers (*Tarsius dianae*) as revealed by radiotracking. *American Journal of Primatology* **68**: 111–125.

Moil, R. J., Millspaugh, J. J., Beringer, J., Sartwell, J., and He, Z. 2007. A new "view" of ecology and conservation through animal-borne video systems. *Trends in Ecology & Evolution* **22**: 660–668.

Nagy, M., Akos, Z., Biro, D., and Vicsek, T. 2010. Hierarchical group dynamics in pigeon flocks. *Nature* **464**: 890–899.

Nagy, M., Vásárhelyi, G., Pettit, B., et al. 2013. Context-dependent hierarchies in pigeons. *Proceedings of the National Academy of Sciences* **110**: 13049–13054.

Nathan, R., Getz, W. M., Revilla, E., et al. 2008. A movement ecology paradigm for unifying organismal movement research. *Proceedings of the National Academy of Sciences of the United States of America* **105**: 19052–19059.

Nathan, R., Spiegel, O., Fortmann-Roe, S., et al. 2012. Using tri-axial acceleration data to identify behavioral modes of free-ranging animals: general concepts and tools illustrated for griffon vultures. *Journal of Experimental Biology* **215**: 986–996.

Newmaster, S. G., Thompson, I. D., Steeves, R. A., et al. 2013. Examination of two new technologies to assess the diet of woodland caribou: video recorders attached to collars and DNA barcoding. *Canadian Journal of Forest Research* **43**: 897–900.

Nowak, K., le Roux, A., Richards, S. A., Scheijen, C. P. J., and Hill, R. A. 2014. Human observers impact habituated samango monkeys' perceived landscape of fear. *Behavioral Ecology* **25**. DOI: 10.1093/beheco/aru110.

Perez-Escudero, A. and de Polavieja, G. G. 2011. Collective animal behavior from Bayesian estimation and probability matching. *PLoS Computational Biology* **7**. DOI: 10.1371/journal. pcbi.1002282.

Pettit, B., Perna, A., Biro, D., and Sumpter, D. J. T. 2013. Interaction rules underlying group decisions in homing pigeons. *Journal of the Royal Society Interface* **10**. DOI: 10.1098/rsif.2013.0529.

Phillips, K. A., Elvey, C. R., and Abercrombie, C. L. 1998. Applying GPS to the study of primate ecology: A useful tool? *American Journal of Primatology* **46**: 167–172.

Qasem, L., Cardew, A., Wilson, A., et al. 2012. Tri-axial dynamic acceleration as a proxy for animal energy expenditure: should we be summing values or calculating the vector? *PLoS ONE* **7**. DOI: 10.1371/journal.pone.0031187.

Rasmussen, D. R. 1991. Observer influence on range use of *Macaca arctoides* after 14 years of observation? *Laboratory Primate Newsletter* **30**: 6–11.

Rattenborg, N. C., Voirin, B., Vyssotski, A. L., et al. 2008. Sleeping outside the box: electro-encephalographic measures of sleep in sloths inhabiting a rainforest. *Biology Letters* **4**: 402–405.

Recio, M. R., Mathieu, R., Denys, P., Sirguey, P., and Seddon, P. J. 2011. Lightweight GPS-tags, one giant leap for wildlife tracking? An assessment approach. *PLoS ONE* **6**. DOI: 10.1371/journal.pone.0028225.

Rempel, R. S., Rodgers, A. R., and Abraham, K. F. 1995. Performance of a GPS animal location system under boreal forest canopy. *Journal of Wildlife Management* **59**: 543–551.

Ren, B., Li, M., Long, Y., Grüter, C. C., and Wei, F. 2008. Measuring daily ranging distances of *Rhinopithecus bieti* via a global positioning system collar at Jinsichang, China: a methodo-logical consideration. *International Journal of Primatology* **29**(3): 783.

Rodgers, A. R. 2001. Recent telemetry technology. Pages 82–121 in *Radio Tracking and Animal Populations*. J. J. Millspaugh and J. M. Marzluff (Eds.). Academic Press, San Diego, CA.

Rodman, P. S. and Mitani, J. C. 1987. Orangutans: sexual dimorphism in a solitary species. Pages 146–154 in *Primate Societies*. B. Smuts, D. L. Cheney, R. M. Seyfarth, T. T. Struhsaker, and R. Wrangham (Eds.). Chicago University Press, Chicago, IL.

Rutz, C. and Troscianko, J. 2013. Programmable, miniature video-loggers for deployment on wild birds and other wildlife. *Methods in Ecology and Evolution* **4**: 114–122.

Sapir, N., Wikelski, M., McCue, M. D., Pinshow, B., and Nathan, R. 2010. Flight modes in migrating European bee-eaters: heart rate may indicate low metabolic rate during soaring and gliding. *PLoS ONE* **5**: e13956.

Sapir, N., Rotics, S., Kaatz, M., et al. 2013. Multi-year tracking of white storks (*Ciconia ciconia*): how the environment shapes the movement and behavior of a soaring-gliding inter-continental migrant. *Integrative and Comparative Biology* **53**: E189–E189.

Shepard, E. L. C., Wilson, R. P., Halsey, L. G., et al. 2009. Derivation of body motion via appropriate smoothing of acceleration data. *Aquatic Biology* **4**: 235–241.

Shumaker, R. 2007. *Orangutans*. Voyager Press, St. Paul, MI.

Sih, A. 2013. Understanding variation in behavioural responses to human-induced rapid environmental change: a conceptual overview. *Animal Behaviour* **85**: 1077–1088.

Singleton, I. and van Schaik, C. P. 2001. Orangutan home range size and its determinants in a Sumatran swamp forest. *International Journal of Primatology* **22**: 877–911.

Spiegel, O., Getz, W. M., and Nathan, R. 2013. Factors influencing foraging search efficiency: why do scarce lappet-faced vultures outperform ubiquitous white-backed vultures? *The American Naturalist* **181**: E102–E115.

Sprague, D. 2004. GPS collars for monkeys: the state of the technology. *American Journal of Physical Anthropology* **186**: 151–154.

Sprague, D. S., Kabaya, M., and Hagihara, K. 2004. Field testing a global positioning system (GPS) collar on a Japanese monkey: reliability of automatic GPS positioning in a Japanese forest. *Primates* **45**: 151–154.

Strandburg-Peshkin, A., Twomey, C. R., Bode, N. W. F., et al. 2013. Visual sensory networks and effective information transfer in animal groups. *Current Biology* **23**: R709–R711.

Strandburg-Peshkin, A., Farine, D. R., Couzin, I. D., and Crofoot, M. C. 2015. Shared decision-making drives collective movement in wild baboons. *Science* **348**: 1358–1361.

Thorington, R. W., Muckenhirn, N. A., and Montgomery, G. G. 1976. Movements of a wild night monkey (*Aotus trivirgatus*). Pages 32–34 in *Neotropical Primates*. R. W. Thorington and P. G. Heltne (Eds.). National Academy of Sciences, Washington, DC.

Tomkiewicz, S. M., Fuller, M. R., Kie, J. G., and Bates, K. K. 2010. Global positioning system and associated technologies in animal behaviour and ecological research. *Philosophical Transactions of the Royal Society B: Biological Sciences* **365**: 2163–2176.

Tomlinson, S., Arnall, S. G., Munn, A., et al. 2014. Applications and implications of ecological energetics. *Trends in Ecology & Evolution* **29**: 280–290.

van Schaik, C. P. 1983. On the ultimate causes of primate social systems. *Behaviour* **85**: 91–117.

Voirin, B., Scriba, M. F., Martinez-Gonzalez, D., et al. 2014. Ecology and neurophysiology of sleep in two wild sloth species. *Sleep* **37**: 753.

Wall, J., Wittemyer, G., Klinkenberg, B., and Douglas-Hamilton, I. 2014. Novel opportunities for wildlife conservation and research with real-time monitoring. *Ecological Applications* **24**: 593–601.

Watts, I., Nagy, M., Biro, T. B., and de Perera, D. 2016. Misinformed leaders lose influence over pigeon flocks. *Biology Letters* **12**: 20160544.

White, E. C., Dikangadissi, J. T., Dimoto, E., et al. 2010. Home-range use by a large horde of wild *Mandrillus sphinx*. *International Journal of Primatology* **31**: 627–645.

Wikelski, M. and Kays, R. 2011. Movebank: archive, analysis and sharing of animal movement data. Available at: www.movebank.org.

Wikelski, M., Kays, R. W., Kasdin, N. J., et al. 2007. Going wild: what a global small-animal tracking system could do for experimental biologists. *Journal of Experimental Biology* **210**: 181–186.

Wilcove, D. S. and Wikelski, M. 2008. Going, going, gone: is animal migration disappearing. *PLOS Biology* **6**: e188.

Williams, D. M., Quinn, A. D., and Porter, W. F. 2012. Impact of habitat-specific GPS positional error on detection of movement scales by first-passage time analysis. *PLoS ONE* **7**. DOI: 10.1371/journal.pone.0048439.

Wilson, A. M., Lowe, J. C., Roskilly, K., et al. 2013. Locomotion dynamics of hunting in wild cheetahs. *Nature* **498**: 185–189.

Wilson, R. P., White, C. R., Quintana, F., et al. 2006. Moving towards acceleration for estimates of activity-specific metabolic rate in free-living animals: the case of the cormorant. *Journal of Animal Ecology* **75**: 1081–1090.

Wilson, R. P., Shepard, E., and Liebsch, N. 2008. Prying into the intimate details of animal lives: use of a daily diary on animals. *Endangered Species Research* **4**: 123–137.

Yoda, K., Murakoshi, M., Tsutsui, K., and Kohno, H. 2011. Social interactions of juvenile brown boobies at sea as observed with animal-borne video cameras. *PLoS ONE* **6**. DOI: 10.1371/journal.pone.0019602.

Zinner, D., Hindahl, J., and Kaumanns, W. 2001. Experimental intergroup encounters in lion-tailed macaques (*Macaca silenus*). *Primate Report* **59**: 77–92.

4 The Ethical Implications, and Practical Consequences, of Attaching Remote Telemetry Apparatus to Macaques

Amy Klegarth, Agustín Fuentes, Lisa Jones-Engel, Greg Marshall, and Kyler Abernathy

Introduction

The use of global positioning system (GPS) units attached to collars is becoming increasingly common in primate studies (Anderson, pers. comm.; Crofoot et al. 2014; Di Fiore & Link 2013; Dore, pers. comm.; Klegarth et al. 2017; Markham & Altmann 2008; Markham et al. 2013; Sprague et al. 2004; Stark, pers. comm.). By deploying GPS collars, researchers can gain enhanced knowledge of primate group whereabouts and overall ranging and landscape use patterns at a high resolution (Crofoot et al. 2014). The utility of these systems has greatly expanded with the increasing spatial accuracy, reliability, and mechanisms (remote data download and drop-off units) of units that facilitate reasonably low impact on study animals (Klegarth et al. 2017; Matthews et al. 2013). While these collars open up new methodological and analytic possibilities for assessing primate ranging patterns and habitat use, they also present a diverse array of technical, structural, and ethical concerns with doing so (Hebblewhite & Haydon 2010; Todd & Shah 2012)

In addition to GPS collars, recently our research team has initiated the use of collar-attached high-definition (HD) camera units (National Geographic Crittercam™). The ability to track primates' activity from their own visual perspective can change the way we study the animals by providing access to a currently unavailable suite of data on their lives and their interactions with humans and other fauna. Crittercams™, developed by the National Geographic Remote Imaging Team (NGRIT), are a microprocessor-controlled camera system affixed to collars. This system provides us a new perspective on how primates navigate their world. These units open avenues for better understanding and analyzing patterns relating to locomotion, path choice, inter-individual interactions, food choice, and bite patterns, as well as "firsthand" data as to what collared animals do immediately, and the 24 hours after, release.

It is often assumed that externally attached devices that weigh under the suggested 5 percent of total bodyweight (American Society of Mammalogists 1998), will have little, or no, negative impact on the animals to which they are attached. Within primates, this has rarely been systematically assessed, but some published studies deploying GPS and radio collars on primates highlight potential impacts (e.g., capuchins in Crofoot et al.

2009; macaques in Sprague et al. 2004; baboons in Markham & Altmann 2008; howler monkeys in Hilpert & Jones 2005; tarsiers in Gursky 1998). Crofoot et al. (2009) reported initial behavioral responses to radio collars that included pulling and manipulating collars up to two weeks post-deployment. Additionally, Crofoot et al. (2010) utilized automated radio-telemetry collars to assess observer impact on capuchin ranging behavior and activity patterns, but did not explicitly test changes in movement patterns relative to the collaring date. Gursky (1998) observed no differences in body condition among tarsiers over a six-month collar deployment that compared collar weights (2.6–4 percent of total body weight versus 5.5–7.6 percent). Similarly, no negative impacts were reported either by Markham and Altmann (2008) nor Sprague et al. (2004); however, no explicit tests for changes in movement or behavior were conducted. To date, the primary negative effect reported among primate collar studies was for a radio-collared female howler who spent more time alone and less time with adult males than other females, and ultimately left her group (Hilpert & Jones 2005). However, owing to the singular nature of that sample, it is imprudent to draw direct links between the individual being collared and the possible social repercussions. Issues of collar attachment and design are discussed throughout a large body of radio-collar literature and are highly species- and sex-specific (e.g., belt designs are poor for females who may become pregnant). More robust measures of health impacts have been reported for non-primates where an initial (1–4 day) acute reduction in movement and activity rate occurred (Todd & Shah 2012), birth sex ratios changed in favor of males for collared individuals compared to control groups (Moorhouse & MacDonald 2005), and increased abandonment of young was reported (Côté et al. 1998). Tuyttens et al.'s (2002) work on badgers demonstrated an acclimation period of ~100 days, below which body condition was impacted and after which it was not. These studies largely highlight trapping, sedation, and handling as the primary stressor over any burden imposed by the collars themselves (Côté et al. 1998; Todd & Shah 2012); as such, we discuss our own trapping methodologies related to collaring in depth, as they relate to minimization of overall stress to the focal individuals.

In this chapter we review the technical and practical aspects of remote telemetry via collar-attached units, with examples based on our work in Singapore and Gibraltar with macaques. We also consider the ethical issues for remote telemetry in general, and provide specific insight from our own case studies. We begin by outlining basic ethical guidelines that we believe must be considered at the onset of any remote telemetry or collar-facilitated study.

Basic Ethical Guidelines

Ethical considerations for embarking on a remote telemetry study that involves collaring primates must begin with the choice of focal individuals and subsequent trapping efforts. While there are a number of good overviews of the methods and practices involved in trapping and handling primates (Setchell & Curtis 2010), there are few that deal directly, and specifically, with ethical concerns in field contexts (Nash 2005). The recent emphasis on primatological ethics (MacKinnon & Riley 2013) is slowly changing the landscape for such research. However, to date, there is little published literature directly dealing with the ethics of the deployment and use of primate-borne telemetry systems. While researchers must always gain Institutional Animal Care and Use Committee (IACUC) approval for their studies, IACUC boards are typically lab-centric and may have little experience with field primatology in particular. Given this, we seek to outline a robust ethical framework for researchers to consider as they develop their own research plans.

One of the current best outlines of the ethical issues faced when trapping and collaring mammals comes from "Refinements in telemetry procedures seventh report of the BVAAWF/FRAME/RSPCA/UFAW Joint Working Group on Refinement, Part A" (Morton et al. 2003). This report focuses on "refinements in the use of internally or externally mounted devices for transmitting or storing (logging) physiological data from experimental animals in the laboratory and in the field," and has sections dealing specifically with externally mounted remote telemetry devices used in the field. First and foremost they remind us that "it is vital to remember that telemetry, like all other procedures on animals, also needs to be refined" (Morton et al. 2003: 3). Here, "refinement" reflects practices that minimize suffering and improve welfare of the target animals during the procedure of interest and to identify, as thoroughly as possible, the potential harms involved in the procedure.

Based on the report we can derive a set of basic ethical practices that must be developed and employed when engaged in projects involving externally mounted remote telemetry devices. These include:

1. Determine that there is a genuine scientific requirement for data obtained by telemetry device.
2. Ensure that the scientific benefits, as well as the benefits to the animals of each study, including the reasons for using telemetry, have been fully set out and weighed against all of the potential harms to animals.
3. Consider the full range of potential harms created by the trapping, sedation, handling, recovery, and release protocols and back-up plans.
4. Consider the physical conformation of the device and its potential to interfere with the full range of locomotion, postures, and behavior of the target individuals.
5. Monitor behavior and physical changes in health or movement to ensure that the physiological burden is minimal, and have a back-up plan to remove the device at minimal risk to the target animal.
6. Have a plan for how to remove the telemetry device at the end of the study, or have a technical facility incorporated into the device such that it will fall off on its own within a specified timeframe. This should be monitored.
7. Monitor device failure rates and incorporate results into overall project evaluation.

There are three basic categories of harm that the deployment of externally borne telemetry units can introduce in primates: (1) potential harms associated with animal capture and telemetry attachment procedures; (2) potential harms during the recovery and release phases post-attachment; and (3) potential physical and social impact of the device on the animal once units are attached and individuals return to their social group.

Here we present a review and assessment of core ethically relevant aspects of trapping/collaring for remote telemetry and the ethical questions the process introduces by drawing examples from our work deploying GPS and Crittercam™ units on macaques in Singapore and Gibraltar. We highlight how we address each of the six specific ethical guidelines as we deal with them throughout the remainder of this chapter. We begin with the benefits to scientific inquiry that are gained by utilizing remote telemetry units.

Determine that there is a genuine scientific requirement for data obtained by telemetry device. For nearly 15 years, our group's research on the human–primate interface has characterized behavior, ecology, and bidirectional pathogen transmission, as well as the varied contexts of human–primate contact across this porous and ever-changing interface (Fuentes et al. 2008; Jones-Engel & Engel 2009; Jones-Engel et al. 2005; Oberste et al. 2013). Over the last five years we have increasingly involved telemetry via collar-attached units as part of our research toolkit. Our study sites in Gibraltar and throughout Southeast Asia are compelling settings owing to the faunal diversity of these regions, which includes a plethora of primate and non-primate species as well as a diverse microbial fauna, some of the world's densest human populations, bustling regional and international commerce, and tourists from around the globe. The heterogeneous landscape in our study sites often has the animals in areas that are difficult to follow or inaccessible (e.g., cliffs, rainforest ravines with unstable slopes), and/or where researcher presence might impact the movement of the animals (e.g., homing to individuals outside of their typical zone of human interface). The data generated from our GPS collaring has allowed us unprecedented and unfettered access to the complex ranging patterns of these animals. Early analyses of these data have given us new insights into the following: (1) the role that urban primates may play as intermediaries between wildlife and human populations; (2) variation in intergroup home and daily ranging patterns; (3) variation in number and use of sleep sites; and (4) the quantitative impact that trapping and collaring may have on study animal ranging patterns. Likewise, footage derived from Crittercam™ collars provided a completely unique perspective on (1) how macaques manipulate collar devices post-deployment and (2) how macaques navigate their environment, particularly in areas researchers might not otherwise have access to.

Ensure that the scientific benefits as well as the benefits to the animals of each study, including the reasons for using telemetry, have been fully set out and weighed against all of the potential harms to animals. Beyond the scientific benefits of increased data consistency and resolution in better characterizing nonhuman primate ranging patterns and habitat use, we embarked upon this work to aid urban primate population management. In both Singapore and Gibraltar, wildlife management frequently deals with macaques as pest species and employs random culls. We deployed GPS collars to (1) evaluate their reliability and efficiency for use by wildlife management and (2) to characterize how these urban primates utilize zones of human interface, to aid in the development of humane, proactive management strategies. Ultimately, these data will be used to help mitigate human–macaque conflict and minimize or eliminate the need for culls within these populations by highlighting interface hot spots for park managers to focus their resources and efforts on. Park rangers typically lack the workforce to employ behavioral modification efforts across all troops (e.g., herding, deterrence), but GPS collar data highlights which troops actually spend a significant amount of time interfacing with humans and the temporal patterns governing that spatial overlap, thus allowing management efforts to be focused on those groups, regions, and times. While the GSM cell network technology was not yet small enough for use on our focal species, GPS collars connected through such GSM cell networks are now viable options for some nonhuman primate species (Dore, pers. comm.). This subset of GPS collars can specifically benefit management efforts by allowing for real-time, long-distance remote data acquisition. One specific example would be if an individual from each troop is tagged around conflict hot-spots, park rangers could access troop whereabouts while off-site and deploy a response team directly to the problem areas and distinguish which troops cause the greatest nuisance.

Upon establishing the benefits not only to science broadly but to the focal species specifically, the next ethical consideration is to ensure that the research team is fully qualified and equipped to safely conduct trapping and collar deployment. Our research on the human–primate interface has benefited from the contributions of team members who possess expertise in a variety of fields: primatology, anthropology, human medicine, veterinary medicine, epidemiology, molecular biology, and remote monitoring. These varied perspectives have proved helpful at all stages of the work from both a practical perspective as well as an ethical one, that of ensuring the work can be conducted safely for all humans and nonhuman primates involved. Safely conducting trapping and collar deployment at the human–macaque interface frequently involves having a large enough workforce to ensure public safety in addition to the safety of the research team and monkeys. In addition to local collaborators and research subjects, researchers must also interact effectively with local and governmental officials and communities, all of whom frequently have their own specific interests and agendas. To this end, it is ethically imperative for researchers to have in place explicit understandings and agreements regarding how such organizations intend to use collected data (MacKinnon & Riley 2013).

Once scientific justification, benefits to the focal species, and a team with the appropriate technical expertise have been assembled, in order to ethically justify trapping and collaring primates, researchers still must meet the following basal criteria: (1) physical and psychological damage to the study animals and their conspecifics will be minimized; (2) researchers will conduct field tests prior to large-scale implementation of telemetry work to provide baselines on study animal behavior and verify no quantifiable deleterious impact on behavior post-deployment; (3) data must meet a predetermined acceptable quantity and quality threshold to justify trapping/collaring (that can be set based on field tests); and (4) collar deployment duration will be limited to answering the specific questions being considered.

*Consider the **full range of potential harms** created by the trapping, sedation, handling, recovery, and release protocols and back-up plans.* Once it is firmly established that capturing the study animals is ethically justified, the basic ethical guidelines for

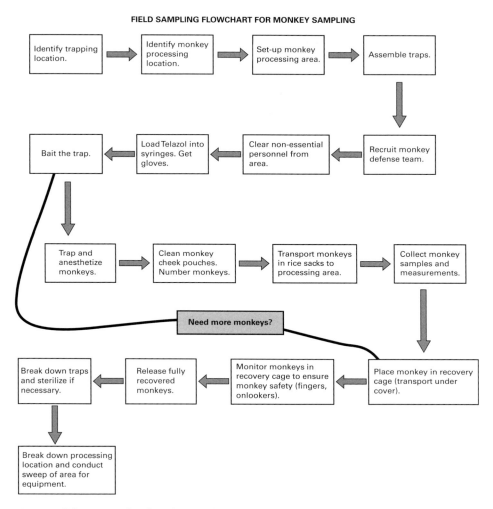

Figure 4.1 Primate trapping flowchart outlining considerations and protocols for researchers embarking on remote telemetry deployment.

trapping procedures should employ methods that: (1) maximize the physical safety of both researchers and target primates; (2) minimize the risk of deleterious physiological and/or psychological impact on target primates; (3) minimize by-catch but maximize data collection for targeted individuals; and (4) measure successful outcomes and revise protocols in response to unsuccessful ones. Our trapping, sampling, and animal handling protocols have evolved with our hypotheses as well as with changing technology. We strongly recommend developing a detailed, step-by-step algorithm for the entire process – from trapping to animal handling to collar attachment to sample acquisition to animal release to data analysis and dissemination. Ours is outlined in Figure 4.1.

Our early methods for trapping wild primates relied on local designs that used natural materials from the forest. However, it became apparent that our methods for trapping wild monkeys were ecologically unsustainable, not portable, and potentially dangerous for both monkeys and researchers: in short, not sufficiently ethically sound. Though the protocols were IACUC-approved and data were successfully collected and no harm had come to either researchers or primates, we recognized that our methods required refinement in order to be more consistent with the ethical imperative that researchers should hold themselves to when handling free-ranging primates. Working with the bioengineers at the Washington National Primate Research Center, we designed a 2 × 2 × 3 m, large trapping cage composed of interlocking aluminum poles and non-porous nylon net that combines portability, durability, reusability, and ease of sterilization – all important considerations for ensuring ideal trapping locations and conditions are achieved in order to promote primate, researcher, and public safety.

We strongly feel that ethical research requires that field trapping teams must include individuals explicitly trained in animal handling and sedation (e.g., veterinarians and/or technicians), ideally with experience handling specific species of interest. It is particularly important to have a trained primate technician/veterinarian on hand as a member of the team as initial undersedation can often lead to repeated sedations which are increasingly dangerous for the animal. Sedation is typically administered within the first five minutes of capture to minimize distress for both the captured individual and the group. Traps are covered with tarps to prevent overheating and to minimize distress to the captured individual's social group. Our animals remain sedated and are monitored continuously during the biological sample collection and collar fittings.

Recognizing that trapping, handling, and anesthesia present inherent risks to these animals, we work quickly and focus our attention first on the physical suitability of the animal for wearing a collar and next on an appropriate collar fit; finally, we collect a full suite of biological and morphometric data. These biological samples (whole blood, plasma, urine, feces, hair, buccal swabs) form a rich dataset that complements the collar-derived data. It is ethically important to maximize the amount of biologically relevant information collected from each individual as it reduces any need for recapture. As such, we collect these metrics from all by-catch individuals as well. At sites with established long-term recapture and monitoring programs, primates are implanted with a unique identifier (AVID microchip) to facilitate future longitudinal studies. Following sample collection, the animals are placed in small recovery cages and allowed to recover fully from anesthesia before being released. Another ethical consideration regarding trapping during collaring efforts is one of trap and recovery cage sterilization. To avoid transfer of pathogens between social groups and geographic sites, it is imperative that research teams be equipped with the supplies to readily sterilize all trap and cage components. We are fortunate to have ready access to running water, bleach, and detergent in both Singapore and Gibraltar, but researchers conducting trapping in more remote areas should consider having water ported to trap sites or otherwise plan on bringing cages back to camps or field stations for decontamination between trap sites.

The trapping procedures described above have been used by our research team since 1998 with no fatalities or significant injuries among >1400 primates we have sampled to date. As such, we believe the trapping method we currently employ is both highly successful and ethically sound, and creates a safe, effective context for attaching collars to nonhuman primates. Heretofore we have provided case-specific contexts for the first three ethical guidelines outlined above. The final three ethical guidelines are considered within the scope of our methods and results. We will end with a comprehensive overview of the outcomes of our GPS and Crittercam™ collar deployments as they relate to the ethical framework as a whole.

Methods

Consider the **physical conformation** *of the device and* **its potential to interfere** *with the full range of locomotion, postures, and behavior of the target individuals.*

GPS Equipment

We deployed Telemetry Solutions Quantum 4000 Medium GPS collars (Telemetry Solutions, Concord, CA) on both long-tailed macaques (*Macaca fascicularis*) in Singapore and Barbary macaques (*M. sylvanus*) in Gibraltar. Collars weighed 160–180 g and we followed American Society of Mammalogists (1998) guidelines for remote telemetry systems (aiming for systems that weighed less than 5 percent of the target animal's total mass). Thus only individuals >3.5 kg were deemed suitable candidates for collar deployment.

The GPS collars were made of waterproofed leather or nylon and affixed with bolts. GPS collars were equipped with store-on-board, ultra-high-frequency (UHF) remote data download capabilities as well as a programmed or remote drop-off mechanism. Both features were deemed necessary as they greatly reduce impact upon the study animals by reducing the need for constant monitoring and the need to recapture individuals for collar removal. Units also emitted very high-frequency (VHF) tracking signals to enable homing to individuals for data retrieval.

Following an initial set of field tests, we added cotton spacers that would degrade over time as a back-up for the drop-off mechanism and an "emergency release" mechanism if the collars were too bothersome for the macaques. Over time the cotton wears and stretches so as to either break away or be easily removed by macaques. The collar material was cut and the cotton spacers were riveted such that 3–4 cm was exposed between collar sections. The use of the cotton spacer was developed after the failure of a pre-programmed release mechanism during the first field test and the successful, but significantly delayed, drop-off experienced during the second. Wires extending from the units were tied down with string and taped over with electrical tape to secure them from chewing and other manipulation after testing that such binding had no discernible impact on signal transmission.

Prior to deployment on the macaques we programmed and tested collar function with researchers wearing programmed collars on their wrists while hiking and downloading collar data from a variety of distances, including with the researchers out of sight from each other. When hiking routes from downloaded data were verified for both units, collar function was deemed suitable for live deployment.

GPS Field Test

We conducted an initial short-term field test in Singapore during summer 2011 to evaluate collar and download equipment in heavily canopied rainforest and under high temperatures and humidity, as well as to assess the tolerance levels of macaques and the health impact of wearing the collars. The first field test was four weeks long and was conducted at Bukit Timah Nature Reserve, Singapore. A second field test was conducted in summer 2012 at Upper Seletar Reservoir, Singapore, to assess a remotely triggered drop-off function prior to engaging in larger-scale long-term deployments. As the primary purpose of the second field test was solely to test the triggered drop-off function, the deployment spanned only four days. The initial field test employed a preset, programmed drop-off and, using the same drop-off hardware but modified software, the subsequent field test assessed a remote trigger function.

GPS: Subjects, Trapping, and Data Collection

Only fully adult *M. fascicularis* and subadult or fully adult *M. sylvanus* were deemed acceptable to collar; no females in advanced pregnancy were collared, nor were individuals who were deemed physically compromised based on examination by the team veterinarian. Collars were fitted only on individuals with chests wide enough that wearing the collar unit did not interfere with a full range of motion in their arms and heads. We paid particular attention to any restrictions of jaw movement, head movement, use of cheek pouches, and the potential for abrasion of the neck area. If any of these seemed to be possible during the fitting of the collar we did not affix the collar to that individual.

Collars were fitted to allow researchers' index and the pointer fingers (adult female, with only a single finger for an adult male researcher) to comfortably fit under, allowing room for maximum mandible movement and full use of cheek pouches. Furthermore, it was deemed important to fit collars using a lax hold on the monkey whereby the individual was held in a variety of natural positions to test fit and comfort. Researchers found that if collars were fitted using standard primate restraint holds, upon relaxation of the hold the fit was compromised. Deployed collars are pictured for both species in Figure 4.2.

In total, 15 macaques were fitted with Quantum 4000 GPS units, including three collared during the Singapore preliminary field tests and six individuals collared in each of two long-term (4–6 months) deployments in Singapore and Gibraltar. Collars were set to collect points every 5–15 minutes (7 a.m. to 7 p.m.) during the field tests and hourly overnight. For long-term deployments collars were programmed to take a GPS fix every half-hour (7 a.m. to 7 p.m.) and every two hours overnight.

Tracking, Monitoring, and Data Download

Individuals were tracked using a three-element Yagi antenna and VHF receiver to their specified frequencies. Upon locating individuals every few days, researchers could download data to a netbook using the program Collar SW 1.74 via a three-element Yagi antenna

(a)

(b)

Figure 4.2 GPS collars deployed on (a) an adult male *Macaca fascicularis* in Singapore and (b) an adult female *M. sylvanus* in Gibraltar.

connected to a remote download unit (Telemetry Solutions, Concord, CA). Researchers also made qualitative behavioral observations to note whether collared individuals were the recipients of aggressive behavior, appeared physically compromised, and whether or not other macaques or the collared individuals themselves manipulated their collar.

Crittercam™ Equipment

Crittercam™ HD video collars were custom-designed and developed by NGRIT and modified based on input from our team using insights from our initial GPS collar field tests. Crittercam™ collars ranged between 240 g and 375 g; thus only individuals >5 kg and >7.5 kg were targeted for small and large Crittercam™ units, respectively. The Crittercam™ units deployed in Singapore were ad hoc attempts employing cameras and cases modified from the NGRIT project with tree kangaroos and attached to small nylon pet collars with an NGRIT-designed pre-programmed release mechanism. The Gibraltar deployment used cameras and casings initially developed for an NGRIT cheetah study with larger nylon collars and a dual release system: the NGRIT-designed release and a back-up self-contained release from Telonics (Mesa, AZ). All units were equipped with VHF tracking signals to enable researchers to locate and observe collared individuals.

All deployments were scheduled to last between 24 and 72 hours, at the end of which the release was programmed to drop the collar/camera assembly off the individual. Recording schedules ranged from a continuous 8–10 hour recording to five two-hour blocks over the course of two days. In addition to analysis of the footage, we made opportunistic, qualitative observations of all individuals following their release. In total, eight individuals were fitted with Crittercam™ units: two in Singapore and six in Gibraltar.

Impact Analysis

*Monitor behavior and appropriate physiological parameters to **ensure that the physiological burden has been minimized** and have a back-up plan to remove the device at minimal risk to the target animal.* For GPS collars, our first assessments of the impact and ethical considerations are based on continuous qualitative observations of what happens upon attachment of the collar, during the animal's recovery in a holding cage, and then upon release. We then assess the impact on the animal wearing the collar with two quantitative valuations: Are ranging patterns impacted? Do any injuries occur during the deployment? We also undertake the following ad libitum qualitative assessments: Does behavior change? How do humans (non-researchers) interacting with/observing the monkeys react?

All GPS collar data were visualized using ESRI (2014) topographic and world imagery basemaps. All Singapore data used the WGS 1984 datum and were projected in WGS 1984 UTM Zone 48N. All Gibraltar data used the WGS 1984 datum and were projected in WGS 1984 UTM Zone 30N. Only three-dimensional fixes were retained; subsequent ranging analysis and field test datasets were cropped to half-hourly fixes to match long-term deployment schedules. The four-day deployment was excluded from the quantitative ranging impact analysis as it was too short to assess significant temporal changes. Two-dimensional fixes derived from less than three connected satellites were removed to increase overall accuracy. The 3D fix dataset was further hand-cropped in ArcMap 10.1 (ESRI 2014) to remove outliers based on either improbable locations (e.g., in oceans or reservoirs) or single points deviating outside the normal home range in a nonlinear fashion before returning to the previous location.

To assess significant changes in ranging across the duration of the collar deployment, means for day range size, daily path length, and movement rate were compared using

ANOVAs and post-hoc Tukey's HSD to explore whether there were significant deviations based on week and month with respect to the initial collaring date across individuals. Day range size was calculated with 95 percent fixed kernel density (FKD) isopleths using a bandwidth determined by least squares cross-validation (LSCV) in the Spatial Ecology Geospatial Modeling Environment SEGME 0.7.3 (2014) and the "ks" package for R 3.1.1. Distance moved between fixes, daily path length, and average movement rate were calculated for all days (7 a.m. to 7 p.m.) using the following formulas, where DM = distance moved, N = northing, E = easting, F = fix, and DH = decimal hour (time hh:mm:ss $\times$ 24):

$$\text{Distance moved} = \ddot{O}((N_1 - N_2)^2 + (E_1 - E_2)^2)$$
$$\text{Total daily distance} = \sum DM \ [F_1 - F_N, \text{for each day}]$$
$$\text{Movement rate} = \sum (DM \ [F_1 - F_2])/(DH_2 - DH_1)$$

Complementing the quantitative ranging metrics collected via the GPS collars, HD footage from Crittercam units™ enabled us to directly view the release and immediate post-release behavior of individuals ($N = 3$). Units that were programmed to delay recording provided a snapshot of behavior after a day of acclimation to wearing the video collars and provided a better approximation for how other individuals might interact with focal, collared animals and the equipment ($N = 5$).

Results

*Monitor device failure rates and **incorporate results into overall project evaluation.***

GPS Collar Connectivity and Drop-off Performance

Telemetry Solution's Quantum 4000 collar connectivity for data download was highly variable across both field sites and short- and long-term deployments. About one-third of the units consistently attained UHF connections near instantaneously across a range of download distances (5–100+ m). In several instances, individuals were only identified via their VHF signal and no apparent line of sight was attained before acquiring UHF connection. Units more typically took 10–30 minutes to establish a UHF connection, even though researchers were frequently within 5–10 m of individuals in open park space when attempting to retrieve data. However, even individual units performed variably with regards to their UHF connections, sporadically fluctuating in their ease of connection. Two units connected extremely poorly, both on individuals who frequently ranged in open park space, and failed to connect over the course of hours spent in extremely close proximity to the collared individual (3–10 m). Upon attaining a UHF connection, data download rates were consistently fast.

Drop-off success was also highly variable across both field tests and long-term deployments (Table 4.1). The initial field test experienced one successful and one unsuccessful pre-programmed drop-off. The second field test yielded a successful, but

Table 4.1 Data tables compiled from all GPS collar deployments (A = Singapore, B = Gibraltar) to determine collar efficiency and used to evaluate whether data quality is high enough to justify further collaring efforts

A.

Macaque ID	SG-BB ♂	SG-BTNR 01 ♀	SG-BTNR 02 ♂	SG-BTRR ♂	SG-MNCF ♂	SG-MNCN ♂	SG-WW ♂	SG-USR ♂	SG-RR ♂
Weeks deployed	22	4	3	23	7	1	24	1	30
Mean HDOP	2.3	1.9	1.3	2.6	2.1	2.2	2.3	2.0	2.3
Mean # satellites connected	5.2	6.4	7.4	4.9	5.5	5.7	5.2	6.5	5.1
3D fix rate (%)	67.1	93.1	98.7	41.5	68.1	85.7	74.0	59.9	60.2
Cotton spacer (Y/N)	Yes	No	No	Yes	Yes	Yes	Yes	No	Yes
Drop-off type and success (Y/N)	Remote trigger; yes	Pre-program; no	Pre-program; yes	Remote trigger; yes	Remote trigger; no	Remote trigger; removed by monkey	Remote trigger; yes*	Remote trigger; yes*	Remote trigger; no

B.

Macaque ID	GIB-AD ♀	GIB-CC ♂	GIB-LBI ♀	GIB-MH ♀	GIB-PPA ♂	GIB-RAW ♀
Weeks deployed	21	5	17	20	14	21
HDOP	3.0	2.8	3.8	3.5	3.1	2.9
Average # satellites connected	4.6	5.0	4.6	4.7	4.7	4.6
3D fix rate (%)	68.0	73.0	60.2	64.2	64.2	53.1
Cotton spacer (Y/N)	Yes	Yes	Yes	Yes	Yes	Yes
Drop-off type and success (Y/N)	Remote trigger; yes	Remote trigger; removed by monkey	Remote trigger; N/A	Remote trigger; N/A	Remote trigger removed by monkey	Remote trigger; N/A

3D fixes are data points collected from 4+ satellite connections, increasing the spatial accuracy as measured by the HDOP. HDOP (horizontal dilution of precision) is a measure of accuracy where HDOP < 2 is ideal and HDOP > 4 is considered poor (Langley 1999).

highly delayed remote trigger drop-off. Telemetry Solutions suggest that the collar should drop off within a 20–120-minute window. However, in our case, the collar dropped off roughly 12 hours after the initial trigger. For the Singapore long-term deployment only two drop-offs functioned as expected, while an additional collar dropped off after several days of continuous triggering. One individual removed its collar within the first three weeks of the study and two collar drop-offs failed completely, including one collar that stopped connecting to the remote base station completely after 2.5 months, despite having an active VHF signal. Overall drop-off success was only 37.5 percent across all Singapore deployments when individual-removed collars were excluded and 62.5 percent if delayed drop-offs are included as successes. Of the Gibraltar long-term deployment, only a single drop-off unit was triggered and it operated as expected. Two subadult males removed their collars via the cotton spacer before the study concluded. Due to on-site administrative decisions made by the local sponsoring agency, two collars were removed and recovered via targeted darting and subsequent health assessment carried out by the macaque management team instead of utilizing the remote trigger mechanism. Also due to local management action the final collar's battery discharged completely before the drop-off could be triggered.

GPS Data Quality

Collar performance metrics are described in Table 4.1, adapted from Klegarth et al. (2017), and included the 3D fix rate, mean number of connected satellites, and mean horizontal dilution of precision (HDOP). Collars across all deployments had an average 3D fix rate of 68.7 percent ($\pm$14.8). Collars connected to 5.3 ($\pm$0.83) satellites on average across deployments and had a mean HDOP of 2.54 ($\pm$0.65).

Crittercam™ Performance

Both small units deployed in Singapore suffered drop-off failures, likely due to the ease with which the focal subjects could access and disrupt connections between the battery and the release mechanism. This failure resulted in one individual wearing the collar-camera unit for an additional ~1.5 months and the second individual removing the camera unit completely, leaving the collar without any battery connection. Both units yielded a full eight hours of HD footage taped over the first two days of each deployment. In Gibraltar all release mechanisms functioned; however, unfortunately some did so prematurely. It is not clear if the early releases were the result of errors in programing or timing faults in the release mechanisms themselves. One focal individual (a subadult male) removed his collar within 24 hours. The camera and collar design was greatly improved due to the initial test in Singapore and serious redesign in collaboration with the NGRIT. Of the six deployments, three units yielded HD footage, one unit failed to record due to a programming error but dropped off successfully via the secondary Telonics drop-off, while two other units were unrecoverable following their drop-off release owing to the difficulties presented by the limestone cliff faces they were located on. One of the three units that yielded HD footage suffered a premature drop-off; as such, only two hours of the recording occurred while the collar was still deployed on the individual.

Table 4.2 Data table summarizing the number of pairwise comparisons between weeks and months, *p*-values derived from ANOVAs, and the number and percentage of significant comparisons for each ANOVA across ranging pattern metrics

	Singapore			Gibraltar		
Species	*M. fascicularis*			*M. sylvanus*		
N = Indv.	5 (7)*			6		
	Day range area	**Daily path length**	**Mean movement rate**	**Day range area**	**Daily path length**	**Mean movement rate**
			Time since collar deployment			
		Week			**Week**	
N = **pairs**	253	253	253	190	190	190
ANOVA sign.	<0.001*	<0.001*	NS*	<0.001	NS	NS
N = **sig. comp. (%)**	4 (1.6%)	5 (2.0%)	0	15 (7.9%)	0	0
		Month			**Month**	
N = **pairs**	15	15	15	10	10	10
ANOVA sign.	<0.001	<0.001	NS	<0.001	NS	<0.05
N = **sig. comp. (%)**	4 (26.7%)	7 (46.7%)	2 (13.3%)	4 (40%)	0	1 (10%)

Impact Analysis

There were significant relationships ($p < 0.05$) in half of the ANOVAs run for daily range area, daily path length, and mean movement rate (Table 4.2). However, the significant relationships were predominately driven by variation between individuals (Figures 4.3 and 4.4). Tukey's HSD post-hoc tests between specific temporal pairwise comparisons (weeks, months) showed no specific impact related to the initial collar deployment date, and the number of significant pairings is detailed in Table 4.2. Percentage of significant pairings increased dramatically based on temporal partition with ranging metrics varying significantly more between months than weeks. This pattern of long-term shifts in ranging paired with a lack of evidence for any initial impact from the collar deployment suggests that seasonal variation is likely driving these differences. There is very little consistency between the three ranging metrics in terms of significant relationships within the ANOVAs, where significant differences in day range area are not directly linked to differences in daily path length or movement rate and vice versa.

Demeanor and Health Effects

In terms of overall health impact, almost all collar deployments were very successful, with little to no collar manipulation observed during the entirety of the deployments for

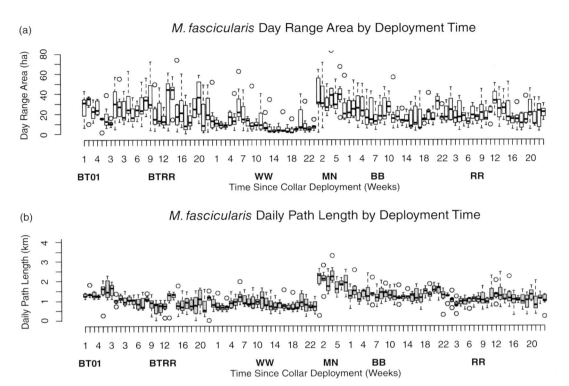

Figure 4.3 Box plots of data distribution for *M. fascicularis* impact analysis of day range area (a; white) and daily path length (b; gray) highlighting variation between individuals. Individual identifiers map to codes in Table 4.1a.

18 of 26 collared individuals (combined GPS and Crittercam™ deployments, >50 collar deployment months). While all individuals manipulated the collar in the recovery cage, none spent more than a few minutes doing so. Post-release, some individuals manipulated the collar more than others during our observations. Manipulation was primarily in the form of spinning or adjusting the collars in a manner similar to adjusting a necktie. Two adult male long-tailed macaques and two subadult male Barbary macaques were periodically observed lightly tugging on their collars. Ultimately both subadult male Barbary macaques removed their units prematurely via the cotton spacer. However, neither adult long-tailed macaque removed their collars via cotton spacers even after the failure of both drop-off units. One adult male long-tailed macaque was missing his collar after what we presume was a fight with another male (owing to newly missing hair patches on his back and legs). We believe the spacer gave way during the skirmish, suggesting cotton spacers can function effectively as safety releases, though the altercation was not directly observed.

One Barbary macaque removed his Crittercam™ unit overnight after his evening release. As such, we could not observe him wearing the collar, and since his unit was unrecoverable there is no footage to indicate if anything in particular prompted the

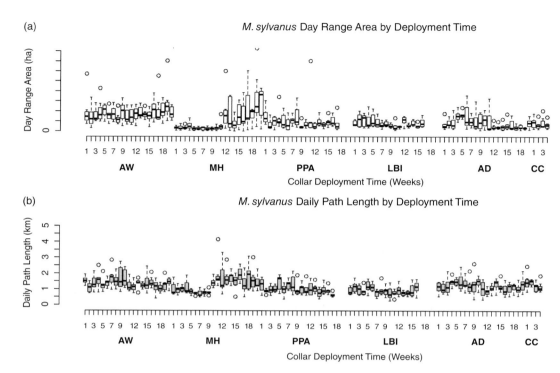

Figure 4.4 Box plots of data distribution for *M. sylvanus* impact analysis of day range area (a; white) and daily path length (b; gray) highlighting variation between individuals. Individual identifiers map to codes in Table 4.1b.

removal. The most significant collar manipulation occurred during one of the two initial long-tailed macaque Crittercam™ deployments, in which the young adult male rejoined his group within five minutes of release and almost immediately began to manipulate and chew on the camera. The tree kangaroo Crittercam™ design had been modified to accommodate vertical–horizontal locomotory and body orientation shifts and this initial redesign resulted in a very loose camera attachment to the collar. The individual's manipulation of his collar resulted in the camera dangling from a single attached end for most of the deployment, further exacerbating his focus on the unit. Eventually this individual completely removed the camera from his collar, rendering the drop-off unit powerless.

No spatial or social peripheralization was observed for any of the collared individuals, and all individuals observed resumed normative social behaviors within 24 hours of their release. We were able to directly observe all but two individuals return to their social groups within 24 hours and all collared individuals returned to the troop they were trapped from. The two we did not observe could simply not be located until after more than 24 hours had elapsed, so we cannot say for certain whether they were with their troops at that juncture. Crittercam™ footage confirmed two individuals spent several hours alone before ultimately rejoining their groups the next morning. We observed no other animals manipulating or directing any attention (visual or physical) to the collars, though we noted conspecifics grooming around and under the collars. During the initial field test in Singapore, neither of the collared adult males nor their social groups displayed any fear of, or aggressive behavior toward, researchers post-collaring, and both calmly fed within a few meters of the research team <24 hours post-deployment. However, the collared female from our initial field test belonged to the least habituated troop and commonly alarm-called at researchers after collaring, though her group did not. Additionally her pre-programmed drop-off unit failed and she is still wearing the collar five years after the initial deployment. She has not suffered any observable physical harm, and has successfully raised and weaned multiple infants during that time period. After consultation with local officials we agreed that the active removal of this device did not warrant the potential risk of trapping or darting this particular animal. This female ranges in tall canopied, dense rainforest and rarely ranges in open, terrestrial landscapes, which makes any potential effort to free-dart her unwarrantedly risky in light of the observed high tolerance and low impact of the collar.

Of the remaining GPS and Crittercam™ deployments, only two individuals alarm-called at researchers. One of these individuals alarm-called only intermittently and ceased calling after two days. The other individual alarm-called more consistently, but still allowed researchers to approach within 5 m. Both of these individuals were from highly habituated troops and both troops ignored researchers completely. Across all deployments only a single individual displayed any aggression toward researchers and the onset of this aggression began three months after his collaring and coincided with government (Singapore) culling that removed all other adult males from his group. The same individual was reported to be aggressive toward the public broadly after the culling and as such we do not believe his aggression was a result of his collaring. We did make every attempt to drop the collar off early as a precaution, but his unit failed to connect after the first two months. Otherwise, all other individuals ($N = 23$) allowed researchers to approach within 1–15 m throughout the duration of the deployments.

Visual inspection from <1 m away revealed no sign of ectoparasite infestation or significant skin irritation, during or after collar removal, for any of the collared individuals across either the *M. fascicularis* field test or the *M. sylvanus* long-term deployments. A single individual experienced moderate contact dermatitis from his collar during the *M. fascicularis* long-term deployment, which was not visible until the collar dropped off. Post drop-off observations showed the affected area healed within a week. Two individuals had minor rub marks (<1 cm), as evidenced from minor fur displacement, near the drop-off mechanism. No other injuries or negative health effects either directly or indirectly associated with wearing the collars were observed during the study for any of the collared individuals. We also observed uninhibited nursing by infants and juveniles on females who were wearing collars ($N = 4$), and observed ventral carrying by those same females. In total, four collars remained deployed on individuals past the study completion dates, three of which are equipped with cotton spacers that should degrade and loosen over time, facilitating drop-off.

Discussion

Both quantitative and qualitative assessments demonstrate that our capture methods have not resulted in significant physical injury or had observable deleterious social impact on trapped animals. The collaring events with both GPS and Crittercam™ remote telemetry devices also had no observable deleterious impact on the social lives of the target animals. While our focal species appear to be socially buffered against physical deterioration, we urge caution and underscore the importance of field tests, particularly when working with more solitary species who may be impacted during an acclimation period, as seen with badgers (Tuyttens et al. 2002). Obviously, it is likely that most of the macaques would have preferred not to be trapped and collared, and thus one could argue that we may be unethical in trapping at all. However, we contend that the data generated via these projects, and its implications for management of the human–macaque interface, combined with the minimal impact on the lives and well-being of the macaques, provides benefits to the focal species and therefore supports our practice.

In terms of amount and quality of collected data, our GPS collars certainly meet performance criteria for considering their use to be ethical. However, this must be tempered by the reality that failed drop-offs present a very real ethical dilemma in terms of freeing individuals from any physical burden presented by the collar units. Our qualitative observations paired with the minimal collar manipulation recorded by Crittercam™ units outside of the initial design flaws suggest that, overall, our units had an acceptably low impact on focal individuals. Attempts were made and are ongoing to dart one individual in Singapore who frequently ranges terrestrially through open park space. All other individuals whose drop-offs failed have been deemed too risky to attempt targeted darting in their mostly arboreal and cliff habitats, given the otherwise low impact observed for these collars. We responded to the first failed pre-programmed drop-off with the deployment of a remote trigger drop-off on all subsequent collars. When the remote trigger drop-off was significantly delayed in the second field test, we deemed it necessary to include a cotton spacer to provide a physical back-up to the electronic drop-off and reduce the amount of time a unit is likely to remain on individuals in the event of drop-off unit failures. Telemetry Solutions products allowed us to recover high-quality data. However, we decided to discontinue their use as they didn't meet our research criteria regarding collar connections and drop-off mechanisms. Owing to the great difficulties and potential dangers associated with the free-darting that is typically required for collar recovery, we strongly encourage researchers to always include a cotton spacer or equivalent break-away mechanism in each deployed collar.

On a temporal scale, there is no quantitative indication whatsoever that collaring has an impact on an individual's ranging patterns. ANOVAs failed to detect any significant relationships consistent with differences between ranging and movement patterns based on time since collar deployment across weeks or months. As such, paired with the minor health impacts observed, we find that GPS collars are an ideal, minimally invasive way to study the spatial ecology of habituated macaques. However, we urge researchers to always conduct a field test on a smaller subset of individuals and to continually assess whether there are any acute changes in movement that would indicate either stress from trapping or a more chronic effect of the collar itself. While we detected neither acute nor chronic effects in our impact analysis of movement patterns, this is likely to be species-specific.

While collar data from Crofoot et al. (2010) did not detect changes in movement based on observer presence, GPS collars help to ensure any potential observer-biased movement is minimized and facilitate simultaneous data collection across multiple groups by reducing the requisite labor power. GPS collars also mitigate challenges presented by rugged terrain that might otherwise hamper VHF triangulation or bias handheld GPS location acquisitions. As GPS becomes an increasingly common tool for primatologists, researchers can use fine-scale collar data to mitigate human–wildlife conflict by identifying conflict hot-spots (Dore, pers. comm.; Klegarth 2017), or answer fundamental questions regarding spatial ecology and group decision-making (Crofoot et al. 2014; Klegarth et al. 2017; Markham et al. 2013).

Conclusion

Evaluating the ethical issues of collaring monkeys: what have we learned? In evaluating what we have learned about collaring monkeys it is important to revisit the basic categories of harm that the deployment of externally borne telemetry units can introduce in primates: potential harms associated with animal capture, telemetry attachment procedures, and with the recovery and release phases post-attachment, and the physical and social impact of the device on the animal once it is attached and returned to the social group.

Obviously, the failures in a few of the cases of our early trials in Singapore are problematic. Overall, field tests resulted in improved collar design and attachment techniques that resulted in subsequent highly successful and demonstrably non-deleterious deployments in Gibraltar and Singapore. However, given the high failure rate and lack of assistance in regards to software and technical malfunctions, we cannot recommend the Telemetry Solutions collars for ongoing research with primates. These initial trials, and their complications, enabled us to observe and assess potential harms associated with animal capture and telemetry attachment/release procedures and modify the device such that the outcomes changed. This allowed for substantive analyses of the physical and social impact of the device on the animal and enabled a more ethical and scientifically valuable methodology.

Given the assessment and validation of the research goals and methodology presented, our current project of trapping and collaring can be considered as meeting the ethical guidelines we set out at the start of this chapter. It is our hope that the process we have described, along with the variation in case studies, enables the creation and use of decision trees (such as Figure 4.5) that will facilitate a more effective, ethical, and productive utilization of remote telemetry devices in primate research.

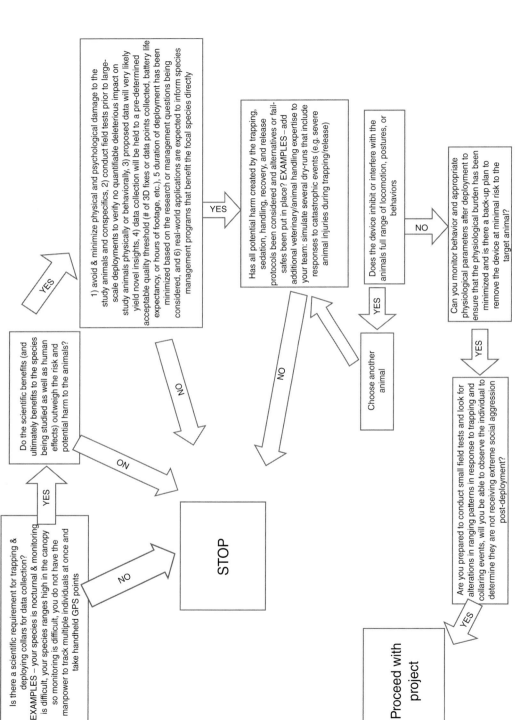

Figure 4.5 A sample decision tree for the use of remote telemetry devices in field primatology with specific examples.

References

American Society of Mammalogists. 1998. Guidelines for the capture, handling, and care of mammals as approved by the American Society of Mammalogists. *Journal of Mammalogy* **74**: 1416–1431.

Côté, S. D., Festa-Bianchet, M., and Fournier, F. 1998. Life-history effects of chemical immobilization and radio collars on mountain goats. *Journal of Wildlife Management* **62**: 745–752.

Crofoot, M. C., Norton, T. M., Lessnau, R. C., et al. 2009. Field anesthesia and health assessment of free ranging white-faced capuchin monkeys (*Cebus capucinus*) in Panama. *International Journal of Primatology* **30**: 125–141.

Crofoot, M. C., Lambert, T. D., Kays, R., and Wikelski, M. R. 2010. Does watching a monkey change its behaviour? Quantifying observer effects in habituated wild primates using automated radiotelemetry. *Animal Behaviour* **80**: 475–480

Crofoot, M. C., Kays, R., Alavi, S., and Wikelski, M. 2014. Democracy or despotism? How do baboons decide? *American Journal of Physical Anthropology* **153**: 99–100.

Di Fiore, A. and Link, A. 2013. Evaluating the utility of GPS collars for studies of ranging by large-bodied, arboreal, forest-dwelling primates. *American Journal of Physical Anthropology* **S56**: 112.

ESRI. 2014. *ArcGIS Desktop: Release 10*. Environmental Systems Research Institute, Redlands, CA.

Fuentes, A., Kalchik, S., Gettler, L., et al. 2008. Characterizing human–macaque interactions in Singapore. *American Journal of Primatology* **70**: 1–5.

Gursky, S. 1998. Effects of radio transmitter weight on a small nocturnal primate. *American Journal of Primatology* **46**: 145–155.

Hebblewhite, M. and Haydon, D. T. 2010. Distinguishing technology from biology: a critical review of the use of GPS telemetry data in ecology. *Philosophical Transactions of the Royal Society of London B: Biological Sciences* **365**: 2303–2312.

Hilpert, A. L. and Jones, C. B. 2005. Possible costs of radio-tracking a young adult female mantled howler monkey (*Alouatta palliata*) in deciduous habitat of Costa Rican tropical dry forest. *Journal of Applied Animal Welfare Science* **8**: 227–232.

Jones-Engel, L. and Engel, G. A. 2009. The risks and contexts of emerging primate-borne zoonoses. Pages 52–77 in *Health, Risk and Adversity*. A. Fuentes and C. Panter-Brick (Eds.). Berghahn Books, Oxford.

Jones-Engel, L., Engel, G. A., Schillaci, M., et al. 2005. Primate to human retroviral transmission in Asia. *Emerging Infectious Diseases* **11**: 1028–1035.

Klegarth, A. R. (2017). Measuring movement: how remote telemetry facilitates our understanding of the human–macaque interface. Pages 70–87 in *Ethnoprimatology: A Practical Guide to Research on the Human–Nonhuman Primate Interface*. K. Dore, E. Riley, and A. Fuentes (Eds.). Cambridge University Press, Cambridge.

Klegarth, A. R., Hollocher, H., Jones-Engel, L., et al. (2017). Urban primate ranging patterns: GPS-collar deployments for *Macaca fascicularis* and *M. sylvanus*. *American Journal of Primatology* **79**. DOI: 10.1002/ajp.22633.

Langley, R. B. 1999. Dilution of precision. *GPS World*. Available at: www.gpsworld.com.

MacKinnon, K. C. and Riley, E. P. 2013. Ethical issues in field primatology. Pages 98–107 in *Ethics in the Field: Contemporary Challenges*. A. Fuentes and J. MacClancy (Eds.). Berghahn Books, New York.

Markham, A. C. and Altmann, J. 2008. Remote monitoring of primates using automated GPS technology in open habitats. *American Journal of Primatology* **70**: 1–5.

Markham, A. C., Guttal, V., Alberts, S. C., and Altmann, J. 2013. When good neighbors don't need fences: temporal landscape partitioning among baboon social groups. *Behavioral Ecology and Sociobiology* **67**: 875–884.

Matthews, A., Ruykys, L., Ellis, B., et al. 2013. The success of GPS collar deployments on mammals in Australia. *Australian Mammalogy* **35**: 65–83.

Moorhouse, T. P. and MacDonald, D. W. J. 2005. Indirect negative impacts of radio-collaring: sex ratio variation in water voles. *Journal of Applied Ecology* **42**: 91–98.

Morton, D. B., Hawkins, P., Bevan, R., et al. 2003. Refinements in telemetry procedures: Seventh Report of the BVAAWF/FRAME/RSPCA/UFAW Joint Working Group on Refinement, Part A. *Laboratory Animals* **37**, 261–299.

Nash, L. T. 2005. Studies of primates in the field and in captivity: similarities and differences in ethical concerns. Pages 27–48 in *Biological Anthropology and Ethics: From Repatriation to Genetic Identity*. T.R. Turner (Ed.). SUNY Press, Albany, NY.

Oberste, M. S., Feeroz, M. M., Maher, K., et al. 2013. Characterizing the picornavirus landscape among synanthropic nonhuman primates in Bangladesh, 2007–2008. *Journal of Virology* **87**: 558–571.

Setchell, J.M. and D.J. Curtis (Eds.). 2010. *Field and Laboratory Methods in Primatology: A Practical Guide*. Cambridge University Press, Cambridge.

Sprague, D. S., Kabaya, H., and Hagihara, K. 2004. Field testing a global positioning systems (GPS) collar on a Japanese monkey: reliability of automatic GPS positioning in a Japanese forest. *Primates* **45**: 151–154.

Todd, D. E. and Shah, S. F. 2012. Assessing acute effects of trapping, handling, and tagging on the behavior of wildlife using GPS telemetry: a case study of the common brushtail possum. *Journal of Applied Animal Welfare Science* **15**: 189–207.

Tuyttens, F. A. M., MacDonald, D. W. J., and Roddam, A. W. 2002. Effects of radio-collars on European badgers (*Meles meles*). *Journal of Zoology* **257**: 37–42.

5 Processing Geospatial Data in R
A Primer

Allison Howard and Roger Mundry

Introduction

Geospatial data are inherently rich and complex, often consisting of large databases and complicated file structures. These data are frequently used to study primate resource use (e.g., Coleman & Hill 2014), social group formation and maintenance (e.g., Qi et al. 2014), and disease transmission (Springer et al. 2016), among many relevant topics. Geospatial data commonly take the form of movement tracks resulting from a researcher following an animal or group of animals and recording their location using handheld GPS units (e.g., Howard et al. 2015; Janmaat et al. 2013; Chapter 6). These movement tracks may also be recorded by GPS tags placed on individual animals (e.g., Patzelt et al. 2014; Chapters 3 and 4). Geospatial data may also result from researchers walking transects to survey primate occurrence (e.g., Araldi et al. 2014; Hicks et al. 2014). This type of data are composed of location coordinates (e.g., the track the primate or the researcher walked) and attribute data, such as time, observed behaviors, or unique identifiers for individuals. Raster and vector areal data (see the section Raster Data) that characterize landscapes of interest also make significant contributions to the study of primatology (e.g., Szantoi et al. 2017). Due to the richness and complexity of geospatial data, automated processing is advantageous, as it reduces processing time and reduces the chance of user error, compared to manual editing.

Commercial or proprietary geographic information systems (GIS) software packages such as Esri ArcGIS, Intergraph GeoMedia, and ERDAS IMAGINE are popular solutions for processing and analysis of spatial data. In addition to these paid packages, open-source, free software solutions such as GRASS GIS, Quantum-GIS (QGIS), and Geospatial Modeling Environment also offer users similar spatial data analysis tools at no cost. The ease of use of both paid and free software packages varies, as does their ability to quickly and efficiently analyze or process large batches of spatial data at once. For example, the conversion of spatial coordinates in many files from one coordinate reference system to another (e.g., decimal degrees to UTM) may require a short line of code or, alternately, many hours of pointing and clicking through a graphical user interface to complete the task.

The statistical program R (R Core Team 2016), in conjunction with R packages or "fundamental units of reproducible R code" (R Packages 2015), provide no-cost, efficient, and peer-reviewed capabilities for processing and analysis of spatial data.

One can use R to open, process, plot, and analyze various geographical data formats such as GPX files (the file format in which GPS data are usually stored), raster data, and shapefiles. The advantages of using R for spatial data analyses are numerous: the program and its packages are free; R can easily be programmed to repeatedly perform the same set of tasks for any number of files; and R offers outstanding graphical capabilities and flexibility. In addition, it is often advantageous to use the same software for multiple tasks within the same project, from reading, merging, and processing data to conducting the desired analyses and creating figures. Porting data between multiple programs introduces the opportunity for error, since programs can differ with regard to how data are read and how missing values are handled. R and its many packages are consistent and there are many resources in the form of books, courses, and online forums suited to introducing the program to users with various levels of proficiency.

This chapter offers an overview of some of the R functions used to process geospatial data. We assume the reader to be familiar with the basics of R (e.g., how to set the working directory, get data into R, and run simple tests. The R novice is referred to works by Crawley [2007], Dalgaard [2002], and Teetor [2011].) We will first introduce how to open geographical data (e.g., GPS tracks, raster data, and shapefiles) in R and then demonstrate solutions for frequently encountered problems using R.

After mastering the skills in the next section of this chapter, readers can visit the webpage associated with this book (www.cambridge.org/9781107062306) to download an R script, a shapefile, and a raster image to practise processing spatial data in R.

Reading Geographical Data in R

Gray text boxes indicate scripts or codes as viewed in a script editor such as Notepad++. Readers can copy and paste the code from these boxes into R to run them as tutorials. Lines that start with a # symbol are notes that do not run as code; rather, they are "commented out" of the functional code and instead provide explanations or examples of output from various commands.

Scripts written in this chapter have been developed and tested using Windows. The use of R on Windows and Mac computers is very similar, with a few exceptions. For example, note that on Macs a relevant file directory is written without the drive letter-colon-slash (e.g., no D:/). Instead it would be: ("~/my_data/NDVI.tif").

Vector Data: GPX Files

GPX files include several data types, such as metadata, tracks, and waypoints. Metadata contain general information about the data in the GPX file, such as the creator of the GPX file, the coordinate system, or the equipment used to collect the data. Tracks store a sequence of location coordinates obtained automatically by the GPS unit as the observer moves through space, usually at a given time or distance interval. Waypoints are points deliberately selected to be stored by the researcher at given locations. In order to read and process multiple GPX files, all the tracks or observation periods (e.g., separate days of focal follows, each consisting of a series of waypoints indicating observation locations) per file must be processed, in addition to processing each GPX file.

GPX files can be opened, read, and analyzed in R using the function `readGPX` of the package `plotKML` (Hengl et al. 2015) or the function `readOGR` of the package `rgdal` (Bivand et al. 2016). The function `readGPX` generates a list composed of five objects: "metadata," "bounds" (the four-corner bounding box coordinates), "waypoints," "tracks," and "routes" (a sequence of points used for planned navigation along a path in the field). The objects "metadata," "waypoints," and "routes" are data frames, "bounds" is a vector object, and "tracks" is a list with one entry for each track.

```
require(plotKML)
#The function readGPX can be executed by assigning a value to the argument,
#'gpx.file', an argument specifying the file name and path.

track1 <- readGPX(gpx.file = "D:/my_tracks/my_first_track.gpx")

#To view the structure of the resulting R object, use str(track1).
str(track1)
# List of 5
# $ metadata : NULL
# $ bounds   : num [ 1:2, 1:2] -45.42 -9.67 -45.4 -9.66
# ..- attr(*, "dimnames")=List of 2
# .. ..$ : chr [ 1:2] "lat" "lon"
# .. ..$ : chr [ 1:2] "min" "max"
# $ waypoints:'data.frame': 426 obs. of  7 variables:
#    ..$ lon : num [ 1:426] -45.4 -45.4 -45.4 -45.4 -45.4 ...
#    ..$ lat : num [ 1:426] -9.66 -9.66 -9.66 -9.66 -9.66 ...
#    ..$ ele : chr [ 1:426] "406.279785" "414.210693" "415.892944" "414.931641"
...
#    ..$ name: chr [ 1:426] "001" "002" "003" "004" ...
#    ..$ cmt : chr [ 1:426] "01-JUL-13 9:46:22" "01-JUL-13 9:49:04" "01-JUL-13
9:52:03" "01-JUL-13 9:55:37" ...
#    ..$ desc: chr [ 1:426] "01-JUL-13 9:46:22" "01-JUL-13 9:49:04" "01-JUL-13
9:52:03" "01-JUL-13 9:55:37" ...
#    ..$ sym : chr [ 1:426] "Flag, Blue" "Flag, Blue" "Flag, Blue" "Flag, Blue"
...
# $ tracks   : NULL
# $ routes   : NULL

#The GPX track can be plotted and inspected as points or as a line.
#as points
plot(x = track1$waypoints$lon, y = track1$waypoints$lat)
#as a line
plot(x = track1$waypoints$lon, y = track1$waypoints$lat, type = "l")
```

Raster Data

Raster data are gridded spatial data dividing the Earth's surface into cells or pixels, with each cell having a value that characterizes that space. Raster data may be digital aerial photographs or satellite images of the Earth's surface. Raster data may represent many characteristics, such as land cover classification, temperature, precipitation, elevation, vegetation index value, or distance from a feature of interest (e.g., roads, water). These data may be discrete, as in the case of land cover classification, or continuous, as in the case of elevation. Raster data may be stored in a variety of file formats, including ASCII grid (.asc), ERDAS Imagine format (.img), geotiff format (.tif), bitmap (.bmp), and JPEG (.jpg), among others.

In the context of spatial analysis for field primatology, raster data may function as a backdrop on which to map other spatial data for display, such as home-range polygons or animal-movement tracks. One may also wish to analyze the characteristics of other spatial data, such as points or polygons, as described by the raster layer. For example, movement track points are frequently analyzed across time to identify patterns in where an animal spends its time. Do animals typically range in areas of higher NDVI (normalized difference vegetation index) during the rainy season? Are their mornings typically spent in areas of lower elevation while afternoons are spent in higher elevations?

To read raster data into R, we use the function `raster` of the package `raster` (Hijmans 2016b). The resulting object is a raster layer with attributes indicating its dimensions (number of rows, number of columns, and number of cells), the cell size or resolution, the spatial extent of the raster, and the coordinate system of the raster (e.g., UTM, decimal degrees). One may also wish to plot the raster data, view a histogram of its distribution, or assign additional attributes to the raster such as its minimum and maximum values.

```
#Code example 1
require(raster)
require(sp)
require(rgdal)

#The function that reads your raster file requires only one argument: the
#file path for your data.
NDVI <- raster("D:/my_data/NDVI.tif")

#Type the name of your raster to see some information about the Raster
#object, this is an example of metadata.

NDVI

# class       : RasterLayer
# dimensions  : 6464, 7269, 46986816  (nrow, ncol, ncell)
# resolution  : 2, 2  (x, y)
# extent      : 449213.1, 463751.1, 8925648, 8938576  (xmin, xmax, ymin,
ymax)
# coord. ref. : +proj=utm +zone=23 +south +ellps=WGS72 +units=m +no_defs
# data source : D:/my_data/NDVI.tif
# names       : NDVI_LandsatTM5RNIR6rededge_72
```

```
#You may wish to use the function setMinMax to compute and store the minimum
#and maximum values of the raster layer into the Raster object.
NDVI <- setMinMax(NDVI)

#Inspect the object again to see that minimum and maximum values have been
#added.
NDVI

# class       : RasterLayer
# dimensions  : 6464, 7269, 46986816  (nrow, ncol, ncell)
# resolution  : 2, 2  (x, y)
# extent      : 449213.1, 463751.1, 8925648, 8938576  (xmin, xmax, ymin,
ymax)
# coord. ref. : +proj=utm +zone=23 +south +ellps=WGS72 +units=m +no_defs
# data source : D:/my_data/NDVI.tif
# names       : NDVI_LandsatTM5RNIR6rededge_72
# values      : -0.9259259, 0.9793814  (min, max)

#The function cellStats can be used to compute statistics for the cells of a
#Raster object.
cellStats(NDVI, mean)
#[ 1]  0.1287617
cellStats(NDVI, sd)
#[ 1]  0.1343234

#You may use the function image to map your raster layer and view its values
#spatially.
image(NDVI)
```

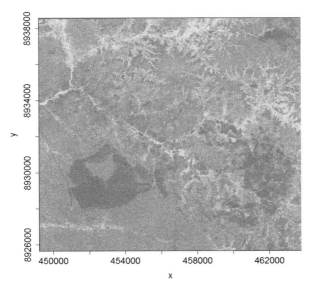

Figure 5.1 Graphical output from code example 1. (A black and white version of this figure will appear in some formats. For the color version, please refer to the plate section.)

```
#Code example 2
#Color palettes can be used to change how raster values are displayed on your
#map. In this example, 8 refers to the number of colors to be included in the
#palette. Using more or fewer colors will change the appearance of your map.
colors <- terrain.colors(8)
image(NDVI, col=colors)
```

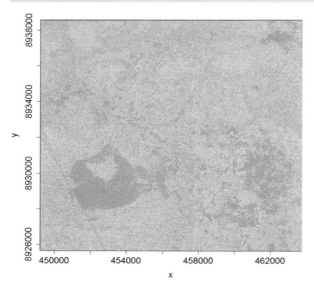

Figure 5.2 Graphical output from code example 2. (A black and white version of this figure will appear in some formats. For the color version, please refer to the plate section.)

```
#Code example 3
#The function hist can be used to plot a histogram of your raster layer's
#values. If your raster layer is particularly large, this function may take
#some time. The argument xlab modifies the label of the x-axis. Similarly,
#the argument ylab can be used to modify the label of the y-axis.

hist(NDVI, main = "Normalized Difference Vegetation Index (NDVI) of Study
Area", xlab = "Pixel Value (NDVI)")
```

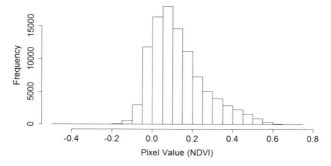

Figure 5.3 Histogram output from code example 3.

Vector Data: Shapefiles

Shapefiles are geospatial vector data that describe spatial objects in the form of points (e.g., locations of villages), lines (e.g., streets, rivers), or polygons (e.g., borders of countries, home ranges, or protected areas). A shapefile consists of a collection of files with the same name prefix stored in a single directory, and having different filename extensions. All shapefiles have at least three components: the shape format file (.shp), the index file (.shx), and the dBase file (.dbf) containing attribute data. In addition, many shapefiles also have other components, such as a coordinate and projection system file (.prj) and a metadata file (.xml) containing information about the source of the data (e.g., spatial extent, how and when the data were collected, legal information about the use of the data). Best practices dictate that all file components pertaining to a shapefile be maintained in the same directory, since their separation into different folders will result in the file failing to function correctly.

The functions `readOGR` and `writeOGR` of the package `rgdal` (Bivand et al. 2016) can be used to read and write shapefiles, GPX files, and other vectorized spatial data. The function `readOGR` reads the projection information associated with the shapefile if this file (.prj) exists in the shapefile's directory.

```
require(rgdal)

#The functions that read and write shapefiles require two arguments:
#the directory in which the shapefile is stored and the name of the
#shapefile without its extension. If a .prj file is located in the
#file directory, this function will read it and associate it with the
#object in R.

homerange <- readOGR("D:/my_data", "homerange")

#If you want to see details about the shapefile, use the ogrInfo
#function with the same two arguments

ogrInfo("D:/my_data", "homerange")

# Source: "D:/my_data", layer: "homerange"
# Driver: ESRI Shapefile; number of rows: 1
# Feature type: wkbPolygon with 2 dimensions
# Extent: (449537.6 8929998) - (456973.1 8935800)
# CRS: +proj=utm +zone=23 +south +datum=WGS84 +units=m +no_defs
# LDID: 87
# Number of fields: 3
# name type length typeName
# 1      Id    0      6   Integer
# 2    Area    2     19      Real
# 3 algebra    0      4   Integer

#A simple map can be created using the plot function. Additional
#shapefile features can be added on top of the existing plot
#using the point and line functions.

plot(homerange, axes = TRUE, border = "black", col = "gray")
```

Frequently Occurring Tasks

When processing GPS tracks and other geographical data, some tasks frequently recur. In this section, we describe solutions for some common tasks.

Projecting and Transforming the Coordinate Reference System of a Dataset

Coordinate reference systems (CRS) provide a method for describing the manner in which the spatial coordinates of a location are described, and the CRS used for a particular dataset will depend upon the source of the data and its purpose (see Lo & Yeung 2007 for an in-depth treatment of this topic). In R, the CRS for spatial data are described by a string of text such as `+proj=utm +zone=23 +south +datum=WGS84 +units=m +no_defs`. The CRS string may show the projection of the reference system (if the data are projected), its datum, the units of the data, and its ellipsoid. R also uses EPSG codes (originally from the European Petroleum Survey Group) to describe the CRS of spatial data, and the proper EPSG code for many commonly used CRS can be found at the website http://spatialreference.org/ref/epsg. When `readOGR` of the package `rgdal` (Bivand et al. 2016) is used to read a shapefile with projection information (.prj) available, R automatically assigns a CRS to the spatial object. To view an object's CRS, the function `proj4string` can be used. When a spatial object lacks a CRS, it can be assigned using the function `CRS`. When a spatial object needs to be transformed from one CRS to another, that transformation is performed using the function `spTransform`. Rasters can also be projected using the function `CRS`, but to transform a raster, the function `projectRaster` must be used.

```
require(plotKML)

#As shown in a previous example, readGPX is used to read a gpx file into R.
track1 <- readGPX(gpx.file = "D:/my_tracks/my_first_track.gpx")
str(track1)

# List of 5
# $ metadata : NULL
# $ bounds    : num [ 1:2, 1:2] -45.42 -9.67 -45.4 -9.66
# ..- attr(*, "dimnames")=List of 2
# .. ..$ : chr [ 1:2] "lat" "lon"
# .. ..$ : chr [ 1:2] "min" "max"
# $ waypoints:'data.frame': 426 obs. of  7 variables:
#    ..$ lon : num [ 1:426] -45.4 -45.4 -45.4 -45.4 -45.4 ...
#    ..$ lat : num [ 1:426] -9.66 -9.66 -9.66 -9.66 -9.66 ...
#    ..$ ele : chr [ 1:426] "406.279785" "414.210693" "415.892944" "414.931641"
...
#    ..$ name: chr [ 1:426] "001" "002" "003" "004" ...
#    ..$ cmt : chr [ 1:426]  "01-JUL-13 9:46:22" "01-JUL-13 9:49:04" "01-JUL-13
9:52:03" "01-JUL-13 9:55:37" ...
#    ..$ desc: chr [ 1:426]  "01-JUL-13 9:46:22" "01-JUL-13 9:49:04" "01-JUL-13
9:52:03" "01-JUL-13 9:55:37" ...
```

```
# ..$ sym : chr [ 1:426] "Flag, Blue" "Flag, Blue" "Flag, Blue" "Flag, Blue"
...
# $ tracks   : NULL
# $ routes   : NULL
```

```
require(rgdal)
#These gps data are in latitude/longitude format and need to be projected. We
#use the package rgdal to project these data, but first, we must create a
#spatial object from the waypoints dataframe we read into the object track1
#in the previous step, and we will define its CRS as lat/long using the
#command CRS.
points.LL = SpatialPoints(cbind(track1$waypoints$lon,   track1$waypoints$lat),
proj4string=CRS("+proj=longlat"))
points.LL
```

```
# class         : SpatialPoints
# features      : 426
# extent        : -45.42427, -45.40287, 9.655607, 9.666413 (xmin, xmax, ymin,
ymax)
# coord. ref. : +proj=longlat +ellps=WGS84
```

```
#The CRS of a dataset can be inspected using the command proj4string
proj4string(points.LL)
```

```
#[ 1] "+proj=longlat +ellps=WGS84"
```

```
#Here we will use the function spTransform and the EPSG code for a desired
#CRS for this data.
points.UTM <- spTransform(points.LL, CRS("+init=epsg:32323"))
points.UTM
```

```
# class         : SpatialPoints
# features      : 426
# extent        : 453454.3, 455802.2, 11067363, 11068558  (xmin, xmax, ymin,
ymax)
# coord. ref. : +init=epsg:32323 +proj=utm +zone=23 +south +ellps=WGS72
#+towgs84=0,0,4.5,0,0,0.554,0.2263 +units=m +no_defs
```

```
#We can also transform or define the CRS of our dataset using the CRS text
#string.
points.UTM <- spTransform(points.LL, CRS("+init=epsg:32723 +proj=utm +zone=23
+south +datum=WGS84 +units=m +no_defs +ellps=WGS84 +towgs84=0,0,0"))
```

```
# points.UTM
# class         : SpatialPoints
# features      : 426
# extent        : 453454.3, 455802.2, 11067364, 11068558  (xmin, xmax, ymin,
ymax)
```

```
#  coord.  ref.  :  +init=epsg:32723  +proj=utm  +zone=23  +south  +datum=WGS84
+units=m +no_defs +ellps=WGS84 +towgs84=0,0,0
```

Measuring the Distance Between Points

Determining the distance between two points can be accomplished via a variety of methods, such as great circle distance, the geodesic (shortest distance between two points on an ellipsoid), and the Vincenty ellipsoid distance, each of which will result in a somewhat different distance estimate. In R, these distances can be calculated using a variety of functions (distCosine, distGeo, distVincentyEllipsoid) from the package geosphere (Hijmans 2016a). The inputs to these functions are the *x* and *y* coordinates of the two points in latitude/longitude. The ellipsoid distance functions default to the WGS84 ellipsoid, although other ellipsoids can be specified.

```
require(geosphere)
#The distance between two points, one located at x = 0, y = 0, and the other
#at x = 90, y = 90, is calculated using the distCosine and
#distVincentyEllipsoid functions. The distance value is in the same units as
#the units of the ellipsoid, in this case, meters.

distCosine(c(0,0), c(90,90))
#[ 1]  10018754

distVincentyEllipsoid(c(0,0), c(90,90))
#[ 1]  10001966
```

Cropping a Raster Dataset

Raster data often represent spatial extents that are broader than the area necessary for analyses. Processing these data and depicting them in maps is often easier if the spatial extent of the data fit their purpose. In these instances, the crop function of the package raster can be used to crop raster data into smaller areas. A spatial object, such as a polygon, can be used to crop the raster. One may also wish to crop the raster interactively, using the drawExtent function of the package raster. This function allows the user to click the corners of a desired rectangular area by which they wish to crop a raster layer.

```
#Code example 4
require(raster)

#We plot the entire NDVI raster to view its spatial extent.
plot(NDVI)
```

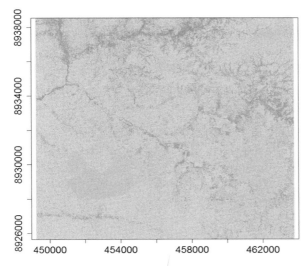

Figure 5.4 Graphical output from code example 4. (A black and white version of this figure will appear in some formats. For the color version, please refer to the plate section.)

```
#Code example 5
#Initiating the drawExtent function from the package raster allows us to
#define a rectangle by which to crop the NDVI raster. Click twice, once in the
#upper left corner of your desired extent, and again the in opposite, lower
#right corner. We assign that extent to the object "e".
e <- drawExtent(show = TRUE)

#A red rectangle appears showing the area you have selected for your extent,
#e.
```

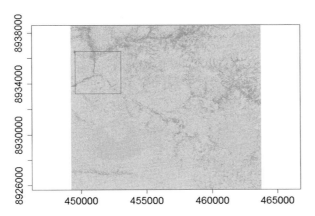

Figure 5.5 Graphical output from code example 5. (A black and white version of this figure will appear in some formats. For the color version, please refer to the plate section.)

```
#Code example 6
#Now, we use the extent e with the function crop from the package raster to
```

```
#crop the NDVI raster. One could also use a shapefile or another spatial
#object in place of e to crop the NDVI raster.
NDVIsub <- crop(NDVI, e)
plot(NDVIsub)
```

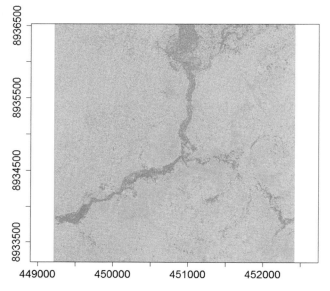

Figure 5.6 Graphical output from code example 6. (A black and white version of this figure will appear in some formats. For the color version, please refer to the plate section.)

Creating a Raster Stack from Raster Layers

Stacks of raster layers are a common format in GIS. These stacks are advantageous because operations can be conducted on individual pixels through the stack of layers. For example, one may wish to calculate summary statistics for a given pixel or manipulate the values of many pixels in a collection of images, such as a vegetation index for the same location at multiple time points or multiple bands of a satellite image. The function `stack` of the package `raster` may be used to create a stack of images from a list of files in a common directory.

```
require(raster)
#First, we create a list of the names of files located in a single directory
list <- list.files(path="D:/my_data/Landsat_images/", full.names=TRUE)
#We create a stack of raster layers using the function stack with the
#argument list.
stackLandsat <- stack(list)
stackLandsat
# class       : RasterStack
# dimensions  : 6941, 7911, 54910251, 7  (nrow, ncol, ncell, nlayers)
# resolution  : 30, 30  (x, y)
# extent      : 366285, 603615, -1223415, -1015185  (xmin, xmax, ymin, ymax)
```

```
# coord. ref. : +proj=utm +zone=23 +datum=WGS84 +units=m +no_defs
#+ellps=WGS84 +towgs84=0,0,0
# names        : LT52200672010035CUB01_B1, LT52200672010035CUB01_B2,
#LT52200672010035CUB01_B3, LT52200672010035CUB01_B4,
#LT52200672010035CUB01_B5, LT52200672010035CUB01_B6, LT52200672010035CUB01_B7
# min values   :                          0,                        0,
#0,                       0,                       0,
#0,                       0
# max values   :                        255,                      255,
#255,                   255,                   255,
```

Determining Home Range Shape

Determining the area utilized by an animal or a group of animals is a complex topic that has been extensively analyzed in the field of spatial ecology and statistics (see Chapter 7). A wide variety of approaches have been used, with one of the simplest techniques, the "minimum convex polygon" (MCP), also being the most common. The MCP is defined as the smallest convex polygon encompassing all observations (Mohr 1947), and is frequently determined by excluding 5 or 10 percent of the points farthest from the polygon's center. The MCP has been highly criticized, however, for overestimating home range (Burgman & Fox 2003). Other methods have been developed to more selectively generate home range estimates. These include Gaussian kernel methods that treat the input points as a utilization distribution (Seaman & Powell 1996) and other non-parametric kernel methods, such as the local convex hull (LoCoH) (Getz & Wilmers 2004). More recently, the problem of range analysis resulting from the use of spatially and temporally autocorrelated movement data (i.e., the animal-movement tracks frequently obtained through focal animal follows or GPS collars) has been addressed in the spatial ecology literature, with the geostatistical tool kriging used to better estimate where animals move (Fleming et al. 2016).

Several R packages provide functions for the determination of home range shape. These include the functions `mcp`, `kernelUD`, and `LoCoH.a` of the package `adeha-bitatHR` (Calenge 2006), and the function `homerange` of the package `ctmm` (Fleming & Calabrese 2017). The reader is directed to the documentation of these packages for demonstration of their proper implementation.

Determining Whether Points Are Inside or Outside a Polygon

The task of testing whether a point or set of points falls inside or outside of an area, for example, testing whether observations occurred within a protected area, is a common problem. This task can be completed using the function `inout` of the package `splancs` (Rowlingson & Diggle 2016). The function takes the coordinates of a point dataset and those of the relevant polygon as input and returns a logical vector (values TRUE/FALSE indicating whether a point is inside or outside the polygon). This function works with lat/long and UTM coordinates.

```
require(splancs)

#In order to check if a set of points falls within a given polygon, the
#coordinates of the points should be assigned to a vector with the x
#coordinates in the first column and the y coordinates in the second column.
#The bounding coordinates of the polygon in question should similarly be
#assigned to a vector.
points <- cbind(points.UTM$coords.x1,points.UTM$coords.x2)
poly.points <- protected.area@polygons[[1]]@Polygons[[1]]@coords

#Below, the function inout tests whether the first argument "points" falls
#within the bounding polygon "poly.points". Each point is assigned a value of
#TRUE or FALSE, and the argument "bound = TRUE" states that any points
#falling exactly on the boundary line of the polygon will return a value of
#"TRUE".
inout.points <- inout(points, poly.points, bound = TRUE)
```

Determining the Size of an Area

The area of a polygon (e.g., a home range) can be calculated using the function `areaPolygon` of the package `geosphere` (Hijmans 2016a). This function calculates the area of a polygon on the ellipsoid when its bounding coordinates are indicated in latitude/longitude.

```
require(geosphere)

#The function areaPolygon can be used to calculate the area of a polygon in
#lat/long coordinates on the ellipsoid. Coordinates must be in
#latitude/longitude in order to use this function. Below, we show how to
#transform the coordinates of a polygon to latitude/longitude, retrieve the
#boundary coordinates of the polygon, and then calculate the area in the
#units of the ellipsoid, in this case square meters.
homerange.LL <- spTransform(homerange, CRS("+proj=longlat"))
poly.points.LL <- homerange.LL@polygons[[1]]@Polygons[[1]]@coords

areaPolygon(poly.points.LL)
#[ 1]  18705931
```

Determining the Distance of Points from the Edge of a Shape

Calculating the distance between points and the edge of a line or a polygon is a common task. One may wish to know how far observation points (e.g., movement tracks, nesting sites) occur from farmland, protected areas, or roads. The function `dist2Line` of the package `geosphere` (Hijmans 2016a) uses a distance function to calculate the distance between a point dataset and the nearest point on a line or polygon feature.

The points and the edges of the line or polygon should be described in latitude/longitude coordinates.

```
require(geosphere)

#The function dist2Line returns a matrix with distance in the first column
#(in the same units as defined by the distance function, default is meters),
#and x and y coordinates of the point in the second and third columns. The
#inputs of the function are points (a vector of two numbers, a matrix of two
#columns: latitude and longitude, or a SpatialPoints object) and a polygon or
#a line (a matrix of two columns: longitude and latitude, or a SpatialLines
#or SpatialPolygons object). A distance function, such as distHaversine can
#be defined by the argument distfun.
dist.points.poly <- dist2Line(points.LL, protected.area.LL, distfun =
distHaversine)

head(dist.points.poly)
#        distance       lon       lat ID
# [1,]  1393.361 -45.42943 -9.674470  1
# [2,]  1427.623 -45.42962 -9.674360  1
# [3,]  1432.617 -45.42966 -9.674331  1
# [4,]  1448.013 -45.42985 -9.674220  1
# [5,]  1450.053 -45.41527 -9.652188  1
# [6,]  1451.391 -45.41530 -9.652166  1
```

Determining Overlap Between Two Areas

One may wish to determine the overlap between two polygon layers – for example, two home ranges. The function `intersect` of the package `raster` (Hijmans 2016b) can be used to generate a new polygon layer depicting the area of overlap. The areaPolygon function applied in the previous example could then be used to calculate the area of this overlap.

```
#Code example 7
require(rgdal)
require(raster)
require(rgeos)

#To determine the extent to which two polygons intersect, the intersect
#function from the package raster can be used. First, we need to read in two
#shapefile datasets using the package rgdal.
agriculture <- readOGR("D:/mydata", "Agriculture1")
AOI <- readOGR("D:/mydata", "AOI")

#We can plot these two polygons together, with the rectangular line showing
#the upper left corner of the AOI polygon.
plot(agriculture, col = "red")
plot(AOI, add = TRUE)
```

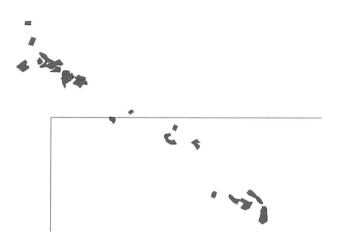

Figure 5.7 Graphical output from code example 7. (A black and white version of this figure will appear in some formats. For the color version, please refer to the plate section.)

```
#Code example 8

#We use the function intersect to create a third polygon object representing
#the area where the AOI and agriculture polygons intersect.
intersect.AOI.ag <- intersect(agriculture, AOI)
intersect.AOI.ag
plot(intersect.AOI.ag, col = "blue", add = TRUE)
```

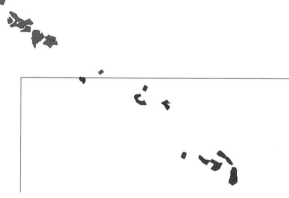

Figure 5.8 Graphical output from code example 8. (A black and white version of this figure will appear in some formats. For the color version, please refer to the plate section.)

Extracting Raster Values to Point Data

It is often necessary to retrieve the values of a raster dataset at the locations for which point, line, or polygon data exist. For example, we may be interested in understanding the relationship between a vegetation index and the points at which we have observed a primate group. In this case, the function `extract` from the package `raster` (Hijmans 2016b) can be used to extract raster cell values to observation points. After extraction of these values, further statistical analyses can be conducted to understand the temporal, spatial, or social patterns behind the animal's association with its landscape.

```
require(raster)

#To extract the values of a raster layer to the locations of other spatial
#data, the extract function can be used. The first argument of this function
#is the raster data, the second is either a points, lines, or polygon
#dataset. Optional arguments may be added including method, which indicates
#whether the value of the extraction should be generated simply ("simple") or
#using a bilinear interpolation ("bilinear"), and whether a buffer should be
#used to extract cell values, and if so, its size. Use of a buffer argument
#will extract cell values from all cells around the point/line/polygon
#dataset for which the cell center falls within the range of the buffer
#distance specified. In the example below, we use a buffer value of 5,
#indicating we wish to take the mean of all cell values within 5 meters of
#each point feature. Since the buffer argument will cause multiple values to
#be extracted for each feature, one must also specify a function by which to
#summarize the values (e.g., mean, min, max) when using the buffer argument.

extract(NDVI, points.UTM, buffer = 5 , fun = mean)
```

Additional Resources

This overview gives a brief introduction into the wide variety of tasks that users may wish to perform using R. Additional information on R, its installation, and over 10,000 associated packages can be found on the Comprehensive R Archive Network (CRAN) page (http://cran.r-project.org). DataCamp is an excellent resource for beginner, intermediate, and advanced video tutorials on writing code and analyzing data in R (www.datacamp.com). Stack Overflow is a forum for programmers writing in many different programming languages, including R (www.stackoverflow.com). Frequently, questions previously asked and answered by other R users can shed light on one's own programming challenges, or one may wish to ask a question of the highly experienced Stack Overflow community and benefit from their expertise. RSeek, a specialized search engine for R and its packages, may also be useful in finding a function to complete a desired task (www.rseek.org), as may be the archive of the R special interest group on geographical data, R-sig-geo (www.mail-archive.com/r-sig-geo@stat.math.ethz.ch).

Concluding Remarks

The use of the statistical computing and graphics software R (R Core Team 2016) can greatly enhance analysis and plotting of geospatial data for field primatology projects.

The strengths of R include its ease of automation, the wealth of resources in print and online for learning to write code, and the fact that R is open-source and free to all users. In addition, R packages are continually developed and reviewed by the large community of R users, lending itself to the rapidly changing nature of scientific best practices. The novice may find R to be less convenient than commercial packages controlled by mouse clicks and graphical interfaces. However, with a small investment of time in learning to write code in R, the user will gain generous returns in the form of ease of processing numerous, complicated files, and avoidance of user-introduced errors.

References

Araldi, A., Barelli, C., Hodges, K., and Rovero, F. 2014. Density estimation of the endangered Udzungwa red colobus (*Procolobus gordonorum*) and other arboreal primates in the Udzungwa Mountains using systematic distance sampling. *International Journal of Primatology* **35**(5): 941–956.

Bivand, R., Keitt, T., and Rowlingson, B. 2016. rgdal: Bindings for the Geospatial Data Abstraction Library. R package version 1.2-4.

Burgman, M. A. and Fox, J. C. 2003. Bias in species range estimates from minimum convex polygons: implications for conservation and options for improved planning. *Animal Conservation* **6**(1): 19–28.

Calenge, C. 2006. The package adehabitat for the R software: a tool for the analysis of space and habitat use by animals. *Ecological Modelling* **197**: 516–519.

Coleman, B. T. and Hill, R. A. 2014. Living in a landscape of fear: the impact of predation, resource availability and habitat structure on primate range use. *Animal Behaviour* **88**: 165–173.

Crawley, M. J. 2007. *The R Book*. Wiley, Chichester.

Dalgaard, P. 2002. *Introductory Statistics with R*. Springer, New York.

Fleming, C. and Calabrese, J. 2017. ctmm: Continuous-Time Movement Modeling. R package version 0.3.5. Available at: https://CRAN.R-project.org/package=ctmm.

Fleming, C. H., Fagan, W. F., Mueller, T., et al. 2016. Estimating where and how animals travel: an optimal framework for path reconstruction from autocorrelated tracking data. *Ecology*. DOI: 10.1890/15-1607.

Getz, W. M. and Wilmers, C. C. 2004. A local nearest-neighbor convex-hull construction of home ranges and utilization distributions. *Ecography* **27**: 489–505.

Hengl, T., Roudier, P., Beaudette, D., and Pebesma, E. 2015. plotKML: scientific visualization of spatio-temporal data. *Journal of Statistical Software* **63**(5): 1–25.

Hicks, T. C., Tranquilli, S., Kuehl, H., et al. 2014. Absence of evidence is not evidence of absence: discovery of a large, continuous population of *Pan troglodytes schweinfurthii* in the Central Uele region of northern DRC. *Biological Conservation* **171**: 107–113.

Hijmans, R. 2016a. geosphere: spherical trigonometry. R package version 1.5-5.

Hijmans, R. 2016b. raster: geographic data analysis and modeling. R package version 2.5-8.

Howard, A. M., Nibbelink, N. P., Madden, M., et al. 2015. Landscape influences on the natural and artificially manipulated movements of bearded capuchin monkeys. *Animal Behaviour* **106**: 59–70.

Janmaat, K. R. L., Ban, S. D., and Boesch, C. 2013. Chimpanzees use long-term spatial memory to monitor large fruit trees and remember feeding experiences across seasons. *Animal Behaviour* **86**: 1183–1205.

Lo, C. P. and Yeung, A. K. 2007. *Concepts and techniques of geographic information systems.* Pearson Prentice Hall, Upper Saddle River, NJ.

Mohr, C. 1947. Table of equivalent populations of North American small mammals. *American Midland Naturalist* **37**: 223–249.

Patzelt, A., Kopp, G. H., Ndaod, I., et al. 2014. Male tolerance and male–male bonds in a multilevel primate society. *PNAS* **41**: 14740–14745.

Qi, X. G., Garber, P. A., Ji, W., et al. 2014. Satellite telemetry and social modeling offer new insights into the origin of primate multilevel societies. *Nature* **5**(5296): DOI: 10.1038/ncomms6296.

R Core Team. 2016. *R: A Language and Environment for Statistical Computing.* R Foundation for Statistical Computing, Vienna.

R packages. 2015. Home page. Available at: http://r-pkgs.had.co.nz.

Rowlingson, B. and Diggle, P. 2016. splancs: spatial and space-time point pattern analysis. R package version 2.01-39. Available at: https://CRAN.R-project.org/package=splancs.

Seaman, D. E. and Powell, R. A. 1996. An evaluation of the accuracy of kernel density estimators for home range analysis. *Ecology* **77** (7): 2075–2085.

Springer, A., Mellmann, A., Fichtel, C., and Kappeler, P. M. 2016. Social structure and *Escherichia coli* sharing in a group-living wild primate, Verreaux's sifaka. *BMC Ecology* **16**(1): 6.

Szantoi, Z., Smith, S. E., Strona, G., Koh, L. P., and Wich, S. A. 2017. Mapping orangutan habitat and agricultural areas using Landsat OLI imagery augmented with unmanned aircraft system aerial photography. *International Journal of Remote Sensing* **38**: 2231–2245.

Teetor, P. 2011. *R Cookbook: Proven Recipes for Data Analysis, Statistics, and Graphics.* O'Reilly Media, Inc., Beijing.

6   Estimating Travel Distance and Linearity of Primate Routes

Ideas on How to Clean and Smooth Track Data Collected with a Handheld GPS

Karline R. L. Janmaat, Simone D. Ban, and Roger Mundry

GPS Accuracy Can Affect the Outcome of a Large Variety of Scientific Conclusions

Primatologists use data collected by GPS devices to answer a wide variety of scientific questions. GPS data on locations where individuals were recorded as present or absent can provide insight into primate genetic diversity, dispersal patterns, densities, and habitat suitability (e.g., Guschanski et al. 2009; Hickey et al. 2012; Junker et al. 2012; Kouakou et al. 2009). GPS data on locations of primates' daily travel paths provide an even wider range of information. Knowing how locations change over time can inform us on disease transmission probabilities, the impact of seasonality in food availability, or differences in social organization (e.g., Lehmann & Boesch 2005; Olupot et al. 1997; Walsh et al. 2005). Calculations of travel distances reveal indices of energy expenditure (e.g., Steudel 2000), while calculations of travel speed provide information on vigilance behavior, levels of food competition, and anticipation of food finding (e.g., Janmaat et al. 2006; Noser & Byrne 2009; Pochron 2001). In addition, travel shape (e.g., linearity of or directional changes in the travel path) can help us reveal cognitive abilities, such as spatio-temporal memory or planning skills (Milton 2000; Noser & Byrne 2007; Valero & Byrne 2007). Lastly, knowledge about directional changes improves our understanding of the importance of specific locations in the habitat, such as fruit trees (Asensio et al. 2011; Byrne et al. 2009). Within this large number of studies, very few reported that GPS devices make errors that can affect the scientific conclusions that are drawn. Even fewer studies investigated how we can limit or correct these errors. In this chapter, we therefore discuss the issues we encountered when using a handheld commercial GPS device (Garmin GPSMAP® 60CSx) to estimate travel locations of wild chimpanzees (*Pan troglodytes verus*) in a West African rain forest. We present methods we used for testing the accuracy of the GPS device and provide primatologists with ideas on how to clean and smooth track data.

Figure 6.1 KJ is following a chimpanzee female on foot in the rain forest of the Taï National Park, Côte d'Ivoire, while automatically tracking her location with a Garmin 60CsX GPS and collecting behavioral data in time and space using a combination of the Waypoint option and voice recorder. Photograph made by Ammie Kalan.

Issues Encountered When Tracking Chimpanzees in Dense Rain Forest

A recommended way to measure the location of an animal that cannot be collared and needs to be followed on foot with a handheld GPS (Figure 6.1) is to wait at the same location until the GPS has made a number of estimations of its location and to save the average value manually. However, when study subjects travel quickly and for long, continuous periods, like chimpanzees (*Pan troglodytes*), observers often do not have time to mark such averaged locations at regular intervals. In our studies, we therefore used the track log function of our GPS that automatically recorded locations in time. We chose a setting that recorded locations "as often as possible," meaning that the GPS automatically stored a location whenever sufficient satellites were around to calculate it. Doing this we found that certain intervals between recorded locations corresponded to exceptionally high travel speeds. After we had checked the maximum speed of one of our observers (KJ; by running a 50 m track in an open area), we discovered that some of the recorded speeds were unrealistic (e.g., 120 km/h) and the GPS was making severe errors that needed to be corrected for (maximum speed of KJ: 18.4 km/h running; 11.16 km/h walking).

Other issues that arose were:

1. At moments when we were with the target chimpanzee and not moving (e.g., sitting under a tree in which the chimpanzee was feeding), the GPS recorded continuous movement. For example, distances between the locations estimated by a GPS that was placed and recording at the same location for 11 days summed up to 52 km of travel (see Figure 6.2).

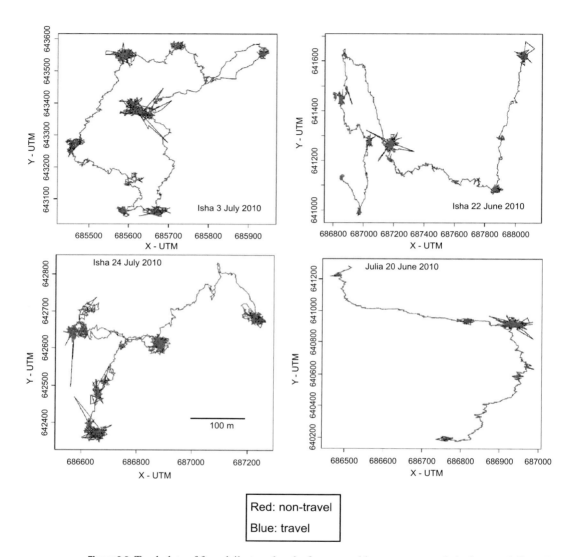

Figure 6.2 Track data of four daily travel paths from two chimpanzees recorded when we followed them with our handheld GPS. The blue and red represent the track data for the times that the chimpanzees were and were not traveling (e.g., during periods when they were grooming), respectively. (A black and white version of this figure will appear in some formats. For the color version, please refer to the plate section.)

2.   The GPS would sporadically record a nest location outside observation hours when we were downloading data in camp.
3.   The GPS would give exactly the same location for a large number of subsequent time points often within a time interval of one minute, as if it had gotten stuck.

Matching our tracking data with behavioral observations recorded in time, in addition, suggested that accuracy during non-travel was lower than during travel (Figure 6.2).

Extreme outliers (>100 m) only occurred when the chimpanzees were stationary. In addition, the track route showed a zig-zag shape while we, in fact, had traveled on a rather straight line. This seemed to occur more often when the animal was traveling slowly.

GPS Accuracy During Non-travel versus Travel

To investigate if indeed there was a difference between the accuracy of locations recorded during travel and non-travel (as suggested in Figure 6.2), we first measured accuracy during non-travel. During our data-collection period, we let one of our GPS devices record 5456 locations at the same place (under the forest canopy) for 11 days. The average distance of all recorded locations to their mean ($N = 5456$ locations) was 11.7 m (mean $= 11.77$ m, SD $= 7.32$ m, min. $= 0$ m, max. $= 65.3$ m). To determine accuracy during travel we marked 64 locations with tags on research trails. We subsequently started walking with the handheld GPS from approximately 50 m before the first tag and continued walking until approximately 50 m after the last tag. During this travel we marked the locations of the tags with the GPS during traveling without interrupting our travel. We subsequently walked the same path back and marked the same locations again in the same way, such that we had two GPS measurements of each marked location. To determine accuracy, we measured the average distance between the pairs of locations and concluded that the accuracy during traveling had a mean of 4.8 m ($N = 64$ locations [pairs of measurements], mean $= 4.79$ m, SD $= 3.14$, min. $= 0.37$ m, max. $= 14.72$ m). This suggests that GPS estimations were much more accurate during travel. We do not know the exact reason for this, since Garmin failed to provide us details on the internal cleaning software. Yet, we suggest increased accuracy during travel is caused by internal software corrections that also use the previous location(s) and movement for estimations of new locations (see Chapter 2). Accuracy may be further increased by the possibility that temporary failures to receive satellite signals may occur less frequently, or be of shorter duration during travel.

GPS Accuracy During Slow versus Fast Travel

To investigate our impression that the GPS was less accurate during slow travel and causing straight-line routes to appear as zig-zag routes, we conducted the following measurements. We walked eight forest routes, once fast and once slow, and compared the distances and linearity (Figure 6.3) of each pair of routes that was estimated by the GPS. Each route was about 2–3 km long and contained travel and a stopping location lasting 10 minutes each (Figure 6.4). The routes were walked along forest trails that were meandering due to tree falls and obstructions.

We found no significant difference between the distance and linearity (Figure 6.5) estimated by the GPS when moving quickly as compared to slow along the eight forest routes (distance: $T^+ = 20$, $N = 8$, $p = 0.84$; linearity: $T^+ = 5$, $N = 8$, $p = 0.66$; slow travel: 352 min, fast travel: 212 min; Figure 6.5). In addition, we walked 20 short travel routes (without stopping points) that had a high variation in linearity (Figure 6.6). For these

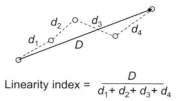

$$\text{Linearity index} = \frac{D}{d_1 + d_2 + d_3 + d_4}$$

Figure 6.3 Linearity was measured by calculating the sum of the distances of the different steps (d_i) that created the animal's route and dividing the straight-line distance between the start and end point of the same route (D) by this sum.

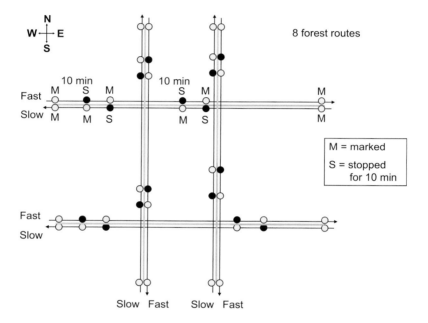

Figure 6.4 Schematic illustration of eight forest routes (four purple and four green lines) of about 2–3 km each. Each route was walked once fast and once slowly in opposite directions and each included a 10 minute stopping point (red dot) and three points (blue dots) at which the route was marked. The points corresponded to the beginning and end of a route and the beginning and end of a trajectory. (A black and white version of this figure will appear in some formats. For the color version, please refer to the plate section.)

routes we had measured the distance and linearity with a tape measure and compass and therefore knew the exact distance (100 m) and linearity of the routes.

We then calculated the difference between the distances estimated by the GPS and the real distances measured with tape and determined what percentage this distance was from the real distance (100 m), and defined this as the "GPS error." We found that despite the large differences presented in Figure 6.7, this GPS error did not differ significantly for routes walked quickly compared to those walked slowly ($T^+ = 107$, $N = 20$, $p = 0.96$; Figure 6.7a). Neither did we find a significant difference for linearity ($T^+ = 145$, $N = 20$, $p = 0.14$; Figure 6.7b; slow travel: 0.69 m/s [SD: 0.22], fast travel: 1.50 m/s [SD: 0.29]).

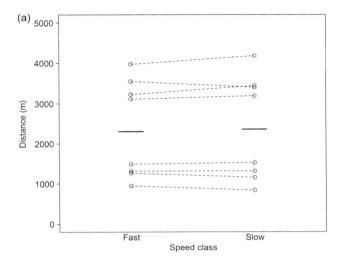

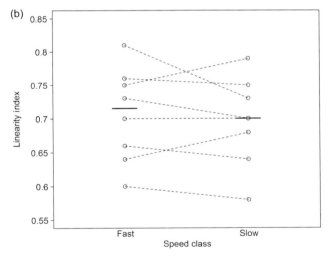

Figure 6.5 Differences between GPS measurements of the same eight forest routes with unknown length (a) and linearity (b) walked at fast and slow speed. Circles represent the estimated measurements (distance or linearity) for each route and the dotted lines in between represent the differences between the measurements at fast or slow speed for the same routes. The thick lines represent the median values.

Developing a Cleaning and Smoothing Method

To account for each of the accuracy issues highlighted above, we developed an automated method to clean and smooth our track data (325,000 track locations). Many studies that have addressed the handling process of GPS track data were developed for studies on animals for which there was uncertainty about the animal's location for considerable time periods (e.g., marine animals that would disappear under the water for up to half an hour; Coyne & Godley 2005). These methods, such as state-space

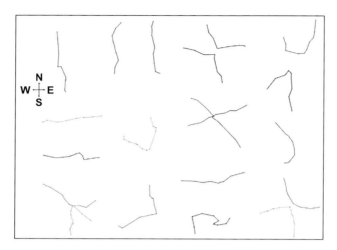

Figure 6.6 Shapes of 20 travel routes (100 m each) with variable linearity. (A black and white version of this figure will appear in some formats. For the color version, please refer to the plate section.)

modeling, were developed to estimate where the animals could have been during these out-of-view periods (Coyne & Godley 2005; Patterson et al. 2008; Tremblay et al. 2009). Our data, however, did not have long time lags between recorded locations. Our GPS device had recorded a sufficient number of locations, even under dense canopy, yet it was unclear to what extent these were reliable. We therefore decided to create the following options to clean and smooth our data.

Cleaning Track Data

First, we created the following options to clean the data by filtering out points identified by:

1.   speeds > maximum speed of our observers (we used 18.4 km/h) as determined from the previous location (points are omitted iteratively in case a single deletion does not lead to a speed smaller than or equal to the maximum speed);
2.   multiple consecutive locations at exactly the same location; and
3.   recorded locations at times outside observation hours.

Smoothing Track Data

Second, we created the option to smooth the data for non-travel and slow travel as described below.

Non-travel

Primatologists are privileged in being able to follow target animals on foot and know from observation when the animal has moved or not (e.g., during resting). We therefore

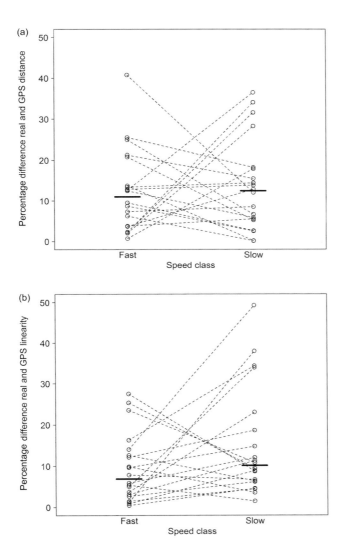

Figure 6.7 GPS errors (percentage difference to the real distance (a) or linearity (b)) made estimating the same 20 travel routes walked quickly and slowly. Circles represent the GPS errors for each route and the dotted lines in between represent the differences between the errors at fast or slow speed for the same routes. The thick lines represent the median values.

decided to use this behavioral information to smooth the GPS data. We identified a non-travel bout in the track data by linking the time of behavioral observations that indicated non-travel with the time of track locations. We then created the option to replace and summarize all locations in these non-travel bouts with the median of all the track locations within the respective bout. To estimate the correct location we took the median instead of the mean since the track locations did not have a normal distribution and included large outliers of up to 100 m (Figure 6.7). This method is similar to what the GPS does when you stand still for some time to manually average your location.

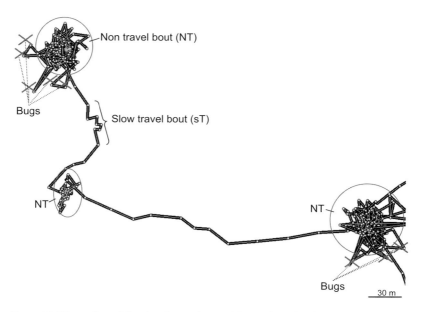

Figure 6.8 Illustration of the cleaning and smoothing options for the track data recorded while following a chimpanzee. The first option is to remove the bugs (red crosses) corresponding to, for example, locations that indicated impossible travel speeds. The second option is to summarize non-travel bouts (all locations within the red circles; NT) and replace all locations within with the median value. Lastly there is the option to summarize slow travel bouts illustrated by a short zig-zag route and to replace all locations within a slow travel bout with one location. (A black and white version of this figure will appear in some formats. For the color version, please refer to the plate section.)

Slow Travel

Dealing with errors made during travel was less straightforward. Despite the finding that the distances and linearity indices that were estimated during fast and slow travel were not significantly different, we decided to create an option to summarize "slow travel bouts" (Figure 6.8). We first defined these as time periods in which all successive locations were closer than twice the mean GPS accuracy (measured during travel) to the subsequent location in the bout. In other words, these were periods in which the GPS locations were so close to each other that the GPS "failed" to detect traveling (if you consider the GPS accuracy; Figure 6.8). We then created the option to replace all locations in these slow travel bouts with one location (the median or the first location). As soon as the next location was further than twice the mean GPS accuracy from the first location in the bout we excluded it from the bout and started determining a new slow travel bout. Hence, long periods of slow travel were "summarized" step by step and were replaced by several locations.

Choice of Smoothing Methods

To find out how to best smooth the track data and what options to choose we investigated the following three approaches (Figure 6.8).

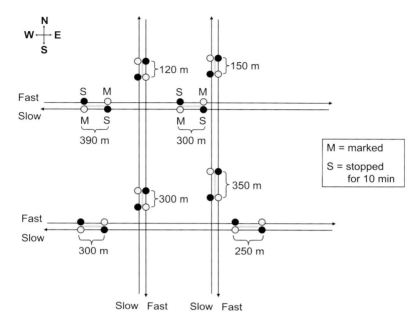

Figure 6.9 Schematic illustration of eight trajectories (yellow lines) of known length and linearity. Each trajectory was walked once fast and once slow in opposite directions, and included a 10 minute stopping point at its beginning (red dot). The blue dots represent the markings of the location of the end of each trajectory. (A black and white version of this figure will appear in some formats. For the color version, please refer to the plate section.)

1.   replace all points in non-travel bouts with the median location;
2.   option 1 and replace all points in slow travel bouts with the first point; and
3.   option 1 and replace all points in slow travel bouts with the median location.

Testing the Smoothing Methods

We compared the performance of each of the three smoothing methods by determining which method gave the best estimates of the real distance and linearity and how these estimates related to the raw GPS data that were not cleaned or smoothed. To measure real distances and linearity we again walked eight different routes/trajectories (Figure 6.9). Each trajectory resembled part of a chimpanzee route by starting with a stationary point of 10 minutes and then continuing with travel, but this time we measured the exact distance and linearity with tape and compass. For each trajectory we calculated the difference between the distances measured with tape and the distances estimated by the GPS when traveling at slow speed and calculated the GPS error as above.

The results indicated that for raw track data collected with the option "as often as possible," the GPS distance estimation was about twice that of the real distance (93 percent; Figure 6.10a). Hence, we concluded that cleaning and smoothing was necessary

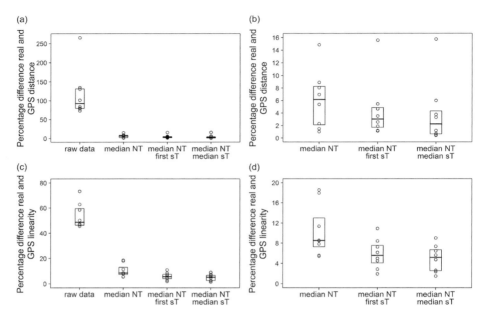

Figure 6.10 The effect of three smoothing methods on GPS errors made during distance and linearity estimation (using a GPS accuracy value of 4.5 m). GPS errors were calculated as the percentage of the differences between the distance (or linearity) estimated by the GPS and the real distance (or linearity) out of the real distance (or linearity) of eight trajectories. We used the data collected during slow travel. Raw data indicates that no cleaning or smoothing had taken place. Median NT indicates the smoothing method whereby only the non-travel data were summarized with the median. First sT and median sT indicate that slow travel bouts were summarized by the first value in the bout or the median value, respectively.

and continued to investigate which smoothing method was best by comparing their effect on the GPS error (Figure 6.10). The best estimate of the real travel distance, with a GPS error of only 2.7 percent, was achieved by summarizing the locations of both the non-travel and slow travel bouts and replacing them by the median of all locations within each bout. For linearity the GPS error was a bit higher (4.9 percent; Figure 6.10c,d). Here again the third smoothing method that summarized the locations of both the non-travel and slow travel bouts and replaced them by the median of all locations within each bout gave the best result. Because our GPS accuracy during travel was based on relatively few measurements (N = 128), and could be argued to be unreliable, we also wanted to investigate whether distance and linearity estimates would change if we assumed a different GPS error. In this way, we tested the reliability of the smoothing method under imperfect knowledge of GPS accuracy. Hence, we smoothed the raw GPS data a second time, but this time we used double the GPS accuracy (9.5 m) as a condition to determine slow travel bouts (see the section Slow Travel). The new smoothed estimates of travel distance and linearity had comparable GPS errors to those in our first analysis (2.3 and 5.2 percent, respectively; Figure 6.11), suggesting that the smoothing program gave relatively stable results, even with uncertainty about the GPS accuracy during travel.

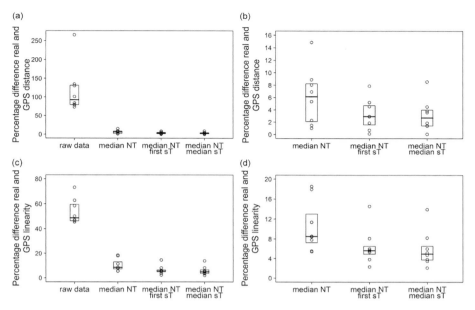

Figure 6.11 The effect of three smoothing methods on GPS errors made during distance and linearity estimation (using a GPS accuracy value of 9.5 m).

R Functions, Programs, and Manuals

All programs, functions, and manuals for cleaning and smoothing of track data were written in R (R Development Core Team 2012) by RM and KJ. The functions expect individual tracks as input, but scripts are also available to apply functions to many tracks at once automatically. Using the manuals as a guide, the user can choose among various functions as required for a particular dataset, either cleaning one or more types of error and/or smoothing as well. The smoothing programs are especially interesting when behavioral data have been recorded simultaneously, allowing the researcher to know when the animal was stationary. If the recording interval is small and GPS inaccuracy is high, one may want to only summarize the non-travel bouts. Since our setting of the GPS was such that it collected locations as often as possible, we also wrote a program that allowed us to extract locations at regular intervals, which was needed to calculate daily path lengths. When a particular time of interest is not present in the data, the program estimates the location at that time, assuming that the animal was walking in a straight line and with continuous speed from the previous location to the unknown location (unweighted linear interpolation). We argue that this is a reasonable assumption since the time interval between known locations was very short (for our data: mean = 20 s, min. = 5 s, max. = 97 s), and chimpanzees are not expected to show much variation in speed and linearity within such short intervals. The functions expect individual tracks as input, but we also provide scripts that can apply them to many tracks automatically.

Implications for Field Primatologists

In this chapter, we discuss issues that we encountered when using a handheld commercial GPS device to estimate travel locations of wild rain forest primates using the tracklog function. We present how we tested the accuracy of the device when estimating location, travel distance, and linearity at variable travel speeds and forest locations. We introduce a set of software programs that enables cleaning up of "bugs" and smoothing the track data during non-travel and slow travel and tested their performance. Cleaning the raw GPS track data and smoothing the non- and slow-travel bouts significantly improved the estimation from the GPS data, such that estimated and real distance and linearity differed only by 2 and 5 percent, respectively. This is excellent news for primatologists who rely on detailed knowledge of the location, length, and speed of daily travel of their study animals. It is similar good news for those who need detailed knowledge on the shape of animals' travel paths – such as studies that analyze significant changes in travel direction (e.g., Byrne et al. 2009) or linearity (Milton 2000; Noser & Byrne 2009) to estimate goal-directedness and mental abilities, although more caution should be used for the latter studies, since the estimated error was twice as high for linearity as for distance.

The results of our study do, however, stress the absolute necessity of cleaning and smoothing raw GPS data. The smoothing programs are especially interesting when behavioral data have been recorded simultaneously, allowing the researcher to know when the animal was stationary. The smoothing method for slow travel can, in addition, be useful for remote sensing data (GPS collar data or gorilla tracking data) where behavioral observations are missing. Despite the fact that GPS data are now collected in almost every primate field study, extremely few studies report on their method of data cleaning or smoothing. In fact, it is often unclear whether any cleaning has occurred at all. From personal communication with primatologists, we know that some researchers simply collect track data less often to avoid them looking "messy" (e.g., the red lines in Figure 6.2). As easy as this option may seem, we hope that this chapter has shown that this is clearly not a solution. Having "messy" data is not necessarily bad. It just makes one aware of the fact that there is a certain level of inaccuracy in each estimated location. The more often one allows the GPS device to collect a location (by, for example, setting the GPS to collect data "most often"), the more positions one has and the better one is able to estimate the "real" location. We hope that our work will make primatologists realize that GPS is not a magic tool, but that its performance can reach very high levels of accuracy when appropriate data handling methods are applied.

References

Asensio, N., Brockelman, W. Y., Malaivijitnond, S., and Reichard, U. H. 2011. Gibbon travel paths are goal oriented. *Animal Cognition* **14**: 395–405.

Byrne, R. W., Noser, R. N., Bates, L. A., and Jupp, P. E. 2009. How did they get here from there? Detecting changes of direction in terrestrial ranging. *Animal Behaviour* **77**: 619–631.

Coyne, M. S. and Godley, B. J. 2005. Satellite tracking and analysis tool (STAT): an integrated system for archiving, analyzing and mapping animal track data. *Marine Ecology Progress Series* **301**: 1–7.

Guschanski, K., Vigilant, L., McNeilage, A., et al. 2009. Counting elusive animals: comparison of a field and genetic census of the entire population of mountain gorillas of Bwindi Impenetrable National Park, Uganda. *Biological Conservation* **142**: 290–300.

Hickey, J. R., Carroll, J. P., and Nibbelink, N. P. 2012. Applying landscape metrics to characterize potential habitat of bonobos (*Pan paniscus*) in the Maringa-Lopori-Wamba landscape, Democratic Republic of Congo. *International Journal of Primatology* **33**: 381–400.

Janmaat, K. R. L., Byrne, R. W., and Zuberbühler, K. 2006. Evidence for spatial memory of fruiting states of rainforest fruit in wild ranging mangabeys. *Animal Behaviour* **71**: 797–807.

Junker, J., Blake, S., Boesch, C., et al. 2012. Recent decline in suitable environmental conditions for African great apes. *Diversity and Distribution* **18**: 1077–1091.

Kouakou, C. Y., Boesch, C., and Kühl, H. 2009. Estimating chimpanzee population size with nest counts: validating methods in Taï National Park. *American Journal of Primatology* **71**(6): 71–76.

Lehmann, J. and Boesch, C. 2005. Bisexually-bonded ranging in chimpanzees (*Pan troglodytes verus*). *Behavioral Ecology and Sociobiology* **57**: 525–535.

Milton, K. 2000. Quo Vadis? Tactics of food search and group movement in primates and other animals. Pages 375–417 in *On the Move: How and Why Animals Travel in Groups*. S. Boinski, and P. A. Garber (Eds.). University of Chicago Press, Chicago, IL.

Noser, R. and Byrne, R. W. 2007. Travel routes and planning of visits to out-of-sight resources in wild chacma baboons (*Papio ursinus*). *Animal Behaviour* **73**: 257–266.

Noser, R. and Byrne, R. W. 2009. How do wild baboons (*Papio ursinus*) plan their routes? Travel among multiple high-quality food sources with inter-group competition. *Animal Cognition* **13**: 145–155.

Olupot, W., Chapman, C. A., Waser, P. M., and Isabirye-Basuta, G. 1997. Mangabey (*Cercocebus albigena*) ranging patterns in relation to fruit availability and the risk of parasite infection in Kibale National Park, Uganda. *American Journal of Primatology* **43**: 65–78.

Patterson, T. A., Thomas, L., Wilcox, C., Ovaskainen, O., and Matthiopoulos, J. 2008. State-space models of individual animal movement. *Trends in Ecology and Evolution* **23**: 87–94.

Pochron, S. 2001. Can concurrent speed and directness of travel indicate purposeful encounter in the yellow baboons (*Papio hamadryas cynocephalus*) of Ruaha National Park, Tanzania? *International Journal of Primatology* **22**(5): 773–785.

R Development Core Team. 2012. *R: A Language and Environment for Statistical Computing*. R Foundation for Statistical Computing, Vienna.

Steudel, K. 2000. The physiology and energetics of movement effects on individual and groups. Pages 9–23 in *On the Move: How and Why Animals Travel in Groups*. S. Boinski and P. A. Garber (Eds.). University of Chicago Press, Chicago, IL.

Tremblay, Y., Robinson, P. W., and Costa, D. P. 2009. A parsimonious approach to modelling animal movement data. *PLoS ONE* **4**(3): 4711.

Valero, A. and Byrne, R. W. 2007. Spider monkey ranging patterns in Mexican subtropical forest: do travel routes reflect planning? *Animal Cognition* **10**: 305–315.

Walsh, P. D., Biek, R., and Real, L. A. 2005. Wave-like spread of ebola Zaire. *PLoS Biology* **3**(11): e371.

Part II

GIS Analysis in Fine-Scale Space

Introduction

Christopher A. Shaffer

The chapters in Part II are intended to provide readers with examples of methods for using GIS to answer fine-scale questions in primate behavioral ecology. Much of the GIS analysis in the primate literature has focused on broad-scale geographic questions (i.e., habitat suitability for a particular primate species), with fine-scale analyses often restricted to home range analysis or daily path lengths. However, the increased accuracy, portability, and affordability of GPS in the past decade, particularly for use on collars (see Chapters 7 and 8), has greatly expanded the types of fine-scale questions that can be addressed with spatial analysis. Further, advances in remote sensing technology, including satellite imagery and LIDAR, have made extremely high-resolution topographical and habitat data much easier to obtain for primate studies. Unfortunately, primatologists are often unsure of how to maximize this technology in their research.

Primatological Questions Suitable for Fine-Scale GIS Analysis

The most common use of fine-scale spatial analysis in the primate literature is for quantifying ranging behavior. Ranging is inherently spatial, so it is unsurprising that many primatologists have incorporated GIS for analysis of both home and day ranges. But relatively few researchers have moved beyond simply documenting the size or length of primate ranges to assess the influence of spatially explicit ecological variables on ranging. One such area of GIS analysis that has proven useful in primate studies is assessing how ranging behavior relates to topography. For example, Gregory et al. (2014) used least cost path analysis to determine whether or not the ranging behavior of bearded sakis was affected by steep slopes in a highly topographical diverse habitat in Suriname. The authors were able to demonstrate that bearded sakis preferentially avoided sloped areas and that topography was one of the most important variables influencing ranging behavior. Sueur et al. (2011a) used data from digital elevation models (DEMs), including slope, solar radiation, and elevation, to determine which of these variables influenced the activity patterns of a semi-free-ranging group of Tonkean macaques. The authors showed that macaques preferred areas of their enclosure that were regularly exposed to the sun but not on a slope and found that they rested and socialized in higher-altitude areas. This type of analysis is relatively easy to conduct – quantifying topographical variables and correlating them with activity patterns – and widely applicable in primate studies. Unfortunately, they are relatively rare in the primate literature. More complex analysis using DEMs and LIDAR-based forest topography maps can be combined with viewshed analysis, particularly for terrestrial, savannah-living primates, to assess the influence of landscape features on movement ecology.

One of the simplest and yet most interesting applications of fine-scale GIS analysis in primatology is assessing spatial variation in behavior. Almost all primate behavioral ecologists incorporate observational data collection in their studies. These behaviors obviously take place in a spatial context – they occur in a location. With the rapidly improving GPS and data-logging technology, it is now easy to simultaneously collect location data at the same time that behavioral sampling occurs. Behavioral data that is spatially explicit can then be easily analyzed in GIS to identify spatial patterns in behavior and test hypotheses. For example, are certain behaviors more likely to occur in certain areas? If so, why? Are certain behaviors, particularly territorial behaviors like scentmarking, loud calling, and vigilance, more likely to occur close to the boundary of a group's home range (Freeman et al. 2012)? Is social behavior more common in some areas of the home range than others, and how might this relate to the distribution of food sources, topography, and proximity to the boundaries of a home range or core area?

GIS can also be used to quantify social spacing, allowing for robust analysis of intragroup interactions. For example, Schmidt and Di Fiore (2015) developed a novel method of analyzing intragroup social organization among woolly monkeys. The authors collected a GPS point at the center of the group during spatial scans and then collected GPS data points for each other member of the group as they walked out from the central location. Using this method, the authors were able to assess how the spacing of adult males related to perceived predation risk, and led them to suggest that woolly monkeys forage in a predation-sensitive manner. Shaffer (2013) used multiple GPS locations collected during five-minute scans to assess how group spread changed in response to ecological variables in bearded saki monkeys. Contrary to predictions, he found that bearded sakis did not adjust group spread in response to changes in patch size throughout their daily paths. With constant improvement in GPS accuracy and, particularly, GPS collar technology, the usefulness of GIS for analyzing both within- and between-group movements in primates is constantly expanding.

Primatologists have also begun to combine spatial analysis with social network analysis (SNA) to make spatially explicit models of primate social networks (Ramoz-Fernández et al. 2011; Sueur et al. 2011b). Social network analysis has become increasingly common in the primate literature over the past decade because of its ability to provide high-resolution data on within-group social interactions. However, few researchers have sought to make social networks spatially explicit. By incorporating the additional variable of space into the network, one can obtain another level of resolution for quantifying primate group structure (Sueur et al. 2011b). In addition to incorporating space into the quantification of social behavior, these analyses allow for improved modeling of disease spread and a better understanding of fission–fusion dynamics.

Fine-scale GIS analysis is also expanding our understanding of one of the most notoriously difficult questions in primate studies – the influence of predation on primate behavioral ecology. For example, Willems and Hill (2009) used the vigilance behavior of vervet monkeys, obtained during scan samples and associated with a GPS point, to construct landscapes of fear – a continuous surface of perceived predation risk. By interpolating these points of vigilance behavior, and using kernel density analysis (see Chapter 8) to produce a density surface, Willems was able to demonstrate how predation risk and resource distribution work synergistically to determine vervet ranging behavior. Similarly, Josephs et al. (2016) explored how sociability, defined spatially using individual GPS locations to infer social proximity, decreased predation risk among vervet monkeys.

Lastly, fine-scale GIS analysis is proving extremely useful for analyzing seed dispersal by primates. Using similar methods to those outlined in Chapter 8, primatologists can quantify the seed shadows of primate-dispersed plants and determine spatial clustering in primate-dispersed seeds. For example, Russo and Augspurger (2004) used spatial autocorrelation to demonstrate that patterns of seed dispersal by spider monkeys, particularly related to their sleeping sites, strongly influenced the spatial structure of *Virola* trees, a common spider monkey food.

The questions reviewed above are just a small sample of the kinds of primatological questions that are well suited to GIS analysis. We encourage the reader to use the chapters in this section as a springboard to other innovative uses of GIS.

Section Summary

The section features a combination of case studies and methods-focused chapters that are designed to provide standardization for some of the most common types of fine-scale GIS analyses and showcase innovative uses of GIS to answer fundamental questions in primate behavioral ecology. It features methods for home range analysis, the quantification of resource abundance and distribution, and daily path analysis. In addition, it shows the potential of relatively simple GIS tools for assessing the way primates encode spatial information and how GIS can be used in captive environments, where GPS and other satellite-based data collection methods are impractical. Finally, this section introduces the use of agent-based modeling for determining the factors that influence primate foraging and ranging patterns.

We begin with chapters that review and attempt to standardize methods for analyzing home range and the spatial distribution of feeding resources. In Chapter 7, Boyle provides a practical guide to the five most commonly used methods in animal studies for quantifying the size of home ranges. As virtually all studies of wild primates conduct some analysis of home range use but few researchers provide detailed justification for their choice of home range calculation method, this chapter provides a much needed set of best practices. Using data from island populations of bearded sakis, she compares the accuracy of these methods and presents the advantages and disadvantages of each. She also makes recommendations for the specific conditions under which each method should be used and specifies the statistics that should be presented for each.

In Chapter 8, Shaffer summarizes useful methods for quantifying resource dispersion in primate studies and shows how GIS allows primatologists to better standardize what constitutes a feeding patch. As Shaffer points out, the food patch is one of the most important concepts in primate behavioral ecology, with most aspects of primate behavior – including home and day range, fission–fusion dynamics, within- and between-group aggression and affiliation – thought to be directly related to the quality and distribution of food patches. However, relatively few primatologists have utilized GIS for quantifying and standardizing resource distribution. Shaffer uses data from a long-term study of bearded sakis to compare several useful spatial statistics for quantifying food patches. Like Boyle, Shaffer provides specific recommendations for when each of the methods should be used.

In Chapter 9, Irwin and Raharison utilize methods described in both Boyle's and Shaffer's chapters to assess the relationship between home range size, daily path length, and habitat choice in sifakas. They demonstrate that, despite the wealth of data made available through technological improvements in GPS and GIS, few primatologists have focused on the issues involved with interpreting these data. Irwin and Raharison illustrate the importance of not only standardizing methodology for quantifying home range size or resource distribution, but also standardizing how we interpret these spatial measurements and what they really tell us about primate behavioral ecology.

The next three chapters, 10–12, focus on analysis of primate daily paths, and show how GIS can be used to assess the type of spatial information that primates use for navigating throughout their ranges. In Chapter 10, Bebko identifies some of the important issues faced by field primatologists attempting to quantify primate daily paths and demonstrates an innovative method for determining the extent to which primates reuse travel routes from a long-term study of orangutans. He also provides valuable recommendations for obtaining the most accurate daily path estimates. Porter et al., in Chapter 11, show the value of GIS for distinguishing between reuse of travel routes and "exploration travel." Using data from chimpanzees and tamarins, the authors demonstrate methods for determining when primates rely on topological spatial information and identifying areas where they may be reorienting their path of travel. Further, they show the utility of GIS for recognizing travel that may be non-deterministic and/or exploratory.

In Chapter 12, Schreier and Grove review the types of search strategies that animals use that do not depend on spatial information. They demonstrate that, depending on the distribution of food resources, animals using non-deterministic foraging strategies can, nevertheless, forage in a highly efficient manner. Using data from a long-term study of free-ranging baboons, they introduce GIS-based methods for identifying nondeterministic foraging behavior in primate studies and distinguishing such patterns from the use of spatial information and other foraging cues.

Chapter 13 provides an entirely different example of the usefulness of spatial analysis in primate studies. In this chapter, Ross and Shender introduce a novel and innovative method for quantifying primate space use in captive apes. The captive environment introduces a number of challenges that make using the types of spatial analysis used in the other chapters in this section impossible (for example, the inaccuracy of GPS units indoors). In addition to showing how space use can be quantified in captivity, we hope that this chapter will expand readers' thinking as to what constitutes a GIS. Ultimately, a GIS is any system that captures and analyzes spatial information. The GIS analysis introduced by Ross and Shender presents an excellent substitute for more traditional GIS methods in environments where satellite-based data collection methods are impossible.

In the final chapter in this section, Chapter 14, Di Fiore reviews the use and promise of spatially explicit agent-based models (ABMs) for primate studies. Much like GIS more generally, agent-based models have been underutilized in primate studies, despite being widely used in ecology. Di Fiore demonstrates how spatially explicit ABM can shed light on primate ranging behavior, social cohesion, spatial memory, disease exchange, and cultural behavior. As Di Fiore points out, because ABMs are often set up as a heterogeneous landscape that influences an agent or multiple agents' behavior, they are particularly well suited for integration with the layered environment of a GIS.

Our intention in this section is not to comprehensively describe all methods for analyzing fine-scale questions in primate behavioral ecology. Instead, we hope to introduce readers to some of the most powerful uses of GIS for fine-scale analysis and, equally importantly, show how primatologists are creatively using the technology to shed new light on fundamental questions in primate behavioral ecology. Particularly for fine-scale primatological questions, analysis often only requires creatively employing relatively simple analysis in novel ways. Therefore, one of the goals of this section is to expand the way that readers think about what constitutes a spatial question.

References

Freeman, N. J., Pasternak, G. M., Rubi, T. L., Barrett, L., and Henzi, S. P. 2012. Evidence for scent marking in vervet monkeys? *Primates* **53**(3): 311–315.

Gregory, T., Mullett, A., and Norconk, M. A. 2014. Strategies for navigating large areas: a GIS spatial ecology analysis of the bearded saki monkey, *Chiropotes sagulatus*, in Suriname. *American Journal of Primatology* **76**(6): 586–595.

Josephs, N., Bonnell, T., Dostie, M., Barrett, L., and Henzi, S.P. 2016. Working the crowd: sociable vervets benefit by reducing exposure to risk. *Behavioral Ecology* **27**(4): 988–994.

Ramos-Fernández, G., Pinacho-Guendulain, B., Miranda-Pérez, A., and Boyer, D. 2011. No evidence of coordination between different subgroups in the fission–fusion society of spider monkeys (*Ateles geoffroyi*). *International Journal of Primatology* **32**: 1367–1382.

Russo, S. E. and Augspurger, C. K. 2004. Aggregated seed dispersal by spider monkeys limits recruitment to clumped patterns in *Virola calophylla*. *Ecology Letters* **7**(11): 1058–1067.

Schmitt, C. A. and Di Fiore, A. 2015. Predation risk sensitivity and the spatial organization of primate groups: a case study using GIS in lowland woolly monkeys (*Lagothrix lagotricha poeppigii*). *American Journal of Physical Anthropology* **156**(1): 158–165.

Shaffer, C. A. 2013. GIS analysis of patch use and group cohesiveness of bearded sakis (*Chiropotes sagulatus*) in the upper Essequibo Conservation Concession, Guyana. *American Journal of Physical Anthropology* **150**(2): 235–246.

Sueur, C., Briard, L., and Petit, O. 2011a. Individual analyses of Lévy walk in semi-free ranging Tonkean macaques (*Macaca tonkeana*). *PLoS One* **6**(10): e26788.

Sueur, C., Jacobs, A., Amblard, F., Petit, O., and King, A. J. 2011b. How can social network analysis improve the study of primate behavior? *American Journal of Primatology* **73**(8): 703–719.

Willems, E. P. and Hill, R. A. 2009. Predator-specific landscapes of fear and resource distribution: effects on spatial range use. *Ecology* **90**(2): 546–555.

7 Home Range Analysis
Why the Methods Matter

Sarah A. Boyle

Introduction

Burt (1943: 351) defined home range as the

area traversed by the individual in its normal activities of food gathering, mating, and caring for young. Occasional sallies outside the area, perhaps exploratory in nature, should not be considered as in part of the home range. The home range need not cover the same area during the life of the individual. Often animals will move from one area to another, thereby abandoning the old home range and setting up a new one.

A quick search on Google Scholar in November 2019 indicated that Burt (1943) has been cited more than 2700 times. Although the general definition of home range by Burt (1943) is commonly referenced in studies that calculate the home range for a particular study group, the definition does not address which data one should use, the duration of data (length of study), the metrics for calculating home range, or (not surprisingly given that it's been 70 years since Burt (1943) coined the definition) the type of software to use.

Accurate estimates of home range are important for understanding a species' behavioral ecology (Hemingway & Bynum 2005; Milton & May 1976; Robbins & McNeilage 2003; Shaffer 2013; Takasaki 1981; Tsuji & Takatsuki 2009) and conservation (Akers et al. 2013; Campbell-Smith et al. 2011; Gerber et al. 2012; Sawyer 2012). Primate species' home ranges vary from <1 ha to >4000 ha (Bartlett 2007; Di Fiore & Campbell 2007; Digby et al. 2007; Enstam & Isbell 2007; Fashing 2007; Fernandez-Duque 2007; Gould & Sauther 2007; Gursky 2007; Kirkpatrick 2007; Nekaris & Bearder 2007; Norconk 2007; Robbins 2007; Stumpf 2007). Even within a primate species, home ranges vary in size (Chaves et al. 2011; Li et al. 2010; Scull et al. 2012). Some of these variations could be attributed to differences in data collection and analyses (Gursky 2007; Ren et al. 2009), but home ranges may actually vary due to ecological and behavioral flexibility of the species under different social conditions, environmental conditions, and different features of the landscape (Boyle et al. 2009a; Chaves et al. 2011; Henzi et al. 2011; Lehmann & Boesch 2003; Palminteri & Peres 2012; Scull et al. 2012).

To date there has been an extensive number of home range methods used in primate studies (see Table 7.1), but overall there has been a lack of standardization of methods. This chapter has three goals: (1) to provide an overview of home range methods, examining how the methods can result in different estimates of home range; (2) to discuss factors to consider when calculating home ranges; and (3) to outline some of the software commonly used for home range estimates. The aim of this chapter is to illustrate not only how the use of different methods can impact home range estimates for primates, but also to demonstrate how the methods one chooses to use should be appropriate for the data one is analyzing. Furthermore, the chapter highlights that information about data analyses should be included in publications in order to facilitate interspecific and intraspecific comparisons.

How Is Home Range Calculated?

Home range can be calculated in a myriad of ways (Figure 7.1). From the 1940s to the 1960s, calculations of home range often involved researchers drawing an amorphous shape to encompass all noted locations of the animal, and determining the area represented by the outlined shape (Burt 1940). Additional early methods, both of which are still used today, included the grid cell (GC) method (Haugen 1942; Siniff & Tester 1965) and the minimum home range, which was coined by Mohr (1947) and is analogous to what is currently called minimum convex polygon (MCP). Since the

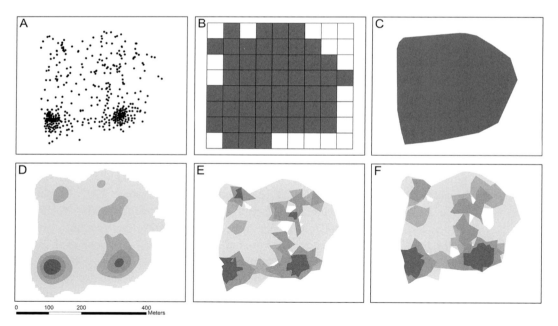

Figure 7.1 Common methods used for quantifying home ranges in primates. Using (a) 500 points that represent the locations of an individual, one may calculate home range using (b) grid cells, (c) minimum convex polygon, (d) fixed kernel, (e) fixed local convex hull, or (f) adaptive local convex hull estimators, to name a few. Note the differences in the size and shape of the outputs, as well as the extent to which core areas of increased use are detectable (darker shades in (d), (e), and (f) indicate greater usage by the animal), and the extent to which areas not traversed by the animal are included as part of its home range. All six examples are at the same scale.

1940s, a variety of other methods have been developed, edited, and modified. Here are some of the most common methods for estimating primate home ranges, with a review of the reasons for and potential drawbacks in using each method.

Grid Cell

The GC method (Figure 7.1b) overlays a grid on top of the study area, and then the number of cells that the animal enters is used to calculate the home range size (Haugen 1942; Siniff & Tester 1965). Blair (1942) modified the GC method to account for the extent to which animals used each cell, so that cells that were visited more received a deeper shading color. In primate studies, most work has focused on using GC to calculate area (Chapman 1988; Hoffman & O'Riain 2011; Matsuda et al. 2009; Tsuji & Takatsuki 2009), not the intensity of use of the cells (but see Garber et al. 1993; Porter et al. 2007). This approach was used for study areas that had grid trail systems and before inexpensive handheld GPS units that functioned in the forest canopy were available.

Grids may be superimposed on paper aerial photographs (Chapman 1988; Fedigan et al. 1988), but with current software a user can make a grid (defining the size and number of cells) using *genvecgrid* or fishnet commands, and use GPS locations to determine the cell that an animal occupied. The user chooses the size of the grid cells and this choice can greatly impact home range estimates: small cells may underestimate and large cells may overestimate the actual area used by the animal (Grueter et al. 2009; Ren et al. 2009; Robbins & McNeilage 2003; Scull et al. 2012; Figure 7.2). Furthermore, the GC method is sensitive to the amount of data collected in relation to the cell size: Isolated, non-continuous locations may be included in the animal's home range if they are used at the moment when data collection occurs, whereas the area in between these locations may be excluded if animals move quickly from one location to another (Li et al. 2010; Powell 2000; Figure 7.2a–c). The appropriate size of the GC can be determined based on the mean spread of the group (Ostro et al. 1999; Figure 7.2a,c,d,f), but there is no standardized method for obtaining the best grid size. It is important to have a large data sample that covers different seasons of the year so that the home range area is not greatly underestimated.

Minimum Convex Polygon (MCP)

Minimum convex polygon (MCP) draws a polygon around data points so that all of the angles of the polygon are convex (Mohr 1947; Figure 7.1c). One may calculate area based on 100 percent of the data points within the polygon or choose lower percentages of the dataset to analyze (e.g., 95 or 50 percent) in order to define core areas, or areas that are used to the greatest extent by the animal. Minimum convex polygon provides a polygon of the home range, but there is no information within the polygon that differentiates areas that are used on a regular basis versus areas that are rarely used by the animal. It is still a very commonly used method in primate studies (Henzi et al. 2011; Lahann 2008; Mekonnen et al. 2010; Mochizuki & Murakami 2013; Spehar et al. 2010),

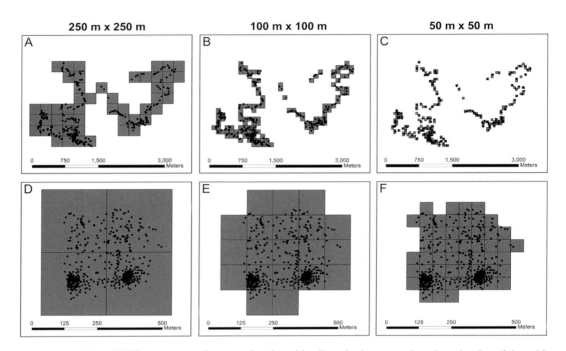

Figure 7.2 Home range estimates using the grid cell method can vary based on the size of the grid cell, the number of data points, and the spread of the points. This example compares home range size and connectivity at different grid cell sizes ((a) and (d) 250 m × 250 m; (b) and (e) 100 m × 100 m; (c) and (f) 50 × 50 m) for two groups of bearded sakis (*Chiropotes sagulatus*). As grid cell size decreases, home range estimates decrease and connectivity decreases.
Appropriate grid cell size will depend on the spread of points, as primate populations vary greatly in the size of their home ranges. Comparisons of the areas estimated by these methods are given later in Table 7.2.

despite criticisms of the method. A variety of software packages and home range extensions (see Table 7.3) allow for quick calculation of MCP.

There have been two main reasons why researchers have recommended avoiding MCP to calculate home range size. First, MCP can overestimate home range size by including areas that the animal does not use (Li et al. 2010), and second, MCP is sensitive to outliers in the data and sample size (Börger et al. 2006; Laver & Kelly 2008; Powell 2000; White et al. 2010). However, these criticisms have not been supported in all studies. For example, Scull et al. (2012) found that MCP was no more sensitive to outliers than was local convex hull (LoCoH; see the later section for details of this home range estimator). In other studies where MCP was used, the researchers showed that as data were added to the analyses the size of the home range reached an asymptote, indicating that larger samples did not further increase range size (Neri-Arboleda et al. 2002; Norscia & Borgognini-Tarli 2008; Robbins & McNeilage 2003). Furthermore, Norscia and Borgognini-Tarli (2008) found that MCP provided smaller estimates than another estimator, the fixed kernel method (see the next section for details on this estimator), and Boyle et al. (2009b) found MCP to be the best method when sample size was low (<300 points) and when the animals were confined to an isolated forest fragment.

Minimum convex polygon may overestimate the size of the home range, especially if areas (e.g., lakes, cliffs) that are inhospitable to the primates are included within the home range calculation. One way to address this issue is to modify the MCP so that uninhabitable areas are clipped out of the polygon (Grueter et al. 2009; Palminteri & Peres 2012). However, it is important to closely examine the data, as modifying the sample size may result in losing important behavioral or ecological data. For example, one may use 95 percent MCP to minimize the number of outliers included in the home range estimation, but Pebsworth et al. (2012b) found that using 95 percent MCP excluded two of the sleeping sites used by the baboons in their study.

Kernel Density Estimation: Fixed Kernel and Adaptive Kernel

Kernel density estimation (KDE) is the most widely used category of home range estimator in ecology (Kie et al. 2010), and it has been used in a variety of primate field studies (Pebsworth et al. 2012a; Raboy & Dietz 2004; Willems & Hill 2009). Kernel density estimation uses location points to calculate a utilization distribution (UD), indicating the probability of finding an animal in a particular location (Silverman 1986; Worton 1989). The most common KDE used for home range analyses is the fixed kernel (FK; Worton, 1989, 1995; Figure 7.1d), followed by the adaptive kernel (AK; Worton, 1989, 1995). In FK, the smoothing parameter (bandwidth, h), which controls the variation or width of the kernel, remains constant (Worton 1989). In AK, h varies based on the density of the data; areas with lower densities of points have greater smoothing (Worton 1989). Overall, FK is more commonly used in primate studies than is AK (Table 7.1), and Seaman and Powell (1996) found FK to perform better than AK, with AK estimates resulting in more error and overestimating home range size.

Although KDE is commonly used for home-range estimates, it is not without problems (Hemson et al. 2005; Moorcroft & Lewis 2006; Row & Blouin-Demers 2006). One of the main critiques of KDE is that an incorrect choice of bandwidth can greatly impact the home range estimate (Blundell et al. 2001; Gitzen & Millspaugh 2003; Hemson et al. 2005; Seaman et al. 1999; Walter et al. 2011; Wauters et al. 2007). Multiple smoothing factors exist, such as the reference bandwidth (h_{ref}; Worton 1995), least squares cross-validation bandwidth (h_{lscv}; Gitzen & Millspaugh 2003; Worton 1989), and ad hoc bandwidth ($h_{ad\ hoc}$; Seaman & Powell 1996; Worton 1989), to name a few. No universal smoothing factor exists (Campos & Fedigan 2009), and there is no best way to choose a bandwidth a priori (Kie et al. 2010; Worton 1989), but choosing the smoothing parameter that is appropriate to the data is critical (Horne & Garton 2006a).

Lichti and Swihart (2011) found KDE bandwidth estimators performed variably based on the sample size and patterns of spatial use. Variations in home range estimates due to bandwidth used have also been documented in a number of primate studies. In a comparison of five methods (GC, MCP, cluster analysis, KDE, and local convex hull), Sawyer (2012) found that KDE had both the largest and smallest estimates of home

Table 7.1 Compilation of primate studies using multiple home range estimation methods

Species	Home range estimates used						Findings of study	Citation
	GC	MCP	FK	AK	LoCoH	Other[a]		
Ateles geoffroyi		x	x		x		LoCoH performed better than FK	Ramos-Fernández et al. (2013)
Chiropotes sagulatus		x	x	x			Similar results among MCP, FK, and AK	Shaffer (2013)
Presbytis potenziani		x	x				Similar results between MCP and FK	Hadi et al. (2012)
Simias concolor		x	x				Similar results, but FK was larger than MCP in the two group comparisons	Hadi et al. (2012)
Pithecia irrorata		x	x				MCP had larger ranges than FK for all five groups of monkeys	Palminteri & Peres (2012)
Papio hamadryas ursinus		x	x		x		FK performed best	Pebsworth et al. (2012b)
Gorilla gorilla diehli	x	x	x[b]		x	x	LoCoH performed best, but other methods have their benefits. If GC is used, it should be used with another method. In general, multiple methods should be used	Sawyer (2012)
Gorilla beringei beringei		x			x		LoCoH better overall but MCP did not differ from LoCoH in sensitivity to outliers	Scull et al. (2012)
Pongo albelii	x	x	x				In 6 of 8 individuals, FK provided a greater range estimate than both GC and MCP	Campbell-Smith et al. (2011)
Eulemur rufifrons		x	x	x			MCP greater than FK and AK for seasonal ranges	Pyritz et al. (2011)
Rhinopithecus roxellana	x	x	x[b]				Kernel performed best	Li et al. (2010)
Pongo pygmaeus wurmbii	x	x	x				FK performed best	Wartmann et al. (2010)
Mandrillus sphinx		x	x			x	Results varied with sample size. FK did better with delineating use within the home range	White et al. (2010)
Allocebus trichotis		x		x			MCP estimated larger ranges than AK	Biebouw (2009)
Chiropotes satanas chiropotes		x	x	x			MCP performed best at small sample sizes in isolated forest fragment. FK and AK overestimated range when sample size was small	Boyle et al. (2009b)
Rhinopithecus bieti	x	x				x	Adaptive MCP performed best. MCP better than GC for monthly or season ranges	Grueter et al. (2009)

Species	GC	MCP	FK	AK	Other	Notes	Reference
Rhinopithecus bieti	x	x				Difference between GC and MCP estimates. Size of grid cell important	Ren et al. (2009)
Propithecus diadema		x	x			MCP greater in 3 of 4 groups; differences <15 percent of greatest estimate	Irwin (2008)
Avahi laniger or *A. meridionalis*		x	x			Did not state which method was preferred. FK had larger estimates than MCP	Norscia & Borgognini-Tarli (2008)
Colobus angolensis ruwenzorii		x	x			MCP and FK produced similar results	Fashing et al. (2007)
Colobus guereza		x	x			Used estimates for feeding ranges. FK did not take into consideration area between some feeding sites	Harris and Chapman (2007)
Tarsius dianae	x	x				Similar results between GC and MCP	Merker (2006)
Perodicticus potto edwardsi		x	x			FK performed better than MCP	Pimley et al. (2005)
Sciurocheirus cameronensis		x	x			FK performed better than MCP	Pimley et al. (2005)
Pan troglodytes verus	x	x				GC gave larger range estimates than MCP	Lehmann & Boesch (2003)
Pan troglodytes		x	x	x		No preference stated, but overall AK > FK > MCP in home range estimates	Newton-Fisher (2003)
Gorilla beringei beringei	x	x				MCP is more appropriate than GC when comparing studies and when sample size is low	Robbins & McNeilage (2003)
Tarsius syrichta		x	x			No differences between MCP and FK	Neri-Arboleda et al. (2002)
Pan troglodytes verus		x	x		x	Estimates varied, with Fourier consistently the smallest	Herbinger et al. (2001)
Alouatta pigra		x	x		x	Home range estimates differed. Digitized polygons preferred by authors	Ostro et al. (1999)

GC, grid cell; MCP, minimum convex polygon; FK, fixed kernel; AK, adaptive kernel; LoCoH, local convex hull. Studies are listed in reverse chronological order.

[a] "Other" included adjusted MCP (Grueter et al. 2009), cluster analysis (Sawyer 2012), digitized polygon (Ostro et al. 1999), Fourier (Herbinger et al. 2001); 95 percent harmonic mean (Ostro et al. 1999), peeled polygon (White et al. 2010), and restrictive polygon (Herbinger et al. 2001).

[b] Kernel type (e.g., fixed, adaptive) was not noted in the methods.

range size for Cross River gorillas (*Gorilla gorilla diehli*) due to the different *h* bandwidths used. Palminteri and Peres (2012) found that data for bald-faced sakis (*Pithecia irrorata*) were over-smoothed and under-smoothed with $h_{ad\ hoc}$ and h_{lscv}, respectively, so they multiplied $h_{ad\ hoc}$ by a constant. A thorough discussion of how and why $h_{ad\ hoc}$ was chosen as a smoothing factor in a study of chacma baboons (*Papio hamadryas ursinus*) was presented by Pebsworth et al. (2012b); home range size for the baboons ranged from 1540 ha to 1880 ha, simply based on the smoothing factor.

Similar to MCP, KDE can also overestimate home range size, particularly when the sample size is small (Boyle et al. 2009b; Wauters et al. 2007), and it can include in its estimation areas within the home range that are not used by the animals, such as in a study by White et al. (2010) of mandrills (*Mandrillus sphinx*). Another critique is that although KDE provides the "utility distribution" of the data, it is not possible to determine the time that samples were collected (Powell 2000), so temporal patterns (e.g., seasonal use of space) are difficult to discern. Lastly, autocorrelation and bias with smoothing parameters are problems associated with KDE (Fieberg 2007a), leading to the use of modified kernel estimators, such as weighted kernel density estimators (Fieberg 2007b). Although autocorrelation among data points has been considered problematic with home range analysis (Cresswell & Smith 1992; Swihart and Slade 1985, 1997; Weber et al. 2001), these autocorrelated data often provide biologically relevant information regarding the animal's behavior and movement patterns (Blundell et al. 2001; Cushman et al. 2005; de Solla et al. 1999; Otis & White 1999).

Local Convex Hull (LoCoH)

Local convex hull (LoCoH) is a non-parametric kernel method (Getz & Wilmers 2004; Getz et al. 2007) that is capable of identifying boundaries for areas that may not be used by the animal (e.g., water bodies, patches of non-habitat land cover). Options for analysis include *k*-LoCoH (which creates the kernels using a fixed number of points, *k* − 1, closest to the root points), *r*-LoCoH (which creates kernels based on the points within a radius, *r*), and *a*-LoCoH (which creates the kernels based on the points within a radius *a* so that the summed distances from the root point is not greater than *a*; Getz et al. 2007). The home range output can vary based on the values chosen for *k*, *r*, or *a* (Getz et al. 2007; Scull et al. 2012; Figure 7.3), so it is important that the user chooses the method and values that are most biologically appropriate for the data, and clearly states these items in the methods. LoCoH can be done in R (adehabitat: Calenge 2006; T-LoCoH: Lyons et al. 2013), or downloaded as a toolbox for use in ArcGIS (ESRI 2013). Although LoCoH is a relatively recent home range method, it has been used in several primate studies (Campos & Fedigan 2009; Pebsworth et al. 2012b; Ramos-Fernández et al. 2013; Sawyer 2012; Scull et al. 2012). For example, Campos and Fedigan (2009) used *a*-LoCoH because the forest habitat of the white-faced capuchin (*Cebus capucinus*) was patchily distributed, and the surrounding clearings and grasslands were not used by the monkeys.

Similar to the KDE smoothing factors, it is not always clear how the parameters for *k* and *a* should be determined (Scull et al. 2012). Furthermore, LoCoH often results in

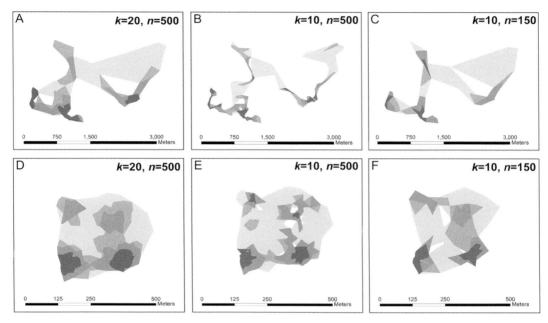

Figure 7.3 Local convex hull (LoCoH) estimates of home range can vary based on the parameters. Here is an example with a fixed k-LoCoH, using the same location points as in Figure 7.2 for two groups of bearded sakis (*Chiropotes sagulatus*). The k value can impact the result, but it is dependent on the number of points and spread of points used for the analysis, as estimates differ for $k = 10$ when 500 points and 150 points are used. The 150-point sample was generated randomly from the 500-point sample. Comparisons of the areas estimated by these methods are given in Table 7.2.

much smaller estimates of home range than when other methods are used (Pebsworth et al. 2012b; Sawyer 2012; Scull et al. 2012). Huck et al. (2008) found LoCoH performed better than FK and MCP, yet suggested that LoCoH should be used in combination with other home range methods because the LoCoH estimates were so small. As with the previously described home range methods, where discrepancies exist in which method is best, LoCoH is not considered the best method for all studies (Pebsworth et al. 2012b).

Comparison of the Common Methods: A Case Study

To illustrate the similarities and differences in home range estimators and sample size, I used a sample of 500 data points (Figure 7.1a) from two groups of bearded saki monkeys (*Chiropotes sagulatus*) at the Biological Dynamics of Forest Fragments Project, Amazonas, Brazil. One group lived in continuous forest while the other group lived in a 12 ha forest fragment. The purpose of this comparison was to illustrate how the most appropriate home range methods can vary even within a primate species, based on the habitat. Additional information regarding the study site, data-collection methods,

Table 7.2 Comparison of home range methods and parameters for two groups of bearded saki monkeys (*Chiropotes sagulatus*) living in continuous forest and a 12 ha forest fragment

Method and parameters[a]	Continuous forest		Forest fragment	
	Home range (ha)	Percentage of MCP value[b]	Home range (ha)	Percentage of MCP value[b]
MCP (100 percent)	444	100	11	100
GC				
50 × 50 m	55	12	13	118
100 × 100 m	124	28	20	182
250 × 250 m	313	70	25	227
500 × 500 m	475	107	25	227
FK	487	110	13	118
LoCoH				
Fixed, $k = 5$	51	11	6	55
Fixed, $k = 10$	118	27	9	82
Fixed, $k = 20$	230	52	10	91
Fixed, $r = 50$ m	8	2	10	91
Fixed, $r = 100$ m	39	9	11	100
Fixed, $r = 250$ m	128	29	11	100
Adaptive, $a = 50$ m	1	0.2	2	18
Adaptive, $a = 100$ m	6	1	5	45
Adaptive, $a = 250$ m	27	6	9	82
Adaptive, $a = 500$ m	54	12	10	91

[a] Home range methods included minimum convex polygon (MCP), grid cell (GC) using different sizes of cells, fixed kernel (FK), and local convex hull (LoCoH) using fixed k, fixed r, and adaptive a with different values for k, r, and a.
[b] Because of the large differences in home range sizes between the two primate groups, the percentage of the minimum convex polygon (MCP) estimate is provided to help with comparison between the two study groups.

and behavior of the groups is available in Boyle et al. (2009a) and Boyle and Smith (2010a).

Based on the 500 point samples, the two bearded saki groups differed greatly in their home range size: the continuous forest group had a home range of 444 ha (calculated with MCP) and the forest fragment group had a home range of 11 ha (calculated with MCP). There were also large differences in home range area within each study group, based on the method used (Table 7.2). These findings highlight that an appropriate size for a grid cell not only depends on the study species, but also on the habitat: a 50 m grid cell was appropriate for the bearded saki group in the small forest fragment, but this size was too small for the group living in the continuous forest, and the 250 m grid cell was too coarse for home range calculations in the small forest fragment (Figure 7.2). Home range size varied greatly based on the size of grid cells (Table 7.2). For MCP and FK, the home range estimates for each group of monkeys were relatively close, in comparison with the extreme home range estimates obtained from some of the GC and LoCoH methods (Table 7.2). For the bearded saki monkeys in the continuous forest, k-LoCoH, *r*-LoCoH, and *a*-LoCoH all provided home range estimates that were considerably smaller than MCP and FK estimates. The estimators *k*-LoCoH and *a*-LoCoH also provided smaller home range estimates for the bearded saki monkeys in the forest fragment, but the differences were not as extreme as with the data from the continuous forest (Table 7.2).

Which method worked best? For the continuous forest data, GC (with a cell size of 500×500 m) and FK both estimated home ranges that were within 10 percent of the MCP estimate (Table 7.2). For the forest fragment data, *r*-LoCoH (with $r = 100$ m and $r = 250$ m) and *a*-LoCoH (with $a = 500$ m) estimated home ranges that were within 10 percent of the MCP estimate. Therefore, while GC and FK were most appropriate for the continuous forest data, these two methods were not the most appropriate for the forest fragment data: they both estimated home range sizes that were larger than the actual size of the forest fragment. In summary, this case study illustrates that it is important to choose home range estimators (and their parameters) that are most appropriate for the data.

Additional Methods

Although GC, MCP, FK, AK, and LoCoH are commonly used to calculate home ranges of primates, many other methods exist. Some of these methods are older and not as commonly used (e.g., ellipses, Jennrich & Turner 1969; harmonic mean, Dixon & Chapman 1980; Fourier series, Anderson 1982) as the methods described above. Other methods are more recent, and they are becoming more prevalent (Kie et al. 2010), such as mechanistic (Moorcroft 2012; Moorcroft et al. 1999) and deterministic (Spencer 2012) home range models. These newer methods are not as commonly included in software programs (Table 7.3) as many of the methods previously mentioned, and have not yet been widely used in primate research. However, these methods are worth examining in greater detail with data from primate field studies. Recent publications have suggested the use of potential path area (PPA) home range analysis, which takes into consideration time attributes (Long & Nelson 2012); kriging (Kie et al. 2010), which is not a new concept but has rarely been applied to home range estimates; Brownian bridges (Horne et al. 2007); and area under the curve (AUC) (Cumming & Cornélis 2012). With the current GPS technology and ability to record large amounts of data almost continuously, it has been proposed that home range estimates should focus on the linear paths of movement, not a set of points, and take temporality of points into consideration (Kie et al. 2010; Steiniger & Hunter 2013; Crofoot, Chapter 3 of this volume).

Which Method Is Best?

For many years, studies have attempted to address the question, "Which method is best?". Mohr (1947) conducted some of the first comparisons of different home range methods (minimum home range and grids), examining differences in the results, while

Table 7.3 Software packages for calculating home range are not identical and they differ in the extent of home range analysis that is possible; it is up to the user to determine which package is most appropriate for the user's data

Name	Free?	Requires other software?[a]	URL for downloading or purchase	Citation
Geospatial Modeling Environment (GME)	Yes	ArcGIS 10.x; R	www.spatialecology.com/gme	Beyer (2010)
ArcGIS	No	No	www.esri.com/software/arcgis	ESRI (2013)
Home Range Extension (HRE)	Yes	ArcView 3.x	http://flash.lakeheadu.ca/~arodgers/hre/	Rodgers & Carr (1998)
Animal Movement	Yes	ArcView 3.x	http://alaska.usgs.gov/science/biology/spatial/gistools/index.php/	Hooge & Eichenlaub (2000)
R (adehabitat)	Yes	No	http://cran.r-project.org/	Calenge (2006)
Local Convex Hull (LoCoH)	Yes	No	http://nature.berkeley.edu/~ajlyons/locoh/	Getz & Wilmers (2004)
Biotas	Free trial	No	www.ecostats.com/web/Biotas	Ecological Software Solutions (2013)
Home Range Tools (HRT)	Yes	ArcGIS 9.x	http://flash.lakeheadu.ca/~arodgers/hre/	Rodgers et al. (2007)
Home Range Analysis and Estimation (HoRAE)	Yes	OpenJUMP (free)	http://146.155.17.19:21080/mediawiki-1.22.7/index.php/Movement_Analysis	Steiniger & Hunter (2012)
Animal Space Use	Yes	No	www.cnr.uidaho.edu/population_ecology/animal_space_use.htm	Horne & Garton (2009)

[a] The availability, home range options, and compatibility with or reliance on other software programs can change quickly. These programs are examples that were available when this book went to press, and it is suggested that the user examines multiple programs prior to choosing one. Inclusion of a program in this table does not constitute an endorsement of the program by the author.

Hayne (1949) discussed the limitations of different methods. Unfortunately, the conclusion of these comparative analyses is that there is no magic home range method that is best to use for all studies (Fieberg & Börger 2012), and different methods often provide different results (Börger et al. 2006; Boyle et al. 2009b; Cumming & Cornélis 2012; Grueter et al. 2009; Gula & Theuerkauf 2013; Huck et al. 2008; Laver & Kelly 2008; Powell 2000). For example, Pebsworth et al. (2012b) compared MCP, FK, and r-LoCoH, and found that the home range estimates for chacma baboons (*Papio hamadryas ursinus*) ranged from 1080 ha to 2310 ha using the exact same dataset. Such differing estimates could greatly impact the understanding of the animal's spatial ecology and behavior in its habitat, potentially impacting how conservation measures are directed.

Across taxa, FK has performed better than MCP in a range of studies (Börger et al. 2006; Pimley et al. 2005; Powell 2000), but in other situations MCP has performed better than kernel density estimators, particularly at low sample sizes (Boyle et al. 2009b; Row & Blouin-Demers 2006). However, comparisons of MCP and FK performance using black and white colobus (*Colobus angolensis ruwenzorii*) data resulted in similar home range estimates (Fashing et al. 2007), as did comparisons of MCP, FK, and AK with bearded saki (*Chiropotes sagulatus*) data (Shaffer 2013). In direct comparisons of a combination of GC, MCP, FK, AK, and LoCoH used for estimating primate home ranges, MCP, FK, and LoCoH were each considered the best choice of estimator at least once (Table 7.1). Although MCP has been criticized for including areas not used by the animal (Worton 1987), most home range estimators have this problem (Gula & Theuerkauf 2013).

The suite of home range estimators that are available can result in different home range estimates, and these differences are not global across all studies. Therefore, many primate studies present results using multiple methods (Table 7.1), allowing for comparisons to previous and future research. Overall it is important to choose the method (or methods) most appropriate for the data (Powell 2000), relevant to the research question that is being asked (Fieberg & Börger 2012), and which minimizes type I (estimate does not include areas that the animals use) and type II (estimate includes areas that are not used by the animals) errors (Fieberg & Börger 2012). Although a particular method may be the best choice for one study, that method may not be the most appropriate for another set of data (Powell 2000).

The Methods Matter: Important Considerations

Standardization of Methods

In a review of 50 published studies, Gula and Theuerkauf (2013) noted the use of 11 different methods and 8 software packages to calculate home range. When studies use different methods to estimate home range, it is nearly impossible to make biologically relevant comparisons between studies (Bearder 1987; Robbins & McNeilage 2003; Sterling et al. 2000). There have been several calls for researchers to standardize the methods used for calculating home range and the reporting of these methods in order to ensure repeatability of the studies and comparisons across studies (Bearder 1987; Fieberg & Börger 2012; Gula & Theuerkauf 2013; Laver & Kelly 2008; Sterling et al. 2000). However, despite the calls for standardization, to date there is no standard for home range estimation.

In the meantime, to address the standardization of the home range methods, it would be helpful to present the results from multiple home-range estimators. Although a particular method may not be the preferred method, it may be best to consider using it in addition to the preferred method if the less-preferred method has been consistently used in the past. For example, traditionally gorilla studies have used the GC method (Robbins & McNeilage 2003), so it may be best to continue to publish GC results along with the results from other estimations so that comparisons can be made with the older studies. In order to prepare for comparisons in the future, it may be worth considering archiving raw data in a data repository (e.g., MoveBank; Fieberg & Börger 2012) so that the data may be analyzed using methods that may become more common in the future.

Reporting Specific Details

Seasonal variations in home range size exist (blue-eyed black lemur, *Eulemur flavifrons*: Volampeno et al. 2011; white-faced capuchin, *Cebus capucinus*: Campos & Fedigan 2009; Sichuan snub-nosed monkey, *Rhinopithecus roxellana*: Li et al. 2010), as do variations in annual ranges (mountain gorilla, *Gorilla beringei beringei*: Robbins & McNeilage 2003; Bornean orangutan, *Pongo pygmaeus wurmbii*: Wartmann et al. 2010; mandrill, *Mandrillus sphinx*: White et al. 2010). Alternatively, the home range may fluctuate throughout the year, but may remain stable in year-to-year comparisons (gray-cheeked mangabey, *Lophocebus albigena*: Janmaat et al. 2009).

It is important that the temporal extent of the data is always clearly defined: Does the home range represent the movements of the animal for a season? One year? Multiple years? For example, in a multi-year study of mountain gorillas (*Gorilla beringei beringei*), home range size was 2100 ha for two consecutive years, and then increased to 4000 ha the following year (Robbins & McNeilage 2003); had these three years of data been presented together as one number representing a total of the three years of data or as an annual average, there would be no indication that home range size doubled from one year to the next. Home ranges can also shift during dispersal and group fission (Janmaat et al. 2009); such details on group dynamics would be important to report with the home range number. Along these lines, it is important that the same temporal scale is used when comparing home ranges from different populations or species, or at least that it is noted that comparisons were made using data from different temporal scales.

In addition, it is also important to present the sample size (Wartmann et al. 2010), and smoothing parameter (Wartmann et al. 2010), given that both items can greatly influence home range estimates. However, there is no magic number for the ideal sample size, as asymptotes can be reached with as few as 100 points (Girard et al. 2002) or may require more than 500 points (Boyle et al. 2009b). If using GC, one should present the size of the cell. By providing detailed information on the data and methods, it will improve comparability among studies, especially when studies are compiled for large edited volumes.

Ecological and Behavioral Variables

It is not possible for one home range method to address all aspects of an organism's biology (Kie et al. 2010); however, understanding the species' behavior and ecology, as well as the habitat and landscape characteristics of the study area, is important. Many species don't use space uniformly, as their movements may be centered along a linear path (Blundell et al. 2001) or in select areas of a heterogeneous landscape (Campos & Fedigan 2009), or defined by a river (Knight et al. 2009). Therefore, it is important to choose the home range method that does not overestimate range by including areas that are not used (or accessible) by the animal. Furthermore, the animals may be confined to an isolated forest fragment (Boyle et al. 2009a), or they may leave the fragment (Boyle & Smith 2010b; Chaves et al. 2011), so unless the animals in the fragments are routinely monitored, one should not assume that the size of the fragment is the home range size of the animals, given that the animals could be using the fragment opportunistically.

Home range should not be thought of solely as a number provided from an estimator; it should have biological context, taking into consideration information on the resources available to the animal, habitat structure, and additional factors of the landscape (Powell & Mitchell 2012). For example, home ranges can be impacted by human influences, such as the impact of cultivated fruit presence on Sumatran orangutan (*Pongo abelii*) foraging and crop-raiding behavior (Campbell-Smith et al. 2011).

Software Options

Technology changes rapidly, and in the past couple of decades there have been (and currently are) a myriad of software programs for calculating home range (Table 7.3). Some software programs have not been updated in more than a decade, other programs rely on the user having specific GIS software, and other programs put a greater emphasis on the user having an understanding of coding. Previous comparisons of software packages have shown variations in home range estimates (Lawson & Rodgers 1997). Although technology changes rapidly, and multiple new software programs will most likely become available after the publication of this current chapter, the overall patterns will likely remain similar for the relatively near future.

Most home range software allow for the use of MCP and kernel analyses; however, even though the names of the methods are identical, the algorithms of the programs differ and as a result the home range area for identical data may differ based on the software used. Furthermore, there are limitations with some of the software packages in calculating home range with some of the methods and/or with some of the smoothing factors (Walter et al. 2011). It is important for the researcher to understand the data and what the data indicate, and not rely solely on the default settings of a software program. Home range software has changed over the years and will likely continue to change, so it is important to understand the main concepts behind the home range methods and then apply this knowledge to future software packages or code.

Conclusion

Horne and Garton (2006b) suggested the use of multiple home range models to better understand movement ecology. Home range estimates can vary with methods (e.g., MCP, kernel, LoCoH), the parameters used (e.g., k values for LoCoH, smoothing factors of FK), and software used (e.g., R, Home Range Tools). Therefore, it is important that primatologists understand the differences in analysis and choose the tools that are most appropriate for their research question and data.

In order for comparisons to be made between studies, it is important to document sample size, temporal definitions (annual, seasonal), smoothing factors used, and overall data-collection methods. Primatologists may want to consider presenting the results from multiple appropriate estimators in order to increase the number of comparisons possible. In summary: The methods matter, but methods should be chosen based on the data (e.g., sample size, geographic spread, number of outliers) and the biological variables associated with the study (e.g., species' behavior and ecology, habitat size, land cover, resource distribution).

References

Akers, A. A., Islam, M. A., and Nijman, V. 2013. Habitat characterization of western hoolock gibbons *Hoolock hoolock* by examining home range microhabitat use. *Primates* **54**: 341–348.

Anderson, D. J. 1982. The home range: a new nonparametric estimation technique. *Ecology* **63**: 103–112.

Bartlett, T. Q. 2007. The Hylobatidae: small apes of Asia. Pages 274–289 in *Primates in Perspective*. C. J. Campbell, A. Fuentes, K. C. MacKinnon, M. Panger, and S. Bearder (Eds.). Oxford University Press, Oxford.

Bearder, S. 1987. Lorises, bushbabies, and tarsiers: diverse societies in solitary foragers. Pages 11–24 in *Primate Societies*. B. B. Smuts, D. L. Cheney, R. M. Seyfarth, R. W. Wrangham, and T. T. Struhsaker (Eds.). University of Chicago Press, Chicago, IL.

Beyer, H. L. 2010. Geospatial modeling environment for ArcGIS. Available at: www.spatialecology.com/gme.

Biebouw, K. 2009. Home range size and use in *Allocebus trichotis* in Analamazaotra Special Reserve, Central Eastern Madagascar. *International Journal of Primatology* **30**: 367–386.

Blair, W. F. 1942. Size of home range and notes on the life history of the woodland deer-mouse and eastern chipmunk in northern Michigan. *Journal of Mammalogy* **23**: 27–36.

Blundell, F. M., Maier, J. A. K., and Debevec, E. M. 2001. Linear home ranges: effects of smoothing, sample size, and autocorrelation on kernel estimates. *Ecological Monographs* **71**: 469–489.

Börger, L., Franconi, N., De Michelle, G., et al. 2006. Effects of sampling regime on the mean and variance of home range size estimates. *Journal of Animal Ecology* **75**: 1393–1405.

Boyle, S. A. and Smith, A. T. 2010a. Behavioral modifications in northern bearded saki monkeys (*Chiropotes satanas chiropotes*) in forest fragments of central Amazonia. *Primates* **51**: 43–51.

Boyle, S. A. and Smith, A. T. 2010b. Can landscape and species characteristics predict primate presence in forest fragments in the Brazilian Amazon? *Biological Conservation* **143**: 1134–1143.

Boyle, S. A., Lourenço, W. C., da Silva, L. R., and Smith, A. T. 2009a. Travel and spatial patterns change when northern bearded saki monkeys (*Chiropotes satanas chiropotes*) live in forest fragments. *International Journal of Primatology* **30**: 515–531.

Boyle, S. A., Lourenço, W. C., da Silva, L. R., and Smith, A. T. 2009b. Home range estimates vary with sample size and methods. *Folia Primatologica* **80**: 33–42.

Burt, W. H. 1940. Territorial behavior and populations of small mammals in southern Michigan. *Miscellaneous Publications Museum of Zoology, University of Michigan* **45**: 1–58.

Burt, W. H. 1943. Territoriality and home range concepts as applied to mammals. *Journal of Mammalogy* **24**: 346–352.

Calenge, C. 2006. The package "adehabitat" for the R software: a tool for the analysis of space and habitat use by animals. *Ecological Modelling* **197**: 516–519.

Campbell-Smith, G., Campbell-Smith, M., Singleton, I., and Linkie, M. 2011. Apes in space: saving an imperiled orangutan population in Sumatra. *PLoS ONE* **6**: e17210.

Campos, F. A. and Fedigan, L. M. 2009. Behavioral adaptations to heat stress and water scarcity in white-faced capuchins (*Cebus capucinus*) in Santa Rosa National Park, Costa Rica. *American Journal of Physical Anthropology* **138**: 101–111.

Chapman, C. 1988. Patterns of foraging and range use by three species of Neotropical primates. *Primates* **29**: 177–194.

Chaves, O. M., Stoner, K. E., and Arroyo-Rodríguez, V. 2011. Seasonal differences in activity patterns of Geoffroyi's spider monkeys (*Ateles geoffroyi*) living in continuous and fragmented forests in southern Mexico. *International Journal of Primatology* **32**: 960–973.

Cresswell, W. J. and Smith, G. C. 1992. The effects of temporally autocorrelated data on methods of home range analysis. Pages 272–284 in *Wildlife Telemetry: Remote Monitoring and Tracking of Animals*. I. G. Priede and S. M. Swift (Eds.). Ellis Horwood, London.

Cumming, G. S. and Cornélis, D. 2012. Quantitative comparison and selection of home range metrics for telemetry data. *Diversity and Distributions* **18**: 1057–1065.

Cushman, S. A., Chase, M., and Griffin, C. 2005. Elephants in space and time. *Oikos* **109**: 331–341.

de Solla, S. R., Bonduriansky, R., and Brooks, R. J. 1999. Eliminating autocorrelation reduces biological relevance of home range estimates. *Journal of Animal Ecology* **68**: 221–234.

Di Fiore, A. and Campbell, C. J. 2007. The Atelines: variation in ecology, behavior, and social organization. Pages 155–185 in *Primates in Perspective*. C. J. Campbell, A. Fuentes, K. C. MacKinnon, M. Panger, and S. Bearder (Eds.). Oxford University Press, Oxford.

Digby, L. J., Ferrari, S. F., and Saltzman, W. 2007. Callitrichines: the role of competition in cooperatively breeding species. Pages 85–106 in *Primates in Perspective*. C. J. Campbell, A. Fuentes, K. C. MacKinnon, M. Panger, and S. Bearder (Eds.). Oxford University Press, Oxford.

Dixon, K. R. and Chapman, J. A. 1980. Harmonic mean measure of animal activity areas. *Ecology* **61**: 1040–1044.

Ecological Software Solutions, LLC. 2013. Biotas. Software.

Enstam, K. L. and Isbell, L. A. (2007. The guenons (genus *Cercopithecus*) and their allies: behavioral ecology of polyspecific associations. Pages 252–274 in *Primates in Perspective*. C. J. Campbell, A. Fuentes, K. C. MacKinnon, M. Panger, and S. Bearder (Eds.). Oxford University Press, Oxford.

ESRI 2013. ArcGIS 10.X. Software.

Fashing, P. J. 2007. African colobine monkeys: patterns of between-group interaction. Pages 201–224 in *Primates in Perspective*. C. J. Campbell, A. Fuentes, K. C. MacKinnon, M. Panger, and S. Bearder (Eds.). Oxford University Press, Oxford.

Fashing, P. J., Mulindahabi, F., Gakima, J. B., et al. 2007. Activity and ranging patterns of *Colobus angolensis ruwenzorii* in Nyungwe Forest, Rwanda: possible costs of large group size. *International Journal of Primatology* **28**: 529–550.

Fedigan, L. M., Fedigan, L., Chapman, C., and Glander, K. E. 1988. Spider monkey home ranges: a comparison of radio telemetry and direct observation. *American Journal of Primatology* **16**: 19–29.

Fernandez-Duque, E. 2007. Aotinae: social monogramy in the only nocturnal haplorhines. Pages 139–154 in *Primates in Perspective*. C. J. Campbell, A. Fuentes, K. C. MacKinnon, M. Panger, and S. Bearder (Eds.). Oxford University Press, Oxford.

Fieberg, J. 2007a. Kernel density estimators of home range: smoothing and the autocorrelation red herring. *Ecology* **88**: 1059–1066.

Fieberg, J. 2007b. Utilization distribution estimation using weighted kernel density estimators. *The Journal of Wildlife Management* **71**: 1669–1675.

Fieberg, J. and Börger, L. B. 2012. Could you please phrase "home range" as a question? *Journal of Mammalogy* **93**: 890–902.

Garber, P. A., Pruetz, J. D., and Isaacson, J. 1993. Patterns of range use, range defense, and intergroup spacing in moustached tamarin monkeys (*Saguinus mystax*). *Primates* **34**: 11–25.

Gerber, B. D., Arrigo-Nelson, S., Karpanty, S. M., Kotschwar, M., and Wright, P. C. 2012. Spatial ecology of the endangered Milne-Edwards' sifaka (*Propithecus edwardsi*): do logging and season affect home range and daily ranging patterns? *International Journal of Primatology* **33**: 305–321.

Getz, W. M. and Wilmers, C. C. 2004. A local nearest-neighbor convex-hull construction of home ranges and utilization distributions. *Ecography* **27**: 489–505.

Getz, W. M., Fortmann-Roe, S., Cross, P. C., et al. 2007. LoCoH: nonparametric kernel methods for constructing home range and utilization distributions. *PLoS ONE* **2**: e207.

Girard, I., Ouellet, J. P., Courtois, R., Dussault, C., and Breton, L. 2002. Effects of sampling effort based on GPS telemetry on home-range size estimations. *Journal of Wildlife Management* **66**: 1290–1300.

Gitzen, R. A. and Millspaugh, J. J. 2003. Comparison of least-squares cross-validation bandwidth options for kernel home-range estimation. *Wildlife Society Bulletin* **31**: 823–831.

Gould, L. and Sauther, M. 2007. Lemuriformes. Pages 46–72 in *Primates in Perspective*. C. J. Campbell, A. Fuentes, K. C. MacKinnon, M. Panger, and S. Bearder (Eds.). Oxford University Press, Oxford.

Grueter, C. C., Li, D., Ren, B., and Wei, F. 2009. Choice of analytical method can have dramatic effects on primate home range estimates. *Primates* **50**: 81–84.

Gula, R. and Theuerkauf, J. 2013. The need for standardization in wildlife science: home range estimators as an example. *European Journal of Wildlife Research* **59**: 713–718.

Gursky, S. 2007. Tarsiiformes. Pages 73–85 in *Primates in Perspective*. C. J. Campbell, A. Fuentes, K. C. MacKinnon, M. Panger, and S. Bearder (Eds.). Oxford University Press, Oxford.

Hadi, S., Ziegler, T., Waltert, M., et al. 2012. Habitat use and trophic niche overlap of two sympatric colobines, *Presbytis potenziani* and *Simias concolor*, on Siberut Island, Indonesia. *International Journal of Primatology* **33**: 218–232.

Harris, T. R. and Chapman, C. A. 2007. Variation in diet and ranging of black and white colobus monkeys in Kibale National Park, Uganda. *Primates* **48**: 208–221.

Haugen, A. O. 1942. Home range of cottontail rabbit. *Ecology* **23**: 354–367.

Hayne, D. W. 1949. Calculation of size of home range. *Journal of Mammalogy* **30**: 1–18.

Hemingway, C. A. and Bynum, N. 2005. The influence of seasonality on primate diet and ranging. Pages 57–104 in *Seasonality in Primates: Studies of Living and Extinct Human and Non-human Primates*. D. K. Brockman and C. P. van Schaik (Eds.). Cambridge University Press, Cambridge.

Hemson, G., Johnson, P., South, A., et al. 2005. Are kernels the mustard? Data from global positioning system (GPS) collars suggest problems for kernel home range analyses with least-squares-cross-validation. *Journal of Animal Ecology* **74**: 455–463.

Henzi, S. P., Brown, L. R., Barrett, L., and Marais, A. J. 2011. Troop size, habitat use, and diet of chacma baboons (*Papio hamadryas ursinus*) in commercial pine plantations: implications for management. *International Journal of Primatology* **32**: 1020–1032.

Herbinger, I., Boesch, C., and Rothe, H. 2001. Territory characteristics among three neighboring chimpanzee communities in the Taï National Park, Côte d'Ivoire. *International Journal of Primatology* **22**: 143–167.

Hoffman, T. S. and O'Riain, M. J. 2011. The spatial ecology of chacma baboons (*Papio ursinus*) in a human-modified environment. *International Journal of Primatology* **32**: 308–328.

Hooge, P. N. and Eichenlaub, B. 2000. Animal movement extension to ArcView. Ver. 2.0. Alaska Science Center, Biological Science Office, U.S. Geological Survey, Anchorage, AK.

Horne, J. S. and Garton, E. O. 2006a. Likelihood cross-validation versus least squares cross-validation for choosing the smoothing parameter in kernel home range analysis. *Journal of Wildlife Management* **70**: 641–648.

Horne, J. S. and Garton, E. O. 2006b. Selecting the best home range model: an information theoretic approach. *Ecology* **87**: 1146–1152.

Horne, J. S. and Garton, E. O. 2009. Animal space use 1.3. Available at: www.cnr.uidaho.edu/population_ecology/animal_space_use.htm.

Horne, J. S., Garton, E. O., Krone, S. S., and Lewis, J. L. 2007. Analyzing animal movements using Brownian bridges. *Ecology* **88**: 2354–2363.

Huck, M., Davison, J., and Roper, T. J. 2008. Comparison of two sampling protocols and four home-range estimators using radio-tracking data from urban badgers *Meles meles*. *Wildlife Biology* **14**: 467–477.

Irwin, M. T. 2008. Diademed sifaka (*Propithecus diadema*) ranging and habitat use in continuous and fragmented forest: higher density but lower viability in fragments? *Biotropica* **40**: 231–240.

Janmaat, K. R. L., Olupot, W., Chancellor, R. L., Arlet, M. E., and Waser, P. M. 2009. Long-term site fidelity and individual home range shifts in *Lophocebus albigena*. *International Journal of Primatology* **30**: 443–466.

Jennrich, R. I. and Turner, F. B. 1969. Measurement of non-circular home range. *Journal of Theoretical Biology* **22**: 227–237.

Kie, J. G., Matthiopoulos, J., Fieberg, J., et al. 2010. The home-range concept: are traditional estimators still relevant with modern telemetry technology? *Philosophical Transactions of the Royal Society B* **365**: 2221–2231.

Kirkpatrick, R. C. 2007. The Asian colobines: diversity among leaf-eating monkeys. Pages 186–200 in *Primates in Perspective*. C. J. Campbell, A. Fuentes, K. C. MacKinnon, M. Panger, and S. Bearder (Eds.). Oxford University Press, Oxford.

Knight, C. M., Kenward, R. E., Gozlan, R. E., et al. 2009. Home range estimation within complex restricted environments: importance of method selection in detecting seasonal change. *Wildlife Research* **36**: 213–224.

Lahann, P. 2008. Habitat utilization of three sympatric cheirogaleid lemur species in a littoral rain forest of southeastern Madagascar. *International Journal of Primatology* **29**: 117–134.

Laver, P. N. and Kelly, M. J. 2008. A critical review of home range studies. *Journal of Wildlife Management* **72**: 290–298.

Lawson, E. J. G. and Rodgers, A. R. 1997. Differences in home-range size computed in commonly used software programs. *Wildlife Society Bulletin* **25**: 721–729.

Lehmann, J. and Boesch, C. 2003. Social influences on ranging patterns among chimpanzees (*Pan troglodytes verus*) in the Taï National Park, Côte d'Ivoire. *Behavioral Ecology* **14**: 642–649.

Li, Y., Jiang, Z., Li, C., and Grueter, C. C. 2010. Effects of seasonal folivory and frugivory on ranging patterns in *Rhinopithecus roxellana*. *International Journal of Primatology* **31**: 609–626.

Lichti, N. I. and Swihart, R. K. 2011. Estimating utilization distributions with kernel versus local convex hull methods. *Journal of Wildlife Management* **75**: 413–422.

Long, J. A. and Nelson, T. A. 2012. Time geography and wildlife home range delineation. *Journal of Wildlife Management* **76**: 407–413.

Lyons, A. J., Turner, W. C., and Getz, W. M. 2013. Home range plus: a space-time characterization of movement over real landscapes. *Movement Ecology* **1**: 2.

Matsuda, I., Tuuga, A., and Higashi, S. 2009. Ranging behavior of proboscis monkeys in a riverine forest with special reference to ranging in inland forest. *International Journal of Primatology* **30**: 313–325.

Mekonnen, A., Bekele, A., Fashing, P. L., Hemson, G., and Atickem, A. 2010. Diet, activity patterns, and ranging ecology of the bale monkey (*Chlorocebus djamdjamensis*) in Odobullu Forest, Ethiopia. *International Journal of Primatology* **31**: 339–362.

Merker, S. 2006. Habitat-specific ranging patterns of Dian's tarsiers (*Tarsius dianae*) as revealed by radiotracking. *American Journal of Primatology* **68**: 111–125.

Milton, K. and May, M. L. 1976. Body weight, diet and home range area in primates. *Nature* **259**: 459–462.

Mochizuki, S. and Murakami, T. 2013. Scale dependent effects in resource selection by crop-raiding Japanese macaques in Niigata Prefecture, Japan. *Applied Geography* **42**: 13–22.

Mohr, C. O. 1947. Table of equivalent populations of North American small mammals. *The American Midland Naturalist* **37**: 223–449.

Moorcroft, P. R. 2012. Mechanistic approaches to understanding and predicting mammalian space use: recent advances, future directions. *Journal of Mammalogy* **93**: 903–916.

Moorcroft, P. R. and Lewis, M. A. 2006. *Mechanistic Home Range Analysis*. Princeton University Press, Princeton, NJ.

Moorcroft, P. R., Lewis, M. A., and Crabtree, R. L. 1999. Home range analysis using a mechanistic home range model. *Ecology*: **80**: 1656–1665.

Nekaris, A. and Bearder, S. K. 2007. The lorisiform primates of Asia and mainland Africa: diversity shrouded in darkness. Pages 24–45 in *Primates in Perspective*. C. J. Campbell, A. Fuentes, K. C. MacKinnon, M. Panger, and S. Bearder (Eds.). Oxford University Press, Oxford.

Neri-Arboleda, I., Stott, P., and Arboleda, N. P. 2002. Home ranges, spatial movements and habitat associations of the Philippine tarsier (*Tarsius syrichta*) in Corella, Bohol. *Journal of Zoology* **257**: 387–402.

Newton-Fisher, N. E. 2003. The home range of the Sonso community of chimpanzees from the Budongo Forest, Uganda. *African Journal of Ecology* **41**: 150–156.

Norconk, M. A. 2007. Sakis, uakaris, and titi monkeys: behavioral diversity in a radiation of primate seed predators. Pages 123–138 in *Primates in Perspective*. C. J. Campbell, A. Fuentes, K. C. MacKinnon, M. Panger, and S. Bearder (Eds.). Oxford University Press, Oxford.

Norscia, I. and Borgognini-Tarli, S. M. 2008. Ranging behavior and possible correlates of pair-living in southeastern avahis (Madagascar). *International Journal of Primatology* **29**: 153–171.

Ostro, L. E. T., Young, T. P., Silver, S. C., and Koontz, F. W. 1999. A geographic information system method for estimating home range size. *Journal of Wildlife Management* **63**: 748–755.

Otis, D. L. and White, G. C. 1999. Autocorrelation of location estimates and the analysis of radiotracking data. *The Journal of Wildlife Management* **63**: 1039–1044.

Palminteri, S. and Peres, C. A. 2012. Habitat selection and use of space by bald-faced sakis (*Pithecia irrorata*) in southwestern Amazonia: lessons from a multiyear, multigroup study. *International Journal of Primatology* **33**: 401–417.

Pebsworth, P. A., MacIntosh, A. J. J., Morgan, H. R., and Huffman, M. A. 2012a. Factors influencing the ranging behavior of chacma baboons (*Papio hamadryas ursinus*) living in a human-modified habitat. *International Journal of Primatology* **33**: 872–887.

Pebsworth, P. A., Morgan, H. R., and Huffman, M. A. 2012b. Evaluating home range techniques: use of global positioning system (GPS) collar data from chacma baboons. *Primates* **53**: 345–355.

Pimley, E. R., Bearder, S. K., and Dixson, A. F. 2005. Home range analysis of *Perodicticus potto edwardsi* and *Sciurocheirus cameronensis*. *International Journal of Primatology* **26**: 191–206.

Porter, L. M., Sterr, S. M., and Garber, P. A. 2007. Habitat use and ranging behavior of *Callimico goeldii*. *International Journal of Primatology* **28**: 1035–1058.

Powell, R. A. 2000. Animal home ranges and territories and home range estimators. Pages 65–110 in *Research Technologies in Animal Ecology: Controversies and Consequences*. L. Boitani and T. K. Fuller (Eds.). Columbia University Press, New York.

Powell, R. A. and Mitchell, M. S. 2012. What is a home range? *Journal of Mammalogy* **93**: 948–958.

Pyritz, L. W., Kappeler, P. M., and Fichtel, C. 2011. Coordination of group movements in wild red-fronted lemurs (*Eulemur rufifrons*): processes and influence of ecological and reproductive seasonality. *International Journal of Primatology* **32**: 1325–1347.

Raboy, B. E. and Dietz, J. M. 2004. Diet, foraging, and use of space in wild golden-headed lion tamarins. *American Journal of Primatology* **63**: 1–15.

Ramos-Fernández, G., Aguilar, S. E. S., Schaffner, C. M., Vick, L. G., and Aureli, F. 2013. Site fidelity in space use by spider monkeys (*Ateles geoffroyi*) in the Yucatan Peninsula, Mexico. *PLoS ONE* **8**: e62813.

Ren, B., Li, M., Long, Y., Wu, R., and Wei, F. 2009. Home range and seasonality of Yunnan snub-nosed monkeys. *Integrative Zoology* **4**: 162–171.

Robbins, M. M. 2007. Gorillas: diversity in ecology and behavior. Pages 305–321 in *Primates in Perspective*. C. J. Campbell, A. Fuentes, K. C. MacKinnon, M. Panger, and S. Bearder (Eds.). Oxford University Press, Oxford.

Robbins, M. M. and McNeilage, A. 2003. Home range and frugivory patterns of mountain gorillas in Bwindi Impenetrable National Park, Uganda. *International Journal of Primatology* **24**: 467–491.

Rodgers, A. R. and Carr, A. P. 1998. HRE: the Home Range Extension for ArcView. Thunder Bay, Ontario: Centre for Northern Forest Ecosystem Research, Ontario Ministry of Natural Resources, Centre for Northern Forest Ecosystem Research, Thunder Bay, Ontario.

Rodgers, A. R., Carr, A. P., Beyer, H. L., Smith, L., and Kie, J. G. 2007. HRT: Home Range Tools for ArcGIS. Version 1.1. Ontario Ministry of Natural Resources, Centre for Northern Forest Ecosystem Research, Thunder Bay, Ontario.

Row, J. R. and Blouin-Demers, G. 2006. Kernels are not accurate estimators of home-range size for herpetofauna. *Copeia* **4**: 797–802.

Sawyer, S. C. 2012. Subpopulation range estimation for conservation planning: a case study of the critically endangered Cross River gorilla. *Biodiversity and Conservation* **21**: 1589–1606.

Scull, P., Palmer, M., Frey, F., and Kraly, E. 2012. A comparison of two home range modeling methods using Ugandan mountain gorilla data. *International Journal of Geographical Information Science* **26**: 2111–2121.

Seaman, D. E. and Powell, R. A. 1996. An evaluation of the accuracy of kernel density estimators for home range analysis. *Ecology* **77**: 2075–2085.

Seaman, D. E., Millspaugh, J. J., Kernohan, B. J., et al. 1999. Effects of sample size on kernel home range estimates. *Journal of Wildlife Management* **63**: 739–747.

Shaffer, C. A. 2013. Ecological correlates of ranging behavior in bearded sakis (*Chiropotes sagulatus*) in a continuous forest in Guyana. *International Journal of Primatology* **34**: 515–532.

Silverman, B. W. 1986. *Density Estimation for Statistics and Data Analysis*. Chapman & Hall, London.

Siniff, D. B. and Tester, J. R. 1965. Computer analysis of animal movement data obtained by telemetry. *BioScience* **15**: 104–108.

Spehar, S. N., Link, A., and Di Fiore, A. 2010. Male and female range use in a group of white-bellied spider monkeys (*Ateles belzebuth*) in Yasuní National Park, Ecuador. *American Journal of Primatology* **72**: 129–141.

Spencer, W. D. 2012. Home range and the value of spatial information. *Journal of Mammalogy* **93**: 929–947.

Steiniger, S. and Hunter, A. J. S. 2012. OpenJUMP HoRAE: a free GIS and toolbox for home range analysis. *Wildlife Society Bulletin* **36**: 600–608.

Steiniger, S. and Hunter, A. J. S. 2013. A scaled line-based kernel density estimator for the retrieval of utilization distributions and home ranges from GPS movement tracks. *Ecological Informatics* **13**: 1–8.

Sterling, E., Nguyen, N., and Fashing, P. 2000. Spatial patterning in nocturnal prosimians: a review of methods and relevance to studies of sociality. *American Journal of Primatology* **51**: 3–19.

Stumpf, R. 2007. Chimpanzees and bonobos: diversity within and between species. Pages 321–344 in *Primates in Perspective*. C. J. Campbell, A. Fuentes, K. C. MacKinnon, M. Panger, and S. Bearder (Eds.). Oxford University Press, Oxford.

Swihart, R. K. and Slade, N. A. 1985. Testing for independence of observations in animal movements. *Ecology* **66**: 1176–1184.

Swihart, R. K. and Slade, N. A. 1997. On testing for independence of animal movements. *Journal of Agricultural, Biological, and Environmental Statistics* **2**: 48–63.

Takasaki, H. 1981. Troop size, habitat quality, and home range area in Japanese macaques. *Behavioral Ecology and Sociobiology* **9**: 277–281.

Tsuji, Y. and Takatsuki, S. 2009. Effects of yearly change in nut fruiting on autumn home-range use by *Macaca fuscata* on Kinkazan Island, northern Japan. *International Journal of Primatology* **30**: 169–181.

Volampeno, M. S. N., Masters, J. C., and Downs, C. T. 2011. Home range size in the blue-eyed black lemur (*Eulemur flavifrons*): a comparison between dry and wet seasons. *Mammalian Biology* **76**: 157–164.

Walter, W. D., Fischer, J. W., Baruch-Mordo, S., and VerCauteren, K. C. 2011. What is the proper method to delineate home range of an animal using today's advanced GPS telemetry systems: the initial step. Pages 249–268 in *Modern Telemetry*. O. Krejcar (Ed.). InTech Open Access Publisher, London.

Wartmann, F. M., Purves, R. S., and van Schaik, C. P. 2010. Modelling ranging behavior of female orang-utans: a case study in Tuanan, Central Kalimantan, Indonesia. *Primates* **51**: 119–130.

Wauters, L. A., Preatoni, D. G., Molinari, A. and Tosi, G. 2007. Radio tracking squirrels: performance of home range density and linkage estimators with small range and sample size. *Ecological Modelling* **3-4**: 333–344.

Weber, K. T., Burcham, M., and Marcum, C. L. 2001. Assessing independence of animal locations with association matrices. *Journal of Range Management* **54**: 21–24.

White, E. C., Dikangadissi, J. T., Dimoto, E., et al. 2010. Home-range use by a large horde of wild *Mandrillus sphinx*. *International Journal of Primatology* **31**: 627–645.

Willems, E. P. and Hill, R. A. 2009. Predator-specific landscapes of fear and resource distribution: effects on spatial range use. *Ecology* **90**: 546–555.

Worton, B. J. 1987. A review of models of home range for animal movement. *Ecological Modelling* **38**: 277–298.

Worton, B. J. 1989. Kernel methods for estimating the utilization distribution in home-range studies. *Ecology* **70**: 164–168.

Worton, B. J. 1995. Using Monte Carlo simulation to evaluate kernel-based home range estimators. *Journal of Wildlife Management* **59**: 794–800.

8 Quantifying Resource Dispersion in Free-Ranging Bearded Sakis in Guyana
What Is a Patch?

Christopher A. Shaffer

Introduction

Few concepts are more central to models of primate socioecology than the food patch. Many aspects of primate behavior are thought to be strongly influenced or even constrained by the distribution and quality of food patches, including group size and cohesiveness, daily path length and home range size, activity patterns, social structure, and patterns of agonistic behavior (Chapman & Chapman 2000; Isbell 1991; Koenig 2002; Nakagawa 1989; Sterk et al. 1997; Symington 1988; van Schaik 1989; Vogel and Janson 2007). According to these models, selection for efficient foraging results in grouping and ranging behaviors that allow primates to maximize feeding rates within a patch (Charnov 1976; Schoener 1971; Stephens & Krebs 1986). As a group of foragers begin to deplete a patch, their mean rate of nutrient intake declines due to reduced densities of food items (scramble competition) or contests with other animals (contest competition). As larger patches contain a greater abundance or density of food items, they can accommodate larger foraging groups. For any patch size, however, a point is reached at which the diminishing returns (i.e., reduced rate of nutrient intake) become high enough that it is more efficient to leave and travel to another patch. When this point is reached is determined by the quality of and distance to the other patches available to the forager (Charnov 1976; Schoener 1971). Therefore, much of the discussion of the role resource dispersion plays in the evolution of primate socioecology revolves around the conditions under which patches are monopolizable and/or depletable. For a patch to be monopolizable, it must be relatively small and/or clumped, allowing dominant individuals to limit access of subordinates (Chapman 1990; Strier 1989; White & Wrangham 1988). In addition, a monopolizable patch should be resource-rich (at least compared to the areas surrounding it), making defending it worthwhile for dominant individuals. A patch is theoretically depletable when the feeding activity of an individual or group leads to the disappearance of all food items (Chapman & Chapman 2000; Charnov 1976). However, patches can be considered functionally depleted when the rate of intake for the forager decreases to a level equal to the average for the rest of the environment (Chapman & Chapman 2000; Charnov 1976; Stephens & Krebs 1986).

Most models of primate socioecology, such as the ecological constraints model, assume that patches are both monopolizable and depletable, at least for frugivore primates (Chapman & Chapman 2000; Chapman et al. 1995; Leighton & Leighton 1982; Pruetz 1999; Stevenson et al. 1998; see Snaith & Chapman 2007 for a discussion of the depletability of patches in folivores). Under these models, when group size increases (or patch size and quality decrease), patch depletion occurs more rapidly, and primate groups will have to travel further to obtain the same intake of food resources. However, despite the centrality of patches to primate behavioral ecology, defining what constitutes a food patch has proven notoriously difficult in studies of wild primates (Chapman 1990; Chapman & Chapman 2000; Chapman et al. 1994; Isbell 1991; Isbell et al. 1998; Pruetz 1999; Shaffer 2013a; Symington 1988; Vogel and Janson 2007; White & Wrangham 1988). At the most basic level, a patch is an area of high resource availability surrounded by areas of low resource availability or a "localized aggregation of food items ... separated from other such aggregations by regions of markedly lower food density" (Temerin & Cant 1983: 336). Operationalizing this definition, however, can be highly problematic. For example, how does one determine what constitutes an area of low resource availability, and who's perspective do we use, that of the researcher or the primate? Also, determining the relative availability of resources will obviously vary by primate species, making it difficult to create measures that apply across all primates. Such standardization is necessary, however, for producing comparative datasets on resource abundance and distribution (Isbell et al. 1998; Pruetz 1999; Vogel and Janson 2007).

Researchers have traditionally solved the patch definition problem by designating each feeding tree as a separate patch (Chapman 1988; Chapman et al. 1994; Dias & Strier 2003; Leighton & Leighton 1982; Phillips 1995; Strier 1989; Symington 1988; White & Wrangham 1988). Patch quality is then determined by the size of the tree, usually measured in DBH (diameter at breast height). This method has many advantages, including the relative ease with which DBH data can be collected and its applicability across all primates. In addition, patch size as measured by this method has been shown to be a strong predictor of several aspects of primate sociality, including group size (Chapman & Chapman 2000; Dias & Strier 2003; Leighton & Leighton 1982; Strier 1989), patch residence time (Chapman 1988; Chapman et al. 1995; Janson 1992), day range (Chapman et al. 1995; Symington 1988), and frequency of agonistic behavior (Janson 1985; Koenig et al. 1998).

However, several researchers have pointed to limitations in this method, especially for species with large group sizes and/or wide group spreads, where individuals in the group may be feeding from multiple trees simultaneously (Isbell et al. 1998; Pruetz 1999; Shaffer 2013a; Vogel and Janson 2007). This is especially problematic for species that may increase group spread as a mechanism for reducing intragroup feeding competition. In addition, defining patches as a single feeding tree tells us little about larger-scale patterns of patchiness, like how clustered are feeding trees, what are the most productive areas of a group's home range, and, returning to the most basic patch definition, what are the areas of high resource abundance surrounded by areas of low resource abundance? In much of the ecological literature, patchiness is determined by the dispersion of individual trees of a given species, with a species being "clumped" or patchy if they have more conspecific neighbors than would be expected if locations of neighbors were chosen randomly (Krebs 1999; Stephens & Krebs 1986). While the methods developed for quantifying patchiness in this manner are useful in primate studies, several issues arise when applying them to feeding trees and resource dispersion. Fortunately for the primatologist, a number of spatial statistics have been developed to both quantify the extent of clustering across geographic areas and to explicitly identify areas with high values that are surrounded by low values.

While defining patches is obviously an inherently spatial question, until recently relatively few researchers utilized GIS in their analysis of primate patch use. However, the increased availability of powerful and relatively easy to use spatial statistics software in the last 10 years gives the primatologist an extremely versatile toolkit for quantifying patch quality in primate studies. Spatial statistics that have been widely used in ecology (and many other disciplines) are easily applied using commercial and open-source GIS software. In this chapter, I summarize useful approaches for quantifying resource dispersion or patchiness using an explicitly GIS-based approach. I discuss several commonly used spatial statistics for quantitatively describing patchiness in a way that can be used to test the relationships between resource dispersion and a variety of behavioral variables. I demonstrate these methods using data from a long-term study of bearded saki (*Chiropotes sagulatus*) ranging behavior in Guyana (Shaffer 2012), showing how they can produce differing results, and which is most appropriate for which socioecological questions. In doing so, I seek to quantitatively define what constitutes a food patch in a manner that allows primatologists to compare how aspects of primate socioecology relate to patch quality and distribution.

It is important to note that this chapter deals with patches as clustered feeding sites and not the broad-scale patches used to define habitat heterogeneity as is often applied in landscape ecology (Forman 1995; Pickett & White 1985). An extensive literature exists on how to identify patches in landscape ecology, some of which is relevant and cited here, but this chapter deals with finer-scale heterogeneity than is referred to in these papers. This inherent ambiguity of "patchiness" shows the importance of standardization in definitions of patches for primate studies.

Methods

Cluster Analysis

Ultimately, quantifying the location, size, and/or quality of food patches involves determining whether primate resources show spatial clustering. An extensive literature exists in forestry and ecology on best practices for assessing the degree of spatial clustering and the location of clusters (see Dale 1999; Everitt et al. 2001; Fortin et al. 2005; Legendre & Fortin 1989; Perry et al. 2002; Upton & Fingleton 1985 for reviews). Cluster analysis involves identifying features found in close proximity to one another (clusters) and/or areas where groups of features with similarly high or low values occur in close proximity (hot- or cold-spots). Cluster analysis is one of the most commonly

Clumped   Uniform   Random

Figure 8.1 Patterns of spatial clustering. The image on the right shows complete spatial randomness (CSR) or a Poisson spatial distribution, the null hypothesis for point pattern analysis.

applied types of GIS analysis and a variety of methods exist for determining whether clusters of features occur more often than would be expected by chance. These methods can be broadly divided into two categories depending on whether the analysis of patterning is based on location alone (point pattern analysis) or on location influenced some attribute (e.g., DBH) (spatial autocorrelation). Both types of analysis are useful for the primatologist interested in quantifying patchiness and the choice of analysis should depend on the specific question being asked and the data available.

Point Pattern Analysis

Point pattern or point process analysis (PPA) involves determining whether or not a set of points exhibit spatial patterning using a null hypothesis of complete spatial randomness (CSR). In other words, do the points exhibit a pattern that is unlikely to result from chance alone? Complete spatial randomness is a Poisson distribution of spatial location (i.e., points are just as likely to be in a location as any other). Point patterns can differ from CSR by being clustered (groups of points are found more closely together than expected) or dispersed (the distance between points is maximized) (Figure 8.1). Understanding the way that points are patterned can tell us something about the underlying process driving that pattern. As tree locations are frequently and easily represented as points in GIS, PPA is commonly used in forestry and ecology to assess tree-to-tree interactions (Dale 1999; Dale and Powell 2001; Diggle 1983; Haase 1995; Haase 2001; Warren 1972). One of the central goals of both disciplines is understanding the underlying biological processes that determine how trees are patterned spatially. While such processes are, of course, of interest to primatologists, primate researchers are equally interested in how the spatial pattern of trees (i.e., patchiness) influences the behavioral characteristics of primates. Point pattern analysis provides a test statistic of patchiness that can be compared to behavioral variables to test questions concerning the influence of ecological processes on primate behavior. Two of the most commonly used methods for PPA are the nearest neighbor index and Ripley's K(d) function.

The Nearest Neighbor Index

The nearest neighbor index calculates the distance between each point and its nearest neighbor and calculates the mean of those distances for the entire dataset (Clark & Evans 1954). The observed average distance is then divided by the expected average distance for a hypothetical random (Poisson) distribution:

$$\text{NNI} = \frac{\text{Observed mean distance}}{\text{Expected mean distance}}.$$

If the means are the same, the ratio equals 1 and the pattern is random; if the ratio is greater than 1, the pattern is dispersed; and if the ratio is less than 1, the pattern is clustered. In addition to the index, the calculated observed mean distance is useful for providing a general idea of the extent of clustering. The test statistic is a Z-score calculated as

$$Z = \frac{\text{Observed mean distance} - \text{Expected mean distance}}{\text{Standard error}}.$$

Z-scores are then compared to the normal distribution to assess significance, with $Z < -1.96$ indicating significant clustering and $Z > 1.96$ indicating significant clustering. The NNI is included in almost all GIS packages and generally requires only two parameters, distance method and size of the study area. In ArcGIS, the GIS output is the NNI statistic, the Z-score, the p-value, and the average nearest neighbor distance. An option is available to produce an .html file with visualization of the results.

Because the NNI is relatively easy to calculate and interpret, it has been used extensively in forestry, ecology, and, to a much lesser extent, primatology. However, it has several disadvantages compared to multi-distance PPA like Ripley's K. One of the most important considerations when employing nearest neighbor analysis is determining the extent of the study area, as this value has a large impact on the index and its associated test statistic. The default value is usually determined by a minimum enclosing rectangle. However, this value is not preferable for use in most primate studies, as it will tend to bias the index toward lower values (higher clustering) due to the non-rectangular shapes of most primate home and day ranges. A more accurate approach is to use the area of a minimum convex polygon (or kernel density home range) that encloses the study area of interest. Another major disadvantage of the NNI is based only on the mean distance to the nearest neighbor and not multiple nearest neighbors. It is, therefore, not useful for assessing clustering at multiple spatial scales.

Ripley's K

In contrast to the NNI, Ripley's K function calculates the clustering of points at a range of distances simultaneously. K is calculated by counting the number of neighboring features within a given distance of a point and summing their values (Ripley 1976). It is a measure of the average density of points at each distance, divided by the average density of points in the entire area. If the number of points found within a given distance is greater than expected compared to a random distribution, clustering is occurring at this distance. Values are calculated at several distances (within a user-defined increment) and these values are displayed in a table to show where clustering is greatest. Because K summarizes clustering (or dispersion) over a range of distances, it is a very useful method for assessing the size of primate food patches (clusters of feeding trees) and the distances between those patches. In addition, because it does not require a predetermined distance threshold or distance band, the K function does not require a-priori assumptions of cluster distance. Instead, clustering can be determined from the feeding tree data itself, allowing for an assessment of patchiness from the perspective of the primate being studied. The most common transformation of the K function is $L(d)$, calculated according to the formula:

$$L(d) = \sqrt{\frac{A\sum_{i=1}^{n}\sum_{j=1,j\neq i}^{n}k_{i,j}}{\pi n(n-1)}},$$

where d is the distance, n equals the total number of features (i.e., trees), A equals the total area of all features (i.e., study area), and $k_{i,j}$ is a weight applied by a boundary correction method. If there is no edge correction used, and the distance between i and j is less than d, $k_{i,j}$ will equal 1. Otherwise it will equal 0. When the $L(d)$ transformation is used, expected K = distance.

When the observed K value is larger than the expected K for a particular distance, the distribution is more clustered than a Poisson distribution for that distance. When the observed K is smaller than the expected K for a particular distance, the distribution is dispersed. The distance at which the difference between observed and expected K is largest is the distance of maximum clustering. To determine significance for Ripley's K, the GIS constructs a 99 percent confidence envelope by distributing points randomly in the specified study area and calculating K for that distribution. In most GIS packages, the user has the option of selecting the number of random distributions or permutations to produce. After the random points are distributed, the GIS selects the lowest and highest K values for each distance and these become the confidence intervals. When no weighting field is specified, Ripley's K calculates whether the location of points at a given distance (or range of distances) is significantly different from CSR. However, Ripley's K can also be weighted by an attribute field, in which case the weight represents the number of coincident points at a given location. For example, a point with a weight of four would be analyzed as four coincident points. The output for a Ripley's K analysis consists of a table summarizing the observed K, expected K, difference between these, and high and low confidence intervals for each of the specified distances in the analysis. Many GIS packages, including ArcGIS, have the option of producing a graph of the results.

While Ripley's K addresses some of the disadvantages associated with the NNI, the size of the study area has a similarly large influence on the results. Points at the edges of the study area can strongly influence Ripley's K values (edge effects). For most K analyses of primate resource dispersion, a buffered minimum convex polygon or other home range polygon is preferable to the default minimum enclosing rectangle. In addition, several boundary correction methods have been produced to account for the problems of edge effects in the calculation of Ripley's K and an extensive literature exists for determining when such correction methods should be applied (Dale and Powell 2001; Dixon 2002; Freeman & Ford 2002; Haase 1995, 2001). One of the most widely used and broadly applicable is "simulate outer boundary values." Whenever these methods are applied, it is imperative that they be reported with the results. Ripley's K function is used extensively in forestry and ecology to characterize habitat heterogeneity but has found very little use in primatology. However, as it is available as a tool in most GIS software, Ripley's K is a useful and robust tool for assessing resource dispersion in primatology datasets.

Spatial Autocorrelation

Spatial autocorrelation is one of the most important concepts in geography, and testing for spatial autocorrelation is often a first step in more complex spatial analyses (Anselin 1995; De Knegt et al. 2010; Everitt et al. 2001; Legendre & Fortin 1989; Perry et al. 2002). As defining patchiness is virtually synonymous with spatial autocorrelation, these analyses are important tools for primatologists. Unlike PPA that only tests for spatial patterns in location, spatial autocorrelation tests whether the characteristics of a feature (the attribute) are more similar (or dissimilar) to features that are close by than to those that are distant. As described by Tobler (1970), "Everything is related to everything else, but near things are more related than distant things." In other words, spatial autocorrelation shows the relationship between a variable and itself across spatial location. If a variable exhibits positive spatial autocorrelation, locations with high values will be surrounded by locations with high values and locations with low values will be surrounded by locations with low values. If it exhibits negative spatial autocorrelation, features with high values will be surrounded by features with low values. In the context of resource dispersion, this means that negative spatial autocorrelation indicates a dispersed pattern, positive spatial autocorrelation indicates a clustered pattern, and no spatial autocorrelation indicates a random pattern.

There is an important distinction between global and local methods for assessing autocorrelation and the difference between these can cause confusion for those new to spatial analysis. Global methods summarize patterns for an entire study area with one statistic, while local methods calculate statistics for each feature to assess if it is dissimilar from its neighbors. Both provide the primatologist with valuable information about the distribution of resources, but the specific questions they address are quite different. Global statistics are very useful for characterizing general habitat heterogeneity or patchiness (i.e., are the resources used over the course of a month, day, or year dispersed, clustered, or random). Because they produce a single statistic for each set of features, global statistics can be used to assess whether behavioral variables that are summarized by day or month (i.e., daily path length, monthly home range size) relate to patchiness. In contrast, local statistics allow for higher-resolution identification of specific patches, and are useful for assessing patch-to-patch changes in behavior.

There are several global statistics for calculating the degree of global spatial autocorrelation, including the joint count statistic, Moran's I, Geary's C, and the General G-statistic (Ebdon 1985). All of these methods produce a single value that summarizes the difference in magnitude of feature attribute values and the spatial distance between these features. The direction and magnitude of the spatial autocorrelation statistic indicates whether values are clustered, random, or dispersed. The statistic that is produced can be compared to behavioral variables to assess whether increased clustering (or patchiness) leads to corresponding increases in daily path length or decreases in group size, as predicted in many models of primate behavioral ecology. Such analyses can be conducted for data parsed by month, day, season, or year for the entire home range of the group being studied.

One of the oldest, most commonly used, and most reliable methods for assessing global spatial autocorrelation is Moran's I (Baily & Gatrell 1995; Ebdon 1985):

$$I = \frac{N\sum_i\sum_j W_{i,j}(X_i - \bar{X})(X_j - \bar{X})}{\left(\sum_i\sum_j W_{i,j}\right)\sum_i(X_i - \bar{X})^2},$$

where N is the number of cases, X_i is the variable value at a particular location, X_j is the variable value at another location, X is the mean of the variable, and $W_{i,j}$ is a weight applied to the comparison between location i and location j. Values for Moran's I vary between 1 and –1, with positive values indicating positive autocorrelation (clustering), and negative values indicating dispersion. Like all statistics used to measure spatial autocorrelation, Moran's I tests the null hypotheses that the spatial distribution of feature values is the result of random spatial processes. Moran's I calculates a Z-score by comparing the expected statistic and variance from a random distribution to those of the observed. Many types of GIS software allow the user to specify the distribution used to compare Z-scores. Moran's I is available as a tool in almost all GIS software. In ArcGIS, the GIS output is the Moran's I statistic, the Z-score, the p-value, and the distance threshold used in the analysis. An option is available to produce an .html file with results.

Most of the methods used for assessing global patterns of spatial autocorrelation have local counterparts. Local methods (local indicators of spatial autocorrelation, or LISA) are more appropriate for identifying where clusters are located and can be combined with global measures to identify which features may be contributing to global auto-correlation. Like the global statistics, these local versions each have strengths and weaknesses. Two of the most commonly used local spatial autocorrelation statistics are the local Moran's I (also called Anselin's LISA) and local Geary's C. Both statistics compare values for a target feature and the neighboring features with the mean for the study area (Anselin 1995). Each feature receives a value for the statistic, with a large positive value indicating the feature value is surrounded by similar values. However, one of the biggest disadvantages of these two statistics for the primatologist interested in determining resource dispersion is that they do not distinguish if clustering is for high or low values. Therefore, if we define a patch as an area of high resource abundance (a cluster of high values) surrounded by areas of low resource abundance (a cluster of low values), neither statistic will distinguish patches from resource-poor areas.

A much more useful approach for this type of question is to use the Getis–Ord G* statistic, as it distinguishes clusters of high values (hot-spots) and low values (cold-spots) (Ord & Getis 1995). As it is explicitly designed to identify the location of high-value clusters (similarly high values for neighboring features), the G* statistic is a valuable tool in the primatologist's geospatial toolkit for identifying patches. To calculate G*, the GIS divides the sum of the values of all features in a neighborhood (within the distance threshold) by the sum of the values for all features in the study area:

$$G_i^*(d) = \frac{\sum_i W_{ij}(d)X_j}{\sum_i X_j},$$

where $W_{ij}(d)$ is a 1/0 spatial weight matrix with 1s for all features defined as being within distance d of a given i (neighbors); all other features are 0. The G* statistic ranges from 0 to 1, with values near 0 indicating no clustering, lower values indicating clustering of low values, and high G* values indicating clustering of high attribute values. To determine statistical significance for the G* test, the GIS calculates Z-scores for each feature by subtracting the expected G* given a random distribution from the observed G* and dividing by the square root of the variance for all features. Positive Z-scores indicate hot-spots and negative Z-scores indicate cold-spots. The G* statistic requires a distance threshold (distance used to look for similar values) to be specified and this can be based on either neighboring features or a set distance. If a set distance is used, there should be a specific biological reason for the choice (e.g., the mean spread of the study group). By manipulating the distance threshold (distance used to look for similar values), the G* statistic can also be used to assess how clustering varies at different spatial scales. The G* test can be applied to either polygon or point data and can, therefore, be used in combination with the patch quality index (PQI) illustrated in the following.

The Getis–Ord G* test is available as a tool in almost all GIS software. For ArcGIS, the output for the test is a new feature layer that consists of the original vector feature locations (points or polygons) with the attribute value used in the analysis, the G* value, the Z-score, and a p-value. If detailed data on the distribution of all feeding trees throughout a particular area are available, the Z-scores from this output feature layer can be interpolated to create a raster surface, showing a generalized view of hot- and cold-spots.

The strength of spatial autocorrelation and hot spot analysis for quantifying resource dispersion (the ability to incorporate attribute values) can also be a limitation, as they require some attribute for each feature in the dataset. In cases where attributes are unknown (i.e., one has locations of feeding trees but not measurements), these methods cannot be used. In addition, one of the biggest concerns in calculating the degree of spatial autocorrelation is the "nearness" problem – how does one determine the appropriate distance within which features are considered nearby versus distant? The method used to determine this distance will strongly effect results and, therefore, should always be based on biologically relevant criteria. For this reason, the distance threshold and the method by which it was determined should always be listed by researchers employing spatial autocorrelation.

Measures of Patch Size and Quality

While PPA and spatial autocorrelation provide quantitative measures of resource dispersion (patchiness), they do not, by themselves, explicitly quantify the size or quality of resources (patch quality). Spatial autocorrelation can indicate where high-quality patches are clustered but it requires some attribute of quality or size for the analysis. Therefore, one is still left with the problem of determining what constitutes a patch. As mentioned above, researchers have traditionally used some characteristic of a single feeding tree to quantify patch size (Chapman 1990; Chapman & Chapman 2000; Symington 1988). The measurement of the tree (DBH, crown volume) becomes the patch value and these values can then be used to determine clustering using a measure of spatial autocorrelation. The most common measure of patch size is DBH. This measure is relatively easy to collect (compared to other measures of tree size), has been shown to be strongly related to several behavioral variables in primates, including group size, and has been argued to be an accurate measure of tree crown size (Chapman et al. 1992).

However, there are several problems with the use of DBH as a measure of patch size. First, DBH alone tells us little about the amount of food available in a tree, as large trees can obviously vary tremendously in the amount of fruit and flowers they produce or the amount of ripe fruit specifically. Therefore, when using DBH as a measure of patch size, it is important to weight it by a phenology score that provides a better measure of how much food is available in that tree. Second, while DBH is strongly correlated with crown volume, there is a great deal of variation in this relationship, both within and across tree species (Coder 2000; Furnival 1961; Peper et al. 2001). Many studies report a broad correlation around $r = 0.6$, indicating DBH is only a gross estimate of the volume of the crown (and therefore, the amount of food items that tree can contain) (Furnival 1961; Masota et al. 2014). Third, and most important for the present study, DBH may not adequately quantify a patch when individuals in a primate group are spread out and feeding from several trees simultaneously. Under this situation, a patch may be better understood as a cluster of several neighboring feeding trees. Isolating one from the others would provide potentially misleading results concerning the amount of food that is available in a specific location. Several species of primate regularly increase group spread as a response to resource scarcity (Di Fiore 1997; Norconk & Kinzey 1994; Peres 1996; Shaffer 2013a). For these primates, the size of one tree taken in isolation may not be especially meaningful if neighboring trees are much larger.

Some researchers have recognized this problem and attempted to produce patch size definitions that incorporate group spread. For example, Vogel and Janson (2007) designed a method for patch quantification using Lloyd's extended index (LEI) that incorporated the primates group spread as the sampling area. Similarly, Pruetz and Isbell (2000) defined patches by using a sample point and plot system based on the size of the study group's home range. In order to address some of the issues involved in using DBH as a measure of patch size for a primate with large group spreads, Shaffer (2013a) produced a simple composite food patch definition using GIS. In this method, a grid system is superimposed over the feeding trees used during each of the daily paths taken by a study group, and tree attributes are spatially joined to the grid cells (Figure 8.2). A food patch is defined as a grid cell that contains at least one feeding tree. Patch size is determined by the combined crown volume of each tree with the grid cell, using the equation:

$$PQI = \sum_{i=1}^{N} VP,$$

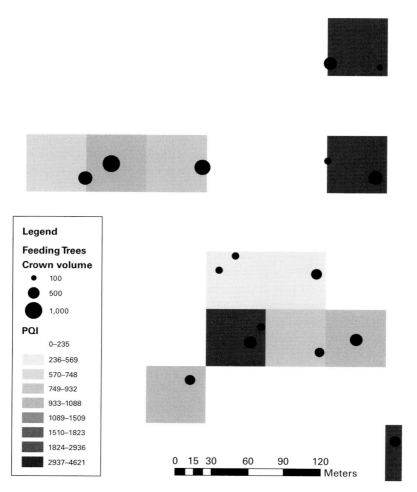

Figure 8.2 Visual representation of patch quality index (PQI). A grid (in this case 50 m²) is superimposed over the feeding trees used for one full-day follow and each grid cell receives a PQI value based on the number of trees it contains, the size of those trees (crown volume), and their phenological state. (A black and white version of this figure will appear in some formats. For the color version, please refer to the plate section.)

where N is the number of trees within the defined food patch, V is crown volume, and P is phenology score. When using a five-point phenological scale (0, 0.25, 0.50, 0.75, 1.0) indicating the approximate percentage of branches bearing fruit (see below), PQI values indicate the total volume of fruit-bearing branches within the patch. A derivation of this method can be used to identify "high-quality" patches (areas significantly higher in food abundance than surrounding areas) by calculating Z-scores for each feeding tree point using the Getis–Ord G* test and creating polygons from those Z-scores using a biologically meaningful cell size (see below). Polygons having values above a certain threshold (i.e., significantly positive) can be defined as high-quality or large patches. Once these high-quality patches are identified, they can be spatially joined with the feeding trees that they contain and their associated crown volumes, producing a PQI. Although the PQI as defined above incorporates data on the relative amount of food items contained in the trees in a patch, it does not account for the relative quality of these food items (e.g., whether they are of a preferred tree species, or nutritionally high quality, or easy to process or mechanically challenging). In cases where this information is available, an additional parameter can be incorporated.

While the PQI method allows for neighboring trees to be identified as the same patch, it introduces the problem of determining the spatial scale used to define patches or clusters (i.e., grid cell size). There are two biologically meaningful ways to address this problem. First, the average group spread (over the course of the day under analysis) of the primate being studied can be used. This method has the advantage of incorporating the behavior of the animals in determining the patch size. The second method is to use Ripley's K function to estimate the distance at which the clustering of feeding trees is most pronounced and use that distance to define patches. Because the spatial scale of clustering is expected to vary for different primate species, Ripley's K provides an excellent tool for determining the appropriate scale to use for defining the grid size for patches. In addition, this method does not require quantitative data on group spread, a variable that is often very difficult to estimate in studies of wild primates. In some cases, the values for each method will be highly correlated (see below). Importantly, combining either method with PQI provides a measure of patch size that can be tailored to the species of interest but simultaneously allows for comparison across studies.

DBH, crown volume, and any other measure of patch size or quality can be used as an attribute for spatial autocorrelation analysis. The polygons created using the PQI method can also be used as features when conducting tests for spatial autocorrelation.

Methods for Assessing Patch Use by Bearded Sakis

Data Collection

To show variation in the results of each of these methods and demonstrate their utility for addressing questions in primate behavioral ecology, I applied them to a dataset collected from a long-term study of bearded sakis in Guyana (Shaffer 2012, 2013a, 2013b). The study site for this research was the Upper Essequibo Conservation Concession in Central Guyana (Shaffer 2012). The concession is located between 3°40′–3°20′ N and 58°25′–58°5′ W on the Essequibo River and consists of undisturbed forest representing a variety of rain forest types characteristic of Central Guyana (Shaffer 2012). All eight of Guyana's primate species (*Chiropotes sagulatus*, *Alouatta macconnelli*, *Sapajus apella*, *Saimiri sciureus*, *Pithecia pithecia*, *Saquinus midas*, *Cebus olivaceus*, and *Ateles paniscus*) are found at the site.

The total dataset consisted of 560 hours of behavioral observation and the locations of 2449 feeding trees collected from January 2008 to January 2009. The following behavioral data were collected using sampling at five-minute intervals (Altmann 1974): activity, food item and species if feeding, and vertical stratification. During each scan, two field assistants and I recorded the approximate spread of the group with a handheld GPS unit (Garmin eTrex VistaHCX). The assistants stayed on either end of the periphery of the group and recorded locations of individuals furthest from the centroid, while I recorded the location of the approximate center (Shaffer 2013a). The distance between the furthest two of these GPS points was then used to calculate a linear group spread distance. I smoothed GPS data using point-center estimation and manual elimination of inaccurate points. GPS accuracy was 4.12 ± 1.70 m based on 100 sample recordings.

In addition to location data collected every five minutes, all feeding trees used by the study group were marked with a GPS point, the phenological state was recorded, and they were later identified to genus or species level. At least four GPS points were recorded for each feeding tree and a point-averaged estimate was obtained to provide maximum accuracy. Phenology scores were assigned based on a five-character scale (0, 0.25, 0.50, 0.75, 1.0) indicating the approximate percentage of branches bearing fruit: (0) indicated no fruit or flowers, (0.25) indicated <25 percent, (0.50) indicated 25–49 percent, (0.75) indicated 50–74 percent, and (1.00) indicated 75–100 percent. This scale was modified from a traditional 0–4 ordinal scale to produce a more biologically meaningful patch quality score (see below). Due to the large number of feeding trees utilized by the study group (over 2400), I was unable to measure all of them. Therefore, for analyses of tree size and food abundance, I chose a sample of the feeding trees by randomly choosing at least one full-day follow per month and measuring the trees used that day. This provided a sample of 1059 trees during 17 full-day follows, representing each month that the study group was observed except April. Crown volume was calculated from measurements of crown breadth (measured with a meter tape), crown depth (estimated using a clinometer taking the height to the first branch of the canopy and subtracting from the overall height), and crown shape (using a standard forestry guide of 10 crown shapes and their associated equations; Coder 2000). Due to my inability to quantify insect abundance, I restricted my analyses to food patches that contained fruit pulp or seeds.

The study group consisted of at least 65 individuals but regularly divided into subgroups throughout the year. In order to quantify subgroup size, I conducted censuses of group membership (number of adults, juveniles, and infants of each sex) at the beginning of each full day. As subgroup size was generally consistent throughout the course of the day (based on six days where multiple censuses were conducted), this provided a reliable measure of daily variation in subgroup size. However, to provide a better estimate of how group size changed during patch to patch movements, I used the number of individuals observed during each five-minute scan as another measure of subgroup size. While this was a relatively gross estimate of group size, as scans almost never included all individuals in the group, it provides another level of resolution in quantifying group cohesiveness.

Data Analysis

I calculated daily path lengths by summing the distances between sequential five-minute scan locations of the approximate center of the bearded saki group during 44 full-day follows. Monthly daily paths were simply the mean daily path length of all full-day follows during that month. I used the fixed kernel method to calculate home range estimates for each month of the study (Chapter 7). To account for variation in sampling effort across months, I multiplied each monthly home range size by a ratio of the observation hours for that month divided by the highest number of monthly hours. I used the least cross-validation smoothing parameter for all kernel analysis.

An important limitation of this demonstration of methods for patch quantification is the lack of data on trees not used for feeding. Therefore, in this study it was impossible to compare the distribution of feeding trees to those that were not used for feeding. In addition, the small sample of days used in this analysis means that the sample distributions of feeding trees, especially when analyzed by month, may not be representative of the actual distributions of feeding trees. However, the methods are illustrated here to show their utility for use in more comprehensive datasets.

To assess resource dispersion throughout the bearded saki home range, I applied PPA using the NNI and Ripley's K function for all feeding trees used by the study group for each month of the study. These analyses provide general characteristics of the resource dispersion over the entirety of the group's home range each month. However, this analysis provides only a very gross estimate of patchiness throughout the monthly range due to the small sample of full-day follows (3–6 full-day follows per month). For both analyses, the study area was a 95 percent isopleth polygon produced by kernel density analysis of study group locations for each month. I buffered each polygon by 100 m to ensure that no feeding trees were at the edges of the study area. For Ripley's K, the "simulate outer boundary values" boundary correction was used. As detailed data on the physical characteristics of most feeding trees were not available, I was unable to conduct a spatial autocorrelation analysis for each month. To compare how well each analysis predicted bearded saki ranging and grouping behavior, I conducted linear regressions using the patchiness statistics (NNI or Ripley's K) to predict monthly home range size, monthly core area size, mean monthly daily path length, mean monthly group size, and mean monthly individuals per scan. For NNI, higher values indicate more dispersed resources. For Ripley's K function, I used the expected K value (distance) where clustering was highest (difference between expected and observed K). Therefore, higher values indicate that trees were more dispersed (larger cluster distances). All data were log transformed to meet the assumption of normality required for linear regression. Variables with negative values (i.e., NNI) were added to a constant (10).

To describe patch-to-patch movements of bearded sakis, I calculated the NNI, Ripley's K function, local Moran's I, mean DBH, and mean PQI for each of 17 full-day follows for which detailed data on feeding tree characteristics were collected. I conducted linear regressions using NNI, Ripley's K, and Moran's I to predict daily path length, group size and individuals per scan, and mean time spent in a patch (patch occupancy) for each day. I chose three of the variables that are argued to be most strongly related to the distribution and quality of food patches, daily path length, subgroup size (measured with two variables), and patch occupancy. Patch occupancy was calculated as the time the group spent feeding in a patch, from the time the first individual in the group entered the patch to the time the last individual departed. If individuals in the group were spread out over multiple patches simultaneously, these patches were combined for estimates of patch occupancy. All variables were log transformed. The study area for both NNI and Ripley's K was calculated as a minimum convex polygon surrounding all feeding trees used during the full-day follow with a 100 m buffer (to adjust for edge effects). A "simulate outer boundary values" edge correction was used for Ripley's K. The attribute value for Moran's I was DBH.

To assess the relationship between patch size and behavioral variables, I conducted linear regressions using DBH and mean PQI to predict group size, individuals per scan, daily path length, and patch occupancy. As DBH alone does not contain information about the dispersion of resources, I also developed a multiple linear regression model using DBH and Ripley's K to predict group size. I used Ripley's K analysis for each full-day follow to estimate the distance at which maximum clustering occurred and used this distance as a grid size for producing PQI. These values ranged from 50 m to 120 m. I also compared these distances to group spread estimates for each of the full-day follows using a Pearson correlation to see if Ripley's K was a useful measure for quantifying patch size from the perspective of the bearded saki group.

To identify statistically significant areas of high resource density across the bearded saki study area, I applied the local Getis–Ord G* to the trees from all 17 daily paths for which detailed data on tree size were available. Because the G* for a particular feature is determined by the values of its neighbors and I only calculated physical characteristics for the trees actually used by the study group, it was necessary to create additional points across the study area that represented trees that were not used for feeding (trees with patch quality values of 0). Therefore, I superimposed a 50×50 m grid over the study area and spatially joined all measured feeding trees with grid cells containing at least one feeding tree receiving a PQI value > 0 and those not containing feeding trees containing a PQI value of 0. I then converted these grid cells into points and ran the local G* test on this dataset. To visualize the results of this analysis, I used ordinary kriging interpolation to create a continuous surface raster of Z-values. To assess the utility of this approach for quantifying patch quality, I compared patch occupancy with G* value for all grid cells where G* Z-score > 1.96 (significant hot-spots) using Spearman rank correlations. All statistical analysis was done in R and all GIS analysis was done in ArcGIS (ESRI). All statistical tests were two-tailed and alpha levels were set a priori at $\alpha = 0.05$.

Results

The results for monthly analysis of resource dispersion are shown in Table 8.1. Using the NNI, bearded saki feeding trees were significantly dispersed during four months, significantly clustered during three months, and randomly distributed during three months. NNI was not a significant predictor of any of the ranging or grouping variables (home range $r = -0.14$, $p = 0.701$; core area $r = -0.42$, $p = 0.229$; day range $r = 0.02$,

$p = 0.960$; group size $r = -0.14$, $p = 0.696$; individuals per scan $r = 0.10$, $p = 0.776$) and NNI was not significantly correlated with maximum clustering distance (Ripley's K) ($r = -0.27$, $p = 0.450$). In contrast, Ripley's K analysis showed that maximum clustering distances (distances where the difference in expected and observed K is greatest) were significantly different from random for all months, indicating a clustered pattern at some spatial scales for each month (Figure 8.3). Ripley's K values showed a large amount of monthly variation in the clustering of feeding trees, with the maximum clustering distance ranging between 113 m and 350 m (Table 8.1). Maximum clustering distance was significantly positively correlated with monthly home range size ($r = 0.72$, $p = 0.019$), monthly core area ($r = 0.64$, $p = -0.048$), and daily path length ($r = 0.70$, $p = 0.025$) but not significantly correlated with group size ($r = 0.50$, $p = 0.138$) or individuals per scan ($r = -0.21$, $p = 0.567$). As higher values of maximum clustering distance indicate more dispersed resources, these results suggest that bearded sakis range over larger distances when resources are more dispersed.

The NNI for the 17 daily paths used in this analysis indicated that feeding trees were significantly clustered for 15 days and randomly distributed for 2 days. In contrast, Moran's I analysis (incorporating DBH as an attribute) indicated feeding trees were significantly clustered for only three study days, significantly dispersed during one day, and randomly distributed for 13 days. Maximum clustering distances identified by Ripley's K analysis ranged from 30 m to 154 m. NNI and Moran's I were significantly positively correlated ($r = 0.59$, $p = 0.020$) and NNI and maximum clustering distance were significantly negatively correlated ($r = -0.52$, $p = 0.033$). NNI was not a significant predictor of any of the ranging or grouping variables for daily paths (Table 8.2). Similarly, maximum clustering distances did not significantly predict any of the behavioral variables tested. Mean daily group spread was strongly positively correlated with maximum clustering distance ($r = 0.65$, $p = 0.005$) (Figure 8.4). Moran's I was a significant predictor of daily path length, group size, and individuals per scan. Both measures of patch size, DBH and PQI, were significant predictors of group size, individuals per scan, and patch occupancy, but neither was a significant predictor of daily path length (Table 8.2). For both grouping variables and patch occupancy, PQI was a better predictor than DBH (Figure 8.5). However, the multiple linear regression model using both DBH and maximum clustering distance to predict group size considerably improved the predictive power of these measures of patchiness and explained approximately the same amount of variation as PQI ($R^2 = 0.58$, $F = 5.53$, $p = 0.003$). The results of the local Getis–Ord G* analysis to identify significant hot- and cold-spots identified 34 statistically significant patches (hot spots) throughout the bearded saki home range (Figure 8.6). Patch occupancy was significantly positively correlated with G* for significant patches ($r = 0.38$, $p = 0.024$).

Discussion

Depending on the way patchiness and/or patch quality were defined, the patch characteristics used in this study were significant predictors of monthly home range size,

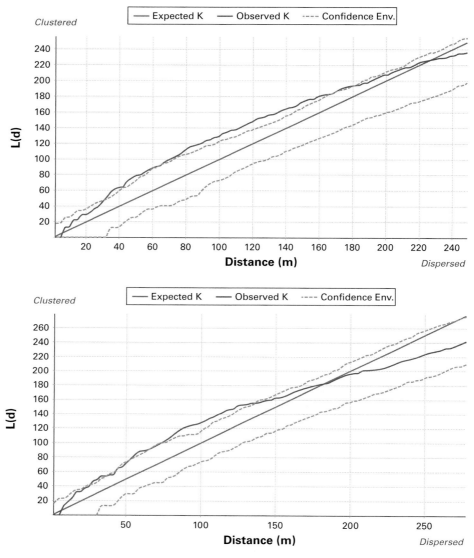

Figure 8.3 Results of Ripley's K analysis for two full-day follows. The trend line represents expected K values based on complete spatial randomness and the red line represents observed K. Gray lines represent 99 percent confidence intervals. When the observed K is above the trend line and the confidence intervals, there is significant clustering at that distance. The distance where the peak occurs in observed K is the distance of maximum clustering. (A black and white version of this figure will appear in some formats. For the color version, please refer to the plate section.)

subgroup size, daily path length, and patch occupancy. As predicted by models of primate socioecological theory, bearded sakis appear to modify the size of their groups according to the size of food patches and spend more time feeding in patches when those patches contain a higher abundance of food items. However, the relationship between ranging

Table 8.1 Measures of resource dispersion and behavioral variables analyzed by month

Month	Day range (m)	Home range (ha)	Core area (ha)	Group size[a]	NNI	Ripley's K (m)[b]
January	4435	578	125	49.8	0.99	178.4
February	4662	751	229	46.5	0.97	226.4
March	4446	618	186	43.8	0.90*	350.3
April	3577	458	96	37	1.13*	113.4
May	3755	618	134	45.8	0.90*	222.5
June	3289	479	115	36.3	0.74**	151.7
September	4309	347	130	22.7	0.98	165.4
October	3538	364	160	26.5	0.95	132.0
November	3454	299	102	19	1.02	214.0
December	3830	378	119	29.7	0.91*	210.1

[a] Number of individuals not including infants
[b] Distance where maximum clustering was observed (i.e., the difference in observed and expected K was highest). All values listed were significantly clustered (i.e., exceeded the 99 percent confidence envelope).
* Significant at $p \leq 0.05$
** Significant at $p \leq 0.01$

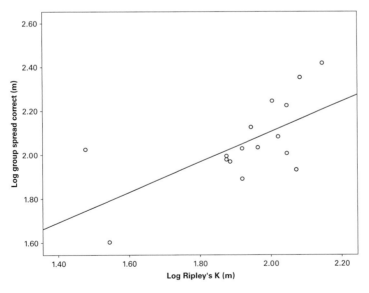

Figure 8.4 Relationship between group spread and maximum clustering distance for 17 full-day follows.

behavior and resource quality and distribution for bearded sakis is more equivocal. While the PPA results indicate the bearded sakis increase daily path length and home range size when resources are more dispersed, they do not appear to increase range size (either daily path length or home range size) when patch quality is low. This may be due to the dietary constraints of a heavily seed-based diet. Therefore, bearded saki ranging behavior may be more strongly related to the type of food they consume than group size or the spatial

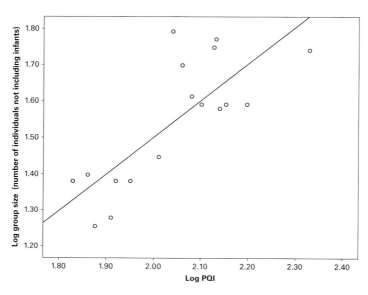

Figure 8.5 Relationship between group size and patch quality index for 17 full-day follows.

distribution of feeding trees, with obtaining the proper mix of nutrients and avoiding secondary compounds being a more important driver of ranging behavior than simply the overall abundance of resources (Shaffer 2013b).

The relationship between patch size and primate behavioral characteristics has been tested for a range of primates under a variety of conditions (Byrne et al. 1990; Chapman 1988; Chapman & Chapman 2000; Chapman et al. 1994, 1995; Dias & Strier 2003; Leighton & Leighton 1982; Phillips 1995; Shaffer 2013a; Stevenson et al. 1998; Strier 1989; Symington 1988; Vogel and Janson 2007, 2011; White & Wrangham 1988). The relationship between group size and patch quality is perhaps the best established empirically. While early studies of this relationship focused on primates with high fission–fusion dynamics, like spider monkeys (Chapman 1990; Symington 1988) and chimpanzees (Chapman et al. 1995; White & Wrangham 1988), a strong relationship between patch size and group size has been reported for many species, including muriquis (Dias & Strier 2003), capuchin monkeys (Phillips 1995), howler monkeys (Chapman 1988; Leighton & Leighton 1982), bearded sakis (Shaffer 2013a), blue monkeys, and more. Almost all of these studies have used DBH as the measure of patch quality. In most, the correlation coefficient between these variables was between 0.40 and 0.70 (Chapman et al. 1995; Dias & Strier 2003; Janson & Goldsmith 1995; Strier 1989; Wrangham et al. 1993). Consistent with the results of these studies, DBH was found to explain approximately 40 percent of the variation in subgroup size for bearded sakis. Therefore, as suggested by several other researchers, DBH is a very effective measure for assessing patch size. However, it may be less useful and less biologically meaningful for species that regularly increase group spread and feed from multiple trees simultaneously. This is especially true for species that adjust group spread to mitigate intragroup feeding competition. Under these conditions, characterizing a

Table 8.2 Results of correlations between measures of resource dispersion and behavioral variables for 17 full-day follows

Variable	NNI	Moran's I	Ripley's K	DBH	PQI
Daily path length (m)	−0.18	0.47[*]	0.35	−0.07	−0.31
Group size[a]	0.35	0.63[**]	−0.20	0.58[*]	0.79[**]
Individuals per scan[b]	0.20	0.69[**]	0.22	0.63[**]	0.76[**]
Patch occupancy (minutes)	0.31	0.34	0.29	0.59[*]	0.73[**]

[a] number of individuals not including infants
[b] not including infants
Values represent Pearson correlation coefficients.
* Indicates significance at the $p < 0.05$ level.
** Indicates significance at the $p < 0.01$ level.

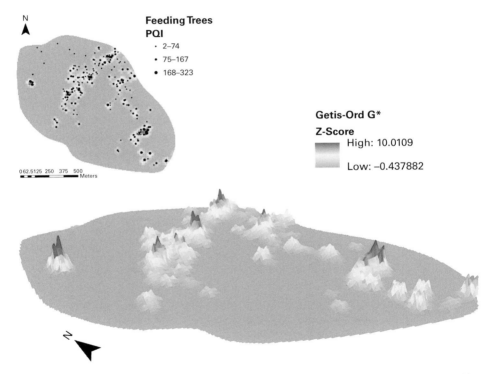

Figure 8.6 Visual representation of Getis–Ord G* analysis for all measured feeding trees used in April. Peaks and red color coding correspond to areas that are statistically significant hot-spots (clusters of high values for PQI). Z-scores were interpolated using an ordinary kriging procedure to produce a continuous surface. (A black and white version of this figure will appear in some formats. For the color version, please refer to the plate section.)

small tree as a single patch when it is surrounded by large, highly productive trees likely does not adequately capture the way individual primates in the group actually perceive food resources. In addition, DBH alone does not provide any information about the dispersion of feeding trees. Consistent with this hypothesis, the composite PQI, which incorporates a biologically meaningful distance of dispersion into the calculation of relative abundance of food items, was a better predictor than DBH of each of the bearded saki behavioral variables tested in this study. Adding a measure of dispersion into the model used to predict the behavioral variables considerably improved the performance of DBH as a predictor. Therefore, when DBH is used to measure patch quality, an additional measure of resource dispersion should be calculated, allowing for a determination of the influence of both patch size and patchiness on behavioral variables. If PQI is used, Ripley's K provides a robust method for determining the size of the grid cells used to define patches.

Two useful tools for quantifying the dispersion of feeding trees are the NNI and Ripley's K. Both statistics provide information about the degree of clustering and the size of clusters, and do not require attribute values, allowing them to be used to analyze patchiness in the absence of detailed data on tree characteristics (although this information can be used to weight the analysis if it is available). Therefore, they are excellent methods for characterizing the patchiness of resources when tree sizes are unknown. The NNI has been used by several primatologists for assessing the relationship between ranging behavior and resource dispersion (Peres 1991; Shaffer 2013b), documenting the spatial distribution of primate groups (Boyle et al. 2009), identifying the spatial patterning of primate intergroup dynamics (Dammhahn and Kappeler 2008), describing spatial patterns in great ape nest building (Fruth and Hohmann 1996), describing the spatial distribution of feeding sites (Lacher et al. 1984; Thompson et al. 2013), and assessing the relationship between resource dispersion and seed predation (Peres 1991). Although widely used in ecology and forestry, Ripley's K has rarely been employed by primatologists. This is unfortunate, given its broad applicability and relative ease of use. A few researchers have used Ripley's K to describe resource dispersion (Thompson et al. 2013) and spatial patterns of primate seed dispersal (Fourrier 2013; Hardesty et al. 2006; Russo and Augspurger 2004; Russo et al. 2006; Sezen et al. 2009), but hopefully this chapter will encourage more uses for this robust method of PPA.

Despite their utility, caution should be exercised when NNI or Ripley's K are applied in primate studies. Both indices are highly dependent on the size of the study area in which they are calculated, and changing the size of the study area for NNI or the shape of the area for Ripley's K can drastically affect results. Therefore, it is extremely important that a biologically relevant study area size is specified (i.e., a kernel density estimated home range polygon) and that these values are published along with the results of the analysis. In addition, while the tests answer similar questions about resource dispersion, and can provide similar results (they were significantly correlated for daily path data in this study), they should be interpreted in very different ways. The NNI provides a general measure of dispersion summarized with a single statistic, while Ripley's K calculates the distances over which resources are clustered or dispersed. NNI is therefore most useful for the primatologists interested in assessing whether feeding trees are clumped, dispersed, or randomly distributed across a home range, day range, or other study area in the absence of data on tree size. In contrast, Ripley's K is useful for assessing the range of distances over which those trees are clumped or dispersed. Thus, it is best used for answering questions about the size of clusters or the spatial scale of clustering, such as: what is the seed shadow for a particular tree species? Or are feeding trees clustered at the same distance over which a primate group spreads itself?

Finally, if these analyses are used without any corresponding measure of patch size, they tell us little about how patch quality influences primate behavior. In this study, neither measure was a significant predictor of any of the behavioral variables when tested for each daily path. Without measures of patch size, one might conclude that the distribution of resources had little effect on the ranging or grouping behavior of bearded sakis. Yet measures that incorporate the abundance of fruit in feeding trees showed that the distribution of resources was significantly related to daily path length, group size, and patch occupancy.

The global Moran's I is an excellent tool for a simultaneous analysis of both patch quality (specified in the attribute field) and patch dispersion. The test produces a single statistic summarizing both distribution and size of resources that can be calculated for each day, month, or even the entire study period and compared to behavioral variables for those same periods. In this study, Moran's I was a significant predictor of daily path length, group size, and patch occupancy. Moran's I has been used in previous primatological studies to quantify resource dispersion for chimpanzees (Anderson et al. 2002) and Samango monkeys (Coleman and Hill 2014), assess habitat preferences of baboons (Hoffman and O'Riain 2012), and describe niche partitioning of capuchins and squirrel monkeys (Levi et al. 2013).

Unfortunately, Moran's I does not distinguish between high–high clustering and low–low clustering, and may lead to spurious or misleading conclusions as a result. For example, in this study Moran's I was significantly positively correlated with daily path length, while all other measures of both resource dispersion and patch size were not significantly related to path length (and were negatively correlated). If only Moran's I was used to assess this relationship, one may conclude that bearded sakis increase foraging effort when high-quality resources (high DBH) are more clustered. However, this result could also mean that bearded sakis increase foraging effort when low-quality resources are more clustered – a very different conclusion. Therefore, for questions that require distinguishing hot-spots from cold-spots, the Getis–Ord G* should be used. Getis–Ord G* is one of the best tools for quantitatively defining patches, especially when conducted on features defined with a composite patch quality index like PQI. Getis–Ord G* provides an estimate of resource-rich versus resource-poor areas of the home range, especially for datasets in which most of the feeding trees used by the study group are mapped (i.e., when groups are followed daily or GPS-collared). In addition, if combined with high-quality remote sensing data (e.g., aerial photographs, LIDAR), Getis–Ord G* can be used to quantify resource distribution in large areas with relatively little sampling effort. This is especially true with the increased availability of relatively accurate methods for estimating tree crown volume and phenological state from remotely sensed images (Drake et al. 2002; Fatoyinbo 2012; Harding et al. 2001). However, limitations of Getis–Ord G* include the need for extremely comprehensive data on the location of feeding trees and detailed data on the phenology of those trees (as the phenological patterns will drastically affect patch richness month to month). If some of the feeding trees are unknown, as in this study, the G* statistic may provide spurious results. For example, it may indicate a statistically significant cold-spot in a resource-rich area simply because that area was not used during the sampled days.

Conclusion

While the results of this study show that each of the methods presented above is useful for quantifying patchiness, they also indicate that the way patchiness and patch quality are defined can drastically impact the conclusions that are drawn concerning the relationship between resource dispersion and primate behavior. In 1999, Pruetz called for standardization in methods of patch quantification, writing "Greater standardization, comparability, and accuracy of measures of food abundance and distribution are required to identify the specific relationships between food availability and primate feeding and social ecology" (Pruetz 1999: 10). Similarly, Vogel and Janson (2011: 738) wrote: "This discrepancy in definitions has led to confusion as to the role food resources play in primate social behavior." In this chapter, I have attempted to move toward standardization by presenting a number of methods for quantifying resource dispersion in studies of wild primates and determining what constitutes a food patch, and showing how each of these are related to behavioral variables in bearded sakis. However, we are still left with the question that opened this chapter: What is a patch? If a patch is a cluster of feeding trees, the most basic and commonly used theoretical definition in ecology, this means that what constitutes a patch (how big the cluster is) and, more importantly, what constitutes a high-quality or productive patch, will vary considerably for different primate species. However, the methods illustrated here provide standardization for how we approach the question of patchiness and give the primatologist tools that can be interpreted across studies. Using these methods, one can directly and quantitatively compare how the patchiness of resources varies for different species, primates with different diets (e.g., folivores versus frugivores), the same species in different habitats, or the same species in the same habitat throughout the year or multiple years. Ultimately, the choice of method, or combination of methods, should depend on the question being asked and the data available. The broad availability of each of these methods in both open-source and commercial GIS software, and their relative ease of application, makes them extremely valuable for addressing fundamental questions in primate socioecology.

References

Altmann, J. 1974. Observational study of behavior: sampling methods. *Behaviour* **49**: 227–267.
Anderson, D. P., Nordheim, E. V., Boesch, C., and Moermond, T. C. 2002. *Factors Influencing Fission-Fusion Grouping in Chimpanzees in the Taï National Park, Côte d'Ivoire: Behavioural Diversity in Chimpanzees and Bonobos*. Cambridge University Press, Cambridge.

Anselin, L. 1995. Local indicators of spatial association: LISA. *Geographical Analysis* **27**: 93–115.

Baily, T. C. and Gatrell, A. C. 1995. *Interactive Spatial Data Analysis*. Longman, New York.

Boyle, S. A., Lourenco, W. C., da Silva, L. R., and Smith, A. T. 2009. Home range estimates vary with sample size and methods. *Folia Primatologica* **80**: 33–42.

Byrne, R. W., Whiten, A., and Henzi, S. P. 1990. Measuring the food constraints of mountain baboons. Pages 105–122 in *Baboons: Behavior and Ecology, Use and Care*. M. T. de Mello, A. Whiten, and R. W. Byrne. International Primatological Society, Brazil.

Chapman, C. A. 1988. Patterns of foraging and range use by three species of neotropical primates. *Primates* **29**(2): 177–194.

Chapman, C. A. 1990. Ecological constraints on group size in three species of neotropical primates. *Folia Primatologica* **55**: 1–9.

Chapman, C. A. and Chapman, L. J. 2000. Determinants of group size in social primates: the importance of travel costs. Pages 24–42 in *On the Move: How and Why Animals Travel in Groups*. S. Boinski and P. Garber (Eds.). University of Chicago Press, Chicago.

Chapman, C. A., Chapman, L. J., Wrangham, R., Gebo, D., and Gardner, L. 1992. Estimators of fruit abundance of tropical trees. *Biotropica* **24**: 527–531.

Chapman, C. A., White, F., Wrangham, R. W. 1994. Party size in chimpanzees and bonobos: a reevaluation of theory based on two similarly forested sites. Pages 45–57 in *Chimpanzee Cultures*. W. C. McGrew, L. F. Marchant, and T. Nishida (Eds.). Harvard University Press, Cambridge, MA.

Chapman, C. A., Wrangham, R. W., and Chapman, L. J. 1995. Ecological constraints on group size: an analysis of spider monkey and chimpanzee subgroups. *Behavioral Ecology and Sociobiology* **36**: 59–70.

Charnov, E. L. 1976. Optimal foraging, the marginal value theorem. *Theoretical Population Biology* **9**: 129–136.

Clark, P. J. and Evans, F. C. 1954. Distance to nearest neighbor as a measure of spatial relationships in populations. *Ecology* **35**: 445–453

Coder, K. D. 2000. *Crown Shape Factors & Volumes*. University of Georgia, Warnell School of Forest Resources, Athens, GA.

Coleman, B. T. and Hill, R. A. 2014. Living in a landscape of fear: the impact of predation, resource availability and habitat structure on primate range use. *Animal Behaviour* **88**: 165–173.

Dale, M. R. T. 1999. *Spatial Pattern Analysis in Plant Ecology*. Cambridge University Press, Cambridge.

Dale, M. R. T. and Powell, R. D. 2001. A new method for characterizing point patterns in plant ecology. *Journal of Vegetation Science* **12**(5): 597–608.

Dale, M. R. T., Dixon, P. M., Fortin, M. J., et al. 2002. Conceptual and mathematical relationships among methods for spatial analysis. *Ecography* **25**: 558–577.

Dammhahn, M. and Kappeler, P. M. 2008. Comparative feeding ecology of sympatric *Microcebus berthae* and *M. murinus*. *International Journal of Primatology* **29**(6): 1567.

De Knegt, H. J., van Langevelde, F., Coughenour, M. B., et al. 2010. Spatial autocorrelation and the scaling of species–environment relationships. *Ecology* **91**: 2455–2465.

Dias, L. G. and Strier, K. B. 2003. Effects of group size on ranging patterns in *Brachyteles arachnoides hypoxanthus*. *International Journal of Primatology* **24**: 209–221.

Di Fiore, A. 1997. Ecology and behavior of lowland woolly monkeys (*Lagothrix lagotricha poeppigii*, Atelinae) in Eastern Ecuador. PhD Thesis. University of California, Davis.

Diggle, P. J. 1983. *The Statistical Analysis of Spatial Point Patterns*. Academic Press, New York.

Dixon, P. M. 2002. Ripley's K function. *Encyclopedia of Environmetrics* **3**: 1796–1803.

Drake, J. B., Dubayah, R. O., Knox, et al. 2002. Sensitivity of large-footprint Lidar to canopy structure and biomass in a neotropical rainforest. *Remote Sensing of Environment*. **81**: 378–392.

Ebdon, D. 1985. *Statistics in Geography*. Blackwell, Malden, MA.

Everitt, B. S., Landau, S., and Leese, M. 2001. *Cluster Analysis*, 4th edition. Arnold, London.

Fatoyinbo, L. 2012. *Remote Sensing of Biomass: Principles and Applications*. Intech, London.

Furnival, G. M. 1961. An index comparing equations used in constructing volume equations. *Forestry Science* **7**: 337–341.

Forman, R. T. T. 1995. *Land Mosaics: The Ecology of Landscapes and Regions*. Cambridge University Press, Cambridge.

Fortin, M., Mark, M. J., and Dale, R. T. 2005. *Spatial Analysis: A Guide for Ecologists*. Cambridge University Press, Cambridge.

Fourrier, M. S. 2013. The spatial and temporal ecology of seed dispersal by gorillas in Lopé National Park, Gabon: linking patterns of disperser behavior and recruitment in an Afrotropical forest. Dissertation, Washington University in St. Louis.

Freeman, E. A. and Ford, E. D. 2002. Effects of data quality on analysis of ecological pattern using the K(d) statistical function. *Ecology* **83**: 35–46.

Fruth, B. and Hohmann, G. 1996. Nest building behavior in the great apes: the great leap forward. Pages 225–240 in *Great Ape Societies*. W. McGrew, L. Marchant, and T. Nishida (Eds.). Cambridge University Press, Cambridge.

Haase, P. 1995. Spatial pattern analysis in ecology based on Ripley's K-function: introduction and methods of edge correction. *Journal of Vegetation Science* **6**: 575–582.

Haase, P. 2001. Can isotropy vs. anisotropy in the spatial association of plant species reveal physical vs. biotic facilitation? *Journal of Vegetation Science* **12**: 127–136.

Hardesty, B. D., Hubbell, S. P., and Bermingham, E. 2006. Genetic evidence of frequent long-distance recruitment in a vertebrate-dispersed tree. *Ecology Letters* **9**: 516–525.

Harding, D. J., Lefsky, M. A., Parker, G. G., and Blair, J. B. 2001. Laser altimeter canopy height profiles: methods and validation for closed-canopy, broadleaf forests. *Remote Sensing of Environment* **76**: 283–297.

Hoffman, T. S. and O'Riain, M. J. 2012. Landscape requirements of a primate population in a human-dominated environment. *Frontiers in Zoology* **9**. DOI: 10.1186/1742-9994-9-1.

Isbell, L. A. 1991. Contest and scramble competition: patterns of female aggression and ranging behavior among primates. *Behavioral Ecology* **2**: 143–155.

Isbell, L. A., Pruetz, J. D., Young, T. P., and Lewis, M. 1998. Movements of vervets (*Cercopithecus aethiops*) and patas monkeys (*Erythrocebus patas*) as estimators of food resource size, density, and distribution. *Behavioral Ecology and Sociobiology* **42**: 123–133.

Janson, C. 1985. Aggressive competition and individual food consumption in wild brown capuchin monkeys (*Cebus apella*). *Behavioral Ecology and Sociobiology* **18**(2): 125–138.

Janson, C. H. 1992. Evolutionary ecology of primate social structure. Pages 95–130 in *Evolutionary Ecology and Human Behavior*. E. A. Smith and B. Winterhalder (Eds.). Aldine, New York.

Janson, C. H. and Goldsmith, M. L. 1995. Predicting group size in primates: foraging costs and predation risks. *Behavioral Ecology* **6**(3): 326–336.

Koenig, A. 2002. Competition for resources and its behavioral consequences among female primates. *International Journal of Primatology* **23**: 759–783.

Koenig, A., Beise, J., Chalise, M. K., and Ganzhorn, J. U. 1998. When females should contest for food: testing hypotheses about resource density, distribution, size, and quality with Hanuman langurs (*Presbytis entellus*). *Behavioral Ecology and Sociobiology* **42**: 225–237.

Krebs, C. 1999. *Ecological Methodology*. Addison-Wesley, Menlo Park, CA.

Lacher, T. E., Bouchardet da Fonseca, G. A., Alves, C., and Magalhaes-Castro, B. 1984. Parasitism of trees by marmosets in a central Brazilian gallery forest. *Biotropica* **16**: 202–209.

Legendre, P. and Fortin, M. J. 1989. Spatial pattern and ecological analysis. *Plant Ecology* **80**: 107–138.

Leighton, M. and Leighton, D. R. 1982. The relationship of size and feeding aggregate size to size of food patch: howler monkeys (*Alouatta palliata*) feeding in *Trichilia cipo* fruit trees on Barro Colorado Island. *Biotropica* **14**: 81–90.

Levi, T., Silvius, K. M., Oliveira, L. F., Cummings, A. R., and Fragoso, J. M. 2013. Competition and facilitation in the capuchin–squirrel monkey relationship. *Biotropica* **45**(5): 636–643.

Masota, A. M., Zahabu, E., Malimbwi, R. E., Bollandsas, O. E. and Eid, R. H. 2014. Volume models for single trees in tropical rainforests in Tanzania. *Journal of Energy and Natural Resources* **3**: 66–76.

Nakagawa, N. 1989. Feeding strategies of Japanese monkeys against the deterioration of habitat quality. *Primates* **30**(1): 1–16.

Norconk, M. A., Kinzey, W. G. 1994. Challenge of neotropical frugivory: travel patterns of spider monkeys and bearded sakis. *Am J Primatol* **34**: 171–183.

Ord, J. K. and Getis, A. 1995. Local spatial autocorrelation statistics: Distributional issues and an application. *Geographical Analysis* **27**: 287–306.

Peper, P. J., McPherson, E. G., and Mori, S. M. 2001. Equations for predicting diameter, height, crown width, and leaf area of San Joaquin Valley street trees. *Journal of Arboriculture* **27**: 306–317.

Peres, C. A. 1991. Seed predation of *Cariniana micrantha* (Lecythidaceae) by brown capuchin monkeys in Central Amazonia. *Biotropica* **23**(3): 262–270.

Peres, C. A. 1996. Use of space, spatial group structure, and foraging group size of gray woolly monkeys (*Lagothrix lagotricha cana*) at Urucu, Brazil. Pages 467–488 in *Adaptive Radiations of Neotropical Primates*. M. A. Norconk, A. L. Rosenberger, and P. A. Garber (Eds.). Plenum Press, New York.

Perry, J. N., Liebhold, A. M., Rosenberg, M. S., et al. 2002. Illustrations and guidelines for selecting statistical methods for quantifying spatial pattern in ecological data. *Ecography* **25**: 578–600.

Phillips, K. A. 1995. Resource patch size and flexible foraging in white-face capuchins (*Cebus capucinus*). *International Journal of Primatology* **16**: 509–521.

Pickett, S. T. A. and White, P. S. 1985. *The Ecology of Natural Disturbance and Patch Dynamics*. Academic Press, New York.

Pruetz, J. D. 1999. Socioecology of adult female vervet (*Cercopithecus aethiops*) and patas monkeys (*Erythrocebus patas*) in Kenya: food availability, feeding competition, and dominance relationships. PhD Thesis. University of Illinois.

Pruetz, J. D. and Isbell, L. A. 2000. Correlations of food distribution and patch size with agonistic interactions in female vervets (*Chlorocebus aethiops*) and patas monkeys (*Erythrocebus patas*) living in simple habitats. *Behavioral Ecology and Sociobiology* **49**(1): 38–47.

Ripley, B. D. 1976. The second-order analysis of stationary point processes. *Journal of Applied Probability* **13**: 255–266.

Russo, S. E. and Augspurger, C. K. 2004. Aggregated seed dispersal by spider monkeys limits recruitment to clumped patterns in *Virola calophylla*. *Ecology Letters* **7**(11): 1058–1067.

Russo, S. E., Portnoy, S., and Augspurger, C. K. 2006. Incorporating animal behavior into seed dispersal models: implications for seed shadows. *Ecology* **87**(12): 3160–3174.

Schoener, T. W. 1971. Theory of feeding strategies. *Annual Review of Ecology and Systems* **2**: 369–403.

Sezen, U. U., Chazdon, R. L., and Holsinger, K. E. 2009. Proximity is not a proxy for parentage in an animal-dispersed Neotropical canopy palm. *Proceedings of the Royal Society B: Biological Sciences* **2761664**: 2037–2044.

Shaffer, C. A. 2012. Ranging behavior, group cohesiveness, and patch use in northern bearded sakis (*Chiropotes sagulatus*) in Guyana. PhD Thesis. Washington University in St. Louis.

Shaffer, C. A. 2013a. GIS analysis of patch use and group cohesiveness of bearded sakis (*Chiropotes sagulatus*) in the Upper Essequibo Conservation Concession, Guyana. *American Journal of Physical Anthropology* **150**: 235–246.

Shaffer, C. A. 2013b. Ecological correlates of ranging behavior in bearded sakis (*Chiropotes sagulatus*) in a continuous forest in Guyana. *International Journal of Primatology* **34**: 515–532.

Snaith, T. V. and Chapman, C. A. 2007. Primate group size and interpreting socioecological models: do folivores really play by different rules? *Evolutionary Anthropology* **16**: 94–106.

Stephens, D. and Krebs, J. 1986. *Foraging Theory*. Princeton University Press, Princeton, NJ.

Sterk, E. A., Watts, D. P. and van Schaik, C. P. 1997. The evolution of female social relationships in primates. *Behavioral Ecology and Sociobiology* **41**: 291–310.

Stevenson, P. R., Quinones, M. J., and Ahumada, J. A. 1998. Effects of fruit patch availability on feeding subgroup size and spacing patterns in four primate species at Tinigua National Park, Colombia. *International Journal of Primatology* **19**(2): 313–324.

Strier, K. B. 1989. Effects of patch size on feeding associations in muriquis (*Brachyteles arachnoides*). *Folia primatologica* **52**: 70–77.

Symington, M. M. 1988. Food competition and foraging party size in the black spider monkey (*Ateles paniscus chamek*). *Behaviour* **105**: 117–134.

Temerin, L. A. and Cant, J. H. 1983. The evolutionary divergence of Old World monkeys and apes. *American Naturalist* **122**: 335–351.

Thompson, C. L., Robl, N. J., Oliveira Melo, L. C., et al. 2013. Spatial distribution and exploitation of trees gouged by common marmosets (*Callithrix jacchus*). *International Journal of Primatology* **34**: 65–85.

Tobler W. 1970. A computer movie simulating urban growth in the Detroit region. *Economic Geography* **46**(Supplement): 234–240.

Upton, G. and Fingleton, B. 1985. *Spatial Data Analysis by Example: Volume 1: Point Pattern and Quantitative Data*. Wiley, Chichester.

van Schaik, C.P. 1989. The ecology of social relationships amongst female primates. Pages 195–218 in *Comparative Socioecology: The Behavioural Ecology of Humans and Other Mammals*. V. Standen and R.A. Foley (Eds.). Blackwell Scientific, Oxford.

Vogel, E. R. and Janson, C. H. 2007. Predicting the frequency of food-related agonism in white-faced capuchin monkeys (*Cebus capucinus*), using a novel focal-tree method. *American Journal of Primatology* **69**: 533–550.

Vogel, E. R. and Janson, C. H. 2011. Quantifying primate food distribution and abundance for socioecological studies: an objective consumer-centered method. *International Journal of Primatology* **32**: 737–754.

Warren, W.G. 1972. Point processes in forestry. Pages 85–116 in *Stochastic Point Processes, Statistical Analysis, Theory and Application*. P.A.W. Lewis (Ed.). Wiley, New York.

White, F. J. and Wrangham, R. W. 1988. Feeding competition and patch size in the chimpanzee species *Pan paniscus* and *Pan troglodytes*. *Behaviour* **105**: 148–164.

Wrangham, R.W., Gittleman, J.L., and Chapman, C.A. 1993. Constraints on group size in primates and carnivores: population density and day-range as assays of exploitation competition. *Behavioral Ecology and Sociobiology* **32**(3): 199–209.

9 Interpreting Small-Scale Patterns of Ranging by Primates

What Does It Mean, and Why Does It Matter?

Mitchell T. Irwin and Jean-Luc Raharison

Introduction

Advances in technologies like GPS units, GPS collars, and GIS software have surged ahead in recent decades, allowing primatologists to quantify many aspects of their study subjects' spatial ecology with increasing ease and accuracy. We have come a long way from the times when pioneering field primatologists would do things like measuring daily path lengths by contorting a piece of string along an animal track hand-drawn on a scale map of their trail system. However, at the same time as welcoming these advances, it is important for primatologists to continue working on the related issue of interpretation. Science, after all, is more than technology, and once the coolness factor wears off we need to ask ourselves what all those data are telling us at the end of the day.

From a strictly applied, conservation management perspective, some rules of interpreting spatial ecological data seem simple. For example, more is better – increases in local population density and/or geographic range size add up to more animals in a global or local population, which is surely good from a conservation perspective. However, many aspects of small-scale ranging data are much more ambiguous in terms of the inferences we can make about the larger population's health and long-term viability. In this chapter, we will discuss three such types of ranging data. For each, we will provide the ecological context that informs our current interpretations, as well as highlighting knowledge gaps and possible future directions to remedy them.

Throughout this chapter, we will review selected examples from the literature, and present new data from our own study of sifakas (*Propithecus diadema*) at Tsinjoarivo, a mid-altitude forest located in central-eastern Madagascar atop the escarpment dividing the central plateau from the eastern coastal lowlands. Tsinjoarivo forest is part of the new Tsinjoarivo-Ambalaomby protected area, currently being created by the NGO SADABE. This study has deliberately targeted lemur groups existing over a wide spectrum of habitat disturbance, made possible by recent historical factors. The Tsinjoarivo region has been settled largely by human populations moving eastward from the central plateau; immigration westward into this region is hampered by low population density and an extremely steep escarpment coincident with the eastern rainforest's eastern boundary. This highly directional invasion has produced a 15 km gradient of habitat disturbance and fragmentation ranging from high (in the west) to low (in the east), while other ecological parameters such as ecology and rainfall are similar.

The Tsinjoarivo sifakas have been the subject of behavioral and ecological research since 2002 (Irwin 2008a, 2008b; Irwin et al. 2010, 2014), centered around three camps. Here we present ranging and behavioral data for four "continuous forest" groups in intact, undisturbed forest (CONT1 and CONT2 at Vatateza: 19°43.25′ S, 47°51.41′ E; 1396 m; CONT4 and CONT5 at Ankadivory: 19°42.98′ S, 47°49.29′ E; 1345 m) and six "fragment" groups in disturbed, fragmented forest (FRAG1, FRAG2, FRAG3, FRAG4, FRAG5, and FRAG6 at Mahatsinjo: 19°40.94′ S, 47°45.46′ E; 1590 m). Forest composition differs between sites, largely due to past disturbance; CONT habitats have higher species richness, higher canopy, fewer (but larger) trees, and higher overall basal area per hectare (Irwin 2006a). The sifakas' diet composition in terms of plant parts is relatively consistent across the study population (53 percent of feeding time on foliage, 24 percent on fruits, 7 percent on seeds, and 15 percent on flowers; Irwin 2008b), but species composition of the diet varies greatly, with FRAG groups relying heavily on mistletoe (a fallback food; Marshall et al. 2009). Groups are capable of persisting in fragments over the short term (fragment groups have survived and reproduced since at least 2000), but indirect signs of stress are evident: a dietary shift with increased reliance on mistletoe (Irwin 2008b) and reduced nutritional intake (Irwin et al. 2015), reduced body mass, especially for juveniles (Irwin 2006a; Irwin et al. 2019), and altered activity patterns including reduction of energetically costly activities such as play and ranging (Irwin 2006a). A previous ranging study (Irwin 2008a) found that two FRAG groups had reduced home range (HR) and daily path length (DPL) compared to two CONT groups, and that CONT groups seemed attracted to forest edges while FRAG groups were repelled from them.

Methods

Behavioral and Density Data

Behavioral data were derived from all-day focal animal follows, and for a subset of these follows ranging data were collected using handheld GPS units (Garmin GPS 76 with external antenna; typical reported error 5–10 m) during day-long focal animal follows conducted by teams of 2–3 people, including local research assistants. Focal animals included only animals >1.5 years old in January 2003, and were selected on a rotating basis to equalize sample sizes. We worked with all assistants and volunteers to standardize data collection and distance estimation. As often as possible, focal animals were located in the morning sleep tree. Data were collected in the form of waypoints; these were recorded at the beginnings and ends of days (sleep sites), and every feeding site for which it was possible to obtain a location (90–97 percent). To prevent intergroup biases related to the spacing of feeding sites, observers also took *ad libitum* locations whenever possible, especially during travel.

HR was calculated from waypoints as a minimum convex polygon (MCP), using Animal Movement Analysis v. 2.04 (Hooge and Eichenlaub, 1997) and ArcGIS 10.1. The MCP HR is the smallest convex polygon that fits around all locations; this method is computationally simple, but can overestimate ranges by including unused areas. In contrast, kernel methods produce more realistic ranges using a probabilistic model (Worton 1989); we did not use kernel HRs because of varying sample size across groups. HRs were manually restricted to forested areas, using a combination of GPS tracking of edges and satellite imagery; HRs determined by the software (especially minimum convex polygons) were clipped to exclude non-forest areas (as these were not used).

Group-specific densities were calculated by dividing average group size (excluding infants) by HR size. Group densities are not adjusted for range overlap, which was only partially quantified in this study (some neighboring study groups overlapped, but overlap could not be ruled out when neighboring groups were unstudied); thus densities reported may be underestimates. Powzyk (1997) suggested that only the outer 20–100 m of her sifaka groups' ranges overlapped with neighbors, and a similar situation seems plausible here; intergroup encounters were rare, with the only observed encounter ~100 m within CONT2's range.

Botanical Data

Botanical data are derived from inventories of 10×100 m plots led by MTI, P. Rasabo, H. Rakotoarimanana, and E. Ranaivoson. Between 7 and 10 plots were sampled within each HR, with the exception of FRAG3: This group was only studied briefly, and two plots sampled in 2001 were used to represent this small HR. Plots were not placed randomly, to avoid sampling areas altered by local people using trail systems. Instead, plot locations were chosen in advance in reference to and away from trails, and evenly spaced within *P. diadema* HRs. The fact that trails were not concentrated along topographical features (e.g., along ridgetops) means that topographic bias due to trail placement is unlikely.

Within each plot, the following data were collected for each stem ≥ 5 cm diameter at breast height (DBH): species identity, DBH, height, crown height, two crown diameters (maximum and perpendicular), and the incidence of hemiparasites (*Bakerella clavata*, *Bakerella* sp., *Viscum* sp.) and hemi-epiphytes (*Medinilla humblotii*, *M. parvifolia*). Lianas were included in the inventory when they exceeded 5 cm DBH, but it proved too difficult to estimate their crown dimensions; therefore they are not represented in crown volume data (lianas represented only 0.19–0.97 percent of stems and 0.049–0.179 percent of basal area per site). One bamboo species that exceeded 5 cm DBH (*Oldeania* sp.) was included in data collection because it makes an important contribution to the forest structure in some plots. Species were identified using published sources (Schatz 2001; Turk 1995), in collaboration with Missouri Botanical Gardens.

Exploration of the dataset revealed that cumulative basal area per hectare (with basal area calculated as $BA = \pi \times (DBH/2)^2$) was a useful correlate of habitat disturbance. Because selective logging was fairly recent (within ~10–20 years), removal of large trees seems to have caused a significant reduction in this variable. Areas with a longer history of human habitation and more active recent hardwood extraction had lower basal area coverage, likely because regrowth is too slow to compensate for the rapid, ongoing loss of large trees (with much of the regrowth comprising trees <5 cm DBH). Although data before human transformation are not available, local informants typically recall the past presence of larger trees in the western parts of Tsinjoarivo, and report a past forest structure similar to what is seen today in the east.

Results and Discussion

Home Range

One of the most fundamental ranging variables that primatologists seek to quantify is the HR size. Simply put, HR is the two-dimensional area used by a primate or a primate group within a certain time period (Burt 1943). Defining the time period is important because increasing the time period or the intensity of sampling often leads to a larger reported HR than would have been detected during a shorter period, or with less intense sampling. It is crucial when reporting HRs, or comparing studies, to bear this effect in mind. It is also crucial to recognize that different analytical methods exist to convert a series of point locations into a "HR" for analysis, ranging from the very inclusive "minimum convex polygon" to more nuanced kernel analyses (Fieberg & Börger 2012; reviewed in Boyle, Chapter 7). This important question is beyond the scope of this chapter; in the text that follows we simply assume that the data under discussion are measurements of an animal's "true" HR. The HR varies across space, time, and individuals (Börger et al. 2006), being greatly influenced by ecological factors such as diet, resource distribution, energetic needs, and locomotor strategy (Kelt and Van Vuren 2001; Marzluff et al. 2004). Understanding how these factors vary within species is important for understanding species–habitat relationships and their conservation implications.

HR is particularly important from a conservation perspective as it is one of the contributing factors influencing overall global or local population size. Very generally, the average group size divided by the average HR size yields an estimate of population density for the broader population. However, the influence of animal or group spacing must also be considered. In situations in which HRs overlap, a simple estimate of population size will be too low, though it can be adjusted when the typical percentage overlap is known (Struhsaker 1981). Conversely, when primate groups do not continuously cover the landscape (i.e., they are patchy), this simple estimate will be too high. When habitat needs are well-understood, this can be easily corrected; for example, in a landscape with patchy forest cover, assuming that only forest is occupied by primates (and this land is fully occupied), one can either present a forest-specific population density, with no adjustment needed, or a landscape-wide population density, which would be the simple estimate multiplied by the proportion of land under forest cover (Ross & Reeve 2011; Struhsaker 1981). However, the patchy distribution of animals in an area is not always conveniently related to easily quantified habitat variation. Often, some "habitat" is occupied and other "habitat" is not, without any clear indication of what the contributing factors are, and without an easily quantified correlate of occupancy that can be detected via remote sensing (Wright et al. 2008). In this case, using typical HR sizes to estimate landscape-wide density or population size is problematic, though where sufficient data exist, ecological niche modeling can be used (Rode et al. 2013).

Despite these complexities, if group size and HR overlap remain constant, and a species is continuously distributed, smaller HRs would correspond to higher densities and population sizes, while larger HRs would correlate with lower densities and population sizes. Leaving the numbers aside and tying these differences to ecological theory leads quickly to the "ideal free distribution" (Fretwell 1972). This theory assumes that animals are unconstrained in terms of moving around the environment (hence, "free"), and have perfect knowledge of the resource potential of the landscape (hence, "ideal"); under these conditions, animals are thought to arrange themselves in a landscape according to the abundance of food. This is usually conceptualized in terms of discrete patches (i.e., a patch with double the food supply should attract twice as many animals), but can be logically extended to a continuous landscape that varies in the local density of food resources. If this extension is valid, then one would expect that "resource-richer" areas should have higher local density (animals per unit area) than "resource-poorer" areas (Milich et al. 2014).

This would lead to an extended interpretation of what "higher population density" (either a change through time, or a comparison across areas) means for the long-term viability of a species. The first inference is that it is good for conservation in the short term simply because more animals are currently preserved within a given area. The second is that it is *especially* good for conservation because that habitat is inferred to be richer – providing more resources per unit area, and giving reason to believe that conservation benefits can be sustained over the long term. The first inference seems straightforward; the more important question is whether the second inference is valid or not.

Ecologists have long warned that local population density can be a "misleading indicator of habitat quality" (van Horne 1983); when habitat quality is measured independently, for example through direct measurements of survival and reproductive success, several counterexamples are known wherein habitat quality and population density are not positively correlated. Van Horne (1983) proposes three main factors that can cause such a relationship. The first is when seasonal migration patterns cause a mismatch between the habitat in which density is measured (e.g., summer habitat) and the habitat in which the most pressing challenges to survival occur (e.g., winter habitat). For primates that maintain a constant HR year-round, this should not occur. A second factor is a time lag in populations' responses to temporal variability in resource density: current densities may reflect previous years' resources and cause a mismatch between current population density and resource density. A third factor stems from social interactions: dominant individuals (or groups) may exclude subordinates from higher-quality habitat, causing surplus individuals to collect in habitat "sinks," which may at times have higher density than preferred habitat.

Two additional complicating factors can arise from habitat loss and the subdivision of once-continuous habitat, as is common in primate habitats around the world (Harper et al. 2007; Laurance et al. 2011). First, short-term crowding can occur when habitat is lost and long-lived primates adjust HR boundaries accordingly. If this causes populations to temporarily exist above carrying capacity, one would expect a future reduction in population density through demographic processes (in some ways analogous to Van Horne's second scenario, above). This appears to match the ranging patterns of saki monkeys (*Chiropotes satanas*) in Brazil (Boyle et al. 2009): When confined to 10 ha fragments (their normal home ranges are 300–559 ha), they use virtually all the available area, and GPS points describing their ranging are uniformly distributed (in contrast to the clumped distribution in continuous forest).

The second scenario is referred to by ecologists as the "fence effect" (Ostfeld 1994), and is based on the observation that small mammals that are physically "fenced in" rise to abnormally high densities, and subsequently overexploit their habitat and experience population crashes. There is much debate over the reason(s) behind the increase, which may be due to stifled emigration out of the habitat, or the fact that "fences" exclude smaller (but not larger) predators. This could impact arboreal primates stranded in fragments, for which forest edges represent a relatively impermeable barrier, via either mechanism. Subadult primates may stay with "stranded" groups longer than they would had they existed in continuous forest, swelling group sizes (but not necessarily HRs), and some evidence suggests altered predator–prey dynamics in fragments (Irwin et al. 2009), likely due to fragmentation's effects on predator movements.

As described above, multiple factors influence any primate group's realized HR, and from a conservation point of view it would be valuable to know what increases or decreases in HR mean for a population's viability. These questions can reflect two directions of causation. First, does the change *reflect* an underlying positive or negative change in the health of individuals or populations? And second, what are the *impacts* of the shift on the health of individuals or populations?

Tsinjoarivo sifakas clearly exhibit reduced HR size in more disturbed habitat (Table 9.1; Figure 9.1). Not only do all six FRAG groups have smaller HRs (10.9–44.1 ha) than CONT groups (62.9–90.2 ha), there is a significant positive relationship between HR size and tree basal area per hectare (HR = $-1.04 + 1.88 \times$ [BA/ha]; linear regression adjusted $R^2 = 0.73$, $p = 0.001$; Figure 9.2). Since basal area per hectare is highest in the least disturbed areas, this implies that forest degradation may have caused HR contraction, while group size has remained relatively constant.

For Tsinjoarivo sifakas, the ideal free distribution (IFD) does not seem to explain the observed change. Taken literally, the IFD would imply that FRAG groups have smaller HRs because their resources are more dense. A logical prediction of this scenario would be increased nutritional inputs and improved health and body condition in the more disturbed habitat, yet these groups actually have reduced nutritional inputs (Irwin et al. 2014, 2015), smaller juveniles (Irwin et al. 2019), and hematology and serum biochemistry values suggesting compromised health (Irwin et al. 2010). The interpretation that habitat disturbance positively impacts health is also contradicted by the greatly reduced activity levels and rates of play among juveniles (Irwin 2006b).

Table 9.1 Sampling, home range, and characteristics of Tsinjoarivo *Propithecus diadema* study groups

Group	Time sampled	Sample size (days/points)	HR (ha)[a]	Animals in group[b]	Local population density (ind./km²)[c]
FRAG1	January–December 2003	71 / 3521	21.2	4	18.87
FRAG2	January–December 2003	65 / 2948	40.1	5	12.47
FRAG3	June–August 2006	14 / 411	10.9	2	18.35
FRAG4	November 2006 to July 2007; June 2008 to August 2009	38 / 1297	44.6	4–5	10.09
FRAG5	September 2008 to September 2009	13 / 285	28.0	2–3	8.93
FRAG6	September 2008 to September 2009	19 / 571	44.1	4	9.07
CONT1	January–December 2003	69 / 2329	83.2	5–6	6.61
CONT2	January–December 2003	73 / 2559	76.0	5–6	7.24
CONT4	September 2008 to September 2009	18 / 329	90.2	6–7	7.21
CONT5	September 2008 to September 2009	17 / 225	62.9	4	6.36

[a] MCP of all waypoints, clipped to exclude non-forest; two detected areas of overlap were FRAG4/FRAG6 (12.1 ha) and CONT4/CONT5 (8.3 ha).
[b] Excluding dependent infants <0.5 years old.
[c] Calculated assuming no overlap; true values may be slightly higher.

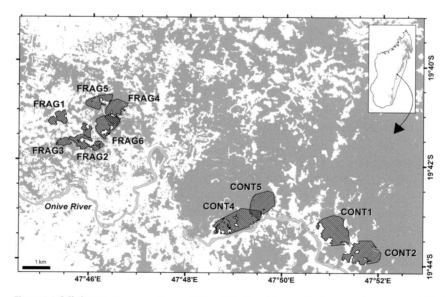

Figure 9.1 Minimum convex polygon HRs of 10 *Propithecus diadema* study groups at Tsinjoarivo (see Table 9.1 for details); gray represents forest cover following IKONOS satellite image (acquisition date November 2001). Other unstudied groups exist near CONT groups, whose overlap with study groups was not quantified.

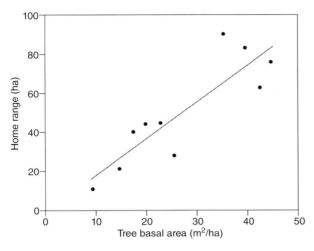

Figure 9.2 Bivariate relationship between *Propithecus diadema* HR size and basal area per hectare in botanical plots (a proxy for habitat disturbance, with selective extraction of trees reducing this variable) at Tsinjoarivo.

The interpretation of disturbed fragments as "demographic sinks" trapping surplus individuals also does not match the observations, as all FRAG groups are full social groups similar in size and composition to CONT groups, rather than collections of non-breeding subadults. Some FRAG groups have been monitored in the same HR, breeding, for >12 years.

As for short-term physical crowding, ideally one would investigate this question by comparing disturbed fragments with disturbed forest areas that were unfragmented, but in reality fragmentation and disturbance are often coupled, and this has been true at Tsinjoarivo. The groups in the smallest fragments (FRAG1, FRAG3) are noteworthy in that they completely occupy forest fragments and have no room to expand, thus crowding seems plausible. Others (FRAG4, FRAG5, and FRAG6) share a larger fragment, though it is still possible that crowding can squeeze multiple groups together as a fragment shrinks. In this way, neighboring groups would, in the short term, each occupy a smaller area until the local population shrinks and re-equilibrates, presumably at a population density similar to pre-fragmentation levels.

This scenario would fit well with the indications of reduced individual health in the more disturbed environments. However, other predictions are not met. If crowding is the sole factor causing HR reductions, one would expect utilization of every corner of available area, and where multiple groups occupy a fragment one would expect increased intergroup encounters and increased agonism. FRAG2 provides a striking example of a group not utilizing all the space available; of the 44.0 ha available, it used 40.1 ha (91 percent), but this figure is misleading since large parts of its fragment were ignored for long periods during a year-long study in 2003. Specifically, the northern-most extent of its fragment (Figure 9.3) is split into two arms, of which the western arm was not entered until the tenth month of the study. This was despite it being at least as intact (if not more so) as most of the realized HR: A single botanical plot from

Table 9.2 Aggression rates (aggressive acts experienced, either as giver or receiver of aggression) during day-long focal animal follows of Tsinjoarivo sifakas

Group	Study period and sample (days)	Aggression rate (/day)
FRAG1	January–December 2003 (167)	0.86
FRAG2	January–December 2003 (162)	0.52
	June 2006 to July 2007 (87)	0.60
FRAG3	June–August 2006 (10)	0
FRAG4	November 2006 to July 2007 (69)	0.54
CONT1	January–December 2003 (157)	1.32
	June 2006 to July 2007 (106)	0.76
CONT2	January–December 2003 (165)	2.22
	June 2006 to July 2007 (91)	0.89

2001 recorded a basal area of 19.49 m^2/ha, higher than the HR-wide average (17.44 m^2/ha). During the two recorded incursions, unusual behavior was noted, including heightened vigilance (often from high vantage points), and less directed, more round-about travel. This is in sharp contrast to the maximized HR use of saki monkeys described by Boyle et al. (2009). In addition, aggression rates were consistently higher in CONT groups than FRAG groups (Table 9.2) – the opposite of the prediction if multiple groups are crowded into a fragment (the case for FRAG4). Intergroup encounters were rare overall (Irwin 2008a); the three neighboring groups, FRAG4, FRAG5, and FRAG6, had little HR overlap and one recorded intergroup encounter in more than 3000 observation hours. It is possible that scentmarking is utilized more heavily in territorial defense than direct encounters and aggression; however, the fact that CONT groups scentmarked at higher rates than FRAG groups (Irwin 2006b) is counter to the prediction if animals are crowded in fragments and thus more motivated to maintain or expand HRs.

Finally, if the fence effect was solely responsible for increased densities via stifled emigration, one would expect a similar HR size per social group, but increased densities through the swelling of groups, while the opposite pattern is observed. The fence effect can also act via altered predation rates in isolated fragments, in this case meaning reduced predation pressure; however, evidence to date suggests higher predation pressure in fragments (Irwin et al. 2009). Thus, in summary, the Tsinjoarivo sifakas' increased HR in disturbed fragments is not cleanly explained by any of the available theories.

Daily Path Length

A second key variable often used to describe the spatial ecology of individuals and groups is daily path length (DPL; "day journey length" and "day range" are often used synonymously). Daily path length generally increases with body mass (Carbone et al. 2005), and there is therefore a degree of interdependence between HR size and daily

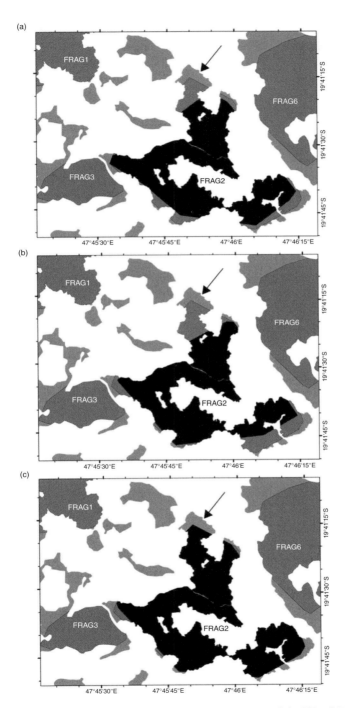

Figure 9.3 Minimum convex polygon representation of the HR of *Propithecus diadema* group FRAG2, during February to June 2003 (a), July to September 2003 (b) and October–December (c), showing underuse of northernmost area available in the forest fragment. Light gray represents ground-truthed fragment boundaries (using GPS tracking), hatched areas represent overall MCP HRs, and black represents MCP HR during the specified period.

path length; metabolic requirements and locomotor abilities mean that gorillas will generally have large HR and DPL, and mouse lemurs low HR and DPL. However, DPL is not a simple function of HR or body mass, and can increase or decrease due to the density and spacing of food resources and the needs of territorial defense (Shaffer 2013a, 2013b). Thus, DPL can be a key ecological variable measured on its own, or as an index by expressing it in relation to HR size.

Very generally, primatologists have suggested that realized DPL primarily represents a balance between two key pressures: the patrolling of territorial boundaries to prevent the penetration of neighboring groups (Peres 2000); and the need to acquire sufficient food resources that day. The latter factor depends on resource density and distribution, as well as group size, which varies greatly across primate species and populations; comparative work has shown that adding additional group members tends to cause increases in DPL via increased feeding competition (the "ecological constraints model": Chapman & Chapman 2000; Teichroeb & Sicotte 2009).

A prevalent model of territorial defense proposed by Mitani and Rodman (1979) and expanded by Lowen and Dunbar (1994) suggests that territoriality will emerge predominantly when the increased cost of patrolling territory boundaries would be small or absent relative to the ranging effort already required for the acquisition of food. Specifically, when typical DPL is similar to or longer than a measure of one's HR diameter, added cost would be minimal because return times for specific parts of the HR are already relatively short. In the opposite case, when DPL is short relative to HR diameter, the added cost of defense would be more onerous; for these populations DPL would depend primarily on food resources and HRs would not be defended.

When differences in DPL are detected among seasons, across habitat variability in a landscape, or through time, it seems natural to turn to this theoretical and empirical work, and consider both food resource distribution and territorial defense as potential underlying factors (Palminteri et al. 2016). First, if changes in active territorial defense drive DPL differences, one would predict that groups with less risk of territorial incursion (e.g., isolated in forest fragments or with fewer neighbors) would show reduced DPL. However, according to the nature of the defensibility index evidence, such differences should be relatively small, as primates should neither tolerate greatly increased ranging costs due solely to territoriality, nor have preexisting territoriality-related ranging costs (far beyond those needed for feeding) that can be reduced.

The second possibility, of variability in DPL arising from variability in food resources, can be manifested in different ways (Hanya & Bernard 2016; Santhosh et al. 2015). One potential framework for evaluating these changes closely parallels the IFD predictions for HR; specifically, if the HR is "richer in resources" (through any combination of increases in patch density, and the richness of individual patches), one could predict both a reduced HR and reduced DPL. Daily path length would be shorter simply because a shorter straight-line distance intersects as many resources as would a longer distance in a poorer habitat. However, it is inadequate to model DPL as simply optimizing food intake; in reality optimum DPL represents a balance between the realized food intake for a given DPL and the specific cost of daily travel (Steudel 2000); for example a 25 percent increase in DPL could cause a 25 percent increase in travel costs but only a 20 percent increase in energy intake, thus being unprofitable. Thus, unraveling causal factors becomes problematic: Does a decreased DPL in a disturbed habitat result from a higher resource density, or increased costs of movement?

The ecological literature provides us with a relevant dichotomy: that between "energy maximizers" and "time minimizers" (Hixon 1982; Schoener 1971). For animals following an "energy maximization" strategy, "potential reproductive success is an increasing function of its net energy gain," while for animals following a "time minimization" strategy, "input beyond a certain net energy gain does not increase potential reproductive success" (Hixon 1982: 596). Unfortunately, this concept has proven relatively hard to test in nature, with most empirical evidence coming from species with more monotonous diets that can be experimentally manipulated (Bergman et al. 2001). However, in the context of primate ranging, the concept could be adapted to correspond with alternative strategies in the face of habitat change (or variability). For example, a habitat whose food resources had been compromised through anthropogenic change may elicit one of two reactions. First, a primate group may expand its DPL (potentially with a concurrent increase in HR) if the increased ranging is necessary to maintain net energy balance (i.e., the cost of the increased ranging is outweighed by the benefit; the daily intake targets should increase slightly due to increased expenditure). This roughly follows an energy maximization strategy. Second, a group may actually decrease its DPL if any costs of increased ranging could not be recouped by additional food inputs that could be gained; in essence, the cost–benefit landscape has changed such that the new optimum DPL is reduced. This roughly follows a time minimization strategy. It is important to note that either of these strategies may fail to bring the animals to the same net energy gain as before; instead the altered DPL is simply the optima in the new landscape, which can be higher or lower than the optima in the previous one.

Previous work on Tsinjoarivo sifakas reported that four groups had reduced DPL during the dry season, and that FRAG groups consistently had 15 percent shorter DPLs relative to CONT groups (Irwin 2008a). It was suggested that the dry season reduction was due primarily to reduced frugivory, but the shorter DPLs in FRAG groups is harder to understand. Reduced DPL is not consistent with the interpretation of a richer habitat (see contradictory evidence suggesting compromised health in the previous section), but more likely reflects increasing adoption of a "time minimization" strategy wherein, due to the compromised food resource landscape, increased rewards of traveling farther would not outweigh the costs of travel.

Habitat Choice

A third key type of GIS analysis that can be derived from individual and group ranging data is that of habitat choice. Within any HR, habitat varies along many axes, such as habitat structure, habitat floristic diversity and species composition, hydrology, local topography, microclimate, and anthropogenic disturbance. These factors can greatly affect diverse aspects of a species' ecology, such as vulnerability to predation, availability and quality of food, locomotor costs, and thermoregulation. Additionally, social factors such as access to mates (Foerster et al. 2017) can also influence ranging. Thus, it seems reasonable to presume that animals will actively divide their time among areas within their HR in such a way that maximizes their fitness (Potts et al. 2016) – in other words, "habitat choice" or "habitat selection." This active choice can be measured; in its most simple form, such a test would compare the proportion of time actually spent in certain defined microhabitats to the expected proportion, with the latter set to equal that microhabitat's proportional contribution to the HR or the broader landscape. This has been done either using encounter rates in a broader landscape (Zeng et al. 2013) or behavioral follows of habituated groups (Akers et al. 2013; Harrison et al. 2010; Irwin 2008a; Palminteri & Peres 2012; Palminteri et al. 2016; Singh et al. 2018).

However, three main factors make such tests problematic. First, the habitat variability itself is often incredibly complex. It may in some cases be very discrete (e.g., grassland versus forest), while in many cases it is relatively continuous (e.g., within continuous forest cover). Even a GIS-assisted division of edge versus interior in a mosaic forested landscape can be problematic, considering that the edges themselves vary considerably in aspect (i.e., the direction the edge faces), local topography, and the abruptness of the ecotone (Kapos et al. 1997; Ries et al. 2004; Turton & Freiburger 1997). Thus, in the worst of cases the GIS-assisted division of habitat types is difficult, *and* the underlying continuous variation hard to quantify; even in the best of cases, when the delineation of habitat types along certain lines is easy, the sheer magnitude of the number of axes on which variation occurs can cloud the true processes going on.

A second difficulty is the fact that the current state of an animal is likely to influence its habitat choice at that moment; these factors include hunger, perceived predation risk (either to oneself or immature group-mates), energetic balance, and thermoregulatory state. A very simple example of this would be actively selecting resting and sleep sites based on habitat structure (to minimize vulnerability to predation), but actively selecting feeding sites based on food availability. Though these two processes of selection might point to the same microhabitat type, there is every reason to think this will often not be the case. This problem can be embraced by measuring the changes in the animal's state (where possible), although some variables will be easier to measure (e.g., activity, ambient temperature), while others will be more difficult (e.g., energetic state, perceived predation risk).

A third difficulty is whether the proportions of habitat types in the HR actually provide an appropriate baseline against which to test ranging choices. In the case where groups are closely packed and unable to strategically expand HRs, this might be a fair assumption. However, for less densely packed species, the HR composition itself may already reflect active choice of habitat; in this case the composition of the broader landscape might be a better benchmark. However, even if a broader sampling of the composition of the landscape is appropriate, it is not clear how widely to cast one's net. The reality will likely often fall somewhere between these two extremes, with animals exerting some control over HRs but additionally making active choices of habitat use within them. One simple way to minimize error is using MCP HRs (which capture actively avoided lacunae within them) versus kernel-based HRs (which exclude such lacunae; Palminteri & Peres 2012).

If one can get past these potential pitfalls, the utility of such information can be great. First, from the point of view of habitat management, letting individual primates "tell" you which habitat is preferred can guide choices about which habitat to preserve or restore. As previous sections have demonstrated, relying simply on "snapshots" of local population density can be misleading; if density is higher in lower-quality habitat, preferentially conserving those habitats would be a conservation misstep. Second, understanding habitat preference can aid in more meaningful interpretations of variation in HR and DPL. For example, if regions differ in the proportion of microhabitats, the one with the higher representation of more preferred microhabitats might allow smaller HRs and DPLs and higher density (following the IFD concept).

We quantified the habitat selection of the Tsinjoarivo sifakas with respect to distance from forest edges (even the CONT groups were not "interior" groups but occupied continuous forest with some edges), using the proportion of their home ranges in different "distance to edge" categories to build expected values for proportions of time (Irwin 2008a). Figure 9.4 illustrates two key aspects of habitat selection in this population. First, groups differ in their treatment of edges: CONT1 spent much more time than expected within 60 m of an edge; CONT2 avoided the outermost edge but spent considerable time in the 20–60 m category; and FRAG groups seemed to show less active selection (though perhaps avoiding the outermost edge). One interpretation of this is increased availability of some foods at edges (Ganzhorn 1995), in this case the edge specialists *Solanum mauritianum* and *Maesa lanceolata* (Irwin 2008b) "attract" the CONT groups, yet the fact that FRAG group home ranges have suffered more pervasive disturbance has reduced the contrast between edge and interior. Second, habitat selection for sleeping differs from selection during feeding: sleep trees are found in "interior" zones more often than expected in FRAG groups, suggesting they seek more intact forest with increased cover, while CONT groups show less active selection (CONT1's apparent preference for middle edge categories might be an artifact of the fact that they often finished daily feeding near edges). Interestingly, this strongly parallels the habitat choices during feeding and sleeping in hoolock gibbons (*Hylobates hoolock*) (Akers et al. 2013), adding more weight to the suggestion that edges provide useful feeding habitat for a variety of species (Ganzhorn 1995; Xiang et al. 2011).

When Preferred Foods Are Lost: An Alternative Model

None of the scenarios outlined in the literature seems to exactly explain the Tsinjoarivo sifakas, who show reductions in HR and DPL with increasing habitat disturbance, yet with independent evidence suggesting they are eating less ideal foods and suffering some health consequences. An alternative hypothesis is proposed here which relates to the dietary shifts seen in FRAG groups (Figure 9.5). Irwin (2008b) described the importance of hemiparasitic mistletoe (Loranthaceae: *Bakerella* cf. *clavata*) in the diet; for CONT groups its flowers and leaves are fallback foods in the lean season, and for FRAG groups it serves a similar lean season role as well as being the main target of rainy season fruit feeding (in sum, the top food in virtually every month). These

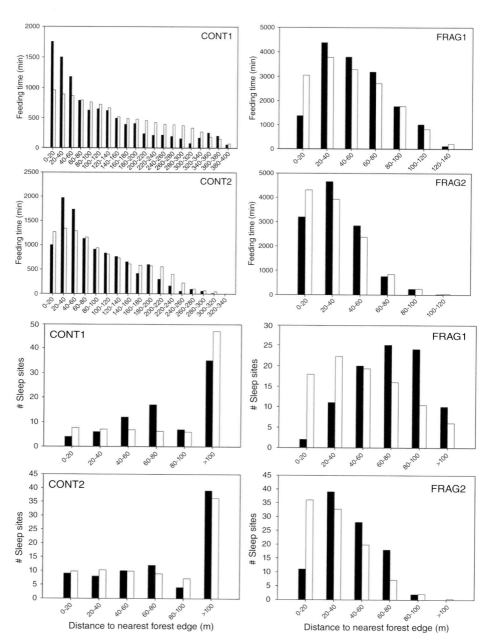

Figure 9.4 Observed versus expected proportions of feeding time (upper four panels) and sleep sites (lower four panels) spent in portions of HR delineated by distance to nearest forest edge for four *Propithecus diadema* study groups at Tsinjoarivo.

mistletoes are especially widespread (Table 9.3). Interestingly, CONT groups have similarly high densities of mistletoes fruiting in the rainy season, but virtually ignore them in favor of large-DBH fruiting hardwood trees (which are rare or absent in fragments due to selective extraction). If it can be reasonably inferred, from the fact

Table 9.3 Botanical characteristics of *Propithecus diadema* home ranges at Tsinjoarivo

Group	Area sampled (ha)	Basal area/ha (m²/ha)	Density of: mistletoe (*Bakerella* cf. *clavata*, individuals/ha)	Density of Preferred Resources (individuals/ha and crown volume/ha)* :				
				Varongy ravinovy (*Ocotea* sp. 1)	Tavolo (*Cryptocarya* sp. 1)	Vahivodiomby (*Salacia madagascariensis*)	Voamalambotaholahy (*Garcinia* sp. 1)	Tsiramiramy (*Abrahamia* cf. *ditimena*)
FRAG1	1.0	14.68	124	1 (2)	58 (882)	0 / absent	0 / absent	0 / absent
FRAG2	1.0	17.44	179	7 (90)	88 (970)	0 / absent	0 / absent	0 / absent
FRAG3	0.2	9.36	110	0 (0)	15 (445)	0 / absent	0 / absent	0 / absent
FRAG4	1.0	22.81	179	13 (224)	84 (1648)	0 / absent	0 / absent	7 (43)
FRAG5	1.0	25.50	248	3 (23)	84 (1000)	0 / absent	0 / absent	3 (24)
FRAG6	1.0	19.85	134	19 (106)	87 (657)	0 / absent	0 / absent	2 (4)
CONT1	1.0	39.58	99	19 (944)	27 (1811)	5 (n/a)	56 (1790)	17 (195)
CONT2	1.0	44.71	98	20 (745)	75 (3944)	5 (n/a)	93 (3410)	7 (217)
CONT4	0.7	35.30	47	26 (778)	26 (1449)	1.4 (36)	49 (491)	71 (933)
CONT5	0.8	42.54	54	30 (1520)	47 (1121)	0 (0)	39 (569)	29 (473)

* Plant species names follow Irwin et al. (2014).

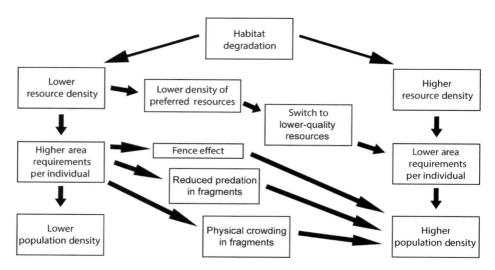

Figure 9.5 Conceptual diagram showing possible population-wide responses to habitat degradation that might lead to either higher or lower population density. Not all concepts found in the literature are included; those excluded are generally not applicable to primates (e.g., seasonal migration; van Horne 1983).

that CONT groups eschew mistletoe, that mistletoe fruits are lower quality (in some way, or a combination of ways) than the hardwood tree fruits, it follows that FRAG groups have switched from rare, preferred foods to common, less-preferred foods. Once that switch has been made, a group's space requirements and their daily foraging effort (DPL) should decrease; both patterns are observed in this population (Irwin 2008a). The home range reduction might simply reflect the fact that a smaller home range "captures" sufficient amounts of mistletoe and other resources; increases would capture more of these less-preferred resources but would not allow significantly better dietary outcomes. The DPL reduction in FRAG groups might reflect the fact that CONT groups often used directed, long-distance travel to move between preferred, large trees whose state they seemed to monitor. Often, research teams would notice them returning to the same 5–10 trees, widely spaced throughout their home range, during a two-week data-collection period. Switching to mistletoes, which are more common and uniformly distributed (Table 9.3), might allow shorter DPLs, as the mistletoes nearby are the same as those on the other side of the home range.

This scenario also matches several other observations in FRAG groups: lower aggression rates (because food patches are lower quality and less worth the cost of defense), lower scentmarking rates (because intergroup competition is less important), reduced health and growth of juveniles, and reduced activity patterns.

Of course, a corollary of this explanation is that CONT groups forego the chance to survive on mistletoe and reduce their ranging costs by decreasing HR size and DPL. This could represent an example of natural selection acting on the individual level; though the regional population size would be larger if they switched to mistletoe, natural selection should favor individuals that opt to defend larger HRs and "capture" more of the rare fruiting trees, if the additional ranging costs are outweighed by the nutritional benefits, with the surplus converted into increased reproductive success. Indeed, the fruits from the hardwood trees are more nutritionally rich, exist in larger fruit crops and are individually considerably larger than mistletoe fruits (Irwin et al. 2014).

If true, this explanation adds to the diversity of ways in which local population density can be increased despite reductions in individual health. These health costs could easily contribute to a reduction in the actual long-term viability of groups and populations, either through a negative population growth rate and slow decline, or increased vulnerability to environmental perturbations (including the stochastic availability of foods) and/or human hunting. These risks will be especially important where the isolation of forest fragments increases. If such habitats are sustained by immigration from other, higher-quality habitats, then they can in the long term make a positive contribution to conservation by storing excess genetic diversity and helping maintain a higher effective population size. When they are isolated, the vulnerability can lead to local extinction and a failure to be recolonized. Either way, the increased local density might be better seen as a "silver lining" in a lower-quality habitat, rather than an all-out conservation victory.

Summary and Future Directions

This review of the literature, and specific examples from the Tsinjoarivo sifakas, illustrates the depressing diversity of ways in which testing of individual spatial ecology hypotheses can falter. Primate individuals and groups balance many intrinsic and extrinsic pressures in their daily ranging decisions, which, scaled up, yield the emergent properties such as HR, DPL, and population density that define their spatial ecology. Given that such a number of factors can contribute to this process, it should not be surprising that differences in these same variables across landscapes or over time can be due to a similarly large variability of underlying processes.

One common theme is that simple inferences cannot easily be drawn from simple observations such as increases or decreases in HR or DPL. Figure 9.6 illustrates how energy intakes and costs (y-axis) might scale with a measure of ranging investment, either HR or DPL (x-axis). The cost of DPL or HR maintenance could be thought to scale in a fairly linear fashion (especially DPL), while the energetic benefit of increased DPL or HR should show diminishing returns. A reduced HR might indicate a richer habitat: Following the reasoning of the IFD, a smaller home range contains as many resources as would a larger home range in poorer habitat (A→B). Alternatively, it could indicate a poorer-quality habitat: If food resources are abundant but lower quality, animals should arrive at the "diminishing returns" part of the curve sooner, and the benefit of maintaining a larger home range would not outweigh the cost (A→C). This should be expected, for example, if animals' intake is limited by chemical defenses (Marsh et al. 2006) or fiber (necessitating longer gut retention times; Clissold et al. 2009); why use more area if the extra food won't do you any good? This seems to match

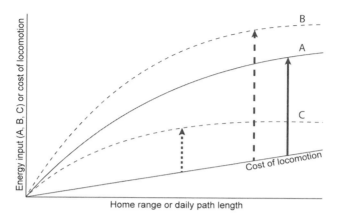

Figure 9.6 Hypothetical modeling of two ways in which habitat change can cause reductions in either HR or DPL. Vertical arrows represent animals' optimization of net energy gain, defined as energetic benefit (food intake, here in three scenarios) minus energetic cost (locomotion or HR maintenance). *A* represents an original state (or baseline), *B* represents a richer habitat in which optimum HR/DPL is reduced while net gain increases, *C* represents a poorer habitat in which optimum HR/DPL is reduced while net gain decreases.

the case of the Tsinjoarivo sifakas, where FRAG groups have switched from preferred foods to common, less-preferred mistletoe. Similarly, for DPL a reduction might indicate a richer habitat (if less ranging is required to meet the same [or a higher] intake target, A→B), or a poorer habitat (if only lower-intake targets are accessible and primates adopt a time minimization strategy, moving to a new, lower optimum DPL, A→C).

Unfortunately, much previous work depends on such monotonic interpretations, particularly with regards to local population density. For example, Johns and Skorupa (1987) and Harcourt (1998) used a "survival ratio" constructed as the population density in disturbed forest divided by density in undisturbed forest, with higher values suggesting higher resilience. Although these were landmark studies at a time when little detail was known of primate lives in disturbed habitat, it now seems inappropriate to continue equating higher local density with higher resilience. More broadly, primatologists need to be wary of using any simple measures of population density as rapidly assessable indicators of habitat change. Though it is reasonable to hope that the future may bring increased understanding that makes this possible, this seems currently out of reach. Though it is tempting, given the limited resources available for research and conservation, to seek shortcuts, the underlying complexity seems too poorly understood – and the costs of mis-speaking too high.

Are we then left in the depressing position of having no working shortcuts? Are we doomed to waiting for generations to pass, while we meticulously record births and deaths, assessing habitat quality through demographic processes (while the forces of habitat destruction march on with their usual swiftness)? Perhaps – but the more optimistic take on the situation is that we are inching ever closer to understanding the mechanisms driving variation in spatial ecology, which surely means that the next generation of research will be better equipped to seek behavioral indicators of population health. Three key areas of research are likely to be especially important. First, quantifying dietary outcomes and how these relate to physiological requirements and respond to habitat variability will fill in the "intake" side of the question. Second, combining veterinary techniques with traditional primatology may yield physiological indicators of health, which can be rapidly assessed and linked to other variations in behavior and spatial ecology. Finally, increasingly sophisticated quantification of habitats, especially the richness and patchiness of their food resources, will build an important context against which to interpret variation in ranging choices.

In sum, GPS and GIS technologies have delivered us an incredible gift – increasingly lower-effort (and in some cases automated) ways to quantify HR size, DPL, habitat preferences, and doubtless other as-yet-unappreciated variables. We have within our grasp a rapidly increasing capacity to test hypotheses about the factors influencing both population phenomena such as population density, and group- or individual-level phenomena such as HR, DPL, and habitat selection. The harder side of the trick might now be knowing which hypotheses and predictions should be part of the picture, and successfully combining ranging data with complementary datasets in search of broader connections.

Acknowledgments

We thank the government of Madagascar, CAFF/CORE, and the Ministry of Environment and Forests for research authorization. All animal capture and observations adhered to the legal requirements of Madagascar, and were approved by McGill University's Animal Care Committee, the University of Queensland's Animal Welfare Unit, and IACUC committees of St. Louis Zoo and Northern Illinois University. For research facilitation we thank P. Wright, B. Andriamihaja, MICET, ICTE, and T. Ranaivoson. We are grateful for funding from Margot Marsh Biodiversity Foundation, National Geographic Society Committee for Research and Exploration, Primate Conservation Inc., Stony Brook University, St. Louis Zoo, Primate Action Fund, Earth and Space Foundation, Eppley Foundation for Research, and an NSERC postdoctoral fellowship to MTI. For invaluable data and sample collection assistance, we thank research assistants E. Razanadrakoto, H. Rakotoarimanana, E. Ranaivoson, J. Rakotofanala, H. Rakotondratsimba, N. Rakotoniaina, A. Rahajasoa, J.-P. Rakotorahalahy, N. Razanadrakoto, C. Razanadrakoto, F. Ranaivomanana, and L. Rakotoarisoa, and for broader assistance we thank the rural communities of Tsinjoarivo. We thank K. Samonds, B. Semel, and P. Garber for useful comments, the editors of this volume for the invitation to participate, and two anonymous reviewers for useful critiques.

References

Akers, A. A., Islam, M. A., and Nijman, V. 2013. Habitat characterization of western hoolock gibbons *Hoolock hoolock* by examining home range microhabitat use. *Primates* **54**: 341–348.

Bergman, C. M., Fryxell, J. M., Gates, C. C., and Fortin, D. 2001. Ungulate foraging strategies: energy maximizing or time minimizing? *Journal of Animal Ecology* **70:** 289–300.

Börger, L., Franconi, N., Ferretti, F., et al. 2006. An integrated approach to identify spatiotemporal and individual-level determinants of animal home range size. *American Naturalist* **168:** 471–485.

Boyle, S. A., Lourenco, W. C., da Silva, L. R., and Smith, A. T. 2009. Travel and spatial patterns change when *Chiropotes satanas chiropotes* inhabit forest fragments. *International Journal of Primatology* **30:** 515–531.

Burt, W. H. 1943. Territoriality and home range concepts as applied to mammals. *Journal of Mammalogy* **24:** 346–352.

Carbone, C., Cowlishaw, G., Isaac, N. J. B., and Rowcliffe, J. M. 2005. How far do animals go? Determinants of day range in mammals. *American Naturalist* **165:** 290–297.

Chapman, C. A. and Chapman, L. J. 2000. Determinants of group size in primates: the importance of travel costs. Pages 24–42 in *On the Move: How and Why Animals Travel in Groups*. S. Boinski and P. A. Garber (Eds.). University of Chicago Press, Chicago, IL.

Clissold, F. J., Sanson, G. D., Read, J., and Simpson, S. J. 2009. Gross vs. net income: how plant toughness affects performance of an insect herbivore. *Ecology* **90:** 3393–3405.

Fieberg, J. and Börger, L. 2012. Could you please phrase "home range" as a question? *Journal of Mammalogy* **93:** 890–902.

Foerster, S., Zhong, Y., Pintea, L., et al. 2017. Feeding habitat quality and behavioral trade-offs in chimpanzees: a case for species distribution models. *Behavioral Ecology* **27:** 1004–1016.

Fretwell, S. D. 1972. *Populations in a Seasonal Environment.* Princeton University Press, Princeton, NJ.

Ganzhorn, J. U. 1995. Low-level forest disturbance effects on primary production, leaf chemistry, and lemur populations. *Ecology* **76:** 2084–2096.

Hanya, G. and Bernard, H. 2016. Seasonally consistent small home range and long ranging distance in *Presbytis rubicunda* in Danum Valley, Borneo. *International Journal of Primatology* **37:** 390–404.

Harcourt, A. 1998. Ecological indicators of risk for primates, as judged by species' susceptibility to logging. Pages 56–79 in *Behavioral Ecology and Conservation Biology*. T. Caro (Ed.). Oxford University Press, Oxford.

Harper, G. J., Steininger, M. K., Tucker, C. J., Juhn, D., and Hawkins, F. 2007. Fifty years of deforestation and forest fragmentation in Madagascar. *Environmental Conservation* **34:** 325–333.

Harrison, M. E., Morrogh-Bernard, H. C., and Chivers, D. J. 2010. Orangutan energetics and the influence of fruit availability in the nonmasting peat-swamp forest of Sabangau, Indonesian Borneo. *International Journal of Primatology* **31:** 585–607.

Hixon, M. A. 1982. Energy maximizers and time minimizers: theory and reality. *American Naturalist* **119:** 596–599.

Hooge, P. N. and Eichenlaub, B. 1997. Animal Movement Extension to ArcView. 2.0 ed. Anchorage, AK: Alaska Science Center – Biological Science Office, US Geological Survey.

Irwin, M. T. 2006a. Ecological impacts of forest fragmentation on diademed sifakas (*Propithecus diadema*) at Tsinjoarivo, eastern Madagascar: implications for conservation in fragmented landscapes. PhD Thesis, Stony Brook University.

Irwin, M. T. 2006b. Ecologically enigmatic lemurs: The sifakas of the eastern forests (*Propithecus candidus, P. diadema, P. edwardsi, P. perrieri,* and *P. tattersalli*). Pages 305–326 in *Lemurs: Ecology and Adaptation*. L. Gould and M. L. Sauther (Ed.). Springer, New York.

Irwin, M. T. 2008a. Diademed sifaka (*Propithecus diadema*) ranging and habitat use in continuous and fragmented forest: higher density but lower viability in fragments? *Biotropica* **40:** 231–240.

Irwin, M. T. 2008b. Feeding ecology of diademed sifakas (*Propithecus diadema*) in forest fragments and continuous forest. *International Journal of Primatology* **29:** 95–115.

Irwin, M. T., Raharison, J.-L., and Wright, P. C. 2009. Spatial and temporal variability in predation on rainforest primates: do forest fragmentation and predation act synergistically? *Animal Conservation* **12:** 220–230.

Irwin, M. T., Junge, R. E., Raharison, J. L., and Samonds, K. E. 2010. Variation in physiological health of diademed sifakas across intact and fragmented forest at Tsinjoarivo, eastern Madagascar. *American Journal of Primatology* **72:** 1013–1025.

Irwin, M. T., Raharison, J.-L., Raubenheimer, D., Chapman, C. A., and Rothman, J. M. 2014. Nutritional correlates of the "lean season": effects of seasonality and frugivory on the nutritional ecology of diademed sifakas. *American Journal of Physical Anthropology* **153:** 78–91.

Irwin, M. T., Raharison, J.-L., Raubenheimer, D. R., Chapman, C. A., and Rothman, J. M. 2015. The nutritional geometry of resource scarcity: effects of lean seasons and habitat disturbance on nutrient intakes and balancing in wild sifakas. *PLoS ONE* **10:** e0128046.

Irwin, M. T., Samonds, K. E., Raharison, J.-L., et al. 2019. Morphometric signals of population decline in diademed sifakas occupying degraded rainforest habitat in Madagascar. *Scientific Reports* **9:** 8776. DOI:10.1038/s41598-019-45426-2.

Johns, A. D. and Skorupa, J. P. 1987. Responses of rain-forest primates to habitat disturbance: a review. *International Journal of Primatology* **8:** 157–191.

Kapos, V., Wandelli, E., Camargo, J. L. and Ganade, G. 1997. Edge-related changes in environment and plant responses due to forest fragmentation in central Amazonia. Pages 33–44 in *Tropical Forest Remnants: Ecology, Management, and Conservation of Fragmented Communities*. W. F. Laurance and R. O. Bierregaard Jr. (Eds.). University of Chicago Press, Chicago, IL.

Kelt, D. A. and Van Vuren, D. H. 2001. The ecology and macroecology of mammalian home range area. *American Naturalist* **157:** 637–645.

Laurance, W. F., Camargo, J. L. C., Luizao, R. C. C., et al. 2011. The fate of Amazonian forest fragments: a 32-year investigation. *Biological Conservation* **144:** 56–67.

Lowen, C. and Dunbar, R. I. M. 1994. Territory size and defendability in primates. *Behavioral Ecology and Sociobiology* **35:** 347–354.

Marsh, K. J., Wallis, I. R., Andrew, R. L., and Foley, W. J. 2006. The detoxification limitation hypothesis: where did it come from and where is it going? *Journal of Chemical Ecology* **32:** 1247–1266.

Marshall, A. J., Boyko, C. M., Feilen, K. L., Boyko, R. H., and Leighton, M. 2009. Defining fallback foods and assessing their importance in primate ecology and evolution. *American Journal of Physical Anthropology* **140:** 603–614.

Marzluff, J. M., Millspaugh, J. J., Hurvitz, P., and Handcock, M. S. 2004. Relating resources to a probabilistic measure of space use: forest fragments and Steller's Jays. *Ecology* **85:** 1411–1427.

Milich, K. M., Stumpf, R. M., Chambers, J. M., and Chapman, C. A. 2014. Female red colobus monkeys maintain their densities through flexible feeding strategies in logged forests in Kibale National Park, Uganda. *American Journal of Physical Anthropology* **154:** 52–60.

Mitani, J. C. and Rodman, P. S. 1979. Territoriality: the relation of ranging pattern and home range size to defendability, with an analysis of territoriality among primate species. *Behavioral Ecology and Sociobiology* **5:** 241–251.

Ostfeld, R. S. 1994. The fence effect reconsidered. *Oikos* **70**: 340–348.

Palminteri, S. and Peres, C. A. 2012. Habitat selection and use of space by bald-faced sakis (*Pithecia irrorata*) in Southwestern Amazonia: lessons from a multiyear, multigroup study. *International Journal of Primatology* **33**: 401–417.

Palminteri, S., Powell, G. V. N., and Peres, C. A. 2016. Determinants of spatial behavior of a tropical forest seed predator: the roles of optimal foraging, dietary diversification, and home range defense. *American Journal of Primatology* **78**: 523–533.

Peres, C. A. 2000. Territorial defense and the ecology of group movements in small-bodied neotropical primates. Pages 100–123 in *On the Move: How and Why Animals Travel in Groups*. S. Boinski and P. A. Garber (Eds.). University of Chicago Press, Chicago, IL.

Potts, K. B., Baken, E., Levang, A., and Watts, D. P. 2016. Ecological factors influencing habitat use by chimpanzees at Ngogo, Kibale National Park, Uganda. *American Journal of Primatology* **78**: 432–440.

Powzyk, J. A. 1997. The socio-ecology of two sympatric indriids: *Propithecus diadema diadema* and *Indri indri*, a comparison of feeding strategies and their possible repercussions on species-specific behaviors. PhD Thesis, Duke University.

Ries, L., Fletcher, Jr., R. J., Battin, J., and Sisk, T. D. 2004. Ecological responses to habitat edges: mechanisms, models, and variability explained. *Annual Review of Ecology, Evolution and Systematics* **35**: 491–522.

Rode, E. J., Stengel, C. J., and Nekaris, K. A.-I. 2013. Habitat assessment and species niche modeling. Pages 79–102 in *Primate Ecology and Conservation: A Handbook of Techniques*. E. J. Sterling, N. Bynum, and M. E. Blair (Eds.). Oxford University Press, Oxford.

Ross, C. and Reeve, N. 2011. Survey and census methods: population distribution and density. Pages 111–131 in *Field and Laboratory Methods in Primatology: A Practical Guide*. J. M. Setchell and D. J. Curtis (Eds.). Cambridge University Press, Cambridge.

Santhosh, K., Kumara, H. N., Velankar, A. D., and Sinha, A. 2015. Ranging behavior and resource use by lion-tailed macaques (*Macaca silenus*) in selectively logged forests. *International Journal of Primatology* **36**: 288–310.

Schatz, G. E. 2001. *Generic Tree Flora of Madagascar*. Surrey: Cromwell Press.

Schoener, T. W. 1971. Theory of feeding strategies. *Annual Review of Ecology and Systematics* **2**: 369–404.

Shaffer, C. A. 2013a. Ecological correlates of ranging behavior in bearded sakis (*Chiropotes sagulatus*) in a continuous forest in Guyana. *International Journal of Primatology* **34**: 515–532.

Shaffer, C. A. 2013b. GIS analysis of patch use and group cohesiveness of bearded sakis (*Chiropotes sagulatus*) in the upper Essequibo Conservation Concession, Guyana. *American Journal of Physical Anthropology* **150**: 235–246.

Singh, M., Cheyne, S. M., and Ehlers Smith, D. A. 2018. How conspecific primates use their habitats: surviving in an anthropogenically-disturbed forest in Central Kalimantan, Indonesia. *Ecological Indicators* **87**: 167–177.

Steudel, K. 2000. The physiology and energetics of movement: effects on individuals and groups. Pages 9–23 in *On the Move: How and Why Animals Travel in Groups*. S. Boinski and P. A. Garber (Eds.). University of Chicago Press, Chicago, IL.

Struhsaker, T. 1981. Census methods for estimating densities. Pages 36–80 in *Techniques for the Study of Primate Population Ecology*. National Research Council (Ed.). National Academy Press, Washington, DC.

Teichroeb, J. A. and Sicotte, P. 2009. Test of the ecological-constraints model on ursine colobus monkeys (*Colobus vellerosus*) in Ghana. *American Journal of Primatology* **71**: 49–59.

Turk, D. 1995. A guide to trees of Ranomafana National Park and Central Eastern Madagascar. Unpublished manuscript.

Turton, S. M. and Freiburger, H. J. 1997. Edge and aspect effects on the microclimate of a small tropical forest remnant on the Atherton Tableland, Northeastern Australia. Pages 45–54 in *Tropical Forest Remnants: Ecology, Management, and Conservation of Fragmented Communities*. W. F. Laurance and R. O. Bierregaard Jr. (Eds.). University of Chicago Press, Chicago, IL.

van Horne, B. 1983. Density as a misleading indicator of habitat quality. *Journal of Wildlife Management* **47:** 893–901.

Worton, B. J. 1989. Kernel methods for estimating the utilization distribution in home-range studies. *Ecology* **70:** 164–168.

Wright, P. C., Johnson, S. E., Irwin, M. T., et al. 2008. The crisis of the critically endangered greater bamboo lemur (*Prolemur simus*). *Primate Conservation* **23:** 5–17.

Xiang, Z. F., Huo, S., and Xiao, W. 2011. Habitat selection of black-and-white snub-nosed monkeys (*Rhinopithecus bieti*) in Tibet: implications for species conservation. *American Journal of Primatology* **73:** 347–355.

Zeng, Y., Xu, J., Wang, Y., and Zhou, C. 2013. Habitat association and conservation implications of endangered Francois' langur (*Trachypithecus francoisi*). *PLoS ONE* **8:** e75661.

10 Determining the Presence of Habitual Travel Route Networks in Orangutans (*Pongo pygmaeus morio*) in Kutai National Park, Borneo

Adam O. Bebko

Introduction

Recent field research has shown that some wild primates possess detailed knowledge of the location and quality of many resources in their home ranges (Janson & Byrne 2007). Understanding how nonhuman primates (hereafter primates) store, organize, and use such information is important for understanding the evolution of human spatial cognition. Knowledge of primate spatial cognition can also inform conservation initiatives for threatened populations by improving protected habitat such that primates are encouraged to travel through desired areas and discouraged from traveling near human development, thereby reducing primate–human conflict.

Many frugivorous primates also inhabit large home ranges and eat at thousands of feeding sites (Di Fiore & Suarez 2007; Janmaat et al. 2006; Knott et al. 2008; Normand & Boesch 2009). A large home range coupled with dispersed, patchy, and relatively unpredictable food resources means that frugivorous primates may have to travel relatively long distances to find food resources. The benefits of efficient travel between dispersed and resource patches may have presented a significant pressure to evolve sophisticated cognitive abilities for spatial processing in primates (Galdikas & Vasey 1992; Milton 1981; Normand & Boesch 2009).

Many captive and wild primates have been found to acquire and store complex spatial information about the location and distance between food resources (Janson & Byrne 2007; Schwartz & Evans 2001). Remembering the location of a large number of resource sites and how to navigate between them could require large amounts of information to be encoded in memory. How primates encode and organize this large quantity of spatial information has been debated heavily and there is currently no consensus on how they do so (Di Fiore & Suarez 2007; Gallistel & Cramer 1996; Poucet 1993).

One hypothesis is that primates navigate using spatial information stored in a Euclidean-based (sometimes referred to as geometric) representation. This type of representation stores spatial information in a coordinate system, including storing relative angles and distances between features (Di Fiore & Suarez 2007; Normand &

Boesch 2009; Poucet 1993). Such Euclidian representations would require remembering all locations individually and the distance, direction, and angles between them.

Primates may also navigate using route-based spatial information. Under this hypothesis, individuals would remember a network of commonly used routes that connect different sites in their territory (Porter & Garber 2012; Poucet 1993). This form of representation may equate to a lower memory burden than a Euclidean representation, because complex geometric relationships need not be memorized between every site. Instead, individuals using route-based navigation would only store basic information about what lies along the routes, locations where the routes intersect each other, and a way (e.g., landmarks) to recognize and follow the routes during travel (Di Fiore & Suarez 2007).

Studying the travel patterns of primates can provide insight into how they store and organize spatial information. Depending on the form of spatial representation that individuals adopt, their travel may result in movement patterns that can provide evidence for or against existing hypotheses regarding spatial cognition. Although it is difficult to assess cognitive processes and mechanisms in field research (Janson & Byrne 2007), these cognitive models can nevertheless provide frameworks within which field studies can be based. However, findings supporting one type of spatial representation in one context may not exclude the possibility that other representations are used in different contexts. Recently, some researchers have postulated that individuals may use a combination of representations at different times for broad- or fine-scale navigation (Dolins et al. 2014). For these reasons, there remains much debate on how primates store and organize spatial information.

Few studies have reported evidence consistent with navigation using a Euclidean representation in primates (but see Dolins 2009; Normand & Boesch 2009). Conversely, there is growing evidence that supports route-based navigation from field studies in several primate species. Some primate species have been observed to travel along networks of repeatedly used, long-term travel routes (habitual routes), and these networks can sometimes be shared by multiple groups and/or individuals (Di Fiore & Suarez 2007; Hopkins 2010; MacKinnon 1974; Noser & Byrne 2010; Porter & Garber 2012).

A habitual route network consists of a set of travel routes that have been reused. These habitual routes connect at "nodes," locations where the routes intersect. In species where the home ranges of several individuals overlap, multiple individuals could share these routes. In some species, habitual routes were found to follow broad topographical features, to connect important resources at nodes, and to be used over long time periods by several individuals (Di Fiore & Suarez 2007; Hopkins 2010; Porter & Garber 2012).

It is important to note that although the presence of habitual route networks supports the hypothesis of an underlying cognitive route-based representation, alternate hypotheses are not ruled out. For example, the presence of habitual routes can sometimes be explained by very basic mechanisms, as observed in honeybees (Cruse & Wehner 2011). Similarly, habitual routes in primates could arise from simple short-distance movement decisions (e.g., moving from one large tree to the next nearest large tree), or by ecological or topographical constraints (arrangement of natural features such as rivers, cliffs, etc.).

Constrained travel could increase the likelihood of travel routes being reused, and therefore could increase the likelihood of habitual routes forming regardless of how individuals represent spatial information. Constrained travel has been found to contribute to repeatedly used travel routes in some non-primate species, including bison and lynx (Bruggeman et al. 2007; Squires et al. 2013). In primates, Di Fiore and Suarez (2007) observed a woolly monkey group expand their range in response to the demise of two neighboring groups. This colonizing group used many of the same habitual routes as the area's previous inhabitants. The fact that the new group's network remained consistent and connected the same resources as the previous groups' networks suggests that ecological and topographical factors may play at least some role in the establishment of habitual route networks.

For arboreal species, the effects of constrained travel might be especially pronounced since navigation through the canopy must be made along branches strong enough to support the individual's weight and must sufficiently overlap with neighboring trees to allow travel across gaps (Hopkins 2010; Thorpe & Crompton 2009). Because of these requirements, the absolute number of possible arboreal paths between resources is likely highly constrained (Lührs et al. 2009). Based on the observation that several different, solitary orangutans used identical supports along arboreal paths, Thorpe and Crompton (2009) suggested that individuals may select travel routes based on known pathways with sufficient arboreal supports available. For these reasons, the additional constraints imposed by arboreal travel may further increase the likelihood of habitual routes forming.

There are some weaknesses in the methodology currently used for detecting habitual route networks. Typically, habitual route networks are identified from examining primate travel routes recorded using GPS devices. However, researchers often do not account for GPS error, which can sometimes be high in densely forested or uneven terrain typical of primate habitat. GPS location data are typically affected by both short-term stochastic error and longer-term systematic errors, which cause GPS location fixes to be slightly different from the genuine locations.

Environmental effects (e.g., atmospheric noise) or the measurement resolution of the equipment can cause stochastic errors. In most cases, these errors are truly random – they are equally likely to be in any direction. The majority of such errors are relatively small ($<$5–20 m on most professional equipment). Such errors cause waypoints taken at a fixed location to scatter about the true location in an approximately two-dimensional normal distribution. As the number of waypoints taken at a location increases, the center of the distribution will approach the true location. Rarely, GPS receivers can momentarily produce very large errors where single waypoints are very far from the actual location ($>$40 m), but these are usually easily flagged as impossibly fast movement and can be deleted. Stochastic errors are worsened by humidity, making GPS accuracy lower in rainy or cloudy conditions.

GPS receivers rely on very accurate time data transmitted from satellites to triangulate a location. However, before being received by the GPS device, signals can reflect off nearby surfaces (called "multipathing"). Compared to open areas, multipathing is more likely to occur near large, dense objects (e.g., vehicles, buildings, cliffs, mountains), large tree trunks, or under dense forest canopy. The slight time delay from reflections causes error in location fixes. Multipathing introduces systematic bias in recorded locations that can last for longer time periods, affecting many waypoints. Such bias can shift an entire GPS track by several meters in one direction. Systematic errors are difficult to notice and correct, since the resulting route appears normal.

As a consequence of error, routes recorded with GPS are noisier, longer, and can be slightly offset compared to the primates' actual travel routes. Therefore, GPS records may incorrectly meander back and forth and backtrack when travel was straight. Similarly, when actual travel meanders or double-backs within distances smaller than the GPS error, these short segments cannot be distinguished from error. For these reasons, field studies of primate travel patterns in fine-scale space must account for GPS error at risk of overestimating travel distance and misidentifying locations.

Another weakness of current methodology for detecting habitual route networks is its reliance on subjective criteria. Early studies described habitual travel routes anecdotally (Galdikas & Vasey 1992; MacKinnon 1974; Milton 1981), and more recent studies with more rigorous methodology detected overlapping travel routes visually on a map (e.g., Di Fiore & Suarez 2007; Noser & Byrne 2010; Porter & Garber 2012). Researchers relied on their own judgment and intuition to decide whether a cluster represents a reused route versus parallel routes close together. However, detecting overlaps by eye is problematic since GPS error could make travel routes appear more clustered or dispersed than in actuality, and it is difficult to assess what designates a cluster (Figure 10.1).

Finally, current methodology has also relied on arbitrary thresholds to determine which overlapping route clusters were deemed habitual routes. Researchers selected arbitrary values for the length and width of such overlapping clusters based on their personal experience with the species, making identification of actual habitual routes subjective. Framing the length and width of routes in reference to values derived from the study population and the measurement equipment would allow for more accurate identification.

There is a need to address these concerns in detecting habitual route networks. Accounting for GPS error would increase confidence in results and reduce false-positives, and reducing the subjectivity of criteria for detection would allow for more meaningful interpretations of the habitual networks that are found. Below, I describe new analyses that reduce these methodological issues.

Current Study

The aim of the study described in this chapter was to build on Di Fiore and Suarez's (2007) method of mapping habitual and shared route networks. I suggest that a better approach would utilize a computer algorithm to detect travel route overlaps and derive cutoff thresholds from movement data of the population being studied and the GPS error of the equipment being used. I describe this new method, called error-overlay, and provide an example application using 21 months of travel data from wild orangutans

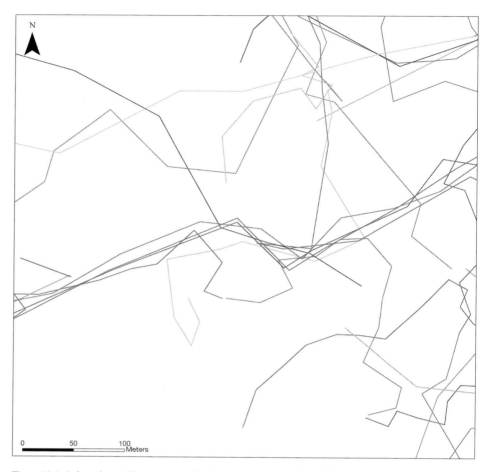

Figure 10.1 A location with many overlapping travel routes. It is difficult to differentiate true overlapping travel routes from those caused by GPS error. (A black and white version of this figure will appear in some formats. For the color version, please refer to the plate section.)

(*Pongo pygmaeus morio*) in Kutai National Park (KNP), East Kalimantan, Borneo, Indonesia.

Among primates, orangutans are among the largest in body size and highly arboreal (Thorpe & Crompton 2009). Little research has been conducted on habitual routes in orangutans, but incidental reports suggest that orangutans may repeatedly use arboreal pathways between resource clusters, and that these pathways are shared by many individuals (Galdikas & Vasey 1992; MacKinnon 1974; Thorpe & Crompton 2009), although this hypothesis has not yet been tested empirically. Orangutans are primarily arboreal, and their large size may limit possible connections between trees, thereby increasing the likelihood that habitual routes will form. Therefore, I predicted that orangutans would use a habitual route network in the study area. Furthermore, orangutans are also semi-solitary (MacKinnon 1974), and therefore are an ideal species to study factors influencing an individual's, rather than a group's, decision to travel along habitual routes since travel decisions are less influenced by conspecifics than in group-living species. Moreover, orangutan home ranges are often highly overlapping (Singleton et al. 2009), so multiple individuals may share the same habitual routes. Examining habitual routes that are reused by multiple individuals at different times may provide further information about factors affecting the formation of habitual routes for a particular population.

Methods

Study Area

The study area is located in KNP, East Kalimantan, Borneo, Indonesia (Figure 10.2) along approximately 8 km of the south bank of the Sangatta River. The study area is divided by a 200 m grid transect system covering approximately 4–5 km^2. Forest in this area has not been seriously commercially logged (Leighton 1993), although there is evidence of small-scale illegal logging and hunting in the recent past (pers. obs.). Borneo-wide forest fires in 1982–1983 and in 1997–1998 heavily damaged the majority of KNP (Setiawan et al. 2009), although small patches of primary forest remain. Burned forest has been regenerating, and the area now consists of a mix of primary and secondary lowland riverine and hill forest. The original forest was a mixture of riverine and upland mixed dipterocarp forest, which experienced masting (Leighton 1993; Morrogh-Bernard et al. 2009).

Subjects and Sampling

As of this study, myself and the site's research staff have observed more than 30 orangutans within the study area, of which 18 have been observed repeatedly, identified, and named. Of the named independent individuals, there are 6 independent females (4 mothers with dependent offspring, and 2 adolescents), and 12 independent males (4 flanged adults, 3 unflanged adults, 5 adolescents).

We found orangutans by surveying the transect system on foot. Once found, we observed the orangutans' behavior during full-day focal individual follows using a continuous event sampling procedure. When possible, observations began at the focal orangutan's overnight nest before it arose in the morning, and continued until it rested in its night nest and ceased activity. We observed individuals up to a maximum of 10 days in a row to limit extended human impact on their activities. When we lost the focal orangutan, we made an effort to relocate it; if successful, we resumed observations and recorded the lost observation time.

Data Collection

For ranging data, we created GPS waypoints every 15 minutes as close as possible to the trunk of the tree occupied by an orangutan using Garmin 60csx and 60cs handheld

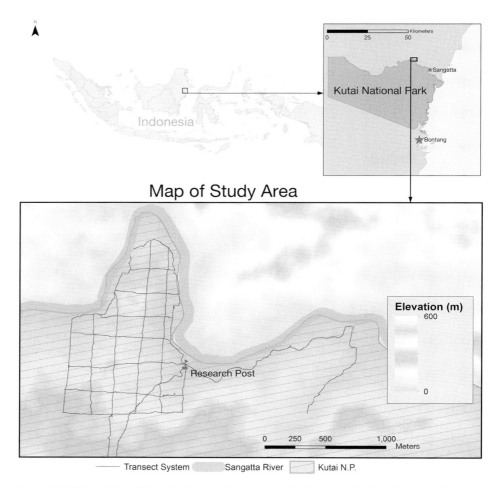

Map of Study Area

Figure 10.2 Kutai National Park in Borneo, Indonesia, with study area indicated. Indonesia Administrative Areas map © GADM 2009. Kutai NP Boundaries Map © Kutai NP Office, used with permission. (A black and white version of this figure will appear in some formats. For the color version, please refer to the plate section.)

units. For each waypoint we described the orangutan's current location and behavior. We recorded orangutan activity (feeding, resting, traveling, other), height in the trees, mode of locomotion, foods eaten (plant/animal species and parts), social partners, if any, and detailed notes on their interactions.

To estimate GPS error, we collected waypoints every 15 minutes from stationary locations for three-hour sessions. We did this 20 times over three months (February, March, July 2011) on 12 different days when normal research duties were being conducted. These sessions occurred at different times of the day during daylight (06:00–18:00). Half of the sessions were collected at the research post in a clearing (two small wooden buildings nearby). The other half were split between two locations with heavy forest cover, one of which was ~30 m from the research post, and the other of which was ~60 m away, next to a stream. The surrounding area had some hills nearby (see elevation in Figure 10.2) but was free of cliffs and large buildings; therefore, any multipathing was likely caused primarily by vegetation.

Measures

Travel Routes

For each day, all GPS waypoints were connected to yield a sequence of travel segments. I defined full-day travel routes as travel routes for which observation spanned the entire day's active period – from the time an orangutan arose from its night nest in the morning to its evening nest site (after daily activity ceased). I defined partial travel routes as any travel routes that did not span the entire day's active period. I constructed multi-day travel routes by combining full-day travel routes when I observed an individual uninterrupted over consecutive days. Multi-day routes avoid the problem of falsely concluding that the ends of travel routes are reused, as is always the case where a travel route begins in the same location it ended at the day before (i.e., a nest).

Daily Travel Distance

I defined the daily travel distance as the distance an orangutan traveled during a full-day travel route, and measured it by summing the length of all travel segments between waypoints, after GPS records were cleaned of noise.

Orangutan Resources

I defined an orangutan resource as any plant (tree, liana, or ground vegetation) of a species that orangutans had been observed to use within the study area (up to the time that this study was conducted). Food resources were any plant species that orangutans were observed to ingest. Nest resources were trees of species in which orangutan nests were found, or in which orangutans were directly observed to build nests.

Habitual Route Network

I defined a habitual route network as a collection of reused route segments (habitual route segments) that interconnected. Locations where these routes intersected were termed nodes. I considered a habitual route shared if it was composed of travel routes from two or more individuals.

   I defined a habitual route segment as the linear area where travel routes overlapped for a length of at least 25 percent of the average daily travel distance of individuals in the local population. I defined nodes as locations where travel routes overlapped at a single location. Overlaps could be from the same individual at different times, or from different individuals. Overlaps, by definition, are areas where two or more travel routes overlapped; however, to ensure the analysis was more conservative, I increased these criteria to three or more segments overlapping for habitual route segments, and five or more overlaps at a location for nodes (ad hoc). I detected these overlapping travel route areas by creating a computer algorithm programmed in Python for ArcGIS 10.0 (described below).

To investigate whether some routes and nodes were more important than others, I further classified both routes and nodes as either "major" or "minor" based on the following ad hoc criteria for number of overlaps: Minor routes had three or four overlaps and minor nodes had five or six overlaps, whereas major routes had more than four overlaps and major nodes had more than six overlaps.

Analyses

Unless otherwise stated, all analyses were completed using ArcGIS 10.x or in Python scripts created as extensions for ArcGIS.

Many of the scripts/analyses described herein are written and packaged to be run directly within the interface of ESRI ArcGIS as Python toolbox plugins. These toolboxes can be obtained by contacting the author.

Estimation of GPS Error

To estimate error, I used waypoints from the three-hour stationary data collection sessions. In many instances, the first waypoints recorded were extremely inaccurate because the GPS signal had not yet been completely acquired. First and second waypoints >40 m away from the centroid of the cluster were deleted. I drew one-standard deviation error ellipses around all remaining waypoints separately for each session (Ministry of Environment BC 2001). I converted the ellipses into estimated 95 percent error circles, which represent the area in which 95 percent of waypoints are expected to fall for each session (Department of Natural Resources WA 2004). I then calculated the mean radius of the 95 percent circles to achieve an overall estimate of the GPS error.

Noise Cleaning of GPS Data

Errors in GPS point data make recorded travel routes "noisy," where recorded points can be slightly offset from the locations they represent. This necessitates "noise cleaning" the data to smooth the travel routes to make them more realistic and to better represent actual travel routes. I created an algorithm that builds on previous methods to remove noise from GPS point data, called the cluster method. The algorithm completes the following steps:

1. A threshold difference was determined from the estimated error of the GPS device.
2. Starting from the first waypoint, any subsequent waypoints within this threshold distance were tagged. Instead of deleting these tagged waypoints, they were added to a "cluster set" including the first tagged waypoint.
3. Once a waypoint was found outside the boundary, all the waypoints in the "cluster set" were used to determine the centroid of this cluster. This centroid waypoint replaced all of its parent waypoints in the noise-cleaned line.
4. The test then started again at the waypoint after the cluster, and continued for every waypoint in the travel route.

Previous studies typically relied on deleting waypoints within a set threshold distance (determined arbitrarily) of previous waypoints (Asensio et al. 2011; Noser & Byrne 2010). In those studies, the deletion was carried out as follows:

1. A threshold difference was determined by selecting a distance the researcher believed to be meaningful for a particular species' travel.
2. Starting from the first waypoint, if the next waypoint was within the threshold distance, it was deleted. If the point after was also within the threshold distance of the first point, it too was deleted, and so on.
3. When a waypoint was found that was not within the threshold distance from the first point, the test started again with this waypoint until all points were scanned.

Although the deletion approach yielded highly simplified routes, it suffered from several problems. First, deletion tended to prioritize the retention of outlying waypoints while deleting more central waypoints (meaning points with the largest error were prioritized over points with the lower error). Also, the deleted waypoints did not influence the final position of retained waypoints in any way; meaning useful data were removed from the final dataset. Finally, in those studies, the threshold distance was often defined arbitrarily, usually based on the researchers' experience with the species under study.

Our cluster method addressed these problems and improved on previous methods (Figure 10.3) because: (1) central points influenced the final dataset more than outlying points, meaning points with lower error were prioritized over points with high error; (2) all recorded points influenced the location of the final dataset, meaning no useful data were lost; and (3) defining the threshold distance based on the estimated GPS error rather than an arbitrary value yielded a more credible outcome because it collapses points that are likely to be indistinguishable from error together into their centroid, thereby "averaging out" the error, while keeping points that are likely to represent separate locations distinct.

Consequently, our cluster method enabled drawing a buffer around the resulting travel route that represented the area where the actual travel route likely resided (i.e., 95 percent confidence that the actual travel route lies within the buffer around the cleaned recorded route). Such error-based buffers provided a useful new method of analyzing the configuration of travel routes that would have hitherto been impossible.

Habitual Route Network

To determine the presence of habitual travel routes, I developed a new method based on computer analysis of travel routes, building on Di Fiore and Suarez's (2007) work. Using ArcGIS 10.0, the method involved noise-cleaning all recorded travel routes to account for GPS error, and then analyzing overlapping areas to determine the presence of habitual routes. For this reason, it was called the error-overlay method.

As described in the previous section, each noise-cleaned GPS travel route was a linear estimation (track) of the individual's actual travel route. To account for the GPS error, a buffer (polygon) was drawn around a track to represent the area of uncertainty

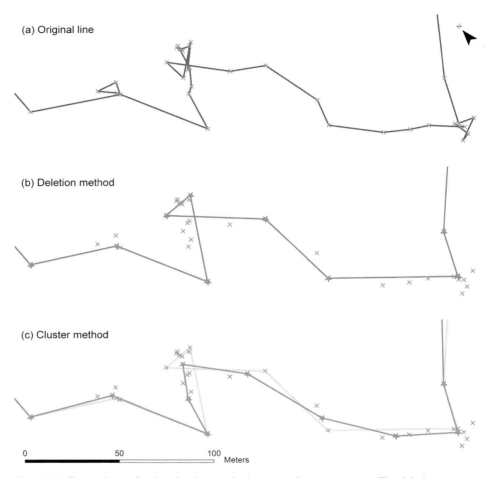

Figure 10.3 Comparison of noise-cleaning methods on travel route segment. The deletion method (b) removed noise from the original (a), but bias toward outlying points misrepresents the travel route, whereas the cluster method (c) improves the estimated travel route. Both methods used a 20 m threshold distance.

around each track wherein the actual travel route lies to some degree of certainty. Many mapping programs (including ArcGIS) have simple built-in functions that can create buffer polygons defined by applying a user-specified distance perpendicular to both sides of the track. However, travel routes can double-back and self-intersect repeatedly, which presents a problem when applying these built-in buffer functions to habitual routes, because they do not recognize self-overlaps. These self-overlaps are important when assessing habitual routes, because they represent areas that are reused. Therefore, I created a custom buffer function that can detect self-overlaps (Figure 10.4). Since two points define a line, our custom buffer function detected self-overlaps occurring at least three waypoints apart, thereby addressing the need to identify areas that are reused within a single travel route.

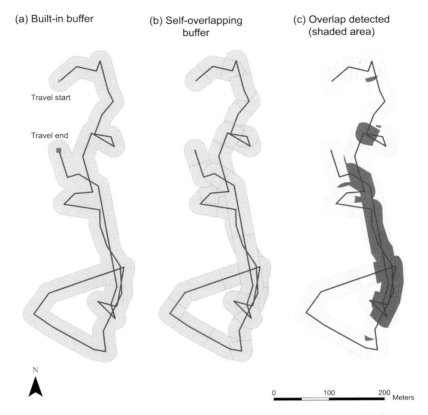

(a) Built-in buffer

(b) Self-overlapping buffer

(c) Overlap detected (shaded area)

Travel start

Travel end

N

0   100   200 Meters

Figure 10.4 Comparison of buffer methods applied to a noise-cleaned multi-day orangutan travel route using 20 m buffers. Built-in buffers create a uniform polygon that cannot detect self-overlaps (a). A custom buffer can overlap itself (b). After analysis, the custom buffer function displays overlaps (c).

After the creation of custom buffers for every travel route, they were arranged on the same map. Overlapping (and self-overlapping) buffers represented places where individuals passed through the same area. The result was an isoline map similar to weather forecasts, where areas were colored based on number of times they were visited. This map displays a visual representation of potential habitual routes within a study area and allows for additional analyses. To create the map, the following algorithm was used:

1.   Self-intersecting buffers were merged to form a set of all buffer polygons.
2.   A union function was applied to the result.
3.   At each overlap (including self-overlaps), the union function created new polygons, an identical polygon for each buffer that overlaps in that area. These identical polygons were stacked at the exact same location with the exact same properties.
4.   The surface area of every polygon in the map was calculated to the maximum number of significant figures possible as a unique identification, which was

shared by identical polygons yet different between non-identical polygons (those that were not created and stacked from the union function).

5. A dissolve function collapsed identical polygons into single output polygons by selecting only polygons with the same identification tag. The dissolve function recorded a count of the number of polygons collapsed into each output polygon, which represented the number of overlaps in that area.

The result is a map of polygons in which each polygon retains the number of overlaps that occurred within it. The map can then be colored and analyzed according to the number of overlapping travel routes in each area.

Applying the Error-Overlay Analysis to Examine Habitual Route Features

I examined the error-overlay map for features of habitual route networks: overlapping travel segments connected together (habitual routes), and nodes where these connected segments intersect each other.

To assess whether overlapping routes were likely habitual travel routes, I compared their length to the average daily travel (ADT) distance, the mean daily travel distance of all individuals in the study population. The ADT provided a reference point for the species and population being studied; travel distances that were proportionally larger relative to the ADT were more likely to represent important distances to individuals than short distances relative to the ADT. Consequently, short overlaps were more likely to represent paths crossing each other at an angle or GPS error, rather than habitual routes. For this reason, large overlaps relative to the ADT were more likely to represent actual habitual travel routes. The width of buffer overlap also informed the likelihood that the overlapping area was actually used as a habitual route. If the width of the overlap was near the width of the buffer (the two buffers appeared on top of one another), then the overlap was more likely to represent travel routes following the same path. Therefore, relatively narrow overlaps where the buffers were barely touching were less likely to represent habitual routes than wider overlaps that approach the buffer width.

Similarly, to identify nodes I used the shape of overlaps to detect locations where travel pathways intersect. Roughly circular areas along habitual routes where there were more overlaps than the habitual routes themselves were identified as nodes if the circular area had a width approximately equal to two times the buffer distance (Figure 10.5). I detected such nodes by placing semi-transparent circles (with radius equal to the buffer distance) on the map at possible node locations, such that the circle completely covered the area where overlaps occurred at a higher rate than the surrounding habitual routes. If a circle did not completely cover the area, or the area was smaller than the circle, this location was not considered a node.

I examined the configurations of detected habitual travel routes and nodes to identify likely habitual route networks. If highly overlapping habitual route segments were joined by nodes, I assumed that they likely represented a habitual-route network. If two or more individuals used these habitual routes, then the network was considered a shared habitual route network.

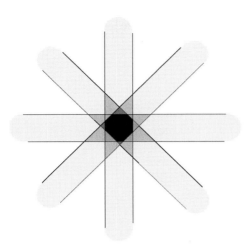

Figure 10.5 An example of a node (hypothetical data): as more buffers intersect, nodes appear roughly circular with a radius approximately equal to the buffer distance (dark shaded area).

Sensitivity of the Error-Overlay Method

When conducting the error-overlay method there is a need to balance the protocol's ability to correctly detect overlapping routes with erroneous detection of overlaps (false-positives). A relatively large buffer distance would detect more overlaps, but would also increase the likelihood of false-positives compared to a relatively small buffer distance, which would detect fewer true overlaps. Furthermore, relatively small buffers are less likely to encompass the correct location of the travel route than relatively large buffers, particularly with increasing GPS error. Therefore, setting the buffer distance to the estimated accuracy of the GPS devices provides a logical interpretation of the buffers, namely that the actual travel route lies somewhere within the buffer.

Results

I recorded a total of 224 daily travel routes from 18 identified and several unidentified orangutans that ranged within the study area between January 2010 and September 2011. Of these, I recorded a total of 113 full-day travel routes representing data from 15 individuals. I participated in ~18 days of observation during June to September 2011. Using only full-day noise-cleaned travel routes, ADT was 475 m (SD = 273 m, range = 0–1231 m).

The average radius of 95 percent GPS error circles was 20.34 m (SD = 9.97 m, range = 6.37–45.20 m) therefore I estimated the GPS error to be 20 m, instead of the error estimate reported by the devices themselves, which usually ranged somewhere between 5 m and 14 m (pers. obs., I did not record data).

The map of relative reuse of orangutan travel routes revealed potential habitual route segments (Figure 10.6). Segments were included in the route network if the length of the overlap was greater than 118 m (25 percent of the 475 m ADT). I detected 45 nodes

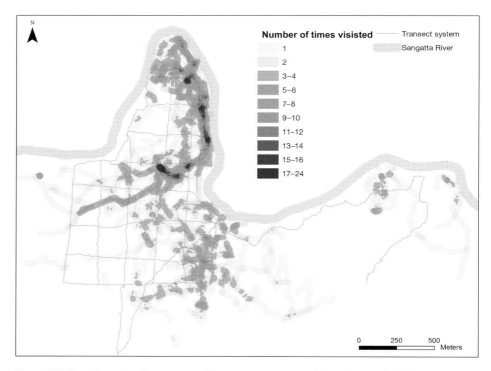

Figure 10.6 Travel routes of orangutans (*Pongo pygmaeus morio*) and areas of relative use as estimated by the error-overlay method, in KNP, Borneo. (A black and white version of this figure will appear in some formats. For the color version, please refer to the plate section.)

(of which 27 were major nodes), and over 8 km of habitual route segments. Habitual route segments often connected at node locations (Figure 10.7).

I found that orangutans repeatedly traveled along a primary corridor of linked major habitual routes and nodes spanning ~2 km. This network ran roughly parallel to the Sangatta River and then diverted west, heading inland and uphill along a ridge. Additionally, multiple individuals used almost every habitual route segment identified, indicating that the habitual route network was shared (Figure 10.8). The majority of orangutans in the study area used at least a portion of the main travel corridor.

I assessed node locations for the presence of orangutan resources. Of the 45 nodes, 43 (96 percent) were within 20 m of at least one orangutan resource (feeding or nesting). Nodes were primarily associated with feeding (38 of 45, 84 percent), and of the 7 nodes not associated with feeding, 5 (71 percent) were associated with at least one orangutan nest.

Furthermore, 27 of the 45 detected nodes (19 major, 8 minor) were situated in areas with previously collected supplemental data on tree size. Very large resource trees, with diameter at breast height (DBH) ≥ 100 cm, are rare in the study area (unpublished data from 38 transects along or near orangutan travel routes), yet 10 of the 27 nodes (37 percent) were associated with at least one of these very large trees. In addition, 22 (81 percent) were within 20 m of at least one large resource tree (DBH ≥ 50 cm). This trend was stronger for major nodes, with 18 of 19 (95 percent) within 20 m of large resource trees.

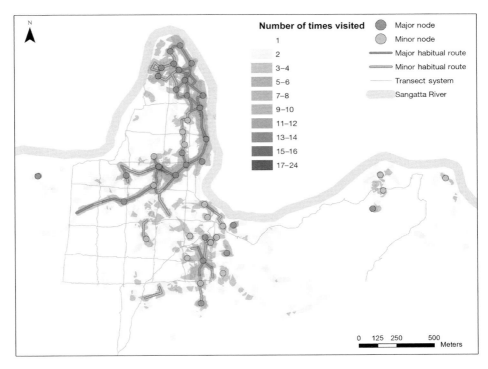

Figure 10.7 The estimated habitual route network of orangutans (*Pongo pygmaeus morio*) in KNP, Borneo, Indonesia, displayed on the map of the corresponding error-overlay. (A black and white version of this figure will appear in some formats. For the color version, please refer to the plate section.)

Discussion

Overall, the algorithm detected a network of habitual travel routes, connected at nodes, and shared by multiple orangutans within the study area. This network was reused over the length of the study period (at least 21 months). The network, identified by an objective computer-driven algorithm and GIS-smoothing process, is consistent with earlier visual reports of "arboreal highways" used by orangutans (Galdikas & Vasey 1992; MacKinnon 1974). The algorithm extended Di Fiore and Suarez's (2007) approach for detecting habitual travel networks by reducing reliance on subjective identification of reused travel routes. I also reduced reliance on arbitrary cutoff values by basing the threshold distance for clustering GPS points on the estimated GPS error and by framing route lengths relative to the average daily travel distance of the study population. Based on these methodological improvements, I have increased confidence that the habitual routes identified here represent true overlaps among orangutan travel routes.

   Despite methodological improvements to detecting reused travel routes, deciding which reused routes and nodes to include in the final habitual route network remains somewhat subjective. Statistically determining areas that are more reused than others

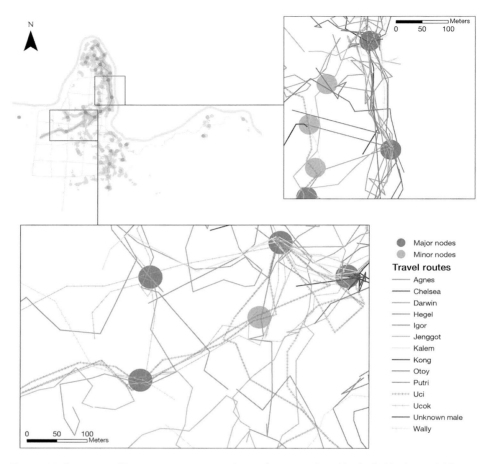

Figure 10.8 Orangutan (*Pongo pygmaeus morio*) travel routes colored by individual, overlaid on nodes of the habitual route network in KNP, Borneo, Indonesia. Multiple individuals used the majority of the habitual routes detected. (A black and white version of this figure will appear in some formats. For the color version, please refer to the plate section.)

nearby, or comparing the detected habitual route network to computer simulations of orangutan versus random movements, could further reduce subjectivity. Currently, the map that results from the algorithm lacks the information to differentiate which habitual routes were shared by more individuals than others, and which routes were reused multiple times by the same individuals. Due to issues with the spatial analysis functions used in the algorithm, to obtain such information one must go back to the original travel routes and identify which individuals contributed to the route. Carrying this information forward to the final map could be useful to analyze why certain routes are preferred over others for particular individuals. Examining individuals' travel preferences may be especially important when examining orangutans and other semi-solitary species whose travel decisions are less influenced by conspecifics compared to group-living species; despite their travel potentially being influenced by other individuals (i.e., avoiding or seeking others), they must make such decisions themselves rather than following the lead of other group members.

Consistent with studies on other primate species, nodes in the route network were predominantly associated with orangutan resources (Di Fiore & Suarez 2007; Porter & Garber 2012). At most node locations, orangutans had eaten or built nests, and nearly all nodes occurred at locations associated with large orangutan resource trees. This was particularly true for major nodes where many routes intersected.

Despite the areas of highly overlapping travel routes, individuals frequently traveled away from detected habitual routes to locations where I had no evidence of other orangutans traveling. This suggests individuals primarily traveled along habitual routes yet also traveled to locations off the main habitual route network. Such off-network travel contrasts with the almost exclusive travel along route networks found in spider and woolly monkeys (Di Fiore & Suarez 2007), and could indicate that orangutans use habitual route networks more flexibly. However, I have insufficient data to assess whether off-network travel was actually along a hitherto undetected habitual route, or along a separate route.

Due to the study site being newly established, travel data from individuals were often separated by months, and some individuals were observed very infrequently. Despite these problems, all observed travel routes were included due to the relatively low quantity of data available. The results of this study are also limited in that data collection spanned only 21 months, so changes in travel patterns or resource availability over longer time periods were not assessed (i.e., masting events). As observations continue at this study site, more data will undoubtedly lead to the detection of more habitual routes in the network, although the overall patterns observed to date will likely remain.

Additionally, the orangutans in the study area were not fully habituated and their movements to evade human observers could have influenced the findings presented here. An attempt to flee could cause individuals to substantially alter their ranging patterns, including travel direction, distance traveled, or choice of travel areas. Subjectively, I observed orangutans fleeing toward open areas with low or no canopy, near steep inclines, where thick lianas or bamboo patches created nearly impenetrable conditions. The orangutans then dropped to the ground and into the brush, where our research team was unable to follow (pers. obs.). In other instances, such as during feeding or resting, orangutans stayed high in trees or stopped traveling and hid to avoid human observers (pers. obs.). Also, data collected at the beginning of the study period (especially in January and February 2010) may be less reliable due to the observers being less experienced. For this reason, caution should be used when generalizing these results to other, more established field sites and other species.

Furthermore, results could be biased due to the unequal distribution of survey effort; observers searched some areas more often than others. Consequently, the habitual routes presented here are predominately clustered in areas were surveys were concentrated. On the other hand, I targeted searches in areas that orangutans tended to visit often, so the concentrated searches may be a relatively accurate reflection of where orangutans tended to travel. However, this could introduce a bias against detecting off-network travel.

Conclusions

In this chapter, I have illustrated what may be considered to be an improved approach to identify and quantify habitual travel networks of primates. Despite the challenges involved in observing partially habituated primates, the error-overlay method was successful in detecting a habitual route network shared by several orangutans that connects important forage and nesting resources. Using the error-overlay method, future studies can examine how other metrics of travel are related to habitual route networks. Such metrics include locations along the habitual route network where travel decisions might be made (Byrne et al. 2009; Porter & Garber 2012) and locations where individuals feed or rest for long periods of time to determine possible travel targets (Bates & Byrne 2009; Galdikas 1988).

Although not possible to evaluate directly, evidence presented here supports the possibility that orangutans may use some form of route-based navigation when traveling in this region. Future studies could further examine such route-based navigation by studying how the use of habitual route networks changes over time. Such temporal changes could inform whether primates can plan travel routes in advance along habitual route networks (Janson & Byrne 2007) and/or use route networks to monitor the availability of temporally sensitive resources (such as ripe fruit) as suggested by Di Fiore and Suarez (2007). Future studies could strengthen the evidence for cognitive processes by including comprehensive ecological data within the study area, including areas where individuals do not tend to travel. For example, Normand and Boesch (2009) conducted ground-based surveys of a large number of trees in their study area, allowing direct quantitative comparisons between areas where individuals travel and areas where they do not. The map derived from the error-overlay method is well suited for combination with such analyses within GIS applications, because the environmental data layers can be queried to compare locations along habitual route networks to locations where individuals infrequently travel.

Knowledge of primate travel patterns could be used by conservation initiatives to improve habitat management. A better understanding of factors that foster the formation of habitual routes could improve habitat corridors connecting fragmented populations by promoting travel along them. Similarly, buffer zones of poor habitat surrounding protected habitat could discourage forays into human settlement, reducing potentially dangerous conflict with humans. Knowledge of key habitual travel routes in threatened primate populations could also be used as a tool to fight development (e.g., logging concessions) by emphasizing the importance of protecting areas essential for their travel. Overall, the findings presented here illustrate the utility of an improved approach to identify and quantify habitual travel networks of primates.

Acknowledgments

I would like to thank Dr. Anne E. Russon for contributing her data and expertise in developing this methodology, and for permission to conduct research at the Orangutans

Kutai Research Project. I would like to thank our research team in Borneo: Agnes Ferisa, Purwo Kuncoro, and the field assistants Pardi, Amat, Yunus, Daman, and Arbain. Research was done with permission and support from Kutai National Park Head Office and the Indonesian Ministry of Research and Technology (RISTEK). This research was funded by grants and donations from: Natural Sciences and Engineering Research Council of Canada (NSERC), L.S.B. Leakey Foundation, and Borneo Orangutan Society Canada.

References

Asensio, N., Brockelman, W. Y., Malaivijitnond, S., and Reichard, U. H. 2011. Gibbon travel paths are goal oriented. *Animal Cognition* **14**(3): 395–405.

Bates, L. A., and Byrne, R. W. 2009. Sex differences in the movement patterns of free-ranging chimpanzees (*Pan troglodytes schweinfurthii*): foraging and border checking. *Behavioral Ecology and Sociobiology* **64**(2): 247–255.

Bruggeman, J. E., Garrott, R. A., White, P. J., Watson, F. G. R., and Wallen, R. 2007. Covariates affecting spatial variability in bison travel behavior in Yellowstone National Park. *Ecological Applications* **17**(5): 1411–1423.

Byrne, R. W., Noser, R., Bates, L. A., and Jupp, P. E. 2009. How did they get here from there? Detecting changes of direction in terrestrial ranging. *Animal Behaviour* **77**(3): 619–631.

Cruse, H., and Wehner, R. 2011. No need for a cognitive map: decentralized memory for insect navigation. *PLoS Computational Biology* **7**(3): e1002009.

Department of Natural Resources WA. 2004. *Standards and Guidelines for Land Surveying Using Global Positioning System Methods*. State Department of Natural Resources, Olympia, WA

Di Fiore, A., and Suarez, S. A. 2007. Route-based travel and shared routes in sympatric spider and woolly monkeys: cognitive and evolutionary implications. *Animal Cognition* **10**(3): 317–329.

Dolins, F. L. 2009. Captive cotton-top tamarins (*Saguinus oedipus oedipus*) use landmarks to localize hidden food items. *American Journal of Primatology* **71**: 316–323.

Dolins, F. L., Klimowicz, C., Kelley, J., and Menzel, C. R. 2014. Using virtual reality to investigate comparative spatial cognitive abilities in chimpanzees and humans. *American Journal of Primatology* **76**: 496–513.

Galdikas, B. M. F. 1988. Orangutan diet, range, and activity at Tanjung Puting, Central Borneo. *International Journal of Primatology* **9**(1): 1–35.

Galdikas, B. M. F. and Vasey, P. 1992. Why are orangutans so smart? Ecological and social hypotheses. Pages 183–224 in *Social Processes and Mental Abilities in Non-Human Primates*. F. D. Burton (Ed.). The Edwin Mellen Press, Lewiston, NY.

Gallistel, C. R. and Cramer, A. E. 1996. Computations on metric maps in mammals: getting oriented and choosing a multi-destination route. *Journal of Experimental Biology* **199**(1): 211–217.

Hopkins, M. E. 2010. Mantled howler (*Alouatta palliata*) arboreal pathway networks: relative impacts of resource availability and forest structure. *International Journal of Primatology* **32**(1): 238–258.

Janmaat, K. R. L., Byrne, R. W., and Zuberbühler, K. 2006. Evidence for a spatial memory of fruiting states of rainforest trees in wild mangabeys. *Animal Behaviour* **72**(4): 797–807.

Janson, C. H. and Byrne, R. 2007. What wild primates know about resources: opening up the black box. *Animal Cognition* **10**(3): 357–367.

Knott, C., Beaudrot, L., Snaith, T., et al. 2008. Female–female competition in Bornean orangutans. *International Journal of Primatology* **29**(4): 975–997.

Leighton, M. 1993. Modeling dietary selectivity by Bornean orangutans: evidence for integration of multiple criteria in fruit selection. *International Journal of Primatology* **14**(2): 257–313.

Lührs, M.-L., Dammhahn, M., Kappeler, P. M., and Fichtel, C. 2009. Spatial memory in the grey mouse lemur (*Microcebus murinus*). *Animal Cognition* **12**(4): 599–609.

MacKinnon, J. 1974. The behaviour and ecology of wild orangutans. *Animal Behaviour* **22**: 3–74.

Milton, K. 1981. Distribution patterns of tropical plant foods as an evolutionary stimulus to primate mental development. *American Anthropologist* **83**: 534–548.

Ministry of Environment BC. 2001. *British Columbia Standards, Specifications and Guidelines for Resource Surveys Using Global Positioning System (GPS) Technology.* Ministry of Environment, Lands and Parks, Victoria, BC.

Morrogh-Bernard, H., Husson, S. J., Knott, C. D., et al. 2009. Orangutan activity budgets and diet. Pages 119–134 in *Orangutans: Geographic Variation in Behavioural Ecology and Conservation.* S. A. Wich, S. S. Utami Atmoko, T. Mitra Setia, and C. P. van Schaik (Eds.). Oxford University Press, Oxford.

Normand, E. and Boesch, C. 2009. Sophisticated Euclidean maps in forest chimpanzees. *Animal Behaviour* **77**(5): 1195–1201.

Noser, R. and Byrne, R. W. 2010. How do wild baboons (*Papio ursinus*) plan their routes? Travel among multiple high-quality food sources with inter-group competition. *Animal Cognition* **13**(1): 145–155.

Porter, L. M. and Garber, P. A. 2012. Foraging and spatial memory in wild Weddell's saddleback tamarins (*Saguinus fuscicollis weddelli*) when moving between distant and out-of-sight goals. *International Journal of Primatology* **34**(1): 30–48.

Poucet, B. 1993. Spatial cognitive maps in animals: new hypotheses on their structure and neural mechanisms. *Psychological Review* **100**(2): 163–182.

Schwartz, B. L. and Evans, S. 2001. Episodic memory in primates. *American Journal of Primatology* **55**(2): 71–85.

Setiawan, A., Nugroho, T. S., and Pudyatmoko, S. 2009. A survey of Miller's grizzled surili, *Presbytis hosei canicrus*, in East Kalimantan, Indonesia. *Primate Conservation* **24**(1): 139–143.

Singleton, I., Knott, C. D., Morrogh-Bernard, H. C., Wich, S. A., and van Schaik, C. P. 2009. Ranging behavior of orangutan females and social organization. Pages 205–214 in *Orangutans: Geographic Variation in Behavioural Ecology and Conservation.* S. A. Wich, S. S. Utami Atmoko, T. Mitra Setia, and C. P. van Schaik (Eds.). Oxford University Press, Oxford.

Squires, J. R., DeCesare, N. J., Olson, L. E., et al. 2013. Combining resource selection and movement behavior to predict corridors for Canada lynx at their southern range periphery. *Biological Conservation* **157**: 187–195.

Thorpe, S. K. and Crompton, R. H. 2009. Orangutan positional behaviour. Pages 33–47 in *Orangutans: Geographic Variation in Behavioural Ecology and Conservation.* S. A. Wich, S. S. Utami Atmoko, T. Mitra Setia, and C. P. van Schaik (Eds.). Oxford University Press, Oxford.

11 Finding Fruit in a Tropical Rainforest

A Comparison of the Foraging Patterns of Two Distinct Fruit-Eating Primates Across Years

Leila M. Porter, Paul Garber, Christopher Boesch, and Karline R. L. Janmaat

Introduction

Tamarins and chimpanzees differ in many aspects of their behavior, biology, and evolutionary history; however, both primates are heavily dependent on a diet of ripe fruits during all months of the year (reviewed in Digby et al. 2011; Stumpf 2011). In addition, previous research on cognition in tamarins and chimpanzees indicates that individuals retain spatial information concerning the location of many feeding sites (e.g., Garber 2000; Janmaat et al. 2013a; Normand et al. 2009). Since primates show a high level of site fidelity (Janmaat et al. 2009) and commonly rely on sessile food sources that are revisited many times over a limited part of the year (such as termite nests and trees producing fruits, leaves, flowers, and/or exudates), one might expect foragers to reuse a limited set of travel routes, return to previously visited feeding sites, and search for new food patches in locations nearby current feeding sites.

In the case of arboreal primates, several species reuse travel routes for periods of months or years, with routes defined as the repeated or habitual movement across the same set of tree crowns in the same sequence or trajectory for a distance of at least 75 m (Di Fiore and Suarez 2007). For example, Di Fiore and Suarez (2007) suggest that spider monkeys (*Ateles belzebuth*) and woolly monkeys (*Lagothrix poeppigii*) disperse seeds along the same travel routes year after year, thereby increasing and perpetuating the density of preferred feeding trees along these routes. Similarly, in the Ituri rain forest of the Congo basin, human foragers consume the pulp of some fruits but discard their seeds: These fruit trees have significantly higher densities along trails than away from trails (Laden 1992). Travel routes, however, are not always foraging routes as animals may travel to the borders of their range to engage in territorial patrols, or reuse routes to move directly between distant feeding sites without stopping to eat along the way. Unfortunately, data on long-term patterns of traveling and foraging for most primate species are not available and, thus, it is unclear if the reuse of travel routes functions primarily for efficient movement to sleeping sites, to monitor range boundaries, to return to areas characterized by a high density of highly productive feeding sites, or some combination of all three.

Ecological factors affect animal ranging patterns in response to temporal changes in resource distribution and productivity. Fruits and floral nectar on individual trees diminish over the course of a few weeks to a few months (Milton 1980), fruiting and flowering seasons end, and although many rainforest trees produce fruits and flowers every year (Adamescu et al. 2018), others do not (Janmaat et al. 2016; Koenig et al. 2003). In addition, not all tree species produce fruit, flowers, or floral nectar at the same time (e.g., *Ficus* spp.), and not all trees produce with the same amplitude or frequency across years (Janmaat et al. 2016; Koenig et al. 2003). Similarly, exudate sites used by primates may vary considerably in their renewal rates and in the quantity of exudates they produce (Garber & Porter 2010). Foragers therefore may encounter changes in resource distribution and productivity on timescales of days, weeks, months, and years, and therefore frequently need to reassess the presence and abundance of resources on individual trees.

To counteract the challenges of finding seasonally available and irregularly produced foods, primates have evolved a variety of foraging patterns to increase encounter rates with productive food sources. For example, individuals in some groups forage in a dispersed fashion and communicate to each other about the location of fruiting trees (e.g., Kalan & Boesch 2015; Schel et al. 2013). This dispersed foraging strategy may increase the group's fruit detection field and increase individuals' food finding success (e.g., Janmaat & Chancellor 2010). Primates also may relocate feeding sites using egocentric and allocentric spatial information related to the location of landmarks and travel routes (e.g., Garber, in press; Janmaat et al. 2014). This may serve to increase foraging efficiency by associating spatial, temporal, and quantity information of trees with color cues, olfactory cues, and phenological patterns (e.g., Ban et al. 2014; Noser & Byrne 2015). Finally, primates may track different rates of food intake or feeding success to exploit species with varying phenological cycles, employing intuitive statistics to decide when and where to feed (e.g., Janmaat et al. 2016; Rakoczy et al. 2014; Tecwyn et al. 2017).

In this study, we compared patterns of foraging and ranging in two distantly related primate species that consume a wide variety of food types. In the case of the Weddell's saddleback tamarins, ripe fruits (49 percent), arthropods (26 percent), exudates (12 percent), and floral nectar (7 percent) account for most of the feeding time (Porter 2001). During a year-long study in northwestern Bolivia, Porter (2001) found that Weddell's saddleback tamarins ate from a total of 81 plant species (fruits, flowers, and exudates), which represented only a small fraction of the plant biodiversity present in the forest (2000 species of vascular plants are estimated to be present in the area: Alverson et al. 2000). In selecting feeding sites, tamarins commonly move between individual flowering and fruiting trees of the same species. Thus, the monkeys tend to focus their immediate foraging efforts on several individual trees of a small number of tree species (Garber 1989).

Western chimpanzees have a diet composed principally of ripe and unripe fruits, seeds, and nuts (85 percent), leaves and pith (14.0 percent), and arthropods (1.7 percent) (Goné Bi 2007). In the Taï forest, Côte d'Ivoire, chimpanzees feed on 150 species of fruit out of the estimated 1300 plant species present in the forest (Janmaat et al. 2016). Even during periods of fruit scarcity, adult females continue to spend 67 percent of their feeding time eating fruits (including nuts), and fruit is consumed daily (unpublished data, KJ). During periods of fruit scarcity, females are known to change travel directions to reach trees that produce fruits that are particularly rich in energy but are rare in their distribution in the forest (Ban et al. 2016; Janmaat et al. 2013a). To discover new fruiting sites, chimpanzees are reported to use two complementary strategies (Janmaat et al. 2013b). Chimpanzee exploitation of certain fruit trees appears to be guided by long-term memory of the location and crop size of these trees (Janmaat et al. 2013a). They also opportunistically inspect trees and are reported to take information on differences in fruiting synchrony into account in determining when to revisit these trees as they travel between targeted sites (Janmaat et al. 2013a, 2013b, 2014).

Adults of these species differ in body mass by more than two orders of magnitude, yet ripe fruits and insects represent major dietary components for each. In this chapter, we identify similarities and differences in the fruit foraging strategies of the two species to test four hypotheses.

H1. If, in general, tropical fruiting cycles vary across years, then we expect both tamarins and chimpanzees to select different fruit feeding sites across years.

H2a. If primates of smaller body mass and group size can satisfy their nutritional requirements by exploiting feeding sites characterized by high as well as low fruit production, whereas larger-bodied primates require feeding sites characterized by high fruit production, then feeding sites revisited by the tamarins are expected to exhibit greater variance in productivity (low, medium, or high) than sites visited by chimpanzees, which should consistently contain high food rewards.

H2b. If highly productive feeding sites are relatively rare and widely scattered across a forested landscape, then we expect chimpanzees to exhibit a stronger positive relationship between the area traveled throughout their home range and the number of productive feeding trees monitored compared to saddleback tamarins.

H3. If primate fruit foragers reuse travel routes principally to assess the availability of current feeding sites and monitor the availability of future feeding sites, then we expect to find a greater density of fruit feeding sites in proximity to travel routes compared to random areas of their home range. If, however, primates principally reuse travel routes to monitor the presence or locations of conspecifics or neighboring groups, then we do not expect to find a greater density of fruit feeding sites in proximity to commonly reused travel routes.

Methods

Tamarin Field Methods

LP and PAG studied a fully habituated group of five Weddell's saddleback tamarins (*Leontocebus weddelli*: for taxonomy see Rylands et al. 2016) during June and July 2009 and the same group (minus one individual who migrated) during June and July 2011 (Table 11.1), in a lowland forest in the Department of the Pando, northern Bolivia (Estación Biológica Tahuamanu – 11°23′ S, 69°06′ W). These months corresponded with the start of the dry season, which typically lasts from June through September (Porter 2001; Porter et al. 2007).

Table 11.1 Study periods and observation hours

Study subject	Year	Study period	Mean observation hours/day ± standard deviation	Number of days with observations	Number of days with no observations
Isha	2009	July 20 to August 16	10 ± 1.7	28	0
Isha	2010	June 21 to August 14	11.4 ± 6.4	52	3
Isha	2011	July 10 to August 30	11.9 ± 2.3	51	0
Julia	2009	June 11 to July 20	9.9 ± 1.3	29	11
Julia	2010	May 7 to June 27	10.9 ± 0.4	52	0
Tamarins	2009	June 5 to July 23	7.8 ± 0.8	29	21
Tamarins	2011	June 9 to July 9	7.9 ± 0.6	23	8

In 2009, we followed one marked focal animal per day and observed a different individual on subsequent days until we had followed all group members. We used focal point samples at two-minute intervals to record data. We observed each group member on seven individual days, except for one male, who was observed for six days. In general, tamarins at this site are active from 07:00 to 16:30. In 2011, we amended the sampling procedure as the animals had lost their identification collars, making focal animal sampling unreliable. Instead, we used group scans at five-minute intervals. In conducting group scans, we recorded the first behavior observed for all visible group members during the first minute of each sample period. On average, we collected data on three of the four tamarins per scan.

We used the following definitions to record feeding and foraging behavior in the study animals: feeding = the animal handled or ingested food; foraging = the animal moved slowly with frequent stops to examine or manipulate objects such as fruits, bark, and/or dried leaves. We marked trees in which the monkeys fed with flagging tape, and if the tree was used on two or more days we recorded its spatial location using a Garmin e-Trex HCx GPS and returned to revisited feeding sites 1–4 times to assess the plants' phenological cycles. We call these "revisited feeding sites." We chose to examine only revisited trees as any tree visited once could have been encountered by chance and not be part of a set of monitored feeding sites. In 2011, we set up a spatial memory field experiment consisting of three feeding platforms each provisioned with a single banana (Garber & Porter 2014); as a result, bananas were part of the group's diet in 2011 (Table 11.2).

Table 11.2 The percentage of different food types in the tamarins' diet based on feeding and foraging time

Year	Ripe fruits	Arthropods	Exudates	Nectar	Banana	Other
2009	60	22	11	6	0	1
2011	61	20	5	4	9	1

Based on an analysis of 14 readings taken at the same location on different days, we found the GPS unit to be accurate in the forest to 10.8 m for one stationary location. The GPS spatial locations were sufficiently accurate for us to relocate the tree, and as such, we did not systematically reject GPS locations based on their error reading. In 2009 we recorded the spatial location of the focal animal at 10-minute intervals, and in 2011 we recorded the spatial position of the study group at 10-minute intervals.

Chimpanzee Field Methods

KJ and Simone Ban observed two fully habituated adult chimpanzee females (*Pan troglodytes verus*; Isha and Julia) belonging to the south community in the old growth lowland rain forest of the Taï National Park, Côte d'Ivoire, West Africa (5°50′20″ N, 7°19′16″ W; Kouakou et al. 2011) in 2009, 2010, and 2011 (Table 11.1). We followed each target female from the point of waking until construction of an evening sleeping nest, and we noted her activity using continuous time sampling (Martin & Bateson 1993), focusing on foraging behaviors (for details, see Janmaat et al. 2013b). In general, chimpanzees at the site are active from 06:00 to 18:00. To document the focal animal's location, we used the track log function of a Garmin 60 CSx GPS and extracted the females' locations every 10 minutes. We identified and removed errors in the GPS data using a method described by Janmaat et al. (2013a; Chapter 6 in this volume). We estimated the accuracy under the forest canopy to be 4.8 m when the chimpanzees were traveling and 11.8 m when they were stationary (Janmaat et al. 2013a). We also marked the spatial position of all fruit trees. The chimpanzee observation periods correspond to the short dry season, which is generally a period of fruit scarcity (Polansky & Boesch 2013). We used the same definitions to record feeding and foraging behavior in the study animals as were used for the tamarins.

We identified fruit exploration behavior in chimpanzees in terms of visual inspection, defined as an upward movement of the study female's head combined with a fixed gaze in the direction of a tree crown (Janmaat et al. 2013b). Most of the recorded inspections occurred after the female came to a halt ($N = 1169$; 95 percent). For analyses we excluded inspections for which the direction was unclear or unlikely to be related to a search for food, such as inspections for which the gaze was not clearly directed at a single tree crown (e.g., distant inspections) or of trees belonging to species for which the fruit was eaten only on the ground. We also excluded inspections for other food or purposes than fruit, namely inspections for sleeping locations, which occurred after the females had emitted a nest grunt (Nishida et al. 2010), or during periods in which monkeys or other chimpanzees were present in the tree (e.g., during hunting). Lastly, we did not include inspections that were immediately followed by feeding on food that grew in the inspected tree. We marked trees that were inspected and/or fed in with paint and recorded their locations using a GPS unit to monitor revisits to these sites.

These research protocols adhered to the principles for the ethical treatment of primates at Northern Illinois University, the University of Illinois, and the Max Planck Institute for Evolutionary Anthropology.

GIS Analyses

We entered all GPS location points into ArcMap version 10.2.2 to map the daily paths of the tamarins and chimpanzees. We used the Minimum Bounding Geometry feature to determine the home range area for the study periods and to determine the area that the study animals covered on each day of the study. This method may overestimate the size of a primate's home range as it potentially includes areas visited rarely by an animal or group (see Boyle, Chapter 7); however, it was appropriate for the analyses as we were interested in daily area coverage and the exploration of new areas.

To investigate the stability of travel routes (length and location) over time, we examined the data for two components of travel: daily paths and route segments. "Daily paths" were defined as the cumulative set of sequential GPS points visited by the primates on a given day. We considered portions of the primates' daily paths that ran parallel to one another – not deviating more than 30 m at any one point – for a distance of $\geq$75 m, on $\geq$2 days to be a "route." A distance of 30 m was selected to account for the horizontal spread of a tamarin group (mean 6 m; as calculated from Lopez-Rebellon 2010), the potential width of travel paths (e.g., animals may consider an entire tree crown to be part of a route rather than a single branch of that tree), and the level of accuracy of the GPS units. To be consistent, we used the same criteria for the chimpanzees. If the tamarins or chimpanzees used the same path on more than two days, we chose the two days with the longest degree of overlap as the route. We chose the 75 m distance following Di Fiore and Suarez (2007) and Porter and Garber (2013) to facilitate interspecific and cross-study comparisons. Future research should examine the effects of changing these criteria on the number of routes identified; however, those analyses are beyond the scope of this chapter (see Bebko, Chapter 10).

To identify routes according to these criteria we added a 30 m wide buffer around each daily path length (creating a polygon with a width of 60 m) and determined where daily paths converged. We then measured the daily paths that overlapped and constructed a line between the two parallel paths to create a route if they ran parallel according to the criteria. We also examined route overlap between years using the same method. If routes from two different years ran parallel to one another for 75 m or more, and did not deviate by more than 30 m, we identified them as the same route used in both years. We also examined the degree of overlap between daily paths and routes by superimposing the daily paths (with their buffers) onto the routes (with their buffers) to identify areas of overlap within a given study period.

Other Analyses

To determine whether routes were positioned near feeding trees more than expected by chance, we compared the number of trees within 30 m of the primates' routes for each study animal/group and study period, and compared these with routes of the same length randomly placed in the home range. For these analyses we used only trees visited two or more times, to make the chimpanzee data directly comparable to the tamarin data. To generate the random routes, we took each of the actual routes, rotated it randomly (0–360°) and moved it to a randomly chosen location within the home range. If the new route did not fit within the home range, we chose a new rotation, until we found a route that was positioned within the home range. We then counted the number of revisited trees located within 30 m of mid-points of the actual routes and of the randomly positioned routes. We compared the mean number of trees along an actual route to the mean trees along random routes for each study year for the tamarins and each of the chimpanzees; as the data were not normally distributed we used the Wilcoxon Signed Rank Test in SPSS v. 24.

We also examined feeding bout lengths in all revisited trees by calculating the number of minutes the foraging party or a solitary chimpanzee or tamarin spent feeding in each revisited fruit tree. A foraging party was defined as two or more animals feeding simultaneously in the same tree. We used the product of "minutes feeding * number of co-feeders" as a proxy measure of food availability in that tree as we assumed that increased time spent feeding was positively related to food consumption.

For the chimpanzees and the tamarins in 2011, the actual feeding party size was known. For the tamarins in 2009, we multiplied the focal animal's foraging minutes by 2.07 (the mean foraging party size of the tamarins in 2011). We grouped data from individual trees belonging to the same species to calculate the mean number of foraging party minutes, the standard deviation, and coefficient of variation for each tree species. We compared the coefficients of variation for each tree species used by the tamarins and each individual chimpanzee using the Mann–Whitney U test in SPSS v. 24.

For analyses of fruit monitoring and fruit exploration, we examined feeding trees visited on two or more occasions for the tamarins, whereas for the chimpanzees we included all feeding trees as sample sizes were too small for analyses if the sample was restricted only to revisited trees. Using this approach, the results are more conservative for the tamarins. At the Taï forest, the mean visibility of trees was 28.1 m for human observers standing on the forest floor ($N = 2150$ trees, range: 5.0–62.1 m; Janmaat et al. 2013a, 2013b). Therefore, we expect chimpanzees to be able to see fruits from 30 m away, as the chimpanzees travel terrestrially most of the time (97 percent of travel bouts occur on the ground: Janmaat et al. 2013a, 2013b), and have a visual acuity similar to humans (reviewed in Janmaat et al. 2013a, 2013b). Therefore, if the primates passed within 30 m of a tree that became a feeding site during a subsequent week, we considered the primate(s) to have "monitored" that site. For consistency, we used the same criterion for the tamarins.

We used only observations from weeks 1–3 to identify monitored trees, as the minimum study period was four weeks (Isha in 2009), and we wanted comparable data for all study periods and animals/groups. We identified a tree as "monitored" if the tree had not been fed in during the current or previous observation week(s), but was fed on in a future observation week. For the tamarins, a tree was only included in the analyses if it was fed on at least two times in a future week. As we only collected phenology data after a tree was fed in, we do not know if the tree was fruiting in the days/weeks before it was fed in. We chose to divide the data by calendar week (rather than by day) to assess resource exploration for two reasons: first, during the initial days of each study period we did not know which trees the primates had already fed in; and second, for the tamarins, we did not have continuous data for each study period (e.g., data were only collected six days per week for the tamarins). Thus, by grouping the data into weeks we hoped to determine more accurately the period during which the primates first used a feeding site that previously had been monitored.

We also investigated how much of its home range each primate traveled through daily by measuring the area of each daily path with its 30 m buffer (described earlier). In addition, during each study period, we investigated whether each group/animal had "expedition days" – days in which the animal/group explored an unusually large area of their home range. To do this, we calculated the minimum convex polygon (MCP) formed from the study subject(s) spatial locations for an entire observation day and compared it to the MCP formed for the year (see above). We opted for this method since the MCP should be larger when primates move using a meandering or circle-shaped travel path that returns to a familiar area, as compared to when they move directly between different feeding trees. Larger MCPs are more likely to indicate explorative behavior than smaller MCPs. We standardized these areas by subtracting the mean daily area used by the tamarin group or the individual chimpanzee from each daily area and divided it by the respective standard deviation of the daily areas visited. An expedition day was defined as a day in which the daily area traversed was more than the standard deviation of all daily areas.

To investigate the effect of the primates' motivation to monitor trees on the probability that animals would embark on an "expedition," we designed a generalized linear mixed model (GLMM) with binomial error structure and logit link function (Baayen 2008) in R (v3.1.3) using the function glmer (R package lme4; Bates et al. 2015). As for our other analyses, we identified a tree as "monitored" if the tree had not been fed in during the current or previous observation week(s) but was fed on in a future observation week. We predicted that searching behavior for new trees would result in primates covering unusually large areas of their home range. To test the interactive effect of the predictor variables (number of monitored trees per meter and primate species) on the probability of going on an expedition (expedition day versus not an expedition day), we first compared the full model with a null model containing all components of the full model without the interaction using likelihood ratio tests (R function "anova"; Dobson & Barnett 2008). We determined the significance of the interaction by comparing the model with the interaction with a model without the interaction but including the main effects, using a likelihood ratio test (R function "drop1"; Barr et al. 2013). To calculate the 95 percent confidence interval of the interactive effect we used a parametric bootstrap simulation based on a custom-written function (R. Mundry, unpublished data). We included one random effect with three levels (individual [for chimpanzees] or group [for tamarins]) to avoid pseudo replication. Having only three levels in a random effect is not ideal, since the mean and the variance of the random effect is more reliably calculated with a larger number of levels. In addition, a low number of levels can lead to stability issues. We opted for this approach instead of running separate models per level to minimize multiple testing issues and to enable us to investigate the interactive effect between primate species and the number of monitored trees, which otherwise would not have been possible. To keep the type I error rate at the nominal level of 5 percent (Barr et al. 2013), we also included the random slope component for the number of monitored trees within individual chimpanzees or the tamarin group, to account for possible individual differences in the effects of this predictor on the response. To fix the model we transformed the number of monitored trees to the third root, to achieve a roughly symmetrical distribution of this variable and z-transformed it to a mean of 0 and standard deviation of 1. Model stability was determined by evaluating model estimates obtained after dropping levels of the random effect one at a time. After completing this procedure, the model was stable, such that the effect of the predictor variables on the probability a primate would go on an expedition was similar irrespective of whether we removed levels of the random effect (e.g., chimpanzee identity). We confirmed the validity of the model results by conducting additional post-hoc Mann–Whitney U tests per level as well as a general linear model (GLM) with the random effect included as a fixed effect.

As the generalized linear regression model was not appropriate for analyzing the visual inspection behavior of the chimpanzees, which had only two levels of random effects, we used the Mann–Whitney U exact test in R (version 2.12.2) using the package "exact-RankTests" (Hothorn & Hornik 2013). This was done to compare the number of fruit trees visually inspected by the chimpanzees on excursion days versus non-excursion days.

Results

Stability in Diet and Reuse of Feeding Trees

In 2009 and 2011, the tamarins' diet was composed primarily of ripe fruit (60–61 percent; Table 11.2). On average, the tamarins fed in 6.1 fruit trees per day (Table 11.3) and 30–61 percent of all trees were revisited at least once during each study period. In contrast, only 7 of the 50 revisited fruit trees (14 percent) used in 2009 were also visited in 2011.

Table 11.3 Fruit tree use by chimpanzees and tamarins

Year	Study subject	Number of days	Number of tree species	Total number of individual trees visited	Number of trees revisited	Mean number of trees revisited/day
2009	Isha	28	29	168	25	0.5
2010	Isha	52	40	362	98	1.9
2011	Isha	51	33	336	96	1.9
2009	Julia	29	18	119	27	0.8
2010	Julia	55	29	226	52	1.0
2009	Tamarins	29	57	82	50	1.7
2011	Tamarins	23	22	109[a]	33[a]	1.4

[a] Includes three artificial feeding platforms.

Table 11.4 The percentage of different food types in the chimpanzee females' diets based on feeding and foraging time

Year	Study subject	Ripe fruits	Unripe fruits	Nuts and seeds	Leaves	Stem and pith	Arthropods	Monkey	Other
2009	Isha	60	2	1	21	14	0	2	1
2010	Isha	68	0	0	17	11	1	1	1
2011	Isha	69	0	1	17	13	0	1	0
2009	Julia	66	0	4	21	7	1	1	1
2010	Julia	64	0	3	17	10	0	4	0

The chimpanzee females' diets also comprised primarily ripe fruit (60–69 percent; Table 11.4). On average, the chimpanzees fed in 8.2 fruit trees per day (Table 11.3) and 15–29 percent of all trees were revisited during each study period. If we restrict the examination to revisited trees, Isha revisited only 13 of these trees across two years and no tree was revisited in all three years. In the case of Julia, only one fruit tree was revisited in each of two study years.

We used the mean number of foraging party minutes per tree species as an estimate of the variance of tree productivity. We found that the mean foraging party bout length (number of feeding minutes × number of foraging party members) across all tree species revisited by the tamarins was 19.8 minutes, with a mean coefficient of variation of 0.52 (range 0–1.42), and for the chimpanzees it was 116 ± 100.4 minutes, with a mean coefficient of variation of 0.89 (range 0–1.85). Tamarins co-fed with 0–4 other animals (mean 2.07), whereas chimpanzees co-fed with 0–19 other animals (mean 3.63). The tamarins exploited trees characterized by a lower variation of food reward than either chimpanzee (tamarins versus Isha: $U = 230$, $p < 0.01$, $n = 57$; tamarins versus Julia: $U = 103$, $p < 0.01$, $n = 48$).

Stability in Daily Path Lengths and Home Range Size

Tamarin daily path lengths were similar across study periods (Table 11.5). In addition, their home range in 2011 was entirely contained within the 2009 home range boundary (Figure 11.1c). Daily path lengths were also similar across study periods for the chimpanzees (Table 11.5). The overlap of Isha's home ranges between years was high: The 2010 range overlapped with the 2009 range by 79 percent; the 2011 range overlapped with the 2010 range by 93 percent; and the 2011 range overlapped with the 2009 range by 95 percent (Figure 11.1f). Home range overlap for Julia between years was lower: the 2010 home range overlapped with the 2009 home range by 43 percent. Julia was in a maximum swelling phase for a large part of the observation period in 2010, and this may have contributed to her increased ranging behavior and lower level of range overlap. The home ranges of Isha and Julia also overlapped with each other, even though we followed them during different fruiting periods (Table 11.1). The overlap of Julia and Isha's home ranges was 80 percent in 2010 and 72 percent in 2009.

Table 11.5 Daily path lengths, home range sizes, routes, and route use

Study animal/group	Year	Mean daily path length (m) ± SD, sample size[a] in parentheses	Home range (ha)	Mean percentage of home range covered per day	Number of routes	Route lengths range (m)	Mean route length ± SD	Percentage overlap of daily paths with routes (range)	Mean percentage overlap of daily paths with routes	Mean number of trees along routes	Z values[b] comparing number of revisited feeding trees on routes versus random routes
Isha	2009	3048 ± 1218 (28)	1988	0.9 ± 0.4	31	76–419	168 ± 84	0–44	17 ± 15	0.5 ± 0.8	−3.066
Isha	2010	2896 ± 1286 (50)	2162	0.8 ± 0.4	94	75–714	200 ± 123	0–68	31 ± 17	0.9 ± 0.4	−5.173
Isha	2011	2989 ± 954 (50)	1707	1.0 ± 0.3	149	76–656	200 ± 102	0–90	45 ± 23	1.4 ± 1.1	−11.750
Julia	2009	2833 ± 1389 (25)	1581	1.0 ± 0.6	29	79–528	203 ± 115	0–29	4 ± 6	0.5 ± 0.7	−2.807
Julia	2010	3327 ± 1365 (50)	2665	0.7 ± 0.3	70	77–715	208 ± 122	0–59	20 ± 13	1.0 ± 1.4	−4.564
Tamarins	2009	1718 ± 333 (15)	35.5	25 ± 13	31	81–444	155 ± 84	13–92	71 ± 19	15.9 ± 12.0	−2.791
Tamarins	2011	1821 ± 274 (15)	28.8	37 ± 12	26	78–241	146 ± 43	28–61	48 ± 10	7.6 ± 4.2	−2.079

[a] Daily path lengths only measured from full-day follows.
[b] Calculated from Wilcoxon sign rank test, n = (# of routes), $p < 0.05$ for all comparisons.

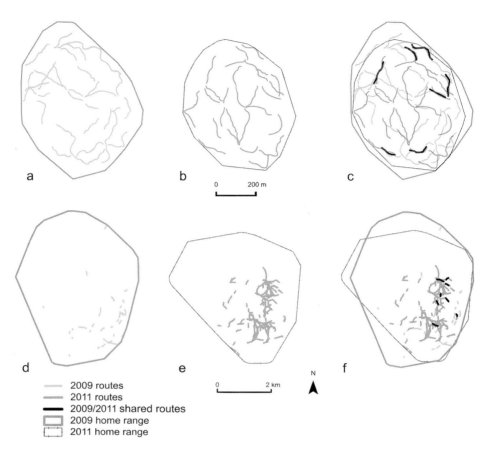

Figure 11.1 Home ranges and route segments for tamarins (top) and chimpanzees (bottom) in 2009 (a, d), 2011 (b, e), and route segment overlap between years (c, f).

Routes and Daily Range Cover

In 2009, the tamarins used 31 routes, and in 2011 they used 26 routes (Figure 11.1a,b; Table 11.5). Between 13 and 92 percent of the tamarins' daily paths were located on these routes (Table 11.5). However, only 14 percent of these routes (n = 8: 78–152 m; mean = 106 ± 22 m) were used during both years by the tamarin study group. Across both study periods, the tamarins covered a mean of 31 ± 14 percent of their home range each day (Table 11.5). For the chimpanzees we identified 31–146 routes per animal per study period, with 0–59 percent of their daily paths located on these routes (Table 11.5). For Julia, there was no route overlap across years. Isha did not reuse any routes from 2009 in 2010, she reused two routes from 2009 in 2011, and she reused seven routes from 2010 in 2011 (range 87–269 m). Female chimpanzees traversed a mean of only 0.9 ± 0.4 percent of their total range per day. In all study periods and for all study groups/animals, the mean number of actual revisited trees, located near the actual travel routes taken was greater than the number of actual revisited trees located near the

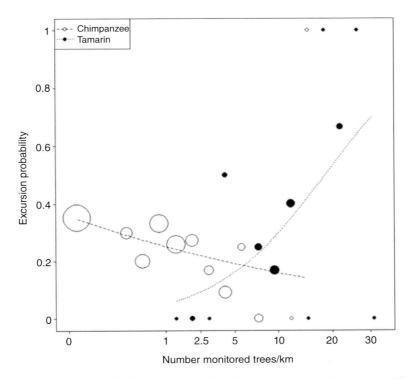

Figure 11.2 The relation between monitoring frequencies and expedition probability in two female chimpanzees (open circles) and one tamarin group (closed circles). The *y*-axis represents the probability that an expedition day occurred, and the *x*-axis represents the number of trees that were monitored per kilometer of travel. The area of the circles represents the sample size per combination of binned predictor and response. The dashed and dotted lines illustrate the expedition probability predicted by the model for chimpanzees and tamarins, respectively.

randomly positioned routes (Table 11.5). There were more revisited feeding trees located near tamarin routes than chimpanzee routes (Table 11.5).

Are Expedition Days Associated with Fruit Monitoring?

The variance in the standardized daily MCP area covered was substantially larger for chimpanzees than for tamarins, despite both species having similar absolute daily travel distances, as well as similar variation in those distances (Figure 11.2). On "expedition days," daily MCP area traversed was more than the standard deviation of all daily MCP; for chimpanzees this was more than 131 ha, while for the tamarins it was more than 13 ha. We found a significant difference between the full model that predicted the probability that the primates went on an expedition day, which contained the interaction of "primate species" and "the number of monitored trees," and the null model which contained only the respective random effect (group/individual) and its respective slopes ($\chi^2 = 5.12$, df $= 1$, $p = 0.0238$, $N_{obs} = 190$, $N_{ind/group} = 3$). The model results indicated

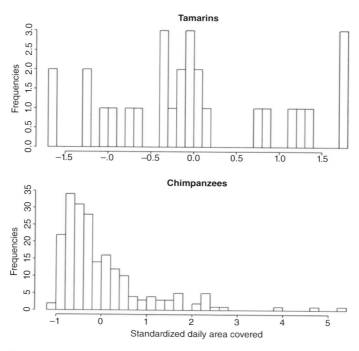

Figure 11.3 Frequency distribution of the standardized new daily area covered by the tamarins and the chimpanzee females.

that the primates monitored a larger number of trees per distance traveled on expedition days in which area coverage was high, but only for tamarins and not for chimpanzees (interactive effect: estimate = 1.76, SE = 0.82, 95 percent CI_{min} = –0.43, 95 percent CI_{max} = 8.07; Figure 11.3, interactive effect of GLM: estimate = 1.68, SE = 0.80, p = 0.036). An additional Mann–Whitney U test indicated that the tamarins monitored a larger number of trees on expedition days (mean = 15.30 ± 7.79, median = 13.15 trees/ km) compared to other days (mean = 9.96 trees ± 7.24, median = 9.74 trees/km, Mann– Whitney U test: U = 50, p = 0.062). However, for the chimpanzees, both females monitored a smaller number of trees per distance traveled on the days in which area coverage was high (Isha's expedition days: mean = 1.65 ± 2.96, median = 0.74 trees/ km; Isha's other days: mean = 1.89 ± 2.44, median = 0.98 trees/km; Julia's expedition days: mean = 0.59 ± 0.98, median = 0 trees/km compared to other days: mean = 0.97 ± 1.23, median = 0.64 trees/km; Mann–Whitney U tests: Julia: U = 354, p = 0.092; but Isha: U = 780, p = 0.637).

For chimpanzees, we also had the opportunity to compare fruit monitoring behavior through behavioral recordings of tree inspections. When we compared the number of visual inspections per distance traveled between expedition days and non-expedition days, we found no indication that chimpanzees inspected more trees on expedition days. We found that the number of trees inspected per distance traveled did not differ between days with high area coverage (1.89 trees/km^2 ± 0.90, median = 1.65) compared to other days (2.01 trees/km^2 ± 1.58, median = 1.64; U = 2277, $N_{>1}$ = 27, $N_{<1}$ = 176, p = 0.7303).

Discussion

Fruit Foraging

In this study, we compared patterns of ranging and foraging in two very distantly related fruit-eating primates with the goal of understanding the challenges each species faces in exploiting fruit resources that vary in space, time, and quantity, and the solutions employed to overcome these challenges. Chimpanzees and tamarins revisited many feeding trees within years, but rarely reused the same individual fruit trees across years despite exploiting the same home range. Tamarins revisited only 7 of 191 fruit trees across both study periods, and chimpanzees revisited only 6 of 1211 fruit trees across three study periods. Thus, the results are consistent with the first hypothesis, that there is considerable variation in the individual fruit feeding sites visited by primates across years, which is likely caused by tropical forests frequently exhibiting irregular fruiting patterns.

Irregular fruiting patterns of individual trees resulting from local environmental perturbation, yearly variation in pollinator effectiveness, and differences in tree species life history traits are likely to require primates to readjust their patterns of ranging and resource monitoring from season to season or year to year (Janmaat et al. 2013a). For example, trees that produced fruit during June and July in one year may not fruit at the same time the following year, with tree fruiting cycles shifting by several weeks or some trees not fruiting each year (Janmaat et al. 2013a; Peñuelas et al. 2004). As the study periods were short, it may be that some of the fruits consumed in one year were consumed in subsequent years but not within the observation periods because of annual shifts in fruiting seasons. However, this cannot fully explain the results. For example, in 2010 the chimpanzee Isha fed on only 20 of the 268 trees that she fed on in 2009, but 83 percent of the fruit species were the same in both years. Thus, she was eating fruits from the same tree species in both study periods, but she exploited different individual trees of those species. A long-term monitoring program of the phenology of individual trees throughout a forest, combined with long-term data on primate foraging patterns, would allow for a more detailed evaluation of how annual variation in the fruiting patterns of individual trees influences primate foraging. However, monitoring every potential feeding site in a forest requires enormous effort, and was beyond the scope of our research projects.

The second hypothesis (H2a) was that given their smaller body mass and smaller group size, the feeding sites revisited by the tamarins were expected to be characterized by greater variance in fruit production than the feeding sites revisited by chimpanzees. That is, whereas tamarins can exploit trees with small, medium, or large fruit crops, chimpanzees are required to preferentially exploit feeding sites that offer a large fruit reward. The analyses showed that tamarin foraging parties were characterized by significantly shorter bout lengths than chimpanzee foraging parties, indicating that, in general, chimpanzees exploited more productive feeding sites than did tamarins. However, variance in tamarin feeding bout length was significantly lower than that of chimpanzees, indicating that tamarin foraging parties received more consistent fruit rewards than did chimpanzee foraging parties.

Several factors may help to explain this finding. Tamarins may obtain a more consistent food reward per feeding bout because, relative to crop size, their smaller gut volume narrowly limits the amount consumed. In addition, tamarins are reported to commonly feed on tree species that fruit in a piecemeal fashion, producing only a small amount of ripe fruit per day (Terborgh 1983). The tamarins revisited 30–61 percent of fruit trees within each study period (Table 11.3). In contrast, each chimpanzee revisited only 15–29 percent of fruit trees within each study period (Table 11.3). In revisiting the same set of trees over the course of consecutive days or weeks, the tamarins might have prioritized individual trees that contained a small yet consistent and predictable food reward (Garber 1988). In exploiting trees with smaller fruit crop size, the tamarins also may avoid interspecific feeding competition with larger-bodied sympatric primate species. Higher levels of variance in chimpanzee feeding bout length may also be explained by differences in fruit size. Chimpanzees may eat fruits which vary more in size (Janmaat et al. 2014), and also eat hard fruits which may take a considerable time to open (e.g., *Treculia africana*): Both factors could increase the duration of feeding bouts. Finally, differences in variance could be explained by species-specific differences in foraging party size. Tamarin foraging party size ranged from 1 to 4; however, chimpanzee foraging party size ranged from 1 to 19. Moreover, chimpanzees appear to focus on fruit trees that produce extremely large crops that can vary in production dramatically across days or weeks (Janmaat et al. 2016), and thus foragers experience more variable food rewards.

The second part of this hypothesis (H2b) posited that if highly productive feeding sites are relatively rare and widely scattered across a forested landscape, then chimpanzees are expected to travel across a larger proportion of their home range each day to locate and monitor these sites. Thus, we expected that chimpanzees would update their knowledge of fruit tree availability and productivity in their home range by going on "expedition days," where they would cover large parts of their range. We found partial support for this prediction. The variation in the daily area covered, and thus the daily area covered on expedition days, was substantially larger for individual chimpanzee females than for the tamarin group, despite similar variation in daily travel distances and similar mean daily travel distances. This is consistent with the idea that the chimpanzees did not travel further on days in which they covered an exceptionally large area (>131 ha) of their range, but traveled in a circular fashion without back tracking, allowing them to explore large parts of their range and to return to familiar areas or food sources at the end of the day. However, contrary to our expectation, chimpanzees failed to monitor more feeding trees on expedition days than on days they covered smaller areas. It is possible that chimpanzees may have been going on these expeditions for social reasons (e.g., to seek out group-mates). Alternatively, they may have been targeting a few productive fruiting trees that they remembered as food sources from previous months or years, after which they returned to familiar food sources in the evening. If chimpanzees maintained long-term memory of the locations of highly productive fruiting trees in their home range across years, then what we initially defined as "excursions" may actually represent goal-oriented travel toward trees used in previous months or years. A recent study found that the same chimpanzee females investigated in this study inspected more trees when they entered less familiar areas of their range (Jang et al. 2019). Thus, chimpanzees may monitor trees through expeditions in less familiar areas of their home range but rely on long-term spatial memory to relocate productive feeding sites in more familiar areas, a possibility that requires further study.

The third hypothesis we tested was that tamarins and chimpanzees reuse travel routes to assess the availability of current and future feeding sites. As such, we expected there to be more revisited sites in proximity to travel routes as compared to other areas of their home range. We found that for both chimpanzees and tamarins, the routes taken passed by more feeding trees than randomly positioned routes. These data support the idea that both the chimpanzees and tamarins reuse travel routes to update resource knowledge. However, given that 48–50 percent of the tamarins' travel was restricted to routes whereas only 4–30 percent of the chimpanzees' travel was restricted to routes (Table 11.5), the tamarins may, to a greater degree than chimpanzees, encode spatial information in a route-based mental representation (i.e., a map) to locate and monitor fruit trees. Furthermore, tamarin routes were located near more fruit trees (mean 7.6–15.9 trees/route) than chimpanzee routes (mean 0.5–1.4 trees/route; Table 11.5). Thus, the tamarin ranging pattern of route-based travel likely facilitated frequent updating of resource knowledge (Porter & Garber 2013). In contrast, the chimpanzees likely rely more on their long-term memory of the location and phenological patterns of trees throughout their home range, allowing them to move directly to those food sources rather than frequently rechecking for fruits along established routes.

If routes are used to monitor fruit resources, and if individual trees are seldom reused across years, it is not surprising that the reuse of route segments was extremely limited across study periods. The long-term utility of any given route will depend on variation in the seasonal or annual distribution of resources. We found that 8 of 55 routes were reused multiple times by tamarins in both 2009 and 2011. Only 9 of 274 of Isha's routes were reused across three different years, and Julia had no routes that were reused for two years. Indeed, these data suggest that the spatial distribution and phenology of feeding trees leads to changes in the location of routes across years.

Our results contrast with those of Di Fiore and Suarez (2007), who showed that spider and woolly monkeys frequently reuse travel paths across years. In addition to potential differences across sites in fruit tree abundance, crop size, and phenological patterns, the sites also differ in their topography. It may be that at hilly sites the energetic demands of moving up and down slopes encourage the use of locating trails along ridges that may provide better sighting visibility or a more reliable set of distant landmark cues, factors that would be less salient for primates in habitats with little change in elevation and reduced sighting distance, like the Estación Biológica Tahuamanu or the Taï forest. Furthermore, the Taï chimpanzees principally travel on the ground. For terrestrial or semi-terrestrial primates, scarce ground vegetation may allow for unobstructed movement, making the reuse of routes unnecessary. Kanyawara chimpanzees use routes more frequently than we found for the Taï chimpanzees, a difference that may be due, in part, to the denser understory found at Kanyawara (Bertolani 2013).

Additional research is needed to examine the influence of foraging party size, group cohesion, and the effectiveness of resource monitoring during route-based travel on primate foraging strategies. For example, given that tamarins forage in a small cohesive group that is spread out over only a few meters, and engage in route-based travel, they may encounter new feeding sites at a lower rate than sympatric primates that live in larger groups or travel larger distances each day. Thus, there may be a trade-off between group size, daily path length, home range area, and resource monitoring that is likely to play a critical role in primate foraging strategies and the cognitive demands of integrating spatial, temporal, social, and ecological information (Garber 2000). In the case of chimpanzees, Janmaat et al. (2013a, 2013b) found that females were more likely to inspect trees in a goal-directed manner when they were alone than when they were in a group. Thus, chimpanzees' opportunities to monitor food sources, and their use of individual memory to update knowledge on future fruit locations, appears to be constrained when moving in a party.

Social factors unrelated to food acquisition also may influence the area of the home range that primates exploit on a given day. In the fission–fusion social organization that characterizes chimpanzees, individuals may adjust their ranging behavior to rejoin or avoid other members of their community to maintain their dominance status in the social hierarchy (Boesch & Boesch 2000). In tamarins, breeding is usually restricted to a single dominant female (reviewed in Garber et al. 2016); thus, subordinate females may monitor parts of their home range that overlap with neighboring groups to assess the availability of reproductive positions (Lledo-Ferrer et al. 2011). The home ranges of neighboring tamarin groups at the Estación Biológica Tahuamanu overlap extensively (mean overlap 66 percent), including parts of their core areas, and therefore cannot be considered exclusive territories (Porter et al. 2015). Therefore, depending on the species, social behaviors such as territorial patrols, male–female consorts, and investigation of breeding opportunities in neighboring groups may influence ranging behavior with the beneficial side-effect of updating resource or ecological information.

Given that virtually all species of primates consume ripe fruits, additional comparisons of ranging and foraging behavior in distinct or distantly related primate species are needed to help elucidate the role of multiple factors, including phylogeny, cognitive abilities, fruit phenology, resource availability, group size, group cohesion, territorial behavior, and reproductive status on patterns of habitat utilization and food search strategies. Long-term studies of individual fruiting trees and their phenological cycles, along with long-term behavioral studies of primates, will help identify adaptations that different primate lineages have evolved to consume fruits with different crop sizes and phenological cycles.

Acknowledgments

LMP and PAG would like to thank E. Nacimento, R. Cuadiay, and C. McKenney for their help with data collection. We also thank the Colección Boliviana de Fauna, Bolivia for their help securing permits for this research and the Ministerio de Medio Ambiente,

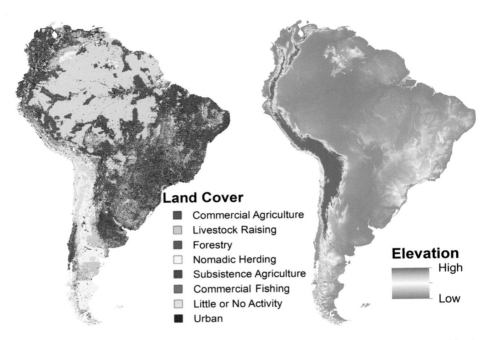

Land Cover

- ■ Commercial Agriculture
- ☐ Livestock Raising
- ■ Forestry
- ☐ Nomadic Herding
- ■ Subsistence Agriculture
- ■ Commercial Fishing
- ☐ Little or No Activity
- ■ Urban

Elevation
High
Low

Figure 2.4 Two raster datasets from South America representing gradients of elevation, and land cover types, respectively. Elevation data are a 30 arc-second DEM (US Geological Survey 1996). Land cover data are clipped from a global mosaic of MODIS-derived land cover classification (Channan et al. 2014). (A black and white version of this figure will appear in some formats.)

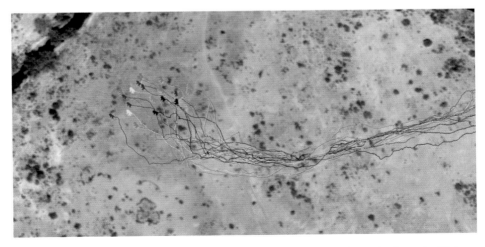

Figure 3.2 Olive baboons (*Papio anubis*) travel together as a more-or-less cohesive unit. High-resolution GPS tracking (1 location/second) of the troop revealed that consensus decision-making governs choices about which direction to move. (A black and white version of this figure will appear in some formats.)

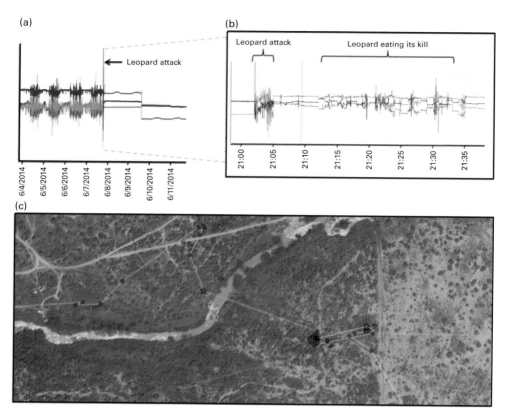

Figure 3.1 Tracking the death of a female baboon. On June 7, 2014 at 21:02, a GPS-tagged female baboon was killed by a GPS-collared leopard. Plots of the baboon's 3D acceleration (sampled for 2 seconds every minute at a rate of 40 Hz) in the days (a) and minutes (b) surrounding her death reveal the exact timing of this predation event, and allow us to infer the amount of time the leopard spent consuming its kill. GPS locations collected at 15-minute intervals (c) show that just prior to the attack (red stars), the baboon (yellow) was stationary on a rocky outcropping (likely asleep, given the time of night), while the leopard was quite a distance away, on the opposite side of a river. In the minutes leading up to the predation event, the leopard (aqua) crossed this river and traveled quickly and directly (>250 meters in 2 minutes) toward the baboon. After the kill, the leopard dragged the baboon approximately 90 meters to another rocky outcropping where the body and collar were eventually recovered. (A black and white version of this figure will appear in some formats.)

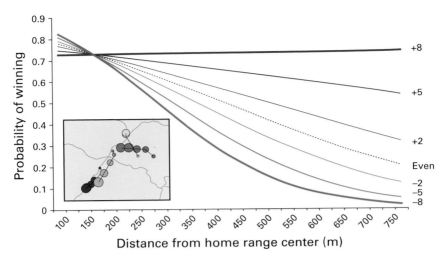

Figure 3.3 Home-field advantage in capuchin intergroup conflict. Automated tracking of six white-faced capuchin (*Cebus capucinus*) social groups revealed that while relative group size (represented by colored lines, top) did influence the odds a group would win in a competitive interaction with a neighbor, the location of the conflict had a larger impact on the outcome (Crofoot 2008). In this study, interactions and their outcomes were defined based on spatial criteria (*see inset*): two groups had to come within 150 m of one another and a clear displacement event had to occur. Using this approach, we identified 58 interactions with a clear winner and loser in 6 months of movement data. In contrast, in 10 months of direct behavioral data collection, we observed 23 intergroup interactions, only 18 of which had a clear outcome (Crofoot 2007). (A black and white version of this figure will appear in some formats.)

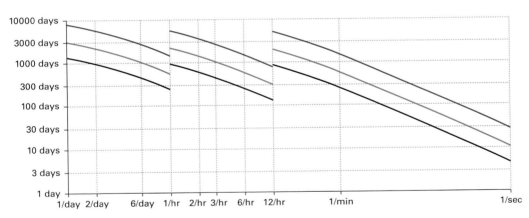

Figure 3.4 Trade-off between sampling frequency and sampling duration. To illustrate this trade-off, I estimated the life span (in days) of GPS collars with small (black; capacity ~2500 mAh), medium (red; capacity ~5800 mAh), and large (blue; capacity ~15,000 mAh) capacity batteries for sampling rates ranging from one location estimate per day to one location estimate per second. Time-to-fix (TTF – the latency between a GPS tag turning on and obtaining a fix) varies with sampling frequency. To account for this, I varied TTF in three stages: TTF = 60 seconds for rates from 1 to 12 fixes/day; TTF decreases monotonically from 60 seconds to 30 seconds for rates from 1 to 12 fixes/hour; TTF = 1 second for rates from 1 fix/5 minutes to 1 fix/second. Note that battery performance varies depending on environmental factors (e.g., temperature), and TTF will be highly dependent on the study site. Predicted collar life spans for low-frequency sampling regimes are likely overestimates. (A black and white version of this figure will appear in some formats.)

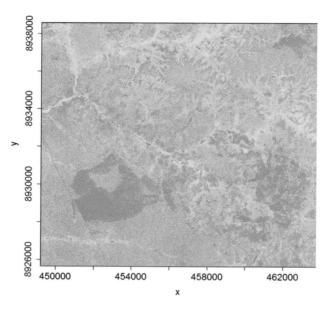

Figure 5.1 Graphical output from code example 1. (A black and white version of this figure will appear in some formats.)

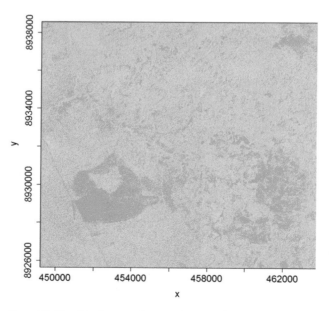

Figure 5.2 Graphical output from code example 2. (A black and white version of this figure will appear in some formats.)

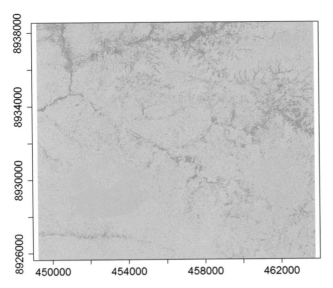

Figure 5.4 Graphical output from code example 4. (A black and white version of this figure will appear in some formats.)

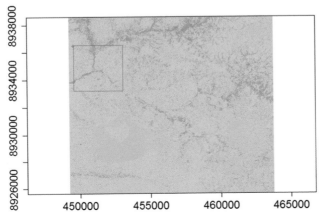

Figure 5.5 Graphical output from code example 5. (A black and white version of this figure will appear in some formats.)

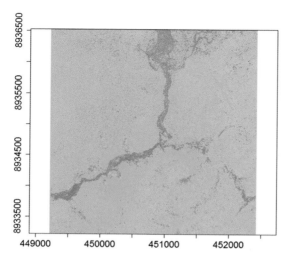

Figure 5.6 Graphical output from code example 6. (A black and white version of this figure will appear in some formats.)

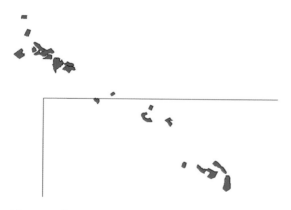

Figure 5.7 Graphical output from code example 7. (A black and white version of this figure will appear in some formats.)

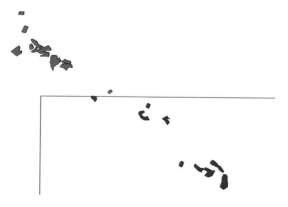

Figure 5.8 Graphical output from code example 8. (A black and white version of this figure will appear in some formats.)

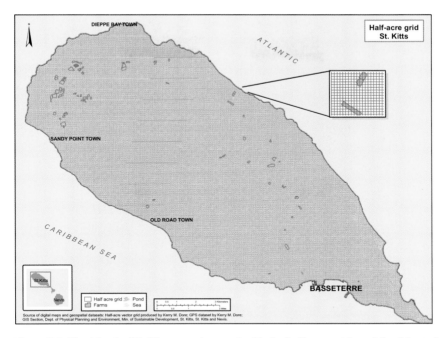

Figure 19.2 The island of St Kitts superimposed with the half-acre grid used for this study (individual grid cells are impossible to see at this scale). (A black and white version of this figure will appear in some formats.)

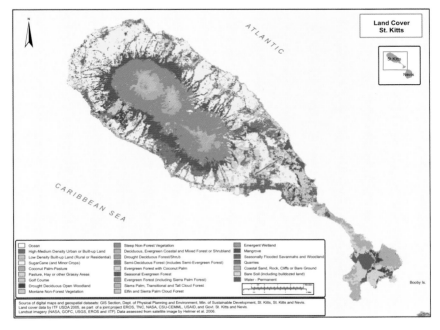

Figure 19.3 Land cover on St Kitts (assessed from satellite images by Helmer et al. 2008). (A black and white version of this figure will appear in some formats.)

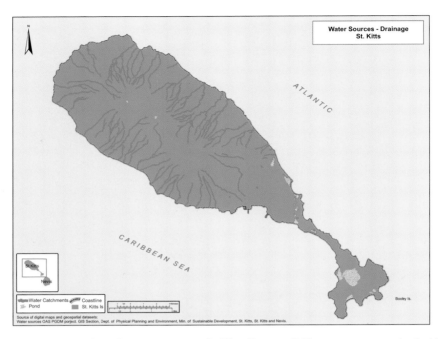

Figure 19.4 Location of water sources on St. Kitts. Data available at: www.oas.org/pgdm/data/gis_ data.htm. (A black and white version of this figure will appear in some formats.)

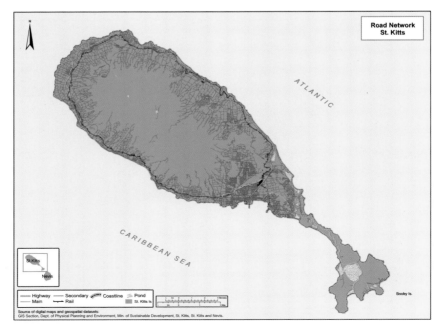

Figure 19.5 Location of roads in St Kitts. Data from the St Kitts Planning Department. (A black and white version of this figure will appear in some formats.)

Bolivia for granting permission to conduct this project. We thank the following institutions for their financial support that made this research possible: Northern Illinois University, University of Illinois, Urbana-Champaign, Fresno Chaffee Zoo, Tinker Foundation Grant from the Center for Latin American and Caribbean Studies, University of Illinois, Center for Latino and Latin American Studies Center, Northern Illinois University. PAG acknowledges Chrissie, Sara, and Jenni for their support and love. LMP thanks Sean for all his help and encouragement.

KRLJ and CB would like to thank the Max Planck Institute for Evolutionary Anthropology for financial support of their research. In Côte d'Ivoire we thank the Ministère de la Recherches Scientifiques, the Ministère de l'Environnement et des Eaux et Forêts, the Office Ivoirien des Parcs et Réserves, the directorship of the Taï National Park, and the Centre Suisse de Recherche Scientifique for logistic support and permission to conduct this research. We are indebted to S. D. Ban, J. Tahou, R. Nabo, L. B. Bally, and V. Gnagnon for invaluable assistance in the field.

References

Adamescu, G. S., Plumptre, A. J., Abernethy, K. A., et al. 2018. Annual cycles are the most common reproductive strategy in African tropical tree communities. *Biotropica* **50**(3): 418–430.

Alverson, W., Moskovitz, D. K., Shopland, J. M. (Eds.). 2000. *Rapid Biological Inventories for Conservation Action: Northwestern Pando, Bolivia*. Field Museum, Chicago, IL.

Baayen, R. H. 2008. *Analyzing Linguistic Data: A Practical Introduction to Statistics Using R.* Cambridge University Press, Cambridge.

Ban, S. D., Boesch, C., and Janmaat, K. R. L. 2014. Taï chimpanzees anticipate revisiting high-valued fruit trees from further distances. *Animal Cognition* **17**: 1353–1364.

Ban, S. D., Boesch, C., N'Guessan, A., et al. 2016. Taï chimpanzees change their travel direction for rare feeding trees providing fatty fruits. *Animal Behaviour* **118**: 135–147.

Barr, D. J., Levy, R., Scheepers, C., and Tily, H. J. 2013. Random effects structure for confirmatory hypothesis testing: keep it maximal. *Journal of Memory and Language* **68**: 255–278.

Bates, D., Mächler, M., Bolker, B., and Walker, S. 2015. Fitting linear mixed-effects models using lme4. *Journal of Statistical Software* **67**: 1–48.

Bertolani, M. P. 2013. Ranging and travelling patterns of wild chimpanzees at Kibale, Uganda: a GIS approach. Doctoral dissertation, University of Cambridge.

Boesch, C. and Boesch, A. 2000. *The Chimpanzees of the Taï Forest: Behavioral Ecology and Evolution*. Oxford University Press, Oxford.

Di Fiore, A. and Suarez, S. A. 2007. Route-based travel and shared routes in sympatric spider and woolly monkeys: cognitive and evolutionary implications. *Animal Cognition* **10**: 317–329.

Digby, L. J., Ferrari, S. F., and Saltzman, W. 2011. The role of competition in cooperatively breeding species. Pages 91–107 in *Primates in Perspective*, 2nd edition. C. J. Campbell, A. Fuentes, K. C. MacKinnon, S. Bearder, and R. M. Stumpf (Eds.). Oxford University Press, New York.

Dobson, A. J. and Barnett, A. 2008. *An Introduction to Generalized Linear Models*. Chapman & Hall/CRC, Boca Raton, FL.

Garber, P. A. 1988. Foraging decisions during nectar feeding by tamarin monkeys (*Saguinus mystax* and *Saguinus fuscicollis*, Callitrichidae, Primates) in Amazonian Peru. *Biotropica* **20**: 100–106.

Garber, P. A. 1989. Role of spatial memory in primate foraging patterns: *Saguinus mystax* and *Saguinus fuscicollis*. *American Journal of Primatology* **19**: 203–216.

Garber, P. A. 2000. The ecology of group movement: evidence for the use of spatial, temporal, and social information in some primate foragers. Pages 261–298 in *On the Move: How and Why Animals Travel in Groups*. S. Boinski and P.A. Garber (Eds.). University of Chicago Press, Chicago, IL.

Garber, P. A. in press. Primate cognitive ecology: challenges and solutions to locating and acquiring resources in social foragers. In *Primate Diet and Nutrition: Needing, Finding, and Using Food*. J. E. Lambert and J. Rothman (Eds.). University of Chicago Press, Chicago, IL.

Garber, P. A., and Porter, L. M. 2010. The ecology of exudate feeding and exudate production in *Saguinus* and *Callimico*. Pages 89–108 in *The Evolution of Exudativory in Primates*. A. Burrows and L. Nash (Eds). Springer, New York.

Garber, P. A., and Porter, L. M. 2014. Navigating in small-scale space: the role of landmarks and resource monitoring in understanding saddleback tamarin travel. *American Journal of Primatology* **76**: 447–459.

Garber, P.A., Porter, L.M., Spross, J., and Di Fiore, A. 2016. Tamarins: insights into monogamous and non-monogamous single female breeding systems. *American Journal of Primatology* **78**: 298–314.

Goné Bi, Z. B. 2007. Régime alimentaire des chimpanzés, distribution spatiale et phénologie des plantes dont les fruits sont consommés par les chimpanzés du Parc National de Taï, en Côte d'Ivoire. PhD Thesis, University of Cocody.

Hothorn, T. and Hornik, K. 2013. exactRankTests: exact distributions for rank and permutation tests. R package version 0.8-24. Available at: http://CRAN.R-project.org/package=exactRankTests.

Jang, H., Boesch, C., Mundry, R., Ban, S. D., and Janmaat, K. R. L. 2019. Travel linearity and speed of human foragers and chimpanzees during their daily search for food in tropical rainforests. *Scientfic Reports* **9**: 11066.

Janmaat, K. R. L. and Chancellor, R. L. 2010. Exploring new areas: how important is long-term spatial memory for mangabey (*Lophocebus albigena johnstonii*) foraging efficiency? *International Journal of Primatology* **31**: 863–886.

Janmaat, K. R. L., Olupot, W., Chancellor, R. L., Arlet, M. E., and Waser, P. M. 2009. Long-term site fidelity and individual home range shifts in *Lophocebus albigena*. *International Journal of Primatology* **30**: 443–466.

Janmaat, K. R. L., Ban, S. D., and Boesch, C. 2013a. Chimpanzees use long-term spatial memory to monitor large fruit trees and remember feeding experiences across seasons. *Animal Behaviour* **86**: 1183–1205.

Janmaat, K. R. L., Ban, S. D. and Boesch, C. 2013b. Taï chimpanzees use botanical skills to discover fruit: what we can learn from their mistakes. *Animal Cognition* **16**: 851–860.

Janmaat, K. R. L., Polansky, L., Ban, S. D., and Boesch, C. 2014. Wild chimpanzees plan their breakfast time, type, and location. *Proceedings of the National Academy of Sciences of the United States of America* **111**: 16343–16348.

Janmaat, K. R. L., Boesch, C., Byrne, R., et al. 2016. The spatio-temporal complexity of chimpanzee food: how cognitive adaptations can counteract the ephemeral nature of ripe fruit. *American Journal of Primatology* **78**: 626–645.

Kalan, A. K. and Boesch, C. 2015. Audience effects in chimpanzee food calls and their potential for recruiting others. *Behavioral Ecology and Sociobiology* **69**: 1701–1712.

Koenig, W. D., Kelly, D., Sork, V. L., et al. 2003. Dissecting components of population-level variation in seed production and the evolution of masting behavior. *Oikos* **102**: 581–591.

Kouakou, C. Y., Boesch, C., and Kuehl, H. 2011. Identifying hotspots of chimpanzee group activity from transect surveys in Taï National Park, Côte d'Ivoire. *Journal of Tropical Ecology* **27**: 621–630.

Laden, G. T. 1992. Ethnoarchaeology and land use ecology of the Efe (pygmies) of the Ituri rain forest, Zaire: a behavioral ecological study of land use patterns and foraging behavior. PhD Thesis, Harvard University.

Lledo-Ferrer, Y., Pelaez, F., and Heymann, E. W. 2011. The equivocal relationship between territoriality and scent marking in wild saddleback tamarins (*Saguinus fuscicollis*). *International Journal of Primatology* **32**: 974–991.

Lopez-Rebellon, N. 2010. Sex and age-based differences in antipredator behavior in saddle-back tamarins (*Saguinus fuscicollis*) in the department of Pando, Bolivia. MA Thesis, DeKalb, Northern Illinois University.

Martin, P. and Bateson, P. 1993. *Measuring Behavior: An Introductory Guide*, 2nd edition. Cambridge University Press, Cambridge.

Milton, K. 1980. *The Foraging Strategy of Howler Monkeys: A Study in Primate Economics*. Columbia University Press, New York.

Nishida, T., Zamma, K., Matsusaka, T., Inaba, A., and McGrew, W. C. 2010. *Chimpanzee Behavior in the Wild: An Audio-Visual Encyclopedia*. Springer, Tokyo.

Normand, E., Ban, S. D., and Boesch, C. 2009. Forest chimpanzees (*Pan troglodytes verus*) remember the location of numerous fruit trees. *Animal Cognition* **12**(6): 797–807.

Noser, R. and Byrne, R. W. 2015. Wild chacma baboons (*Papio ursinus*) remember single foraging episodes. *Animal Cognition* **18**, 921–929.

Peñuelas, J., Filella, I., Xiaoyang, Z., et al. 2004. Complex spatiotemporal phenological shifts as a response to rainfall changes. *New Phytologist* **161**: 837–846.

Polansky, L. and Boesch, C. 2013. Long-term fruit phenology and rainfall trends conflict in a West African lowland tropical rainforest. *Journal of Tropical Ecology* **45**: 409–535.

Porter, L. M. 2001. Dietary differences among sympatric Callitrichinae in northern Bolivia: *Callimico goeldii, Saguinus fuscicollis* and *S. labiatus. International Journal of Primatology* **22**: 961–992.

Porter, L. M. and Garber, P. A. 2013. Foraging and spatial memory in wild Weddell's saddleback tamarins (*Saguinus fuscicollis weddelli*) when moving between distant and out-of-sight goals. *International Journal of Primatology* **34**: 30–48.

Porter, L. M., Sterr, S. M., and Garber, P. A. 2007. Habitat use and ranging behavior of *Callimico goeldii. International Journal of Primatology* **28**: 1035–1058.

Porter, L. M., Erb, W. M., Saire, C. L., et al. 2015. Temporal changes in the composition of saddleback tamarin (*Saguinus fuscicollis weddelli*) groups over time. *American Association of Physical Anthropologists* **156**(60): 255–256.

Rakoczy, H., Clüver, A., Saucke, L., et al. 2014. Apes are intuitive statisticians. *Cognition* **131**(1): 60–68.

Rylands, A., Heymann, E., Matauschek, C., et al. 2016. Taxonomic review of the New World tamarins (Primates: Callitrichidae). *Zoological Journal of the Linnean Society* **177** (4): 1003–1028.

Schel, A. M., Machanda, Z., Townsend, S. W., Zuberbühler, K., and Slocombe, K. E. 2013. Chimpanzee food calls are directed at specific individuals. *Animal Behaviour* **86**: 955–965.

Stumpf, R. M. 2011. Chimpanzees and bonobos: inter- and intraspecies diversity. Pages 340–356 in *Primates in Perspective*, 2nd edition. C. J. Campbell, A. Fuentes, K. C. MacKinnon, S. Bearder, and R. M. Stumpf (Eds.) Oxford University Press, New York.

Tecwyn, E. C., Denison, S., Messer, E. J., and Buchsbaum, D. 2017. Intuitive probabilistic inference in capuchin monkeys. *Animal Cognition* **20**(2): 243–256.

Terborgh, J. 1983. *Five New World Primates: A Study in Comparative Ecology.* Princeton University Press, Princeton, NJ.

12 Random Walk Analyses in Primates

Amy L. Schreier and Matt Grove

Models of foraging behavior often assume that foragers either have no information about the spatial distribution of resources that they seek or, at the other extreme, that they are omniscient with regard to the locations of those resources. This is paralleled by a distinction between the optimization of search behavior (which assumes no knowledge of resource locations) and the pursuit of efficient routes between multiple resource patches (often explicitly considered to be a cognitive task). In this chapter we discuss a variety of movement models that have recently become common in animal ecology. We then use a population of hamadryas baboons as a case study to investigate the relevance of these models to a species possessing spatial memory and learning capabilities.

Simple, Biased, and Correlated Random Walks

Random walks, as a generic class of movement models, have long been used in ecology and biology. They have often formed the basis for theoretical advances based on simulation, and have been the default class of models for fitting to empirical movement data. All forms of random walk are composed of three probabilistic distributions: those of the step lengths, the turning angles, and the residency (or "waiting") times (Berg 1983). In field studies these are empirical distributions culled most often from GPS or telemetry data, while in simulation studies they are the theoretical (statistical) distributions from which a walk is generated. GPS data are thus crucial for the analysis of primate ranging patterns: not only do they provide a clear, spatial depiction of movement via a GIS, but they also provide raw data that can be "collapsed" into univariate series (such as step lengths) for more in-depth analyses. Although random walk analyses can be more rapidly undertaken outside the framework of a GIS, the dialogue between spatially explicit GIS analyses and spatially implicit statistical analyses is one that provides particularly robust conclusions. This becomes particularly clear when the results of statistical analyses performed on data extracted from a GIS are related back to the spatial context to aid interpretation.

The relationships between the three elements of a random walk are shown schematically in Figure 12.1. The simplest form of random walk (often called literally the simple random walk, or SRW) involves a constant step length of 1 and a turning angle distribution which is "circular uniform" (i.e., any angle is equally likely to occur as the next turning angle).

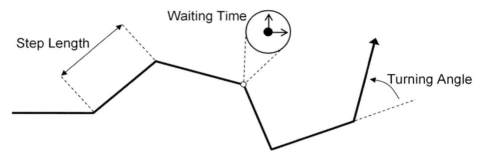

Figure 12.1 The three components of a random walk (after Grove 2010).

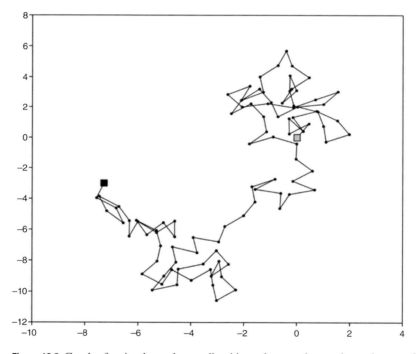

Figure 12.2 Graph of a simple random walk with random turning angles and steps of unit length. Gray and black squares denote the start and end of the walk respectively.

An example of 100 steps of a SRW is shown in Figure 12.2. Residency times are often disregarded in this context, or considered to be constant, though this can be a limitation when discussing some forms of random walks. In the analyses of Schreier and Grove (2010), for example, waiting times were power-law distributed; if waiting times had been assumed to be constant in this case, it could have led to the (erroneous) conclusion that the step lengths themselves were power-law distributed. It is thus often useful to analyze waiting times as a separate variable, since they reveal the structure of the resource base; power-law distributed waiting times, for example, imply a power-law distribution in patch value, rather than a power-law distribution in inter-patch distance.

The SRW first entered theoretical biology via particle physics as a means of studying animal dispersal (e.g., Skellam 1951; Patlak 1953a, 1953b; Reid 1953); it remains a useful model in theoretical studies due to its relationship to the normal distribution and the derivation of "traveling wave" models of dispersal (see Turchin 1998). The SRW is also highly prevalent as a model for empirical movement data, where it has proved useful in studying the movement patterns of a range of animals, including gophers (Benedix 1993), gazelles (Ward & Saltz 1994), wood mice (Blackwell 1997), and caribou (Schaefer et al. 2000). Until relatively recently, most modifications of the SRW involved adding an element of correlation to the turning angles of the walk, allowing researchers to examine animal movements on resource gradients or toward specific goals. To this end, the two main classes of models developed are referred to as *biased* and *correlated* random walks.

Biased random walks (BRWs) are used to describe movement toward specific goals, the locations of which are detected or known from relatively large distances away. Biased random walks are often used to describe the movement trajectories of avian and aquatic foragers (e.g., Bailey & Thompson 2006; Faugeras & Maury 2007; Grunbaum 1998; Reynolds et al. 2007a), as their truly three-dimensional environments allow for detection of resources at greater distances than would be possible in most terrestrial environments. In contrast to BRWs, correlated random walks (CRWs) display high correlations between series of turning angles, with directly adjacent turning angles often being very similar. Thus, BRWs tend to show relatively long-term persistence toward a goal, indicated by a series of turning angles close to zero and thus by relatively straight-line travel; CRWs, by contrast, show high similarity between adjacent turning angles, even when these differ substantially from zero. A CRW can in fact display long-term persistence, but it is important to note that, unlike a BRW, it will not necessarily do so. Due to their flexibility in producing everything from straight-line searches to spiral searches, CRWs are one of the most common means of modeling animal movement (e.g., Bergman et al. 2000; Bovet & Benhamou 1988; Crist et al. 1992; Johnson et al. 1992, 2008; Kareiva & Shigesada 1983; Skellam 1973).

Lévy Walks

Unlike BRWs and CRWs, both of which concern modified turning angle distributions, the Lévy walk (LW) involves a modification of the step length distribution. Formally, the probability of a step of length l is distributed as

$$p(l) = cl^{-\mu}, \, l \geq l_{min}, \, 1 \leq \mu < 3, \qquad [1]$$

where l_{min} is the minimum step length and $c = (\mu - 1)l_{min}^{\mu-1}$ is a normalizing constant. Within the specified exponent range the additive distribution converges to a power-law (Lévy 1937), producing the scale-free behavior that has prompted such interest among ecologists. Lévy walks were first introduced as a model for animal movement by

Shlesinger and Klafter (1986; see also Shlesinger et al. 1993), who suggested that ants found to be following this pattern might be afforded "a slight evolutionary advantage over ants performing other walks" (Shlesinger & Klafter 1986: 283). Despite this early – and prescient – contribution, few further ecological papers on LWs appeared until the late 1990s (but see Levandowsky et al. 1988a, 1988b).

The current interest in LW within ecology was spurred by a series of papers published by Viswanathan and colleagues (e.g., 1996, 1999, 2002) that successfully combined theoretical and empirical analyses of this particular form of random walk. Viswanathan et al. (1996) found that the flights of wandering albatrosses conformed to a Lévy distribution, hypothesizing that this pattern was an evolutionary adaptation enabling the efficient harvest of ocean surface resources that were fractally distributed. Subsequent papers focused on this generic evolutionary hypothesis, with an important simulation study (Viswanathan et al. 1999) demonstrating that an LW with an exponent of 2 is an optimal search pattern for a forager searching without prior information for randomly distributed, static, non-depleting, low-density resources. These simulations were coupled with new empirical data demonstrating LW in bumblebees and deer; additional data on soil amoebas (Levandowsky et al. 1997), reindeer (Marell et al. 2002), jackals (Atkinson et al. 2002), albatrosses (Fritz et al. 2003), microzooplankton (Bartumeus et al. 2003), arctic seals (Austin et al. 2004), moths (Reynolds et al. 2007a), elephants (Dai et al. 2007), goats (de Knegt et al. 2007), and bees (Reynolds et al. 2007b, 2007c) confirmed the prevalence of LW patterns in foraging organisms.

In the past decade, studies of LW in primates including humans have also sporadically appeared. Ramos-Fernández et al. (2004) found LW patterns in the foraging of spider monkeys in the forest of the Yucatan Peninsula, Mexico, with an exponent close to the value of 2 considered optimal by Viswanathan et al. (1999). In a detailed analysis they also found different exponents for monkeys foraging individually and in subgroups, and demonstrated that the majority of the long-distance relocations forming the tail of the power-law distribution were made by males. These authors further considered the possibility that spider monkeys were not "searching" for food, but rather following routes between fruiting trees, the locations of which were known in advance; this is a possibility to which we will return in some detail below. Sueur (2011; Sueur et al. 2011) found that movements of Tonkean macaques conformed to LW, but that those of chacma baboons did not; again, these authors raise the possibility of prior knowledge as opposed to random search as a factor structuring movement patterns.

Studies of human foragers have been largely equivocal. Brown and colleagues (2007) argued that the Dobe !Kung of Botswana and Namibia relocate according to an LW pattern, but a reanalysis of these data using likelihood methods (Grove 2010) suggests that a log-normal distribution provides a better fit. Miramontes et al. (2012) found no evidence for LWs in the movement patterns of Mexican Me'Phaa peasants searching for firewood, but Raichlen et al. (2014) argue that Tanzanian Hadza hunter-gatherers perform LWs when foraging for a number of food items, including underground tubers. Brantingham (2006) argued that the mobility of early Upper Paleolithic humans in western France, as reconstructed from the distances that they moved raw materials, followed a power-law with an exponent slightly below the Lévy range, while a number of studies of modern Western populations have suggested that, even in an age of air travel and long-distance diffusion, human movements follow a long-term Lévy mobility pattern (Brockmann et al. 2006; Gonzalez et al. 2008; Rhee et al. 2011).

Doubts About Lévy Walks

Since the initial proliferation of papers on LW reviewed above, a number of doubts have surfaced regarding the validity of the "Lévy Hypothesis" (Bartumeus 2007). Such doubts can be divided into those about the methods used to fit models to data, and those concerning the important distinction between the finding of an LW *pattern*, and the *process* actually responsible for the generation of that pattern. Simplistic regression methods, employed by many early studies, have been shown to misrepresent the actual step length distributions (Edwards et al. 2007; Grove 2010; Sims et al. 2007), with likelihood methods for exponent derivation now favored (see the methodological summaries in Grove 2010 and Schreier & Grove 2010). Despite these doubts, likelihood methods demonstrate that some, if not all, of the studies outlined above do reflect LW in foraging organisms (see Sims et al. 2008; Viswanathan et al. 2008). The doubts over the relationship between pattern and process, however, remain, and are particularly germane to the study of primates and other organisms that may retain detailed "mental maps" of their habitats.

A number of researchers exploring LW and other random walks in primates (Ramos-Fernández et al. 2004; Schreier & Grove 2010; Sueur 2011; Sueur et al. 2011) have voiced the opinion that the very notion of "search" may not properly describe the foraging patterns of cognitively sophisticated animals such as primates. It is clear (Boyer et al. 2006; Ramos-Fernández et al. 2004) that what appears to be an LW pattern can emerge simply from an animal's interaction with a resource base that is already familiar to it; this becomes relatively likely a priori when we consider that the distribution of primary feeding resources may itself show fractal structure (Brown et al. 2002; Condit et al. 2000; de Jager and Rohweder 2011). Thus the idea implicit (and occasionally explicit) in much of the LW literature, of a pre-programmed search algorithm acting independently of interaction with the environment, must be questioned. This is particularly the case when what is being tested or described is simply the conformity of a given dataset to a particular pattern. Chapleau and colleagues (1988:136) argue that "the study of patterns must be free from any assumptions about processes" if we are to accurately test evolutionary hypotheses. Thus, even when an LW pattern is found through reliable methods, we are far from demonstrating the existence of an innate algorithm.

Of particular value in this context are recent papers by Benhamou (2007) and Gautestad and Mysterud (2005; see also Gautestad 2013), both of which suggest that alternative processes could produce what appear to be LWs. Benhamou (2007) adopts a model in which the forager alternates between two search modes depending upon whether it is moving within a patch or between patches. Both modes are described by exponentially distributed step length distributions, with the between-patch step length

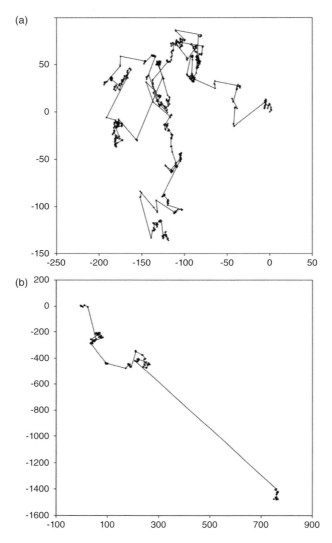

Figure 12.3 One thousand steps of (a) a composite Brownian walk and (b) a Lévy walk. While both walks produce apparently clustered distributions, the LW occasionally produces much longer step lengths than are found in the composite Brownian walk. Note difference in scale.

mean ($\lambda = 15$) being substantially higher than the within-patch step length mean ($\lambda = 1$). Simulating this pattern when the forager spends 90 percent of its time within patches and the remaining 10 percent traveling between patches leads to a composite step length distribution very similar to that created by simulating an LW with Viswanathan et al.'s (1999) optimal exponent value of $\mu = 2$. Examples of the resulting walk patterns, with random turning angles, are graphed in Figure 12.3.

Figure 12.4 shows analyses of these step length distributions (as per Benhamou 2007); it is clear from this figure that employing the technique prevalent in early LW

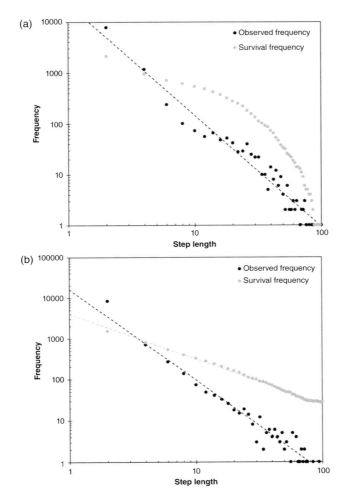

Figure 12.4 Analysis of 10,000 step lengths generated via (a) a composite Brownian walk (CBW) and (b) a Lévy walk. The CBW is created by sampling from two exponential distributions: the first has unit mean and is chosen with probability 0.9; the second has a mean of 15 and is chosen with probability 0.1. The graphs show both the observed frequencies (black circles) and the survival frequencies (gray circles); only the latter adequately distinguishes between the CBW and the LW. After Benhamou (2007:1964).

studies, of plotting frequencies of step lengths and fitting regression lines, will readily identify an LW pattern in the data generated via the two-mode process. Graphing the data as survival curves – that is, as the cumulative number of step lengths greater than any given value – avoids this problem and is recommended for future studies (Benhamou 2007; see also Clauset et al. 2009; Newman 2005; Schreier & Grove 2010; see Figure 12.4).

Gautestad and Mysterud (2005) provide an alternative process that involves a forager engaging in movements at multiple scales, complete with occasional memory-based returns to previously visited locations. This model has the advantage of creating walk patterns that mimic the establishment of gradually shifting home ranges as seen in most empirical datasets, and demonstrates that the two-mode search pattern advocated by Benhamou (2007) may in fact extend to a greater range of modes, depending on environmental complexity (see also de Jager and Rohweder 2011). For example, a valuable study by Boyer et al. (2006) extends the study of spider monkeys by Ramos-Fernández et al. (2004) to show that an LW-like pattern may emerge directly from the animals' interactions with the environment. In this model system, resource patches were Poisson distributed in space but power-law distributed in size, with agents visiting each patch only once and choosing the next patch so as to minimize the ratio of patch size ($\approx$ energetic input) to distance traveled ($\approx$ energetic output). With values of the exponent of the patch size distribution between 3 and 4, resultant forager step length distributions following power-laws with exponents between 2 and 3 were recovered. These results duplicate the patterns observed in spider monkeys by Ramos-Fernández et al. (2004); perhaps more importantly, they also show that an animal that has full knowledge of its resource base can produce an LW-like step length distribution due to interaction with its environment rather than via an innate algorithm.

Area-Restricted Search

The two-mode model proposed by Benhamou (2007) draws on a long history of research into a model of foraging dynamics commonly referred to as "area-restricted search" (ARS; see Benhamou 1992; Bond 1980; Kareiva & Odell 1987; Knell & Codling 2012; Laing 1938). Area-restricted search is a highly intuitive model in which a forager alternates between within-patch and between-patch movement patterns, with the two patterns showing quite distinct step length and turning angle distributions, as well as contrasting movement speeds. Upon encountering a resource item, a forager conforming to ARS will begin traveling more slowly, will adopt a more tortuous (i.e., less linear) path, and will reduce average step length. All of these changes in movement pattern should increase the probability of further resource detection, under the assumption that resources occur in patches. When an area or patch becomes unproductive, as indicated by a relatively long period without resource encounter, the forager will revert to the "extensive" mode of movement in which step lengths are long, turning angles are small, and travel speed is high, so as to facilitate the discovery of another, more profitable patch.

Area-restricted search has been documented in chalcid parasites (Laing 1937, 1938), lacewings (Bond 1980), pocket gophers (Benedix 1993), bees (Keasar et al. 1996), polecats (Lode 2000), and humans (Hills et al. 2013), among others, and has been subject to a considerable degree of theoretical study (e.g., Benhamou 1992; Ford 1983; Kareiva & Odell 1987; Knell & Codling 2012). Within the field of primatology, researchers have tended to focus on specific aspects of the theory, demonstrating for example that capuchin monkeys are more likely to detect resources when traveling at lower speeds (Janson & DiBitetti 1997), or that both chacma baboons and chimpanzees travel rapidly and in linear fashion between resource patches (Byrne et al. 2009).

Schreier and Grove (2014; see below) show that hamadryas baboons follow what is essentially an ARS pattern, but focus on the potential cognitive correlates of the theory as it relates to primates with a developed knowledge of their habitat.

The cognitive slant on ARS involves viewing the pattern as indicating an interaction between areas of the home range known to be resource-rich ("patches," broadly construed) and the paths between those patches, along which few resources will be found. In the traditional view of ARS (e.g., Benhamou 1992; Knell & Codling 2012), the animal is searching during both the intensive (area-restricted) and the extensive phases. As discussed above in relation to LW and CBW, primates with a knowledge of their habitat will spend at least some of their time moving between *known* locations rather than "searching" for those locations. Grove (2013) has demonstrated analytically that when resources are detectable from relatively long distances and are at relatively high density, there is no advantage gained by the forager from remembering their locations. Though initially proposed as a general foraging model independent of ARS, Grove's model (2013) can be reinterpreted as predicting what needs to be remembered by a forager with particular perceptual capacities in a given habitat type (Schreier & Grove 2014). As a general rule, foragers will benefit more from remembering the location of a patch (or resource-rich area) than they will from remembering the specific contents or qualities of that patch. In terms of ARS, the most appropriate model for primates involves alternating between an extensive phase of movements *between known patches* and an intensive phase of *searching within patches*. This dichotomy is explored further below, in relation to the foraging movements of hamadryas baboons (*Papio hamadryas*).

A Case Study: Hamadryas Baboons

Hypothesis

A two-mode movement pattern – distinguishing between travel within patches versus travel between patches – may produce an LW pattern (Benhamou 2007). In accordance with the concept of ARS (Benhamou 1992; Bond 1980; Curio 1976; Kareiva & Odell 1987), we hypothesized that hamadryas baboons in Awash National Park, Ethiopia might switch between periods in which they travel slowly and search within patches (i.e., palm forest and *Acacia* scrublands habitat types, see below) and travel greater distances between known locations (i.e., between patches, e.g., from cliff to *Acacia* scrublands, palm forest to cliff, etc.).

Study Site and Subjects

We examined movement patterns in a population of hamadryas baboons inhabiting the area surrounding the Filoha outpost of Awash National Park in central Ethiopia (9°6′27″ N, 40°0′50″ E). The outpost is surrounded by about 2 km² of natural hot springs, doum palm forests, swamp vegetation, and a 1.5 km-long cliff (Swedell 2002b,

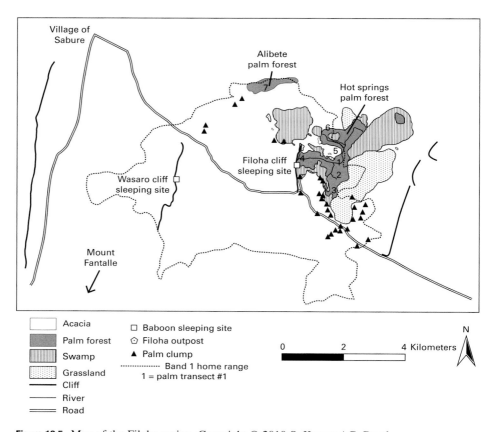

Figure 12.5. Map of the Filoha region, Copyright © 2010 S. Karger AG, Basel.

2006), while the larger area consists of *Acacia* scrublands, open grasslands, and additional cliffs, which are typical of hamadryas habitat in other parts of their geographic range (Al-Safadi 1994; Biquand et al. 1992; Kummer 1968; Sigg & Stolba 1981; Swedell 2006; Zinner et al. 2001). There are at least four cliffs in the Filoha vicinity, although the baboons regularly slept on just two during the March 2005 to February 2006 study period contributing to this analysis: the Filoha cliff and the Wasaro cliff (Figure 12.5). Several bands of hamadryas baboons populate the Filoha region. The study group, Band 1 (aka "Group 1"), has been observed intermittently since 1996 (Schreier and Swedell 2008, 2009, 2012a, 2012b; Swedell 2000, 2002a, 2002b, 2006; Swedell & Schreier 2009; Swedell et al. 2008, 2011). In February 2006, Band 1 consisted of approximately 210 individuals, including 24 leader males, 7 follower males, about 20 adult and subadult solitary males, 53 adult females, 13 subadult females, and at least 90 juveniles and infants.

Four of the five habitat types – *Acacia* scrublands, palm forests, swamps, and open grasslands – constitute patches in that they are distinct from one another and are dominated by particular plant resources that the baboons feed on (the flowers, leaves, and seeds of *Acacia* spp., the fruit of *Hyphaene thebaica*, the blades, flowers, roots, and stems of *Cyperus* spp., and the blades, flowers, roots, and stems of *Sporobolus* spp., respectively). During the study period, the Filoha region was characterized by 23 *Acacia* scrublands patches, 7 palm forests, 7 open grassland patches, and 4 swamps (Schreier 2009). The fifth habitat type – cliffs – does not contain food resources but is an essential resource for the baboons as they sleep together on a cliff each night. The baboons spent almost 65 percent of daytime hours in *Acacia* scrublands and palm forests, the majority of which was spent traveling and feeding, and about one-quarter of their time (24 percent) resting and grooming on cliffs (Schreier 2009). They consistently spent the early part of the day on a cliff before traveling into the other habitat types to forage, and eventually returned to a cliff in the afternoon. As the baboons used only two sleeping cliffs during the study period, there are four overall travel routes: Filoha–Filoha, Filoha–Wasaro, Wasaro–Filoha, and Wasaro–Wasaro.

Data Collection and Analysis

Data on movement patterns were collected by conducting all-day follows of Band 1. Accompanied by a field assistant, AS located the baboons at their sleeping cliff at 06:00 and followed them until 18:00, or for as long as possible until we had to leave them in order to arrive at camp before dark. We followed the baboons after nights when they slept on the Filoha cliff, and sometimes after they slept on the Wasaro cliff. During all-day follows, AS mapped the geographic center of the band every 15 minutes using a Garmin eTrex Legend handheld global positioning system (GPS) unit. Daily path lengths were determined based on days ($N = 105$) for which we recorded complete daily routes (i.e., from the morning sleeping site to the evening sleeping site) (e.g., Altmann & Altmann 1970; Sigg & Stolba 1981). We calculated daily path lengths by summing the distance between all mapped locations using ArcView GIS 3.1 software. To compute complete daily paths on days when we had to leave the baboons to return to Filoha before they actually reached the Wasaro cliff, we calculated the straight-line distance from where we left the baboons to their usual Wasaro cliff sleeping site (confirming this location the following morning).

We tested whether the baboons' travel patterns conformed to a Lévy distribution by comparing the power-law and exponential distributions of both step length and waiting time data (Schreier & Grove 2010). To calculate step lengths, we first transformed our data from latitudinal and longitudinal coordinates into great circle distances between pairs of points using the haversine. Each step length, defined as the distance between two successive GPS points at 15-minute intervals, is thus scaled to a consistent ratio that takes into account the curvature of the Earth. Waiting times were calculated as multiples of the 15-minute periods used for sampling (e.g., if the band was stationary for three successive sampling periods, a waiting time of 45 minutes was recorded). Both datasets were divided based on the sleeping cliff at which the band began and completed their daily foraging route (see Schreier & Grove 2010 for details).

To distinguish between travel within patches versus travel between patches, we fitted exponential and normal distributions to step lengths from each 15-minute segment of the day individually (i.e., 06:00–06:15, 06:15–06:30, etc.), with each 15-minute segment represented by all the GPS points recorded for that segment across days (see Schreier & Grove 2014 for details). Furthermore, the partial sum method (Knell & Codling 2012) allowed us to identify "tipping points" – or transitions – between periods of high-speed and low-speed foraging (the assumption being that high-speed foraging corresponds to travel between patches and low-speed foraging to travel within patches; Schreier & Grove 2014).

Results

For the step length dataset, three of the four travel routes were best approximated by an exponential distribution (indicating random travel), and not the power-law distribution. Only the Wasaro–Wasaro route was best approximated by the power-law distribution, and thus conforms to LW. In contrast, all four of the waiting times on the travel routes followed Lévy distributions (Schreier & Grove 2010).

While none of the individual segments of the Filoha–Filoha travel route conformed to a normal distribution, 10 segments of the Filoha–Wasaro route, 5 segments of the Wasaro–Filoha route, and 7 segments of the Wasaro–Wasaro route did conform to a normal distribution. This reveals that there were phases of these three travel routes that were consistently spent moving between known resource locations. These normally distributed segments involved significantly longer-distance movements on all three of the Filoha–Wasaro, Wasaro–Filoha, and Wasaro–Wasaro travel routes, indicating that, in line with ARS theory, the baboons were alternately traveling long distances between known patches and short distances within patches (Schreier & Grove 2014).

For the Filoha–Filoha travel route ($N = 49$), the partial sum analysis suggested two major tipping points at 08:00 and 14:00 (Schreier & Grove 2010). These correspond to the points at which distances covered in each 15-minute segment consistently rise above and fall below the average distance traveled per segment on this route. These transitions neatly bracket the middle period of the day of travel and forage, and generally correspond with when the baboons departed from the Filoha cliff in the morning and when they began their travel back to the cliff in the afternoon (Schreier 2009). Thus, these tipping points indicate transitions between travel within patches (i.e., within *Acacia* scrublands or palm forests) and travel between patches (i.e., between the cliff and palm forests or *Acacia* scrubland in the morning, and vice versa in the afternoon).

For the Filoha–Wasaro travel route ($N = 29$), the partial sum analysis suggested five tipping points during the course of the daily route which correspond with the baboons' on-the-ground travel from the Filoha cliff to the Wasaro cliff (Schreier & Grove 2014). On these days, the baboons' travel included three peaks: travel from the Filoha cliff into the Hot Springs palm forest, followed by travel into and through *Acacia* scrublands, and finally travel to the Wasaro cliff (Schreier 2009). The five tipping points therefore correspond to the beginning and end of the first two of these travel peaks, and the beginning of the third one. The end of the last travel peak (i.e., travel to the Wasaro cliff) probably did not emerge as a tipping point because the last hour of the Filoha–Wasaro route usually had to be estimated as a direct path from where we had to leave the baboons in order to return to camp by dark.

For the Wasaro–Filoha travel route ($N = 12$), tipping points occurred at 07:45 and 12:00, marking the transitions between travel within patches (i.e., travel within *Acacia* scrublands) versus travel between patches (i.e., cliff to *Acacia* scrublands and vice versa). The segments conforming to normal distributions occur in two clusters, between 08:00 and 09:45 and between 14:45 and 15:45 (Schreier & Grove 2014), corresponding to when the baboons left the Wasaro cliff in the morning and approached the Filoha cliff in the afternoon. Finally, partial sum analysis of the Wasaro–Wasaro route ($N = 15$) indicated tipping points at 07:15 and 10:15 (Schreier & Grove 2014), which correspond to the beginning and end of the first peak in travel activity (i.e., departure from the Wasaro cliff and "settling in" to forage in the *Acacia*) and at 14:45 which corresponds to the baboons departing the *Acacia* en route to the Wasaro cliff.

Discussion

The movement pattern in which step lengths are exponentially distributed while waiting times follow a power-law suggests that the patches used by the baboons are randomly distributed in space but power-law distributed in size (Schreier & Grove 2010). As mentioned above, an LW with exponent of 2 is an optimal search pattern for a forager searching with no prior information about the resources in its environment (Viswanathan et al. 1999). There is, however, abundant evidence that primates' abilities to learn about and monitor aspects of their environments far exceed those of other animals (Shettleworth 1998). For example, Normand and Boesch (2009) argue that chimpanzees in Taï forest were aware of the distances and directions they were traveling, as evidenced by approaching the same resources from various directions. Noser and Byrne (2007, 2010) suggest that chacma baboons navigate through their environment using route-based maps, relying on landmarks to travel from one place to another. Furthermore, to choose efficient paths, tamarins compare the distances and directions from their current location to a large number of potential foraging trees (Garber & Porter 2014; Porter & Garber 2013).

Particularly relevant to the present case study, Kummer (1968) reported that hamadryas baboons seemed to remember specific locations in their natural environment and appeared to travel between them via the shortest route. When in search of water sources, the baboons appeared to use least-distance strategies to travel from one location to another, and they sped up as they approached a water source even before it was in view (Kummer 1968). Similarly, Sigg and Stolba (1981) reported several lines of evidence suggesting that hamadryas baboons know the spatial layout of their home range. First, they found a strong correlation between departure direction from the sleeping cliff and the location (relative to the sleeping cliff) of the midday water hole. Members of bands often split up after leaving the sleeping cliff but reunited at midday water holes, arriving from an assortment of directions and morning travel sequences (Sigg 1986). Second, the baboons reached frequently visited resources from a wider variety of departure directions than sites visited less commonly. In addition, the baboons' travel speed increased more frequently before reaching such resources than would be expected by chance, even when those resources were not in sight (Sigg & Stolba 1981).

The assumption inherent in the LW of no prior information about resource distribution is thus almost certainly violated in hamadryas baboons, and the concept of "search" itself likely does not apply to animals with advanced cognitive abilities, such as primates. Optimal behaviors in familiar habitat will necessarily differ from those when true search is being employed. As discussed above, an LW pattern can emerge due to animals' interactions with resources with which they are already familiar. The LW pattern that was produced from the baboon waiting time data may be due to the fractal structure of the baboons' resources and thus would not in and of itself demonstrate the existence of an innate search algorithm.

The tipping points suggested by the partial sum analyses of all four travel routes effectively differentiate between two modes of travel, and indicate that the baboons do indeed display different movement strategies when traveling within as opposed to between patches. Their daily travel routes are thus consistent with periods of ARS, or searching within patches, as well as longer movement between known patches. The baboons are thus searching only intermittently at restricted scales while they travel directly between these resource-rich patches. The LW pattern described by Schreier and Grove (2010) and discussed above therefore more likely reflects the baboons' interactions with their known environment than an innate search algorithm suggested by the Lévy hypothesis. The hamadryas baboon movement patterns provide a clear example of how an LW pattern may emerge even when the animals are not only engaged in search. Their travel patterns better fit the two-mode model which distinguishes between search at the local scale and long-distance movement between known locations, and this may also be true for other animals with knowledge of the distribution of resources in their home range.

The interface between GPS data, their presentation in a spatially explicit GIS, and their analysis with spatially implicit statistical models provides a wealth of tools for the characterization of primate movement patterns. A key methodological conclusion to be drawn from the above analyses is that while data from a GIS can be extracted in univariate form for further statistical testing, the results of such testing can only be fully interpreted by returning to the GIS as a record of movement patterns "on the ground." Statistics in this instance provide simple, informative metrics concerning the movement pattern *in general*; to examine the *specifics* of the movement pattern – and in particular to understand the effects of habitat structure on that pattern – we must return to the spatial record embodied within the GIS. In this way, data collected via GPS can be interrogated in multiple formats, allowing us both to test existing hypotheses and to formulate further research questions.

Acknowledgments

We thank Christopher Shaffer, Francine Dolins, Jena Hickey, Nathan Nibbelink, and Leila Porter for inviting us to contribute a chapter to this volume. AS thanks Larissa Swedell for help at all stages of the field project as well as for funding, and the Wildlife Conservation Authority of Ethiopia for permission to conduct research at Filoha.

Funding was provided by the City University of New York PSC-CUNY Research Award Program (award #66588-0035 to L. Swedell), the New York Consortium in Evolutionary Primatology, and the City University of New York PhD Program in Anthropology. For support and assistance in the field, thanks to Getenet Hailemeskel, Demekech Woldearegay, Teklu Tesfaye, Getu Mamush, Denberu Tesfaye, Getu Kifle, and Julian Saunders. MG thanks Robin Dunbar for comments on the underlying model, and Charles Janson for discussions regarding the mathematics of spatial memory.

References

Al-Safadi, M. M. 1994. The hamadryas baboon, *Papio hamadryas* (Linnaeus, 1758) in Yemen (Mammalia: Primates: Cercopithecidae). *Zoology in the Middle East* **10**: 5–16.

Altmann, S. A. and Altmann, J. 1970. *Baboon Ecology*. University of Chicago Press, Chicago, IL.

Atkinson, R. P. D., Rhodes, C. J., Macdonald, D. W., and Anderson, R. M. 2002. Scale-free dynamics in the movement patterns of jackals. *Oikos* **98**: 134–140.

Austin, D., Bowen, W. D., and McMillan, J. I. 2004. Intraspecific variation in movement patterns: modeling individual behaviour in a large marine predator. *Oikos* **105**: 15–30.

Bailey, H. and Thompson, P. 2006. Quantitative analysis of bottlenose dolphin movement patterns and their relationship with foraging. *Journal of Animal Ecology* **75**: 456–465.

Bartumeus, F. 2007. Levy processes in animal movement: an evolutionary hypothesis. *Fractals: Complex Geometry Patterns and Scaling in Nature and Society* **15**: 151–162.

Bartumeus, F., Peters, F., Pueyo, S., Marrase, C., and Catalan, J. 2003. Helical Levy walks: adjusting searching statistics to resource availability in microzooplankton. *Proceedings of the National Academy of Sciences of the United States of America* **100**: 12771–12775.

Benedix, J. H. 1993. Area-restricted search by the plains pocket gopher (*Geomys bursarius*) in tallgrass prairie habitat. *Behavioral Ecology* **4**: 318–324.

Benhamou, S. 1992. Efficiency of area-concentrated searching behavior in a continuous patchy environment. *Journal of Theoretical Biology* **159**: 67–81.

Benhamou, S. 2007. How many animals really do the Lévy walk? *Ecology* **88**: 1962–1969.

Berg, H. C. 1983. *Random Walks in Biology*. Princeton University Press, Princeton, NJ.

Bergman, C. M., Schaefer, J. A., and Luttich, S. N. 2000. Caribou movement as a correlated random walk. *Oecologia* **123**: 364–374.

Biquand, S., Biquand-Guyot, V., Boug, A., and Gautier, J.-P. 1992. Group composition in wild and commensal hamadryas baboons: a comparative study in Saudi Arabia. *International Journal of Primatology* **13**: 533–543.

Blackwell, P. G. 1997. Random diffusion models for animal movement. *Ecological Modelling* **100**: 87–102.

Bond, A. B. 1980. Optimal foraging in a uniform habitat: search mechanism of the green lacewing. *Animal Behaviour* **28**: 10–19.

Bovet, P. and Benhamou, S. 1988. Spatial analysis of animals' movements using a correlated random walk model. *Journal of Theoretical Biology* **131**: 419–433.

Boyer, D., Ramos-Fernández, G., Miramontes, O., et al. 2006. Scale-free foraging by primates emerges from their interaction with a complex environment. *Proceedings of the Royal Society B: Biological Sciences* **273**: 1743–1750.

Brantingham, P. J. 2006. Measuring forager mobility. *Current Anthropology* **47**: 435–459.

Brockmann, D., Hufnagel, L., and Geisel, T. 2006. The scaling laws of human travel. *Nature* **439**: 462–465.

Brown, C. T., Liebovitch, L. S., and Glendon, R. 2007. Lévy flights in Dobe Ju/'hoansi foraging patterns. *Human Ecology* **35**: 129–138.

Brown, J. H., Gupta, V. K., Li, B.-L., et al. 2002. The fractal nature of nature: power laws, ecological complexity and biodiversity. *Philosophical Transactions of the Royal Society B: Biological Sciences* **357**: 619–626.

Byrne, R. W., Noser, R., Bates, L. A., and Jupp, P. E. 2009. How did they get here from there? Detecting changes of direction in terrestrial ranging. *Animal Behaviour* **77**: 619–631.

Chapleau, F., Johansen, P. H., and Williamson, M. 1988. The use and abuse of the term strategy. *Oikos* **53**: 136–138.

Clauset, A., Shalizi, C. R., and Newman, M. E. J. 2009. Power-law distributions in empirical data. *SIAM Review* **51**: 661–703.

Condit, R., Ashton, P. S., Baker, P., et al. 2000. Spatial patterns in the distribution of tropical tree species. *Science* **288**: 1414–1418.

Crist, T. O., Guertin, D. S., Wiens, J. A., and Milne, B. T. 1992. Animal movement in heterogeneous landscapes: an experiment with *Eleodes* beetles in shortgrass prairie. *Functional Ecology* **6**: 536–544.

Curio, E. 1976. *The Ethology of Predation*. Springer, New York.

Dai, X., Shannon, G., Slotow, R., Page, B., and Duffy, K. J. 2007. Short-duration daytime movements of a cow herd of African elephants. *Journal of Mammalogy* **88**: 151–157.

de Jager, N. R. and Rohweder, J. J. 2011. Spatial scaling of core and dominant forest cover in the Upper Mississippi and Illinois River floodplains, USA. *Landscape Ecology* **26**: 697–708.

de Knegt, H. J., Hengeveld, G. M., van Langevelde, F., et al. 2007. Patch density determines movement patterns and foraging efficiency of large herbivores. *Behavioral Ecology* **18**: 1065–1072.

Edwards, A. M., Phillips, R. A., Watkins, N. W., et al. 2007. Revisiting Lévy flight search patterns of wandering albatrosses, bumblebees and deer. *Nature* **449**: 1044–1045.

Faugeras, B. and Maury, O. 2007. Modeling fish population movements: from an individual-based representation to an advection–diffusion equation. *Journal of Theoretical Biology* **247**: 837–848.

Ford, R. G. 1983. Home range in a patchy environment: optimal foraging predictions. *American Zoologist* **23**: 315–326.

Fritz, H., Said, S., and Weimerskirch, H. 2003. Scale-dependent hierarchical adjustments of movement patterns in a long-range foraging seabird. *Proceedings of the Royal Society B: Biological Sciences* **270**: 1143–1148.

Garber, P. A. and Porter, L. 2014. Navigating in small-scale space: the role of landmarks and resource monitoring in understanding saddleback tamarin travel. *American Journal of Primatology* **76**: 447–459.

Gautestad, A. O. 2013. Animal space use: distinguishing a two-level superposition of scale-specific walks from scale-free Levy walk. *Oikos* **122**: 612–620.

Gautestad, A. O. and Mysterud, I. 2005. Intrinsic scaling complexity in animal dispersion and abundance. *American Naturalist* **165**: 44–55.

Gonzalez, M. C., Hidalgo, C. A., and Barabasi, A.-L. 2008. Understanding individual human mobility patterns. *Nature* **453**: 779–782.

Grove, M. 2010. The quantitative analysis of mobility: ecological techniques and archaeological extensions. Pages 83–118 in *New Perspectives on Old Stones: Analytical Approaches to Palaeolithic Technologies*. S. Lycett and P. Chuahan (Eds.). Springer, Dordrecht.

Grove, M. 2013. The evolution of spatial memory. *Mathematical Biosciences* **242**: 25–32.

Grunbaum, D. 1998. Using spatially explicit models to characterize foraging performance in heterogeneous landscapes. *American Naturalist* **151**: 97–115.

Hills, T. T., Kalff, C., and Wiener, J. M. 2013. Adaptive Levy processes and area-restricted search in human foraging. *PLoS ONE* **8**. DOI: 10.1371/journal.pone.0060488.

Janson, C. H. and DiBitetti, M. S. 1997. Experimental analysis of food detection in capuchin monkeys: effects of distance, travel speed, and resource size. *Behavioral Ecology and Sociobiology* **41**: 17–24.

Johnson, A. R., Milne, B. T., and Wiens, J. A. 1992. Diffusion in fractal landscapes: simulations and experimental studies of tenebrionid beetle movements. *Ecology* **73**: 1968–1983.

Johnson, D. S., London, J. M., Lea, M.-A., and Durban, J. W. 2008. Continuous-time correlated random walk model for animal telemetry data. *Ecology* **89**: 1208–1215.

Kareiva, P. and Odell, G. 1987. Swarms of predators exhibit preytaxis if individual predators use area-restricted search. *American Naturalist* **130**: 233–270.

Kareiva, P. M. and Shigesada, N. 1983. Analyzing insect movement as a correlated random walk. *Oecologia* **56**: 234–238.

Keasar, T., Shmida, A., and Motro, U. 1996. Innate movement rules in foraging bees: flight distances are affected by recent rewards and are correlated with choice of flower type. *Behavioral Ecology and Sociobiology* **39**: 381–388.

Knell, A. S. and Codling, E. A. 2012. Classifying area-restricted search (ARS) using a partial sum approach. *Theoretical Ecology* **5**: 325–339.

Kummer, H. 1968. *Social Organization of Hamadryas Baboons*. University of Chicago Press, Chicago, IL.

Laing, J. 1937. Host-finding by insect parasites: I. Observations on the finding of hosts by *Alysia manducator, Mormoniella vitripennis* and *Trichogramma evanescens*. *Journal of Animal Ecology* **6**: 298–317.

Laing, J. 1938. Host-finding by insect parasites: II. The chance of *Trichogramma evanescens* finding its hosts. *Journal of Experimental Biology* **15**: 281–302.

Levandowsky, M., Klafter, J., and White, B. S. 1988a. Feeding and swimming behavior in grazing microzooplankton. *Journal of Protozoology* **35**: 243–246.

Levandowsky, M., Klafter, J., and White, B. S. 1988b. Swimming behavior and chemosensory responses in the protistan microzooplankton as a function of the hydrodynamic regime. *Bulletin of Marine Science* **43**: 758–763.

Levandowsky, M., White, B. S., and Schuster, F. L. 1997. Random movements of soil amebas. *Acta Protozoologica* **36**: 237–248.

Lévy, P. 1937. *Theorie de l'Addition des Variables Aleatoires*. Paris: Gauthier-Villars.

Lode, T. 2000. Functional response and area-restricted search in a predator: seasonal exploitation of anurans by the European polecat, *Mustela putorius*. *Austral Ecology* **25**: 223–231.

Marell, A., Ball, J. P., and Hofgaard, A. 2002. Foraging and movement paths of female reindeer: insights from fractal analysis, correlated random walks, and Lévy flights. *Canadian Journal of Zoology/Revue Canadienne De Zoologie* **80**: 854–865.

Miramontes, O., DeSouza, O., Hernandez, D., and Ceccon, E. 2012. Non-Levy mobility patterns of Mexican Me'Phaa peasants searching for fuel wood. *Human Ecology* **40**: 167–174.

Newman, M. E. J. 2005. Power laws, Pareto distributions and Zipf's law. *Contemporary Physics* **46**: 323–351.

Normand, E. and Boesch, C. 2009. Sophisticated Euclidean maps in forest chimpanzees. *Animal Behaviour* **77**: 1195–1201.

Noser, R. and Byrne, R. W. 2007. Travel routes and planning of visits to out-of-sight resources in wild chacma baboons, *Papio ursinus*. *Animal Behaviour* **73**: 257–266.

Noser, R. and Byrne, R. W. 2010. How do wild baboobs (*Papio ursinus*) plan their routes? Travel among multiple high-quality food sources with inter-group competition. *Animal Cognition* **13**, 145–155.

Patlak, C. S. 1953a. Random walk with persistence and external bias. *Bulletin of Mathematical Biophysics* **15**: 311–318.

Patlak, C. S. 1953b. A mathematical contribution to the study of orientation of organisms. *Bulletin of Mathematical Biophysics* **15**: 431–476.

Porter, L. and Garber, P. 2013. Foraging and spatial memory in wild Weddell's saddleback tamarins (*Saguinus fuscicollis weddelli*) when moving between distant and out-of-sight goals. *International Journal of Primatology* **34**: 30–48.

Raichlen, D. A., Wood, B. M., Gordon, A. D., et al. 2014. Evidence of Lévy walk foraging patterns in human hunter-gatherers. *Proceedings of the National Academy of Sciences USA* **111**(2): 728–733.

Ramos-Fernández, G., Mateos, J. L., Miramontes, O., et al. 2004. Lévy walk patterns in the foraging movements of spider monkeys (*Ateles geoffroyi*). *Behavioral Ecology and Sociobiology* **55**: 223–230.

Reid, A. T. 1953. On stochastic processes in biology. *Biometrics* **9**: 275–289.

Reynolds, A. M., Reynolds, D. R., Smith, A. D., Svensson, G. P., and Lofstedt, C. 2007a. Appetitive flight patterns of male *Agrotis segetum* moths over landscape scales. *Journal of Theoretical Biology* **245**: 141–149.

Reynolds, A. M., Smith, A. D., Menzel, R., et al. 2007b. Displaced honey bees perform optimal scale-free search flights. *Ecology* **88**: 1955–1961.

Reynolds, A. M., Smith, A. D., Reynolds, D. R., Carreck, N. L., and Osborne, J. L. 2007c. Honeybees perform optimal scale-free searching flights when attempting to locate a food source. *Journal of Experimental Biology* **210**: 3763–3770.

Rhee, I., Shin, M., Hong, S., et al. 2011. On the Lévy-walk nature of human mobility. *IEEE–ACM Transactions on Networking* **19**: 630–643.

Schaefer, J. A., Bergman, C. M., and Luttich, S. N. 2000. Site fidelity of female caribou at multiple spatial scales. *Landscape Ecology* **15**: 731–739.

Schreier, A. L. 2009. The influence of resource distribution on the social structure and travel patterns of wild hamadryas baboons (*Papio hamadryas*) in Filoha, Awash National Park, Ethiopia. Dissertation, City University of New York.

Schreier, A. L. and Grove, M. 2010. Ranging patterns of hamadryas baboons: random walk analyses. *Animal Behaviour* **80**: 75–87.

Schreier, A. L. and Grove, M. 2014. Recurrent patterning in the daily foraging routes of hamadryas baboons (*Papio hamadryas*): spatial memory in large- versus small-scale space. *American Journal of Primatology* **76**: 421–435.

Schreier, A. and Swedell, L. 2008. Use of palm trees as a sleeping site for hamadryas baboons (*Papio hamadryas*) in Ethiopia. *American Journal of Primatology* **70**: 107–113.

Schreier, A. L. and Swedell, L. 2009. The fourth level of social structure in a multi-level society: ecological and social functions of clans in hamadryas baboons. *American Journal of Primatology* **71**: 948–955.

Schreier, A. L. and Swedell, L. 2012a. The socioecology of network scaling ratios in the multilevel society of hamadryas baboons. *International Journal of Primatology* **33**: 1069–1080.

Schreier, A. L. and Swedell, L. 2012b. Ecology and sociality in a multilevel society: ecological determinants of social cohesion in hamadryas baboons. *American Journal of Physical Anthropology* **148**: 580–588.

Shettleworth, S. J. 1998. *Cognition, Evolution, and Behavior*. Oxford University Press, New York.

Shlesinger, M. F. and Klafter, J. 1986. Lévy walks versus Lévy flights. Pages 279–283 in *On Growth and Form*. H. E. Stanley and N. Ostrowski (Eds.). Martinus Nijhof, Amsterdam.

Shlesinger, M. F., Zaslavsky, G. M., and Klafter, J. 1993. Strange kinetics. *Nature* **363**: 31–37.

Sigg, H. 1986. Ranging patterns in hamadryas baboons: evidence for a mental map. Pages 87–91 in *Primate Ontogeny, Cognition, and Social Behaviour*, Vol. 3, J. G. Else and P. C. Lee (Eds.). Cambridge University Press, Cambridge.

Sigg, H. and Stolba, A. 1981. Home range and daily march in a hamadryas baboon troop. *Folia Primatologica* **26**: 40–75.

Sims, D. W., Righton, D., and Pitchford, J. W. 2007. Minimizing errors in identifying Lévy flight behaviour of organisms. *Journal of Animal Ecology* **76**: 222–229.

Sims, D. W., Southall, E. J., Humphries, N. E., et al. 2008. Scaling laws of marine predator search behaviour. *Nature* **451**: 1098–1102.

Skellam, J. G. 1951. Random dispersal in theoretical populations. *Biometrika* **38**: 196–218.

Skellam, J. G. 1973. The formulation and interpretation of mathematical models of diffusionary processes in population biology. Pages 63–85 in *The Mathematical Theory of the Dynamics of Biological Populations*. M. S. Bartlett and R. W. Hiorns (Eds.). Academic Press, New York.

Sueur, C. 2011. A non-Lévy random walk in chacma baboons: what does it mean? *PLoS ONE* **6**. DOI: 10.1371/journal.pone.0016131.

Sueur, C., Briard, L., and Petit, O. 2011. Individual analyses of Lévy walk in semi-free ranging tonkean macaques (*Macaca tonkeana*). *PLoS ONE* **6**. DOI: 10.1371/journal.pone.0026788.

Swedell, L. 2000. Two takeovers in wild hamadryas baboons. *Folia Primatologica* **71**: 169–172.

Swedell, L. 2002a. Affiliation among females in wild hamadryas baboons (*Papio hamadryas hamadryas*). *International Journal of Primatology* **23**: 1205–1226.

Swedell, L. 2002b. Ranging behavior, group size and behavioral flexibility in Ethiopian hamadryas baboons (*Papio hamadryas hamadryas*). *Folia Primatologica* **73**: 95–103.

Swedell, L. 2006. *Strategies of Sex and Survival in Hamadryas Baboons: Through a Female Lens*. Prentice Hall, Upper Saddle River, NJ.

Swedell, L. and Schreier, A. 2009. Male aggression towards females in hamadryas baboons: conditioning, coercion, and control. Pages 244–268 in *Sexual Coercion in Primates: An Evolutionary Perspective on Male Aggression Against Females*. M. N. Muller and R. Wrangham (Eds.). Harvard University Press, Cambridge, MA.

Swedell, L., Hailemeskel, G., and Schreier, A. 2008. Composition and seasonality of diet in adult male hamadryas baboons: preliminary findings from Filoha. *Folia Primatologica* **79**: 476–490.

Swedell, L., Saunders, J., Schreier, A., et al. 2011. Female "dispersal" in hamadryas baboons: transfer among social units in a multi-level society. *American Journal of Physical Anthropology* **145**: 360–370.

Turchin, P. 1998. *Quantitative Analysis of Movement*. Sinauer Associates, Sunderland, MA.

Viswanathan, G. M., Afanasyev, V., Buldyrev, S. V., et al. 1996. Levy flight search patterns of wandering albatrosses. *Nature* **381**: 413–415.

Viswanathan, G. M., Bartumeus, F., Buldyrev, S. V., et al. 2002. Levy flight random searches in biological phenomena. *Physica A: Statistical Mechanics and Its Applications* **314**: 208–213.

Viswanathan, G. M., Buldyrev, S. V., Havlin, S., et al. 1999. Optimizing the success of random searches. *Nature* **401**: 911–914.

Viswanathan, G. M., Raposo, E. P., and da Luz, M. G. E. 2008. Levy flights and superdiffusion in the context of biological encounters and random searches. *Physics of Life Reviews* **5**: 133–150.

Ward, D. and Saltz, D. 1994. Foraging at different spatial scales: dorcas gazelles foraging for lilies in the Negev Desert. *Ecology* **75**: 48–58.

Zinner, D., Pelaez, F., and Torkler, F. 2001. Distribution and habitat associations of baboons (*Papio hamadryas*) in central Eritrea. *International Journal of Primatology* **22**: 397–413.

13 The Use of Small-Scale Spatial Analysis to Evaluate Primate Behavior and Welfare in Captive Settings

Stephen R. Ross and Marisa A. Shender

Introduction

The manner in which wild, free-ranging primates spatially utilize their environment is useful for studies of home ranges, environmental variability, territoriality, climate change effects, ecology, and travel patterns. The emergence of satellite-based technologies including global positioning systems (GPS) and geographic information systems (GIS) has provided an invaluable set of resources with which to track the movement of primates and other animals across vast landscapes with great detail. The strength of these systems, as described elsewhere in this volume, is the increasingly accurate ability to record the use of space by individuals and groups over distances that would be difficult to cover using other technologies. There are circumstances, however, in which satellite-based systems are unnecessary, ineffective, or simply not tenable for use. Most notably, they are problematic when spatial analysis is required within small captive settings such as laboratories, zoos, or sanctuaries.

An understanding of how captive primates utilize the spaces provided to them can help elucidate a range of basic and applied research questions. For instance, in rigid, experimental settings, space-use analysis can be used to track how subjects perform in navigation and spatial memory-related tasks. Implementing systems such as space-use analysis could aid in exploration of the neural basis for the control of particular behaviors as they relate to the manipulation of sensory feedback. Other studies might track how animals explore available space during their daily activities, thereby providing new insight into how the welfare of captive primates is affected by their artificial built environments. Space in captive settings is relatively small as compared to wild settings, and the degree to which satellite-based systems are effective or necessary is an important issue for investigators to consider. In this chapter we will review options for collecting spatial data in small-scale settings and discuss how both technology-based and traditional methodologies can meet the needs of researchers studying primates' use of space and their behaviors within those enclosures.

When and Why Might One *Not* Need GPS Methodologies?

While the advancement of GPS technology has facilitated broader implementation of studies of wild primates in natural settings, there remain several factors that tend to make the use of GPS technology less ideal for studies of primates in captive settings. Though no single factor may eliminate the use of GPS transmitters as a potential tool for collating spatial data in these settings, other methods may be more appropriate.

The first limitation of GPS technology is its resolution. In almost all cases, captive primate habitats are exponentially smaller than those experienced by their wild counterparts. Wild home ranges vary from as small as 0.3 ha for mouse lemurs (Radespiel 2007) to 4000 ha ranges for terrestrial baboon species (Markham & Altmann 2008). Captive environments, whether in laboratories, zoos, or sanctuaries, are only a fraction of these sizes. For instance, while wild chimpanzee home ranges generally cover 5–15 km^2 (mean = 12 km^2; Chapman & Pavelka 2005; Clutton-Brock & Harvey 1977; Newton-Fisher, 2003), the largest captive facilities pale in comparison. Even the relatively expansive outdoor habitats at the Chimp Haven sanctuary in Louisiana top out at about 0.02 km^2, or about 0.2 percent of the wild range sizes. Due to these smaller sizes, measurements of space use by captive primates are often in meters or even fractions of meters rather than kilometers or hectares. For example, the typical measure of proximity is often simply the arm's length of the subject species being observed. While the arm span of gorillas may reach close to a meter, most primate species have substantially smaller arm spans and even high-resolution GPS imagery is unlikely to reliably capture distinctions at that level.

A second limitation of GPS technology is that many artificial primate environments include, and in some cases are limited to, indoor areas where GPS signals may be rendered less optimal. The use of GPS tracking for wild primates seems to work best in open environments such as savannahs and open grasslands, and attempts to utilize GPS tracking in heavily forested areas have been less effective (D'Eon et al. 2002; Phillips et al. 1998; Reutebuch et al. 2003). Even when GPS signals can penetrate indoor areas, those signals are generally more sporadic, and given that the greatest drain on GPS collar batteries occurs when the system searches for satellite signals to acquire a location fix, this issue likely has significant detriment to transmitter longevity.

The practical and logistical considerations of placing GPS collars on captive primates is another issue that may give pause to those considering satellite-based solutions for studies of captive primate space use. While there is some indirect evidence that the administration of radio-collars causes no undue disruption to primate subjects wearing them (Markham et al. 2013), the considerations for captive primates are likely measured in different terms. For primates in publicly viewable areas such as in zoo exhibits, staff are likely to be reluctant to have animals wearing equipment that may be (inaccurately or not) perceived by the public as harmful, cumbersome, or obtrusive (M. Leahy, pers. comm., November 19, 2013). There are also safety concerns with collars. First, an animal with a collar may become entangled on structural hardware in the exhibit. Second, given that some GPS collars automatically detach following the end of their battery life (time-in-mortality), an untethered electronic device in a glass-fronted exhibit might lead to damage to the exhibit, the animals, and/or visitors.

Finally, in comparison to the direct observation methods we will describe later in this chapter, the cost of GPS collar systems may be prohibitive for many researchers. Wildlife GPS devices can cost up to tens of thousands of dollars (Matthews et al.

2013) including a receiver, software, cables, and extra batteries, and can push the limits of most captive-based research programs.

Though the advantages of an automated data collection system remain attractive to those interested in how captive primates utilize the space of artificial environments, the aforementioned restrictions often render GPS-based solutions untenable. Non-automated methods, using human observers, have become the norm for this field of study and in this chapter we describe how several of these methods have been used to study primate space use in artificial environments.

Non-Automated Methods of Tracking Space Use

The vast majority of micro-scale studies rely on direct observations of individuals. Observations such as these focus on individuals' locations on a proxy map from which their movements can be inferred. Understanding the manner in which captive primates utilize the artificial environments in which they live can provide important insight into the relative appropriateness of those spaces. As such, most studies of captive primate space use are specifically interested in the characteristics of the areas utilized by the subjects. In other words, researchers are interested in discerning animal preferences for particular elements of their habitat by recording which parts of the enclosure are used most frequently. This association between space use and enclosure characteristics has been measured both directly and indirectly, and here we will describe the primary methods that have been utilized.

Categorization of Space

One of the key characterizations of captive space use studies is the manner by which the environment is defined. At any given moment in time, a primate subject might inhabit a unit of space and this unit of space can be defined a priori (in advance of data collection) or post hoc (as part of the analysis process). While the former method involves hypothesis-driven categorization of areas which define how data are collected, the latter process may be considered akin to the use of GIS information in which secondary layers of information are overlayed on an otherwise neutral set of grid points. We hereafter term these approaches as *functional categorization* and *neutral categorization* systems.

An example of a functional categorization system comes from Roberts and Kohn (1993) and their study of captive tarsiers (*Tarsius bancanus*). Prior to data collection, the tarsiers' environment was categorized based on the investigators' interests and hypotheses on how the primates might use the space. For instance, the space was divided into vertical tiers, and the authors found the tarsiers used small-diameter vertical elements and mid-level enclosure heights at proportions that differed from the avail-ability of those features. The diminutive size of this species (rarely above 150 g), and the relatively small enclosure (approximately 18.4 m^2) also illustrates well the working environments in which more direct observational methods are necessary.

Similar work has been done with apes in which space use is recorded on maps with areas of interest that differ in size and composition but are selected based on some functional aspect of the building or the animal's behavior. For instance, Traylor-Holzer and Fritz (1985) observed four groups of chimpanzees in indoor spaces composed of three connected cages totaling approximately 21.4 m^2 in size. Data were collected on which room they chose, whether they positioned themselves on an upper or lower section of the room, to what barrier they were closest, and whether they were positioned in a corner, edge, or the center of the cage. Of note, these spaces were uniform in neither shape nor size. They were defined in advance of data collection and observers used these predefined spaces to record the location of the subjects. Here, the authors expressed hypotheses about the use of particular areas of the enclosure and found that adult (but not juvenile) chimpanzees showed preferences for the smaller cages, upper levels, and preferred to be near the perimeter of the areas.

An alternative approach is to use a neutral grid system in which uniformly spaced and sized units of space compose the entire environment. Such a system provides some advantages over a functional approach in that, much like the implementation of layers of GIS data, a variety of questions of varying complexity can be addressed at the analysis phase without being unduly restricted by predefined categories of space. Ogden et al. (1993) observed several groups of gorillas living in the naturalistic exhibits (ranging from 1100 to 2100 m^2) at three zoological parks, with the objective of determining preferences for specific structural environmental features. To do so, they recorded the location of subjects using maps of the enclosures that were divided into equal 3×3 m quadrats. As part of the analysis process, each quadrat was categorized based on factors such as slope, proximity to holding areas, and the presence of specific environmental features such as trees, rocks, and bushes. The authors were able to conclude that the gorillas preferred quadrats that were both flat and near the indoor holding area where they were fed and housed for the night – findings that have influenced exhibit design for this species since the paper was published.

Case Study: Ape Space Use Studies at Lincoln Park Zoo

In order to illustrate the range of primate space use studies conducted in artificial environments such as zoo exhibits, we here review the body of work generated by the Lester E. Fisher Center for the Study and Conservation of Apes at Lincoln Park Zoo (Chicago, IL). Here, our lab has been studying the spatial patterns of their chimpanzees and gorillas continuously for over a decade. We present an overview of this body of work to illustrate the multifaceted potential of this dataset and to highlight how the direct observation methodologies are particularly well suited to our research objectives.

In 2000, Lincoln Park Zoo initiated planning to design and construct a new exhibit for their resident gorillas and chimpanzees. At the core of the planning process was the idea that research could and should play a formative role in the design of the facility; as a result, we initiated a post-occupancy evaluation program. Post-occupancy evaluations are intended to allow managers to make effective decisions about planning and designing environments. Maple and Finlay (1987) describe the process as "using systematic models to find out exactly what makes designed environments work well for their users." Environmental psychologists have used these methods to help design high-traffic service environments, such as hospitals and post offices, for decades, but only more recently have these techniques been used to design animal-based environments. Here, scientific studies can be conducted on how animal inhabitants utilize their space in order to best inform future design.

Under this post-occupancy design philosophy, we sought to understand exactly how apes use their surroundings. This knowledge was then applied to the design of the new environment, and we subsequently evaluated the changes in space use that resulted from the new design. In this light, the study of captive primate space use is an important tool in informing not only exhibit design, but ultimately animal welfare and, in the case of zoos, the visitor experience (Ross & Lukas 2000).

Over the 10-year history of ape space use evaluation at Lincoln Park Zoo, the methodologies have evolved considerably. Though all data have always been collected electronically, there has been a gradual shift from methods that address very specific questions to more flexible and powerful means to evaluate a range of inquiries, including post-hoc questions. Consistent across methodology has been the overriding philosophy of understanding how apes utilize their artificial environments, which can provide insights into how these spaces meet their behavioral and psychological needs. In the case of species that have less overtly displayed behavioral repertoires (e.g., gorillas compared to chimpanzees), space use evaluations may be especially advantageous over traditional ethogram-based behavioral studies.

Functional Categorization of Space Use

When the post-occupancy evaluation process began, the gorillas and chimpanzees at Lincoln Park Zoo were housed at the Lester E. Fisher Great Ape House (GAH; Figure 13.1). At the time of its construction in the mid-1970s it was revolutionary for both its ape residents and visitors to the zoo. A series of indoor day rooms stretched two stories in height, providing apes with new climbing opportunities and visitors with unique views. The rooms themselves were complex and featured myriad permanent and moveable structures around which the apes could move. By 2000, the weaknesses of the building's design were evident and planning for a new, more naturalistic exhibit started. As part of this process, it was important to understand how the apes utilized this environment in order to inform that future design. In particular, we sought to identify measurable environmental preferences demonstrated by the apes. For example, did they prefer areas up high or down low? Were they spending more time watching zoo visitors by the tall glass windows or did they prefer to watch the keeper staff preparing meals in the building's core?

Initial space use evaluations were conducted in concert with behavioral data collection such that the adjacency of the focal ape to particular environmental features (doors, glass, water features, etc.) was recorded as part of timed interval scans. These methods were advantageous as they did not require any graphical representation of the space;

Figure 13.1 Indoor dayroom at the Lester Fisher Great Ape House (GAH) at Lincoln Park Zoo *ca.* 1999. Photo courtesy of Lincoln Park Zoo.

each element adjacency was an individual option to be selected on the interval. The weakness of this functional approach, however, is that it requires spaces to be categorized, and as such limits what data are recorded. For example, if an ape is recorded as being adjacent to a glass wall there is no information about where along the glass wall they are positioned. Nonetheless, Ross and Lukas (2006) recorded the location of 20 apes in relation to categories of environmental elements over a two-year period and compared these positional frequencies to volumetric measurements of the enclosures. This comparison of "observed" and "expected" frequencies allowed them to conclude that the apes demonstrated preferences for particular features of the space (wire mesh walls, doorways, corners) while avoiding other aspects (open spaces).

Neutral Grid and Post-Hoc Categorization

In 2004, the new Regenstein Center for African Apes (RCAA; Figure 13.2) was opened at Lincoln Park Zoo. Though the design of the exhibit was highly influenced by the findings from the evaluation of GAH, it also featured a range of innovations including mulch-bedding floors and flexible environments in which animals could better control their own access to outdoor yards. Importantly, the design of RCAA also included specialized second-story observation decks for researchers, providing comprehensive views that ensured animal locations could be accurately and consistently recorded.

The initial objective of space use studies in RCAA was to evaluate if and how the apes' environmental preferences were affected by the new design. We recognized some of the restrictions of our previous methodologies, and implemented a more flexible system based on the neutral grid paradigm and the need for a map interface. Observers used tablet computers on which representations of the actual exhibit space could be overlayed with a grid representing 1 m^2 quadrats. Users collected information on the

Figure 13.2 Indoor dayroom at the Regenstein Center for African Apes (RCAA) at Lincoln Park Zoo (*ca.* 2004). Photo courtesy of Lincoln Park Zoo.

location of the animal every 30 seconds by selecting the grid space on the map with a stylus. These methods allowed for very precise locating of the animal within its indoor and outdoor environments with a level of precision that would be difficult to achieve with satellite-based methods.

To facilitate the comparison with the element-adjacency data from the older facility, data from the new facility were transformed to characterize each grid by its proximity to the same set of features used in the previous analysis (Ross et al. 2009). The authors utilized an electivity index (Vanderploeg & Scavia 1979) to measure the utilization of specific elements in relation to their availability in the environment, which helped determine the degree to which the old and new exhibits structurally fulfilled the apes' preferences and spatial needs. Chimpanzees and gorillas showed significant differences in how they used certain structural elements in the new facility. For instance, gorillas tended to show less preference for areas adjacent to doorways in the new facility compared to the former facility, in which those resources were highly preferred. By demonstrating how changes in exhibit design can alter, and hopefully improve, the manner in which captive primates utilize their environments, these data can be useful in future enclosure design.

Neutral Grid and Spread of Participation Index

The subsequent analysis of space utilization data for the apes at RCAA leveraged the quantitative power of a neutral grid system (Ross et al. 2011a). The spatial locations of 23 ape subjects were recorded over a four-year period after moving to the new facility, giving a total of almost 15,000 data points. At each sampling interval, the location of the focal animal was recorded on the electronic map interface in which each cell represented a space of approximately 1 m^2. The observer also noted the vertical placement of the subject within a set of five vertical tiers of approximately 2 m increments. To determine the degree to which ape subjects selectively utilized their available space, the authors used a spread of participation index (SPI; Dickens 1955), which is a descriptor of how evenly the available space is used. They compared the apes' indoor space use dependent on whether they had access to an adjacent outdoor yard, as well as a comparison of how the apes used their indoor versus outdoor space. Overall, the apes were found to be very selective in how they used their enclosures. Over the four years of the study, chimpanzees were only recorded in 56.5 percent of the possible three-dimensional locations and gorillas in only 28.5 percent. Of this time, chimpanzees spent 50 percent of their time in only 3.2 percent of their total space and gorillas spent half their time in only 1.5 percent of their available space. When considering only ground-level use, the chimpanzees and gorillas used a higher proportion of the spaces: 98.6 percent and 97.9 percent respectively. Chimpanzees spent approximately 33 percent of their observed time outdoors when that opportunity was available and the gorilla group even less: only 7.1 percent.

Additional Uses of Ape Spatial Data at RCAA

For over a decade, our lab has collected near-data observation on the spatial patterns of the chimpanzees and gorillas living at the RCAA. This represents among the densest datasets of its kind in the world, and not only helps facilitate applied science endeavors but is also available to inform care and management staff in the building. Along with analyses that extricate patterns of exhibit use, we have found the location-based data to be useful in a number of ways and complementary to our behavior-based evaluations that demonstrated the behavioral effects of the exhibit change (Ross et al. 2011b). In this study we found chimpanzees showed decreases in the frequency of abnormal behaviors and gorillas exhibited reduced agonism – both changes indicative of positive welfare states that could be attributed to the careful design that was influenced by spatial studies.

An additional utilization of the fine-grained spatial data generated by direct observation by Fisher Center scientists is the ability to calculate travel distances for captive apes. Broad spatial investigations of home ranges and daily travel distances have been conducted on wild primates for many years using both direct observational (e.g., Amsler 2010; Bates & Byrne 2009) and satellite-based (Janmaat et al. 2013; Markham & Altmann 2008) methods. As we have discussed, captive environments are just a fraction of the size of wild habitats, but studies of captive primate travel distances can provide interesting insights into animal welfare, enclosure design, and animal health and obesity. For instance, Shender and Ross (2013) estimated the daily travel distances for 6 chimpanzees and 11 gorillas living at RCAA by calculating straight-line distances between consecutive positions recorded on the map interface. They found that, like their wild counterparts, captive chimpanzees tended to travel longer distances than gorillas (chimpanzees 1.2 km/day; gorillas 0.8 km/day). Additionally, daily travel was increased when individuals were provided access to their large outdoor yards, especially evident in chimpanzees.

In another recent adaptation of the spatial use data at RCAA, observers now collect data in group scans rather than focal follows – a prospect that would be nearly impossible in almost any wild environment. However, these group-scan data allow for simultaneous analysis of both spatial utilization patterns and social network evaluation. Collecting information on the spatial location of multiple individuals provides the exciting opportunity to record, at high precision, interindividual distances which may provide important insights into group cohesion questions (Kurtycz et al. 2014; Shender et al. 2012).

Future Directions

Our lab at Lincoln Park Zoo has invested considerably in our investigations of ape spatial patterns and the results of our work have helped influence exhibit design and animal management practices. A large part of the investment in collecting these data is the personnel involved. We are fortunate to have a consistent staff of research assistants who help coordinate dozens of carefully trained research interns to collect the thousands of hours of data we have used in the studies described above. Clearly not every organization has the means to recruit, train, and coordinate this many human observers and, as such, automated systems to measure and track primate space use are attractive. As with GPS-based technology, the benefits of an automated tracking system to record the space use of individuals include reduction in transcription errors, minimizing human workload, and broadening of data-collection periods to include 24-hour coverage of subjects. We have outlined why satellite-based systems may not be feasible in many captive and micro-scale environments, but other technology-based alternatives that do not rely on human observers may be viable options.

Embedded Devices

The use of embedded devices, which use radio-frequency identification (RFID) technology, converting radio waves into a medium of data storage and transmission, provides a relatively low-impact foray into automated data collection. The small devices (<1 cm) can be easily implanted under the skin of the animal and are widely utilized as a means of identifying pets and livestock (Landt 2005), as well as for disease control, breeding, and stock management (Ng et al. 2005). The embedded microchips work by relaying information directly to a local base station throughout the day and night, providing data coverage that would be untenable for a team of human observers to achieve. Embedded devices have a relatively long lifespan due to the fact they lie dormant until a communication is made with a base station, whereas most collars are in a perpetual "on" state, which drains batteries. Such devices have been successfully utilized with GPS-based systems, most notably as part of tracking the success of individuals that have been recently reintroduced to wild environments (Trayford & Farmer 2012). Currently, we are unable to predict how a system such as this would function for space use monitoring in captive primates, though clearly the potential exists. For instance, an RFID monitoring system has been implemented at Dallas Zoo (Lipton 2012) with great success monitoring their elephant herd, providing their staff with continuous travel and space use data.

Stereo Cameras and Tracking Software

Despite the relatively low invasiveness of small, embedded tracking tags, there are many settings in which these techniques would be considered unacceptable because of the need to sedate the animal to embed the device. An alternative automated approach is the use of a matrix of stereo cameras that recognize and track animal movement through specialized software. Most video-tracking software works through the use of a system of stereo cameras set up strategically around the enclosure, which track the animal's movement, activity, and behavior. Data are collected in real-time and collated offline, allowing researchers to gather a full day's worth of spatial activity remotely. Once collected, the data output can be visualized on a map interface, allowing the researcher to track multiple individuals or points of interest simultaneously. Although such a system offers a non-invasive monitoring technique, it does require more initial set-up and preparation of the infrastructure (both with time and money) prior to the commencement of data collection.

Although most automated video-tracking applications have been used in a controlled laboratory environment (mosquitoes: Gomez-Marin et al. 2012; Spitzen et al. 2013; and zebrafish: Cachat et al. 2011), recently there have been implementations in larger environments, looking at activity measures with livestock (Spink et al. 2001). The applications with primates are even rarer, but Khan et al. (2005) describe a camera-based system that tracked the three-dimensional trajectory of rhesus macaques (*Macaca mulatta*) performing a spatial navigation task in an outdoor laboratory setting. Here, the system provides trajectories, path length, speeds, and other quantitative variables that would be impossible to record through human observation alone. These applications and further iterations of these technologies (see Ghadar et al. 2013) show great promise for accurate and automated spatial tracking of primates and other species.

Conclusion

As evidenced by their widespread implementation, GPS-based systems are an excellent tool to study the space use patterns of animals traversing wide ranges. However, much smaller settings, such as those in laboratories, zoos, and sanctuaries, represent conditions in which the benefits of a satellite-based system may be lost. In this chapter, we have outlined the primary reasons why GPS-based systems may be untenable for micro-scale environments and have described a brief history of observer-based methods to study space use. Human-based methods have worked very well for sites such as the RCAA, but there remains a strong need to develop automated solutions that bring with them the benefits of GPS systems (continuous, automated data) without the need for vast teams of observers. It is this gap in technology-based solutions that may perhaps be slowing the growth of studies in captive animal space use. That gap can be filled either by addressing weaknesses of GPS-based systems or the development of new technologies that can work under micro-scale conditions. In either case, the growth of this field stands to contribute substantially to our understanding of the animal–environment association that is so important for improving the care, management, and welfare of captive primates.

References

Amsler, S. J. 2010. Energetic costs of territorial boundary patrols by wild chimpanzees. *American Journal of Primatology* **72**(2): 93–103.

Bates, L. A., and Byrne, R. W. 2009. Sex differences in the movement patterns of free-ranging chimpanzees (*Pan troglodytes schweinfurthii*): foraging and border checking. *Behavioral Ecology and Sociobiology* **64**(2): 247–255.

Cachat, J. M., Stewart, A., Utterback, E., et al. 2011. Three-dimensional neurophenotyping of adult zebrafish behavior. *PloS One* **6**(3): e17597.

Chapman, C. A. and Pavelka, M. S. 2005. Group size in folivorous primates: ecological constraints and the possible influence of social factors. *Primates* **46**(1): 1–9.

Clutton-Brock, T. H. and Harvey, P. H. 1977. Primate ecology and social organization. *Journal of Zoology* **183**(1): 1–39.

D'Eon, R. G., Serrouya, R., Smith, G., and Kochanny, C. O. 2002. GPS radiotelemetry error and bias in mountainous terrain. *Wildlife Society Bulletin* **30**: 430–439.

Dickens, M. 1955. A statistical formula to quantify the "spread-of-participation" in group discussion. *Speech Monographs* **22**: 28–31.

Ghadar, N., Zhang, X., Li, K., et al. 2013. Visual hull reconstruction for automated primate behavior observation. Pages 1–6 in *2013 IEEE International Workshop on Machine Learning for Signal Processing (MLSP)*. IEEE, Piscataway, NJ.

Gomez-Marin, A., Partoune, N., Stephens, G. J., and Louis, M. 2012. Automated tracking of animal posture and movement during exploration and sensory orientation behaviors. *PLoS ONE* **7**(8): e41642.

Janmaat, K. R., Ban, S. D., and Boesch, C. 2013. Chimpanzees use long-term spatial memory to monitor large fruit trees and remember feeding experiences across seasons. *Animal Behaviour* **86**(6): 1183–1205.

Khan, Z., Herman, R. A., Wallen, K., and Balch, T. 2005. An outdoor 3-D visual tracking system for the study of spatial navigation and memory in rhesus monkeys. *Behavior Research Methods* **37**(3): 453–463.

Kurtycz, L. M., Shender, M. A., and Ross, S. R. 2014. The birth of an infant decreases group spacing in a zoo-housed lowland gorilla group (*Gorilla gorilla gorilla*). *Zoo Biology* **33**: 471–474.

Landt, J. 2005. The history of RFID. *IEEE Potentials* **24**(4): 8–11.

Lipton, A. 2012. RFID goes on Safari. *RFiD Journal* **9**(3).

Maple, T. L. and Finlay, T. W. 1987. Post-occupancy evaluation in the zoo. *Applied Animal Behaviour Science* **18**(1): 5–18.

Markham, A. C. and Altmann, J. 2008. Remote monitoring of primates using automated GPS technology in open habitats. *American Journal of Primatology* **70**(5): 495–499.

Markham, A. C., Guttal, V., Alberts, S. C., and Altmann, J. 2013. When good neighbors don't need fences: temporal landscape partitioning among baboon social groups. *Behavioral Ecology and Sociobiology* **67**: 875–884.

Matthews, A., Ruykys, L., Ellis, B., et al. 2013. The success of GPS collar deployments on mammals in Australia. *Australian Mammalogy* **35**: 65–83.

Newton-Fisher, N. E. 2003. The home range of the Sonso community of chimpanzees from the Budongo Forest, Uganda. *African Journal of Ecology* **41**(2): 150–156.

Ng, M. L., Leong, K. S., Hall, D. M., and Cole, P. H. 2005. A small passive UHF RFID tag for livestock identification. Pages 67–70 in *MAPE 2005. IEEE International Symposium on Microwave, Antenna, Propagation and EMC Technologies for Wireless Communications*, Vol. 1. IEEE, Piscataway, NJ.

Ogden, J. J., Lindburg, D. G., and Maple, T. L. 1993. Preference for structural environmental features in captive lowland gorillas (*Gorilla gorilla gorilla*). *Zoo Biology* **12**(4): 381–395.

Phillips, K. A., Elvey, C. R., and Abercrombie, C. L. 1998. Applying GPS to the study of primate ecology: a useful tool?. *American Journal of Primatology* **46**(2): 167–172.

Radespiel, U. 2007. Ecological diversity and seasonal adaptations of mouse lemurs (*Microcebus* spp.). Pages 211–234 in *Lemurs*. L. Gould and M. Sauther (Eds.). Springer, New York.

Reutebuch, S. E., McGaughey, R. J., Andersen, H. E., and Carson, W. W. 2003. Accuracy of a high-resolution lidar terrain model under a conifer forest canopy. *Canadian Journal of Remote Sensing* **29**(5): 527–535.

Roberts, M. and Kohn, F. 1993. Habitat use, foraging behavior, and activity patterns in reproducing western tarsiers, *Tarsius bancanus*, in captivity: a management synthesis. *Zoo Biology* **12**(2): 217–232.

Ross, S. R. and Lukas, K. E. 2000. Conducting a post-occupancy evaluation as part of the design process for a new great ape facility. Pages 140–141 in *The Apes: Challenges for the 21st Century*, Conference Proceedings, May 10–13, 2000, Brookfield, IL.

Ross, S. R., and Lukas, K. E. 2006. Use of space in a non-naturalistic environment by chimpanzees (*Pan troglodytes*) and lowland gorillas (*Gorilla gorilla gorilla*). *Applied Animal Behaviour Science* **96**(1): 143–152.

Ross, S. R., Schapiro, S. J., Hau, J., and Lukas, K. E. 2009. Space use as an indicator of enclosure appropriateness: a novel measure of captive animal welfare. *Applied Animal Behaviour Science* **121**(1): 42–50.

Ross, S. R., Calcutt, S., Schapiro, S. J., and Hau, J. 2011a. Space use selectivity by chimpanzees and gorillas in an indoor–outdoor enclosure. *American Journal of Primatology* **73**(2): 197–208.

Ross, S. R., Wagner, K. E., Schapiro, S. J., and Hau, J. 2011b. Transfer and acclimation effects on the behavior of two species of African great apes moved to a novel and naturalistic zoo environment. *International Journal of Primatology* **32**: 99–117.

Shender, M. A. and Ross, S. R. 2013. The effects of available space on a group of captive gorillas (*Gorilla gorilla gorilla*) and chimpanzees (*Pan troglodytes*) living in a naturalistic zoo-setting. *American Journal of Primatology* **75**(S1): 51.

Shender, M. A., Anderson, K. E., and Ross, S. R. 2012. Group cohesion in captive gorillas (*Gorilla gorilla gorilla*) and chimpanzees (*Pan troglodytes*) living in a naturalistic zoo exhibit. *American Journal of Primatology* **74**(S1): 75.

Spink, A. J., Tegelenbosch, R. A. J., Buma, M. O. S., and Noldus, L. P. J. J. 2001. The EthoVision video tracking system: a tool for behavioral phenotyping of transgenic mice. *Physiology & Behavior* **73**(5): 731–744.

Spitzen, J., Spoor, C. W., Grieco, F., et al. 2013. A 3D analysis of flight behavior of *Anopheles gambiae* sensu stricto malaria mosquitoes in response to human odor and heat. *PLoS ONE* **8**(5): e62995.

Trayford, H. R. and Farmer, K. H. 2012. An assessment of the use of telemetry for primate reintroductions. *Journal for Nature Conservation* **20**: 311–325.

Traylor-Holzer, K. and Fritz, P. 1985. Utilization of space by adult and juvenile groups of captive chimpanzees (*Pan troglodytes*). *Zoo Biology* **4**(2): 115–127.

Vanderploeg, H. A. and Scavia, D. 1979. Two electivity indices for feeding with special reference to zooplankton grazing. *Journal of the Fisheries Board of Canada* **36**(4): 362–365.

14 The Promise of Spatially Explicit Agent-Based Models for Primatology Research

Anthony Di Fiore

Introduction

It is a rare moment when one is given the chance to proselytize for a methodological approach, and I am grateful for this opportunity to advocate for a particular way of studying natural phenomena that affords researchers almost unlimited creativity to design, explore, and generate predictions about a system. Almost 25 years ago, as a first-year graduate student, I read a paper that wormed its way into my head and has remained influential to this day. That paper – by Irenaeus te Boekhorst and Paulien Hogeweg, published in 1994 in the journal *Behavior* – was radical because it offered a countervailing hypothesis to the standard socioecological model proposed to explain the flexible association and subgrouping patterns of chimpanzees. The "standard" model posited that the benefits of cooperation among male kin in defending access to females and territory were key in explaining why male chimpanzees were commonly found in parties with other males, while female chimpanzees were more often solitary because of the costs of feeding competition.

What te Boekhost and Hogeweg demonstrated, using a spatially explicit agent-based simulation model, was that simple differences in the programmed behaviors of males versus females, which were informed by observations of wild chimpanzees, could result in both highly dynamic subgroups (e.g., "fissioning" and "fusing") and self-structuring (e.g., males being found in larger parties and more commonly in association with other males). However, these grouping patterns emerged *without* positing a specific benefit for cooperation or any particular pattern of genetic relatedness among group members. Moreover, the male and female agents in the simulation model also recapitulated some of the sex differences in ranging behavior seen in chimpanzees, such as males moving farther, on average, during their daily travels than females. The point of te Boekhost and Hogeweg's paper was not so much to explain the behavioral biology of chimpanzees in terms of adaptive function; rather, they asked a fundamentally different question: "Can chimpanzee-like party structures emerge from simple rules that specify nothing more than direct interactions between the behavior of individuals on the one hand and the structure of their local environment on the other hand?" (te Boekhorst & Hogeweg 1994a: 234–235). Based on their agent-based simulation, the answer was "yes!"

Models and Modeling

Researchers trying to understand natural phenomena, such as the subgrouping dynamics of chimpanzees in the example above, are often interested in developing models that represent the key components and processes of a system in a simplified form. Models, obviously, are not the real world, but they are like it in some important respects, and their main purpose is to help us evaluate our ideas and intuition about how the world works – if our model is correct, what would we expect to see happen in this world under conditions x, y, or z? Agent-based simulation modeling is one modeling approach that is particularly suited to understanding complex systems that involve multiple components that interact with one another in different ways and on different timescales. In contrast to verbal models (which provide qualitative or abstract explanations for natural phenomena) and formal mathematical models (which describe natural processes and outcomes by means of logical expressions and mathematical relationships), simulation models in general – and ABMs in particular – seek to understand the dynamics of a natural system as the emergent outcome of interactions between sets of actors and the environments in which those interactions take place. Agent-based modeling is thus a bottom-up approach that accommodates dynamic systems involving multiple actors (e.g., the shifting social connections among a set of individuals) and is primarily concerned with how global patterns emerge from local interactions. This approach contrasts with more formal, mathematical modeling approaches, which tend to emphasize equilibrium conditions and are more focused on understanding the relationship among system-level variables (e.g., rainfall and animal activity budgets, or food availability and ranging behavior) than with the states and behaviors of individual actors in the system.

Various authors have described the key elements, advantages, and limitations of the agent-based modeling approach, particularly as it applies to the social, behavioral, and ecological sciences (e.g., Billari et al. 2006; Crooks & Heppenstall 2012; DeAngelis & Mooij 2005; Epstein 1999; Gilbert & Troitzsch 2005; Gilbert 2008; Gilbert & Terna 2000; Grimm & Railsback 2005; Grimm et al. 2006, 2010; Macal & North 2009, 2010; Miller & Page 2007). I summarize this information here, but encourage the curious reader to consult the excellent aforementioned reviews for additional detail and discussion.

Central to agent-based models (ABMs) are, of course, the constituent actors – the eponymous *agents* – which can be either animate (e.g., individual animals) or inanimate (e.g., patches of resources) and which are endowed with "attributes" (e.g., *age, sex, weight, status, crop size*) that can either be static or vary in response to the agent's experiences and interactions with other actors and with the environment (Figure 14.1). Animate agents (e.g., simulated "monkeys") are often characterized as being *autonomous*; they are responsible for their own behavior and can make decisions about what course of action to pursue in a given situation. These decisions are often based on the presumption of *rational choice*. Typically, the set of agents in any given model is *heterogeneous* – that is, individual agents can vary in their attribute values and in the rules that govern their behaviors. In the parlance of contemporary computer

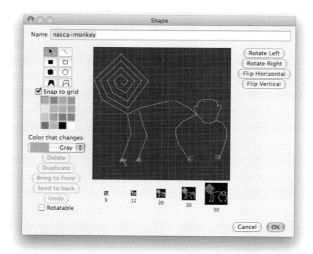

Figure 14.1 Graphical representation of agents in the author's "SIM-PRIMATE" model (Di Fiore 2009). In this model, "PRIMATE" agents possess a suite of attributes defining their nutritional needs (*sex, age, daily-food-requirements*), digestive physiology (*gut-volume, digestion-rate, ingestion-rate*), movement behavior (*travel-step-length*), competitive ability (*rank*), sociability (*min-separation-distance, social-radius*), and mortality risk (*risk-of-predation*).

programming, agents can be conceived of, and are treated in modeling software, as "objects" – individual instantiations of a particular class (e.g., "Rover" as an instantiation of the general class "DOG").

In addition to their individuality, agents are also generally presumed to be both *perceptive*, i.e., able to acquire information about the environment and about the states, qualities, needs, or motivations of other agents, and *reactive*, i.e., their behavior is not fixed but rather can be modified in response to acquired information. Agents can also be *interactive* and *communicative*; they can choose to seek out, avoid, fight, mate, cooperate, or exchange information with one another, and their behavior may be influenced by these interactions. Agents are generally programed to follow particular behavioral rules (e.g., to perform behavior x in situation y with probability z). In some models, agents may be able to *learn* or *adapt*, modifying their behavior on the basis of prior experience. Finally, in most ABMs, agents are *mobile*; they exist in a heterogeneous world within which they can move around and have the opportunity to interact with other actors or with features of the environment. Their behavior, then, can also be contingent upon or sensitive to environmental conditions at their precise location in the model world. The fact that agent-based simulations typically take place within an explicitly spatial framework lends the approach an immediate connection, at least conceptually, to the world of GIS and other tools of spatial analysis.

In any ABM, the *modeler* is responsible for defining the agents – their perceptual abilities, cognitive capacities, desires, and goals – as well as for setting out the behavioral rules that they may follow. The modeler also designs the environment and its features – its spatial dimensions, the components of interest, and the range of phenomena that can occur within it. For example, an ABM of primate foraging behavior might involve agents that differ in *age*, *sex*, and *nutritional requirements*. Those agents could also be endowed with additional attributes such as *dominance rank*, *search strategy*, *travel speed*, *resource detection distance*, or *memory capacity*, any of which might reasonably affect an individual's success at finding and competing over food in the model world. A modeler might be interested in exploring what effect these agent attributes may have, alone or in combination, on agents' foraging success, and in how that foraging success is simultaneously influenced by environmental variables (e.g., food distribution in space or time). She might ask, for example, if particular classes of individuals who differ from one another on multiple attribute dimensions can nonetheless enjoy similar foraging success. Or, she might wish to explore whether agents with particular characteristics (e.g., large memory capacity and low rank versus low memory capacity and high rank) do better in particular kinds of environments (e.g., those with more evenly versus more patchily distributed foods, or those where temporal changes in food availability are predictable versus unpredictable).

Apart from the flexibility afforded by allowing us to include heterogeneous agents and environments in a model, agent-based simulation has several important advantages that make it particularly useful for studying biological systems. First, the approach *forces us to be very explicit about our assumptions* about how (we think) the world works. This is because the behavioral rules that agents are programmed to follow when interacting with one another or with the environment are specified programmatically, typically as a set of formal conditional statements – e.g., *IF <a predator is detected within my range of perception> THEN <turn away from it and flee>* or *IF <the amount of food I have eaten> IS GREATER THAN <the capacity of my belly> THEN <stop eating>*. Second, when compared to formal analytical modeling, the agent-based approach is immediately more suited to systems in which *individuals can manifest complex behavior* (such as individual learning and adaptation), *where they differ from one another in dimensions that are difficult to operationalize* (such as in their capacity for behaving rationally), and *where the outcome of interactions among agents is influenced by spatial and/or social factors* (e.g., agents' relative position, orientation, and distance, or their past history of interaction) (Bonabeau 2002; Crooks & Heppenstall 2012). While it may be quite difficult to develop formal mathematical models to describe the relationships among multiple, simultaneously varying individual attributes and environmental variables (especially if those relationships are nonlinear), these can often be explored effectively and easily through simulation. Finally, several contemporary agent-based simulation platforms allow for *immediate visual feedback* about the state of the system and/or its constituent agents, thus facilitating model debugging and validation as well as making its workings more accessible to users of the model.

Agent-based simulation modeling of course has its limitations. A familiar one is that models tend to be too complex, with so many assumptions and parameters that they lack generalizability and have only limited predictive power (Bryson et al. 2007; Kokko 2007). This, however, is a common critique of modeling generally, where it is important (but often difficult) to strike the right balance between simplicity and complexity. As with other modeling approaches, it is crucial that a modeler be very clear about the purpose of developing a particular simulation: Is the goal to explore general phenomena (e.g., how does resource distribution influence group cohesion), or is the aim to allow precise quantitative predictions to be made? Likewise, modelers need to be very concerned about both *verification* of a model's implementation in software (i.e., whether the model behaves as expected, given the assumptions made about how the world works) and *validation* of the model (i.e., whether predictions or emergent patterns generated by the model are supported by new or independent datasets). Apropos of this point, Bryson et al. (2007) provide a cogent argument as to how ABMs in behavioral biology represent valid scientific hypotheses that can be tested and evaluated as such. Here, the process of model validation and subsequent refinement – i.e., confirming that the behavior of a model appropriately reflects that of the natural system being modeled and that the attributes and capacities of agents are grounded in biological reality, and then testing whether predictions generated by the model are supported by independent datasets – is tantamount to the traditional hypothetico-deductive method in science and can be an important tool for social science research (Bryson et al. 2007).

In their two books on agent-based modeling in the biological sciences, Volker Grimm and Steve Railsback emphasize how all scientific modeling is an iterative process (Figure 14.2), involving successive rounds of hypothesis testing and refinement (Grimm & Railsback 2005; Railsback & Grimm 2012). For agent-based modeling, however, iterative testing is particularly important because our models are software algorithms (often complicated ones with multiple decision points) and the process of verification mentioned above – i.e., confirming that our programs and the agents in them perform as we mean them to – is absolutely crucial. Thus, ABM development typically involves coding and testing separate pieces of a model individually (to break the code into discrete, manageable pieces), monitoring the states of select agents during test runs of a simulation (to confirm that agents are indeed making decisions in the manner that we think we have programmed them to), and performing statistical analyses on the outputs of test runs (to confirm that the model indeed reproduces patterns we would expect based on how it was formulated) (Railsback & Grimm 2012). Graphical user interfaces (GUIs) associated with some of the software toolkits for agent-based modeling discussed in the rest of this chapter can facilitate this iterative process.

Another important aspect of agent-based modeling is to be able to communicate not only the results of a model, but also its rationale and its implementation, in such a way that, like other methods in biology, any particular ABM can be understood as more than just a "black box" and can be replicated by other researchers. To this end, Grimm and colleagues (2006, 2010) proposed a standard for describing and documenting ABMs: the *ODD (overview, design concepts, and details) protocol*, the dual purpose of which is "to make writing and reading model descriptions easier and more efficient" and to produce "more complete model descriptions, making ABMs easier to replicate and hence less easily dismissed as unscientific" (Grimm et al. 2010; 2760). Briefly, the ODD protocol suggests that all ABM descriptions should include, first, an "Overview" that describes the purpose of the model, identifies the constituent entities (e.g., individual agents, collections of agents, or the environment) and their relevant attributes, and provides a high-level description of the processes being modeled (e.g., *foraging*,

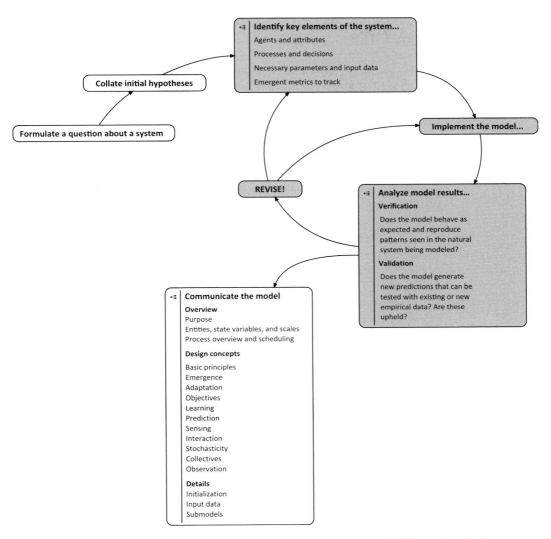

Figure 14.2 Summary of the agent-based modeling cycle and the ODD (*overview, design concepts, details*) protocol for describing and documenting agent-based models (modified from Grimm & Railsback 2005; Grimm et al. 2010; Railsback & Grimm 2012). Steps that are shaded gray are those that typically require multiple iteration during model development and testing.

reproduction, dispersal) and how they are scheduled in relation to one another. Following that, the ABM description should include information about all of the relevant "design concepts" that the model implements, including, among other things, information about the agents' sensory capabilities, what results are tracked as emerging from the agents' behavior, whether agents are capable of learning, etc. Finally, the description should include "details" about how the model is initialized, what input data are specified for the model (e.g., what landscape a model runs in), and the algorithms underlying all of the different processes included in the model. Readers are encouraged to consult Grimm et al. (2010) for a more complete discussion of the ODD protocol for describing and documenting ABMs.

History of Agent-Based Simulation Modeling in Primatology

Many basic features of primate biology make this group particularly well suited to the use of agent-based approaches for modeling behavior. For example, most primates are long-lived and reside in social groups comprising overlapping generations of animals, where they have recurring social interactions with many of the same individuals over long time periods. Moreover, at any given time, a great deal of variation exists among the individuals within these groups in terms of basic physical attributes (e.g., body size, sex), as well as age, prior experiences, the size and structure of their kin networks, etc. Perhaps most importantly, primates show a range of seemingly complex social behaviors – e.g., coalitions and alliances, collective actions (such as coordinated travel or group defense), reciprocity, and reconciliation – which primatologists, in general, are very interested in explaining. Agent-based modeling is a powerful tool for exploring whether some of these social phenomena can emerge from interactions among individuals acting in a self-interested fashion and following simple behavioral rules (Goldstone & Janssen 2005). Since the decision rules that agents follow are defined precisely, the approach also allows us to test, *in silico*, among alternative rules. For example, in a hypothetical primate foraging model, we might explore whether agents' food acquisition rate co-varies with some aspect of their perceptual abilities or whether their survival in the simulation is related to attributes describing their capacity for spatial memory.

The promise and utility of agent-based modeling notwithstanding, its use in primatology thus far has been surprisingly limited. To date, only a handful of studies have employed ABMs to explore different aspects of primate behavioral biology. Below, I give a brief overview of this history, highlighting a few key studies that illustrate some of the broad range of topics to which agent-based modeling may be applied.

Great Ape MIRROR Worlds

As mentioned above, one of the first applications of agent-based modeling in primatology was the fascinating work of Paulien Hogeweg, a computational systems biologist interested in artificial life. In a series of papers in the late 1980s and early 1990s, Hogeweg and colleagues developed and applied an agent-based approach in an attempt to better understand the variation and complexity in great ape association patterns, in particular the dynamic and variable party composition of chimpanzees (Hogeweg 1988; Hogeweg & Hesper 1985, 1990; te Boekhorst & Hogeweg 1994a, 1994b). At the time, chimpanzee association patterns were suggested to be related to kinship among males and to the importance of male–male cooperation in range defense, but Hogeweg's research group was interested in asking whether the so-called complexity in association patterns could instead "emerge through self structuring" from a limited set of wholly deterministic rules that governed individual behavior. That is, was it necessary to posit social complexity or nepotism, or complex cognition, in order to arrive at a (superficially) complex set of social dynamics?

To evaluate this idea, te Boekhorst and Hogeweg (1994a) developed a chimpanzee "MIRROR" world in which male and female computer agents (CHIMPs) were programmed to follow different behavioral rules and were then left to move and interact in a simulated environment. This simulated environment was similar in some respects to the environment in which natural populations of chimpanzees are found – a forest containing feeding trees and protein sources. Female CHIMPs were programmed to move and forage in the environment according to simple rules: search for a food patch; if one is detected, approach it and feed until sated and then leave. If a female depleted a patch before being sated, she would move on and search for alternative feeding sites. Male CHIMPs followed similar rules, except that they first looked around for another CHIMP agent. If one was found, the male CHIMP would move toward it and inspect if it was a female CHIMP in estrus; if so, the male would follow the female, and, if not, he would instead move on in search of food.

During runs of the simulation, te Boekhorst and Hogeweg (1994a) kept track of the time CHIMP agents spent moving and feeding and in association with one or more other agents. The results of the simulations mimic many of the patterns of aggregation and association seen in natural populations of chimpanzees: female CHIMPs were found to spend more time alone and in smaller parties than male CHIMPs, males were more commonly found in mixed-sex parties than females, and male daily travel distances tended to be greater than those of females.

In a parallel MIRROR world populated with ORANG agents (resembling, after a fashion, orangutans at the Sumatran site of Ketambe), te Boekhorst and Hogeweg (1994b) explored the consequence of different resource distributions on ORANG grouping patterns. ORANGs were programmed to move through the environment searching first for food (either in very large FIG trees, which were unlikely to be depleted by single or small numbers of foragers, or in other smaller, more depletable FRUIT patches) and then for other individuals. Associations of ORANGs could occur when more than one individual wound up feeding in the same FRUIT or FIG patches. Once an individual was sated, or once the patch it was in was depleted, the ORANG would move off to the next closest food patch. "Travel bands" thus arose when two or more animals were feeding in the same patch and emptied it out; they would then move off together to the next feeding patch. These travel bands, not surprisingly, formed more commonly in smaller FRUIT patches than in large FIG patches as they were more likely to be depleted during foraging bouts.

Running their simulations in different "seasons" – a FRUIT season (when the number of fruit patches in the habitat was high) and a NONFRUIT season (when this number was low) – te Boekhorst and Hogeweg (1994b) found that travel parties were more common and larger in the former, the result of animals tending to leave depleted patches together. ORANGs were also less likely to be solitary during the fruiting season, and, regardless of season, they tended to travel farther on days when they were in travel bands versus on days when they were alone. All of these results from the simulation model are consistent with what is known of the behavior of wild orangutans, but that is not the key point. Rather, the results suggest that fundamental aspects of habitat structure, in combination with simple behavioral rules, may be sufficient for explaining orangutan grouping dynamics, without assuming that animals actively either maintain contact with or avoid one another.

Modeling Social Behavior: The DOM-WORLD and Its Descendants

Since these seminal projects in the early 1990s, several other research teams have employed agent-based modeling to gain insight into other aspects of primate sociality. The best known of these is a series of studies into the formation, stability, and steepness of dominance hierarchies by Charlotte Hemelrijk and colleagues, who modified Hogeweg's MIRROR world to examine whether these properties of hierarchies might likewise emerge from the interactions that take place among a set of agents following explicitly stated behavioral rules. In Hemelrijk's (1999a) DOM-WORLD model, for example, agents follow a few simple rules regarding aggregation and spacing. Briefly, a fixed number of agents live and interact in a continuous world where, if an agent strays too far from other individuals, it searches for and moves back toward those others, but if it detects another individual too close by (inside the agent's "personal space"), then it first evaluates its likelihood of winning a dominance interaction with that other individual and, if victory seems likely, initiates such an interaction. In the model, the outcome of any particular dominance interaction is stochastic, based on the relative values of the two agents' dominance ("DOM") attributes: individuals with higher current dominance are more likely to win, but unexpected reversals are nonetheless possible. After an interaction, the value of each agent's DOM attribute is modified up or down, based on whether it won or lost. The actual amount that DOM values change is determined by the relative dominance of the interactants (winning by a "subordinate" has a larger effect on DOM values than winning by a "dominant") and is also modulated by a scaling parameter ("STEP-DOM"), where higher values imply that single dominance interactions can have more of an effect. After the interaction, the spacing between the two agents is also adjusted: the "winner" chases the "loser" a short distance and then turns away. Hemelrijk (1999a) then used this very simple model to explore some aspects of the system's emergent dynamics. Interestingly, modifying the single parameter STEP-DOM (which she argued reflects a difference in the intensity of aggression) resulted in a host of differences in group-level descriptors of dominance behavior and spatial structure, and these differences mirror those argued to exist between more "despotic" and more "egalitarian" species of macaques.

In parallel and subsequent work, Hemelrijk and colleagues, as well as other research groups, have used the DOM-WORLD model to explore various other aspects of primate social biology, including the phenomenon of female dominance over males (Hemelrijk 1999b, 2001, 2002; Hemelrijk et al. 2003), the spatial organization of social groups (Evers et al. 2011, 2012; Hemelrijk 1999b, 2000), and, more recently, the phenomenon of reciprocity in various social relationships (Hemelrijk & Puga-Gonzalez 2012; Puga-Gonzalez et al. 2009).

For example, Puga-Gonzalez et al. (2009) extended the basic DOM-WORLD model to include grooming and an additional individual state attribute, an "anxiety" score. In their "GrooFi" (for "grooming plus fighting") world, agents were programmed to consider grooming as a behavioral option to perform in lieu of initiating a dominance interaction when encountering another individual at close range. Specifically, an agent can choose to groom another animal when it perceives the risk of losing a fight with that individual to be high. The likelihood that an animal chooses to groom (versus simply to not initiate any social interaction) depends on its anxiety level; animals are more likely to groom when their anxiety level is high, and grooming reduces the anxiety level of both the groomer and the recipient of grooming. When run, the model generates some patterns of social affiliation among animals akin to those seen in natural populations (e.g., a certain degree of reciprocity in grooming interactions). Moreover, as in the DOM-WORLD simulations, when the model is run with high versus low values for the STEP-DOM parameter (which, again, is presumed to reflect the intensity of aggressive interactions), different patterns of affiliative behavior emerge that are consistent with those seen in "despotic" versus "egalitarian" macaques (e.g., more grooming up the hierarchy and more grooming directed among similarly ranked animals when the intensity of aggression is greater) (Puga-Gonzalez et al. 2009). Dolado and Beltran (2012) subsequently compared empirical patterns of grooming and aggression seen in captive *Cercocebus torquatus* to those predicted by the GrooFi model under both low- and high-intensity aggression parameter values, and they found that some observed patterns matched each of these conditions, providing a nice example of the utility of the model outside of the system for which is was originally conceived. In a further exploration of the emergent features of the GrooFi model, Hemelrijk and Puga-Gonzalez (2012) found that patterns reminiscent of various types of coalitionary behavior reciprocated support among dyads, and "exchange" of grooming for support also arose. The take-home point is that a variety of social interactions that are often presumed to require sophisticated cognition (e.g., triadic awareness or an ability to remember and keep track of prior interactions) may instead emerge as self-structured by-products of individuals following a set of simple behavioral rules.

More recently, Evers et al. (2014) developed an alternative ABM of primate social behavior in which an agent's interactions with other specific individuals are mediated by its emotional state as well as its history of prior interactions with those individuals. In their so-called "EMO-model," agents' overall emotional states are characterized and tracked along three variable dimensions, one reflecting "ANXIETY" (as in the GrooFi model), one "SATISFACTION," and one "AROUSAL." Agents' attitudes toward other group members are also characterized along two dimensions, "LIKE" and "FEAR." Social interactions impact the values of most of these agent attributes. For example, an agent's LIKE for a partner increases following grooming with that individual and declines slowly when grooming does not occur; an agent's AROUSAL increases when it is close to a more dominant animal or after it observes, receives, or directs aggression toward another animal, and it decreases after participating in affiliative interactions or after receiving submissive signals. An agent's FEAR of every other group member is fixed and depends on the rank difference between the agent pair (in this model, ranks are stable and unchanging, unlike in the DOM-WORLD and GrooFi models).

Evers et al. (2014) parameterized and tuned the model using empirical data from free-ranging macaques and then partially validated it, demonstrating that the model generates several emergent, higher-order patterns of behavior that are consistent with additional empirical data. For example, subordinates in the model, as in empirical studies, received and gave less aggressive behavior than dominants, gave more submissive behavior than dominants, groomed other animals more than dominants, and had higher AROUSAL scores. Similarly, model agents, like real macaques, tended to direct their affiliative behavior (and their aggression, under certain parameter conditions) toward similarly ranked individuals and their submissive behavior toward distantly ranked animals, and the overall extent of reciprocity in grooming seen among model agents fell within the range reported in empirical studies. Notably, the EMO-model is quite a bit more complex than its predecessors and posits a specific form of "emotional bookkeeping" as a mechanism shaping social interactions among pairs of individuals in primate social groups. Given the model's reasonable validation, it can now be used as a tool to generate additional predictions that can be tested against empirical data and it provides a promising framework for exploring the possible emotional regulation of social relationships.

Foraging Ecology and Association Patterns

One of the fundamental tenets of behavioral ecology is that resource distribution is a key variable that can influence the aggregation and association patterns of animals, and, as described above, te Boekhorst and Hogeweg's (1994a, 1994b) MIRROR world models of CHIMPs and ORANGs reinforce that idea by demonstrating that autonomous individual agents following simple behavioral rules can self-organize in rather complex and dynamic association patterns. Another more recently developed model provides a further demonstration. Ramos-Fernández et al. (2006) built a spatially explicit ABM of primate foraging, which was focused, conceptually, on species like spider monkeys and chimpanzees that feed on patchily distributed high-quality resources and show a high degree of fission–fusion dynamics. In their model, the distribution of food patches in the environment, together with the amount of food located in those patches, can be adjusted by modifying a single parameter, β, which is the exponent for an inverse power-law function that summarizes the distribution of food patch sizes. The β parameter thus expresses the degree of heterogeneity among possible food patches. Into this world, they placed a set number of foraging agents, who each began at a randomly selected patch. Agents then foraged in the world for a set number of time steps, moving among food patches according to the following rules: (1) when leaving a depleted food patch, move to the patch that minimizes the ratio of travel cost (i.e., distance to the patch) to expected gain (i.e., amount of food anticipated to be in that patch); and (2) do not return to a previously visited patch. During simulation runs, as in the great ape MIRROR world models, agents can coalesce (or "fuse") into subgroups if they meet up at the same patch, and they can leave patches as they become depleted and travel together if they both select the same next patch to visit. However, because different agents may have different foraging trajectories before coming together at a particular patch, they might also "fission" from one another upon leaving a patch if the next patch chosen by one agent has already been visited by another subgroup member.

Ramos-Fernández et al. (2006) ran simulations in this world under different values for β and then examined the emergent patterns of association among agents (e.g., the distribution of subgroup sizes that agents were found in, the average length of time that subgroups of various size lasted, the number of other agents encountered, etc.). Even though their model contains no "rules" as to how agents should interact with one another, it nonetheless generates rich and temporally variable subgrouping dynamics that are quite markedly influenced by the value chosen for β, i.e., by the degree of heterogeneity among possible food patches. Interestingly, the model additionally revealed that preferential associations can arise among subsets of foraging agents, simply by virtue of the combination of how resources of different value are distributed in space and how agents are programmed to forage. That is, both *complex social dynamics* and *differentiated social relationships* emerge from a very simple model that specifies nothing about how agents interact "socially" with one another. As Ramos-Fernández et al. (2006: 537) note, the point of their modeling exercise was not to test specific hypotheses about the factors that might affect subgroup formation and size, but rather to generate a "null model of social grouping that predicts the way in which subgroup size will vary when confronted with a realistic foraging environment."

Group Coordination, Navigation, and Spatial Memory

For the foraging model described above, Ramos-Fernández and colleagues made some important simplifications. First, agents were assumed to have expansive knowledge of the locations and expected fruit content either of all ("complete knowledge") or of a random half ("partial knowledge") of the thousands of trees in the simulated environment. Second, agents could move in a single time step to any tree in the habitat. Third, the behavioral decisions of any particular agent did not (directly) influence the behavioral decisions of others. Several other ABMs of primate foraging and activity have also been developed that do not make these less-than-realistic assumptions (and consequently the models are a good deal more complex). Sellers et al. (2007), for example, developed an ABM designed to look at group-level decision-making in baboons (see also Hill et al. 2014). The model is run in an environment constructed based on empirical data on vegetation and habitat structure from the De Hoop Nature Reserve in South Africa, where the researchers have conducted studies of the behavioral biology of wild chacma baboons (*Papio ursinus*). The model world thus consists of a matrix of grid cells, each corresponding to a particular habitat type and concomitant level of food resources, with some cells also containing water sources and sleeping sites. Baboon agents placed in this world are characterized by attributes that track their daily water and energy intake and the amount of time spent in social activity. Based on the current state of their attribute scores, agents make behavioral decisions at each time step about whether it is better to *forage, rest,* or *socialize* in their current location or *move* to a different location within a given search radius, where they perceive that they can perform one of those behaviors more efficiently. Before their action is determined, however, agents *vote* whether or not to move, and will only do so if a sufficient proportion of group members vote in favor of doing so. If the group-level decision is to stay put, then individual agents who voted to move instead perform their next-most-preferred behavior. The model, parameterized with empirical data from wild baboons at De Hoop, is run over a simulation period of seven months, during which time the environment varies, due both to the actions of the baboon agents (foraging reduces the amount of food available in each grid cell) and to the rate of resource growth in different habitat types, which can vary from month to month. Thus, agents are faced with a spatially explicit but dynamic environment that changes in response to their behavioral choices, and the preferred actions of other agents can have a direct impact on the behavior of any particular agent.

A likewise complex ABM of primate foraging was developed by Bonnell and colleagues (2010, 2013) and was recently used to explore the effects of different types of spatial memory, memory capacities, and social rules on patterns of group-level navigation for simulated red colobus monkeys (*Procolobus rufomitratus*). As in the baboon model, red colobus monkey agents are placed in a spatially explicit resource landscape modeled after a particular study site (Kibale National Park, Uganda) and must make decisions at each time step, in this case about how to behave in order to balance set food intake needs versus safety requirements. In contrast to the baboon "voting" model, however, individuals had ultimate control over their own movements, and these are shaped by their individual compromises between sometimes competing drives: When personal energy reserves are sufficient, monkey agents prioritize moving to keep close to conspecifics as a hedge against the risk of predation, but when their reserves are low, monkey agents can sacrifice safety in favor of moving away from group-mates into areas with better resource access. Bonnell et al. (2013) ran a suite of different simulations involving agents with different styles of spatial memory (a *Euclidean* mental map in which animals remember and can navigate among the locations of key resource sites habitat-wide versus a *landmark-based* mental map in which animals remember the locations of key resources only relative to a smaller number of landmarks positioned throughout the habitat), different memory capacities (i.e., the absolute number of sites that the animal agents could remember), and social rules that they follow (either weighing other group-mates equally or prioritizing one "leader" individual in the group when making decisions about who to keep close to for safety).

For both of these models, the researchers evaluated their simulation results by comparing them to empirical data from their respective field studies. In the case of the baboon study, the model was not terribly successful in generating simulated activity budgets or patterns of range use that matched empirical data closely (Sellers et al. 2007). The modelers concluded that this was due, in part, to the spatial and temporal scale at which the model was designed, and they suggest that refinements to incorporate both a finer-grained environmental landscape and more frequent decisions on the part of agents might yield a better-validated model. The red colobus model was successfully tuned to reproduce certain group-level behaviors expected based on field observations (e.g., larger groups of simulated monkeys traveled farther per day and had larger home ranges than smaller groups, while range size, daily travel distance, daily travel time, and group spread all increased as habitat quality decreased) across a broad range of parameter conditions (Bonnell et al. 2010). When simulation results were compared to empirical data on group-level movement patterns, the best fit was for those models in which agents utilized landmark-based memory and a leader-following social rule (Bonnell et al. 2013).

Social Systems, Landscapes, and Population Genetic Structure

Spatially explicit agent-based modeling has also been used to explore how aspects of primate social organization and features of the landscape together shape the population genetic structure of primates (Di Fiore & Valencia 2013, 2014). The GENESYS simulation toolkit (Di Fiore 2010a, 2010b, 2012) allows users to create a population of simulated primate agents that follow a user-defined set of social, mating, and dispersal rules, which can be tuned to what is known of a species' natural biology. For instance, among other options, users can provide age-specific reproductive and mortality rates, specify the proportion of adults of each sex who are allowed to breed in a group along with the degree of reproductive skew, and set the proportion of individuals of each sex who disperse. Individual agents in the model are also assigned multilocus genotypes at a suite of neutral markers (these can be specified by the user or assigned randomly based on population-level allele frequencies) and assembled into social groups in a spatially explicit landscape, which is also input into the model by a user. Once initialized, simulation runs then track the population forward in time across multiple generations to examine how population genetic structure emerges from the agents' interactions with one another as well as their distribution and dispersal across the landscape.

Di Fiore and Valencia (2013, 2014) verified the toolkit by undertaking studies of the effects of mating system and habitat fragmentation on the population genetic structure of simulated "tamarin" monkeys. For example, the model generated levels of average intragroup relatedness comparable to those seen in genetic studies of wild tamarins as well as theoretically expected patterns of genetic differentiation across the landscape (i.e., a very clear effect of isolation by distance and additional, rapidly accumulating genetic divergence between areas of the landscape separated by regions of restricted gene flow, such as on opposite sides of a river) (Di Fiore & Valencia 2013, 2014). As with the other models discussed above, however, the point was not to generate quantitative predictions about any particular taxon but rather to provide a flexible modeling framework within which users can explore, *in silico*, the population genetic consequences of different animal social systems and how these consequences are simultaneously influenced by landscape factors.

Additional Applications where ABMs Show Promise

As noted above, because ABMs are concerned with dynamic systems and how these are generated from the bottom up, they can be particularly useful for exploring systems with many types of actors interacting in complex ways. As a result, the agent-based approach has applications in many fields in the natural (DeAngelis & Mooij 2005; Grimm & Railsback 2005) and social sciences (Axelrod 1997; Epstein 2007; Epstein & Axtell

1996; Gilbert & Troitzsch 2005). In the social sciences, for example, agent-based modeling has been applied to modeling a wide range of problems in anthropology (e.g., biocultural evolution: Barton et al. 2011; Barton & Riel-Salvatore 2012; hominin paleobiology: Griffith et al. 2010; the development of Balinese water temple networks: Lansing & Kremer 1993), archeology (e.g., the fate of Puebloan cultures in the Four Corners region of the US Southwest: Axtell et al. 2002; Kolher et al. 2009; Janssen 2009; the socioecological system of the ancient Maya: Heckbert 2013), economics (e.g., the emergence of economic markets and trade networks, governance of common-pool resources: see reviews by Tesfatsion 2002, 2003 and examples in Tesfatsion & Judd 2006), geography (e.g., shifting patterns of land-use land cover: Bithell & Brasington 2009; Parker et al. 2003), psychology (e.g., human mate choice: Smaldino & Schank 2012), and sociology (see review by Macy & Willer 2002). The approach has also been applied to real-world business problems (e.g., traffic simulation, changes to stock market policy: Bonabeau 2002), ecosystem management (e.g., Bousquet & Le Page 2004), urban planning (e.g., Batty 2005), disaster management (e.g., Hashemi & Alesheikh 2013), epidemiology (e.g., Roche et al. 2008; Perez & Dragocevic 2009), medicine and physiology (e.g., An & Wilensky 2009; Chiacchio et al. 2014), and to a wide range of ecological issues (e.g., optimal foraging theory: Barton 2008, 2015; predator–prey population dynamics in fragmented landscapes: Baggio et al. 2011; herbivore foraging in terrestrial ecosystems: Oom et al. 2004; ecosystem-level tropic interactions: Parrott & Kok 2002; nutrient transport among ecosystems: Albeke et al. 2015; human adaptations to climate change: e.g., Balbi & Giupponi 2009; Berger & Troost 2014; Bharwani et al. 2005; Janssen & de Vries 1998; Wang et al. 2013). Within animal behavior and primatology, in addition to the case studies described above, ABMs have been effectively applied to modeling animal searching behavior (e.g., Conradt et al. 2003), the evolution of cooperation and collective behavior (e.g., Pepper & Smuts 1999; Ward et al. 2001), the spatial organization of animal groups (e.g., Couzin et al. 2002; Dumont & Hill 2004), disease transmission (e.g., Bonnell et al. 2010; Nunn 2009), the interplay between foraging behavior and predation risk (e.g., Nibbelink & Carpenter 1998; Ward et al. 2000), and the emergence of cultural differences in diets between groups (e.g., van der Post & Hogeweg 2008, 2009), among other topics. Readers interested in the range of phenomena to which ABMs can be applied and in materials for learning agent-based modeling are encouraged to visit the OpenABM section of the Computational Modeling for SocioEcological Science Network (CoMSES Net, www.comses.net), a research network that aims to foster and expand the use of computational modeling across the sciences. The network also maintains an online repository for archiving and sharing ABMs, which is an excellent source of examples to study (Rollins et al. 2014).

Agent-Based Modeling and Spatial Analysis

Importantly, each and every one of the primate ABM case studies described above takes an explicitly *spatial* perspective on agents' interactions with one another. In the

DOM-WORLD, GrooFi, and EMO-model world, for example, even though the simulation environment is homogeneous, the interactions that take place among mobile agents are explicitly mediated by their separation distance and relative orientation. In all of the other models mentioned, simulations are played out in explicitly heterogeneous environments, where agents' behaviors are influenced by the distribution of resources and/or features of the landscape and where the results of the simulations are used for subsequent spatial analysis. Thus, agent-based approaches and spatial analysis often naturally go hand-in-hand, and for some time researchers have commented on the promise of more closely integrating agent-based modeling with tools for geospatial analysis, such as those provided by GIS (Brown et al. 2005; Crooks & Castle 2012). Close integration of agent-based modeling and GIS, however, is complicated by several factors, particularly the different underlying philosophical perspectives and goals that typically characterize ABMs versus GIS. In an ABM, researchers are particularly interested in *how the states of mobile individual agents change over time*. Simulation models typically track agents through time, and spatial information (e.g., the location of an agent in the landscape) is just one of potentially many attributes that define an agent's state at a particular moment. Still, the spatial state of the system as a whole is often not represented in the data model (though it might be pieced together by integrating across agents' spatial attributes). By contrast, GIS is explicitly concerned with efficiently *representing and facilitating analysis of spatial information*, but often at the expense of the temporal dimension. Temporal changes can be incorporated into GIS databases in several ways (Peuquet 2005), but systems capable of performing sophisticated and powerful queries on spatio-temporal data, analogous to those that most modern GIS frameworks can do with geospatial data, have yet to be developed. Thus, integrating ABMs and GIS usually involves either linking existing systems together programmatically (through data transfer or database sharing) or embedding some of the functionality of one of these environments within the other.

Brown et al. (2005) and Crooks and Castle (2012) offer nice overviews of the issues associated with integrating ABMs and GIS, and they each categorize possible integrated systems along a continuum from "loosely" to "tightly" coupled. Loosely coupled systems involve the transfer of data back and forth between agent-based modeling and GIS software to accomplish specific functions best performed in one environment or the other. For example, an ABM developed to explore altitudinal range use of snub-nosed monkeys might want to take advantage of a digital elevation model of the monkeys' habitat and use the functionality of GIS to estimate the cost of the movement from one point to another along different possible paths, which then might factor into agents' decisions over which route to take. In this case, a simulation running in the ABM environment would be suspended periodically and information about the agents' positions and targets passed to a GIS to be used for the movement-cost analysis, the results of which are then returned to the ABM for the simulation to continue. Because in such a system the ABM and GIS operate asynchronously, and because repeated back-and-forth data transfer between the systems can require significant processing time (particularly for models with a large number of agents), loosely coupled ABM–GIS systems tend to be inefficient. An example of a more moderately coupled system would be one that uses a common database to store both spatial information used by the GIS and attribute information about agents' states used by the ABM. Here, although the two systems might still be called on asynchronously to perform certain functions, the time costs associated with repeated data transfers is lessened because the underlying database is shared. Finally, a tightly coupled system would be one that allows the ABM and GIS environments to communicate and share data with one another directly and seamlessly, and one that, ideally, allows modelers to access the functionality of both systems from a single API (application programming interface) (Crooks & Castle 2012).

In practice, coupling existing ABMs and GIS often requires considerable programming or scripting skills, which may be beyond the reach of many modelers. However, some software tools have been developed that either allow users to incorporate agent-based modeling approaches within an existing GIS platform (i.e., a GIS-centric approach) or to implement certain spatial data manipulation and analysis algorithms within an existing ABM toolkit (i.e., an ABM-centric approach) (Brown et al. 2005; Crooks & Castle 2012). Such systems can allow users to work in a familiar environment and take advantage of programming tools they may already be accustomed to. For example, the *Agent Analyst* tool for the proprietary software *ArcGIS* (ESRI) is an example of a GIS-centric integrated system. The tool basically installs and allows users to seamlessly connect to a version of the open-source agent-based modeling toolkit *Repast* (North et al. 2013), described below, from within the ArcGIS environment. Users can thus create ABMs directly within ArcGIS, treating any spatial objects (points, polygons, raster cells) as agents and programming their behavior through the use of a simple Python-like scripting language (Johnston 2013). By contrast, as an example of an ABM-centric system, the *GIS* extension adds basic GIS functionality to the agent-based modeling software *NetLogo* (Wilensky 1999), also described below. Possibilities also exist for embedding certain spatial data manipulation and analysis algorithms within other ABM toolkits. For example, *GeoMASON*, an extension for the ABM toolkit *MASON* (Luke et al. 2005), allows users to import geospatial data in vector and raster formats, and current versions of the *Repast* and *GAMA* toolkits also include possibilities for working with geospatial data.

Agent-Based Modeling Software Toolkits

Currently, a large number of software toolkits, for various computer operating systems, are available for agent-based modeling: As of this writing, for example, the Wikipedia entry for "Comparison of agent-based modeling software" lists over a dozen of these, though many are no longer in active development. Below, and in Table 14.1, I briefly describe a few of these toolkits, focusing on those that are non-commercial, enjoy active user communities, and have some capacity or promise for integrating geospatial data and/ or performing geospatial analyses. Further discussion of these and other toolkits, including several commercial alternatives, are provided by Railsback et al. (2006), Berryman (2008), Nikolai and Madey (2009), Allan (2010), and Crooks and Castle (2012).

Table 14.1 Summary of non-proprietary agent-based modeling toolkits discussed in the text

Toolkit	URL	Programming language(s)	Open-source license	GIS capabilities	Key strengths
Repast	https://repast.github.io/index.html	Java; C# (and other .NET languages), Python, ReLogo; some ability to visually design model classes	New BSD	A built-in plugin provides the ability to import vector and raster data in a variety of formats; geospatial data can be used to create model agents	Mature, comprehensive development platform; supports programming in a variety of languages
MASON	http://cs.gmu.edu/~eclab/projects/mason/	Java	Academic free license	*GeoMASON* plugin provides the ability to work with vector and raster data in a variety of formats	Size, speed, and ability to deal with very large numbers of agents; ability to suspend and move models among computers
SeSAm	www.simsesam.org/	Own visual programming language	GNU LGPL	A forthcoming plugin is expected to allow import and export of vector (ESRI shapefile) and raster data	Ability to design models visually
GAMA	https://gama-platform.github.io/	GAML and own visual programming language	GNU GPL	Support is built in for loading vector data (ESRI shapefiles) into simulations and for creating agents from GIS data; as yet, does not support raster data	Comprehensive development platform; modeling-oriented language; ability to design models visually
Processing	http://processing.org/	Java, JavaScript, CoffeeScript, Python	GNU LGPL and GPL	External libraries provide support for incorporating various geospatial data into programs (e.g., map tiles, vector data in GeoJSON or GPX format)	Ease of creating quick "sketches" with immediate visual feedback; sketches can be deployed to web; ability to use web-friendly geospatial data formats

Table 14.1 (*cont.*)

Toolkit	URL	Programming language(s)	Open-source license	GIS capabilities	Key strengths
NetLogo	http://ccl.northwestern.edu/netlogo/	NetLogo	GNU GPL	The *gis* extension allows importing of vector (ESRI shapefiles) and raster (ESRI ASCII grid files) data, plus simple geoprocessing and export of raster files	Immediate visual feedback, interactivity, easy to learn programming language; large user community

Note: each of these toolkits is available for a variety of computer operating systems (MacOS, Windows, Linux).

Repast (for "REcursive Porous Agent Simulation Toolkit") is a free, open-source, cross-platform toolkit for agent-based modeling originally created at the University of Chicago and currently being developed by researchers at the Argonne National Laboratory (North et al. 2013). Earlier versions of *Repast* supported model development in three different programming languages: Java (*RepastJ*), C# (*Repast.NET*), and the Python-like "Not Quite Python" (*RepastPy*). The latest iteration, *Repast Simphony* (North et al. 2013), is designed to be completely object-oriented and modular. Standard plugins are included in the basic toolkit to extend its functionality, e.g., to support visualization of running models and to allow models to incorporate geospatial data employing standard GIS tools. Other plugins allow *Repast Simphony* to interface with other third-party software, such as the statistical programming language *R*, the network visualization tool *Pajek*, and the open-source GIS, *GRASS*. In addition to being backward compatible with models developed in earlier versions of *Repast* in other programming languages, the *Repast Simphony* toolkit introduces a new modeling language, ReLogo, based on the high-level easy-to-learn language, Logo. *Repast Simphony* itself is distributed as a plugin for *Eclipse*, a free, open-source integrated development environment that supports a variety of programming languages. As discussed above, *Agent Analyst* – a tool for the GIS software package *ArcGIS* – now allows *Repast* ABMs to be developed and run from within the *ArcGIS* environment (Johnston 2013).

MASON (for "Multi-Agent Simulator of Neighborhoods") is a free, open-source, cross-platform software for running agent-based models written in the object-oriented programming language Java. The toolkit was developed jointly by the *Evolutionary Computation Laboratory* and the *Center for Social Complexity* at George Mason University (Luke et al. 2005). *MASON* combines a simulation library core with a graphical user interface console and a set of tools for visualizing simulation runs. As mentioned above, an extension, *GeoMASON*, now makes it possible to import geospatial data in vector and raster format for characterizing environments in which simulations take place (Sullivan et al. 2010).

SeSAm (for "Shell for Simulated Agent Systems") is a free, cross-platform tool for agent-based simulation, in which models and data visualizations can be designed entirely using a visual interface that does not require users to know a programming language (Klügl et al. 2006). For example, attributes of agents are specified using the "Edit Agent" dialogue box and popup menus, and the possible behaviors of those agents, as well as the rules governing when particular behaviors should be performed, are graphically configured in the various tabs of the dialogue box. *SeSAm* was first developed at the University of Würzburg (Germany), and current development continues at Örebro University (Sweden). At present, *SeSAm* does not support importing of spatial data, but a forthcoming GIS plugin is expected to add this feature.

GAMA (for "Generic Agent-based Modelling Architecture") is a free, open-source, cross-platform toolkit for agent-based modeling that is under joint development by various research teams in France and at Can Tho University in Vietnam (Grignard et al. 2013). *GAMA*, like *Repast*, is built on the *Eclipse* platform and provides an integrated environment for designing and running models and for visualization. Models are developed in a unique, object-oriented programming language called GAML (for "GAMA Modeling Language") that has parallels with both Java and the dialect of Logo used in the *NetLogo* modeling environment (see below). A plugin also allows models to be designed graphically and then converted into GAML. The *GAMA* toolkit aims to be a comprehensive ecosystem for model development and for running simulation experiments. The toolkit, for example, allows models to access external database management systems (e.g., SQLite, MySQL, PostgreSQL) and to call *R* code, and it also already allows modelers to incorporate geospatial information into models and to build agents from geospatial data. As such, it is a very promising candidate as an ABM-centric integrated system.

Processing is a free, open-source, cross-platform programming language and development environment that was created at MIT's Media Lab for visual artists to be able to easily use software as a medium for designing interactive graphics and visualizations (Reas & Fry 2007, 2010). The syntax of the original *Processing* programming language draws heavily from (but simplifies) other well-developed object-oriented languages, particularly Java. While not developed specifically for agent-based modeling, the object-oriented nature of *Processing* programs (typically referred to as "sketches," highlighting the philosophy that software is a medium for artistic creativity) provides the potential for quick visual prototyping, and, with recent releases, the ability to program in different "modes" inspired by other languages (e.g., Python and JavaScript) in addition to Java makes the environment a candidate worth considering as a tool for developing ABMs. External software libraries, including *giCentre* and *Unfolding Maps*, allow use and visualization of geospatial data within *Processing*.

NetLogo is a free, open-source, cross-platform integrated environment for creating and visualizing agent-based models (Wilensky 1999). It was developed at the *Center for Connected Learning and Computer-Based Modeling*, first at Tufts University and currently at Northwestern University. *NetLogo* includes both a code editor for programming models (in a dialect of the high-level language, Logo) and a graphical interface window where modelers can design visualizations for running models as well as ways for users to interact with models as they are set up and run. A large number of extensions, distributed both by the developers and by the user community, add functionality to the modeling environment. For example, the *GIS* extension, bundled with current versions of *NetLogo*, allows users to import spatial data (in both vector and raster format) for use in a model or to run simple geoprocessing tasks and queries on these data within the modeling environment. Similarly, the *r* extension allows users to call functions from the statistical programming environment, *R*, and utilize them in ABMs. *NetLogo* currently enjoys a very large and active user community, and the environment can be used not just for model development but also for teaching basic programming skills, as the language is simple enough that beginners can start writing code with little prior experience and the user interface provides immediate visual feedback on running code. In terms of its ease of use, availability of online resources for learning, capacity to incorporate geospatial data, and ability to integrate with a variety of other software, *NetLogo* is likely to be the most interesting of these alternatives for novice modelers, especially those new to computer programming.

Conclusions

Agent-based modeling is a powerful, flexible, and creative tool that has been used widely in the natural and social sciences for exploring questions about the dynamics of complex systems and about how those systems can emerge, bottom-up, from the myriad interactions of their constituents with one another and with the environment. Agent-based approaches are oftentimes *spatially explicit*, meaning that simulations are situated in a particular landscape and that the behavioral decisions of individual agents depend in part on their location within that landscape and/or on the spatial configuration among agents. Thus, the approach is inherently tied, conceptually, to many of the themes discussed elsewhere in this volume. Agent-based modeling also now has a long (if not very deep) history in primatology, but *its promise is nowhere near tapped*. Here, I have highlighted areas where agent-based modeling has been used to good effect to explore a range of topics of interest to primatologists, and introduced a few of the mature software environments that can be used for developing agent-based simulations, several of which are accessible even to novice programmers. I enthusiastically encourage curious readers to explore some of these resources!

References

Albeke, S. E., Nibbelink, N. P., and Ben-David, M. 2015. Modeling behavior by coastal river otter (*Lontra canadensis*) in response to prey availability in Prince William Sound, Alaska: a spatially-explicit individual-based approach. *PLoS ONE* **10**: e0126208.
Allan, R. J. 2010. Survey of agent based modelling and simulation tools. Technical Report DL-TR-2010-007. Science and Technology Facilities Council.

An, G., and Wilensky, U. 2009. From artificial life to *in silico* medicine: NetLogo as a means of translational knowledge representation in biomedical research. Pages 183–214 in *Artificial Life Models in Software*. M. Komosinski and A. Adamatzky (Eds.). Springer-Verlag, London.

Axelrod, R. M. 1997. *The Complexity of Cooperation: Agent-Based Models of Competition and Collaboration*. Princeton University Press, Princeton, NJ.

Axtell, R. L., Epstein, J. M., Dean, J. S., et al. 2002. Population growth and collapse in a multi-agent model of the Kayenta Anasazi in Long House Valley. *Proceedings of the National Academy of Sciences USA* **99**: 7275–7279.

Baggio, J. A., Salau, K., Janssen, M. A., Schoon, M. L., and Bodin, Ö. 2011. Landscape connectivity and predator–prey population dynamics. *Landscape Ecology* **26**: 33–45.

Balbi, S. and Giupponi, C. 2009. Reviewing agent-based modelling of socio-ecosystems: a methodology for the analysis of climate change adaptation and sustainability. Working Paper 15. Department of Economics, Ca' Foscari University of Venice.

Barton, C. M. 2008. Patch choice model from optimal foraging theory (Human Behavioral Ecology) (Version 1). CoMSES Computational Model Library. Available at: www.openabm.org/model/2221/version/1.

Barton, C. M. 2015. Diet breadth model from optimal foraging theory (Human Behavioral Ecology) (Version 2). CoMSES Computational Model Library. Available at: www.openabm.org/model/2225/version/2.

Barton, C. M. and Riel-Salvatore, J. 2012. Agents of change: modeling biocultural evolution in Upper Pleistocene western Eurasia. *Advances in Complex Systems* **15**: 1150003.

Barton, C. M., Riel-Salvatore, J., Anderies, J. M., and Popescu, G. 2011. Modeling human ecodynamics and biocultural interactions in the Late Pleistocene of western Eurasia. *Human Ecology* **39**: 705–725.

Batty, M. 2005. *Cities and Complexity: Understanding Cities with Cellular Automata, Agent-Based Models, and Fractals*. MIT Press, Cambridge, MA.

Berger, T. and Troost, C. 2014. Agent-based modelling of climate adaptation and mitigation options in agriculture. *Journal of Agricultural Economics* **65**: 323–348.

Berryman, M. 2008. Review of software platforms for agent based models. Report DSTO-GD-0532. Australian Government Department of Defense, Land Operations Division, Defence Science and Technology Organisation.

Bharwani, S., Bithell, M., Downing, T. E., et al. 2005. Multi-agent modelling of climate outlooks and food security on a community garden scheme in Limpopo, South Africa. *Philosophical Transactions of the Royal Society B: Biological Sciences* **360**: 2183–2194.

Billari, F. C., Fent, T., Prskawetz, A., Scheffran, J. 2006. Agent-based computational modelling: an introduction. Pages 1–16 in *Agent-Based Computational Modelling: Applications in Demography, Social, Economic and Environmental Sciences*. F. C. Billari, T. Fent, A. Prskawetz, and J. Scheffran (Eds.). Physica-Verlag, Heidelberg.

Bithell, M. and Brasington, J. 2009. Coupling agent-based models of subsistence farming with individual-based forest models and dynamic models of water distribution. *Environmental Modelling & Software* **24**: 173–190.

Bonabeau, E. 2002. Agent-based modeling: methods and techniques for simulating human systems. *Proceedings of the National Academy of Sciences USA* **99**(S3): 7280–7287.

Bonnell, T. R., Sengupta, R. R., Chapman, C. A., and Goldberg, T. L. 2010. An agent-based model of red colobus resources and disease dynamics implicates key resource sites as hot spots of disease transmission. *Ecological Modelling* **221**: 2491–2500.

Bonnell, T. R., Campennì, M., Chapman, C. A., et al. 2013. Emergent group level navigation: an agent-based evaluation of movement patterns in a folivorous primate. *PLoS ONE* **8**: e78264.

Bousquet, F. and Le Page, C. 2004. Multi-agent simulations and ecosystem management: a review. *Ecological Modelling* **176**: 313–332.

Brown, D. G., Riolo, R., Robinson, D. T., North, M., and Rand, W. 2005. Spatial process and data models: toward integration of agent-based models and GIS. *Journal of Geographical Systems* **7**: 25–47.

Bryson, J. J., Ando, Y., and Lehmann, H. 2007. Agent-based modelling as scientific method: a case study analysing primate social behaviour. *Philosophical Transactions of the Royal Society B: Biological Sciences* **362**: 1685–1699.

Chiacchio, F., Pennisi, M., Russo, G., Motta, S., and Pappalardo, F. 2014. Agent-based modeling of the immune system: NetLogo, a promising framework. *BioMed Research International* **2014**: 1–6.

Conradt, L., Zollner, P., Roper, T., Frank, K., and Thomas, C. 2003. Foray search: an effective systematic dispersal strategy in fragmented landscapes. *The American Naturalist* **161**: 905–915.

Couzin, I. D., Krause, J., James, R., Ruxton, G. D., and Franks, N. R. 2002. Collective memory and spatial sorting in animal groups. *Journal of Theoretical Biology* **218**: 1–11.

Crooks, A. T. and Castle, C. J. E. 2012. The integration of agent-based modelling and geographical information for geospatial simulation. Pages 219–251 in *Agent-Based Models of Geographical Systems*. Springer, Dordrecht.

Crooks, A. T. and Heppenstall, A. J. 2012. Introduction to agent-based modelling. Pages 85–105 in Agent-Based Models of Geographical Systems. Springer, Dordrecht.

DeAngelis, D. L. and Mooij, W. M. 2005. Individual-based modeling of ecological and evolutionary processes. *Annual Review of Ecology and Systematics* **36**: 147–168.

Di Fiore, A. 2009. Agent-based simulation modeling of primate sociality. *American Journal of Physical Anthropology Supplement* **48**: 118–119.

Di Fiore, A. 2010a. Forward-time, individual-based simulations and their use in primate landscape genetics. 23rd Congress of the International Primatological Society, August 2010, Kyoto, Japan.

Di Fiore, A. 2010b. The influence of social systems on primate population genetic structure: an agent-based modeling approach. SOCIOR Conference on Social Systems: Demographic and Genetic Issues, September 2010, University of Rennes, Paimpont, France.

Di Fiore, A. 2012. The interplay between primate social organization and population genetic structure: insights from agent-based simulation models. 24th Congress of the International Primatological Society, August 2012, Cancun, Mexico.

Di Fiore, A. and Valencia, L. M. 2013. Monogamy, polygyny, and polyandry: exploring the genetic consequences of callitrichine social systems using agent-based simulation. 36th Annual Meeting of the American Society of Primatologists, June 2013, San Juan, Puerto Rico.

Di Fiore, A. and Valencia, L. M. 2014. The interplay of landscape features and social system on the genetic structure of a primate population: a simulation study using "tamarin" monkeys. *International Journal of Primatology* **35**: 226–257.

Dolado, R. and Beltran, F. S. 2012. Emergent patterns of social organization in captive *Cercocebus torquatus*: testing the GrooFiWorld agent-based model. *Journal of Biosciences* **37**: 777–784.

Dumont, B. and Hill, D. R. C. 2004. Spatially explicit models of group foraging by herbivores: what can agent-based models offer? *Animal Research* **53**: 419–428.

Epstein, J. M. 1999. Agent-based computational models and generative social science. *Complexity* **5**: 41–60.

Epstein, J. M. 2007. *Generative Social Science: Studies in Agent-Based Computational Modeling*. Princeton University Press, Princeton, NJ.

Epstein, J. M. and Axtell, R. 1996. *Growing Artificial Societies: Social Science from the Bottom Up*. MIT Press, Cambridge, MA.

Evers, E., de Vries, H., Spruijt, B. M., and Sterck, E. H. M. 2011. Better safe than sorry: socio-spatial group structure emerges from individual variation in fleeing, avoidance or velocity in an agent-based model. *PLoS ONE* **6**: e26189.

Evers, E., de Vries, H., Spruijt, B. M., and Sterck, E. H. M. 2012. Look before you leap: individual variation in social vigilance shapes socio-spatial group properties in an agent-based model. *Behavioural Ecology and Sociobiology* **66**: 931–945.

Evers, E., de Vries, H., Spruijt, B. M., and Sterck, E. H. M. 2014. The EMO-model: an agent-based model of primate social behavior regulated by two emotional dimensions, anxiety-FEAR and satisfaction-LIKE. *PLoS ONE* **9**: e87955.

Gilbert, N. 2008. The idea of agent-based modeling. Pages 1–20 in *Agent-Based Models*. Sage, Thousand Oaks, CA.

Gilbert, N. and Terna, P. 2000. How to build and use agent-based models in social science. *Mind & Society* **2000**: 57–72.

Gilbert, N. and Troitzsch, K. G. 2005. *Simulation for the Social Scientist*, 2nd edition. Open University Press (McGraw-Hill Education), Glasgow.

Goldstone, R. L. and Janssen, M. A. 2005. Computational models of collective behavior. *Trends in Cognitive Sciences* **9**: 424–430.

Griffith, C., Long, B., and Sept, J. 2010. HOMINIDS: an agent-based spatial simulation model to evaluate behavioral patterns of early Pleistocene hominids. *Ecological Modelling* **221**: 738–760.

Grignard, A., Taillandier, P., Gaudou, B., et al. 2013. GAMA 1.6: Advancing the art of complex agent-based modeling and simulation. Pages 117–131 in *PRIMA 2013: Principles and Practice of Multi-Agent Systems*. Springer, New York.

Grimm, V. and Railsback, S. F. 2005. *Individual-Based Modeling and Ecology*. Princeton University Press, Princeton, NJ.

Grimm, V., Berger, U., Bastiansen, F., et al. 2006. A standard protocol for describing individual-based and agent-based models. *Ecological Modelling* **198**: 115–126.

Grimm, V., Berger, U., DeAngelis, D. L., et al. 2010. The ODD protocol: a review and first update. *Ecological Modelling* **221**: 2760–2768.

Hashemi, M. and Alesheikh, A. A. 2013. GIS: agent-based modeling and evaluation of an earthquake-stricken area with a case study in Tehran, Iran. *Natural Hazards* **69**: 1895–1917.

Heckbert, S. 2013. MayaSim: An agent-based model of the ancient Maya social-ecological system. *Journal of Artificial Societies and Social Simulation* **16**: 11.

Hemelrijk, C. K. 1999a. An individual-orientated model of the emergence of despotic and egalitarian societies. *Proceedings of the Royal Society of London Series B: Biological Sciences* **266**: 361–369.

Hemelrijk, C. 1999b. Effects of cohesiveness on inter-sexual dominance relationships and spatial structure among group-living virtual entities. Pages 524–534 in *Advances in Artificial Life: Fifth European Conference on Artificial Life*. D. Floreano, J.-D. Nicoud, and F. Mondana (Eds.). Springer-Verlag, Berlin.

Hemelrijk, C. K. 2000. Towards the integration of social dominance and spatial structure. *Animal Behaviour* **59**: 1035–1048.

Hemelrijk, C. 2001. Sexual attraction and inter-sexual dominance among virtual agents. *Lecture Notes in Computer Science* **1979**: 167–180.

Hemelrijk, C. 2002. Despotic societies, sexual attraction and the emergence of male "tolerance": an agent-based model. *Behaviour* **139**: 729–747.

Hemelrijk, C. and Puga-Gonzalez, I. I. 2012. An individual-oriented model on the emergence of support in fights, its reciprocation and exchange. *PLoS One* **7**: e37271.

Hemelrijk, C., Wantia, J., and Dätwyler, M. 2003. Female co-dominance in a virtual world: ecological, cognitive, social and sexual causes. *Behaviour* **140**: 1247–1273.

Hill, R. A., Logan, B. S., Sellers, W. I., and Zappala, J. 2014. An agent-based model of group decision making in baboons. Pages 454–476 in *Modelling Natural Action Selection*. A. K. Seth, T. J. Prescott, and J. J. Bryson (Eds.). Cambridge University Press, Cambridge.

Hogeweg, P. 1988. MIRROR beyond MIRROR, puddles of Life. Pages 297–315 in *Artificial Life I*. C. G. Langton (Ed.). Addison-Wesley, Redwood City, CA.

Hogeweg, P. and Hesper, B. 1985. Socioinformatic processes, a MIRROR modelling methodology. *Journal of Theoretical Biology* **113**: 311–330.

Hogeweg, P. and Hesper, B. 1990. Individual oriented modelling in ecology. *Mathematical and Computer Modelling* **13**: 83–90.

Janssen, M. 2009. Understanding artificial anasazi. *Journal of Artificial Societies and Social Simulation* **12**: 13.

Janssen, M. and de Vries, B. 1998. The battle of perspectives: a multi-agent model with adaptive responses to climate change. *Ecological Economics* **26**: 43–65.

Johnston, K. M. 2013. *Agent Analyst: Agent-Based Modeling in ArcGIS*. ESRI Press, Redlands, CA.

Klügl, F., Herrler, R., and Fehler, M. 2006. SeSAm: Implementation of agent-based simulation using visual programming. Pages 1439–1440 in *Proceedings of the Fifth International Joint Conference on Autonomous Agents and Multiagent Systems*. Association for Computing Machinery, New York.

Kokko, H. 2007. *Modelling for Field Biologists and Other Interesting People*. Cambridge University Press, Cambridge.

Kolher, T. A., Varien, M. D., Wright, A., and Kuckelman, K. A. 2009. Mesa Verde migrations: new archaeological research and computer simulation suggest why ancestral Puebloans deserted the northern Southwest United States. *American Scientist* **96**: 145–153.

Lansing, J. S. and Kremer, J. N. 1993. Emergent properties of Balinese water temple networks: coadaptation on a rugged fitness landscape. *American Anthropologist* **95**: 97–114.

Luke, S., Cioffi-Revilla, C., Panait, L., Sullivan, K., and Balan, G. 2005. MASON: a multi-agent simulation environment. *Simulation* **81**: 517–527.

Macal, C. M. and North, M. J. 2009. Agent-based modeling and simulation. Pages 86–98 in *Proceedings of the 2009 Winter Simulation Conference*. M. D. Rossetti, R. R. Hill, B. Johansson, et al. (Eds.). IEE, Piscataway, NJ.

Macal, C. M. and North, M. J. 2010. Toward teaching agent-based simulation. Pages 1–10 in *Proceedings of the 2010 Winter Simulation Conference*, B. Johansson, S. Jain, J. Montoya-Torres, J. Hugan, and E. Yücesan (Eds.).

Macy, M. W. and Willer, R. 2002. From factors to actors: computational sociology and agent-based modeling. *Annual Review of Sociology* **28**: 143–166.

Miller, J. H. and Page, S. E. 2007. *Complex Adaptive Systems: An Introduction to Computational Models of Social Life*. Princeton University Press, Princeton, NJ.

Nibbelink, N. P. and Carpenter, S. R. 1998. Interlake variation in growth and size structure of bluegill (*Lepomis macrochirus*): inverse analysis of an individual-based model. *Canadian Journal of Fisheries and Aquatic Sciences* **55**: 387–396.

Nikolai, C. and Madey, G. 2009. Tools of the trade: a survey of various agent based modeling platforms. *Journal of Artificial Societies and Social Simulation* **12**: 2.

North, M. J., Collier, N. T., Ozik, J., et al. 2013. *Complex Adaptive Systems Modeling With Repast Simphony. Complex Adaptive Systems Modeling.* Springer, Heidelberg.

Nunn, C. L. 2009. Using agent-based models to investigate primate disease ecology. Pages 83–110 in *Primate Parasite Ecology.* M. A. Huffman and C. A. Chapman (Eds.). Cambridge University Press, Cambridge.

Oom, S., Beecham, J., Legg, C., and Hester, A. 2004. Foraging in a complex environment: from foraging strategies to emergent spatial properties. *Ecological Complexity* **1**: 299–327.

Parker, D. C., Manson, S. M., Janssen, M. A., Hoffmann, M. J., and Deadman, P. 2003. Multi-agent systems for the simulation of land-use and land-cover change: a review. *Annals of the Association of American Geographers* **93**: 314–337.

Parrott, L. and Kok, R. 2002. A generic, individual-based approach to modelling higher trophic levels in simulation of terrestrial ecosystems. *Ecological Modelling* **151**: 154–178.

Pepper, J. W. and Smuts, B. B. 1999. The evolution of cooperation in an ecological context: an agent-based model. Pages 45–76 in *Dynamics in Human and Primate Societies.* T. Kohler and G. Gumerman (Eds.). Oxford University Press, Oxford.

Perez, L. and Dragocevic, S. 2009. An agent-based approach for modeling dynamics of contagious disease spread. *International Journal of Health Geographics* **8**: 50.

Peuquet, D. J. 2005. Time in GIS and geographical databases. Pages 91–103 in *Geographical Information Systems: Principles, Techniques, Management and Applications (Abridged Edition),* P. A. Longley, M. F. Goodchild, D. J. Maguire, and D. W. Rhind (Eds.). Wiley, Hoboken, NJ.

Puga-Gonzalez, I. I., Hildenbrandt, H. H., and Hemelrijk, C. K. C. 2009. Emergent patterns of social affiliation in primates, a model. *PLoS Computational Biology* **5**: e1000630.

Railsback, S. F. and Grimm, V. 2012. *Agent-Based and Individual-Based Modeling: A Practical Introduction.* Princeton University Press, Princeton, NJ.

Railsback, S. F., Lytinen, S. L., and Jackson, S. K. 2006. Agent-based simulation platforms: Review and development recommendations. *Simulation* **82**: 609–623.

Ramos-Fernández, G., Boyer, D., and Gomez, V. P. 2006. A complex social structure with fission–fusion properties can emerge from a simple foraging model. *Behavioural Ecology and Sociobiology* **60**: 536–549.

Reas, C. and Fry, B. 2007. *Processing: A Programming Handbook for Visual Designers and Artists.* MIT Press, Cambridge, MA.

Reas, C. and Fry, B. 2010. *Getting Started with Processing.* O'Reilly Media, Cambridge, MA.

Roche, B., Guégan, J.-F., and Bousquet, F. 2008. Multi-agent systems in epidemiology: a first step for computational biology in the study of vector-borne disease transmission. *BMC Bioinformatics* **9**: 435.

Rollins, N. D., Barton, C. M., Bergin, S., Janssen, M. A., and Lee, A. 2014. A computational model library for publishing model documentation and code. *Environmental Modelling & Software* **61**: 59–64.

Sellers, W., Hill, R., and Logan, B. 2007. An agent-based model of group decision making in baboons. *Philosophical Transactions of the Royal Society Series B: Biological Sciences* **362**: 1699–1710.

Smaldino, P. E. and Schank, J. C. 2012. Human mate choice is a complex system. *Complexity* **17**: 11–22.

Sullivan, K., Coletti, M., and Luke, S. 2010. GeoMason: GeoSpatial support for MASON. Technical Report GMU-CS-TR-2010–16. Department of Computer Science, George Mason University.

te Boekhorst, I. J. A. and Hogeweg, P. 1994a. Self-structuring in artificial "chimps" offers new hypotheses for male grouping in chimpanzees. *Behaviour* **130**: 229–252.

te Boekhorst, I. and Hogeweg, P. 1994b. Effect of tree size on travel band formation in orang-utans: data analysis suggested by a model study. Pages 119–129 in *Artificial Life IV: Proceedings of the Fourth International Workshop on the Synthesis and Simulation of Living Systems.* R. A. Brooks and P. Maes (Eds.). MIT Press, Cambridge, MA.

Tesfatsion, L. 2002. Agent-based computational economics: growing economies from the bottom up. *Artificial Life* **8**: 55–82.

Tesfatsion, L. 2003. Agent-based computational economics: modeling economies as complex adaptive systems. *Information Sciences* **149**: 262–268.

Tesfatsion, L. and Judd, K. L. (Eds.). 2006. *Handbook of Computational Economics: Volume 2: Agent-Based Computational Economics*. Elsevier, Amsterdam.

van der Post, D. J. and Hogeweg, P. 2008. Diet traditions and cumulative cultural processes as side-effects of grouping. *Animal Behaviour* **75**: 133–144.

van der Post, D. J. and Hogeweg, P. 2009. Cultural inheritance and diversification of diet in variable environments. *Animal Behaviour* **78**: 155–166.

Wang, J., Brown, D. G., Riolo, R. L., Page, S. E., and Agrawal, A. 2013. Exploratory analyses of local institutions for climate change adaptation in the Mongolian grasslands: an agent-based modeling approach. *Global Environmental Change* **23**: 1266–1276.

Ward, J., Austin, R., and Macdonald, D. 2000. A simulation model of foraging behaviour and the effect of predation risk. *Journal of Animal Ecology* **69**: 16–30.

Ward, C., Gobet, F., and Kendall, G. 2001. Evolving collective behavior in an artificial ecology. *Artificial Life* **7**: 191–209.

Wilensky, U. 1999. NetLogo. Center for Connected Learning and Computer-Based Modeling, Northwestern University, Evanston, IL. Available at: http://ccl.northwestern.edu/netlogo/.

Part III

GIS Analysis in Broad-Scale Space

Introduction

Francine L. Dolins

Primatologists take it for granted that it is important to study primates. We rarely consider the unique quality of the information that we uncover, because we expect to be intrigued and surprised by what we find; we expect to be able to put together more of the puzzle pieces as well as to identify additional parts of the puzzle. The individual primates we observe and test, and the groups, populations, and species to which they belong, teach us about their day-to-day lives and the distinctive ways they survive, and help us uncover their specific past and the shared past of our common ancestors. Geospatial technology is critical to aiding primatologists in these efforts. Compared to previous technologies (e.g., a Brunton compass, tripod, a 50 m tape measure, onion paper, ruler and a good pencil with an eraser to hand-draw maps and paths), it is much easier, collects more accurate data and allows more accurate analyses using geographic information systems (GIS), and allows greater flexibility in terms of how to effectively implement these data for multiple types of analyses.

Geospatial technology of all types enables a focus on broad-scale space for larger geographic questions, such as assessing the quality, size, and general suitability of a habitat for a specific primate species. Particularly important in the present day of primate species decline, is identifying the conservation requirements for populations and species to survive, often near to or with human populations, and their needs for resources. It is with this in mind that we include the six chapters in this section, to help guide primatologists to maximize the full functionality of the often underutilized current technology for their research and conservation efforts. We compare and contrast fine scale (local scale) and broad scale (landscape scale) in these various chapters, as in the previous section.

More journals have emerged in the last few decades that highlight projects using GIS analyses and other specialized and related geospatial technology (e.g., remote sensing technology, LIDAR) (see Table III.1 for examples). Older journals that focus on biogeography now also highlight articles using GIS and remote sensing data.

Questions in Field Primatology Suited for Broad-Scale Space Analysis

Using geospatial technology, we can ask questions about broad-scale space that apply to habitat use, suitability, ranging behavior, and dynamic changes in landscape that affect behavior. We can address specific questions about movement and foraging ecology, the socioecological dynamics of groups, and behaviors reflecting resource dispersion. Importantly, with broad-scale space analysis, we can track, monitor, and assess

Table III.1 Examples of geospatial technology and GIS-related journals

Journal name	Year started	Aims and focus
International Journal of Remote Sensing	1980	The focus is on the theoretical aspects of remote sensing and applications of remotely sensed data from the atmosphere, biosphere, cryosphere, and terrestrial Earth.
Transactions in GIS	1996	Publishes the latest advances and best practices in spatial sciences, including ways in which GIS is applied to organize, represent, store, analyze, model, and visualize information.
Environmental Modelling & Software	1997	Aims to improve scientists' capacity to represent, understand, predict, and manage the dynamics of behavioral systems at a range of scales, including describing model development, evaluation, and outcomes from applications.
International Journal of Geographical Information Science	1997	To provide a forum for the exchange of original ideas, approaches, methods, and experiences in the field of GIS science.
Nature Geoscience	2008	Aims to publish quality research across a broad spectrum of Earth sciences in areas such as atmospheric science, biogeochemistry, climate science, geobiology, geoinformatics, and remote sensing.
Remote Sensing	2009	Aims to include all types of remote sensing science, including sensor design, application in the geosciences, environmental sciences, ecology, and civil engineering.

conservation issues for primates, such as habitat loss, groups movement within and across fragmented forests, intrusion of new roads or logging into primate habitat, and other human activity that affects primate groups' wellbeing.

We can track the movement and foraging ecology of nonhuman primates as well as humans to study the ecological and sociocultural factors involved in foraging decisions, group transfer, fission–fusion, and other important socioecological factors. For example, we can quantify the movements of a primate species that ingests seeds and disperses them in their habitat, assessing the quality and viability of seedlings from primate dispersal compared to that of birds and other mammals, as well as wind-blown seed dispersal. These data have important ramifications for understanding the health of a forest structure and habitat for long-term support of multiple species. We can also address questions in broad-scale space to investigate and quantify the anthropogenic effects on a habitat and on the species dependent on the resources within that affected habitat. This has wide-ranging applications for conservation of the multitude of the world's primate species (approximately 60 percent) that are or soon will be endangered and considered under significant threat for extinction in the next few years (Estrada et al. 2017, 2018).

A further application of GIS is to help to distinguish the types of spatial cognitive strategies and spatial memory that species possess, and which the same or different species may use in diverse types of landscapes. An essential question in primate behavioral ecology is how prosimians, monkeys, apes, and humans internally represent and apply spatial, temporal, and quantity information to identify and recall feeding sites to forage efficiently. With the significant differences in primate species characteristics, from body size and gut requirements to diet, home range size, group size and cohesion, daily ranging length, and movement strategies, the challenges and requirements will also differ substantially. Of great interest is how these factors apply to the cognitive capacities of different primate species and also individuals, and ultimately their foraging and navigational strategies. When navigating both short and long distances in foraging bouts, does a female chimpanzee compared to a pygmy marmoset, for example, parse the space differently, dependent on body size differences and disparities in home and day ranges and quality and distribution of their respective resources? Is space encoded and recalled as multiple connected units of fine-scale space, or as one broad-scale space, or both, depending on the tasks and requirements of the tasks in that space? What is the impact on spatial memory and recall (Garber & Dolins, 2014), and can we assess this with geospatial technology?

Section Summary

This section presents studies using multiple types of spatial data combined with ecological niche modeling by which to assess the biogeography, macroecology, and primate populations. The approach taken and type of spatial data for each study is dependent on the research questions being addressed. In the chapter by Chiou and Blair (Chapter 15), these authors provide an in-depth review of ecological niche modeling as it relates to multiple types of investigations to deepen our understanding of primate behavioral ecology, evolution of primates, and species conservation. Applying ecological niche modeling can assist in predicting species distributions, which is foundational to conservation efforts, tracking the spread of disease among primates, and understanding the relationship of behavioral flexibility to the habitat and biogeography. The authors review the various types of ecological niche modeling, such as habitat suitability models. They also explore the utility of ecological niche modeling for assessing the effects of climate change on an array of taxonomic groups as well as the effects of anthropogenic incursions into habitats. A further application of ecological niche modeling is in evaluating speciation. For example, the authors describe how it is applied in evaluating eight species of *Eulemur* to determine the degree of ecological niche divergence among these species.

On a related set of topics, using Madagascar as a kind of "case study," Steffens and Lehman write about landscape ecology of deforestation processes and lemur biogeography in Madagascar (Chapter 17). In the face of so many species' extinctions occurring across taxa and regions globally, these authors work within the new and very necessary applied area of conservation biogeography. Taking into account the foundations of classic biogeographic modeling, the goals of this new field are to apply unique conceptual and technological approaches to generate predictive models of environmental degradation and changes in biodiversity. Spatial data form the basis for much of the analyses, including the dynamic responses by flora and fauna to changes occurring as a result of deforestation leading to fragmented habitats, climate change, and other, significant anthropogenic effects. The authors apply landscape-level analyses to determine the deforestation patterns and the remaining lemur forest habitats remaining east and west, and at both high and low elevation levels for comparison and predictive modeling. Their analyses reveal that five lemur species (one Critically Endangered) select lowland forests, habitats which are most at risk of deforestation. This broad-scale study and its concomitant analyses serve as an example for future and further studies in high-risk conservation areas that can assist with directing efforts to protect forested habitats, responses to the extremes of climate change, and the anthropogenic pressures of deforestation, including hunting and poaching.

Illegal hunting and habitat fragmentation are two of the main risk factors for a primate species to become Threatened, Endangered or to go Extinct. In Chapter 16, Hickey and Conroy present a significant example of how data derived from geospatial technology and GIS analyses aid our understanding of conservation requirements for bonobos in the Democratic Republic of Congo, a highly endangered primate species. Importantly, this chapter demonstrates how fragmented habitats and the presence of humans, even from a distance, can impact the routes and path use, and other bonobo behaviors. The authors' evaluate forest edge density data in combination with quantified evidence of human encroachment near and in the forest; they find that higher forest edge density signals greater levels of forest fragmentation. The authors address the question of the effects of higher forest edge density. Specifically, by applying GIS analyses, they estimate the bonobo density and site occupancy in these fragmented forests. They ask whether, on its own, a higher forest edge density leads to worse conditions for the bonobos, if hunting is taken out of the equation? They also address the question of what then is the impact of hunting on its own, or the occurrence of humans' presence in bonobo habitat (measures include distance from agricultural sites, distance from roads, distance from rivers, machete cuts, traps, hunting camps, log-cut trees, etc.). Their analyses demonstrate that, individually, these anthropogenic factors are destructive and undermine the quality of bonobo populations. Together, the reduced quality of the habitat and increased hunting pressures magnify the negative effects on this highly endangered species. Recommendations for further studies include calculating nest occurrences long term with repeated studies at the same sites for comparisons of empty to bonobo-occupied forests. The authors recommend that studies should incorporate both fine-scale (local-scale) and broad-scale (landscape-scale) data collection in order to gauge causal factors involved. Their chapter provides details of how to conduct such studies with spatially explicit data and the related GIS analyses to reveal dominant spatial patterns of forest use and avoidance by bonobos as effected by levels of human encroachment into these forests. This case study provides a demonstration of the structural factors necessary to address the potential consequences on populations of threatened or endangered populations of primates.

In studying primate behavioral ecology through the interrelated fields of biogeography and macroecology as described in Chapter 18, Kamilar and Beaudrot provide details of data-collection methods and analyses for assessment of primate species' distributions, comparisons of abiotic and biotic environments, and the evolutionary histories and distributions of extinct taxa. They present the application of various statistical models that make use of GPS data via GIS analyses to ascertain and quantify patterns of ecological community composition across multiple locations over a broad-scale spatial area. They address the questions of community composition across four questions: (1) Why do some similar communities have the same species while others do not (species co-occurrence patterns and community nestedness)? (2) How do communities differ across habitats (identifying biogeographic regions through cluster analyses)? (3) What environmental factors (e.g., local climate, temperature, moisture, plants, and soil quality) affect species' occurrences in spatially explicit locations (quantifying species niche space: ordination and ecological niche models)? And (4) can we use spatially explicit data to determine geographic variation and predict variation in biological traits in community structures (Mantel tests, canonical correspondence analysis and spatial regression models)? In the latter, spatially explicit analyses via Mantel tests and canonical correspondence analysis can, if applied without confounding effects, identify critical influences of spatial and environmental factors on phylogeny. For example, one study of lemurs found that the most accurate predictor of body mass for closely related species was not site-specific climate or dietary variables. Instead, closely related species were more similar to each other based on body mass independent of the site-specific environmental factors.

This chapter presents a breadth of statistical tools available to field primatologists for multiple types of spatial analyses. These tools can address critical questions for understanding species' requirements in habitats, the composition of the ecological communities of which they are part, and how these communities may differ across regions for the same primate species. For example, the objective in conducting cluster analysis, which can be conducted on a local or a global scale, is to objectively evaluate patterns of biological communities' composition; its power lies in its identification of which species are necessary for the foundational structure of these biological communities. Analyses of the spatially explicit data using the various statistical models described in this chapter provide insight into species distributions and species' ecological requirements.

As human populations increase globally, and as more natural habitats are turned into agricultural land to support these growing populations, there will be increased tensions and negative encounters between the wildlife who had relied on the resources of those habitats and the humans growing and tending the crops. The ultimate loser in these interactions will mainly be the wildlife, including many primates. There is an increasing need for strategies to reduce these tensions while also enabling both humans and the nonhuman primates to survive and thrive. Moreover, effective conservation efforts always include the local human community, their needs, their cultural requirements, and importantly, their cultural perspectives. The ethnoprimatological approach incorporates these human cultural and survival requirements, with the local community members being partners in developing management plans for their crops and reducing tensions with the nonhuman primates. The management strategies are created based on spatial and ethnographic tools for the goals of shared space and resources. In Chapter 19, Dore et al. detail their own ethnoprimatological investigation as a demonstration. In St. Kitt's, they evaluated the local community's needs, wants, and attitudes toward the vervet monkeys who raid their crops (crop-foraging); the monkeys are considered to be pests. The authors developed a predictive model of crop-raiding that takes into account variables such as proximity to the forest boundary, distance from the road, from neighboring farms, from water sources, the types of crops grown, farmers' planting behavior, and the availability of natural foods in the forest seasonally. Crop-raiding occurs most often of mangoes, which is a favorite food resource for vervet monkeys. The authors first monitor and document typical crop damage done by raiding vervet monkeys, and then develop a model to predict monkey crop damage. The authors also use ethnographic methods to understand the interactions of the local community with the monkeys and their conceptualization of the human–monkey conflict. They then quantify the land-cover of forest and agricultural land on a map with grid cells and distance attributes, adding in the observed frequency of monkey crop raids and preferences, presence, and time spent by farmers with or without dogs protecting their crops, and evaluations of seasonal food availability in the forests. The authors use hierarchical linear and hierarchical generalized linear modeling to generate predictive models, which provides a predictive model at a higher resolution spatial scale. For example, assessing the impact of environmental variables on a smaller scale while also working on a multilevel model to take into account the entire farm area. The predictive models are found to be viable and effective. The final part of this study evaluates whether attitudes have changed together with the actual reduction in monkey crop-raiding. Through interviews with the farmers it is revealed that they are not as bothered by the crop-raiding behavior but more the wastefulness of the way the monkeys eat the food; the farmers do not like to see one bite out of a fruit or vegetable. They view the monkeys as being similar to humans and therefore they should not have a wasteful attitude toward food. They acknowledge that animals other than monkeys do more damage to their crops. The reduction in sugar crops in St. Kitts also affected monkeys' behavior, leading to more crop raiding. They develop sustainable management plans that take into account these agricultural changes and cultural attitudes toward the monkeys.

In the concluding chapter, Chapter 20, the overarching theme of the volume is described, the application of spatial analysis technology and its potential for addressing questions foundational to research conducted by field primatologists. The final consideration and focus are on the increasing number of primate species globally who are on the brink of ecological disaster due to anthropogenic disturbances and pressures. We, as scientists, can rely on spatially explicit data derived by GPS technology, GIS analyses, and detailed statistical modeling to provide enough information to develop effective and predictive strategies, to attempt to slow and even halt primate habitat destruction globally, and to protect parcels of habitat necessary to maintain viable primate populations and for the local human communities who are often equally at risk.

References

Estrada, A., Garber, P. A., Rylands, A. B., et al. 2017. Impending extinction crisis of the world's primates: why primates matter. *Science Advances* **3**: e1600946.

Estrada, A., Garber, P. A., Mittermeier, R. A., et al. 2018. Primates in peril: the significance of Brazil, Madagascar, Indonesia and the Democratic Republic of the Congo for global primate conservation. *PeerJ* DOI: 10.7717/peerj.4869.

Garber, P. A. and Dolins, F. L. 2014. Primate spatial strategies and cognition: introduction to the special issue. *American Journal of Primatology* DOI: 10.1002/ajp.22257.

15 Modeling Niches and Mapping Distributions

Progress and Promise of Ecological Niche Models for Primate Research

Kenneth L. Chiou and Mary E. Blair

Introduction

In this chapter we briefly review the burgeoning field of ecological niche modeling and explore its relevance to studies of primate ecology, evolution, and conservation. Recent years have witnessed an explosion of interest in ecological niche models, spurred on by the increasing availability of occurrence data and spatially explicit environmental data, as well as GIS tools and technologies appropriate for processing the increasingly high-resolution and multidimensional data typical of this field.

Ecological niche models (ENMs), sometimes known as species distribution models (SDMs), relate observed points of occurrence to spatially explicit environmental variables thought to be relevant in shaping the ecological tolerances of a given taxon or population (Franklin 2009; Peterson et al. 2011). These models are often used to predict species distributions – such as in biogeography, conservation management (including climate change assessment), or pathogen modeling – or they can focus on the models themselves as representations of species ecological niches. When strong associations are found between occurrences and environmental predictors, ENMs can provide important insights into the ecological tolerances or habitat preferences of species or populations.

While newcomers can surely appreciate the exciting applications made possible by ENMs, the deluge of alternative methods and implementations can be overwhelming. Some of these methods emphasize distinct theoretical issues concerning the nature of ecological niches. Others emphasize statistical or computational issues. In light of the abundance of considerations, many newcomers simply run the most available software, usually without modifying the default settings. In doing so, they may overlook more suitable methods or fail to correct for biases or other shortcomings in their datasets.

In this chapter, we review previous applications of ENMs in primate studies and highlight areas of primatology for which ENMs can offer valuable insights. We also review some of the factors to consider when selecting and running models, and attempt to illustrate this with a brief case study. Our goal is to minimize the difficulties that many encounter while learning to develop, employ, and interpret ENMs and to encourage others to explore this promising tool for applications in primatology.

Ecological Niche Models in Primatology

Despite the recent expansion of ENM approaches and their relevance to our understanding of primate ecology, evolution, and conservation, as of this writing (December 2015), applications to primate populations are still relatively rare in comparison to other taxonomic groups. Here we briefly review some of the ways in which ENMs are being used in studies of primate populations.

Habitat Suitability Models

The most common application of ENMs to studies of primate populations has been through the approach of habitat suitability modeling (reviewed by Rode et al. 2013), which focuses on the likelihood of occurrence rather than the fitness of species (Hirzel & Le Lay 2008). The outputs of habitat suitability models are often incorporated into gap analyses – a method for identifying spatial "gaps" in existing protected area management plans by determining whether particular environments are poorly represented in existing areas (Scott et al. 1987) – that can be used for species-, site-, country-, or regional-level conservation planning (Morales-Jimenez et al. 2005; Rode et al. 2013). Also, for rare and elusive species for which complete distribution data are unavailable, habitat suitability models can be useful for directing future survey efforts (Rode et al. 2013).

In addition to gap analyses, studies have inferred suitable habitat for regional and site-level conservation planning (Campos & Jack 2013; Hickey et al. 2013; Junker et al. 2012; Peck et al. 2011; Pintea et al. 2014; Vidal-García & Serio-Silva 2011). Coudrat and Nekaris (2013), for instance, used Maxent to model suitable habitat for four macaque species (*Macaca arctoides*, *M. assamensis*, *M. leonina*, and *M. mulatta*) in Nakai-Nam Theun National Protected Area, central-eastern Laos, and found important differences in characteristics of suitable habitats across species, with implications for conservation management. Hickey et al. (2013) used biotic and abiotic data (including fragmentation) associated with bonobo (*Pan paniscus*) nests to predict suitable conditions across the species' range.

For rare and elusive species, ENMs can be used to help locate areas that might provide suitable habitat for a species but have not yet been surveyed. Boubli and de Lima (2009), for example, modeled the suitable habitat of brown-backed bearded sakis (*Chiropotes israelita*) and black uakaris (*Cacajao melanocephalus*, *C. hosomi*, and *C. ayresi*) in remote regions of western Amazonas, Brazil using Maxent to guide future survey expeditions into these remote areas. Also, Thorn et al. (2009) and Voskamp et al. (2014) modeled suitable habitat in Maxent for Asian slow lorises in Borneo, Java, and Sumatra, and compared the model to protected area and land use information to define areas that should be high-priority survey sites, sites for reintroduction, or sites for possible protected area extensions. Similar approaches may be useful for identifying priority areas for archeological or paleontological surveys by predicting site distributions using ENMs (Beeton et al. 2013), which can help complement other GIS approaches (e.g., Conroy et al. 2012).

Modeling the Potential Effects of Future Climate Change

Although threats such as hunting and habitat disturbance may be more immediate concerns for primate population persistence as compared to stressors related to climate change, assessing likely future exposure to climate change across a species' range can nevertheless play an important role in conservation prioritization and planning for the long-term survival of species (Blair et al. 2012). Models and empirical analyses of range shifts in other taxonomic groups suggest that species show individualistic responses to changing climates (Peterson et al. 2011). Future climate projection data from the Intergovernmental Panel on Climate Change (IPCC) are available for at least three emissions scenarios (A1, A2, B2), seven general circulation models (GCMs), and seven time periods (www.ccafs-climate.org). Ecological niche models can be calibrated in the current climate and then projected into the future using IPCC scenarios to identify the parts of a species' range that are expected to be most exposed to changes in temperature and precipitation.

A growing number of studies project primate ENMs into the future using IPCC scenarios. Most studies focus on projecting shifts in climatically suitable areas for a species or group of species, allowing an estimation of potential future habitat loss as well as refuge areas that might be prioritized in conservation efforts. Examples include studies of Francois' langurs and Tonkin snub-nosed monkeys (Vu et al. 2010, 2011), Sichuan snub-nosed monkeys (Luo et al. 2014), lion tamarins (Meyer et al. 2014), and Bornean orangutans (Struebig et al. 2015). Another application to primate populations is the use of ENMs to project climatic suitability for vegetation species providing key habitat, rather than to project climatic suitability for the individual species themselves. Wong et al. (2013), for example, used Maxent to model and project the distribution of key vegetation types of importance to the Yunnan snub-nosed monkey under IPCC scenarios to infer and plan for the potential effects of climate change on this species. Common criticism of these applications of ENMs include failure to capture uncertainty across model algorithms and scenarios and a limited ability for validation of future projections. One approach to improve validation is to use a two-step modeling process, forecasting from the recent historical past (when such data are available) and validating the forecast with present occurrence data, then forecasting to the future; Chatterjee et al. (2012) modeled gibbon distributions in China across three time intervals using fossil and historical data, current data, and IPCC scenarios, providing additional validation for their projections across time. Further, ensemble forecasting has been presented as a method that better captures the uncertainty of modeling into the future by calibrating ensembles, or sets of ENMs, using various algorithms projected to a suite of future climate scenarios and exploring the resulting range of uncertainties (Araújo & New 2007). This approach has been theoretically and empirically shown to outperform forecasts by individual models in predictive ability. Brown and Yoder (2015) modeled ENMs for 57 lemur species under future climate scenarios using an ensemble approach. They found that 60 percent of the lemur species modeled will experience considerable range reductions entirely due to future climate change. When taking into account the uncertainties, climate change projections can be useful to determine general trends in terms of areas and species likely to be the most affected by habitat loss due to climate change. In order to most accurately estimate local extinction risks due to climate change, however, it may be important to couple ENMs with models of dispersal, demography, or interactions among species (Peterson et al. 2011; Sterling et al. 2013).

Biogeography, Niche Evolution, and Ecological Speciation

Ecological niche models can provide considerable insight into the biogeographic history of organisms, including species' environmental requirements, potential barriers that limit dispersal, and the degree to which ecological niches change over evolutionary timescales (Bett et al. 2012; Blair et al. 2013b; MacColl 2011; Raxworthy et al. 2007; Wiens 2004).

Bett et al. (2012) constructed ENMs for gray-, red-, and black-shanked doucs (*Pygathrix cinerea, P. nemaeus,* and *P. nigripes*) to investigate the north-to-south distribution turnover common across several primate groups in Vietnam, Laos, and Cambodia. The ENMs successfully predicted the north-to-south gradient based only on climatic variables, and the authors used the differences between the most important variables in each model to discuss whether a zoogeographic barrier or current or historical climatic shifts are most likely to explain the biogeographic history of this group. A similar approach was applied to explain the parapatric distribution of brown and black-and-gold howler monkeys (Holzmann et al. 2015). Paleoclimate layers are increasingly available and may further inform questions of primate biogeographic histories by facilitating the modeling of past species distributions, calibrated with fossil data.

Blair et al. (2013b) produced ENMs for eight species of *Eulemur* to test for ecological niche conservatism or divergence between sister species pairs, defined as species that are the only descendants of a common ancestral species. Ecological niche divergence refers to the tendency for related species to differ more ecologically than expected by random drift (or simple Brownian motion descent with modification [Losos 2008]), while ecological niche conservatism refers to the tendency for related species to differ less ecologically than expected by random drift. Blair and colleagues tested for ecological niche divergence or conservatism using the null model developed by Warren et al. (2008), in which observed ENM overlap was compared to a null distribution of overlap values generated from random points within the geographic range of the species pair. For three sister-pair comparisons, the tests supported the null model that niches are no more divergent than the available background region. Combined with the presence of a riverine barrier between these pairs, the null results are consistent with an allopatric speciation model. For the sister pair *E. flavifrons–E. macaco,* however, Blair and colleagues found support for significant niche divergence (Figure 15.1). Consistent with their parapatric distribution on an ecotone and the lack of obvious geographic barriers, these findings support a parapatric model of speciation and support overall the idea that multiple speciation processes are at work among these closely related lemurs.

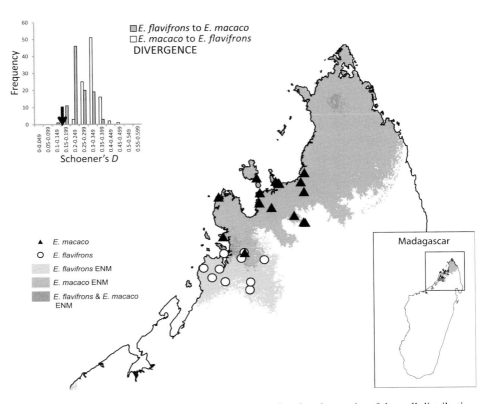

Figure 15.1 ENMs, occurrence records, and histograms showing the results of the null distribution test with 100 replicates for *Eulemur flavifrons–Eulemur macaco*. The black arrow on the histograms shows where the actual overlap between the two ENMs falls compared to the null distribution of pseudo-replicated niche overlap values. Adapted from Blair et al. (2013b). (A black and white version of this figure will appear in some formats. For the color version, please refer to the plate section.)

Niche models can also be used to predict the geography of hybrid zones. Indeed, the overlap between the above ENMs (Blair et al. 2013b) coincides with known hybrid zones between *Eulemur* species, including the known hybrid zone between *E. macaco* and *E. flavifrons* (Figure 15.1). Innovative work is being done in other taxa to predict hybrid zones and other species interactions in recognition of the fact that biotic interactions may be as prominent as climate in determining species distributions. A recent study, for instance, attempted to disentangle the roles of biotic interactions and climate in determining the location of a moving hybrid zone between the breeding ranges of two parapatric passerines in Europe, and found that interspecific interactions, not climate, accounted for the present location of the contact zone (Engler et al. 2013).

Researchers have also used ENMs to identify cryptic species lineages for which processes of morphological differentiation, lineage sorting, and the formation of reproductive barriers may be incomplete, but ecological attributes have differentiated. This approach has been most commonly applied to reptiles, amphibians, and birds (e.g., Raxworthy et al. 2007), but has also been applied to primate populations. Kumara et al. (2009), for example, mapped the distribution of various subspecies of slender lorises in peninsular India using ENMs. Their results indicated the presence of a previously undescribed, geographically disjunct, and ecologically unique subspecies occupying a distinct and intermediate climate region running along the eastern fringe of the southern Western Ghats. The study also described morphological differences, and recommended an urgent need for detailed exploration and conservation action. Other recent studies have documented how both environmental variation and rivers shape patterns of genetic differentiation between chimpanzee subspecies (Mitchell et al. 2015; Sesink Clee et al. 2015).

Which Ecological Niche Model?

Selecting and implementing a particular type of ENM for any given research question can be an intimidating task requiring rumination over issues such as sample size, sample bias, spatial scale, environmental correlations, model complexity, desired statistical metrics, and accessibility of algorithms and software. The process of model selection can be particularly agonizing due to the abundance of methods to choose from (Table 15.1 and Figure 15.2) and the knowledge that discrepancies among model performances can sometimes be very large, particularly for the projection of species distributions into independent or unknown circumstances (Pearson et al. 2006; Peterson et al. 2007; Thuiller 2003). Our goal in this section is not to cover all of these methods, but rather to highlight how they differ and to indicate important issues to consider when choosing among them. We hope that this review will encourage readers to explore available methods, justify their choices, and apply them effectively. Because our focus is on the practical implementation of ENMs, we use the terms "methods" and "models" broadly to refer to modeling approaches that have been published and are generally available as software. This encompasses not only their algorithms but also the factors that influence other key elements of the modeling process, such as characteristics of occurrence data, choice of environmental variables, selection of decision thresholds, and prevention of overfitting.

The majority of studies discussed in this chapter thus far have used correlative ENMs, which use associations between species occurrence records and environmental variables to characterize the environments within which species can exist or are likely to exist. The advantages and disadvantages of these correlative ENMs as compared to mechanistic or process-based ENMs (Kearney & Porter 2009) have been widely discussed in the literature (e.g., Dawson et al. 2011; Pearson & Dawson 2003). Criticisms of correlative ENMs have commonly focused on their inability to yield information about the underlying mechanisms that limit species distributions. An important advantage of correlative ENMs, however, is that detailed knowledge of the functional traits of organisms is not required. Correlative methods therefore have the potential to be applied rapidly to a large number of species, as well as to rare or poorly understood species,

Table 15.1 Partial list of ecological niche modeling methods.

Method	Description	Statistical approach	Data[a]	Software[b]	References
ANN	Artificial neural networks	Machine learning	PA*/Ab	R (nnet), SNNS, openModeller, ModEco	Manel et al. 1999 Pearson et al. 2002
BIOCLIM	Bioclimatic envelope model	Distance	PO	R (dismo, biomod2), openModeller, DIVA-GIS, ModEco	Nix 1986 Busby 1991
BN	Bayesian networks	Machine learning	PA*	ModEco, Elvira	Friedman et al. 1997 Aguilera et al. 2010
BRT	Boosted regression trees	Machine learning	PA*	R (gbm, dismo)	Leathwick et al. 2006b Elith et al. 2008
BRUTO	Generalized additive model with adaptive back-fitting	Regression	PA*/Ab	R (mda)	Leathwick et al. 2006a
CART	Classification and regression trees (also known as decision trees)	Machine learning	PA*/Ab	R (rpart), ModEco	De'ath & Fabricius 2000 Rouget et al. 2001
DOMAIN	Continuous point-to-point similarity metric (Gower metric)	Distance	PO	R (dismo), openModeller, DIVA-GIS, ModEco	Carpenter et al. 1993
ENFA	Ecological niche factor analysis	Distance	PB	Biomapper, openModeller	Hirzel et al. 2002
GAM	Generalized additive models	Regression	PA*/Ab	R (mgcv, gam)	Guisan et al. 2002
GARP	Genetic algorithm for rule set production	Machine learning	PP	openModeller, DesktopGarp	Stockwell & Peters 1999
GDM	Generalized dissimilarity models (including community and single-species implementations; see Elith et al. 2006)	Regression	PA*/Ab	Unreleased	Ferrier et al. 2002 Elith et al. 2006
GLM	Generalized linear models	Regression	PA*/Ab	R (stats), ModEco	Guisan et al. 2002
HABITAT	HABITAT envelope procedure	Distance	PO	Unreleased	Walker & Cocks 1991

Table 15.1 (*cont.*)

Method	Description	Statistical approach	Data[a]	Software[b]	References
LIVES	Limiting variable and environmental suitability	Distance	PO	Unreleased	Li & Hilbert 2008
MARS	Multivariate adaptive regression splines (including community and interaction implementations; see Elith et al. 2006)	Regression	PA*/Ab	R (mda)	Friedman 1991 Moisen & Frescino 2002
MAXENT	Maximum entropy	Machine learning	PB	Maxent, R (dismo via maxent.jar), openModeller, ModEco	Phillips et al. 2006 Phillips & Dudík 2008
MD	Mahalanobis distance	Distance	PO	R (dismo)	Farber & Kadmon 2003 Rotenberry et al. 2006
PPM	Point process models	Regression	PO	R (spatstat, ppmlasso), Maxent	Renner et al. 2015
RF	Random forests	Machine learning	PA*	R (randomForest), openModeller	Cutler et al. 2007
RS	Rough set	Machine learning	PA*	ModEco	Pawlak 1991 Guo & Liu 2010
SVM	Support vector machines	Machine learning	PO (one-class SVM); PA*/Ab (rest)	R (e1071, kernlab), openModeller, ModEco	Guo et al. 2005 Drake et al. 2006

* Presence/absence methods can be applied to presence-only datasets through the generation of pseudo-absences.

[a] PO = presence only; PA = presence/absence; PP = presence/pseudo-absence; PB = presence/background; Ab = abundance data;

[b] All software in this list is freely available. For methods implemented in R, relevant packages are listed in parentheses.

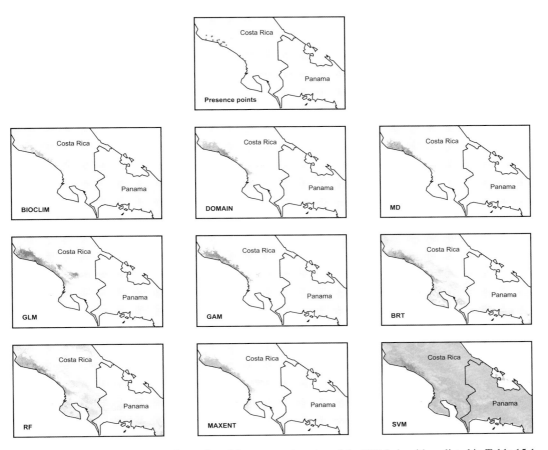

Figure 15.2 A comparison of model outputs using nine of the ENM algorithms listed in Table 15.1. Models were trained using presence points for *Saimiri oerstedii citrinellus*, shown in red, that were compiled from several sources. Modeling generally followed procedures described in Box 15.1. The values mapped represent the model outputs, but their interpretations depend on the method used. For envelope methods, they represent distance values. For other methods, they represent suitability scores, but not necessarily occurrence probabilities. Green pixels represent higher values, but scales are not shown because values are relative. (A black and white version of this figure will appear in some formats. For the color version, please refer to the plate section.)

including many primates. Lehmann et al. (2010) used a mechanistic (time-budget) model to link climate variables to the behavior and biogeography of great apes, for which detailed information is available. Another recent study, however, compared a mechanistic time-budget model to a correlative Maxent model for vervets and reported that the two approaches produced remarkably similar predictions for vervet distribution despite the conceptual and methodological differences between these two modeling approaches (Willems & Hill 2009). The remainder of this chapter focuses on correlative approaches, which we anticipate to be more readily applicable to primate datasets in the near term.

Box 15.1 Case Study: Testing for Niche Divergence Among Subspecies of the Central American Squirrel Monkey

Squirrel monkeys (genus *Saimiri*) occur throughout the Amazon, and also in a disjunct, highly restricted area along the Pacific coast of Central America. A recent biogeographical analysis of the genus suggests that the Central American species *S. oerstedii* is a northern ancestral remnant of a population expansion event from the *S. ustus* A group approximately 1.35 and 1 Ma (Lynch Alfaro et al. 2015). The two subspecies of *S. oerstedii* (*S. oerstedii oerstedii* and *S. oerstedii citrinellus*) are distinguished by pelage differences (Hershkovitz 1984; Rylands & Mittermeier 2009) and have disjunct geographic distributions on either side of the large Térraba River. Recent genetic studies have lent support for the reciprocal monophyly of these subspecies (Blair et al. 2013a; Lynch Alfaro et al. 2015). The split between the subspecies has been dated to between 0.25 and 0.15 Ma (Lynch Alfaro et al. 2015) or 0.16 and 0.11 Ma (Chiou et al. 2011), consistent with the hypothesis that the subspecies separated during a sea-level rise of *ca.* 100 m in the Middle–Upper Pleistocene (Ford 2006; Nores 1999). *S. oerstedii* are restricted to lowland settings (below 500 m asl) and are therefore constrained to the Central and Southern Pacific coasts by the Central and Talamanca Cordilleras. High water levels in the Pleistocene would thus have resulted in their isolation (Ford 2006), which is now maintained by the Térraba River.

In this case study, we use ENMs to test hypotheses about ecological niche divergence between the two subspecies of *S. oerstedii*. The timing of genetic divergence coincides with a potential isolation event due to sea-level rise in the Middle–Upper Pleistocene, suggesting an allopatric divergence process for these populations. An allopatric process is essentially a spatial process, which may be facilitated by ecological niche conservatism, where failure to adapt to new environments maintains separation between populations (Wiens 2004). An allopatric divergence process would be most supported by a finding of niche conservatism, or a failure to reject a null model (Blair et al. 2013b; Losos 2008). By contrast, a finding of niche divergence might suggest a process of ecological divergence, if distributed along an ecotone, or post-divergence ecological specialization.

We sourced occurrence data for *S. o. citrinellus* from prior fieldwork (Blair & Melnick, 2012a, 2012b) and for *S. o. oerstedii* from published (Rodríguez-Vargas 2003; Solano Rojas 2007) and unpublished sources (A. Mora & G. Gutiérrez-Espeleta, unpubl. data). Presence points were assessed visually for obvious errors. We used 19 bioclimatic variables in the WorldClim dataset (Hijmans et al. 2005) to characterize the environmental background of our study region. We set a window encompassing the study area, then ran a principal components analysis (Peterson et al. 2007) to create a final environmental dataset of eight independent variables encompassing most (>99 percent) of the bioclimatic variation. To minimize spatial autocorrelation, we filtered presence records by sampling for environmentally equidistant points (i.e., points that were most distant from other records in environmental space) (Oliveira et al. 2014). The final dataset comprised 23 presence records for

Box 15.1 (*cont.*)

S. o. citrinellus and 206 presence records for *S. o. oerstedii*. For methods requiring absence information, we generated pseudo-absences randomly from the background for each species with a ratio of nine pseudo-absences per presence.

Modeling was complicated by differences in spatial bias in the occurrence datasets. Points for *S. o. citrinellus* were few, but reasonably well distributed and representative of the restricted range of the subspecies. Points for *S. o. oerstedii* were more numerous, but exhibited much more uneven coverage, even following filtering.

For both species, we ran five algorithms to model the ecological niche (Table 15.2), calculating predictions across the study region for each model. To evaluate the predictions, we cross-validated the models via five-fold partitioning using two measures of model performance: area under the receiver operating characteristic curve (AUC) and the maximum (i.e., threshold-independent) true skill statistic (Allouche et al. 2006).

As expected, model performance measures were generally higher for *S. o. citrinellus* (Table 15.2), reflecting the more even sampling design. Because of the biases in our occurrence dataset, we created a more robust model for each species by combining all five models into an ensemble forecast of subspecies distributions, using the minimum training presence as a classification threshold (Figure 15.3).

To test for niche overlap, we calculated similarity statistics (Warren et al. 2008) and conducted background randomization tests (Warren et al. 2010) to assess whether inferred niches were more or less different than expected by chance based on differences in the environmental backgrounds in which they occur. Background areas for each subspecies were defined based on areas falling within 10 km of a known occurrence. Randomization tests in both directions using 100 replicates with Maxent models revealed significant niche divergence for the D similarity statistic ($p < 0.01$, $p < 0.01$), but not the I similarity statistic ($p = 0.33$, $p = 0.33$).

Based on these results, we find support for significant niche divergence under one statistic, but cannot reject the null hypothesis under the other statistic. Given a lack of a clear ecological gradient between the distributions of two subspecies, our results are most consistent with an allopatric divergence scenario. A cautious interpretation is needed, however, given known biases in the sampling of each subspecies. Ultimately, these models illustrate the limitations of inferences based on incomplete or biased sampling. A reasonable conclusion, therefore, is that even the best models may fail when there are unaddressed shortcomings in the data.

Accessibility

One of the most important considerations for selecting ENMs is more practical than methodological. While many methods have been published, not all are equally accessible. Some software implementations are not made available. Others may be disseminated as software extensions or libraries, or as standalone programs, but nevertheless

Table 15.2 Model evaluation results for two subspecies using five algorithms.

Subspecies	Method	AUC	TSS (maximum)
S. o. citrinellus	MD	0.9861668	0.9251109
S. o. citrinellus	ANN	0.9779671	0.8973745
S. o. citrinellus	SVM	0.9781707	0.9562147
S. o. citrinellus	BRT	0.9817845	0.8986909
S. o. citrinellus	MAXENT	0.9863144	0.9213667
S. o. oerstedii	MD	0.9777778	0.9625000
S. o. oerstedii	ANN	0.9983673	0.9959184
S. o. oerstedii	SVM	0.9942857	0.9755102
S. o. oerstedii	BRT	0.9979167	0.9875000
S. o. oerstedii	MAXENT	0.9975510	0.9877551

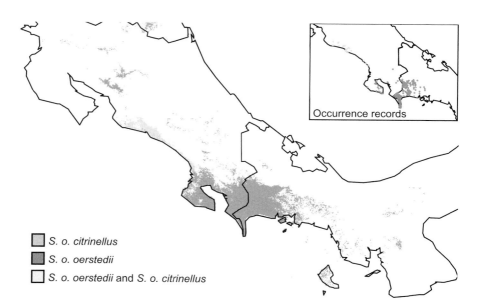

Figure 15.3 Projected distributions for *Saimiri oerstedii oerstedii* and *Saimiri citrinellus citrinellus* using an ensemble approach (Box 15.1). (A black and white version of this figure will appear in some formats. For the color version, please refer to the plate section.)

remain inaccessible due to cost (e.g., software is proprietary), system requirements (e.g., software is platform-specific), or difficulty of use. For some projects, certain methods may be undesirable due to the computational time involved.

The most accessible methods are released as software that is freely available and cross-platform, with detailed documentation on model algorithms, settings, and parameters. The inclusion of tutorials or sample datasets can be an effective complement to other documentation (e.g., Phillips 2009). The availability of a graphical user interface (GUI) can also increase accessibility by reducing the learning curve for operating the tool. Maxent and GARP, for instance, both have standalone GUI versions (Phillips et al.

2006; Scachetti-Pereira 2002) while ModEco (Guo & Liu 2010) is a relatively recent GUI application employing a wide range of algorithms. Despite these advantages, however, an active community of users and developers continue to support non-GUI systems. The most prominent of these systems is R (R Core Team 2013), which is both a programming language and a command-line statistical program. R's use of the command line can be intimidating for novices, but we find that the command line provides greater control over analysis and fosters a greater understanding and appreciation of model settings and parameters. This helps avoid the blunder common to novice GUI users of hitting "go" without changing or even checking the default settings.

A growing number of ENM methods are supported in R through packages such as *dismo* and *biomod2*. Many of these methods, especially those included in the same packages, share many details of their implementation and can therefore be readily run together with other methods, which is very helpful for comparing or combining models (Thuiller et al. 2009). When prepared as scripts, analyses can be generalized and reused such that a series of procedures can be reapplied to evolving or independent datasets, thereby reducing considerably the time and effort needed to set up, adjust, and rerun analyses. Because of its power, flexibility, and popularity in the ENM community, we strongly encourage readers to consider using R for running ENMs. Hijmans and Elith (2013) and Georges and Thuiller (2013) provide excellent guidance for getting started.

Treatment of Presence, Absence, and Abundance

All ENM methods require *a priori* information on species distributions as part of their approaches. The methods can be classified according to two criteria: (1) whether the input data are treated as continuous measures of abundance or as binary measures of presence/absence; and (2) how absence data are provided and interpreted (particularly for presence/absence methods).

Abundance-based methods require prior data not only on *whether* species occur, but also on the number (or relative number) of individuals present. Estimates of relative abundance are virtually impossible to obtain without intensive sampling and seldom cover extensive geographic space due to practical considerations. For primates and other animals, abundance comparisons are further confounded by factors such as range shifts, group size/structure, activity patterns, and detection ability. Abundance methods are best-suited for sampling designs for which abundance information is recorded and the detection probability can be addressed. For primates and other animals, these methods may therefore be effectively employed together with field methods such as camera-trap surveys, capture–recapture sampling, or sight–resight of animals with individually identifiable features. Abundance methods are also well-suited for modeling plant distributions from plot data (Potts & Elith 2006) and may therefore have useful applications for assessing primate habitats (see also Rode et al. 2013).

Presence/absence approaches treat their input data as binary (i.e., species are either recorded or not recorded) and are therefore more appropriate for occurrence data lacking information on abundance. An inherent challenge with presence/absence approaches, however, relates to detection probability and the relative reliability of presences compared to absences. Notwithstanding any errors in identification or geo-referencing, geographic presences are in general more reliable than absences because of the possibility that "absent" species are in fact present but undetected (e.g., Kéry et al. 2010). Several analytical approaches attempt to address this uncertainty by eliminating the need to provide information on absences. Because most data on primate distributions are likely to be geographically biased with relatively small samples, approaches not requiring absence information may be of great utility. While these approaches are sometimes labeled as "presence-only" methods in the literature, this label can be misleading when applied to certain methods that nevertheless incorporate indirect measures of absence into their models (e.g., "background" points in Maxent). In our discussion, we reserve the label "presence-only" for methods not involving any form of absence. Presence-only data, in contrast, refer to data for which absence and abundance information is not available.

The Mahalanobis distance (Farber & Kadmon 2003) is one illustrative example of a true presence-only method. In this method, environmental values across the study region are positioned in environmental space and a mean vector representing optimal conditions is computed for presence records only. The covariance of the presence sample is also used to compute an ellipsoidal distribution surrounding the data. The suitability of all cells (the Mahalanobis distance) is calculated according to their proximity to this vector in environmental space, scaled by the width of the ellipsoid in the test cell's direction. The Mahalanobis distance thus provides an intuitive scale-invariant means of comparing an unknown sample to a known sample while taking into account covariance in the dataset.

Presence/absence approaches, in contrast, incorporate both presence and absence into their models. These methods include traditional statistical models such as generalized linear models (GLMs) and generalized additive models (GAMs), both of which use linear regression to fit a main presence–absence pattern. When absence data are not available, presence/absence methods can nevertheless be used with presence-only datasets by randomly generating "pseudo-absences" in place of true absences. The pseudo-absences can be randomly derived from the entire study area (i.e., the background) or from a subset of it, such as all non-presence cells. The software GARP, for instance, randomly generates pseudo-absences from the total study area in lieu of user-defined absences (Stockwell & Peters 1999). This strategy is similar to presence/background methods (described below) but differs in that the pseudo-absences representing the background are still treated as absences in the building of the model.

Presence/background approaches use presence records together with data from the entire study area without treating any parts of the background as absences. Maxent, for instance, uses sample points and background samples to generate a distribution that maximizes the relative entropy between the probability densities estimated from each (Elith et al. 2011). Ecological niche factor analysis (ENFA), by contrast, uses factor analysis to compare the distribution of ecological values associated with presence records to the distribution of values comprising the full background in multidimensional space (Hirzel et al. 2002). Because the background distribution is based on the defined study area, presence/background methods can be considerably affected by the choice of study extent (Anderson & Raza 2010).

Model Approach, Evaluation, and Performance

Every ENM method will generate a prediction when properly run. Understanding how good a model is and how suitable it is for a particular purpose is considerably more difficult (e.g., Lozier et al. 2009). The manner in which a method is implemented dictates how its results should be interpreted. Choosing a model based on its statistical or ecological suitability is an important but difficult task that is covered in more detail elsewhere (Franklin 2009; Peterson et al. 2011). When comparing models, however, we find it useful to ask whether models make sense geometrically (does the shape of the modeled relationships make sense?), ecologically (is the model sensible given the ecological relationships being modeled?), and spatially (are the model's predictions plausible when mapped out in geographic space?).

The simplest ENM approaches use a distance-based "envelope" to define the boundaries of suitable habitat in multidimensional environmental space. These include the BIOCLIM model (Busby 1991; Nix 1986), which defines the envelope as the space delimited by the minimum and maximum values for all presences, the DOMAIN model (Carpenter et al. 1993), which uses a multivariate point-to-point similarity coefficient known as the Gower metric to assign classification values to sites based on the proximity of the most similar record in environmental space, and the Mahalanobis distance (Farber & Kadmon 2003), which is the standardized difference between the environmental values for any point and the mean values for the same variables across all presence points. Distance methods do not estimate a response function and cannot tease apart the relative importance of environmental predictors. They also assume that organisms are found in optimal habitats, are well-sampled in environmental space, and that their habitat variables are not dynamic. Despite these assumptions and limitations, distance methods continue to be widely used (e.g., Booth et al. 2014).

A number of ENM approaches use statistical methods such as regression to estimate fitted response functions in their models. These include GLMs, GAMs, and multivariate adaptive regression splines (MARS). A GLM is an extension of basic linear regression that uses link functions to fit linear predictors to a flexible range of distributions (e.g., Gaussian, Poisson, binomial, negative binomial, gamma) in the response variable. Through transformations of predictor variables, GLMs can be made to accommodate nonlinear relationships between predictors and responses. A GAM is a nonparametric (or semi-parametric) extension of a GLM that uses smooth functions to fit predictors to complex, nonlinear, and nonmonotonic responses. A MARS is similar to a GAM in that it makes fewer assumptions about the form of the response function. Unlike a GAM, however, a MARS fits the response in a stepwise, adaptive manner, resulting in a series of connected linear segments rather than smooth curves in a GAM (Friedman 1991). Unlike distance approaches, regression models can accommodate categorical predictors and can address individually the contributions of environmental variables to habitat suitability due to additivity in the models.

A diverse group of ENM approaches are derived from the field of machine learning and are hence referred to as machine learning methods. There is considerable overlap, however, between the fields of machine learning and inferential statistics, and the classification of these ENMs is not without ambiguity (Franklin 2009). In general, machine learning approaches differ in that they learn the mapping function (or classification rules) inductively from the training data while statistical approaches estimate parameters from the data but require that distributions be set by the user (Breiman 2001). While machine learning models can require a shift in thinking for researchers accustomed to statistical paradigms, some have well-formed statistical properties that have been dissected for ecological applications (e.g., Elith et al. 2008, 2011). Machine learning methods include decision trees, genetic algorithms, and maximum entropy. We describe these methods below because they are commonly used and have accessible software implementations.

Decision trees, or classification and regression trees (CART), refer to two related algorithms and their outputs: classification trees (CT) and regression trees (RT). Both CT and RT are assembled as recursive binary splits that classify observations based on threshold values of single predictors (De'ath & Fabricius 2000). In other words, the model can be thought of as a tree-shaped series of rules which at each branching point (node) uses a conditional statement (e.g., annual rainfall < 15 cm) to divide the response into two classes, each of which is relatively homogeneous. Decision trees partition the predictor space using a series of rules to identify areas having the most homogeneous responses. At each node, the responses then take as their values either the majority class (for CT) or the average value (for RT) of the training data. Decision trees are particularly effective at modeling complex (nonlinear and nonadditive) relationships between predictors and responses, including categorical predictors, which are difficult to parameterize using linear models when they have many categories. Decision trees are also very robust at handling missing values and outliers (De'ath & Fabricius 2000). They do have some drawbacks, however, including poor categorization of linear or smooth species responses, poor categorization of rare classes, especially with limited observations, and potential instability to changing inputs (Franklin 2009). Ensemble techniques that combine decision trees with algorithms for boosting, such as boosted regression trees (Elith et al. 2008), and bagging, such as random forests (Cutler et al. 2007), have been shown to improve performance by compensating for some of these deficiencies.

Genetic algorithms have been extensively used for niche modeling through the use of the genetic algorithm for rule set production (GARP) software (Stockwell & Peters 1999). Like decision trees, genetic algorithm models are expressed in terms of conditional decision rules. Unlike decision trees, however, the rules are generated as part of a population of rules that are "evolved" iteratively through modifications (i.e., "mutation") and evaluation based on ability to predict known cases (i.e., "natural selection"). Through successive iterations, an optimal set of rules emerge. In GARP, the population of rules includes several different kinds of models (e.g., envelope, logistic regression) from which the algorithm chooses the optimal set (Stockwell & Peters 1999). GARP and other genetic algorithms are stochastic algorithms that produce different results when applied to the same data. A more robust model can be produced by running the algorithm multiple times and summarizing across runs (Anderson et al. 2003).

Maximum entropy is a machine learning model that has been widely applied to ENM research through the Maxent algorithm and software (Phillips & Dudík 2008; Phillips et al. 2006). It is based on the principle that, given limited information about a set of features, the probability distribution that best models that information is the distribution of maximum entropy (i.e., that is most spread out, or closest to uniform), subject to the constraint that the expected value of each feature matches its empirical mean. Applied to ENMs, environmental variables are the features comprising the space upon which the probability distribution is defined and the values found at presence locations supply the constraints. The maximum entropy distribution is effective at modeling incomplete information because it agrees with everything that is known without assuming anything that is not known (Phillips et al. 2006).

Point process models (PPMs) have recently emerged as highly promising tools for presence-only modeling (Renner et al. 2015). By demonstrating close connections with both Maxent and traditional GLMs (Renner & Warton 2013), PPMs can claim the performance benefits of Maxent while clarifying important points of statistical interpretation and implementation. Because the target of interest in PPMs is intensity, however, these models may be most appropriate for modeling abundance based on suitably sampled presence data.

Aside from algorithms such as those described in this chapter, a number of methods are available for improving model accuracy, minimizing overfitting, and evaluating model performance. These methods are in general not restricted to particular models, and we cover some of them in the following section on "Implementing ecological niche models." We mention them here, however, because modeling approaches and (particularly) software vary in the availability and implementation of these additional methods and this can be an important consideration when choosing an ENM method.

Finally, another factor to consider is how well methods perform in comparison to one another. A number of studies have systematically compared ENM methods (e.g., Elith & Graham 2009; Elith et al. 2006; Loiselle et al. 2003; Pearson et al. 2006; Segurado & Araújo 2004; Wisz et al. 2008) and have consistently demonstrated differences in performance among methods. These studies differ in their focus on different applications – for instance, projections into future climate scenarios (Araújo et al. 2005; Pearson et al. 2006), projections into unsampled areas (Peterson et al. 2007), modeling of presence-only data (Elith et al. 2006; Tsoar et al. 2007), or modeling with small sample sizes (Pearson et al. 2007).

Elith et al. (2006) conducted one of the most comprehensive comparative ENM studies to date in terms of the number of models compared (16), global coverage (6 regions across the globe), and number of species (226). For each species, they trained models based on presence-only occurrence records (such as those typical from unplanned surveys or museum collections) and evaluated models based on presence and absence records collected from planned surveys of the same regions. They found that machine learning models such as Maxent and boosted regression trees performed relatively well due to their ability to predict species distributions. A number of publications, however, caution against simplistic interpretations of these comparisons (e.g., Peterson et al. 2011), as different evaluation strategies emphasize different goals and consequently make different assumptions. Elith and colleagues, for instance, evaluated models based on their predictions of species-occupied areas rather than all abiotically suitable areas, the latter of which is more expansive since abiotically suitable areas may nevertheless be unsuitable due to biotic factors. Evaluation based on species-occupied areas assumes that species are in equilibrium with their environment and is therefore problematic for applications such as projections into future climate scenarios (Araújo & New 2007), modeling niche evolution (Warren et al. 2008), or predicting range shifts in non-native species (Peterson 2003).

Ecological Niche Models in Practice

Whereas the previous section focused on the diversity of ENM approaches, in this section we describe the practice of designing and running ENMs. Our review below is largely model-independent, but in some cases we concentrate our discussion on Maxent because of its popularity, high performance, and suitability for presence-only data.

Before beginning the modeling process, the model objectives should be clearly expressed. What is being modeled? Is the focus on modeling niches or distributions? Is the focus on the fundamental niche or the realized niche? The fundamental niche (or potential niche) refers to the set of all environmental states that permit a species to survive, while the realized niche refers to the set of all environmental states that permit a species to survive in the presence of competitors or other biotic or movement factors. Whereas the fundamental niche represents the range of theoretical possibilities, the realized niche represents the range that is observable in nature due to real-world circumstances, which may be spatially or temporally specific. While the realized niche is often understood as a subset of the fundamental niche, this is not necessarily the case – for instance, in sink habitats (low-quality patches where species occupancy is maintained by an influx of individuals from high-quality patches) or in cases where there is facilitation among species (see Levi et al. 2013 for a primate example). In general, the fundamental niche is more relevant for assessing potential distributions, while the realized niche is more relevant for assessing occupied distributions. We recommend that readers consult Soberón and Peterson (2005) and Peterson et al. (2011) for a more thorough discussion.

Sample Data

Sample data provide information relevant for characterizing areas of environmental space as being part of, or not part of, the ecological niche. They virtually always take the form of geographic presence/absence/abundance locations that provide training information for the models through their spatially associated environmental values, which we discuss in the following section.

Absence and abundance data generally take the form of areas, usually grid cells, rather than points. Unlike presence data, absence and abundance areas require considerable survey effort in order to minimize false-negatives, i.e., calling species absent when they are in fact present. Rigorous survey data are also beneficial for presence-only data – for instance by minimizing spatial bias or by increasing coverage of areas where species are rare but present – but are frequently not available.

Presence data are often provided as geo-referenced points in space, but not always. Presence data can also exist as areas, such as in the case of home range data or distributional data with well-defined boundaries (e.g., islands or national parks). If presence areas are smaller than the resolution of the environmental data, they can be treated as points. If they are larger, however, the environmental values of pixels from across each presence area may be required in order to characterize the occurrence in terms of their mean, range, variance, etc. (Franklin 2009). Presence data can also be expressed as implicit, but non-geo-referenced, points of varying precision (e.g., "in Kaohsiung, Taiwan" or "1.2 km southwest of Fibwe Hide, Kasanka National Park"). These occurrences can be interpreted as areas conservatively encompassing the occurrence point. If these areas are small, like presence areas they can be treated as point data. If they are large, however, additional judgments must be made. In many cases, the data may be deemed unusable.

There are many sources for occurrence data, but the most reliable are from field studies. Geo-referenced occurrences are often obtained from the literature or from colleagues working in the field. Natural history collections are another major source of data on species distributions and are particularly invaluable as a source of information on historical distributions. These records vary in their accuracy, both geographic and taxonomic. These issues, however, are sometimes documented through metadata and in many cases the primary source material (i.e., "vouchered specimen") has been retained and can be reexamined. Occurrence data may also be obtained from secondary sources such as scanned distribution maps, although this is seldom advisable due to numerous issues, including mapmaking precision and geo-referencing errors.

The Internet is a major source of occurrence data, both through scientific and community sources. The Global Biodiversity Information Facility (GBIF) is the most prominent repository and includes occurrence data from many natural history collections. Other sources are newer and less established, but have the potential to be of great utility for primate ENM studies. GPS collars are being increasingly deployed and their data are beginning to be deposited in repositories such as Movebank (http://movebank.org). These data are especially promising for high-resolution local studies. Camera-trap surveys are a promising source of occurrence data for rare or elusive species, as are newer methods such as metagenomic DNA surveys (e.g., Calvignac-Spencer et al. 2013). Repositories for these kinds of data do not yet exist to our knowledge, but could become invaluable. Aside from scientific sources, occurrence data are also available through photo-sharing websites such as Flickr (http://flickr.com) or citizen science efforts such as Project Noah (http://projectnoah.org). We caution, however, that many of the photos on these websites are of captive animals, are not geo-referenced, or are geo-referenced using imprecise methods that are not necessarily indicated in the metadata (e.g., smartphone location services with wide errors or visual geotagging applied post hoc). These websites also contain numerous errors in taxonomic assignment, although these can sometimes be corrected based on the photos themselves. These issues are important and may ultimately turn researchers away from incorporating these data into their projects. We note, however, that the same issues are prevalent in scientific repositories such as GBIF (Newbold 2010; Yesson et al. 2007), and we remain altogether enthusiastic about the promise of citizen science approaches to ENM research (see also Hochachka et al. 2012).

Creating a good occurrence dataset ultimately requires a balance between the desire for an adequate sample size, the avoidance of positional or taxonomic errors, and the minimization of sample bias. While large samples may seem desirable, some studies (e.g., Pearson et al. 2007) have shown that acceptable models can be built from small samples, especially using certain methods (Elith et al. 2006; Stockwell & Peterson 2002; Wisz et al. 2008). A recent study (Beck et al. 2013) compared GBIF data to independent compilation efforts for European hawkmoths and found that GBIF contributed less information for niche modeling despite containing many more distribution records. It is therefore better to have small, well-distributed samples with low bias/error than to have large samples for which bias/error is prevalent. At least 50 presence observations per species (Kadmon et al. 2003) seems to work well as a rule of thumb, with lower targets for restricted, rare, or elusive species (Pearson et al. 2007). For presence–absence methods, previous studies have suggested targeting a ratio of one absence point for every presence point (e.g., McPherson et al. 2004). This suggested ratio, however, depends on species prevalence and should be higher for rare species (Franklin 2009). This ratio also does not apply to presence–background methods involving randomly generated pseudo-absences, as selection of these pseudo-absences follows other considerations (VanDerWal et al. 2009).

It is less important for the sample size to be large than for it to be representative of the niche distribution. In reality, most ENM datasets are biased in both geographic and environmental space (Figure 15.4). In a recent literature review, for instance, Yackulic et al. (2013) found that 87 percent of datasets used in Maxent studies were subject to sample selection bias and that few studies attempted to correct for it. Spatial bias can result from many factors, such as from concentrating survey effort around areas of convenience such as roads or campsites, or from skewed representation of areas and taxa that have historically received greater attention. A few methods exist for reducing these biases or for taking them into account. When measures of sampling effort are available, this information can be incorporated into models. In Maxent, this is accomplished using a "bias file" that specifies the relative sampling effort across cells. When information on sampling effort is not available, the density of occurrence records can be used as a proxy for relative sampling effort (Kramer-Schadt et al. 2013). For datasets with uneven sample density, spatial bias can also be reduced through spatial filtering, i.e., by randomly filtering records from areas with high record density (e.g., Boria et al. 2014; Oliveira et al. 2014). Kramer-Schadt et al. (2013) compared the bias file and spatial filtering approaches and found that both improved model predictions and were

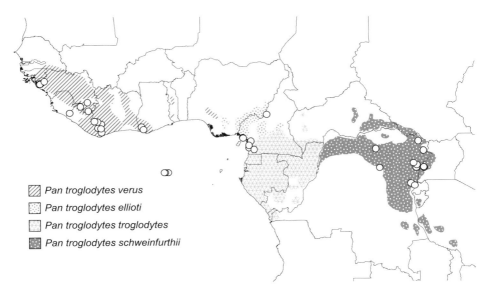

Figure 15.4 Spatial bias and positional errors in sample locales are evident in occurrence data for common chimpanzees (*Pan troglodytes* spp.) downloaded from the Global Biodiversity Information Facility (http://gbif.org; accessed December 15, 2013). In total, 116 records had spatial coordinates. These sample points (white circles) are shown superimposed over a chimpanzee distribution map adapted from Bjork et al. (2011). Not shown are six points located on other continents. Notice that some points occur in the middle of the Atlantic Ocean, indicating that errors are present in the dataset (there are no marine chimpanzees). Not all errors, unfortunately, can be so easily identified. (A black and white version of this figure will appear in some formats. For the color version, please refer to the plate section.)

therefore preferable to not correcting for biases at all. Of the two methods, they found spatial filtering to be more effective.

Environmental Data

Environmental data are composed of the features that might influence occupancy across time and space. Stated another way, environmental data constitute the mathematical space upon which ENMs are defined. In the model training stage, they provide the values at sample locations that are used to develop the model, as well as for the background sample locations required for some approaches. In the model prediction stage, they provide the values used to calculate suitability scores across the test region. The environmental data for the training region and test region are often equivalent, but they can differ, such as when models are projected into different regions or time periods.

Environmental variables are ultimately important for ENMs because of the expectation that they are related to aspects of niches and distributions. One goal of variable selection is therefore to identify which variables best provide this information. This is affected to a great extent by the spatial scale of the study. Climatic variables, for instance, are widely acknowledged to be important determinants of thermal, moisture, and light regimes that influence range limits at coarse scales, while factors such as land cover, habitat structure, vegetation phenology, and competitor or predator density are likely to be more relevant at medium and fine scales.

The decision regarding which variables to include in the analysis should take into account whether the model focuses on the potential or realized niche/distribution. If the focus is on the potential distribution, variables that remain relatively static over large scales and timeframes may be more relevant. Conversely, if the focus is on the occupied distribution, variables that are more dynamic and local may become important.

In the past, one of the biggest barriers to ENM research was the scarcity of suitable environmental datasets. Now digital environmental datasets are quite common and their availability has helped spur the explosion of interest in ENMs in recent years. The most influential datasets have succeeded due to their high, often global coverage, the standardization of methodology across broad areas, and their ability to provide meaningful information for niche models. This includes the WorldClim dataset (Hijmans et al. 2005), which provides high-resolution (30 arc-seconds, or about 1 km) temperature and precipitation surfaces for land areas covering the entire Earth. These surfaces have been used to derive a set of 19 bioclimatic variables known as Bioclim variables because they were first developed for early bioclimatic envelope modeling studies using the BIOCLIM method and software (Booth et al. 2014). These 19 variables are intended to represent annual trends, seasonality, and extremes in temperature and precipitation conditions.

While the availability of these datasets is exciting, it is important that users be mindful of possible quality issues and of the pitfalls of using the data incorrectly (Barry & Elith 2006). Values from the Worldclim dataset, for example, were interpolated from data collected by weather stations across the world. These weather stations are not distributed evenly across space and in many cases the tropical regions inhabited by most primates have the poorest coverage (Figure 15.5). Areas with low coverage are not only prone to missing potentially important information on aspects of microclimate, but they are also disproportionately impacted by errors in weather station data. It is therefore advisable to dedicate at least some effort toward understanding how much trust to place in these data for applications. In some cases, data products from downscaled regional climate models might be available or more appropriate for a given area of interest, particularly for areas with considerable topographic complexity.

Aside from climatic variables, variables derived from satellite or aerial imagery are widely used for ENM research. This includes digital elevation models, land cover classifications, and vegetation indices. Vegetation is likely to be of particular importance for primate distributions as both a source of food and as a critical habitat component. Vegetation and other habitat variables can be classified from multispectral or hyperspectral imagery or from data collected in the field (Rode et al. 2013). For these data, however, it can be challenging to describe a meaningful relationship between vegetation classifications and habitat suitability, especially at greater geographic scales (e.g., Chapman et al. 2002). Distributions of other species are also sometimes used as predictors (e.g., Heikkinen et al. 2007). While they suffer from similar scale issues, such predictors may nevertheless provide meaningful information on biotic interactions such as with food resources, competitors, predators, or facilitators.

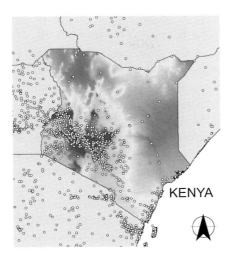

Figure 15.5 An example of low or uneven spatial coverage of weather stations contributing data to interpolated climate datasets. Here, annual mean temperature (BIO1) from the Worldclim dataset (Hijmans et al. 2005) is visualized in Kenya at 30 arc-second (~1 km) resolution along with the locations of weather stations (white circles) contributing raw data to the interpolation. Temperatures are displayed on a red–blue (hot–cold) color scale, with a 2.5 standard deviation stretch function applied in order to increase contrast. (A black and white version of this figure will appear in some formats. For the color version, please refer to the plate section.)

After determining what variables are available for niche modeling, it is important to ask how many and which variables to include. In some cases, it may be necessary to eliminate variables that do not correspond temporally with other variables or with the sample data. Variables may also prove to be unusable due to spatial issues, such as with incompatible projections, resolutions, or extents, although methods exist for resolving these issues.

Many of the primate ENM studies reviewed in this chapter ran their models using all 19 Bioclim variables in the Worldclim dataset. This "all but the kitchen sink" approach is understandable, given that information on key factors limiting primate species is rarely known. It leads, however, to high degrees of collinearity among variables, which can have adverse effects on statistically based methods (Dormann et al. 2013). Further-more, inclusion of many variables tends to result in overfit models or a loss of degrees of freedom (Peterson & Nakazawa 2008). It is generally advisable to select among variables when they correlate. The decision regarding which variables to include, however, can have important impacts on the model. Braunisch et al. (2013) demon-strated this to be the case particularly for projections into future climate change scenarios, where correlative relationships among climate parameters do not necessarily persist. They found that, even when collinearity among variables was maintained across time periods, selecting different variables resulted in different predictions.

When information is available regarding life history and physiological tolerances, the best approach is to use that information to choose an appropriate set of variables (e.g., Blair et al. 2013b). In the absence of a-priori information, there are some existing methods that have been used to reduce dimensionality in ENMs and to explore relationships among variables (reviewed by Dormann et al. 2013). One approach is to use correlation analysis to identify a set of least-correlated variables, although this approach does not necessarily correct for collinearity (Dormann et al. 2013). Another approach is to use principal components analysis or similar ordination techniques to transform the variables onto new orthogonal axes, then to use the most important dimensions as modeling inputs (e.g., Peterson et al. 2007).

While reducing the number of variables is generally desirable, this can also have adverse effects. Using too few variables can cause the model to miss important factors and to estimate overly broad distributional areas. For some methods, particularly machine learning methods, collinearity may not be such an important issue (Elith et al. 2011; Guisan & Thuiller 2005). One effective strategy might be to run the ENM using many variables with collinear relationships, then to let the model determine which variables contribute the most information relevant to the model. Maxent, for instance, iteratively changes coefficients of environmental features and assigns the increases in the model gain (fit) to the variables the features depend on. These cumulative gains are then used to assess percentage contribution to the models. Additionally, the jackknife test in Maxent measures variable contributions to the models when they are the only variable included in the model and when they are the only variable excluded from the model. This helps shed light on how much relevant information each variable provides as well as how much relevant information each variable *uniquely* provides (i.e., that is not provided by other variables).

Because Maxent and other presence–background (or presence–pseudo-absence) approaches train their models by incorporating a sample of cells taken from the study region, they potentially require additional consideration regarding the extent of the training region used. Anderson and Raza (2010) demonstrated that study regions that were too wide resulted in predictions that were overfit to conditions found near occupied localities. This occurs because wide regions are more likely to include areas that are suitable for species, but that are not occupied due to movement limitations or biotic interactions. In Maxent, "clamping" (i.e., treating variables outside the training range as if they were at the limit of the training range) can be used to help overcome this problem.

Spatial autocorrelation is another important potential issue affecting environmental datasets (Keitt et al. 2002). Spatial autocorrelation results from sample points in space having values that are more similar than expected by chance. When it is positive, points that are nearer exhibit more similar values than those that are far apart. The use of autocorrelated variables may place undue emphasis on environmental factors that may not be important influences on niches and distributions. Several methods have been proposed to correct for this problem (reviewed in Dormann et al. 2007). One method that has been widely adopted corrects for spatial correlation by calculating a measure of autocorrelation, the autocovariate, as a new term and including it as an additional variable in the environmental dataset (Dormann et al. 2007). The procedure of correcting for spatial autocorrelation may be more important for regression approaches than for machine learning methods. Václavík et al. (2011) found that while accounting for spatial autocorrelation using multiple methods and geographic scales improved the performance of both a Maxent and GLM model, it reduced spatial autocorrelation in the residuals of only the GLM model.

Evaluating Model Performance

Once the model inputs have been determined and the model has been run, several measures exist for assessing performance and significance. Performance is generally assessed based on the ability of the model to predict occurrences in geographical or, less commonly, environmental space. High-performing models should be expected to minimize commission (false-positive) and omission (false-negative) errors. Of these two error categories, omission errors are more worrisome because they indicate either model failure or erroneous training data, with a few exceptions (e.g., sink populations). Commission errors are more difficult to interpret due to uncertainty over whether negative data reflect true absences or an absence of knowledge.

Evaluation datasets can take the form of fully independent occurrence data, but we anticipate that these will rarely be available for primate research. A more practical approach to evaluation and one of the most widely used is known as *k*-fold cross-validation, or cross-partitioning. In this evaluation scheme, the occurrences are divided into *k* random subsets of even size. In successive stages, new models are run using each subset as evaluation data and the remaining subsets as training data. In this manner, a distribution of *k* estimates of commission/omission error can be estimated.

Estimating commission/omission requires the use of a discrimination threshold (cutoff value) to determine which cells should be judged as suitable or unsuitable habitats for species. Thresholds are also necessary for the mapping of predicted distributions into geographic space. A number of thresholds have been proposed and employed in ENM research (Liu et al. 2005). One intuitive threshold that is well-suited for presence-only data is the "minimum training presence" (MTP). The MTP sets as a threshold the lowest prediction value corresponding with a known presence. A predicted distribution based on the MTP as a threshold can be interpreted as encompassing the areas that are at least as suitable as the least suitable location the species is known to inhabit. It is therefore a conservative measure that identifies the minimum possible area while maintaining zero omission error (Pearson et al. 2007). The MTP, however, can perform poorly if questionable presence observations exist in the dataset or if presence observations are not otherwise representative of suitable habitats. Still more conservative thresholds such as the 10 percent MTP and the equal training sensitivity and specificity are useful in these cases.

One goal of evaluation, however, might be to assess model performance independent of thresholds. The receiver operating characteristic (ROC) curve is commonly used for this purpose. The ROC plots the lack of omission error (true-positive rate) on the *y*-axis against the commission error (false-positive rate) on the *x*-axis. In contrast to threshold-based evaluation measures, the ROC calculates numerous omission and commission errors across a range of prediction strengths. The area under the curve (AUC) of the ROC plot represents an overall measure of the performance of the model across a range of thresholds. Its characteristics make it a popular choice as a performance metric

(Peterson et al. 2011). Care should be taken to use appropriate settings (e.g., Muscarella et al. 2014), however, as AUC can be inflated in presence-only models.

Evaluation methods and metrics make possible critical assessments of factors influencing model performance and strategies for improving performance. These include topics already discussed, such as choosing effective sample sizes, minimizing sample selection bias, correcting for collinearity among environmental variables, and correcting for spatial autocorrelation. Performance can also sometimes be improved by modifying model parameters usually treated as defaults. In Maxent, for example, default parameters were set using average values judged to be optimal using extensive empirical "tuning" (Phillips & Dudík 2008). Species-specific tuning of parameters shows promise as another method for increasing performance in Maxent, particularly for applications where generality and transferability are desirable (Radosavljevic & Anderson 2014).

Conclusion

Many questions of interest to primatologists can be explored using ENMs, from incorporating climate change into conservation plans to predicting the geographies of hybridization and mixed species associations. Paired with coalescent models or genetic data including next-generation genetic sequencing, ENMs can be used for even more robust inferences about biogeography and population histories. Ecological niche models hold great promise for primatologists, and we hope this chapter will encourage expanded use of the approach among our colleagues.

Acknowledgments

We are grateful to the editors for inviting us to contribute to this volume and to two anonymous reviewers for their helpful feedback. We also thank G. Gutiérrez-Espeleta, A. Rojas, and D. Solano for contributing squirrel monkey occurrence data. MEB thanks P. Galante, R. Pearson, and the New York Regional Species Distribution Modeling discussion group for inspiration and dialogue. During the writing of this chapter KLC was partially supported by a National Science Foundation Graduate Research Fellowship (DGE-1143954) and MEB was partially supported by a National Science Foundation Science, Engineering, and Education for Sustainability Fellowship (CHE-1313908).

References

Aguilera, P. A., Fernández, A., Reche, F., and Rumí, R. 2010. Hybrid Bayesian network classifiers: application to species distribution models. *Environmental Modelling and Software* **25**: 1630–1639.

Allouche, O., Tsoar, A., and Kadmon, R. 2006. Assessing the accuracy of species distribution models: prevalence, kappa and the true skill statistic (TSS). *Journal of Applied Ecology* **43**: 1223–1232.

Anderson, R. P. and Raza, A. 2010. The effect of the extent of the study region on GIS models of species geographic distributions and estimates of niche evolution: preliminary tests with montane rodents (genus *Nephelomys*) in Venezuela. *Journal of Biogeography* **37**: 1378–1393.

Anderson, R. P., Lew, D., and Peterson, A. T. 2003. Evaluating predictive models of species' distributions: criteria for selecting optimal models. *Ecological Modelling* **162**: 211–232.

Araújo, M. B. and New, M. 2007. Ensemble forecasting of species distributions. *Trends in Ecology & Evolution* **22**: 42–47.

Araújo, M. B., Pearson, R. G., Thuiller, W., and Erhard, M. 2005. Validation of species–climate impact models under climate change. *Global Change Biology* **11**: 1504–1513.

Barry, S. and Elith, J. 2006. Error and uncertainty in habitat models. *Journal of Applied Ecology* **43**: 413–423.

Beck, J., Ballesteros-Mejia, L., Nagel, P., and Kitching, I. J. 2013. Online solutions and the "Wallacean shortfall": what does GBIF contribute to our knowledge of species' ranges? *Diversity and Distributions* **19**: 1043–1050.

Beeton, T. A., Glantz, M. M., Trainer, A. K., Temirbekov, S. S., and Reich, R. M. 2013. The fundamental hominin niche in late Pleistocene Central Asia: a preliminary refugium model. *Journal of Biogeography* **41**: 95–110.

Bett, N. N., Blair, M. E., and Sterling, E. J. 2012. Ecological niche conservatism in doucs (genus *Pygathrix*). *International Journal of Primatology* **33**: 972–988.

Bjork, A., Liu, W., Wertheim, J. O., Hahn, B. H., and Worobey, M. 2011. Evolutionary history of chimpanzees inferred from complete mitochondrial genomes. *Molecular Biology and Evolution* **28**: 615–623.

Blair, M. E. and Melnick, D. J. 2012a. Genetic evidence for dispersal by both sexes in the Central American squirrel monkey, *Saimiri oerstedii citrinellus*. *American Journal of Primatology* **74**: 37–47.

Blair, M. E. and Melnick, D. J. 2012b. Scale-dependent effects of a heterogeneous landscape on genetic differentiation in the Central American squirrel monkey (*Saimiri oerstedii*). *PLoS ONE* **7**: e43027.

Blair, M. E., Rose, R. A., Ersts, P. J., et al. 2012. Incorporating climate change into conservation planning: identifying priority areas across a species' range. *Frontiers of Biogeography* **4**: 157–167.

Blair, M. E., Gutiérrez-Espeleta, G. A., and Melnick, D. J. 2013a. Subspecies of the Central American squirrel monkey (*Saimiri oerstedii*) as units for conservation. *International Journal of Primatology* **34**: 86–98.

Blair, M. E., Sterling, E. J., Dusch, M., Raxworthy, C. J., and Pearson, R. G. 2013b. Ecological divergence and speciation between lemur (*Eulemur*) sister species in Madagascar. *Journal of Evolutionary Biology* **26**: 1790–1801.

Booth, T. H., Nix, H. A., Busby, J. R., and Hutchinson, M. F. 2014. BIOCLIM: the first species distribution modelling package, its early applications and relevance to most current MaxEnt studies. *Diversity and Distributions* **20**: 1–9.

Boria, R. A., Olson, L. E., Goodman, S. M., and Anderson, R. P. 2014. Spatial filtering to reduce sampling bias can improve the performance of ecological niche models. *Ecological Modelling* **275**: 73–77.

Boubli, J. P., and de Lima, M. G. 2009. Modeling the geographical distribution and fundamental niches of *Cacajao* spp. and *Chiropotes israelita* in northwestern Amazonia via a maximum entropy algorithm. *International Journal of Primatology* **30**: 217–228.

Braunisch, V., Coppes, J., Arlettaz, R., et al. 2013. Selecting from correlated climate variables: a major source of uncertainty for predicting species distributions under climate change. *Ecography* **36**: 971–983.

Breiman, L. 2001. Statistical modeling: the two cultures. *Statistical Science* **16**: 199–215.

Brown, J. L., and Yoder, A. D. 2015. Shifting ranges and conservation challenges for lemurs in the face of climate change. *Ecology and Evolution* **5**: 1131–1142.

Busby, J. R. 1991. BIOCLIM: a bioclimate analysis and prediction system. *Plant Protection Quarterly* **6**: 8–9.

Calvignac-Spencer, S., Merkel, K., Kutzner, N., et al. 2013. Carrion fly-derived DNA as a tool for comprehensive and cost-effective assessment of mammalian biodiversity. *Molecular Ecology* **22**: 915–924.

Campos, F. A. and Jack, K. M. 2013. A potential distribution model and conservation plan for the critically endangered Ecuadorian capuchin, *Cebus albifrons aequatorialis*. *International Journal of Primatology* **34**: 899–916.

Carpenter, G., Gillison, A. N., and Winter, J. 1993. DOMAIN: a flexible modelling procedure for mapping potential distributions of plants and animals. *Biodiversity and Conservation* **2**: 667–680.

Chapman, C. A., Chapman, L. J., and Gillespie, T. R. 2002. Scale issues in the study of primate foraging: red colobus of Kibale National Park. *American Journal of Physical Anthropology* **117**: 349–363.

Chatterjee, H. J., Tse, J. S. Y., and Turvey, S. T. 2012. Using ecological niche modelling to predict spatial and temporal distribution patterns in Chinese gibbons: lessons from the present and the past. *Folia Primatologica* **83**: 85–99.

Chiou, K. L., Pozzi, L., Lynch Alfaro, J. W., and Di Fiore, A. 2011. Pleistocene diversification of living squirrel monkeys (*Saimiri* spp.) inferred from complete mitochondrial genome sequences. *Molecular Phylogenetics and Evolution* **59**: 736–745.

Conroy, G. C., Emerson, C. W., Anemone, R. L., and Townsend, K. E. B. 2012. Let your fingers do the walking: a simple spectral signature model for "remote" fossil prospecting. *Journal of Human Evolution* **63**: 79–84.

Coudrat, C. and Nekaris, K. A.-I. 2013. Modelling niche differentiation of co-existing, elusive and morphologically similar species: a case study of four macaque species in Nakai-Nam Theun National Protected Area, Laos. *Animals* **3**: 45–62.

Cutler, D. R., Edwards, T. C., Jr, Beard, K. H., et al. 2007. Random forests for classification in ecology. *Ecology* **88**: 2783–2792.

Dawson, T. P., Jackson, S. T., House, J. I., Prentice, I. C., and Mace, G. M. 2011. Beyond predictions: biodiversity conservation in a changing climate. *Science* **332**: 53–58.

De'ath, G. and Fabricius, K. E. 2000. Classification and regression trees: a powerful yet simple technique for ecological data analysis. *Ecology* **81**: 3178–3192.

Dormann, C. F., McPherson, J. M., Araújo, M. B., et al. 2007. Methods to account for spatial autocorrelation in the analysis of species distributional data: a review. *Ecography* **30**: 609–628.

Dormann, C. F., Elith, J., Bacher, S., et al. 2013. Collinearity: a review of methods to deal with it and a simulation study evaluating their performance. *Ecography* **36**: 27–46.

Drake, J. M., Randin, C., and Guisan, A. 2006. Modelling ecological niches with support vector machines. *Journal of Applied Ecology* **43**: 424–432.

Elith, J. and Graham, C. H. 2009. Do they? How do they? WHY do they differ? On finding reasons for differing performances of species distribution models. *Ecography* **32**: 66–77.

Elith, J., Graham, C. H., Anderson, R. P., et al. 2006. Novel methods improve prediction of species' distributions from occurrence data. *Ecography* **29**: 129–151.

Elith, J., Leathwick, J. R., and Hastie, T. 2008. A working guide to boosted regression trees. *Journal of Animal Ecology* **77**: 802–813.

Elith, J., Phillips, S. J., Hastie, T., et al. 2011. A statistical explanation of MaxEnt for ecologists. *Diversity and Distributions* **17**: 43–57.

Engler, J. O., Rödder, D., Elle, O., Hochkirch, A., and Secondi, J. 2013. Species distribution models contribute to determine the effect of climate and interspecific interactions in moving hybrid zones. *Journal of Evolutionary Biology* **26**: 2487–2496.

Farber, O. and Kadmon, R. 2003. Assessment of alternative approaches for bioclimatic modeling with special emphasis on the Mahalanobis distance. *Ecological Modelling* **160**: 115–130.

Ferrier, S., Drielsma, M., Manion, G., and Watson, G. 2002. Extended statistical approaches to modelling spatial pattern in biodiversity in northeast New South Wales: II. Community-level modelling. *Biodiversity and Conservation* **11**: 2309–2338.

Ford, S. M. 2006. The biogeographic history of Mesoamerican primates. Pages 81–114 in *New Perspectives in the Study of Mesoamerican Primates*. A. Estrada, P. A. Garber, M. Pavelka, and L. Luecke (Eds.). Springer, New York.

Franklin, J. 2009. *Mapping Species Distributions: Spatial Inference and Prediction*. Cambridge University Press, Cambridge.

Friedman, J. H. 1991. Multivariate adaptive regression splines. *The Annals of Statistics* **19**: 1–67.

Friedman, N., Geiger, D., and Goldszmidt, M. 1997. Bayesian network classifiers. *Machine Learning* **29**: 131–163.

Georges, D. and Thuiller, W. 2013. An example of species distribution modeling with biomod2. R CRAN Project. Tutorial supplied with the "biomod2" package.

Guisan, A. and Thuiller, W. 2005. Predicting species distribution: offering more than simple habitat models. *Ecology Letters* **8**: 993–1009.

Guisan, A., Edwards, T. C., Jr., and Hastie, T. 2002. Generalized linear and generalized additive models in studies of species distributions: setting the scene. *Ecological Modelling* **157**: 89–100.

Guo, Q. and Liu, Y. 2010. ModEco: an integrated software package for ecological niche modeling. *Ecography* **33**: 637–642.

Guo, Q., Kelly, M. and Graham, C. H. 2005. Support vector machines for predicting distribution of Sudden Oak Death in California. *Ecological Modelling* **182**: 75–90.

Heikkinen, R. K., Luoto, M., Virkkala, R., Pearson, R. G., and Körber, J.-H. 2007. Biotic interactions improve prediction of boreal bird distributions at macro-scales. *Global Ecology and Biogeography* **16**: 754–763.

Hershkovitz, P. 1984. Taxonomy of squirrel monkeys genus *Saimiri* (Cebidae, Platyrrhini): a preliminary report with description of a hitherto unnamed form. *American Journal of Primatology* **7**: 155–210.

Hickey, J. R., Nackoney, J., Nibbelink, N. P., et al. 2013. Human proximity and habitat fragmentation are key drivers of the rangewide bonobo distribution. *Biodiversity and Conservation* **22**: 3085–3104.

Hijmans, R. J., Cameron, S. E., Parra, J. L., Jones, P. G., and Jarvis, A. 2005. Very high resolution interpolated climate surfaces for global land areas. *International Journal of Climatology* **25**: 1965–1978.

Hijmans, R. J. and Elith, J. 2013. Species distribution modeling with R. R CRAN Project. Tutorial supplied with the "dismo" package.

Hirzel, A. H. and Le Lay, G. 2008. Habitat suitability modelling and niche theory. *Journal of Applied Ecology* **45**: 1372–1381.

Hirzel, A. H., Hausser, J., Chessel, D., and Perrin, N. 2002. Ecological-niche factor analysis: how to compute habitat-suitability maps without absence data? *Ecology* **83**: 2027–2036.

Hochachka, W. M., Fink, D., Hutchinson, R. A., et al. 2012. Data-intensive science applied to broad-scale citizen science. *Trends in Ecology & Evolution* **27**: 130–137.

Holzmann, I., Agostini, I., DeMatteo, K., et al. 2015. Using species distribution modeling to assess factors that determine the distribution of two parapatric howlers (*Alouatta* spp.) in South America. *International Journal of Primatology* **36**: 18–32.

Junker, J., Blake, S., Boesch, C., et al. 2012. Recent decline in suitable environmental conditions for African great apes. *Diversity and Distributions* **18**: 1077–1091.

Kadmon, R., Farber, O., and Danin, A. 2003. A systematic analysis of factors affecting the performance of climatic envelope models. *Ecological Applications* **13**: 853–867.

Kearney, M. and Porter, W. 2009. Mechanistic niche modelling: combining physiological and spatial data to predict species' ranges. *Ecology Letters* **12**: 334–350.

Keitt, T. H., Bjornstad, O. N., Dixon, P. M., and Citron-Pousty, S. 2002. Accounting for spatial pattern when modeling organism–environment interactions. *Ecography* **25**: 616–625.

Kéry, M., Gardner, B., and Monnerat, C. 2010. Predicting species distributions from checklist data using site-occupancy models. *Journal of Biogeography* **37**: 1851–1862.

Kramer-Schadt, S., Niedballa, J., Pilgrim, J. D., et al. 2013. The importance of correcting for sampling bias in MaxEnt species distribution models. *Diversity and Distributions* **19**: 1366–1379.

Kumara, H. N., Irfan-Ullah, M., and Kumar, S. 2009. Mapping potential distribution of slender loris subspecies in peninsular India. *Endangered Species Research* **7**: 29–38.

Leathwick, J. R., Elith, J., and Hastie, T. 2006a. Comparative performance of generalized additive models and multivariate adaptive regression splines for statistical modelling of species distributions. *Ecological Modelling* **199**: 188–196.

Leathwick, J. R., Elith, J., Francis, M. P., Hastie, T., and Taylor, P. 2006b. Variation in demersal fish species richness in the oceans surrounding New Zealand: an analysis using boosted regression trees. *Marine Ecology Progress Series* **321**: 267–281.

Lehmann, J., Korstjens, A. H., and Dunbar, R. I. M. 2010. Apes in a changing world: the effects of global warming on the behaviour and distribution of African apes. *Journal of Biogeography* **37**: 2217–2231.

Levi, T., Silvius, K. M., Oliveira, L. F. B., Cummings, A. R., and Fragoso, J. M. V. 2013. Competition and facilitation in the capuchin–squirrel monkey relationship. *Biotropica* **45**: 636–643.

Li, J. and Hilbert, D. W. 2008. LIVES: a new habitat modelling technique for predicting the distribution of species' occurrences using presence-only data based on limiting factor theory. *Biodiversity and Conservation* **17**: 3079–3095.

Liu, C., Berry, P. M., Dawson, T. P., and Pearson, R. G. 2005. Selecting thresholds of occurrence in the prediction of species distributions. *Ecography* **28**: 385–393.

Loiselle, B. A., Howell, C. A., Graham, C. H., et al. 2003. Avoiding pitfalls of using species distribution models in conservation planning. *Conservation Biology* **17**: 1591–1600.

Losos, J. B. 2008. Phylogenetic niche conservatism, phylogenetic signal and the relationship between phylogenetic relatedness and ecological similarity among species. *Ecology Letters* **11**: 995–1003.

Lozier, J. D., Aniello, P., and Hickerson, M. J. 2009. Predicting the distribution of Sasquatch in western North America: anything goes with ecological niche modelling. *Journal of Biogeography* **36**: 1623–1627.

Luo, Z., Zhou, S., Yu, W., et al. 2014. Impacts of climate change on the distribution of Sichuan snub-nosed monkeys (*Rhinopithecus roxellana*) in Shennongjia area, China. *American Journal of Primatology* **77**: 135–151.

Lynch Alfaro, J. W., Boubli, J. P., Paim, F. P., et al. 2015. Biogeography of squirrel monkeys (genus *Saimiri*): south-central Amazon origin and pan-Amazonian diversification of a lowland primate. *Molecular Phylogenetics and Evolution* **82B**: 436–454.

MacColl, A. D. C. 2011. The ecological causes of evolution. *Trends in Ecology & Evolution* **26**: 514–522.

Manel, S., Dias, J.-M., and Ormerod, S. J. 1999. Comparing discriminant analysis, neural networks and logistic regression for predicting species distributions: a case study with a Himalayan river bird. *Ecological Modelling* **120**: 337–347.

McPherson, J. M., Jetz, W., and Rogers, D. J. 2004. The effects of species' range sizes on the accuracy of distribution models: ecological phenomenon or statistical artefact? *Journal of Applied Ecology* **41**: 811–823.

Meyer, A. L. S., Pie, M. R., and Passos, F. C. 2014. Assessing the exposure of lion tamarins (*Leontopithecus* spp.) to future climate change. *American Journal of Primatology* **76**: 551–562.

Mitchell, M. W., Locatelli, S., Sesink Clee, P. R., Thomassen, H. A., and Gonder, M. 2015. Environmental variation and rivers govern the structure of chimpanzee genetic diversity in a biodiversity hotspot. *BMC Evolutionary Biology* **15**: 1.

Moisen, G. G. and Frescino, T. S. 2002. Comparing five modelling techniques for predicting forest characteristics. *Ecological Modelling* **157**: 209–225.

Morales-Jimenez, A. L., Nekaris, A., Lee, J., and Thompson, S. 2005. Modeling distributions for Colombian spider monkeys (*Ateles* spp.) to find priorities for conservation. *American Journal of Primatology* **66** (Suppl. 1): 131.

Muscarella, R., Galante, P. J., Soley-Guardia, M., et al. 2014. ENMeval: an R package for conducting spatially independent evaluations and estimating optimal model complexity for Maxent ecological niche models. *Methods in Ecology and Evolution* **5**: 1198–1205.

Newbold, T. 2010. Applications and limitations of museum data for conservation and ecology, with particular attention to species distribution models. *Progress in Physical Geography* **34**: 3–22.

Nix, H. A. 1986. A biogeographic analysis of Australian elapid snakes. Pages 4–15 in *Atlas of Elapid Snakes of Australia*. R. Longmore (Ed.). Australian Government Publishing Service, Canberra.

Nores, M. 1999. An alternative hypothesis for the origin of Amazonian bird diversity. *Journal of Biogeography* **26**: 475–485.

Oliveira, G. de, Rangel, T. F., Lima-Ribeiro, M. S., Terribile, L. C., and Diniz-Filho, J. A. F. 2014. Evaluating, partitioning, and mapping the spatial autocorrelation component in ecological niche modeling: a new approach based on environmentally equidistant records. *Ecography* **37**: 637–647.

Pawlak, Z. 1991. *Rough Sets: Theoretical Aspects of Reasoning about Data*. Kluwer, Dordrecht.

Pearson, R. G. and Dawson, T. P. 2003. Predicting the impacts of climate change on the distribution of species: are bioclimate envelope models useful? *Global Ecology and Biogeography* **12**: 361–371.

Pearson, R. G., Dawson, T. P., Berry, P. M., and Harrison, P. A. 2002. SPECIES: a spatial evaluation of climate impact on the envelope of species. *Ecological Modelling* **154**: 289–300.

Pearson, R. G., Thuiller, W., Araújo, M. B., et al. 2006. Model-based uncertainty in species range prediction. *Journal of Biogeography* **33**: 1704–1711.

Pearson, R. G., Raxworthy, C. J., Nakamura, M., and Peterson, A. T. 2007. Predicting species distributions from small numbers of occurrence records: a test case using cryptic geckos in Madagascar. *Journal of Biogeography* **34**: 102–117.

Peck, M., Thorn, J., Mariscal, A., et al. 2011. Focusing conservation efforts for the critically endangered brown-headed spider monkey (*Ateles fusciceps*) using remote sensing, modeling, and playback survey methods. *International Journal of Primatology* **32**: 134–148.

Peterson, A. T. 2003. Predicting the geography of species' invasions via ecological niche modeling. *Quarterly Review of Biology* **78**: 419–433.

Peterson, A. T. and Nakazawa, Y. 2008. Environmental data sets matter in ecological niche modelling: an example with *Solenopsis invicta* and *Solenopsis richteri*. *Global Ecology and Biogeography* **17**: 135–144.

Peterson, A. T., Papes, M., and Eaton, M. 2007. Transferability and model evaluation in ecological niche modeling: a comparison of GARP and Maxent. *Ecography* **30**: 550–560.

Peterson, A. T., Soberón, J., Pearson, R. G., et al. 2011. *Ecological Niches and Geographic Distributions*. Princeton University Press, Princeton, NJ.

Phillips, S. J. 2009. A brief tutorial on MaxEnt. Available at: https://biodiversityinformatics .amnh.org/open_source/maxent/Maxent_tutorial2017.pdf.

Phillips, S. J. and Dudík, M. 2008. Modeling of species distributions with Maxent: new extensions and a comprehensive evaluation. *Ecography* **31**: 161–175.

Phillips, S. J., Anderson, R. P., and Schapire, R. E. 2006. Maximum entropy modeling of species geographic distributions. *Ecological Modelling* **190**: 231–259.

Pintea, L., Jantz, S., Nackoney, J. R., and Hansen, M. C. 2014. The first high resolution maps of chimpanzee habitat health in Africa. In *IUCN World Parks Congress*, November 12–19, 2014. Sydney, Australia.

Potts, J. M. and Elith, J. 2006. Comparing species abundance models. *Ecological Modelling* **199**: 153–163.

R Core Team. 2013. *R: A Language and Environment for Statistical Computing*. R Foundation for Statistical Computing, Vienna.

Radosavljevic, A. and Anderson, R. P. 2014. Making better Maxent models of species distributions: complexity, overfitting and evaluation. *Journal of Biogeography* **41**: 629–643.

Raxworthy, C. J., Ingram, C. M., Rabibisoa, N., and Pearson, R. G. 2007. Applications of ecological niche modeling for species delimitation: a review and empirical evaluation using day geckos (*Phelsuma*) from Madagascar. *Systematic Biology* **56**: 907–923.

Renner, I. W. and Warton, D. I. 2013. Equivalence of MAXENT and Poisson point process models for species distribution modeling in ecology. *Biometrics* **69**: 274–281.

Renner, I. W., Elith, J., Baddeley, A., et al. 2015. Point process models for presence-only analysis. *Methods in Ecology and Evolution* **6**: 366–379.

Rode, E. J., Stengel, C. J., and Nekaris, K. A.-I. 2013. Habitat assessment and species niche modeling. Pages 79–102 in *Primate Ecology and Conservation: A Handbook of Techniques*. E. J. Sterling, N. Bynum, and M. E. Blair (Eds.). Oxford University Press, Oxford.

Rodríguez-Vargas, A. R. 2003. Analysis of the hypothetical population structure of the squirrel monkey (*Saimiri oerstedii*) in Panamá. Pages 53–62 in *Primates in Fragments: Ecology and Conservation*. L.K. Marsh (Ed.). Kluwer, New York.

Rotenberry, J. T., Preston, K. L., and Knick, S. T. 2006. GIS-based niche modeling for mapping species' habitat. *Ecology* **87**: 1458–1464.

Rouget, M., Richardson, D. M., Lavorel, S., et al. 2001. Determinants of distribution of six *Pinus* species in Catalonia, Spain. *Journal of Vegetation Science* **12**: 491–502.

Rylands, A. B. and Mittermeier, R. A. 2009. The diversity of the New World primates (Platyrrhini): an annotated taxonomy. Pages 23–54 in *South American Primates*. P. A. Garber, A. Estrada, J. C. Bicca-Marques, E. W. Heymann, and K. B. Strier (Eds.). Springer, New York.

Scachetti-Pereira, R. 2002. DesktopGarp v1.1.6. Available at www.nhm.ku.edu/desktopgarp.

Scott, J. M., Csuti, B., Jacobi, J. D., and Estes, J. E. 1987. Species richness: a geographic approach to protecting future biological diversity. *BioScience* **37**: 782–788.

Segurado, P. and Araújo, M. B. 2004. An evaluation of methods for modelling species distributions. *Journal of Biogeography* **31**: 1555–1568.

Sesink Clee, P. R., Abwe, E. E., Ambahe, R. D., et al. 2015. Chimpanzee population structure in Cameroon and Nigeria is associated with habitat variation that may be lost under climate change. *BMC Evolutionary Biology* **15**: 2.

Soberón, J. and Peterson, A. T. 2005. Interpretation of models of fundamental ecological niches and species' distributional areas. *Biodiversity Informatics* **2**: 1–10.

Solano Rojas, D. 2007. Evaluación del hábitat, el paisaje y la población del mono tití (Cebidae, Platyrrhini: *Saimiri oerstedii oerstedii*) en la Península de Osa, Costa Rica. Master's Thesis. Universidad Nacional de Costa Rica.

Sterling, E. J., Bynum, N., and Blair, M. E. 2013. Conclusion: the future of studying primates in a changing world. Pages 346–350 in *Primate Ecology and Conservation: A Handbook of Techniques*. E. J. Sterling, N. Bynum, and M. E. Blair. (Eds.). Oxford University Press, Oxford.

Stockwell, D. and Peters, D. 1999. The GARP modeling system: problems and solutions to automated spatial prediction. *International Journal of Geographical Information Science* **13**: 143–158.

Stockwell, D. R. B. and Peterson, A. T. 2002. Effects of sample size on accuracy of species distribution models. *Ecological Modelling* **148**: 1–13.

Struebig, M. J., Fischer, M., Gaveau, D. L. A., et al. 2015. Anticipated climate and land-cover changes reveal refuge areas for Borneo's orang-utans. *Global Change Biology* **21**: 2891–2904.

Thorn, J. S., Nijman, V., Smith, D., and Nekaris, K. A.-I. 2009. Ecological niche modelling as a technique for assessing threats and setting conservation priorities for Asian slow lorises (Primates: *Nycticebus*). *Diversity and Distributions* **15**: 289–298.

Thuiller, W. 2003. BIOMOD: optimizing predictions of species distributions and projecting potential future shifts under global change. *Global Change Biology* **9**: 1353–1362.

Thuiller, W., Lafourcade, B., Engler, R., and Araújo, M. B. 2009. BIOMOD: a platform for ensemble forecasting of species distributions. *Ecography* **32**: 369–373.

Tsoar, A., Allouche, O., Steinitz, O., Rotem, D., and Kadmon, R. 2007. A comparative evaluation of presence-only methods for modelling species distribution. *Diversity and Distributions* **13**: 397–405.

Václavík, T., Kupfer, J. A., and Meentemeyer, R. K. 2011. Accounting for multi-scale spatial autocorrelation improves performance of invasive species distribution modelling (iSDM). *Journal of Biogeography* **39**: 42–55.

VanDerWal, J., Shoo, L. P., Graham, C., and Williams, S. E. 2009. Selecting pseudo-absence data for presence-only distribution modeling: how far should you stray from what you know? *Ecological Modelling* **220**: 589–594.

Vidal-García, F. and Serio-Silva, J. C. 2011. Potential distribution of Mexican primates: modeling the ecological niche with the maximum entropy algorithm. *Primates* **52**: 261–270.

Voskamp, A., Rode, E. J., Coudrat, C. N. Z., et al. 2014. Modelling the habitat use and distribution of the threatened Javan slow loris *Nycticebus javanicus*. *Endangered Species Research* **23**: 277–286.

Vu, M. V., Thach, H. M., and Pham, V. T. 2010. Using environmental niche model to study the distribution of Tonkin snub-nosed monkey (*Rhinopithecus avunculus*) in Northeastern Vietnam under some climate change scenarios. Pages 156–164 in *Proceedings of the 24th International Conference on Informatics for Environmental Protection, Cologne/Bonn, Germany.*

Vu, M. V., Thach, H. M., Le, M. T. T., and Pham, V. T. 2011. Study on the using of environmental niche model Bioclim to estimate the distribution of Francois's Langur (*Trachypithecus francoisi*) in Northern of Vietnam under climate change of IPCC scenario A$_2$. *VNU Journal of Science: Natural Sciences & Technology* **27**: 70–76.

Walker, P. A. and Cocks, K. D. 1991. HABITAT: a procedure for modelling a disjoint environmental envelope for a plant or animal species. *Global Ecology and Biogeography Letters* **1**: 108–118.

Warren, D. L., Glor, R. E., and Turelli, M. 2008. Environmental niche equivalency versus conservatism: quantitative approaches to niche evolution. *Evolution* **62**: 2868–2883.

Warren, D. L., Glor, R. E. and Turelli, M. 2010. ENMTools: a toolbox for comparative studies of environmental niche models. *Ecography* **33**: 607–611.

Wiens, J. J. 2004. Speciation and ecology revisited: phylogenetic niche conservatism and the origin of species. *Evolution* **58**: 193–197.

Willems, E. P. and Hill, R. A. 2009. A critical assessment of two species distribution models: a case study of the vervet monkey (*Cercopithecus aethiops*). *Journal of Biogeography* **36**: 2300–2312.

Wisz, M. S., Hijmans, R. J., Li, J., et al. 2008. Effects of sample size on the performance of species distribution models. *Diversity and Distributions* **14**: 763–773.

Wong, M. H. G., Li, R., Xu, M., and Long, Y. 2013. An integrative approach to assessing the potential impacts of climate change on the Yunnan snub-nosed monkey. *Biological Conservation* **158**: 401–409.

Yackulic, C. B., Chandler, R., Zipkin, E. F., et al. 2013. Presence-only modelling using MAXENT: when can we trust the inferences? *Methods in Ecology and Evolution* **4**: 236–243.

Yesson, C., Brewer, P. W., Sutton, T., et al. 2007. How global is the Global Biodiversity Information Facility? *PLoS ONE* **2**: e1124.

16 Does Reduced Habitat Quality or Increased Hunter Access Explain Defaunation of Fragmented Forests?
Bonobos as a Case Study

Jena R. Hickey and Michael J. Conroy

Introduction

Primatologists require tools to better understand primate habitat use and occurrence at broad spatial scales in order to address the potential consequences of accelerated land use change on many threatened or endangered primate populations. Landscape-level variables derived from remote sensing can contribute to more informed conservation planning decisions, yet need to be grounded in established relationships with local field data. Landscape-level variables necessarily are measured at different scales than GPS-level variables, thereby confounding our understanding of the causal mechanisms that relate them. For example, the mechanism causing empty forest syndrome, a condition in which relatively intact stands of forest are devoid of most fauna, has generally been attributed to local hunting (Fa & Brown 2009; Redford 1992; Wilkie et al. 2011). Wilkie et al. (1992) made a convincing case that forest fragmentation via roads and transects from logging activities exacerbated hunting pressure on forest fauna in the Republic of Congo. Therefore, we (Hickey et al. 2012, 2013) hypothesized that remotely sensed data measuring forest fragmentation and landscape-level proxies of hunter access (distance from agriculture, distance from road, distance from rivers) may correspond to relative hunting pressure for many hunted species because areas near agriculture, roads, and rivers are necessarily near areas of higher human concentration. However, it remains untested whether those landscape metrics actually relate to relative hunting pressure. Approaches using geographic information systems (GIS) and global positioning systems (GPS) are essential to answering such important questions.

Bonobos (*Pan paniscus*) are endangered great apes that are in jeopardy due to illegal hunting (poaching) and habitat fragmentation (Fruth et al. 2008). Hickey et al. (2013) demonstrated that habitat fragmentation as measured by edge density (ED) and relative hunter access as measured by distance from agriculture, distance from road, and distance from rivers effectively predicted rangewide occurrence of bonobo nest blocks. Yet, the pervasiveness of hunting throughout the bonobo's range – including areas that are legally protected (Dupain and Van Elsacker 2001; Hart et al. 2008) – precluded a rangewide assessment of the predictive importance of landscape-level factors in the absence of hunting (Hickey et al. 2013). The difficulty is that, at the rangewide scale, there are essentially no areas without hunting. Therefore, there is a need for fine-scale analyses in areas that differ in relative hunting pressure in order to compare the utility of both remotely sensed and field-derived data in predicting bonobo occupancy and to assess the conservation implications of those factors. Over the long term, it will be important to clarify the mechanism by which landscape-level predictors relate to bonobo occupancy. Based on previous studies (Hickey et al. 2012, 2013; Wilkie et al. 2011), the assumed causal mechanism is hunting.

We evaluated bonobo site occupancy within the Maringa–Lopori–Wamba (MLW) landscape in relation to both landscape-level predictors, as well as local evidence of human presence. We quantified and compared the influence of these factors on probability of bonobo site occupancy, and suggest that this information can inform and focus bonobo conservation efforts. Additionally, we anticipated imperfect detection of bonobo nests seen on the transect line (0 m distance), violating a key assumption of density estimation via distance sampling (Buckland et al. 2001). Thus, we employed double-independent observer techniques (Williams et al. 2002) to estimate detection probability and to correct estimates or abundance accordingly. Given that humans in this landscape must hunt, farm, and harvest trees to shape their livelihoods, this project seeks to provide data that decision-makers can use to optimally zone sylvo-agro-pastoral (Dupain et al. 2009) activities and protected areas in order to ensure the persistence of bonobos. In addition, these results provide a baseline for long-term studies striving to elucidate causal mechanisms relating bonobo occupancy to remotely derived data.

Methods

Study Area

Maringa–Lopori–Wamba (Figure 16.1) is an area designated as a conservation landscape by the Central African Regional Program for the Environment (CARPE), a branch of the US Agency for International Development (USAID) (Hickey & Sidle 2006). It was selected as a CARPE landscape specifically for the conservation of bonobos in conjunction with alleviation of poverty (Hickey & Sidle 2006). Maringa–Lopori–Wamba is approximately 74,000 km^2 and is characterized by large areas of intact lowland rainforest, human settlement, slash-and-burn agriculture, and numerous large timber concessions (totaling >6000 km^2) in different states of harvest rotation or harvest planning (Dupain et al. 2009). We conducted our field research both inside and outside of a recently designated protected area known as the Lomako–Yokokala Faunal Reserve (LYFR) and a logged area near the town of Kee, DRC (Figure 16.1).

Field Data Collection

From February to July 2009, we surveyed 68 km of line-transects and recorded locations of all detected bonobo nests and human signs (machete cuts, traps, hunting

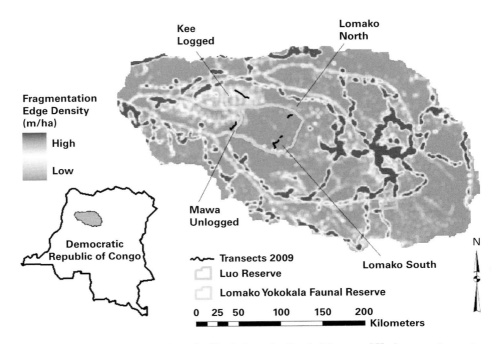

Figure 16.1 Four study regions (Lomako North, Lomako South, Mawa, and Kee), survey transects, protected areas, and edge density in the Maringa–Lopori–Wamba landscape, Democratic Republic of Congo. (A black and white version of this figure will appear in some formats. For the color version, please refer to the plate section.)

camps, paths, roads, and log-cut trees). We used double independent-observer search methods (Williams et al. 2002), thereby surveying all transects twice in order to quantify and address detection probability, which is critical for unbiased estimates of occupancy with imperfect detection (MacKenzie et al. 2006). We conducted transects in four major regions stratified by forest fragmentation as measured by ED (m/ha) (see the section GIS Methods). They ranked from lowest to highest ED as follows: (1) Lomako South, inside the southern portion of LYFR; (2) Lomako North, inside the northern portion of LYFR; (3) Mawa, an unlogged region west of Lomako South; and (4) Kee, a logged area northwest of LYFR (Figure 16.1). All regions differed significantly in ED (see Figure 16.3) except the two Lomako regions, which shared similarly low ED (intact forest). We further stratified random start and end points of all transects a priori in ArcGIS 9.3 (ESRI, Redlands) using "distance from fire" (see GIS Methods), a measure expected to correlate with the proximity of human presence. We found that fire points corresponded more accurately to the locations of roads, villages, and slash-and-burn agriculture than the available layer on human settlements. In this landscape, all communities practice slash-and-burn agriculture, creating fires sufficiently large that satellites detect them. In stratifying by distance from fire, we attempted to collect site-occupancy data along a gradient of potential human threat in every region with strata further from fire expected to experience lower likelihood of hunting pressure.

GIS Methods

In ArcGIS 9.3, we separated the surveyed transects into 542 sites. In order to define the size of bonobo sites, we applied previously documented nest group distances to the size of the raster pixels. When assigning nests to nest groups, the suggested cutoff distance between nests within a single nest group is 30 m (Mulavwa et al. 2010). Our raster pixels were 57 × 57 m; consequently sites for this study were 120 m long and corresponded approximately to pixel length buffered by 30 m (the estimated distance between nest groups) on either side. For each site, we conducted a select-by-location in ArcGIS and separately selected all bonobo nests and human signs within 100 m of the center of each site. We then summed the total count of bonobo nests, as well as each type of human sign (machete cuts, traps, hunting camps, log-cut trees, paths, and roads) per site.

Our objective was to evaluate the relative magnitude of effect of landscape variables versus local human activities, the former derived from remotely sensed data and the latter measured by counts of human signs from field surveys. Therefore, we created three metrics (ED, distance from river, and distance from fire) thought to represent habitat fragmentation, relative hunting pressure, or both. ED captured the fragmentation from rivers, roads, timber harvest, and agriculture, thereby relating not only to habitat degradation, but also to potential hunter access via any of these human-created or natural access routes (Laurance et al. 2009). For example, in MLW rivers are the primary travel corridors, hence areas closer to rivers are also closer to potential hunter access. To develop specific GIS layers for distance from river and distance from fire as proxies for relative hunting pressure, we calculated the Euclidean distance from rivers (USGS 2000) and fire points (Davies et al. 2009). Using the "extract values to points" tool in the Spatial Analyst extension of ArcGIS, we then extracted the values from these three raster data layers to our sites in order to analyze them as covariates to predict bonobo site occupancy. We defined forest ED as the linear edge between forest and non-forest in a given area and used ED as a measure of habitat fragmentation. ED was shown to be a strong predictor of bonobo nest occurrence in MLW as well as rangewide (Hickey et al. 2012, 2013), and specific methods for calculating ED may be found in Hickey et al. (2012). Fire points were detected via LANDSAT imagery and then interpreted and provided by the University of Maryland (Davies et al. 2009). The fire points database included a rating of relative confidence (0–100 percent) in the accuracy of its classification as a fire. Based on guidance in the associated metadata, we used fire points rated ≥50 percent confidence in determining distance from fire strata for our study design. However, during the field season we noted that even low-confidence fire points tended to be actual slash-and-burn fields, therefore the distance from fire predictor variable includes fire points of all confidence levels in lieu of spatial data on village locations.

Population Estimation, Detection Probability, and Occupancy Estimation Methods

Viewed from the forest floor, fresh bonobo nests are large, green leafy clusters occurring at various heights amid equally green foliage of the forest canopy. Lack of dramatic color or texture contrast and potential for vegetation to obstruct viewing can cause some nests to go undetected; thus nondetection cannot be equated to nonoccurrence. Therefore, we analyzed individual nest mark–recapture (sight–resight) histories with Huggins closed-capture population estimation models (Huggins 1989) in Program MARK (version 6.1). This allowed us to provide unbiased estimates of N, the total number of nests along all transects surveyed, and to assess potential heterogeneity in detection probability (p) based on observer (Team A or B) and time (survey occasion 1 or 2). Following Mohneke and Fruth (2008), we estimated density of bonobo nests using the following formulas:

$$\hat{D}_1 = \frac{n}{dr \times pr \times L \times 2w} \tag{1}$$

and

$$\hat{D}_2 = \frac{\hat{N}}{dr \times pr \times L \times 2w}, \tag{2}$$

thereby incorporating the estimated number of nests (either the naïve count of n detections or the unbiased estimate of nests $\hat{N}$ from Program MARK), nest decomposition rate (dr), nest production rate (pr), total length of all transects surveyed (L), and approximate mean viewing distance along either side of the transects ($2w$). To develop a range of estimates for D, we applied two different estimates of dr, 99 d and 75.5 d (Eriksson 1999 in Mohneke & Fruth 2008 and Mohneke & Fruth 2008, respectively) and pr, 1.37 and 1 (Mohneke & Fruth 2008 and Reinartz et al. 2006, respectively). To determine w, we measured perpendicular distance to detected nests along 13 km of transect and selected the distance at which frequency of observations declined sharply.

Ideally, when modeling the effect of landscape and local variables on bonobo site occupancy (ψ), we would have again used models that account for detection probability, p. Our sight–resight field procedure allowed the computation of p to estimate the combined probabilities that a given site was either: (1) occupied and detected, (2) occupied but not detected, or (3) not occupied. Therefore, we built models of site occupancy in both Program MARK (a likelihood analysis) and in WinBUGS (version 1.4.3; a Bayesian analysis). Although Program MARK and Bayes analysis both provided consistent estimates of p and ψ across all models, the addition of environmental covariates to the site occupancy models caused unreliable results (see Hickey 2012 for more details). Therefore, we collapsed occupancy histories into binary ("presence–absence") data combining data from both occasions 1 and 2 in order to conduct logistic regression models to evaluate the influence of environmental predictor variables on bonobo site occupancy (for more explanation, see Logistic Regression).

Logistic Regression and Multi-Model Inference

We ranked all logistic regression models (program R) using an information-theoretic (Akaike's information criteria, or AIC) approach to model selection as discussed by

Table 16.1 Remotely sensed and field-derived data used in logistic regression models to predict the probability of bonobo site occupancy in the Maringa–Lopori–Wamba landscape, Democratic Republic of Congo.

Source	Predictor variable	Units	Measure of	Expected relationship with bonobo occupancy
Remotely sensed (Hansen et al. 2008; Hickey et al. 2012)	Edge density	m/ha (km/10km^2)	Forest fragmentation	–
Remotely sensed (Davies et al. 2009)	Distance from fire	km	Proximity to human settlements and, potentially, relative hunting pressure	+
Remotely sensed (USGS 2000)	Distance from river	km	Proximity to human travel corridors	+
Field-collected	Machete cuts	Count/site	Human activity in forest	–
Field-collected	Traps	Count/site	Hunting activity in forest	–
Field-collected	Hunting camps	Count/site	Hunting activity in forest	–
Field-collected	Log-cut trees	Count/site	Human alteration of forest and potentially increased human access via log-extraction trails	–
Field-collected	Paths	Number of intersections/ site	Human access	–
Field-collected	Roads	Number of intersections/ site	Human access	–

Akaike (1973) and Anderson et al. (2000). We developed a candidate set of models describing potential relationships between site occupancy and landscape and local variables (Table 16.1). Information-theoretic methods (Anderson et al. 2000) evaluate the relative plausibility of different models using estimates of likelihood. To reduce the potential for overfitting, we examined the parameter estimates of univariate models for nine predictors and retained those exhibiting potential significance at $\alpha \leq 0.1$ for use in a global logistic regression model (Millington et al. 2010). In order to avoid multi-collinearity, we calculated Pearson's correlation coefficient, r, on all pairs of predictors and eliminated the weaker predictor of any two correlated ($r > 0.49$) variables from the global model. We built a set of candidate models to predict site occupancy from all possible combinations of non-correlated parameters contained in the global model. We calculated AIC (Akaike 1973) with the small-sample bias adjustment (AICc; Hurvich & Tsai 1989) to evaluate the fit of each candidate model. To compare models, we assessed the relative fit of each candidate model by calculating Akaike weights (Anderson et al. 2000), with the best-fitting candidate model having the greatest Akaike weight. We created a confidence set of models that included only those candidate models with Akaike weights greater than 10 percent of the largest Akaike weight, as suggested by

Royall (1997). We considered models with Akaike weights less than 10 percent of the greatest weight to have too little evidence to be plausible explanations for bonobo site occupancy. We described general patterns among models in the confidence set and provided parameter estimates from the top model.

In logistic regression, predictions are expressed in log-odds, and odds ratios are used to interpret the relative strength of factors affecting the response, assuming the other factors are held constant. In order to calculate an odds ratio, the parameter estimate for each coefficient must be back-transformed with the exponential function, e^x, where x is the logit-linear parameter estimate. This procedure allows inference of the relationship between the predictor and response variables (Hosmer & Lemeshow 1989). We then calculated the odds ratio for each predictor in the top model in order to infer the direction and magnitude of the relationships with bonobo site occupancy. Odds ratios >1 indicate positive relationships, such that with each unit increase in the variable, the probability of occupancy is e^x times greater. Odds ratios <1 indicate a negative relationship and are interpreted more easily by taking the inverse and stating "sites are $1/e^x$ times" *less* likely to be occupied with each unit increase in the parameter.

ANOVA Corrected for Multiple Comparisons

We used one-way ANOVAs to test whether there were differences among regions with respect to each variable (machete cuts, traps, roads, ED, distance from fire, and distance from river), applying the Tukey correction for multiple comparisons. Results were then compared to bonobo occupancy in each of the regions to help explain the pattern of occupancy relative to regional conditions.

Results

Field Surveys, Detection Probability, Density and Occupancy Estimation

We detected a total of 338 nests of which 319 were usable for this analysis, the others being opportunistically sighted during hikes to or from transects. We found no nests in Kee, the previously logged region, and we detected none in Lomako North. The latter is an area where abundant hunting signs (fresh, set traps) were found, despite its official designation as a protected area (see Figure 16.3). Examined in Program MARK, occasion histories per individual nest resulted in stable models and estimates of p and $\hat{N}$. Huggins closed-capture population estimation calculated $\hat{N}(\pm SD)$ as 352.7 (± 12.98). Using the naïve count for number of nests $n = 319$ and an effective strip width $2w = 0.06$ km, the density of nest-building bonobos from equation (1) equals:

$$\hat{D}_1 = \frac{319}{99 \times 1.37 \times 68 \times 0.06} = 0.576 \, \text{bonobos/km}^2,$$

Table 16.2 A range of naïve and detection-adjusted density estimates ($\hat{D}$, bonobos/km^2) based on bonobo nest surveys conducted during 2009 in the Maringa–Lopori–Wamba landscape, Democratic Republic of Congo, using alternate estimates of number of nests (n and $\hat{N}$), nest decomposition rates (dr), and nest production rates (pr).

		$\hat{D}_1$ (naïve)	$\hat{D}_2$ (adjusted for detection probability)
		n	$\hat{N}$
pr_1	dr_1 (99 d)	0.576	0.638
	dr_2 (75.5 d)	0.756	0.837
pr_2	dr_1 (99 d)	0.790	0.874
	dr_2 (75.5 d)	1.04	1.15

$n = 319$ naïve (raw) nest count.
$\hat{N} = 353$ number of nests adjusted for detection probability.
dr_1 from Eriksson (1999).
dr_2 from Mohneke and Fruth (2008).
$pr_1 = 1.37$ nests built per bonobo/d; from Mohneke and Fruth (2008).
$pr_2 = 1$ nest built per bonobo/d; from Reinartz et al. (2006).

whereas holding all other estimates constant and employing the number of nests corrected for p, $\hat{N} = 353$, the $\hat{D}$ from equation (2) equals:

$$\hat{D}_2 = \frac{353}{99 \times 1.37 \times 68 \times 0.06} = 0.638\,\text{bonobos}/\text{km}^2.$$

Because the values of dr and pr can vary by location and season, we calculated a range of estimates for $\hat{D}_1$ and $\hat{D}_2$ (Table 16.2).

We found individual nest-detection probability varied significantly by observer but not by survey occasion. Mean detection rates of Teams A and B were 0.78 and 0.58, respectively. Teams A and B differed significantly from each other during occasion 1 (t-statistic = 2.43, d.f. = 317, $p = 0.016$) and occasion 2 (t-statistic = 3.46, d.f. = 317, $p < 0.001$). However, the difference in observer detection rates was homogenized over occasion histories, because the survey protocol included periodically alternating Teams A and B between occasion times 1 and 2, thereby creating an effectively constant p among survey occasions (see Hickey 2012 for more details). Assuming a constant p among survey occasions, Program MARK and the Bayesian analysis agreed, producing similar values for p ($\pm$SD) of 0.745 ($\pm$0.047) and 0.737 ($\pm$0.047), respectively.

Similarly, modeling a constant p and ψ, the Program MARK estimate and the Bayesian analysis result (mean of the posterior distribution) concurred with ψ ($\pm$SD) of 0.136 ($\pm$0.016) and 0.138 ($\pm$0.016), respectively. We determined the minimum convex polygon (MCP) around surveyed transects (Figure 16.2), which encompasses 3115 km^2, 79 percent of which falls within the protection of the LYFR. Extrapolating the mean of the ψ values to the MCP gives:

$$3115 \text{ km}^2 \times 0.137 = 426.8 \text{ km}^2$$

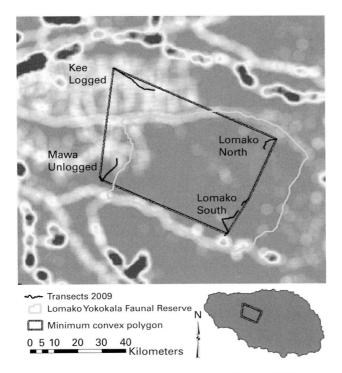

Transects 2009
Lomako Yokokala Faunal Reserve
Minimum convex polygon
0 5 10   20   30   40
Kilometers

N

Figure 16.2 Minimum convex polygon containing the 2009 survey transects in four regions of the Maringa–Lopori–Wamba landscape, Democratic Republic of Congo. (A black and white version of this figure will appear in some formats. For the color version, please refer to the plate section.)

occupied within the MCP. Inverting the occupancy estimate, we can see that at any given time approximately $(1 - 0.137) \times 100 = 86.3$ percent of the MCP is *un*occupied by bonobos, despite being predominantly protected lowland rainforest.

Logistic Regression

We collapsed occupancy histories into presence–absence data combining data from both occasions 1 and 2 in order to conduct logistic regression. This procedure increases the power of the data to detect a pattern with the covariates; however, it also eliminates consideration of detection probability (p). Yet, we reasoned that most occupied sites were detected with our protocol. Since p is the probability of detecting a nest, given it is there, the probability of *not* detecting a nest given it is there equals $(1 - p)$. In general, nondetection at a site that contains at least one nest (false absence) can be estimated by $(1 - p)^i$, where i is the number of survey occasions. In this case, the best-ranked occupancy model had constant p between occasions, therefore we estimated the probability of false absences as:

$$(1 - \bar{p})^2 = (1 - 0.74)^2 = 0.068,$$

where $\bar{p}$ was the mean of Program MARK and Bayesian analysis estimates for site-level detection probability. The corresponding probability that we *correctly* determined site occupancy was $1 - 0.068 = 0.932$. Based on this high probability of correct site classification, relatively few occupied sites went undetected, therefore we analyzed the effect of predictors on presence–absence using logistic regression.

In R, we constructed a global model with six of nine possible predictors. There was no evidence of multicollinearity (all Pearson's $|r| < 0.44$); however, we excluded hunting camps due to low occurrence ($n = 7$), log-cut trees due to abnormal behavior caused by zero variance at occupied sites (100 percent of occupied sites had zero log-cut trees within 100 m), and paths due to non-significance in the univariate model ($p = 0.9$). Out of 64 models, 13 had Akaike weights ≥ 10 percent of the best model (Table 16.3). ED was the most prevalent parameter, being present in all models in the confidence set. Machete cuts occurred in 11 and distance from river occurred in 10 of the top 13 models. Together, ED, distance from river, and machete cuts were the most important predictors of site occupancy. As expected, all models predicted that sites were consistently less likely to be occupied with increasing ED and machete cuts, whereas sites were more likely to be occupied with increasing distance from rivers (Table 16.4). There was nearly no relationship between bonobo site occupancy and distance from fire, although occupancy appeared to decline weakly with increasing distance from fire.

Table 16.3 Model rank, predictor variables, number of parameters (K), AICc, ΔAICc, Akaike weights (w) for each model (i) in the confidence set of models predicting bonobo site occupancy in the Maringa–Lopori–Wamba landscape, Democratic Republic of Congo.

Rank	Candidate model	K	AICc	ΔAICc	w_i	Percentage max. w_i
1	ED+FIRE+RIVER+CUT	5	345.692	0.0000	0.1926	100.0
2	ED+RIVER+CUT	4	346.26	0.5678	0.1450	75.3
3	ED+RIVER+CUT+TRAP	5	346.907	1.2148	0.1049	54.5
4	ED+FIRE+RIVER+CUT+TRAP	6	347.008	1.3157	0.0998	51.8
5	ED+FIRE+RIVER+CUT+ROAD	6	347.732	2.0396	0.0695	36.1
6	ED+CUT	3	348.009	2.3168	0.0605	31.4
7	ED+RIVER+CUT+ROAD	5	348.294	2.6020	0.0524	27.2
8	ED+RIVER+CUT+TRAP+ROAD	6	348.947	3.2543	0.0378	19.6
9	ED+FIRE+RIVER+CUT+TRAP	7	349.053	3.3606	0.0359	18.6
10	ED+CUT+TRAP	4	349.506	3.8138	0.0286	14.9
11	ED+FIRE+RIVER+TRAP	5	349.639	3.9464	0.0268	13.9
12	ED+FIRE+CUT	4	349.817	4.1244	0.0245	12.7
13	ED+FIRE+RIVER	4	349.819	4.1272	0.0245	12.7

Akaike weights are interpreted as the relative plausibility of candidate models.
ED = edge density (m/ha); CUT = number of machete cuts; FIRE = distance from fire (km); RIVER = distance from river (km); ROAD = number of road crossings; TRAP = number of traps.

Table 16.4 Number of models that contained the parameter from the confidence set of 13 models, and the parameter estimates, odds ratios, and interpretation of the top model predicting bonobo site occupancy in the Maringa–Lopori–Wamba landscape, Democratic Republic of Congo.

	Number of models parameter occurs in	Parameter estimate	Odds[a] ratio	Interpretation[b] For each unit increase the odds of bonobos occupying the site are
(Intercept)	13	−1.812	0.176	
ED (m/ha)	13	−0.239	0.787	1.27 times lower
CUTS	11	−0.234	0.791	1.26 times lower
RIVER (km)	10	0.497	1.644	1.64 times greater
FIRE (km)	7	−0.054	0.947	1.06 times lower

[a] Back-transforming the parameter estimate of ED produced the odds ratio $e^{-0.239} = 0.787$; and because 0.787 is less than 1 the odds ratio indicates a negative relationship between ED and site occupancy.

[b] Therefore, sites were $(1/0.787) = 1.27$ times less likely to be occupied for each additional m/ha (or scaled to the approximate size of a bonobo home range: 1.27 times less likely to be occupied for each 2 km increase of edge in the surrounding 20 km^2).

ED = edge density (m/ha); CUTS = number of machete cuts; RIVER = distance from river (km); FIRE = distance from fire (km).

Back-transforming the parameter estimates of the top model produced the odds ratio $e^{-0.239} = 0.787$ for ED; and because 0.787 is less than 1, the odds ratio indicates a negative relationship between ED and site occupancy. Therefore, the odds of bonobos occupying a site were $(1/0.787) = 1.27$ times *lower* for each additional m/ha (or scaled to the approximate size of a bonobo's home range, 1.27 times *lower* for each 2 km increase of edge in the surrounding 20 km^2; Table 16.4). Similarly, sites were 1.26 times *less* likely to be occupied for each additional machete cut within a 120 m site. Sites were 1.64 times *more* likely to be occupied for each 1 km increase in distance away from a river. Parameter estimates for all other coefficients had values near 0 such that the relationship (positive or negative) with site occupancy was inconclusive.

Analysis of Environmental Factors

One-way ANOVAs showed differences in landscape-scale and local-scale variables among sample regions. Overlaying bonobo occupancy allowed us to tease out potential differences due to hunting versus habitat structure alone (Figure 16.3). For instance, Lomako North is within an officially designated protected area, with a low mean (±SD) ED of 1.74 (±1.6) m/ha, that was significantly farther from fires than the other regions (mean [±SD] fire distance 20.08 [±1.41] km, $F = 196.24$, d.f. 3, 538, $p < 0.0001$ for all comparisons). Despite these qualities, Lomako North had zero detected nests and very high numbers of machete cuts and traps, many of which still had animals captured in them. Lomako North and the logging area, Kee, did not differ significantly in mean

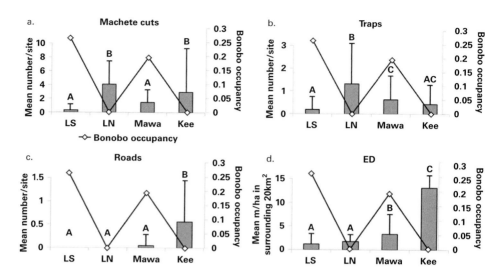

Figure 16.3 Bonobo site occupancy (◊), mean number of human signs, and mean edge density (ED) by region in the Maringa–Lopori–Wamba landscape, Democratic Republic of Congo. Region names abbreviated as follows: LS = Lomako South and LN = Lomako North.

number of machete cuts per site, and these two regions had significantly more machete cuts than either Lomako South or Mawa (Figure 16.3a). Lomako North and Kee, both of which had zero bonobo nests detected, had significantly more traps than Lomako South (Figure 16.3b). In fact, Lomako North had significantly more traps than all other regions. Lomako North and Lomako South were the most similar in terms of mean ED (Figure 16.3d); however, these two regions were the most dissimilar in mean number of traps per site ($F = 20.00$, d.f. 3, 538, $p < 0.0001$) (Figure 16.3b).

Comparing the bonobo-occupied regions of Lomako South and Mawa to the unoccupied logged region of Kee indicated that neither of the former regions differed significantly in mean number of traps from Kee. While not a significant difference, Mawa actually had a higher mean number (±SD) of traps per site than Kee, 0.63 (±1.06) and 0.44 (±0.86), respectively. The attribute that did differ between Kee and the two bonobo-occupied regions was ED (Figure 16.3d), with Kee exhibiting significantly greater ED ($F = 633.03$, d.f. 3, 538, $p < 0.0001$).

Interestingly, the two bonobo-occupied sites, Lomako South and Mawa, differed significantly in mean number (±SD) of traps per site, 0.19 (±1.32) and 0.63 (±1.06), respectively (Figure 16.3b). Lomako South exhibited the fewest traps of all the regions and the highest site occupancy by bonobos.

Discussion

We estimated overall bonobo density and site occupancy within the MCP around our transects, and quantified important influences of hunting pressure on bonobo occupancy from both remotely sensed and field-derived data. Our survey design included sampling large tracts of forest unoccupied by bonobos, thereby avoiding inflated estimates of occupancy. In addition, we demonstrated that line-transect bonobo nest surveys involve imperfect detection (including at 0 m distance from the transect where traditional distance methods assume $p = 1$) and adjusted estimates of nest counts accordingly. Regional comparisons of bonobo occupancy revealed the important negative effect of hunting in the absence of fragmentation and the important negative effect of fragmentation when hunting pressure is similar.

This study generally supported estimates of bonobo density generated by studies employing distance methods (Buckland et al. 2001). Using two different nest decomposition rates and nest production rates from the literature, we computed four estimates of detection-corrected bonobo density, D, ranging from 0.638–1.15 bonobos/km^2, all of which fell within the range of values reported in estimates for MLW (0.28 bonobos/km^2 to 1.4 weaned bonobos/km^2; Hashimoto & Furuichi 2001 and Eriksson 1999, respectively).

Just as it is important to sample areas of both low and high bonobo occupancy in order to avoid inflated or deflated density estimates, we believe it is also important to appropriately incorporate detection probability, p, in sample design to avoid biased estimates of occupancy, abundance, and density. Traditional distance-sampling techniques for estimating density incorporate functions for declining p based on increasing distance from the transect, but assume perfect detection at 0 m distance from the transect. We offer an alternate survey approach that addresses imperfect detection at 0 m from the transect. Our estimate of $\hat{p} = 0.74$ based on mark–recapture (sight–resight) analysis of nests provides a reference point for comparisons to future estimates by other teams of observers.

Comparisons between regions underscore the importance of both local-scale and landscape-scale predictors. Consider Lomako North, a region that contained no detected nests despite having apparent outward characteristics of favorable habitat, including low fragmentation and large distance from fire. Based on these landscape characteristics, we might have expected bonobo occupancy to be high, or at least detected. Instead, this area had zero detected nests and significantly higher numbers of traps than any other region. For Lomako North, the number of traps was the prevailing attribute correlated with the observed low occupancy by bonobos. These results substantiate previous reports that hunting is a major problem even in intact forest (Hart et al. 2008; Redford 1992; Wilkie et al. 2011), and can lead to the empty forest syndrome in which a forest appears otherwise suitable yet is depauperate of fauna.

Results from Lomako North demonstrate that bonobos inhabiting a nationally designated protected area are not necessarily effectively protected *per se*, and that extensive improvements are needed in law enforcement as well as in proactive efforts to provide alternatives for local peoples. For this site specifically, we recommend additional financial and capacity-building support for a guard station located on the Yokokala River in the Ekombe territory. We envision such a station employing and training locals as guards, thereby contributing to increased employment opportunities. We expect that regular patrols of the northeastern quadrant of LYFR, as well as inspections of boats commuting on the Yokokala River, would decrease hunting pressure in this portion of the reserve. We assume that since important drains on wildlife populations come from non-local commercial hunters (Fa & Brown 2009; Hart et al. 2008), finding and confiscating bushmeat derived from protected areas is an essential element to reducing the problem of poaching.

Because fragmentation can increase hunter access to forest areas, it can be difficult to demonstrate whether the negative effect of fragmentation on bonobo occupancy is due to habitat preference or confounded by hunting pressure. This study provides one example supporting forest fragmentation as a negative effect on bonobo occupancy under apparently low hunting pressure. In the case of the logged area compared to the two bonobo-occupied regions, the logged area differed significantly in fragmentation (ED) but not in mean number of traps. Because the logged area had similar hunting pressure, but high ED and zero nests detected, we concluded that fragmentation is important to consider for bonobo distributions even in the absence of hunting. Conversely, Lomako North and Lomako South did not differ significantly in ED, yet Lomako North had significantly more traps. Having detected zero nests in Lomako North, we concluded that hunting is an important variable to consider for bonobo distributions regardless of fragmentation. Essentially, both landscape- and local-level variables are important in shaping bonobo distributions, and both are important to consider in landscape management in order to protect this species.

A weakness in this study is that we do not have nest- or trap-occurrence data prior to the logging event, hence our study represents a snapshot in time. For example, based on our data alone, we cannot know whether Kee had higher bonobo occupancy prior to logging. If it did, we cannot discern from our single-season data whether Kee was hunted and drained of bonobos (perhaps during or immediately after logging), or if bonobos have extremely low occupancy there now because of the high ED itself. For this reason, we advocate long-term repeated studies in these and other regions in order to build datasets that can detect factors related both to empty forests as well as factors contributing to high bonobo occupancy. This study highlights the importance of both forest fragmentation and indirect measures of hunting pressure as factors relating to bonobo occupancy, and quantifies the effects of each of these variables on the probability of bonobo occupancy. Studies that employ GIS to incorporate both local-scale (GPS) and broad-scale (landscape) data into ecological analyses allow more in-depth understanding of causal mechanisms at play.

Acknowledgments

We thank R. K. Tshombe, J. Dupain, T. Senga, Pasteur C. W. Balongelwa, G. T. Muda, Principal Conservator Nayifilua, F. Botamba, the Congolese Institute for the Conservation of Nature (ICCN), the Congolese Ministry of Scientific Research, the Lomako–Yokokala Faunal Reserve, the African Wildlife Foundation, and the Wildlife Conservation Society (WCS). We warmly thank G. Reinartz, S. McLaughlin, P. Guislain, N. Etienne, T. Hart, T. Eppley, S. Iloko-Nsonge, S. Boongo, J. Lokuli-Lokuli, Chief

Administrator R. Mujinga, and L. Kembo. Funding for field research was provided by: the US Fish and Wildlife Service – Great Ape Conservation Fund (98210-8-G654); a research fellowship to J. Hickey from the Wildlife Conservation Society; and a small grant from Global Forest Science. Idea Wild provided essential field gear. J. Hickey held an American Fellowship from the American Association of University Women (AAUW) during a portion of this study.

References

Akaike, H. 1973. Information theory and an extension of the maximum likelihood principle. Pages 267–281 in *Second International Symposium on Information Theory*. B. N. Petrov and F. Csaki (Eds.). Akademiai Kiado, Budapest.

Anderson, D. R., Burnham, K. P., and Thompson, W. L. 2000. Null hypothesis testing: problems, prevalence, and an alternative. *Journal of Wildlife Management* **64**: 912–923.

Buckland, S. T., Anderson, D. R., Burnham, K. P., et al. 2001. *Introduction to Distance Sampling: Estimating Abundance of Biological Populations*. Oxford University Press, New York.

Davies, D. K., Ilavajhala, S., Wong, M. M., and Justice, C. O. 2009. Fire information for resource management system: archiving and distributing MODIS active fire data. *IEEE Transactions on Geoscience and Remote Sensing* **47**: 72–79.

Dupain, J. and Van Elsacker, L. 2001. The status of the bonobo in the Democratic Republic of Congo. Pages 57–74 in *All Apes Great and Small Volume 1: African Apes*. B. M. F. Galdikas, N. Erickson Briggs, L. K. Sheeran, G. L. Shapiro and J. Goodall (Eds.). Kluwer Academic/ Plenum Publishers, New York.

Dupain, J., Nackoney, J., Kibambe, J., Bokelo, D., and Williams, D. 2009. Maringa–Lopori– Wamba Landscape. Pages 329–338 in *The Forests of the Congo Basin: State of the Forest 2008*. C. de Wasseige, D. Devers, P. de Marcken, et al. (Eds.). Publications Office of the European Union, Luxembourg.

Eriksson, J. 1999. A survey of the forest and census of the bonobo (*Pan paniscus*) population between the Lomako and the Yekokora rivers in the Equateru province, D R Congo. MSc Thesis. University of Uppsala.

Fa, J. E. and Brown, D. 2009. Impacts of hunting on mammals of African tropical moist forests: a review and synthesis. *Mammal Review* **39**: 231–264.

Fruth, B., Benishay, J. M., Bila-Isia, I., et al. 2008. *Pan paniscus*. In *IUCN Red List of Threatened Species, Version 2010.4*. Available at: www.iucnredlist.org.

Hansen, M. C., Roy, D., Lindquist, E., et al. 2008. A method for integrating MODIS and Landsat data for systematic monitoring of forest cover and change in the Congo Basin. *Remote Sensing of Environment* **112**: 2495–2513.

Hart, J., Grossmann, F., Vosper, A., and Ilanga, J. 2008. Human hunting and its impact on bonobos in the Salonga National Park, D.R. Congo. Pages 245–271 in *The Bonobos Behavior, Ecology, and Conservation*. T. Furuichi and J. Thompson (Eds.). Springer, New York.

Hashimoto, C. and Furuichi, T. 2001. Current situation of bonobos in the Luo reserve, Equateur, Democratic Republic of Congo. Pages 83–93 in *All Apes Great and Small Volume 1: African Apes*. B. Galdikas, N. Briggs, L. Sheeran, G. Shapiro, and J. Goodall (Eds.). Kluwer Academic/ Plenum Press, New York.

Hickey, J. R. 2012. Modeling bonobo (*Pan paniscus*) occurrence in relation to bushmeat hunting, slash-and-burn agriculture, and timber harvest: harmonizing bonobo conservation with sustainable development. Dissertation. University of Georgia.

Hickey, J. R. and Sidle, J. G. 2006. *USDA Forest Service Office of International Programs Trip Report: Mission to Support Landscape Planning in the Maringa-Lopori-Wamba Landscape, Democratic Republic of Congo.* Available at http://carpe.umd.edu/Documents/2006/MLWTripReportFinal.pdf.

Hickey, J., Carroll, J. P., and Nibbelink, N. P. 2012. Applying landscape metrics to characterize potential habitat of bonobos (*Pan paniscus*) in the Maringa–Lopori–Wamba landscape, Democratic Republic of Congo. *International Journal of Primatology* **33**: 381–400.

Hickey, J. R., Nackoney, J., Nibbelink, N. P., et al. 2013. Human proximity and habitat fragmentation are key drivers of the rangewide bonobo distribution. *Biodiversity & Conservation* **23**: 3085–3104.

Hosmer, D. W. and Lemeshow, S. 1989. *Applied Logistic Regression.* Wiley, New York.

Huggins, R. M. 1989. On the statistical analysis of capture experiments. *Biometrika Trust* **76**: 133–140.

Hurvich, C. M. and Tsai, C. 1989. Regression and time series model selection in small samples. *Biometrika* **76**: 297–307.

Laurance, W. F., Goosem, M., and Laurance, G. W. 2009. Impacts of roads and linear clearings on tropical forests. *Trends in Ecology and Evolution* **24**: 659–669.

MacKenzie, D. I., Nichols, J. D., Royle, J. A., et al. 2006. *Occupancy Estimation and Modeling: Inferring Patterns and Dynamics of Species Occurrence.* Elsevier, Burlington, MA.

Millington, J. D. A., Walters, M. B., Matonis, M. S., and Liu, J. 2010. Effects of local and regional landscape characteristics on wildlife distribution across managed forests. *Forest Ecology and Management* **259**: 1102–1110.

Mohneke, M. and Fruth, B. 2008. Bonobo (*Pan paniscus*) density estimation in the SW-Salonga National Park, Democratic Republic of Congo: common methodology revisited. Pages 151–166 in *The Bonobos Behavior, Ecology, and Conservation.* T. Furuichi and J. Thompson. (Eds.). Springer, New York.

Mulavwa, M. N., Yangozene, K., Yamba-Yamba, M., et al. 2010. Nest groups of wild bonobos at Wamba: selection of vegetation and tree species and relationships between nest group size and party size. *American Journal of Primatology* **72**: 575–586.

Redford, K. H. 1992. The empty forest. *BioScience* **42**: 412–422.

Reinartz, G. E., Isia, I. B., Ngamankosi, M., and Wema, L. W. 2006. Effects of forest type and human presence on bonobo (*Pan paniscus*) density in the Salonga National Park. *International Journal of Primatology* **27**: 603–634.

Royall, R. M. 1997. *Statistical Evidence: A Likelihood Paradigm.* Chapman & Hall, New York.

USGS. 2000. HYDRO1k Elevation Derivative Database. Available at http://eros.usgs.gov/#/Find_Data/Products_and_Data_Available/gtopo30/hydro/africa.

Wilkie, D. S., Sidle, J. G., and Boundzanga, G. C. 1992. Mechanized logging, market hunting and a bank loan in Congo. *Conservation Biology* **6**: 570–580.

Wilkie, D. S., Bennett, E. L., Peres, C. A., and Cunningham, A. A. 2011. The empty forest revisited. *Annual New York Academy of Sciences* **1223**: 120–128.

Williams, B. K., Nichols, J. D., and Conroy, M. J. 2002. *Analysis and Management of Animal Populations.* Academic Press, San Diego, CA.

17 Landscape Ecology of Deforestation Processes and Lemur Biogeography in Madagascar

Travis S. Steffens and Shawn M. Lehman

Introduction

Although it is now axiomatic that global biodiversity is threatened and that species are going extinct at an accelerating rate (Ceballos et al. 2015), remarkably little is known about the distribution dynamics of many threatened taxa (Brook et al. 2006; Fahrig 2003; Grenouillet & Comte 2014; Guisan et al. 2013). This conservation crisis has spurred the development of new fields of applied research, such as conservation biogeography. Conservation biogeography applies novel conceptual approaches to classic biogeographic models to determine how environmental and anthropogenic changes influence biodiversity (Whittaker et al. 2005). At its core, conservation biogeography focuses on the theory and statistical analyses of spatial dynamics of taxa within a changing environment (Franklin 2010). These dynamic processes include critical questions on how plants and animals respond to changes in habitat availability and use, due to the effects of global warming, forest loss and fragmentation, and anthropogenic pressures (Malcolm et al. 2006; Riitters et al. 2000; Woodroffe & Ginsberg 1998).

A fundamental issue in conservation biogeography is determining how deforestation processes at differing scales influence the distribution of threatened plants and animals (Tscharntke et al. 2012). This is a fundamental issue because numerous theoretical and empirical studies have revealed that deforestation processes and their effects on plants and animals vary among, for example, patch, landscape, and regional levels (Debinski & Holt 2000; Saunders et al. 1991; Tscharntke et al. 2012; Turner 1989; Urban & Keitt 2001). A landscape can be defined as a set of spatially complex ecosystems, habitats, or land use types (Gustafson & Gardner 1996). Thus, a typical deforested landscape can be operationally defined as a set of forest fragments (i.e., patches) embedded in a habitat matrix that contains relatively fewer, lower-quality resources as well as varying patterns of plant species composition within and connectivity between fragments (Urban & Keitt 2001; Watling et al. 2011). The interrelated network of adjoining landscapes then forms a region, which also often involves broader macroclimatic and anthropogenic dynamics (Pickett & Cadenasso 1995). This notion of a low-quality but useable matrix separates conservation biogeography from classic biogeography, where most models implicitly assume an inhospitable matrix (Lomolino et al. 2005). For example, classic island biogeography is a theory on how immigration and extinction rates of organisms interact with the size and location of islands surrounded by a water matrix to affect biodiversity (MacArthur & Wilson 1967). In an oceanic-island model, the matrix is inhospitable, and therefore not the subject of resource exploitation by the organisms being studied. Conversely, revised models in conservation biogeography consider the matrix to vary in quality, and in some cases the available resources in the matrix actually attract organisms from their natural habitats, such as food resources in croplands bordering intact forests (Ricketts 2001; Watling et al. 2011). This matrix distinction is a relatively new idea that resulted from observations of functionally forest-dependent species that traversed the matrix between forest fragments (Kupfer et al. 2006). Although the matrix may serve as a supplemental resource or travel route for some animals, other species avoid matrix and edge habitats (Ewers & Didham 2008). Thus, studies of the landscape ecology of plants and animals in fragmented forest landscapes have been the subject of considerable research interest in recent years (Arroyo-Rodríguez et al. 2017; Porensky & Young 2013; Tscharntke et al. 2012).

Deforestation of fragmented landscapes has typically been investigated in protected areas, experimental plots, and along river courses and roads in lowland tropical regions (Tscharntke et al. 2012; Turner 1996). There is, however, less known about landscape conversion of forests in tropical montane regions (Kinnaird et al. 2003). When deforestation occurs due to anthropogenic activities, then the general model is for upslope deforestation in mountainous regions (Pounds et al. 1999; Tapia-Armijos et al. 2015). Put differently, forest habitats tend to be removed in a "bottom-up" process, due to anthropogenic activities first in more easily accessible, low-lying areas, such as fertile valleys, followed by deforestation at increasingly higher and less accessible elevations. Although rarely studied in the tropics, a reverse deforestation pattern, which can be termed "top-down," has been observed in low-lying areas in which remaining forests are exploited last along river bottoms, in valleys, or along scenic corridors (Barros & Uhl 1995). Determining which of these two deforestation patterns exist in anthropogenic landscapes is critical for conservation planning, reforestation efforts, and forest management. For example, upslope deforestation causes seasonal slides and rapid flows of debris and soil material into low-lying areas, greatly reducing arable land and preventing seedling growth and development (Veerle et al. 2003). Although high-slope areas above the deforestation and slide zones will experience fewer direct impacts, forests overlying laterite soils can develop erosional gullies, called *lavakas* in Madagascar, on steep terrains due to groundwater sapping (Cox et al. 2009). Conversely, "top-down" deforestation in high-slope areas can cause massive slides that deforest all lower-slope zones, catastrophically changing forest habitats and water chemistry (Veerle et al. 2003). Despite the importance of understanding the relationship between deforestation patterns and elevation for conservation planning, there have been few landscape-level comparisons of forest loss in lower versus higher elevations within a tropical region.

Another important biogeographic effect of deforestation in high elevations is an increased probability of upslope distribution displacement (UDD). Upslope distribution displacement results from varying abiotic and biotic processes, such as changes in ambient humidity and forest habitats, which lead to plants and animals increasing their median or maximal elevation ranges (Chen et al. 2009). As lower-elevation plants and animals move upslope, they can displace or even extirpate taxa specialized for high-elevation habitats. Climate change has been suggested to be the primary cause of these changes in abiotic and biotic responses in plants and animals (Feeley et al. 2011; Raxworthy et al. 2008). For example, Feeley et al. (2011) documented that increased ambient temperatures resulted in almost two-thirds of 250 tree genera shifting their mean distributions upslope by 2.5–3.5 meters per year over the course of only four years in the tropical Andes. Furthermore, this upslope movement resulted in an increased number of tree genera previously found only at lower elevations in most of the high-elevation plots. Although there has been increased research effort into studies of the effects of global warming on primate biology and biogeography (Dunham et al. 2008, 2011; Struebig et al. 2015), there is little information on how forests and primates respond to UDD at the landscape level in tropical regions.

The biota of Madagascar is ideally suited for studies of the landscape ecology of deforestation patterns. A biodiversity review indicated that almost 70 percent of the 12,000 plant species and all the primate species are found only on Madagascar (Goodman & Benstead 2005). Despite these remarkable levels of biodiversity and endemism, Madagascar lost 44 percent of its forest cover between 1953 and 2014 (Vieilledent et al. 2018), which has been converted to either agricultural fields or deforested grasslands (Allnutt et al. 2008; Green & Sussman 1990; Harper et al. 2007). Furthermore, there is marked regional variation in forest types across the island, due in part to a high-elevation central plateau that bisects the island into western and eastern regions (Goodman & Rakotondravony 2006). Western Madagascar is composed primarily of vast tracts of grasslands surrounding fragments of tropical dry forest, both of which slope down from the central plateau to the western shore (Ganzhorn et al. 1999; Waeber et al. 2015). Studies of deforestation patterns indicate that approximately 3 percent of the original western dry forest remains as of the year 2000 (Allnutt et al. 2008; Ganzhorn et al. 2001; Whitmore & Sayer 1992).

The eastern region lies atop a steep escarpment that maintains most of the remaining tropical forest (Du Puy & Moat 1996). Eastern humid forest can be further subdivided into lowland, montane, and cloud forest types based on elevation, abiotic factors, and plant community structure (Brown & Gurevitch 2004; Consiglio et al. 2006; Dumetz 1999). Lowland forest occurs from sea level to 800 m above sea level (asl) and represents a biologically rich ecosystem with high annual rainfall (*ca.* 200 cm/year) and a well-developed, continuous canopy. Montane forest (800–1300 m asl) is characterized by cooler ambient temperatures and a lower, less continuous forest canopy. Cloud forest occurs only above 1300 m asl and is characterized by a low canopy rarely reaching above 15 m and a ground layer dominated by terrestrial herbaceous vegetation. Although anthropogenic disturbance of remaining forests occurs across the island (Brown & Gurevitch 2004), a fundamental issue is to determine whether deforestation operates in a downslope pattern in the low-lying western dry forest versus an upslope pattern in the more altitudinally complex eastern humid forest. Understanding directionality of deforestation patterns is an important conservation issue because of the increasing rarity of forests at higher elevations, lack of data on elevational range limits for many lemur taxa, and model predictions of range reduction for many lemurs due to climate change (Brown & Yoder 2015).

Lemurs are widely recognized as one of the world's highest conservation priorities, due primarily to deforestation and hunting pressures (Schwitzer et al. 2014). Of the 111 extant lemur species recognized and monitored under the International Union for Conservation of Nature (IUCN) Red List in 2018, 95 percent ($N = 105$ species) are threatened with extinction. However, most publications, including the IUCN Red List maps, provide only flat, two-dimensional maps of lemur distribution patterns in fragmented landscapes, despite the fact that the underlying forest habitats may differ markedly due to elevation variations. Although clearly useful for demarcating conservation areas to maximize biodiversity, these maps fail to capture critical information on how lemur distribution varies along elevational gradients. For example, Goodman and Ganzhorn (2003, 2004) investigated elevational variation and lemur biogeography, concluding that the 24 lemur taxa included in their study showed a broader range of elevation midpoints compared to primates in other tropical montane regions. Lemur diversity peaked at 800–1200 m asl, whereas the species diversity of monkey and ape communities was highest at elevations below 400 m asl. These differences likely reflect the fact that Madagascar, in general, and the eastern humid forest in particular, maintain fewer tracts of lowland forest relative to the larger, more ecologically stochastic montane forest. A recent study of lemur biogeography across montane and cloud forests in southeast Madagascar found that lemur species diversity significantly declined with increasing elevation up to 1500 m asl (Lehman 2013). Above this elevational threshold, lemur community dynamics became stochastic and unpredictable, which might complicate predictive models on lemur responses to deforestation processes and climate change, particularly when these models are based on data collected primarily in low-elevation areas (i.e., relatively stable community dynamics). For example, recent geospatial models estimate range contractions and shifts of at least 600 km in length (north to south) for 12 species of lemurs in the mid-elevation eastern rainforests (Brown & Yoder 2015). Despite the critical importance of these predictions for setting conservation priorities, models such as this one assume species presence and static community dynamics in elevationally complex forest landscapes irrespective of species-specific elevational limits. Thus, there is a crucial need for further research into the distribution patterns of lemurs in fragmented forest landscapes that occur across elevationally complex forest areas.

In this chapter, we use landscape-level analyses of spatial data to test two hypotheses on deforestation patterns in Madagascar. Our first hypothesis is that in the western region, intact dry forest will be found at lower elevations than deforested areas across randomly sampled landscapes. This hypothesis implies a "top-down" deforestation process, such that remaining dry forest should be found in low-lying areas containing waterways important for rice culture and trees exploited by local people for firewood and building materials (e.g., along rivers and in valleys). Our second hypothesis is that in eastern humid forest, intact forest will exist at higher elevations than deforested areas across landscapes, indicating that deforestation is occurring in a "bottom-up" pattern. In this region, the steep slopes on which existing forest can be found result in deforestation by local people to create *tavy* (slash-and-burn agriculture) starting at the more accessible low-altitude areas (Green & Sussman 1990). Concomitantly, we sought to determine how deforestation patterns affected lemur habitat availability in the more altitudinally complex eastern humid forests.

Methods

To determine if western dry forest has undergone a "top-down" deforestation process and eastern humid forest a "bottom-up" deforestation process, we measured forest and non-forest elevation within randomly distributed landscapes of 80–100 km^2 each (40 in western dry forest and 40 in eastern humid forest). We randomly selected the location of the landscapes within two regions, western dry forest and eastern humid forest. The regions exclusively comprised a single forest type (dry or humid), and we excluded regions of overlap such as in the northern portion of the country, where dry forest and humid forest come into contact. In the west, we only included western dry deciduous forest and excluded areas containing spiny dry forest or western humid forest. In the east, we only included humid forest in the analysis. We created shapefiles of the randomly selected landscapes in each region in ArcGIS, resulting in 40 western and 40 eastern landscapes. To measure the amount of forest versus non-forest in each landscape we used the geoprocessing tool in ArcGIS to clip a Madagascar Vegetation Map shapefile created by the Royal Botanical Gardens, Kew (Moat & Smith 2007) by the 40 eastern and 40 western landscape shapefiles. We used the selection by attribute function to determine how much forest and non-forest was within each landscape. Using these selections, we created separate shapefiles for forest and non-forest within each of the 80 landscapes.

For our elevation data we used the WorldClim dataset (Hijmans et al. 2005). We clipped a 30-second (0.86 km^2) resolution raster elevation file by a shapefile of the Madagascar country boundary. We used the raster extract-by-polygon tool to determine the elevation of forest versus non-forest within each landscape shapefile. The elevation raster data was extracted from the WorldClim elevation raster based on polygon shapefiles of forest and non-forest for each landscape. This tool uses the center of the raster cell to determine whether the cell falls inside or outside of the polygon, regardless of the proportion of the cell that was actually forested. Consequently, the raster extraction between forest and non-forest shapefiles of the same landscape may result in some degree of overlap. The final output contains 1–131 cells of 0.86 km^2 size, each representing an elevation value (m asl).

In order to test our hypotheses and deal with issues of pseudo-replication, we first ran a logistic mixed effects model on forest presence/absence against elevation in eastern humid and then western dry forests. The elevation data came from raster cells within each of the 80 landscapes (total number of cells = east and west). We used Student's *t*-tests to determine any differences in the mean elevation of eastern forest versus eastern non-forest, eastern forest versus western forest, eastern non-forest versus western non-forest, and western forest versus western non-forest. With 40 or 100 cells randomly chosen from each of the 40 landscapes in the east and west (total sample size is 80 or 200), we took the mean elevation of all forest and non-forest cells in each landscape and ran a *t*-test on the landscape means for all 80 landscapes for eastern forest versus eastern non-forest, eastern forest versus western forest, eastern non-forest versus western non-forest, and western forest versus western non-forest.

We tested for spatial autocorrelation in our elevation data using both the cell data within landscapes and the aggregated data for each landscape to determine whether the spatial distribution of our selected landscapes influenced our results. We assessed spatial autocorrelation of elevation of forest and non-forest cells within and their mean among the 80 total landscapes using the Moran's *I* calculator in ArcMap. This statistic tests for patterns of spatial dispersion among cells between the randomly selected landscapes, which in theory should not be clustered in terms of elevations for forest and non-forested data. Statistical significance was determined using a Z-score dispersion. Spatial data are considered clustered when Moran's *I* test statistic approaches +1.0 and dispersed when the test statistic nears −1.0.

To determine how lemur species distributions are affected by elevational gradients of eastern humid forest, we selected 12 lemur species of 7 genera whose ranges were mainly confined to eastern humid forest: *Avahi laniger*, *Eulemur rubriventer*, *Hapalemur aureus*, *Hapalemur griseus*, *Hapalemur simus*, *Indri indri*, *Propithecus candidus*, *Propithecus diadema*, *Propithecus edwardsi*, *Phaner furcifer*, *Varecia rubra*, and *Varecia v. variegata*. Although many other lemur species have been described in the last 10 years, these designations are based primarily on genetics data collected from only a few individuals in limited or even single localities, and thus lack critical information on geographic ranges (Tattersall & Species 2007). Geographic ranges for each of the 12 lemur species we used were digitized in ArcMap based on jpeg images from Mittermeier et al. (2006) and saved as shapefiles. Based on these shapefiles, forest versus non-forest elevations were extracted using the same methods as for the 80 landscapes above.

Using habitat characteristics described by Lehman (2013), we selected three different elevation categories that represent ecological shifts in vegetation, including lowland forest (0–800 m), montane forest (801–1300 m), and cloud forest (1300+ m). We then randomly sampled 40, 100, and 500 forest and non-forest cells from each of the 12 lemur species ranges and ran a *t*-test on the mean elevation of forest versus non-forest in each range. Finally, we calculated the proportion of each species range that was in the three elevation categories (0–800 m, 801–1300 m, and 1300+ m) using all the cells within each species range.

Results

We found that occurrence of forest in the east and west are significantly related to elevation (Table 17.1). Moreover, eastern humid forests occurred at significantly higher elevations than eastern non-forest using a subsample of 200 cells, and we found the same trend using a subsample of 80 cells (Table 17.2), supporting the hypothesis of a "bottom-up" deforestation process in the east. Eastern humid forest occurred at

Table 17.1 Logistic mixed model results for elevation effects on forest/non-forest occurrence in all landscapes combined.

Model	Variables	Estimate	Standard error	Z-value	p-value
East	Intercept	−8.99	0.81	−11.15	<0.01
	Elevation	0.011	0.0006	18.85	<0.01
West	Intercept	−2.84	0.26	−9.92	<0.01
	Elevation	0.005	0.0007	7.73	<0.01
All	Intercept	−5.51	0.44	−12.48	<0.01
	Elevation	0.009	0.0004	20.18	<0.01

Table 17.2 Descriptive and comparative statistics of forest and non-forest cells subsampled from landscapes in the east and west.

Landscapes	Area 1 (km^2)	Mean 1	N	Area 2 (km^2)	Mean 2	N	t-statistic	p-value
Eastern forest versus	34.40	904.33	40	34.40	720.50	40	1.92	0.06
eastern non-forest	86.00	828.64	100	86.00	638.81	100	3.14	<0.01
Eastern forest versus	34.40	799.45	40	34.40	773.00	40	8.77	<0.01
western forest	86.00	828.40	100	86.00	179.67	100	14.14	<0.01
Eastern non-forest versus	34.40	653.30	40	34.40	157.90	40	6.57	<0.01
western Non-forest	86.00	561.94	100	86.00	185.47	100	8.56	<0.01
Western forest versus	34.40	165.95	40	34.40	197.90	40	−1.04	0.30
western non-forest	86.00	154.50	100	86.00	198.29	100	−1.85	0.07

significantly higher elevations than western dry forest, and the same pattern holds when comparing non-forested areas in eastern and western Madagascar (Table 17.2). Therefore, eastern forests occur at higher elevations than eastern non-forests and eastern forests and non-forests are higher than western forests and non-forests, respectively. However, there was no significant difference in elevation between western dry forest and western non-forest using a subsample of 80 cells, but there is a non-significant trend that western forests occurred at lower elevations than western non-forests using a subsample of 200 cells (Table 17.2).

Contrary to our non-aggregated data analysis, when aggregated by landscape, we found there was no significant difference in mean elevation between eastern humid forest and eastern non-forest, which does not support the "bottom-up" deforestation process in the east (Table 17.3). Similar to the non-aggregated data analysis, we found eastern humid forest occurred at significantly higher elevation than western dry forest, and eastern non-forest existed at significantly higher elevation than western non-forest (Table 17.3). In the western region, dry forest was found at approximately the same elevation as non-forest (Table 17.3).

When looking at the aggregated data, we found that there was no spatial autocorrelation among eastern (Moran's $I = 0.05$; $p = 0.10$) or western (Moran's $I = 0.04$; $p = 0.07$) forest landscapes. However, there were low levels of significant spatial autocorrelation

Table 17.3 Descriptive and comparative statistics of forest and non-forest cells aggregated within landscapes.

Landscapes	Area 1 (km²)	Mean 1	N	Area 2 (km²)	Mean 2	N	t-statistic	p-value
Eastern forest versus eastern non-forest	4000	742.13	40	4000	628.08	40	1.22	0.23
Eastern forest versus western forest	4000	742.13	40	4000	185.18	40	7.73	<0.01
Eastern non-forest versus western non-forest	4000	628.08	40	4000	171.51	40	6.62	<0.01
Western forest versus western non-forest	4000	185.18	40	4000	171.51	40	0.39	0.70

among eastern (Moran's $I = -0.02$; $p = 0.05$) or western (Moran's $I = 0.07$; $p = 0.004$) non-forest landscapes. There was no spatial autocorrelation among cells within western dry deciduous forest landscapes (Moran's $I = -0.05$; $p = 0.80$) or western non-forest landscapes (Moran's $I = -0.03$; $p = 0.96$), confirming that cells within western plots were randomly distributed with respect to elevation. However, there was significant, positive spatial autocorrelation among cells in eastern humid forest landscapes (Moran's $I = 0.38$; $p < 0.01$) and eastern non-forest landscapes (Moran's $I = 0.32$; $p < 0.01$). The positive spatial autocorrelation in the cell data in the east versus in the west reflects the fact that the underlying topography of the east is more mountainous and thus spatially clustered with respect to elevation. When aggregated, the spatial autocorrelation between eastern and western non-forest may reflect non-random deforestation processes.

For the species range tests conducted using subsamples of cells, there were significant differences in the elevation of eastern humid forest and eastern non-forest within each species range (Table 17.4). Eastern humid forest was at higher elevations than eastern non-forest in all species ranges accept *Hapalemur griseus*, where eastern humid forest (mean = 573.69 m) was significantly lower than non-forest (mean = 841.05 m). When looking at only 40 forest and 40 non-forest cells within each species range, we found the same pattern as for 100 forest and 100 non-forest cells, except for within two species ranges, *V. v. variagata* and *P. edwardsi*, which had non-significant results at this sample size (Table 17.4). There were considerable interspecific differences in the proportion of the three elevational habitats exploited by each species across the 40 landscapes (Figure 17.1). The ranges of five lemur species (*H. aureus*, *H. griseus*, *P. candidus*, *P. furcifer*, and *V. rubra*) were predominantly lowland forest. Montane forest accounted for the majority of the species' range for seven species (*A. laniger*, *E. rubriventer*, *H. simus*, *I. indri*, *P. diadema*, *P. edwardsi*, and *V. v. variegata*). No lemur species had ranges dominated by cloud forest, and only *E. rubriventer* had an appreciable, but not dominant, portion of its forested range in this spatially rare habitat. We found that forest within *H. aureus*, *H. griseus*, *P. furcifer*, and *V. rubra* ranges occurred near or below the mean elevation of non-forest in eastern Madagascar. Having ranges with forest with lower mean elevation than the mean elevation of non-forest in eastern Madagascar suggests that these four species are at greater risk from deforestation processes (Figure 17.2).

Table 17.4 Descriptive and comparative statistics of the mean elevation of forest and non-forest within the randomly sampled geographic ranges of 12 lemur species.

Species	Mean elevation forest	N	Mean elevation non-forest	N	t-statistic	p-value
Avahi laniger	849.05	40	535.55	40	4.02	<0.01
	782.22	100	601.50	100	3.51	<0.01
	827.33	500	785.65	500	13.45	<0.01
Eulemur rubriventer	1181.28	40	839.60	40	4.29	<0.01
	1113.68	100	909.77	100	3.99	<0.01
	1097.69	500	908.64	500	9.03	<0.01
Hapalemur aureus	552.58	40	460.13	40	3.92	<0.01
	557.80	100	464.56	100	6.01	<0.01
	N/A	N/A	N/A	N/A	N/A	N/A
Hapalemur griseus	523.20	40	785.65	40	−3.05	<0.01
	573.69	100	841.05	100	−5.28	<0.01
	553.73	500	851.85	500	−13.54	<0.01
Hapalemur simus	769.25	40	345.75	40	6.06	<0.01
	746.32	100	445.47	100	6.51	<0.01
	N/A	N/A	N/A	N/A	N/A	N/A
Indri indri	967.10	40	673.28	40	5.38	<0.01
	962.75	100	641.57	100	8.55	<0.01
	897.76	500	652.93	500	14.64	<0.01
Propithecus candidus	785.05	40	451.05	40	4.71	<0.01
	730.89	100	491.95	100	6.03	<0.01
	771.22	500	470.00	500	15.17	<0.01
Propithecus diadema	891.75	40	523.53	40	6.69	<0.01
	844.21	100	570.41	100	7.40	<0.01
	899.04	500	610.58	500	18.09	<0.01
Propithecus edwardsi	1092.75	40	988.23	40	1.68	0.09
	1142.96	100	905.05	100	5.79	<0.01
	11136.85	500	889.77	500	11.48	<0.01
Phaner furcifer	384.73	40	163.13	40	3.80	<0.01
	405.17	100	135.35	100	8.45	<0.01
	410.90	500	172.01	500	15.01	<0.01
Varecia rubra	537.38	40	314	40	3.29	<0.01
	565.67	100	363.63	100	4.56	<0.01
	524.27	500	324.36	500	10.68	<0.01
Varecia v. variegata	842.25	40	874.10	40	-0.54	0.59
	856.48	100	790.38	100	1.54	<0.01
	893.81	500	827.38	500	3.51	<0.01

Discussion

The main objectives of our study were to determine if there was "top-down" deforestation occurring in western dry forests and "bottom-up" deforestation in eastern humid forests, and how these processes may influence lemur species ranges in eastern Madagascar. There was no significant difference and thus no statistical support for the

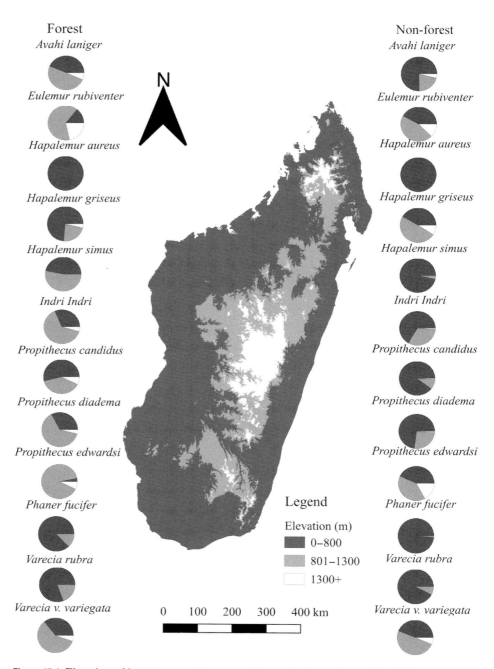

Figure 17.1 Elevation of lemur geographic ranges (forested and non-forested) in Madagascar.

"top-down" hypothesis in western dry forests. Although traveling through western Madagascar leads to inferences that remaining forest is relegated to drainage lines, valleys, and other low-lying areas (Lehman & Steffens, pers. obs.), there is little actual difference in elevation between low-lying areas containing forest and the higher areas of

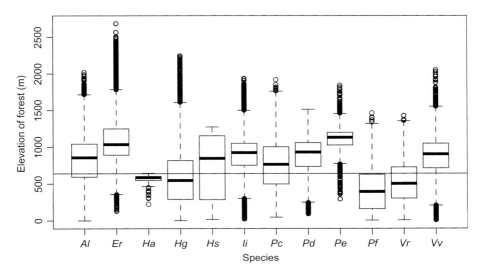

Figure 17.2 Elevation of forest within lemur species ranges in eastern humid forest. Al = *Avahi laniger*; Er = *Eulemur rubiventer*; Ha = *Hapalemur aureus*; Hg = *Hapalemur griseus*; Ii = *Indri indi*; Pc = *Propithecus candidus*; Pd = *Propithecus diadema*; Pe = *Propithecus edwardsi*; Pf = *Phaner furcifer*; Vr = *Varecia rubra*; Vv = *Varecia v. variegate*. Horizontal line is the mean elevation.

non-forest at the landscape level. Consequently, we would not expect lemur species in the west to suffer negatively from "top-down" deforestation processes at the landscape and regional scale.

Although our landscape analysis of western deforestation processes did not support our "top-down" hypothesis, deforestation is ongoing in this region. Thus, the question arises as to how this process is operating in western dry forests (Elmqvist et al. 2007). Attempts to answer this question have not been done using landscape-level data; rather, most research has employed GIS analyses of satellite data to investigate temporal patterns of deforestation in what amounts to a single landscape or as part of an island-wide assessment (Whitehurst et al. 2009). Zinner et al. (2014) analyzed deforestation rates from 1963 to 2010 in the Menabe region, which encompasses approximately 120 km^2 of western dry forest (i.e., slightly larger than one of the study landscapes we sampled). Deforestation rates were highest in 2000–2010 and most intense in edge habitats bordering this region. Deforestation was suggested to result predominantly from local people clearing forest for (in decreasing order) zebu (*Bos indicus*) pastures, agriculture, and selective logging. Gorenflo et al. (2011) conducted a more geographic study of broader regional deforestation patterns from 1990 to 2000 in Madagascar. Across the entire western dry forest region, they found numerous statistically significant but low-impact determinants of deforestation, such as accessibility by trails or roads, elevation, protected status of the land, and income inequality. Differences in sampling resolutions and selection of independent variables between these two studies result in largely disparate conservation recommendations, with the within-region study focusing on anthropogenic effects and the across-region study listing various geographic and economic indicators of deforestation rates. We suggest, therefore, that the ultimate question of what is driving deforestation of western dry forests will result from a comprehensive landscape study incorporating geographic, ecological, economic, and anthropological data into a GIS.

Our results demonstrate some support for the "bottom-up" pattern of deforestation at a local scale but not at a regional scale in eastern humid forests. Specifically, deforestation was most prevalent in areas that once contained lowland forest (0–800 m asl), but less of an issue for montane forest (801–1300 m asl) and cloud forest (1300+ m asl) throughout eastern humid forests. However, the same results were not found when we aggregated data at a more regional scale, which likely reflected positive spatial autocorrelation. Positive spatial autocorrelation occurred because non-forested areas tended to be clustered, and forested areas are clustered together. In other words, deforestation has occurred in a non-random spatial pattern due to localized, anthropogenic deforestation of small areas in eastern humid forests (i.e., perforated forest). Forest perforation is a problematic issue in GIS and remote sensing because small, isolated perforation areas can be "joined," resulting in a large deforested area due to natural and anthropogenic activities (e.g., cyclonic wind damage, erosion, and slash-and-burn agriculture). These localized patterns of deforestation then tend to be swamped in analyses of satellite imagery by edge effects and fragmentation at larger spatial scales (Riitters et al. 2000). Moreover, additive edge effects in forested areas between perforations can cause complex changes in forest composition even in the absence of anthropogenic deforestation, further complicating analyses of remote imaging data (Malcolm et al. 2017; Vogt et al. 2007). For example, edge effects between perforated areas can overlap, causing dynamic changes in forest structure and plant reproductive dynamics (Fernandez et al. 2002). Thus, our models indicate that there may be complex patterns of forest dynamics in eastern humid forests, with a strong likelihood that deforested areas will continue to expand into remaining forest, but that the spatial patterns inherent in these processes require more complex, thematic accuracy in image processing and analyses.

Issues with spatial autocorrelation may explain, in part, why statistical models used in earlier studies have succeeded more in explaining where, how, and at what rate deforestation has occurred, but not necessarily why this process has occurred in eastern humid forests (Agarwal et al. 2005; Green & Sussman 1990; Harper et al. 2007). For example, Harper et al. (2007) compared aerial photographs from the 1950s to Landsat images in the later part of the twentieth century to estimate deforestation rates and levels of forest fragmentation in Madagascar. Despite a reduction in deforestation rates from 1.7 percent per year during 1970–1990 to 0.8 percent per year in 1990–2000, there was a reduced number of fragments larger than 5000 km^2 and a major increase in edge effects in the remaining fragments over the same time period in eastern humid forests. Forest loss may have slowed in that time period, but that may result from less interior forest being available for anthropogenic disturbance in the eastern region.

Deforestation processes have been overly simplified in some conservation studies by invoking only slash-and-burn agriculture as the ultimate driver of forest loss and fragmentation in eastern humid forests (Seddon et al. 2000; Smith et al. 1997). Rather, slash-and-burn agriculture should be seen as a proximate component of deforestation, with equal emphasis placed on understanding how ecology, culture, and politics relate to the ultimate factors driving deforestation in eastern Madagascar (Styger et al. 2007). For example, Agarwal et al. (2005) used spatial hierarchical and Bayesian models to understand how four geographic and economic factors, such as slope and human population density, related to deforestation patterns in eastern Madagascar. Their novel approach highlighted the strong role of human population pressure on deforestation processes. However, few researchers have determined how unique habitats that exist at differing elevational levels are related to human density and thus to altered forest landscapes. One of the methodological issues with this approach is that human density cannot be extrapolated from satellite imagery, necessitating longitudinal direct census work of isolated communities in remote forested regions, many of which are new settlements and thus lacking longitudinal demographic data (Brinkmann et al. 2014).

Our final objective was to determine how deforestation patterns affected lemur habitat availability in the more elevationally complex eastern humid forests. Based on our sampling methods, five lemur species have mostly lowland forests within their range and are therefore at increased risk of extirpations due to further habitat loss (*H. aureus*, *H. griseus*, *P. candidus*, *P. furcifer*, and *V. rubra*). Put differently, these five species prefer lowland forests (0–800 m asl), which are likely to be deforested first in eastern humid forests. Moreover, of the five lemur species that our analyses indicate have mostly lowland forests within their range, two (*H. aureus* and *V. rubra*) are endangered and *P. candidus* is critically endangered. Previous research into biogeographic patterns of lemur diversity along elevational gradients highlights a major concern with population viability in eastern humid forests. For example, Lehman (2013) studied lemur assemblage patterns along elevational gradients at 16 sites in southeastern Madagascar. Although lemur species diversity was highest at sites within the elevation range of 810–1019 m asl, none of the lemur taxa listed as endangered or critically endangered were found at sites above 1500 m asl. Therefore, there is a very real possibility for a wave of lemur extirpations or even extinctions if deforestation processes move into higher-elevation habitats throughout eastern Madagascar.

An implication of climate change for the movement of forests upslope is the increased potential for UDD of lemur species in eastern humid forest. The concomitant effects of UDD on lemur species is unknown, although potential effects include increased competition resulting in the potential loss of high-elevation specialists (Pounds et al. 1999; Raxworthy et al. 2008). The "bottom-up" deforestation processes we found at some spatial levels in the east can result in habitat fragmentation following classical biogeographic patterns such as Island Biogeography Theory (MacArthur & Wilson 1967). The resulting pattern of habitat, where forests are relegated to the highest-elevation areas, can create habitat islands on mountain peaks separated by a matrix of non-habitat, analogous to oceanic islands. Depending on the size of the remaining habitat, the distance between habitat fragments, and the nature of the matrix between fragments, the implications for lemur species would include reduced dispersal success and decreased species richness (Diamond 1975; MacArthur & Wilson 1967). "Bottom-up" deforestation processes may influence lemur species that are sensitive to changes in abiotic features, such as temperature, that are dependent on factors such as elevation. For example, some lemur species, such as *Cheirogaleus* spp., require particular temperatures to maintain a healthy metabolic state during periods of torpor (Dausmann et al. 2005). Dausmann et al. (2005) suggest that *Cheirogaleus medius* (occurring in western dry forests) require some periods in which temperature exceeds 30°C, otherwise they will need to be wakened to maintain a healthy metabolic state. Blanco and Rahalinarivo (2010) confirmed that the eastern *Cheirogaleus crossleyi* required more arousals to maintain homeostasis in areas where temperatures do not exceed 30°C than did *Cheirogeleus medius* in the west. However, they also suggested that due to the lower temperatures in eastern high-elevation forest, *Cheirogaleus crossleyi* can actually enter deep hibernation. Thus, "bottom-up" deforestation may influence hibernating primates by forcing them to undergo increased arousals at higher elevations than at lower elevations due to increasingly higher ambient temperatures at higher elevations.

Although there has been increased use of GIS and associated technologies in primatology, few studies have employed these tools at the landscape level in primates in general, and lemurs in particular. Conversely, the vast majority of research on primates has been conducted only at the patch level. Nonetheless, recent theoretical research indicates that many of the main issues in conservation biogeography are best studied using a landscape approach (Pickett & Cadenasso 1995; Turner 1989; Urban & Keitt 2001). For example, Tscharntke et al. (2012) have outlined eight hypotheses on how landscape processes affect biodiversity patterns and ecological processes at varying biogeographic scales experiencing anthropogenic disturbance. Testing these hypotheses using GIS at the landscape scale will answer critical conservation biogeography questions on how primates and their forested habitats respond to global warming, forest loss and fragmentation, and anthropogenic pressures.

Acknowledgments

We thank Christopher Shaffer, Francine Dolins, Jena Hickey, Nathan Nibbelink, and Leila Porter for their kind invitation to participate in this edited volume. We also thank the reviewers for their insightful comments that improved our chapter. We also thank the Repoblikani'i Madagasikara Ministère de l'Environment et des Forêts Madagascar and University of Antananarivo for permission to conduct our research in Madagascar. For their support, advice, and hospitality, we thank Patricia Wright, Benjamin Andriamahaja, Jonah Ratsimbazafy, the amazing staff at ICTE/MICET, Fanja Raoelinirina, and the staff at La Maison du Pyla. We are grateful to the many men and women who have assisted us with our research in Madagascar, particularly Andry Rajaonson, Mamy Razafitsalama, Rindra Rakotoarivony, and Keriann McGoogan. Our research is supported by the University of Toronto and a Discovery Grant from the Natural Sciences and Engineering Research Council of Canada.

References

Agarwal, D. K., Silander, J. A., Gelfand, A. E., Dewar, R. E., and Mickelson, J. G. 2005. Tropical deforestation in Madagascar: next term analysis using hierarchical, spatially explicit, Bayesian regression models. *Ecological Modelling* **185**(1): 105–131.

Allnutt, T., Ferrier, S., Manion, G., et al. 2008. A method for quantifying biodiversity loss and its application to a 50-year record of deforestation across Madagascar. *Conservation Letters* **1**(4): 173–181.

Arroyo-Rodríguez, V., Melo, F. P., Martínez-Ramos, M., et al. 2017. Multiple successional pathways in human-modified tropical landscapes: new insights from forest succession, forest fragmentation and landscape ecology research. *Biological Reviews* **92**(1): 326–340.

Barros, A. C. and Uhl, C. 1995. Logging along the Amazon River and estuary: patterns, problems and potential. *Forest Ecology and Management* **77**(1): 87–105.

Blanco, M. B. and Rahalinarivo, V. 2010. First direct evidence of hibernation in an eastern dwarf lemur species (*Cheirogaleus crossleyi*) from the high-altitude forest of Tsinjoarivo, central-eastern Madagascar. *Naturwissenschaften* **97**(10): 945–950.

Brinkmann, K., Noromiarilanto, F., Ratovonamana, R. Y., and Buerkert, A. 2014. Deforestation processes in south-western Madagascar over the past 40 years: what can we learn from settlement characteristics? *Agriculture, Ecosystems & Environment* **195**: 231–243.

Brook, B. W., Traill, L. W., and Bradshaw, C. J. A. 2006. Minimum viable population sizes and global extinction risk are unrelated. *Ecology Letters* **9**(4): 375–382.

Brown, K. A. and Gurevitch, J. 2004. Long-term impacts of logging on forest diversity in Madagascar. *PNAS* **101**(16): 6045–6049.

Brown, J. L. and Yoder, A. D. 2015. Shifting ranges and conservation challenges for lemurs in the face of climate change. *Ecology and Evolution* **5**(6): 1131–1142.

Ceballos, G., Ehrlich, P. R., Barnosky, A. D., et al. 2015. Accelerated modern human-induced species losses: entering the sixth mass extinction. *Science Advances* **1**(5): e1400253.

Chen, I.-C., Shiu, H.-J., Benedick, S., et al. 2009. Elevation increases in moth assemblages over 42 years on a tropical mountain. *Proceedings of the National Academy of Sciences* **106**(5): 1479–1483.

Consiglio, T., Schatz, G. E., McPherson, G., et al. 2006. Deforestation and plant diversity of Madagascar's littoral forests. *Conservation Biology* **20**(6): 1799–1803.

Cox, R., Bierman, P., Jungers, M. C., and Rakotondrazafy, A. M. 2009. Erosion rates and sediment sources in Madagascar inferred from ^{10}Be analysis of lavaka, slope, and river sediment. *Journal of Geology* **117**(4): 363–376.

Dausmann, K. H., Glos, J., Ganzhorn, J. U., and Heldmaier, G. 2005. Hibernation in the tropics: lessons from a primate. *Journal of Comparative Physiology* **B175**(3): 147–155.

Debinski, D. M. and Holt, R. D. 2000. A survey and overview of habitat fragmentation experiments. *Conservation Biology* **14**(2): 342–355.

Diamond, J. M. 1975. Assembly of species communities. *Ecology and Evolution of Communities* **342**: 444.

Du Puy, D. J., and Moat, J. 1996. A refined classification of the primary vegetation of Madagascar based on the underlying geology: using GIS to map its distribution and to assess its conservation status. Pages 205–218 in *Proceedings of the International Symposium on the Biogeography of Madagascar*. W. R. Lourenço (Ed.). Editions de l'ORSTOM, Paris.

Dumetz, N. 1999. High plant diversity of lowland rainforest vestiges in eastern Madagascar. *Biodiversity and Conservation* **8**(2): 273–315.

Dunham, A. E., Erhart, E. M., Overdorff, D. J., and Wright, P. C. 2008. Evaluating effects of deforestation, hunting, and El Niño events on a threatened lemur. *Biological Conservation* **141**(1): 287–297.

Dunham, A. E., Erhart, E. M., and Wright, P. C. 2011. Global climate cycles and cyclones: consequences for rainfall patterns and lemur reproduction in southeastern Madagascar. *Global Change Biology* **17**(1): 219–227.

Elmqvist, T., Pyykönen, M., Tengö, M., et al. 2007. Patterns of loss and regeneration of tropical dry forest in Madagascar: the social institutional context. *PLoS ONE* **2**(5): e402.

Ewers, R. M. and Didham, R. K. 2008. Pervasive impact of large-scale edge effects on a beetle community. *PNAS* **105**(14): 5426–5429.

Fahrig, L. 2003. Effects of habitat fragmentation on biodiversity. *Annual Review of Ecology, Evolution, and Systematics* **34**(1): 487–515.

Feeley, K. J., Silman, M. R., Bush, M. B., et al. 2011. Upslope migration of Andean trees. *Journal of Biogeography* **38**(4): 783–791.

Fernandez, C., Acosta, F. J., Abella, G., Lopez, F., and Diaz, M. 2002. Complex edge effect fields as additive processes in patches of ecological systems. *Ecological Modeling* **149**: 273–283.

Franklin, J. 2010. Moving beyond static species distribution models in support of conservation biogeography. *Diversity and Distributions* **16**(3): 321–330.

Ganzhorn, J. U., Fietz, J., Rakotovao, E., Schwab, D., and Zinner, D. 1999. Lemurs and the regeneration of dry deciduous forest in Madagascar. *Conservation Biology* **13**(4): 794–804.

Ganzhorn, J. U., Lowry, P. P., Schatz, G. E., and Sommer, S. 2001. The biodiversity of Madagascar: one of the world's hottest hotspots on its way out. *Oryx* **35**(4): 346–348.

Goodman, S. M. and Benstead, J. 2005. Updated estimates of biotic diversity and endemism for Madagascar. *Oryx* **39**(1): 73–77.

Goodman, S. M. and Ganzhorn, J. 2003. Biogeography of lemurs in the humid forests of Madagascar: the role of elevational distribution and rivers. *Journal of Biogeography* **31**(1): 47–56.

Goodman, S. M. and Ganzhorn, J. 2004. Elevational ranges of lemurs in the humid forests of Madagascar. *International Journal of Primatology* **25**(2): 331–350.

Goodman, S. M. and Rakotondravony, D. 2006. The effects of forest fragmentation and isolation on insectivorous small mammals (Lipotyphla) on the Central High Plateau of Madagascar. *Journal of Zoology* **250**(2): 193–200.

Gorenflo, L. J., Corson, C., Chomitz, K. M., et al. 2011. Exploring the association between people and deforestation in Madagascar. Pages 197–221 in *Human Population* Volume **1650**. R. P. Cincotta and L. J. Gorenflo (Eds.). Springer, Berlin.

Green, G. M. and Sussman, R. W. 1990. Deforestation history of the eastern rain forests of Madagascar from satellite images. *Science* **248**(4952): 212–215.

Grenouillet, G. and Comte, L. 2014. Illuminating geographical patterns in species' range shifts. *Global Change Biology* **20**(10): 3080–3091.

Guisan, A., Tingley, R., Baumgartner, J. B., et al. 2013. Predicting species distributions for conservation decisions. *Ecology Letters* **16**(12): 1424–1435.

Gustafson, E. J. and Gardner, R. H. 1996. The effect of landscape heterogeneity on the probability of patch colonization. *Ecology* **77**(1): 94–107.

Harper, G. J., Steininger, M. K., Tucker, C. J., Juhn, D., and Hawkins, F. 2007. Fifty years of deforestation and forest fragmentation in Madagascar. *Environmental Conservation* **34**(4): 325–333.

Hijmans, R. J., Cameron, S. E., Parra, J. L., Jones, P. G. and Jarvis, A. 2005. Very high resolution interpolated climate surfaces for global land areas. *International Journal of Climatology* **25**(15): 1965–1978.

Kinnaird, M. F., Sanderson, E. W., O'Brien, T. G., Wibisono, H. T., and Woolmer, G. 2003. Deforestation trends in a tropical landscape and implications for endangered large mammals. *Conservation Biology* **17**(1): 245–257.

Kupfer, J. A., Malanson, G. P., and Franklin, S. B. 2006. Not seeing the ocean for the islands: the mediating influence of matrix-based processes on forest fragmentation effects. *Global Ecology and Biogeography* **15**(1): 8–20.

Lehman, S. M. 2013. Effects of altitude on the conservation biogeography of lemurs in south east Madagascar. Pages 1–20 in *High Altitude Primates*. S. Gursky, A. Krzton, and N. Grows (Eds.). Springer, New York.

Lomolino, M. V., Riddle, B. R., and Brown, J. H. 2005. *Biogeography*, 3rd edition. Sinauer Associates, Sunderland, MA.

MacArthur, R. H. and Wilson, E. O. 1967. *The Theory of Island Biogeography*. Princeton University Press, Princeton, NJ.

Malcolm, J. R., Liu, C., Neilson, R. P., Hansen, L., and Hannah, L. 2006. Global warming and extinctions of endemic species from biodiversity hotspots. *Conservation Biology* **20**(2): 538–548.

Malcolm, J. R., Valenta, K., and Lehman, S. M. 2017. Edge effects in tropical dry forests of Madagascar: additivity or synergy? *Landscape Ecology* **32**(2): 327–341.

Mittermeier, R. A., Konstant, W. R., Hawkins, F., et al. 2006. *Lemurs of Madagascar*, 2nd edition. Conservation International, Washington, DC.

Moat, J. and Smith, P. P. 2007. *Atlas of the Vegetation of Madagascar*. Royal Botanic Gardens, Kew, London.

Pickett, S. and Cadenasso, M. 1995. Landscape ecology: spatial heterogeneity in ecological systems. *Science* **269**(5222): 331–334.

Porensky, L. M. and Young, T. P. 2013. Edge-effect interactions in fragmented and patchy landscapes. *Conservation Biology* **27**(3): 509–519.

Pounds, J. A., Fogden, M. P. L., and Campbell, J. H. 1999. Biological response to climate change on a tropical mountain. *Nature* **398**(6728): 611–615.

Raxworthy, C., Pearson, R., Rabibisoa, N., et al. 2008. Extinction vulnerability of tropical montane endemism from warming and upslope displacement: a preliminary appraisal for the highest massif in Madagascar. *Global Change Biology* **14**(8): 1703–1720.

Ricketts, T. 2001. The matrix matters: effective isolation in fragmented landscapes. *American Society of Naturalists* **135**(1): 212–222.

Riitters, K., Wickham, J., O'Neill, R., Jones, B., and Smith, E. 2000. Global-scale patterns of forest fragmentation. *Conservation Ecology* **4**(2): 3.

Saunders, D. A., Hobbs, R. J., and Margules, C. R. 1991. Biological consequences of ecosystem fragmentation: a review. *Conservation Biology* **5**(1): 18–32.

Schwitzer, C., Mittermeier, R. A., Johnson, S. E., et al. 2014. Averting lemur extinctions amid Madagascar's political crisis. *Science* **343**(6173): 842–843.

Seddon, N., Butchart, S., Tobias, J., et al. 2000. Conservation issues and priorities in the Mikea Forest of south-west Madagascar. *Oryx* **34**(4): 287–304.

Smith, A. P., Horning, N., and Moore, D. 1997. Regional biodiversity planning and lemur conservation with GIS in Western Madagascar. *Conservation Biology* **11**: 498–512.

Struebig, M. J., Fischer, M., Gaveau, D. L., et al. 2015. Anticipated climate and land-cover changes reveal refuge areas for Borneo's orangutans. *Global Change Biology* **21**(8): 2891–2904.

Styger, E., Rakotondramasy, H. M., Pfeffer, M. J., Fernandes, E., and Bates, D. M. 2007. Influence of slash-and-burn farming practices on fallow succession and land degradation in the rainforest region of Madagascar. *Agriculture, Ecosystems & Environment* **119**(3): 257–269.

Tapia-Armijos, M. F., Homeier, J., Espinosa, C. I., Leuschner, C., and de la Cruz, M. 2015. Deforestation and forest fragmentation in South Ecuador since the 1970s: losing a hotspot of biodiversity. *PLoS ONE* **10**(9): e0133701.

Tattersall, I. and Species, W. 2007. Madagascar's lemurs: cryptic diversity or taxonomic inflation? *Evolutionary Anthropology* **16**: 12–23.

Tscharntke, T., Tylianakis, J. M., Rand, T. A., et al. 2012. Landscape moderation of biodiversity patterns and processes: eight hypotheses. *Biological Reviews* **87**(3): 661–685.

Turner, I. M. 1996. Species loss in fragments of tropical rain forest: a review of the evidence. *Journal of Applied Ecology* **33**(2): 200–209.

Turner, M. G. 1989. Landscape ecology: the effect of pattern on process. *Annual Review of Ecology and Systematics* **20**: 171–197.

Urban, D. and Keitt, T. 2001. Landscape connectivity: a graph-theoretic perspective. *Ecology* **82**(5): 1205–1218.

Veerle, V., Michiel, V., Gerard, G., et al. 2003. Linking hydrological, infinite slope stability and land-use change models through GIS for assessing the impact of deforestation on slope stability in high Andean watersheds. *Geomorphology* **52**(3–4): 299–315.

Vieilledent, G., Grinand, C., Rakotomalala, F. A., et al. 2018. Combining global tree cover loss data with historical national forest cover maps to look at six decades of deforestation and forest fragmentation in Madagascar. *Biological Conservation* **222**: 189–197.

Vogt, P., Riitters, K. H., Estreguil, C., et al. 2007. Mapping spatial patterns with morphological image processing. *Landscape Ecology* **22**(2): 171–177.

Waeber, P. O., Wilmé, L., Ramamonjisoa, B., et al. 2015. Dry forests in Madagascar: neglected and under pressure. *International Forestry Review* **17**(2): 127–148.

Watling, J. I., Nowakowski, A. J., Donnelly, M. A., and Orrock, J. L. 2011. Meta-analysis reveals the importance of matrix composition for animals in fragmented habitat. *Global Ecology and Biogeography* **20**(2): 209–217.

Whitehurst, A. S., Sexton, J. O., and Dollar, L. 2009. Land cover change in western Madagascar's dry deciduous forests: a comparison of forest changes in and around Kirindy Mite National Park. *Oryx* **43**(2): 275–283.

Whitmore, T. C. and Sayer, J. A. 1992. *Tropical Deforestation and Species Extinction.* Chapman & Hall, New York.

Whittaker, R. J., Araujo, M. B., Paul, J., et al. 2005. Conservation biogeography: assessment and prospect. *Diversity and Distributions* **11**(1): 3–23.

Woodroffe, R. and Ginsberg, J. R. 1998. Edge effects and the extinction of populations inside protected areas. *Science* **280**(5372): 2126–2128.

Zinner, D., Wygoda, C., Razafimanantsoa, L., et al. 2014. Analysis of deforestation patterns in the central Menabe, Madagascar, between 1973 and 2010. *Regional Environmental Change* **14**: 1–10.

18 Quantitative Methods for Primate Biogeography and Macroecology

Jason M. Kamilar and Lydia Beaudrot

Introduction

Technological advances have brought a wealth of new data and analytical approaches to biogeography and macroecology (Graham et al. 2004; Kamilar & Beaudrot 2013). Many of these advances are centered on spatially explicit data analyses enabled by global positioning systems (GPS) and geographic information systems (GIS). In particular, geographic coordinates of species locales can be obtained through field surveys using GPS devices, triangulation with radio-telemetry transmitters, as well as through museum specimens with reliable collection locations (Graham et al. 2004). Although most studies using geographic data from point occurrence have focused on extant primates, there is increasing interest in the distribution of extinct species (Anemone et al. 2011). Known occurrence data of fossil taxa can be similarly acquired with GPS devices upon discovery or via specific and unambiguous descriptions of collection-site locations. In contrast, primate distributions were traditionally defined via range maps based on known or hypothesized occurrences (e.g., Wolfheim 1983). Range maps assume that a species is found throughout its range, when in reality we know that they are replete with gaps because not all terrain is suitable habitat for occupancy. Known localities from geographic point-location data obtained with GPS and GIS technology better represent species distributions and allow for more rigorous spatial and ecological modeling.

In addition to establishing reliably known species occurrence distributions, GPS coordinate data allow scientists to describe the abiotic and biotic environments in which the species are found. A wide variety of geo-referenced environmental variables are publicly available and can be used to understand how species distributions and traits vary across space and time. Some of the most commonly used variables estimate climate, vegetation, soil, and anthropogenic characteristics (Batjes 2009; Carroll et al. 2009; Hijmans et al. 2005). Combining species occurrence data with environmental datasets allows researchers to understand the range of climate variation that species can inhabit in the wild, connect climate and habitat characteristics to species' presences and absences as well as co-occurrences (beta diversity, i.e., turnover in the species found in communities based on geographic distance), and investigate anthropogenic effects on primate distributions and abundance. These data can be analyzed using commonly implemented methods (e.g., principal component analysis, Mantel tests), as well as more specialized analytical approaches such as ecological niche models and phylogenetic comparative methods. The specific data and analytical approach selected are dependent on the research questions of interest.

In this chapter, we discuss multiple types of spatial data and analyses that can be used to answer questions regarding the biogeography and macroecology of primates using spatially explicit data on (1) primate species occurrence only and (2) primate species occurrence integrated with other data (e.g., climate, trait, phylogenetic data). This research has important implications for understanding the ecology and evolution of extant and extinct primate species distributions as well as biological diversity more generally. Many of these data and methods can be applied to conservation questions and to investigate how primates fit within the broader community of sympatric vertebrates.

Methods Using Spatially Explicit Data on Species Occurrences Only Quantifying Species and Community Distributions

We begin by describing several methods that quantify patterns in the community composition of species at multiple spatial locations over large spatial extents. Quantifying biogeographic patterns with these methods contributes to our understanding of why communities contain the species that they do and how community composition varies across space.

Species Co-occurrence Patterns

In 1975, Jared Diamond first proposed a set of assembly rules that he argued could be examined to evaluate whether communities at different sites are composed of random assemblages of organisms or if interactions between species result in predictable patterns of co-occurring species across sites. Diamond's assembly rules are evaluated by comparing the presence and absence of species at a number of different spatial locations; the rules test to what extent interactions between species at a site influence community assembly (Diamond 1975). A number of quantitative co-occurrence patterns have been investigated, in particular guild proportionality (Wilson 1989), Fox's assembly rule for favored states (Fox 1987), nestedness (Atmar & Patterson 1993), and body size structure (Hutchinson 1959). Most notably, Diamond's rules fueled widespread investigation of checkerboard distributions, which have been studied across many taxonomic groups and ecological systems using a null model approach (Gotelli & McCabe 2002; Kamilar & Ledogar 2011). A checkerboard distribution refers to the alternating presence of ecologically similar species on islands or other habitat patches, which is argued to be the result of competitive exclusion. In a maximally checkerboarded distribution, two species never co-occur because competition has resulted in the exclusion of the inferior competitor, whereas in a minimally checkerboarded distribution, two species consistently co-occur because they are able to co-exist and thus competitive exclusion has not occurred.

After many years of debate about how to construct appropriate null models with which to examine assembly rules (Strong et al. 1984), Stone and Roberts (1990) developed the "C-score," or checkerboard score, which quantifies the "checkerboarded-ness" of a community and is still in widespread use today. The C-score is calculated as $CU_{ij} = (r_i - S_{ij})(r_j - S_{ij})$ where r_i and r_j are the total number of occurrences across sites of species i and j and S is the number of sites where the two species co-occur. The C-score is then calculated as the mean of the CU values for all species pairs in a matrix. The C-score calculated from the observed data is then compared to a distribution of C-scores calculated based on a null model. If the observed matrix has a significantly higher C-score than matrices under the null model, then the community exhibits significant ecological structure and the investigator can conclude that the community is not a random assemblage of organisms but that interactions between species may have led to the observed significant structure in the data. We note causality cannot be inferred from such observational results in the absence of experimental data.

The R package EcoSimR (Gotelli et al. 2015) can be used to test for significantly checkerboarded distributions as well as a number of other co-occurrence patterns. EcoSimR has functions that permute the community presence–absence matrix to create a null distribution. A variety of options are available for choices about whether to maintain the row and column totals and guidelines for best practices are provided.

Because the analyses of species presence–absence data currently available through EcoSimR are unable to differentiate between multiple drivers of co-occurrence patterns, including segregated, aggregated, or nested distributions (Ulrich & Gotelli 2012), an increasing number of studies have focused on co-occurrence patterns at the species-pair level (Cardillo & Meijaard 2010; Sanderson et al. 2009; Sfenthourakis et al. 2005). Rather than summing and averaging the values for all species pairs in a community, a species-pair approach restricts the level of analysis to two species and evaluates the checkerboardedness of each pair in comparison to a null distribution for that pair. The species-pair approach therefore provides a better approximation of the potential role of negative (e.g., competition) or positive interactions (e.g., mutualism, facilitation) between species because it identifies significantly high or low checkerboard scores for each species pair, respectively.

At least two programs, PAIRS (Ulrich 2008) and COOC (Sfenthourakis et al. 2004), have been developed for species-pair analyses. We note that PAIRS is limited to a maximum of 150 species and COOC uses only 5000 simulations, which can result in high type I error rates when species richness is high (Fayle & Manica 2010). For analyses of more than 150 species, we recommend adapting functions from the vegan package in R (Oksanen et al. 2013). For example R code, see Beaudrot et al. (2013).

Community Nestedness

Analysis of the level of nestedness in a set of communities provides information on the amount of hierarchical structure across the spatial extent of the sites. Like species analyses of co-occurrence patterns, nestedness requires data on the presence and absence of species at a number of different spatial locations. A set of communities

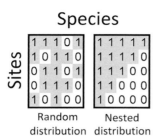

Figure 18.1 Two datasets representing random and nested structures. Species are represented by columns and study sites are represented by rows. Cells are the presence (1) or absence (0) of a species at a particular site.

may exhibit significant nestedness if small communities contain species that are a nested subset of increasingly larger communities (Atmar & Patterson 1993; Guimarães & Guimarães 2006; Patterson 1987) (Figure 18.1). A common explanation for this pattern is the differential dispersal ability of species. In addition, extirpations that occur in an ordered fashion may also result in a nested set of communities. In particular, species could exhibit varying levels of extinction risk, such that some species can only survive in a few communities, while other species can persist in many or all communities. Finally, if communities are found in a variety of habitat types, then the habitats themselves may exhibit some form of hierarchical structure, e.g., a simple habitat containing few ecological niches and species may be found within a complex habitat that contains diverse ecological niches and many species.

Nested patterns of community structure in primates have received limited attention. Ganzhorn (1998) found that primate communities in eastern and western Madagascar exhibited a significant nested pattern. In addition, he found that geographic distance was the best predictor of community composition in western communities. Therefore, he argued that the differential dispersal of species in this region resulted in nested assemblages. Later work by Lehman (2006) found that primate communities in Guyana exhibited a significantly nested pattern. Finally, a novel application of this method was recently applied to cultural assemblages of humans, chimpanzees, and orangutans. Kamilar and Atkinson (2013) found that human and chimpanzee cultural repertoires exhibited significant nested patterns, yet this was not present for orangutans. This may suggest that nested cultural repertoires were present in the last common ancestor of humans and chimpanzees. Orangutans may not exhibit this pattern due to their less gregarious social organization or their widespread extinction across much of southeast Asia during the last several thousand years.

Software packages available to calculate nestedness are varied and have improved over time. For example, Nestcalc (Atmar & Patterson 1993) was developed to quantify the nestedness of communities in the early 1990s. More recently the ANINHADO package was developed (Almeida-Neto et al. 2007, 2008). This method offers some improvements over the original technique, as it is less sensitive to the size of the community matrix (species by site dataset) as well as matrix fill (i.e., the number of "presences" in the data matrix).

Identifying Biogeographic Regions

Cluster Analysis

When the spatial extent of the study area is large and a research question requires identifying regions or patches with similar species composition in the study area, cluster analysis is a useful tool. Cluster analysis generates spatial clusters based on locations that have similar species composition (or other attributes designated as the variable of interest) (Fortin & Dale 2005).

While the goal of cluster analysis is to attain objectivity in the grouping of biological communities, it is nevertheless both a science and an art that requires a number of subjective decisions based on the question of interest. Thus, as Krebs (1999) describes, the central paradox of clustering methods is that they are objective in their calculations, but only after subjective decisions have been made. When carefully implemented, however, cluster analyses provide a useful tool for identifying which species are important for structuring biological communities and for identifying similar groups in the absence of a-priori assumptions. Cluster analysis can be used to identify groups at any spatial scale, ranging from local to global.

Once the objectives of a study have been identified, input data are needed in the form of a species by site matrix where species are the columns and sites are the rows. The matrix can be populated with either presence–absence or abundance data. The next step is to select a dissimilarity index to calculate the distance between sites. When a dissimilarity index is applied to the species by site matrix, it produces a matrix of values representing the distances for each pairwise site composition comparison. For example, a distance matrix will contain one distance measure for each comparison between site A and B, A and C, A and D, etc. Careful attention must be paid to the appropriate selection of the distance matrix based on the question of interest because different metrics have different properties. Some indices can be applied to presence–absence data, whereas others can be used for abundance data. There is an extensive literature available elsewhere on the properties of similarity indices (Baselga et al. 2007; Carvalho et al. 2012; Koleff et al. 2003; Magurran 1988; Tuomisto 2010a, 2010b). The majority of clustering methods then identify clusters using the distance values from the dissimilarity index rather than the raw input data matrix.

Clustering methods include both non-hierarchical classifications and hierarchical classifications. Non-hierarchical techniques produce a single partition that maximizes similarity within groups and are most useful for summarizing differences. Common non-hierarchical methods include K-means partitioning, in which the number of clusters is identified a priori, as well as ordination techniques (Legendre and Legendre 1998).

Hierarchical classification cluster methods produce a series of hierarchical partitions that represent the relationships between samples. These can take the form of either divisive or agglomerative methods. Divisive hierarchical methods begin with a single group and make divisions repeatedly from the "top down," whereas agglomerative hierarchical algorithms work from the "bottom up" by starting with an individual sample and searching for the most similar samples to make a group (Legendre and Legendre 1998). There are a number of different agglomerative linkage methods for

Tree diagram for nine cases
Unweighted pair-group average
Euclidean distances

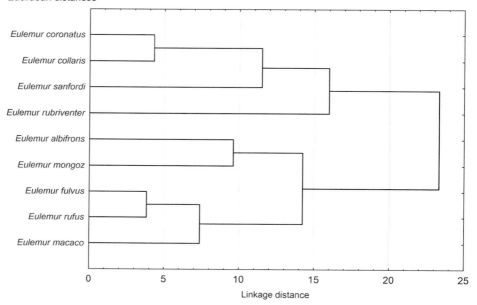

Figure 18.2 A hierarchical UPGMA cluster analysis based on Euclidian distances of social group size and composition and dietary data. The dendrogram illustrates population-level spatial variation in *Eulemur* behavior and ecology. Data obtained from Ossi and Kamilar (2006).

identifying clusters. Kreft and Jetz (2010) provide a quantitative examination of nine hierarchical agglomerative clustering methods and conclude that the unweighted pair-group method using arithmetic averages (UPGMA) outperforms other commonly used techniques. The UPGMA clustering method calculates the average distance between two clusters as the distance between each cluster point and all other points in a different cluster (Figure 18.2). A new cluster is formed from the two clusters with the lowest average distance (Fielding 2007).

A longstanding weakness of cluster methods has been that the methods produce a result but without any measures about uncertainty surrounding the result (Fielding 2007). New methods, however, have been developed to quantify uncertainty via bootstrapping. For example, the "recluster" package in R calculates the relative strength of clusters by shuffling the row order in the input data matrix, creating new cluster dendrogram trees from the resampled data and then quantifying the percentage of times that each of the cluster nodes are recovered (Dapporto et al. 2013). The output "consensus tree" provides information on the cluster strength and therefore can be used to draw stronger conclusions about the grouping of biological communities.

Clusters, once identified, provide the foundation for further quantitative analysis of ecological and evolutionary patterns at a range of spatial scales. For example,

Carstensen et al. (2013) highlight how cluster analysis can be used to identify broad biogeographic regions that can then function as regional species pools for further analysis of macroecological patterns. Beaudrot et al. (2014) use this method to identify regions in which to study the relative influences of environmental filtering and dispersal limitation on primate community composition throughout sub-Saharan Africa. Cluster analysis resulted in nine biogeographic regions. Partial Mantel tests within each region revealed that dispersal limitation was a stronger determinant of primate communities, but that the strength of the dispersal limitation was strongest near the equator and declined with increasing absolute latitude. Thus, identification of biologically meaningful samples is central to understanding the factors that influence species distributions and community composition.

Methods Incorporating Spatially Explicit Covariate Data

In this section we describe a number of methods that use geographically referenced data on species occurrences and covariates, such as environmental data (e.g., temperature, rainfall, soil conditions, vegetation, etc.). Like the species occurrences, the covariate data are from explicit spatial locations (e.g., x, y coordinates obtained by GPS or GIS), which are used in the analyses.

Quantifying Species Niche Space

Ordination
Ordination methods, such as principal components analysis (PCA) and principal coordinates analysis (PCoA) (Manly 2005; McGarigal et al. 2000; Tabachnick & Fidell 1989), have a long tradition in ecological research. These methods reduce the dimensionality of a complex dataset, thereby allowing the information contained in numerous variables to be examined in fewer (often two or three) dimensions. The mathematical mechanics of these methods are based on the idea that most variables co-vary to some extent. A dataset with correlated variables contains redundant information that can be removed through ordination analysis. New variables can be created that are a combination of the original variables, yet are independent from each other and explain most of the variation in the original dataset. These new variables can be plotted visually, enabling two or three axes to represent a more complex multidimensional space (Figure 18.3). Reducing complex datasets to a few important variables is useful because it makes data interpretation easier and can reveal important biological patterns that may be more difficult to detect otherwise. In addition, many statistical techniques may be more difficult to implement and/or interpret if variables are highly correlated. Macroecological datasets often contain correlated variables (e.g., annual rainfall and rain seasonality, temperature and elevation), and therefore are commonly analyzed using ordination techniques (Kamilar & Muldoon 2010; Peres 1997).

GIS-based climate data are now widely available and enable researchers to easily collect a large amount of abiotic environmental information for many locations. For

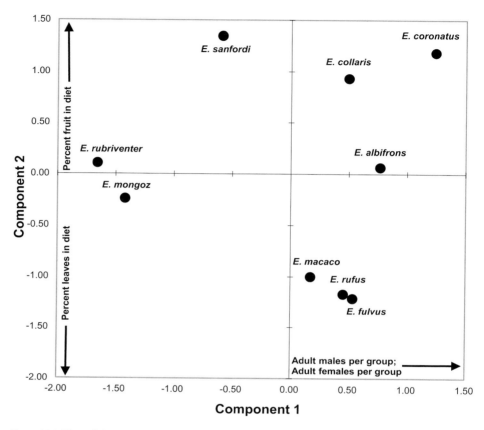

Figure 18.3 Plot of the first two principal components analyses illustrating spatial variation in social group size and composition and diet data across *Eulemur* populations. Data obtained from Ossi and Kamilar (2006).

instance, the WorldClim database (Hijmans et al. 2005) contains 19 bioclimatic variables that quantify various aspects of temperature and rainfall variation for nearly every terrestrial location in the world. Not surprisingly, many of these climate variables are highly correlated, and therefore contain redundant information. Principal component analysis can be used to summarize all or a subset of WorldClim's bioclimatic variables into only a few axes. Several studies have used this approach to quantify the multidimensional climatic niche space occupied by species. This research involves using the known locations for multiple species and extracting climate data for each occurrence. In one study, Kamilar and Muldoon (2010) used a PCA to quantify the climatic niche space of Malagasy primates. Their dataset comprised more than 1000 known localities from 43 taxa, with nine abiotic variables for each site. The abiotic variables quantified various aspects of rainfall and temperature variation, as well as elevation. The two most important components produced by the PCA resulted in a rainfall niche axis and a temperature niche axis. The authors then used these results to calculate the mean climatic niche space of each species and examined this variation in a phylogenetic context. Asking the question of whether closely related species tend to exhibit similar climatic niche spaces, their results showed that this was not the case. In fact, closely related species usually exhibited distinct climatic niches and distantly related species often converged on the similar climatic niche spaces.

Other studies have used PCA to quantify the niche space of primate communities based on the biological traits of their species. For instance, Fleagle and Reed (1996) used a PCA to quantify 10 traits (including those related to body mass, diet, and positional behavior) for all species living in eight communities distributed across each of the four major regions inhabited by primates. They found that communities displayed substantial overlap in their ecospace within continents. In contrast, there was a noticeable difference in the ecospace exhibited by communities on different continents. Their results largely reflect differences in the historical biogeography of primates and the subsequent endemism and associated biological diversity of species within each continent.

It is important to note that although PCA is designed to deal with collinearity among variables, some authors suggest that including several highly correlated variables in a PCA may produce spurious results (McGarigal et al. 2000). Therefore, they recommend removing highly correlated variables before analysis.

Principal component analysis and other ordination techniques (e.g., PCoA, factor analysis, canonical correspondence analysis, multidimensional scaling, etc.) are commonly found in many comprehensive statistical packages (e.g., SPSS, Statistica, SAS) and can also be implemented in R using vegan (Oksanen et al. 2013) and other packages.

Ecological Niche Models

Predicting the potential distribution of species using ecological niche modeling (i.e., species distribution modeling) has been an increasingly popular goal in ecology, though this is only beginning to take hold in primate-focused research. Typically, scientists predict the potential distribution of a species based on known species occurrences and the climatic and other abiotic factors (e.g., soil pH, topography) that a species is known to experience. However, other factors, such as competition with other species occupying similar niches, may also influence species distributions. Importantly, recent research in niche modeling is beginning to incorporate the effects of biotic interactions (Kissling et al. 2012). At a basic level, niche modeling analyses can provide insights into the particular environmental factors that are associated with known species occurrences. This approach has been used by Boubli and de Lima (2009) and Vidal-García and Serio-Silva (2011) for Neotropical primates and Thorn et al. (2009) for lorises. In addition, niche models can be used to predict shifts in species ranges under different climate change scenarios (Junker et al. 2012; Thorne et al. 2013), which could have important conservation implications. Finally, some researchers have used niche models as evidence for delineating species boundaries and modifying taxonomic schemes. For example, Blair et al. (2013) examined the ecological divergence and species diversity of *Eulemur*. A similar study by Kamilar et al. (2016) focused on *Microcebus* taxa (Figure 18.4).

(a)   (b)

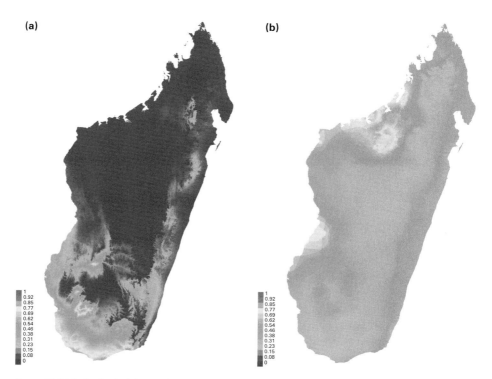

Figure 18.4 Ecological niche models of (a) *Microcebus griseorufus* and (b) *Microcebus murinus* based on temperature and rainfall variables. Warmer colors indicate a higher probability of the species being present. Cooler colors indicate areas of low probability of being present.
Adapted from Kamilar et al. (2016), © Cambridge University Press 2016, with permission.
(A black and white version of this figure will appear in some formats. For the color version, please refer to the plate section.)

Several methods exist to perform ecological niche modeling, including generalized additive models, boosted regression trees, GARP (genetic algorithm for rule set prediction), and MaxEnt (maximum entropy) (Elith & Graham 2009). One of the most commonly used and best-performing methods for niche modeling is MaxEnt (Elith et al. 2006; Phillips & Dudík 2008; Phillips et al. 2006). One important benefit of this method is that it can predict species distributions based on known occurrences, and without data about known absences. Therefore, the challenges associated with being certain about locations where species do not exist is less important compared to other methods. Further details about niche modeling are presented in Chapter 15 and by Merow et al. (2013).

Predicting Spatial Variation in Community Structure and Biological Traits

Spatially explicit data can be used to examine geographic variation in biological traits (at the intraspecific and interspecific levels) and community structure. In particular, researchers are often interested in how geographic distance, environmental factors, and genetics influence geographic variation in biological traits and community-level characteristics. A wide variety of methods are available to address these topics.

Mantel Tests

One of the most commonly implemented statistical methods is the Mantel test (Mantel 1967). The traditional version of a Mantel test uses one independent and one dependent variable, with the variables arranged as either a dissimilarity/distance or similarity matrix. This arrangement is particularly useful for spatial data since one matrix usually represents geographic distance among sites or populations. Statistical significance is obtained via a randomization approach. Therefore, this test is useful for data that do not satisfy the assumptions of parametric statistics. Mantel tests can also be modified to include more than one predictor matrix (Smouse et al. 1986). The partial Mantel test allows for two or more predictor matrices, which accounts for covariation among predictors, and can therefore reveal the independent effect of each predictor on the dependent variable. Several studies have used this latter approach to examine various questions in biological anthropology and primatology. However, we should note that some recent papers have discussed several weaknesses of the method (Guillot & Rousset 2013).

Several studies have used a similar approach to examine nonhuman primate diversity. Ossi and Kamilar (2006) used partial Mantel tests to investigate the relative importance of phylogeny and local environmental factors on the behavior and ecology of *Eulemur* populations. They found that phylogeny best predicted variation in social organization, while controlling for local environmental factors. In contrast, local environment best predicted activity budgets, independent of phylogeny. At a broader spatial and taxonomic scale, Beaudrot and Marshall (2011) used partial Mantel tests to tease apart the relative importance of geographic distance and environmental factors for predicting the species composition of primate communities. They found that geographic distance was consistently a stronger predictor of community structure in Africa, South America, and Borneo, but that environmental distance was more important for primate communities within Madagascar.

In addition to using data, hypotheses themselves can be represented as a distance matrix and used in Mantel tests. Sokal et al. (1997) used this approach to test alternative hypotheses related to the dispersal of early humans throughout Africa and Eurasia. Matrices were designed to represent different ideas about human dispersal, including hypotheses of regional continuity, out of Africa, and single origin out of southwest Asia. These design matrices were correlated to a matrix based on cranial traits of fossil hominin taxa. Interestingly, the single origin out of southwest Asia hypothesis of humans best predicted the cranial morphology matrix.

Several options are available to conduct Mantel tests. Some of the most popular software packages that can perform both Mantel and partial Mantel tests are the standalone spatial statistics program PASSAGE (Rosenberg 2001) or the vegan (Oksanen et al. 2013) and ecodist (Goslee & Urban 2013) packages in R.

Canonical Correspondence Analysis

Another method used to predict the species composition of communities is canonical correspondence analysis (CCA). This method is both an ordination technique and a predictive analysis, utilizing a set of independent variables to predict a set of dependent variables while accounting for covariation within and between datasets. Therefore, it is possible to account for spatial effects by including geographic variables as predictors in the model. Traditionally this method was limited because it requires a relatively large dataset that conforms to parametric statistical assumptions. More recent versions can use a randomization approach to generate p-values, allowing for a relaxation of these assumptions (ter Braak & Smilauer 2002). The results of CCA can be visually displayed as a biplot (Gower & Hand 1995) that displays the predictor variables as vectors, with the length of each vector being proportional to its importance in predicting the dependent variables. The dependent variables are displayed as points in multidimensional space, similar to a PCA plot. Dependent variables are best predicted by independent variables whose vectors are in the same plane (Figure 18.5).

Some authors argue that CCA is more powerful than Mantel tests because the raw data are used in CCA, as opposed to distance matrices (Legendre 2000; Legendre et al. 2005). Canonical correspondence analysis also has the advantage of being able to discern the specific independent variables responsible for explaining variation in the dependent variables. For example, using partial Mantel tests can reveal a negative association between geographic distance and community similarity. Using a CCA, geographic distance is represented as two variables: latitude and longitude. Therefore, using this approach could show that latitude in particular was the most important geographic variable, and that it best explained variation in the presence/absence of a particular set of species within the communities.

Canonical correspondence analysis was used by Kamilar (2009) to predict continental variation in the species composition of primate communities from geographic (latitude and longitude) and climate variables. He found that both latitude and longitude were significant predictors of community composition in Africa, Asia, and the Neotropics, whereas only longitude was a significant predictor for Malagasy communities. In all cases, these geographic effects were independent of climate. In addition, several climatic variables were significant predictors of primate community structure in all regions except Asia.

This method was also applied to a putative cultural dataset of chimpanzees. Numerous cultural traits have been identified for chimpanzees, but the number and frequency of traits varies across sites (Whiten et al. 2001). Kamilar and Marshack (2012) used CCA to investigate the relative importance of geographic distance and local ecological factors for explaining across-site cultural variation. They found that sites in close proximity to each other exhibited similar cultural repertoires, independent of ecological effects. This similarity declined as the distance between sites increased.

For many years, the only available program that conducted a CCA using randomization was CANOCO (ter Braak & Smilauer 2002). With the increasing popularity of R in recent years, other options are available, including the vegan package (Oksanen et al. 2013). To our knowledge, this analysis is not currently available in SPSS.

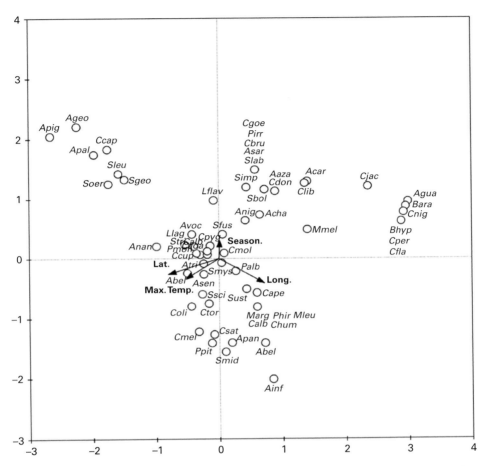

Figure 18.5 Biplot representing the relative importance of latitude, longitude, and climate variables for predicting the species composition of Neotropical primate communities. This figure was originally published in the electronic supplement of: Kamilar JM (2009) Environmental and geographic correlates of the taxonomic structure of primate communities. *American Journal of Physical Anthropology* 139:382–393. The figure is reproduced here courtesy of Wiley-Liss, Inc. Copyright © 2008 Wiley-Liss, Inc.

Spatial Regression Models

Whereas CCA models directly examine spatial effects by including geographic variables as predictors, many spatial regression models use an indirect approach to incorporate spatial effects. For example, a CCA analysis may include the latitude and longitude of each study site as predictors and variables such as the presence/absence of species as dependent variables. In contrast, spatial regression models, such as simultaneous autoregressive models, may account for spatial effects by adjusting the model's error structure using a spatially explicit variance–covariance matrix. This has the effect of down-weighting samples that are in close proximity to each other. There are several statistical techniques available to account for spatially autocorrelated datasets, including generalized linear models, generalized estimating equations, and conditional auto-regressive models. These and other methods (including those that directly incorporate spatial variables into the models, such as eigenvector mapping), are thoroughly reviewed in Dormann et al. (2007).

Spatial regression models have not been commonly used in primatological research. Some recent exceptions are studies conducted by Kamilar et al. (2014, 2015). These papers examined the potential importance of climatic variables for predicting the phylo-genetic structure of primate and mammal communities across African parks and protected areas. In particular, several simultaneous autoregressive models were used to predict various measures of community structure while accounting for spatial autocorrelation in the residual structure of the models. Accounting for spatial autocorrelation is potentially important because sites in close proximity to each other are more likely to exhibit similar climatic and community structures than sites that are found far away. Interestingly, both studies found that climatic variables are important predictors of community structure, but the specific climate variables that are important vary across clade (haplorrhines versus strepsirrhines and primates versus carnivorans versus ungulates).

Regression models that explicitly account for spatial effects are likely to increase in popularity with the increased availability of recently developed statistical software. Presently, a variety of spatial regression models can be conducted using the Spatial Analysis for Macroecology program (Rangel et al. 2010). This program is a "point and click" software package that has been commonly used in ecological research. Add-itional options can be found in the R computing environment, especially in the spdep package (Bivand 2013).

Distinguishing the Influences of Space and Phylogeny

We have discussed several methods that can be used for spatially explicit analyses and account for possible confounding effects of spatial autocorrelation (e.g., partial Mantel tests and CCA). Increasing availability of well-resolved phylogenies has enabled explicit evolutionary approaches to studying community structure and, in some cases, a compara-tive analysis can be both spatial and phylogenetic in nature. For instance, a model's error structure may show phylogenetic or spatial autocorrelation in the case of examining the potential effects of abiotic factors on interspecific trait variation. A generalized linear model developed by Freckleton and Jetz (2009) addresses this issue by using a geo-graphic distance matrix and a phylogenetic variance–covariance matrix (i.e., a matrix representing the phylogenetic distance between species in the dataset) to weigh the residuals of the model. In addition, their model quantifies the effects of space and phylogeny in the error structure. Importantly, if space and phylogeny have no influence on the model, then the analysis is identical to a normal linear model.

Freckleton and Jetz's method to separate spatial and phylogenetic effects was recently used in two publications examining different aspects of primate biogeography. In a dataset comprising more than 100 primate species, Kamilar and Bradley (2011) found a negative relationship between the actual evapotranspiration (as opposed to potential evapotranspiration) within a species' geographic range and the brightness of their hair. In addition, both phylogeny and space had very little effect on the model. The method was also used by Kamilar et al. (2012) to investigate whether Bergmann's rule (i.e., increased body size associated with high latitudes, usually corresponding to lower temperatures) or resource seasonality best explained body mass variation in Malagasy primate species. They used site-specific geo-referenced climate data and dietary information as independent variables in a model predicting species body mass. Neither climatic nor dietary variables were strong predictors of body mass. In addition, phylogeny, but not space, had a significant effect in the models. Additional analyses showed that closely related species exhibited similar body mass, independent of the environmental conditions they experienced.

Final Thoughts

The aim of this chapter has been to provide a broad illustration of the statistical tools available for spatial analyses in biogeographic and macroecological research, as well as the diversity of questions that can be answered with these tools. While our review has not been exhaustive in its coverage of methods or published research, we hope it will provide an introductory reference to general methodological concepts and examples in primates that will be useful to readers. Extant primates are particularly well-suited to serve as the focal taxon for these questions because their distributions and biology are better known than most other tropical mammals (Primack & Corlett 2005; Reed & Bidner 2004). This is important because more insight into the mechanisms that drive species distributions can be gained when occurrences are known with a high degree of confidence. In contrast, if occurrences are not well known, then false absences are likely to bias results. While we focused mostly on extant primate studies, we note that many of the methods and questions discussed in this chapter can also be applied to paleoecological research. In sum, the time is ripe to address biogeographic and macroecological questions in primates, given the wealth of spatially explicit data available and rapidly developing quantitative techniques.

Acknowledgments

JMK thanks John Fleagle, Charles Janson, Pat Wright, Charlie Nunn, Catherine Graham, Bob Sussman, Rich Smith, Brenda Bradley, Kaye Reed, Natalie Cooper, and Kathleen Muldoon for their insights into biogeography, macroecology, and macroevolution. In addition, he thanks Jim Rohlf and Bob Sokal for many helpful discussions about multivariate and spatial statistics. LB thanks Andy Marshall, Sandy Harcourt, Marcel Rejmánek, Kaye Reed, and Sharon Lawler for influential discussions.

References

Almeida-Neto, M., Guimaraes, P. R., and Lewinsohn, T. M. 2007. On nestedness analyses: rethinking matrix temperature and anti-nestedness. *Oikos* **116**: 716–722.

Almeida-Neto, M., Guimarães, P., Guimarães, Jr. P. R., Loyola, R. D., and Ulrich, W. 2008. A consistent metric for nestedness analysis in ecological systems: reconciling concept and measurement. *Oikos* **117**: 1227–1239.

Anemone, R. L., Conroy, G. C., and Emerson, C. W. 2011. GIS and paleoanthropology: incorporating new approaches from the geospatial sciences in the analysis of primate and human evolution. *Yearbook of Physical Anthropology* **54**: 19–46.

Atmar, W. and Patterson, B. D. 1993. The measure of order and disorder in the distribution of fragmented habitat. *Oecologia* **96**: 373–382.

Baselga, A., Jimenez-Valverde, A., and Niccolini, G. 2007. A multiple-site similarity measure independent of richness. *Biology Letters* **3** (6): 642–645.

Batjes, N. H. 2009. Harmonized soil profile data for applications at global and continental scales: updates to the WISE database. *Soil Use and Management* **25**: 124–127.

Beaudrot, L. H. and Marshall, A. J. 2011. Primate communities are structured more by dispersal limitation than by niches. *Journal of Animal Ecology* **80**: 332–341.

Beaudrot, L., Struebig, M. J., Meijaard, E., et al. 2013. Co-occurrence patterns of Bornean vertebrates suggest competitive exclusion is strongest in distantly related taxa. *Oecologia* **173**: 1053–1062.

Beaudrot, L., Kamilar, J. M., Marshall, A. J., and Reed, K. E. 2014. African primate assemblages exhibit a latitudinal gradient in dispersal limitation. *International Journal of Primatology* **35**: 1088–1104.

Bivand, R. 2013. spdep. R package.

Blair, M. E., Sterling, E. J., Dusch, M., Raxworthy, C. J., and Pearson, R. G. 2013. Ecological divergence and speciation between lemur (*Eulemur*) sister species in Madagascar. *Journal of Evolutionary Biology* **26**: 1790–1801.

Boubli, J. P. and de Lima, M. G. 2009. Modeling the geographical distribution and fundamental niches of *Cacajao* spp. and *Chiropotes israelita* in northwestern Amazonia via a maximum entropy algorithm. *International Journal of Primatology* **30**: 217–228.

Cardillo, M. and Meijaard, E. 2010. Phylogeny and co-occurrence of mammal species on Southeast Asian islands. *Global Ecology and Biogeography* **19**(4): 465–474.

Carroll, M. L., Townshend, J. R., DiMiceli, C. M., Noojipady, P., and Sohlberg, R. A. 2009. A new global raster water mask at 250 m resolution. *International Journal of Digital Earth* **2**: 291–308.

Carstensen, D. W., Lessard, J. P., Holt, B. G., Borregaard, M. K., and Rahbek, C. 2013. Introducing the biogeographic species pool. *Ecography* **36**: 1–9.

Carvalho, J. C., Cardoso, P., and Gomes, P. 2012. Determining the relative roles of species replacement and species richness differences in generating beta-diversity patterns. *Global Ecology and Biogeography* **21** (7): 760–771.

Dapporto, L., Ramazzotti, M., Fattorini, S., et al. 2013. recluster: an unbiased clustering procedure for beta-diversity turnover. *Ecography*. DOI: 10.1111/j.1600-0587.2013.00444.x.

Diamond, J. M. 1975. Assembly of species communities. Pages 342–444 in *Ecology and Evolution of Communities*, M. L. Cody and J. M. Diamond (Eds.). Cambridge, MA: Harvard University Press.

Dormann, C. F., McPherson, J. M., Araujo, M. B., et al. 2007. Methods to account for spatial autocorrelation in the analysis of species distributional data: a review. *Ecography* **30**: 609–628.

Elith, J. and Graham, C. H. (2009) Do they? How do they? WHY do they differ? On finding reasons for differing performances of species distribution models. *Ecography* **32**: 66–77.

Elith, J., Graham, C. H., Anderson, R. P., et al. 2006. Novel methods improve prediction of species' distributions from occurrence data. *Ecography* **29**: 129–151.

Fayle, T. M. and Manica, A. 2010. Reducing over-reporting of deterministic co-occurrence patterns in biotic communities. *Ecological Modelling* **221**: 2237–2242.

Fielding, A. H. 2007. *Cluster and Classification Techniques for the Biosciences*. Cambridge University Press, New York.

Fleagle, J. G. and Reed, K. E. 1996. Comparing primate communities: a multivariate approach. *Journal of Human Evolution* **30**: 489–510.

Fortin, M.-J. and Dale, M. R. T. 2005. *Spatial Analysis: A Guide for Ecologists*. Cambridge University Press, Cambridge.

Fox, B. J. 1987. Species assembly and the evolution of community structure. *Evolutionary Ecology* **1**: 201–213.

Freckleton, R. P. and Jetz, W. 2009. Space versus phylogeny: disentangling phylogenetic and spatial signals in comparative data. *Proceedings of the Royal Society B* **276**: 21–30.

Ganzhorn, J. U. 1998. Nested patterns of species composition and their implications for lemur biogeography in Madagascar. *Folia Primatologica* **69** (Suppl. 1): 332–341.

Goslee, S. and Urban, D. 2013. ecodist: Dissimilarity-based functions for ecological analysis. R package.

Gotelli, N. J. and McCabe, D. J. 2002. Species co-occurrence: a meta-analysis of J. M. Diamond's assembly rules model. *Ecology Letters* **83**: 2091–2096.

Gotelli, N. J., Hart, E. M., and Ellison, A. M. 2015. EcoSimR: null model analysis for ecological data. R package.

Gower, J. C. and Hand, D. J. 1995. *Biplots*. Chapman and Hall/CRC, London.

Graham, C. H., Ferrier, S., Huettman, F., Moritz, C., and Peterson, A. T. 2004. New developments in museum-based informatics and applications in biodiversity analysis. *Trends in Ecology and Evolution* **19** (9): 497–503.

Guillot, G. and Rousset, F. 2013. Dismantling the Mantel tests. *Methods in Ecology and Evolution*. DOI: 10.1111/2041-210x.12018.

Guimarães, P. R. and Guimarães, P. 2006. Improving the analyses of nestedness for large sets of matrices. *Environmental Modelling and Software* **21**: 1512–1513.

Hijmans, R. J., Cameron, S. E., Parra, J. L., Jones, P. G., and Jarvis, A. 2005. Very high resolution interpolated climate surfaces for global land areas. *International Journal of Climatology* **25**: 1965–1978.

Hutchinson, G. E. 1959. Homage to Santa Rosalia, or why are there so many kinds of animals? *American Naturalist* **93**: 145–159.

Junker, J., Blake, S., Boesch, C., et al. 2012. Recent decline in suitable environmental conditions for African great apes. *Diversity and Distributions* **18**: 1077–1091.

Kamilar, J. M. 2009. Environmental and geographic correlates of the taxonomic structure of primate communities. *American Journal of Physical Anthropology* **139**: 382–393.

Kamilar, J. M. and Atkinson, Q. D. 2013. Cultural assemblages show nested structure in humans and chimpanzees but not orangutans. *PNAS* **111**: 111–115.

Kamilar, J. M. and Beaudrot, L. 2013. Understanding primate communities: recent developments and future directions. *Evolution and Anthropology* **22**: 174–185.

Kamilar, J. M. and Bradley, B. J. 2011. Interspecific variation in primate coat color supports Gloger's rule. *Journal of Biogeography* **38**: 2270–2277.

Kamilar, J. M. and Ledogar, J. A. 2011. Species co-occurrence patterns and dietary resource competition in primates. *American Journal of Physical Anthropology* **144**: 131–139.

Kamilar, J. M. and Marshack, J. L. 2012. Does geography or ecology best explain "cultural" variation among chimpanzee communities? *Journal of Human Evolution* **62**: 256–260.

Kamilar, J. M. and Muldoon, K. M. 2010. The climatic niche diversity of Malagasy primates: a phylogenetic approach. *PLoS ONE* **5**: e11073.

Kamilar, J. M., Muldoon, K. M., Lehman, S. M., and Herrera, J. P. 2012. Testing Bergmann's rule and the resource seasonality hypothesis in Malagasy primates using GIS-based climate data. *American Journal of Physical Anthropology* **147**: 401–408.

Kamilar, J. M., Beaudrot, L., and Reed, K. E. 2014. The influences of species richness and climate on the phylogenetic structure of African haplorhine and strepsirrhine primate communities. *International Journal of Primatology* **35**: 1105–1121.

Kamilar, J. M., Beaudrot, L., and Reed, K. E. 2015. Climate and species richness predict the phylogenetic structure of African mammal communities. *PLoS ONE* **10**: e0121808.

Kamilar, J. M., Blanco, M., and Muldoon, K. M. 2016. Ecological niche modeling of mouse lemurs (*Microcebus* spp.) and its implications for their species diversity and biogeography. Pages 449–461 in *Dwarf and Mouse Lemurs of Madagascar: Biology, Behavior and Conservation Biogeography of the Cheirogaleidae.* S. M. Lehman, U. Radespiel, and E. Zimmermann (Eds.). Cambridge University Press, Cambridge.

Kissling, W. D., Dormann, C. F., and Groeneveld, J., et al. 2012. Towards novel approaches to modelling biotic interactions in multispecies assemblages at large spatial extents. *Journal of Biogeography* **39**: 2163–2178.

Koleff, P., Gaston, K. J., and Lennon, J. J. 2003. Measuring beta diversity for presence–absence data. *Journal of Animal Ecology* **72**(3): 367–382.

Krebs, C. J. 1999. *Ecological Methodology*, 2nd edition. Benjamin Cummings, Menlo Park, CA.

Kreft, H. and Jetz, W. 2010. A framework for delineating biogeographical regions based on species distributions. *Journal of Biogeography* **37** (11): 2029–2053.

Legendre, P. 2000. Comparison of permutation methods for the partial correlation and partial Mantel tests. *Journal of Statistical Computation and Simulation* **67**: 37–73.

Legendre, P. and Legendre, L. 1998. *Numerical Ecology*. Elsevier Science BV, Amsterdam.

Legendre, P., Borcard, D., Peres-Neto, P. R. 2005. Analyzing beta diversity: partitioning the spatial variation of community composition data. *Ecological Monographs* **75** (4): 435–450.

Lehman, S. M. 2006. Nested distribution patterns and the historical biogeography of the primates of Guyana. Pages 63–80 in *Primate Biogeography*. S. M. Lehman and J. G. Fleagle (Eds.). Springer, New York.

Magurran, A. E. 1988. *Ecological Diversity and Its Measurements*. Princeton University Press, Princeton.

Manly, B. F. 2005. *Multivariate Statistical Methods: a Primer*. CRC Press, Boca Raton, FL.

Mantel, N. 1967. The detection of disease clustering and a generalized regression approach. *Cancer Research* **27**: 209–220.

McGarigal, K., Cushman, S., and Stafford, S. 2000. *Multivariate Statistics for Wildlife and Ecology Research*. Springer, New York.

Merow, C., Smith, M. J., and Silander, J. A. 2013. A practical guide to MaxEnt for modeling species' distributions: what it does, and why inputs and settings matter. *Ecography*. DOI: 10.1111/j.1600-0587.2013.07872.x.

Oksanen, J., Blanchet, F. G., Kindt, R., et al. 2013. vegan: community ecology package. R package.

Ossi, K. M. and Kamilar, J. M. 2006. Environmental and phylogenetic correlates of *Eulemur* behavior and ecology (Primates: Lemuridae). *Behavioral Ecology and Sociobiology* **61**: 53–64.

Patterson, B. D. 1987. The principle of nested subsets and its implications for biological conservation. *Conservation and Biology* **1**(4): 323–334.

Peres, C. A. 1997. Primate community structure at twenty western Amazonian flooded and unflooded forests. *Journal of Tropical Ecology* **13**: 381–405.

Phillips, S. J. and Dudík, M. 2008. Modeling of species distributions with Maxent: new extensions and a comprehensive evaluation. *Ecography* **31**: 161–175.

Phillips, S. J., Anderson, R. P., and Schapire, R. E. 2006. Maximum entropy modeling of species geographic distributions. *Ecological Modeling* **190**: 231–259.

Primack, R. and Corlett, R. 2005. *Tropical Rain Forests: An Ecological and Biogeographical Comparison*. Blackwell Publishing, New York.

Rangel, T. F. L. V. B., Diniz-Filho, J. A. F., and Bini, L. M. 2010. SAM: a comprehensive application for Spatial Analysis in Macroecology. *Ecography* **33**: 46–50.

Reed, K. E. and Bidner, L. R. 2004. Primate communities: past, present, and possible future. *American Journal of Physical Anthropology* **47**: 2–39.

Rosenberg, M. 2001. PASSAGE: Pattern Analysis, Spatial Statistics, and Geographic Exegesis Version 1.0. Arizona State University.

Sanderson, J. G., Diamond, J. M., and Pimm, S. L. 2009. Pairwise co-existence of Bismark and Solomon landbird species. *Evolutionary Ecology Research* **11**: 771–786.

Sfenthourakis, S., Giokas, S., and Tzanatos, E. 2004. From sampling stations to archipelagos: investigating aspects of the assemblage of insular biota. *Global Ecology and Biogeography* **13**: 23–35.

Sfenthourakis, S., Tzanatos, E., and Giokas, S. 2005. Species co-occurrence: the case of congeneric species and a causal approach to patterns of species association. *Global Ecology and Biogeography* **15**: 39–49.

Smouse, P., Long, J., and Sokal, R. R. 1986. Multiple regression and correlation extensions of the Mantel test of matrix correspondence. *Systematic Zoology* **35**: 627–632.

Sokal, R. R., Oden, N. L., Walker, J., and Waddle, D. M. 1997. Using distance matrices to choose between competing theories and an application to the origin of modern humans. *Journal of Human Evolution* **32**: 501–522.

Stone, L. and Roberts, A., 1990. The checkerboard score and species distributions. *Oecologia*, **85**(1): 74–79.

Strong, D. R., Simberloff, D., Abele, L. G., and Thistle, A. B. (Eds.). 1984. *Ecological Communities*. Princeton University Press, Princeton.

Tabachnick, B. G. and Fidell, L. S. 1989. *Using Multivariate Statistics*, 2nd edition. Harper and Row, New York.

ter Braak, C. J. F. and Smilauer, P. 2002. CANOCO for Windows Version 4.5. Microcomputer Power.

Thorn, J. S., Nijman, V., Smith, D., and Nekaris, K. A. I. 2009. Ecological niche modelling as a technique for assessing threats and setting conservation priorities for Asian slow lorises (Primates: Nycticebus). *Diversity and Distributions* **15**: 289–298.

Thorne, J. H., Seo, C., and Basabose, A., et al. 2013. Alternative biological assumptions strongly influence models of climate change effects on mountain gorillas. *Ecosphere* **4**: 108.

Tuomisto, H. 2010a. A diversity of beta diversities: straightening up a concept gone awry. Part 1. Defining beta diversity as a function of alpha and gamma diversity. *Ecography* **33**(1): 2–22.

Tuomisto, H. 2010b. A diversity of beta diversities: straightening up a concept gone awry. Part 2. Quantifying beta diversity and related phenomena. *Ecography* **33**(1): 23–45.

Ulrich, W. 2008. Pairs: a FORTRAN program for studying pair-wise species associations in ecological matrices. Available at: www.uni.torun.pl/~ulrichw.

Ulrich, W. and Gotelli, N. J. 2012. Pattern detection in null model analysis. *Oikos*. DOI: 10.1111/j.1600-0706.2012.20325.x.

Vidal-García, F. and Serio-Silva, J. C. 2011. Potential distribution of Mexican primates: modeling the ecological niche with the maximum entropy algorithm. *Primates* **52**: 261–270.

Whiten, A., Goodall, J., McGrew, W. C., et al. 2001. Charting cultural variation in chimpanzees. *Behaviour* **138**: 1481–1516.

Wilson, J. B. 1989. A null model of guild proportionality, applied to stratification of a New-Zealand temperate rain-forest. *Oecologia* **80**(2): 263–267.

Wolfheim, J. H. 1983. *Primates of the World: Distribution, Abundance, and Conservation*. University of Washington Press, Seattle.

19 GIS and GPS Techniques in an Ethnoprimatological Investigation of St Kitts Green Monkey (*Chlorocebus sabaeus*) Crop-Foraging Behavior

Kerry M. Dore, Daniel Sewell, Eduardo M. Mattenet, and Trudy R. Turner

Introduction

Over 350 years ago, the ecology of St Kitts, an island in the West Indies, was dramatically altered when Europeans arrived. The English and later French introduced sugar cane production, brought in a large African slave workforce, and (unintentionally) introduced a highly intelligent and adaptable invasive animal species, the green monkey (*Chlorocebus sabaeus*). Ever since green monkeys arrived in St Kitts, they have thrived on the island, in part by foraging on farmers' crops. In this chapter, we utilize GIS and GPS techniques to generate a predictive model of this crop-foraging behavior. Additionally, we use ethnographic techniques to understand the nuanced ways in which historic land use changes in St Kitts have altered green monkey movements, and, in turn, Kittitians' cultural conceptualization of monkeys. Our work shows the benefits of utilizing an ethnoprimatological framework and combining quantitative and qualitative data collection techniques in assessing human–nonhuman primate (NHP) conflict situations, which are inherently highly spatial in nature.

Predicting St Kitts Green Monkey Crop Foraging

The general behaviors of St Kitts green monkeys were well studied in the 1970s and 1980s (Chapman 1985, 1987; Chapman & Fedigan 1984; Chapman et al. 1988; Fairbanks & Bird 1978; McGuire 1974; Petto & Povinelli 1985; Poirier 1972; Sade & Hildrech 1965), yet descriptions of the monkeys' crop foraging have always been anecdotal. Sade and Hildrech (1965), Poirier (1972), and McGuire (1974) explain that even in the early days of habitation on St Kitts, green monkeys were serious crop foragers, but relatively little was written about their patterns of crop damage.

A number of methods have been used to quantify NHP crop damage. These include measurements of the damage to crops (1) in an area overlaid with a grid system (Linkie et al. 2007; Naughton-Treves 1996); (2) within specific crop stands (Hill 2000; Naughton-Treves 1997; Naughton-Treves et al. 1998; Warren et al. 2007); (3) along vegetation transects or plots (Priston 2005; Siex & Struhsaker 1999); (4) using questionnaires (Gillingham & Lee 2003; Tweyho et al. 2005); and (5) evaluating farmers' records which are subsequently checked by enumerators (Linkie et al. 2007). For this project, a grid system was used because of the broad distribution of farms in St Kitts and the goal to survey the entire island. More specifically, the grid-based system used in this study is adapted from Sitati et al. (2003), who investigated the variables that predicted human–elephant conflict in a 1000 km^2 area adjacent to Masai Mara National Reserve in Kenya.

Previous studies of crop-foraging NHPs in Africa and Asia show that farms are more vulnerable to crop damage when they are closer to the forest boundary, further from roads, have fewer neighboring farms, when farmers spend less time guarding their crops, when preferred crops are grown, and when there is less alternative food available in the animal's environment (Gillingham & Lee 2003; Hill 1997, 2000; Maples et al. 1976; Naughton-Treves 1997, 1998; Naughton-Treves et al. 1998; Newmark et al. 1994; Priston 2005; Siex & Struhsaker 1999; Strum 1994). This study tests whether the factors identified as predictors of NHP crop damage on other continents are also predictors of crop damage by green monkeys on St Kitts.

The rationale for including several additional covariates as possible predictors of crop damage is specific to the environment of St Kitts. With regard to season/alternative food availability, the important factor is the mango season. During the months of May through August, thousands of mango trees produce fruit in the forest and ravines of St Kitts. Mangoes are known to be a favorite food source for St Kitts green monkeys (McGuire 1974). Therefore, we hypothesize that during the mango season, farms will have a lower risk of crop damage by green monkeys because there is a significant amount of preferred, alternative food during this limited time period. McGuire (1974) has also shown that St Kitts green monkeys utilize ravines for cover and water. Therefore, we hypothesize that farms closer to ravines will be more likely to experience crop damage by monkeys. Finally, as St Kitts farmers' planting behavior is highly variable, two additional variables are included: the number of months the farm contained crops in the mango season (May–August) and the number of months the farm contained crops in the non-mango season (September–April). For both variables, we hypothesize that farms with crops planted more often will be more likely to experience crop damage from monkeys (see Table 19.1 for all of the hypotheses tested).

The goal of the first stage of this investigation is to methodically document crop damage and evaluate the possible role of these environmental variables in predicting a farm's risk of crop damage. Nonhuman primate crop foraging has been extensively studied within the fields of primatology and human–NHP conflict; however, there are few models that *predict* NHP crop damage. This work builds upon preliminary GIS approaches (Hashim et al. 2009; Webber 2006) and epidemiological approaches that use incidence rates to predict patterns of NHP crop damage (Nijman & Nekaris 2010; Priston & Underdown 2009). Webber (2006) and Hashim et al. (2009) show that certain environmental variables can be used to effectively predict NHP crop foraging, but they do not generate models that have been tested and proven effective on new data. Priston and Underdown's (2009) and Nijman and Nekaris' (2010) models work with only a subset of variables deemed important a priori (mainly crop type and distance to the

Table 19.1 Hypotheses tested.

H1: Farms will be more vulnerable to primate crop damage the closer they are to the forest boundary.

H2: Farms will be more vulnerable to primate crop damage the further they are from roads.

H3: Farms will be more vulnerable to primate crop damage the fewer neighbors they have.

H4: Farms will be more vulnerable to primate crop damage when the farmers spend less time guarding their crops.

H5: Farms will be more vulnerable to primate crop damage when they contain crops preferred by monkeys.

H6: Farms will be more vulnerable to primate crop damage when there is less alternative food available (i.e., during the non-mango season).

H7: Farms will be more vulnerable to primate crop damage the closer they are to water sources.

H8: Farms will be more vulnerable to primate crop damage when they have crops planted during more months of the mango season.

H9: Farms will be more vulnerable to primate crop damage when they have crops planted during more months of the non-mango season.

forest boundary). This study aims to assess the risk to any farm or piece of land in St Kitts and to utilize information on all possible predictive variables.

Incorporating Ethnoprimatology

Ethnoprimatologists argue that humans and NHPs mutually impact each other. Thus, practitioners of ethnoprimatology actively assess this mutual interaction and the perspectives of each of these groups at their field sites. An ethnoprimatological approach combines primatology and cultural anthropology and considers ethnographic methods as integral components of understanding the ecological contexts of primates. Ethnoprimatologists ask: How do humans affect NHP behavior and ecological patterns and how do NHPs affect human cultural conceptualizations (Fuentes 2006)? Since the inception of ethnoprimatology, it has become clear that it is necessary to understand human interactions with and conceptualizations of the NHP groups in their environment in order to fully understand NHP behavior, ecology, and conservation (Cormier 2002, 2003; Fuentes 2006, 2012; Fuentes & Hockings 2010; Fuentes & Wolfe 2002; Hardin & Remis 2006; Hill & Webber 2010; Paterson & Wallis 2005; Riley 2007; Riley & Priston 2010; Wheatley 1999).

Thus, the goal of the second stage of this investigation is to use ethnographic techniques to understand Kittitian farmers' relationship to monkeys and how this may have changed over time. Understanding the factors that influence a farm's likelihood of crop damage by monkeys via GIS and GPS techniques will provide some perspective on how farmers influence one aspect of monkey behavior (i.e., crop foraging), and this qualitative data will expose the ways that green monkeys influence farmers' behaviors and beliefs. While it is clear that a farm's vulnerability to crop damage is spatial in nature, our results will show how the human–NHP interface at the heart of ethnoprimatological research is also spatial in nature. Additionally, while the quantitative techniques employed in this study can tell us about the proximate causes of crop damage, the historic data obtained through an ethnographic approach can shed light on the ultimate causes of this conflict. Together, these techniques can generate a more robust picture of green monkey crop-foraging in St Kitts and better inform future management strategies.

Methods

Site Selection

Lists of registered farmers were provided by the St Kitts Department of Agriculture. The department's crop extension officers, who visit farms regularly and provide technical assistance to farmers, generated these lists. Two crop extension officers were assigned to this project and were present during almost all data collection. This was especially important in the early stages of the project when KMD and field assistants were learning how to identify young crops.

St Kitts has nine parishes, some of which have significantly more farms than others. One-third of the farms in each parish ($n = 65$) were selected to be in the study (Figure 19.1). This sample size was the largest that could be monitored accurately

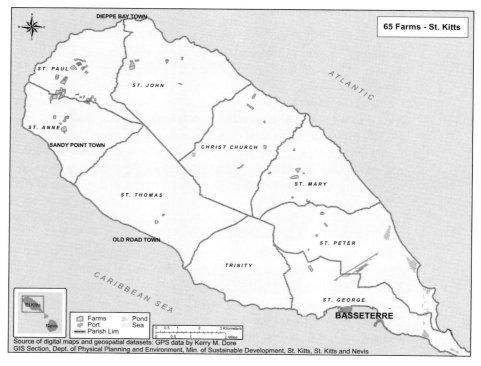

Figure 19.1 The nine parishes in St Kitts and the 65 farms selected to be in the study. (A black and white version of this figure will appear in some formats. For the color version, please refer to the plate section.)

and represent all of the farms in St Kitts. These farms were chosen at random, with the exception that farms larger than 15 acres were not included as there was not enough time or personnel to monitor farms this large (only 5 farms were not included in the study because they were too large, and only 10 farms in total in St Kitts were listed as 15 acres or larger). All of the farms in each parish were assigned a number, and the numbers were randomized using the statistical program R (R Core Team 2008). Starting with the farm that was randomly assigned number 1 in each parish, the farmer was contacted and asked if he or she would be willing to participate in the study. If the farmer declined, or the farm was no longer in use, the next farmer on the list was contacted until farmers from 33 percent of the farms in each parish granted their permission. Participating farmers were told the details of the study and informed that the research was purely academic and scientific, and that the data would be used to determine which farms and crops are at greatest risk of NHP crop damage. They were told that there was no guarantee that any action would take place as a result of this research, including compensation for crop loss, in order to minimize the likelihood of damage being exaggerated.

Monitoring Crop Loss

A polygon (vector) grid (Figure 19.2) composed of half-acre (~45 × 45 m) squares (the approximate size of the smallest participating farm) was constructed and placed over the entire island using ArcMap version 9.3, a geographic information system (GIS), prior to the start of data collection (ESRI ArcGIS). Crop damage was assessed at the level of the grid cell and at the level of the farm on each farm for 12 sequential months. Farms were visited in the same order each month. This order was determined randomly, again with the statistical program R (R Core Team 2008). Farms were visited Monday to Friday each week. On average, four or five farms were monitored daily for 16 days each month.

On the initial visit to each farm, the farm's location and area were recorded with handheld Garmin Venture HC GPS units. Often, the farmer described the crops that were being grown, at what times each crop was planted, and when it was going to be harvested (see Table 19.2 for a list of all the crops mapped during the course of the study).

On each farm visit, the entire farm was checked for crop damage, often with the farmer's assistance. If crop damage was only superficial and the farmer could still reap the crop item or it could spring back, then the item was not counted as damaged. If any part of the crop item was damaged, then the entire item was considered damaged (the percentage of the individual crop item, e.g., number of corn kernels on one ear of corn, was not recorded). Green monkey crop damage is easy to identify, as the animals typically only take a few bites out of the item. While green monkeys are significant crop-foragers, wild pigs, cows, sheep, and goats also forage on crops in St Kitts. Therefore, evidence of pig and livestock damage was also collected with these methods. This damage is distinct from that of the green monkeys, who take a few bites of fruit and leave the rest: wild pigs uproot ground vegetables and sheep and goats eat the vegetation.

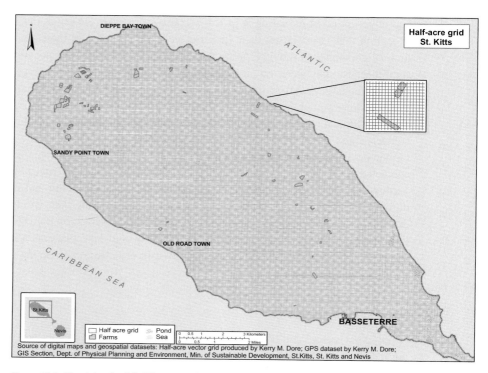

Figure 19.2 The island of St Kitts superimposed with the half-acre grid used for this study (individual grid cells are impossible to see at this scale). (A black and white version of this figure will appear in some formats. For the color version, please refer to the plate section.)

The percentage of crop damage was assessed at two levels: on the farm as a whole and within each individual grid cell. At the farm level, the percentage of crop loss to each crop was calculated by dividing the number of damaged crop items by the total number of crop items on the farm. If, for example, we found damaged tomatoes on the farm, every damaged and undamaged tomato on the farm was individually counted. For ground crops (e.g., sweet potato), the percentage of crop loss was calculated as the area uprooted over the total area of the crop on the farm. The area calculation function on the GPS unit was used for this purpose: One selects this function on the unit and then walks the perimeter of the area to be calculated, pressing a button at the start and end of the polygon.

At the individual cell level, crop damage was recorded in grid cells that fell within the farm and did not contain crops from any other farm (any grid cells that contained crops from multiple farms were excluded from the study). Using the GPS units, the coordinates of the corners of each grid cell were located on the ground and marked with yellow ribbons that were removed after each visit. A printed map of each farm with the location of all grid cell coordinates helped ensure the accuracy of the locations provided by the GPS unit. Then, the percentage of each damaged crop in the cell was determined using the same methods as at the farm level. On the rare occasion that crop damage was so

Table 19.2 Crops mapped on study farms (September 2010 to August 2011).

5 finger (Carambola)	Ginger	Plantains
Ackee	Golden apple	Pomegranate
Atney	Gooseberry	Pontserrat
Avocado	Grapes	Pumella grapefruit
Basil	Greens	Pumpkin
Bok choi	Guava	Red peas
Breadfruit	Hot pepper	Sea grape
Breadnut	Irish potato	Seasoning pepper
Broccoli	Lemon	Shaddock
Cabbage	Lettuce	Skinny tree (canape)
Callaloo	Lime	Sorrel
Carrot	Mango	Soursap
Cashew	Morocco	Spinach
Cassava	Noni	Squash
Cauliflower	Nuff nuff	String beans
Celery	Okra	Sugar apple
Chives	Onion	Sun melon
Coconut	Orange	Sweet pepper
Collards	Papaya	Sweet potato
Corn	Passion fruit	Tangerine
Cucumber	Peanuts	Tea bush
Custard apple	Peas	Thyme
DET (dasheen, eddo, tannia)	Pigeon peas	Tomato
Eggplant	Pineapple	Watermelon
Fig	Pink grapefruit	Yams
		Zucchini

Data compiled by field assistant Lindsay Mahovetz.

severe that the farmer had already re-plowed and replanted the field with a different crop at the time of the monthly visit, the incident was noted, but the degree of damage was not estimated and the data were not included in the analyses. After each monthly visit, all of the damaged crops were collected and taken off of the farm to avoid counting the same crop as damaged on more than one occasion.

Quantifying Environmental Predictors

GIS maps of St Kitts' land cover (Figure 19.3), water drainage (Figure 19.4), and roads (Figure 19.5) were obtained from the St Kitts Department of Physical Planning and Environment within the Ministry of Sustainable Development. The forest boundary was digitized from the land cover map, which defines the apron of forest surrounding the volcano, Mt. Liamuiga. The program Hawth's Tools (Beyer 2004) was used to calculate the center point of each grid cell in ArcMap. The map with grid cell center points was spatially joined to the forest boundary, water source, and road maps, prompting the GIS to give each point the attributes of the closest line. This created a large table with all grid cell centers and distance attributes (to the nearest forest boundary, water source, and

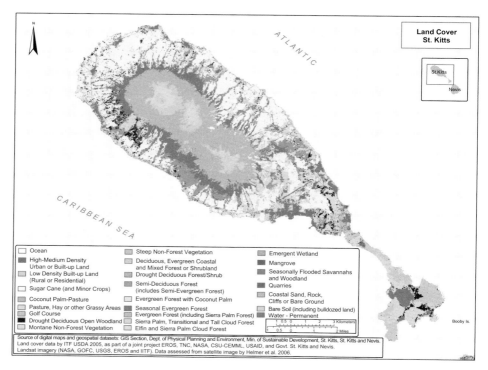

Figure 19.3 Land cover on St Kitts (assessed from satellite images by Helmer et al. 2008). (A black and white version of this figure will appear in some formats. For the color version, please refer to the plate section.)

road, respectively). These distances were transferred to a separate data file containing the 699 grid cells contained within the 64 farms specific to the study. The number of months the cell contained crops was counted and this number was also transferred to the database file, categorized into two groups: the mango and non-mango season. The three distances and the two seasons of number of months with crops planted were specific to each grid cell.

Naughton-Treves' (1998) technique to compare observed to expected frequencies of crop foraging was utilized to obtain crop preferences for the predictive model (Table 19.3). The observed frequency was calculated monthly as the percentage of damage to the damaged crop divided by the percentage of damage to all crops that were damaged during that monthly visit. The expected frequency of foraging events for each crop was calculated monthly as the area of the damaged crop divided by the area of all crops available on the farm that month. The most preferred crops have the highest positive deviations of observed from expected frequencies. For the purposes of the predictive model, each cell was assigned a preference value that corresponded to the most preferred crop in the cell that month. Like the three distances and the number of months with crops planted, crop preference was specific to each grid cell.

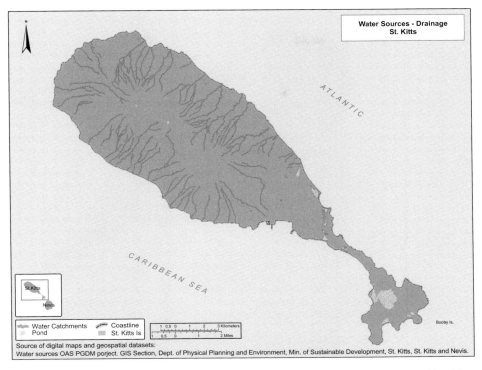

Figure 19.4 Location of water sources on St Kitts. Data available at: www.oas.org/pgdm/data/gis_data.htm. (A black and white version of this figure will appear in some formats. For the color version, please refer to the plate section.)

To measure the effect of neighboring farms, the surroundings for each farm were visually inspected for neighbors and assigned a value of 1–4, with 4 being the greatest number of possible neighbors. All grid cells that fell within the farm were assigned the same value for "neighbors," so this variable is specific to each farm. To measure the effect of guarding behavior on crop damage, during interviews, farmers were asked the number of hours per week they spent on their farm. Based on this number, confirmed with personal observation and whether or not they also used dogs, farms were assigned a number out of 8, with 8 designated for farmers that spent the most time protecting their crops (1 = 0–20 h/wk, no dogs; 2 = 0–20 h/wk, dogs; 3 = 21–40 h/wk, no dogs; 4 = 21–40 h/wk, dogs; 5 = 41–60 h/wk, no dogs; 6 = 41–60 h/wk, dogs; 7 = 61+ h/wk, no dogs; 8= 61+ h/wk, dogs). All grid cells that fell within the farm were assigned the same value for guarding.

In addition to the aforementioned spatial predictors, the temporal effect of season/alternative food availability was also evaluated. Crop loss during September–April was considered to have occurred in the non-mango season and crop loss during May–August was considered to have occurred in the mango season. The effect of season was assessed at the grid cell level in order to determine the effect of season on crop damage for each grid cell.

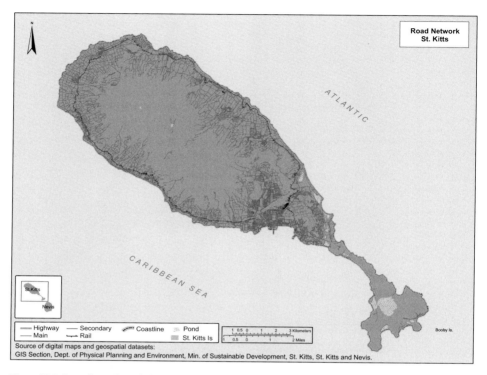

Figure 19.5 Location of roads in St Kitts. Data from the St Kitts Planning Department. (A black and white version of this figure will appear in some formats. For the color version, please refer to the plate section.)

Model Development: Hierarchical Linear Models and Hierarchical General Linear Models

Hierarchical Linear Models

Due to the nature of data collection techniques utilized in this study, a standard linear regression assessing the contribution of the predictive variables to crop damage was not appropriate. This is because data were collected at the level of the grid cell, and grid cells are nested within farms. In other words, the similarity among grid cells within a particular farm induces additional dependencies that violate the assumption of independent observations required by linear regression.

Hierarchical linear modeling (HLM), or multilevel modeling, is applicable to situations in which the data have a nested structure. In HLM, the individuals and their groups are conceptualized as a hierarchical system of sampling units, or experimental units as the case may be, nested in groups. The distributions of these individual units and groups are defined at separate levels of this hierarchical system, typically in terms of linear combinations of predictive variables and random error terms.

Table 19.3 Crop preference data.

Crop	Incidents	Crop	Obs./Exp.	Value assigned
Pumpkin	22	Pink grapefruit	12158.63	10
Watermelon	16	Orange	1728.2	10
Tomato	16	Soursap	1035.1	10
Peanut	15	Atney	270.5	10
Okra	14	Papaya	116.19	10
Eggplant	12	Passion fruit	113.03	10
Sweet pepper	11	Squash	70.6	9
Cucumber	11	Eggplant	64.09	9
Sweet potato	8	Cucumber	48.03	8
Cabbage	8	Corn	26.78	7
Squash	6	Watermelon	13.56	6
Fig	6	Okra	9.17	5
Corn	4	Pumpkin	8.54	5
Sea pepper	2	Sweet pepper	7.19	4
Passion fruit	2	Tomato	4.48	4
Papaya	2	Peanut	2.59	3
Pink grapefruit	2	Cabbage	2.53	3
Onion	2	Fig	2.26	2
Atney	2	Sweet potato	1.79	2
Dasheen/eddo/tannia	1	Yam		1
Zucchini	1	Noni		1
Yam	1	Sea pepper		1
Soursap	1	Onion		1
Orange	1	Dasheen/eddo/tannia		1
Noni	1	Zucchini		1
Lime	1	Lime		1
		No preferred		0

For the predictive models generated for this study, crop loss was quantified at two levels: the entire farm and within individual half-acre grid cells. Thus, using a multilevel model means that one can examine how a farm's likelihood of experiencing crop damage is influenced by both the characteristics of the grid cell (e.g., distance to the nearest water source) and characteristics of the farm (e.g., how much time the farmer spends guarding his or her crops; this variable is the same for all grid cells on the farm). The grid cell is measured and modeled at Level 1 and the farm at Level 2. The following multilevel model shows this two-level structure with one predictor variable at each level:

$$\text{Level 1}: \quad Y_{ij} = \beta_{0j} + \beta_{1j} X_{ij} + r_{ij}$$

$$\text{Level 2}: \quad Y_{p0} + Y_{p1} W_j + u_{pj}, p = 0, 1$$

Hierarchical Generalized Linear Models

Most of the grid cells monitored during the course of this study did not receive damage, which necessitated two predictive models to account for this large number of zeros. The first predictive model that will be described has a binary dependent variable (presence/absence of damage; 1/0). The HLM can be generalized to our context by replacing Y_{ij} in the left-hand side of the Level 1 equation with the logit of the probability of receiving damage, where $\text{logit}(p) = \ln(p/1 - p)$. In this framework, Level 2 is unchanged.

Using this hierarchical approach gives this predictive model a higher resolution spatial scale than previous models. It assesses the impact of environmental variables down to individual half-acre sections of individual farms, but the multilevel nature of the model also considers the characteristics of the farms in their entirety.

Predictive Models

With our model, we wish to see how well the model fits the data, and also to see how well the model predicts new data. The model fit will be evaluated by using the area under the curve (AUC) for a receiver operating characteristic (ROC) curve. Receiver operating characteristic curves will be used to determine cutoff values for prediction, i.e., the value above which an estimated probability of incurring damage will lead the researcher to formally predict damage. To find this cutoff value, the closest top-left criteria will be considered (Perkins & Schisterman 2006), using a cost of 15. This means that the financial cost of predicting no damage and actually getting damage is 15 times more than the cost of predicting damage and actually not getting damage. The value of 15 gives a good balance between sensitivity and specificity and is sufficiently high to reflect the difference in importance of the two types of misclassifications.

Estimation of the data was done via the h-likelihood method. For more details, see Lee and Nelder (1996) and Rönnegård et al. (2010).

Ethnographic Methods

Ethnographic methods were utilized to investigate the dynamics of the human–NHP interface in St Kitts. Each of the 64 farmers participating in this study were interviewed, using an open-ended approach, about their experiences with green monkeys as a whole and on their farm as well as their personal and farm histories, their daily struggles, and issues in Kittitian society (these questions were approved by the University of Wisconsin-Milwaukee's Institutional Review Board). Many of these questions were generated after arriving in St Kitts and learning more about "the monkey problem" by speaking with members of the agricultural community (see Dore 2017). The interviews occurred during the same 12 months the farms were being monitored (September 2010 to August 2011). The order of interviews occurred as the comfort level with the farmer increased; farmers who were more open and communicative were interviewed at the beginning of the study, and those that were more reserved were interviewed later, after KMD had established a relationship with them. In addition, conversations about monkeys were initiated at every possible opportunity. Cab drivers, people at the grocery store, local friends, farmers not in the study, members of the agriculture department, and anyone else KMD ran into were asked about their feelings on monkeys, how the situation has changed over time, the effects of the end of the sugar industry, and so on.

Results

Crop Damage

A total of 87.1 hectares on 64 farms were monitored (one farm was not cultivated during the study period). Crop damage from monkeys was recorded on 53 percent (34/64) of the farms in the study. Compared to pigs and other livestock, incidents of crop damage by monkeys occurred much more frequently: 176 incidents of crop damage by monkeys were recorded compared to 16 by pigs and 12 by livestock (see Tables 19.4 and 19.5 for means and standard deviations). Importantly, however, while monkeys destroyed 4853 pounds of ground crops and 7860 individual crop items during 12 months of

Table 19.4 Mean crop damage by crop pest (monk = monkey, live = livestock), differentiated between above-ground crops (measured by individual crop item) and below-ground crops (measured in acres).

	Monk above	Monk below	Pig above	Pig below	Live above	Live below
Jan.	33.31	0.00	0.00	0.00	0.00	0.01
Feb.	10.45	0.00	0.00	0.00	0.55	0.00
Mar.	8.30	0.00	0.00	0.00	0.00	0.00
Apr.	7.63	0.00	0.00	0.00	0.00	0.00
May	1.02	0.00	0.00	0.02	0.00	0.00
Jun.	1.17	0.00	0.00	0.00	0.00	0.00
Jul.	0.47	0.00	0.00	0.00	1.88	0.00
Aug.	0.17	0.00	0.00	0.00	0.00	0.00
Sep.	5.36	0.00	0.80	0.00	0.00	0.00
Oct.	24.80	0.00	0.00	0.00	0.00	0.00
Nov	10.89	0.01	0.00	0.00	0.00	0.00
Dec.	19.47	0.00	0.00	0.00	13.69	0.00

Table 19.5 Standard deviation in crop damage by crop pest (monk = monkey, live = livestock), differentiated between above-ground crops (measured by individual crop item) and below-ground crops (measured in acres).

	Monk above	Monk below	Pig above	Pig below	Live above	Live below
Jan.	123.24	0.00	0.00	0.00	0.00	0.04
Feb.	65.76	0.02	0.00	0.02	4.38	0.00
Mar.	43.10	0.00	0.00	0.00	0.00	0.00
Apr.	28.36	0.04	0.00	0.01	0.00	0.00
May	3.62	0.00	0.00	0.10	0.00	0.00
Jun.	7.55	0.00	0.00	0.00	0.00	0.00
Jul.	3.75	0.00	0.00	0.00	15.00	0.00
Aug.	1.38	0.00	0.00	0.00	0.00	0.00
Sep	20.83	0.04	6.25	0.01	0.00	0.00
Oct.	99.85	0.00	0.00	0.03	0.00	0.00
Nov.	39.87	0.03	0.00	0.01	0.00	0.00
Dec.	68.86	0.01	0.00	0.00	109.50	0.00

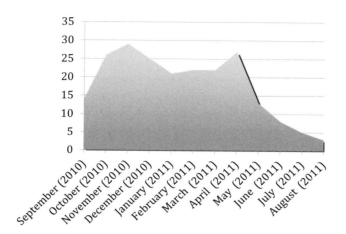

Figure 19.6 Number of grid cells affected by monkey crop damage during the twelve-month study period.

visits, pigs destroyed 10,475 pounds of ground crops and 51 individual crop items during the same time period (livestock destroyed 1021 individual crop items and 2834 pounds of ground crops). This shows that while monkey damage occurs much more frequently, pigs do significantly more damage per foraging event.

Damage was monitored on a total of 699 grid cells nested within the 64 farms. Of these 699 cells, 125 were affected by crop damage by monkeys at some point during the year (18 percent). Damage in cells did not occur evenly across months. Figure 19.6 shows the decline in the number of cells affected by crop damage during the mango season (from May to August).

Tree fruits were the most preferred crop, followed by squash, eggplant, cucumber, corn, watermelon, okra, pumpkin, sweet pepper, tomato, peanut, cabbage, fig, and sweet potato (Table 19.3). Crops with only one incident were placed low on the scale regardless of their observed/expected ratio, with the exception of tree fruits, which were combined into one category. "Mango" is not included as a cultivated tree fruit because it was cultivated on only one farm. The "value assigned" column explains how the values were assigned to crops based on their observed/expected ratios. These are the values that were assigned to individual grid cells each month.

Predicting the Likelihood and Severity of Crop Damage

Part 1: Predicting the Likelihood of Damage

The HGLM considers that the way each of the nine variables affect the probability of damage varies somewhat by farm. This means that in the model, the intercept and slopes of the seven Level 1 variables (distance to water source "water," distance to nearest road "road," distance to forest "forest," most preferred crop in cell "pref," number of months with crops planted in the non-mango season [months of September to April] "moSA," number of months with crops planted in the mango season [months of May to August] "moMA," and whether the measurement was taken during the mango season "mango") will vary to some degree, though the mean effect of each of these variables will be a linear function of the two farm variables: the number of neighbors the farm has ("neighbors") and how much time the farmer spends guarding the farm ("guarding"). How these variables vary by farm is dependent on the random noise associated with Level 2. Additionally, the interaction between each Level 1 predictor variable and "mango" is included to test whether the variables that predict crop damage vary seasonally.

The results show very small collinearity between the predictor variables (all variance inflation factors [VIFs] were under 1.24), implying that we are not losing power due to correlations between predictors. Due to the large number of interaction terms in the models, there are no obvious interpretations that come from the fixed effects (see Dore [2013] for model details). Variable selection was performed on the full model to obtain a reduced model with fewer predictor variables. With the exceptions "distance to road" and "number of months with crops planted in the non-mango season," all of the original variables have significant main effects and thus are shown to be important in making predictions. The variance components from both the full and reduced models show that the extent to which mango season affects the probability of a farm receiving damage varies more than how the other variables affect the probability of receiving damage.

Making Predictions

The AUC for an ROC curve for the full and reduced models was 0.8678 and 0.8583 respectively (they are not statistically significantly different). The resulting cutoff values for making hard predictions are 0.0323 and 0.0269 for the full and reduced models, respectively. To avoid overfitting the data, the choice of making predictions based on the full or reduced model was determined by leave-one-out cross-validation (LOOCV).

The mean squared error (MSE) from the LOOCV was very similar for the full and reduced models, yielding the values 0.03184 and 0.03174 for full and reduced models respectively. Using the cutoff values from the ROC closest top-left criteria, Tables 19.6 and 19.7 were obtained (again using the cross-validated predictions). This gives a

Table 19.6 Predicted/actual table for full model

	True is 0	True is 1
Predicted is 0	4595	47
Predicted is 1	1305	168

Table 19.7 Predicted/actual table for reduced model.

	True is 0	True is 1
Predicted is 0	4517	43
Predicted is 1	1383	172

sensitivity (specificity) of 0.7788 (0.7814) and 0.7656 (0.8000) for the full and reduced
models respectively. These results imply that by using fewer variables we are obtaining
nearly equivalent, and with respect to MSE and specificity better, prediction results.

A script usable in R or Excel has been created which allows one to input the values of
all of the predictive variables and generate both the probability that damage will occur
on the specific plot of land, and, using the cutoff values from the ROC closest top
criteria, whether damage is predicted (YES) or not (NO).

Part 2: Predicting the Severity of Damage

Here the dataset was narrowed down to only the grid cells that received damage. This
makes it possible to use the detailed information on the percentage of crop damage in
each grid cell and to investigate which variables help predict the severity of damage,
given that crop damage has occurred. The predictive variables implemented in the HLM
are the same as in Part 1 (see Dore [2013] for the full model). Not unexpectedly, the data
violated the assumption of normality. However, we were able to satisfy this assumption
by utilizing a Box–Cox transformation of the response variable.

The variable selection procedure was again performed to obtain a reduced model with
fewer variables. There was no evidence of collinearity between any of the independent
variables that would affect the variable selection procedure. The effect of spatial
correlation among the residuals was tested and determined to be insignificant. This
implies that the spatial dependency is fully accounted for in the hierarchical structure of
the model. The final reduced model is:

$$
\begin{aligned}
y_{ij}|&damage \\
&= \gamma_{0,0} + y_{4,0}cropPref + \gamma_{5,0}moSA + \gamma_{7,0}mango + \gamma_{11,0}mango : cropPref \\
&+ \gamma_{12,0}mango : moSA + r_{0j} + r_{(1j)}water + r_{2j}road + r_{3j}forest + r_{4j}cropPref \\
&+ r_{5j}moSA + r_{6j}moMA + r_{7j}mango + r_{8j}mango : water + r_{9j}mango : road \\
&+ r_{10j}mango : forest + r_{11j}mango : cropPref + r_{12j}mango : moSA \\
&+ r_{13j}mango : moMA + \epsilon_{ij}
\end{aligned}
$$

Tables 19.8 and 19.9 show the fixed and random effects for the reduced models (data for
the full model not shown). The question of whether to use the full or reduced model was

Table 19.8 The fixed effects for the reduced model.

Fixed effect	Estimate	Standard error	t-value	Pr($>$|t|)
(Intercept)	−1.5279	0.379762	−4.0233	9.18E-05
pref	0.020159	0.026886	0.749775	0.454597
moSA	−0.05465	0.051757	−1.05585	0.292779
mango	−0.25444	0.907762	−0.2803	0.779647
m:p	0.36539	0.180259	2.027032	0.044479
m:moSA	−0.42587	0.160634	−2.65115	0.008907

Variables with p-values greater than 0.10 are included because they are significant (at $p < 0.10$) in
an interaction.

Table 19.9 The random effects' variance components for the reduced model

Variance component	Estimate
Intercept	0.000559
water	9.55E-07
road	1.99E-06
forest	9.49E-08
pref	0.002109
moSA	0.000416
moMA	0.002646
mango	0.001716
m:w	3.66E-06
m:r	3.05E-06
m:f	1.68E-06
m:p	9.83E-05
m:moSA	0.00011
m:moMA	0.000263

again answered by using LOOCV. As a measure of how well the model fits, the square of the prediction errors, i.e.

$$\sum_{i,j} \left(\gamma_{ij} - \hat{\gamma}_{ij} \right)^2,$$

is computed for both the full and reduced models. The values for the full and reduced models respectively are 133.9 and 86.71, indicating that the reduced model is dramatically better at predicting the extent of damage incurred by monkeys.

There are several conclusions that can be drawn from the reduced model. During the non-mango season, both crop preference (pref) and the number of months with crops planted during the non-mango season (moSA) have a statistically significant effect, and that effect is amplified during the mango season. So higher crop preference leads to more damage, especially during the mango season. Similarly, having crops planted during more months of the non-mango season leads to a decrease in damage, especially in the mango season. The effect of mango season is slightly more difficult to interpret since it is confounded in the two interaction terms, but one can derive from the model output a table like the following:

moSA	pref
2	≤ 3
3	≤ 4
4	≤ 5
5	≤ 6
6	≤ 7
7	≤ 8
8	Anything

Each row of this table gives conditions based on "moSA" and "pref" for which a farm will receive less damage. For example, the first row implies that if crops were planted for two months during the non-mango season and "pref" is ≤3, there will be less damage to the grid cell during the mango season. Similarly, for the next five rows, the last row implies that if crops were planted for eight months during the non-mango season, then regardless of the value of "pref," there will be less damage to the grid cell during the mango season.

The variability in how predictor variables affect crop damage is largest for crop preference and mango season, as seen by the large variance components for these two variables. Thus, for example, the way in which mango season affects damage on farms varies from farm to farm more so than, say, distance to the forest boundary. On average, however, the interpretations of the significant fixed effects (crop preference, number of months with crops planted in the non-mango season, and mango season) still hold. A script usable in R and Excel has been created which allows one to input the values for these variables and generate the predicted severity of damage once damage has been predicted.

Ethnographic Results

The results of these predictive models show that green monkey crop foraging behavior is predictable. However, this approach does not take into account the historical/temporal aspect of St Kitts' landscape, and the fact that it has undergone tremendous changes since the collapse of the sugar industry in 2005. Data from interviews and conversations with Kittitian farmers and members of the agricultural community, described below (and in more detail in Dore 2013, 2018; Dore et al. 2018), show that the sugar industry has played a large role with regard to green monkey movements and Kittitian farmers' cultural conceptualizations of monkeys.

From the 1600s until 2005, an organized system of sugar cane production dominated the arable land on the island, and small-scale farmers worked in ravines and at the base of the mountain, above the cane apron, which wrapped around a high-altitude forest in the center of the island. This activity created a barrier, preventing most mainland monkeys from leaving the forest (monkeys are also found on the southeast peninsula, where crops have never been grown in significant amounts). After the industry closed in 2005, thousands of acres opened up for small-scale farming on this government-owned land. There are now more farmers than ever, but few that work at the base of the forest, where they used to maintain important food sources for monkeys (i.e., fruit trees and crops – primarily fruits, vegetables, and root crops). Additionally, there is no longer the kind of full-time, large-scale activity on the agricultural land that existed during sugar production, including the presence of forest rangers with guns. This situation means that monkey presence in agricultural areas is no longer restricted to the base of the forest; monkeys have come out of the mountain in search of food and now damage crops all over St Kitts, including in gardens in the villages and downtown.

The ethnographic data also highlight the effect of the sugar industry on human–green monkey interconnections. The predictive model shows that human agricultural practices currently affect monkey behaviors, and the ethnographic data on the role of the sugar industry on green monkey movements provides context about how humans have historically affected NHP behavior. With regard to how green monkeys have affected Kittitians' cultural conceptualizations, the ethnographic data show that these conceptualizations are inextricably linked to the sugar industry. Monkeys have always been vilified as crop "raiders," and in order to protect their crops from monkeys, farmers have always had to expend a significant amount of energy. However, during the time of the sugar industry, monkeys were only pests in a buffer zone around the forest–farm boundary, and only to the small set of smallholding farmers that cultivated crops along this boundary and in the ravines. Most Kittitians involved in agriculture worked in the well-protected cane fields, and their primary experience with monkeys was "in the pot" as food. Since the end of the sugar industry, large-scale agriculture no longer serves as a barrier to monkey movements. Monkeys now damage crops all over the island, so many more farmers are dealing with this problem and farmers have become more conscious of green monkey behavioral patterns and intelligence. As a result, the similarity between humans and monkeys has become increasingly apparent, and while many Kittitians still eat monkeys, the ethnographic data show that this number has decreased significantly. For example:

(Kerry Dore: When people in St Kitts are talking about monkeys, what kinds of things are they saying about them?) Well most people, like they used to, they will catch them and eat them. *(OK, yeah. What do you think about that? Do you think it's OK to eat monkey?)* Well, I ate it when I was younger, but now I'm a man, I won't. *(Now you won't eat it? Why not?)* Because of what I see. *(What do you mean?)* Like the one having the menstruation and looking like people, I'm saying "no man." It turn my mind. (Kerry Dore, farmer interview, July 15, 2011).

Finally, the ethnographic data show the effect of the sugar industry on the unique nature of green monkey pestilence discourse in St Kitts. The pestilence discourse regarding monkeys is unique (compared to humans, pigs, and livestock, who also eat crops) for three reasons. First, there is some leniency with regard to monkeys foraging crops because farmers recognize that monkeys only do this because they are hungry because of insufficient food in the mountain as a repercussion of the sugar industry closure. Second, monkeys are considered "natural" animals compared to the domestic livestock that have owners who should be taking responsibility for them. Third, monkeys' similarity to humans exacerbates conflict because farmers expect monkeys to behave with human-like manners in their crop foraging. Monkeys are "school boys," they are "educated," they have "gone to college," they are "half people," they are "just like people," they "are people," and they "do everything like a human," so monkeys are "willful" and are conscious of their crop-foraging behavior, they are "wasteful" or "bad minded" when they take one bite out of 20 different cucumbers instead of eating one whole cucumber, and when your crops get damaged the day after you chase monkeys off your farm, they are "spiteful" (Dore et al. 2018).

Discussion

St Kitts Green Monkey Crop-Foraging Behavior

The results of the predictive models of St Kitts green monkey crop-foraging behavior can be compared to previous studies of NHP crop foraging worldwide. This work confirms that distance to the forest boundary, season/alternative food availability, preventative strategies, crop type, number of neighboring farms, and the amount of crops under cultivation are important variables in determining which farms are damaged by monkeys. Additionally, the models show that distance to nearby water sources is important. This variable has not been assessed in previous studies of NHP crop foraging; however, Sitati et al. (2003) show that it is a significant factor with regard to elephant crop foraging. This study does not support the influence of roads on the locations of NHP crop damage.

In addition, the results of the predictive models generated here must be interpreted in the context of what is known about St Kitts green monkey crop-foraging behavior. The first predictive model provides evidence that a farm's likelihood of experiencing damage is related to all of the variables investigated (except distance to road and number of months with crops planted in the non-mango season): mango season, distance to the forest boundary, distance to water, crop preference, number of neighboring farms, the farmer's guarding behavior, and how often the farmer plants crops (in the mango season). It is not possible to determine the exact nature of the relationships between these variables and whether a farm will experience crop damage (i.e., to support or reject the hypotheses on the relationship between these variables and crop damage) because of the large number of interaction terms, but it is clear that knowledge of all of these variables is necessary to make the most accurate predictions of a farm's likelihood of experiencing crop foraging by green monkeys.

The results of the second predictive model generated for this analysis show that three variables – crop preference, the number of months with crops planted (in the non-mango season, September to April), and mango season – are important in predicting the severity of crop damage a farm will receive. The effect of crop preference on crop damage supports hypothesis 5 that more crop damage will occur on farms containing the monkeys' preferred crops. This effect is amplified during the mango season, when the animals can afford to be choosier with regard to what they will eat because uncultivated mango fruit is readily available in the forest and ravines.

The effect of the number of months with crops planted (in the non-mango season) does not support hypothesis 9. The results show that *less* crop damage occurs on farms with crops planted during more months of the non-mango season, and this effect is amplified in the mango season. In other words, from September to April, the more often a farmer plants crops, the less likely he or she is to receive monkey crop damage, especially during the mango season (May to August). One explanation for this effect may be farmer presence: While this study accounted for farmer presence by asking farmers the number of hours per week they spend on their farm and what type of other guarding measures they use, these behaviors were not broken down seasonally. Generally speaking, the more often a farmer plants crops, the more likely he or she is to be present on their farm. These results indicate that if farmers plant more crops in the non-mango season (and it is assumed they are therefore present on their farm more often), they are less susceptible to crop damage, especially in the mango season, when again the monkeys can afford to be choosier in what they eat. This indicates that during the mango season, monkeys are less likely to forage in farms that had more crops planted, and an associated active farmer presence, during the longer non-mango season.

The effect of mango season is not as straightforward due to the interactions with crop preference and number of months with crops planted (during the non-mango season). Generally speaking, the data support hypothesis 6 that farms will receive more crop damage during the non-mango season, but this effect is related to the monkeys' preference for crops on the farm and the number of months the farm has crops planted. While farms generally have more crop damage during the non-mango season, if they have crops planted in very few months of the non-mango season and plant crops highly preferred by monkeys, then this trend does not hold. Collectively, these results indicate that, of the farms likely to experience crop damage from green monkeys, seasonal fruiting plays a role in which farms will experience the most severe damage, but that farmers' planting behavior, specifically the consistency of their cultivation and the crops they plant, have the ability to offset this effect (i.e., if farmers plant non-preferred crops consistently over many months of the year, they will not see a reduction in damage during the non-mango season, because damage will be low all year long).

The Ethnoprimatological Context

Conversations with Kittitian farmers and members of the agricultural community reveal the novelty of the current patterns of agricultural production in St Kitts. Previously, virtually all of the island's arable land was taken up in sugar cane, so smallholding farmers were limited to the marginal areas below the forest boundary and in the ravines. It has only been 13 years since the government has allocated plots of former sugar cane land to farmers. Prior to 2005, these lands were under continuous production and protection, restricting monkeys from entering and controlling their population size.

While statistical restrictions necessitated differentiating between the likelihood and severity of crop damage, an ethnoprimatological approach provides the opportunity to explore these two aspects of primate crop damage and their role in farmers' attitudes toward green monkeys. The ethnographic data show that the severity of the monkeys' crop foraging plays a greater role in farmers' negative perceptions of green monkeys than does the likelihood of the monkeys' crop foraging. Again, the sugar industry plays a significant role in this result. Kittitian farmers are keenly aware of the significant changes that have occurred since the closure of the sugar industry and how they have affected the monkeys. They recognize that the animals are eating crops because they can no longer find the food necessary to sustain themselves in the mountains as they could during the days of the sugar cane industry. This plays a role in the fact that farmers are willing to share some of their crops with the monkeys. When farmers are asked about the nature of NHP crop foraging, they respond that they are primarily frustrated by the monkeys' "wasteful" behavior, not necessarily the act of eating crops. Farmers can spare three cucumbers, but the severe, negative perception of monkeys results when the farmer comes to his or her farm to find that the monkeys have taken one bite out of 30 different cucumbers. Because farmers now see monkeys on a regular basis, they recognize their human-like qualities and thus expect them to behave with human manners (Dore et al. 2018).

Conclusion

This study exposes the limitations of primatological research projects that do not take into account anthropogenic context. While the results of the predictive models are highly informative with regard to managing the current problem of crop damage by monkeys in St Kitts, it does not consider the historical context of this issue or how Kittitian farmers' perceptions of monkeys have changed over time. Attending to these issues through an ethnoprimatological framework provides a much more holistic view of this environmental issue.

From the first stage of analysis, we know that data on a farm/grid cell's distance to the forest boundary, distance to water sources, number of neighboring farms, guarding behavior, and planting frequency, as well as monkeys' crop preference and alternative food availability (mangoes in this case), are necessary to make the most accurate predictions of a farm's likelihood of receiving crop damage. With regard to the severity of this damage, three variables are particularly important: crop preference, number of months with crops planted, and mango season, and the relationship between these variables and crop damage is more straightforward. Farmers working in areas predicted to have severe monkey crop damage can limit the severity of the damage by consistently planting crops that are low on the scale of monkey preference. Farms that do this will not see a decrease in crop damage during the mango season because their rates of crop damage will be low all year long.

The ethnographic data reveal that while crop damage by monkeys has been a problem in St Kitts for over 350 years, it is really only in the last 15 years, since the sugar industry closed in 2005, that this problem has gotten out of control. The sugar industry and its infrastructure were highly effective at preventing monkeys from entering the lowlands. Now, the monkeys are all over the island, most notably on former cane land now filled with the smallholding farms where this research took place. These results expose the important point that not all relevant spatial data can be revealed via quantitative spatial analysis; qualitative data may also reveal important spatial aspects of the human–NHP interface.

Conversations with the agricultural community of St Kitts show that farmers are fully aware of how recent land use changes have exacerbated human–NHP conflict, and they are, in some ways, sympathetic to the fact that the monkeys no longer have the food needed to sustain themselves in the mountains. Thus, it is really the severe crop damage, not the damage itself, which is responsible for negative perceptions of monkeys in St Kitts. This work has narrowed down the factors responsible for severe crop damage, and thus will hopefully be able to improve Kittitians' perceptions of green monkeys over time, along with scientifically backed, sustained management strategies.

Our future plans include working with the St Kitts government to manage "the monkey problem." We now know which factors are responsible for severe damage, and the ethnographic data have shown that the sugar industry was highly effective at keeping monkey damage at bay. Thus, part of this management strategy may include mimicking the sugar industry infrastructure, which includes systematically protecting large plots of land containing multiple farms. In totality, this work shows that while

quantitative methods like GIS and GPS are highly informative with regard to primatological questions, qualitative data are necessary to place these questions in cultural
context and most effectively conserve (or manage) nonhuman primates.

References

Beyer, H. L. 2004. Hawth's analysis tools for ArcGIS. Available at www.spatialecology.com/
htools.

Chapman, C. A. 1985. The influence of habitat on behavior in a group of St. Kitts green monkeys.
Journal of Zoology, London **206**: 311–320.

Chapman, C. A. 1987. Selection of secondary growth areas by vervet monkeys (*Cercopithecus
aethiops*). *American Journal of Primatology* **12**: 217–221.

Chapman, C. A. and Fedigan, L. M. 1984. Territoriality in the St. Kitts vervet, *Cercopithecus
aethiops*. *Journal of Human Evolution* **13**: 677–686.

Chapman, C. A., Fedigan, L. M., and Fedigan, L. 1988. Ecological and demographic influences
on the pattern of association in St. Kitts vervets. *Primates* **29**: 417–421.

Cormier, L. A. 2002. Monkey as food, monkey as child: Guaja symbolic cannibalism. Pages 63–84
in *Primates Face to Face: The Conservation Implications of Human and Nonhuman Primate
Interconnections*. A. Fuentes and L. D. Wolfe. Cambridge University Press, Cambridge.

Cormier, L. A. 2003. *Kinship with Monkeys: The Guaja Foragers of Eastern Amazonia*. Columbia University Press, New York.

Dore, K. M. 2013. An anthropological investigation of the dynamic human–vervet monkey
(*Chlorocebus aethiops sabaeus*) interface in St. Kitts, West Indies. Dissertation. University
of Wisconsin-Milwaukee.

Dore, K. M. 2017. Navigating the methodological landscape: ethnographic data expose the
nuances of "the monkey problem" in St. Kitts, West Indies. Pages 219–231 in *Ethnoprimatology: A Practical Guide to Research at the Human–Nonhuman Primate Interface*. K. M. Dore,
E. P. Riley, and A. Fuentes. Cambridge University Press, Cambridge.

Dore, K. M. 2018. Ethnoprimatology without conservation: the political ecology of farmer-green
monkey (*Chlorocebus aethiops sabaeus*) relations in St. Kitts, West Indies. *International
Journal of Primatology* **39**: 918–944.

Dore, K. M., Eller, A. R., Eller, J. L. 2018. Identity construction and symbolic association in
farmer–vervet monkey (*Chlorocebus aethiops sabaeus*) interconnections in St. Kitts. *Folia
Primatologica* **89**: 63–80.

Fairbanks, L. A. and Bird, J. 1978. Ecological correlates of interindividual distance in the St. Kitts
vervet (*Cercopithecus aethiops sabaeus*). *Primates* **19**: 605–614.

Fuentes, A. 2006. Human–nonhuman primate interconnections and their relevance to anthropology. *Ecological and Environmental Anthropology* **2**(2): 1–11.

Fuentes, A. 2012. Ethnoprimatology and the anthropology of the human–primate interface.
Annual Review of Anthropology **41**: 101–117.

Fuentes, A. and Hockings, K. 2010. The ethnoprimatological approach in primatology. *American
Journal of Primatology* **72**: 841–847.

Fuentes, A. and Wolfe, L. 2002. *Primates Face to Face: Conservation Implications of Human–
Nonhuman Primate Interconnections*. Cambridge University Press, Cambridge.

Gillingham, S. and Lee, P. C. 2003. People and protected areas: a study of local perceptions of wildlife
crop-damage conflict in an area bordering the Selous Game Reserve, Tanzania. *Oryx* **3**: 316–325.

Hardin, R. and Remis, M. J. 2006. Biological and cultural anthropology of a changing tropical forest: a fruitful collaboration across subfields. *American Anthropologist* **108**: 273–285.

Hashim, N. R., Abdul Manan, M. S., and Nazli, M. F. 2009. Using geographic information system to predict primate crop raiding in peninsular Malaysia. *IUP Journal of Environmental Sciences* 3(4): 39–46.

Helmer, E. H., Kennaway, T. A., Pedreros, D. H., et al. 2008. Land cover and forest formation distributions for St. Kitts, Nevis, St. Eustatius, Grenada and Barbados from decision tree classification of cloud-cleared satellite imagery. *Caribbean Journal of Science* **44**: 175–198.

Hill, C. M. 1997. Crop-raiding by wild vertebrates: the farmer's perspective in an agricultural community in western Uganda. *International Journal of Pest Management* **43**: 77–84.

Hill, C. M. 2000. Conflict of interest between people and baboons: crop raiding in Uganda. *International Journal of Primatology* **21**: 299–315.

Hill, C. M. and Webber, A. D. 2010. Perceptions of nonhuman primates in human–wildlife conflict scenarios. *American Journal of Primatology* **72**: 919–924.

Lee, Y. and Nelder, J. A. 1996. Hierarchical generalized linear models with discussion. *Journal of the Royal Statistical Society B* **58**: 619–678.

Linkie, M., Dinata, Y., Nofrianto, A., and Leader-Williams, N. 2007. Patterns and perceptions of wildlife crop raiding in and around Kerinci Seblat National Park, Sumatra. *Animal Conservation* **10**: 127–135.

Maples, W. R., Maples, M. K., Greenhood, W. F., and Walek, M. L. 1976. Adaptations of crop-raiding baboons in Kenya. *American Journal of Physical Anthropology* **45**: 309–316.

McGuire, M. T. 1974. *The St. Kitts Vervet.* Karger, New York.

Naughton-Treves, L. 1996. Uneasy neighbors: wildlife and farmers around Kibale National Park, Uganda. Dissertation. University of Florida.

Naughton-Treves, L. 1997. Farming the forest edge: vulnerable places and people around Kibale National Park, Uganda. *Geographical Review* **87**: 27–46.

Naughton-Treves, L. 1998. Predicting patterns of crop damage by wildlife around Kibale National Park, Uganda. *Conservation Biology* **12**: 156–169.

Naughton-Treves, L., Treves, A., Chapman, C., and Wrangham, R. 1998. Temporal patterns of crop-raiding by primates: linking food availability in croplands and adjacent forest. *Journal of Applied Ecology* **35**: 596–606.

Newmark, W. D., Manyanza, D. N., Gamassa, D.-G. M., and Sariko, H. I. 1994. The conflict between wildlife and local people living adjacent to protected areas in Tanzania: human density as a predictor. *Conservation Biology* **8**: 249–255.

Nijman, V. and Nekaris, K. A. I. 2010. Testing a model for predicting primate crop-raiding using crop- and farm-specific risk values. *Animal Behaviour Science* **127**: 125–129.

Paterson, J. and Wallis, J. 2005. *Commensalism and Conflict: The Primate–Human Interface.* American Society of Primatologists, Norman, OK.

Perkins, N. J. and Schisterman, E. F. 2006. The inconsistency of "optimal" cutpoints obtained using two criteria based on the receiver operating characteristic curve. *American Journal of Epidemiology* **163**: 670–675.

Petto, A. J. and Povinelli, D. J. 1985. Some preliminary observations of vervets (*Cercopithecus aethiops*) from the Greatheeds Pond Area on St. Kitts, WI. *Canadian Journal of Anthropology* 4(2): 77–81.

Poirier, F. E. 1972. The St. Kitts green monkey (*Cercopithecus aethiops sabaeus*): ecology, population dynamics, and selected behavioral traits. *Folia Primatologica* **17**: 20–55.

Priston, N. E. C. 2005. Crop raiding by *Macaca ochreata brunnescens* in Sulawesi: reality, perceptions and outcomes for conservation. Dissertation. University of Cambridge.

Priston, N. E. C. and Underdown, S. J. 2009. A simple method for calculating the likelihood of crop damage by primates: an epidemiological approach. *International Journal of Pest Management* **55**: 51–56.

R Core Team. 2008. R: *A Language and Environment for Statistical Computing*. R Foundation for Statistical Computing, Vienna.

Riley, E. P. 2007. The human–macaque interface: conservation implications of current and future overlap and conflict in Lore Lindu National Park, Sulawesi, Indonesia. *American Anthropologist* **109**: 473–484.

Riley, E. P. and Priston, N. E. C. 2010. Macaques in farms and folklore: exploring the human–nonhuman primate interface in Sulawesi, Indonesia. *American Journal of Primatology* **72**: 848–854.

Rönnegård, L., Shen, X., and Alam, M. 2010. HGLM: a package for fitting hierarchical generalized linear models. *R Journal* **2**(2): 20–28.

Sade, D. S. and Hildrech, R. W. 1965. Notes on the green monkey (*Cercopithecus aethiops sabaeus*) on St. Kitts, West Indies. *Caribbean Journal of Science* **5**: 67–81.

Siex, K. S. and Struhsaker, T. T. 1999. Colobus monkeys and coconuts: a study of perceived human–wildlife conflicts. *Journal of Applied Ecology* **36**: 1009–1020.

Sitati, N. W., Walpole, M. J., Smith, R. J., and Leader-Williams, N. 2003. Predicting spatial aspects of human–elephant conflict. *Journal of Applied Ecology* **40**: 667–677.

Strum, S. C. 1994. Prospects for managing primate pests. *Revue d'Ecologie: La Terre et la Vie* **49**: 295–306.

Tweyho, M., Hill, C. M., and Obua, J. 2005. Patterns of crop raiding by primates around the Budongo Forest Reserve, Uganda. *Wildlife Biology* **11**: 327–347.

Warren, Y., Buba, B., and Ross, C. 2007. Patterns of crop-raiding near a Nigerian National Park. *International Journal of Pest Management* **53**: 207–216.

Webber, A. D. 2006. Primate crop raiding in Uganda: actual and perceived risks around Budongo Forest Reserve. Dissertation. Oxford Brookes University.

Wheatley, B. P. 1999. *The Sacred Monkeys of Bali*. Waveland, Prospect Heights, NY.

20 Conclusion

Francine L. Dolins

Introduction

The overarching theme of this volume is the application of spatial analysis technology and its potential for tackling major questions foundational to research conducted by field primatologists. In the series of chapters that comprise this volume, the goal of the editors and chapter authors was to provide a thorough reference for "best" as well as innovative practices in collecting and analyzing data using global positioning systems (GPS) and geographic information systems (GIS), including also the use of geo-tracking and remote telemetry apparatus via collars. The processes described are aimed at providing the most accurate measurements and interpretation of movement aligned with other forms of behavior. The authors have presented detailed mapping systems of multiple species and terrains that were distinct from one another and varied as examples for different types of field sites and their study requirements. Distinct ways in which mapping data might be collected, analyzed, and visualized, such that these examples provide models and insights for other researchers, were also discussed. These methods include studies that address theoretical and practical questions about life history strategies, individual and group movement, ecological problem solving, resource knowledge, foraging behavior, predator avoidance, social interactions and competition, and reproductive strategies. The application of GIS data provides insight into the interaction of biogeographical factors with behavior and also population-level genetics. Importantly, GPS data provide the foundation for detailed studies for conservation. A majority of primate species globally are on the brink of ecological disaster due to anthropogenic disturbances and pressures. Increasingly, scientists rely on the data provided by GPS technology to inform our attempts to stem habitat destruction and to protect parcels of habitat necessary to maintain viable primate populations and for the local human communities who are often equally at risk.

This book is presented in three sections, each integrating research reflecting a diverse set of perspectives, species, and habitats, and incorporating multiple techniques in the use of GPS data and spatial analyses. Each of these sections involves discussions of key research questions central to understanding the ecological and biogeographical variables that influence primate behavior, and ultimately the conservation status of species. Many of the kinds of questions addressed in primate field and captive research have a spatial basis. The scale and geographic range may span several countries, the full diameter of a tree's crown, or the interior exhibit of a group of primates at a zoological park. To understand how individuals or those in a group perceive and use space, travel, and conduct cognitive operations resulting in efficient navigation and foraging requires precise methodology. GPS data and GIS analyses provide precision in spatial information gathering and analytic tools that enhance the accuracy in addressing these space-based issues. GPS and GIS have, in the past two decades, considerably increased our ability to ask and answer questions in theoretical and applied ways in behavioral ecology (including movement patterns), nutrition, foraging behavior, social behavior including patterns of fission–fusion, spatial and other types of perceptual cognition, the interaction of biogeographical factors aligned with behavior and population genetics, conservation issues, and responses to habitat loss and hunting in particular, and animal husbandry. The importance of GPS and GIS to current scientific techniques and investigations in field primatology cannot be overstated.

GPS, Spatial Analyses, and Conservation: The Present and the Future

When the editors and chapter authors began working on this volume, we were aware of the primate extinction crisis looming and that this was sadly predicted to occur on a large scale (Peres 1999, 2001). However, as we progressed in completing the manuscript to further advance research methods for field primatologists, the rapid pace of peril for wild primates has become unbounded, even by comparison with the original predictions. Due to purely human activity, approximately 60 percent of all wild primate species are projected to be at risk of extinction in the next few years and 75 percent of wild primate populations are in decline (Estrada et al. 2017, 2018; IUCN 2019; Muller et al. 2012). The anthropogenic activity includes logging and extraction of rare and endangered tree species (e.g., rosewood), slash and burn for agricultural clearing, bushmeat hunting and snaring, poaching, and even the presence of humans passing through areas of forest. All of these negative human activities and their effects have been mapped using GPS data and spatial analyses.

In primate habitat countries, the principal reason for forest clearance is agricultural, mostly for the behemoth multinational corporations that produce commodities ("forest-risk" products) largely consumed in the USA, Canada, China, Japan, and the European Union (Estrada et al. 2017; Garber 2019). These "forest-risk" products include beef, soy, palm oil, and natural rubber, principally grown in primate-habitat countries (Garber 2019). Spatial analyses provide the data to predict that at the rate of current forest destruction, 68 percent of the forest areas inhabited by extant species of prosimians, monkeys, and apes will be converted to support "forest-risk" agriculture before the turn of the next century (Estrada et al. 2017). These data were based on spatial modeling, which as a formative method is described in a number of the chapters in this volume (Chapters 8, 14, 15, 17, and 18).

With these very stark predictions of ecological destruction, it is apparent that the scientific community must tackle and attempt to reverse the extreme decline and potential extinction of many wild animal populations and species, including the many primate species at risk. Further studies to support conservation efforts, using the GPS data-collection techniques and GIS analyses as outlined and described in the chapters of this book, are presented for reference and guidance. Compared to two or more decades ago, through the use of GPS and GIS, primatologists can effectively monitor species and even individual animals not only to address questions in basic research that provide information for conservation purposes but also to monitor specific populations of primates and their habitats (Muller et al. 2012). Each of the chapters in this book provides examples and reference scenarios. For example, in a case study examining causal factors in bonobo population decline, Hickey and Conroy (Chapter 16) demonstrate that fragmented forests (due to logging) together with the effects of hunting negatively impact bonobo occupancy of that forest. Using GPS data and GIS analyses to determine causal relationships, the authors separately examined the impact of intact forests and fragmented forests with multiple levels of hunting pressures, low to high. They showed that for each factor alone, forest fragmentation or any level of hunting pressure, can negatively influence bonobo presence in a given area. Together, the combination of these factors significantly negatively impacted the wild bonobo populations and their behavior. Even a machete cut in a tree had an impact on the travel behavior of a group of bonobos. The authors' precise use of GPS data collection and spatial analysis enabled this type of causal investigation (quasi-experimental) that led to invaluable conclusions about what levels of anthropogenic pressures can cause disturbance to an endangered species.

A crucial part of any effective conservation effort always includes the local human community. The ethnoprimatological approach is an exceptional way to provide insight into how to incorporate the human needs of the local community members as partners in conservation with that of the nonhuman primates. In Chapter 19, an ethnoprimatological investigation provides an example of how to evaluate local communities' needs, wants, and attitudes toward the primates who raid their crops and are considered to be pests, and to provide viable solutions.

Interestingly, of the more than 500 species of primates, only a handful are generally represented in peer-reviewed journal articles, affecting funding for further research on wild primates and giving a biased impression that there are only a few primate species in existence (Bezanson & McNamara 2019; Rodrigues 2019). Approximately half of all manuscripts published in a prominent primatological journal were on the same few genera: *Macaca, Pan, Cebus/Sapajus, Papio, Alouatta, Gorilla,* and *Callithrix*. Moreover, there is a bias in primatological and other scientific journals, with almost twice as many papers published based on captive studies compared to those on field-based studies or field experiments (Janmaat 2019). Captive studies were also cited at a much higher rate than field studies (Janmaat 2019), generally affecting future funding for more field research as well as the careers of those field primatologists. Despite this, we must recognize that there is a crucial need for an expansion of field studies of more wild primate species. The natural habitat of primates is disappearing at such a rapid rate, particularly the tropical forests, and with these habitats also goes the behaviors that are expressed within them. Behaviors do not fossilize nor do they transfer, unchanged, to primates who comprise the captive populations. Indeed, even as a scientist who conducts both captive and field research on primate behavior and cognition,

I recognize that collecting data with captive primates may reflect artifacts of their captivity and possible human enculturation.

In this present time, we have available enhanced capabilities to collect spatial and behavioral data on wild primates using advanced technologies, including GPS systems and techniques (as described in all of the chapters of this book), as well as advanced methods for analyzing the data (see Chapters 5 and 6 in particular). These new technologies also include GPS integration into collars worn by individual primates as described in Chapters 3 and 4. Additionally, using other noninvasive methods, we can gather data with camera traps, audio triangulation (Kalan et al. 2016), and heat sensors for thermal imaging or thermography (as used with wild elephants in *The Elephant Listening Project*, http://elephantlisteningproject.org/thermal-imaging). The latter produces images of the full body of the animal in a color scale, with the core body temperatures apparent by comparison with temperatures closer to the skin. There are multiple ways that these data-collection techniques can be used for monitoring animals, as well as in conjunction with each other. Thermography, for example, can be used for evaluating numbers of individuals at locations, social behavior, the health status of an individual as well as their reproductive state (for females).

The central question in conservation often is: *When is a forest fragment too small to support a genetically diverse and healthy (primate) population?* What the particular power of GPS data and the related spatial analyses can provide in field studies is to identify and parse the landscape variables necessary for the survival of primate populations. These include identifying the biogeographical features that make up the space (the quality and quantity of the home range size per group and potentially more) and the foraging and social interaction requirements for multiple groups sufficient to buffer them from drought and disease, as well as to maintain a healthy genetic population in that habitat. In this volume, Steffens and Lehman (Chapter 17) and Kamilar and Beaudrot (Chapter 18) provide excellent examples of techniques to assess forest fragments and the ecological features in the biogeography necessary to support primate populations. These types of field studies and analyses are crucial for protecting the survival of primates globally.

Field studies themselves are also protective for the primate populations being studied. Logging and poaching decrease in and around study sites (Janmaat 2019). At many field sites, conservation education, community education, and related projects in support of the local human communities have been initiated by field primatologists to enhance their welfare and to partner with them on conservation efforts (e.g., Dolins et al. 2010; Savage et al. 2010). Thus, field studies are crucial for the survival and continuity of many wild primate populations globally.

With improvements in field methods, such as the implementation of existing high-quality GPS technology and GIS analyses, and insightful study designs such as those employed by the contributing chapter authors in this volume, more and varied species, and particularly those at risk of extinction, can and should be studied in depth. Obtaining this breadth of knowledge about extant primate species may serve to sustain their populations against the threats of extinction. Our knowledge about these individual primates, populations, and species may be the principal way of saving them.

Addendum

The Amazon rainforest is burning. The fires are a human-made event (a tragedy), with fringes of the forest set alight, charcoaling out of existence (Evans 2019; Pecanha & Wallace 2019). The question is: *Can science and the use of technology conserve primates and their habitats, and simultaneously reduce local human impact while improving their lives?* As outlined in this book, we can and should advance the goal of implementing high-quality scientific methods and technology to save primate populations and entire species and to improve the lives of the humans in local communities of primate-habitat countries. In tandem, through accumulated facts about these primate species and the ecological systems they inhabit, scientists and primatologists in particular should use strong advocacy and even activism to promote policy changes for the benefit of primate conservation.

References

Bezanson, M. and McNamara, A. 2019. The what and where of primate field research may be failing primate conservation. *Evolutionary Anthropology* **28**: 166–178.

Dolins F. L., Jolly, A., Ratsimbazafy, J., et al. 2010. Conservation education in Madagascar: three case studies in the biologically diverse island-continent. *American Journal of Primatology* **72**(5): 391–406.

Estrada, A., Garber, P. A., Rylands, A. B., et al. 2017. Impending extinction crisis of the world's primates: why primates matter. *Science Advances* **3**: e1600946.

Estrada, A., Garber, P. A., Mittermeier, R. A., et al. 2018. Primates in peril: the significance of Brazil, Madagascar, Indonesia and the Democratic Republic of the Congo for global primate conservation. *PeerJ.* DOI 10.7717/peerj.4869.

Evans, K. 2019. Ancient farmers burned the Amazon, but today's fires are very different. *National Geographic.* Available at www.nationalgeographic.com/environment/2019/09/ancient-humans-burned-amazon-fires-today-entirely-different.

Garber, P. A. 2019. Commentary, Distinguished Primatologist Address: moving from advocacy to activism – changing views of primate field research and conservation over the past 40 years. *American Journal of Primatology.* DOI: 10.1002/ajp.23052

IUCN. 2019. The IUCN Red List of Threatened Species. Version 2018-2. Available at www.iucnredlist.org.

Janmaat, K. R. L. 2019. What animals do not do or fail to find: a novel observational approach for studying cognition in the wild. *Evolutionary Anthropology.* DOI: 10.1002/evan.21794,

Kalan, A. K., Piel, A. K., Mundry, R., et al. 2016. Passive acoustic monitoring reveals group ranging and territory use: a case study of wild chimpanzees (*Pan troglodytes*). *Frontiers in Zoology* **13**(1): 34.

Muller, R. D., Muller, D., Schierhorn, F., Gerold, G., and Pacheco, P. 2012. Proximate causes of deforestation in the Bolivian lowlands: an analysis of spatial dynamics. *Regional Environmental Change* **12**(3): 445–459.

Pecanha, S. and Wallace, T. 2019. We're thinking about the Amazon fires all wrong: these maps show why. *Washington Post.* Available at: www.washingtonpost.com/opinions/2019/09/05/were-thinking-about-amazon-fires-all-wrong-these-maps-show-why.

Peres, C. A. 1999. Ground fires as agents of mortality in a Central Amazonian forest. *Journal of Tropical Ecology* **15**(4): 535–541.

Peres, C. A. 2001. The fire next time: the potential for a catastrophic blaze threatens the Amazon. *Time Magazine*, 8 January: 48.

Rodrigues, M. A. 2019. Is science failing the world's primates? *The Revelator: Wild, Incisive, Fearless*. Available at https://therevelator.org/primates-research.

Savage, A., Guillen, R., Lamilla, I., and Soto, L. 2010. Developing an effective community conservation program for cotton-top tamarins (*Saguinus oedipus*) in Colombia. *American Journal of Primatology* **72**(5): 379–390.

Index